Novum Testamentum et Orbis Antiquus
Series Archaeologica 5b

Edited by Martin Ebner (Bonn), Heidrun Mader (Köln), Peter Lampe (Heidelberg),
Stefan Schreiber (Augsburg) and Jürgen Zangenberg (Leiden)

Advisory Board
Helen K. Bond (Edinburgh), Thomas Schumacher (Fribourg), John Barclay (Durham),
Armand Puig i Tàrrech (Barcelona), Ronny Reich (Haifa), Edmondo F. Lupieri (Chicago),
Stefan Münger (Bern)

Khirbet Qumran and Ain-Feshkha

Roland de Vaux' excavations

(1951–1956)

III A

in English translation

Translated by David ORTON

The Archaeology of Qumran

Reassessment of the interpretation
Peripheral constructions of the site

Jean-Baptiste HUMBERT o.p.
Correspondant of the *Inscriptions et Belles-Lettres* Academy
and
Alain CHAMBON

Notice by Hervé MONCHOT, UMR 8167

Qumran Terracotta Oil Lamps

Jolanta Młynarczyk
Institute of Archaeology, University of Warsaw

École biblique et archéologique française de Jérusalem
and
General direction of the international cooperation
of the French Foreign and European Affairs Ministry

VANDENHOECK & RUPRECHT

This book was created by the

DEPARTMENT OF ARCHEOLOGY
EDITING OFFICE

at the
École biblique et archéologique française de Jérusalem

Layout editing by Kiyoshi Inoue, graphic designer.
According to the model of the authors.

Jerusalem 2023

Including 179 figures and 113 plates

Bibliographic information published by the Deutsche Nationalbibliothek:
The Deutsche Nationalbibliothek lists this publication in the Deutsche
Nationalbibliographie; detailed bibliographic data available online: https://dnb.de.

© 2024 by Vandenhoeck & Ruprecht, Robert-Bosch-Breite 10, 37079 Göttingen, Germany,
an imprint of the Brill-Group
(Koninklijke Brill NV, Leiden, The Netherlands; Brill USA Inc., Boston MA, USA;
Brill Asia Pte Ltd, Singapore; Brill Deutschland GmbH, Paderborn, Germany,
Brill Österreich GmbH, Vienna, Austria)
Koninklijke Brill NV incorporates the imprints Brill, Brill Nijhoff, Brill Schöningh,
Brill Fink, Brill mentis, Brill Wageningen Academic, Vandenhoeck & Ruprecht,
Böhlau and V&R unipress.

All rights reserved. No part of this work may be reproduced or utilized in any form or by
any means, electronic or mechanical, including photocopying, recording, or any information
storage and retrieval system, without prior written permission from the publisher.

Initial layout editing and typesetting by Lionel Mochamps
Printed and bound by Hubert & Co, Göttingen
Printed in the EU

Vandenhoeck & Ruprecht Verlage | www.vandenhoeck-ruprecht-verlage.com

ISSN 1420-4622
ISBN 978-3-525-57090-6

Fr. Roland Guérin de Vaux o.p., Qumrân camp site, 1956
By courtesy © Sabine Weiss

fig. 1.   The Qumran site in its untouched environment, in 1951

Dedicated to

Jean Prignaud o.p.
1928 - 2015

who introduced us to archaeology

In Memory

of

Max and Helen Rosenbaum

by Glen Rosenbaum, a longtime supporter
of publication of the Dead Sea Scrolls

and

Weston Fields

with gratitude for his significant work,
fundraising and scholarship in support of
Dead Sea Scrolls research and its dissemination

Table of contents

Introduction 13

Part One
Review of the interpretation of the archaeology of Qumran

First chapter	Earthquake, fire and exile	25
Chapter 2	The long walls of Qumran	35
Chapter 3	Ashes and traces of fire	47
Chapter 4	Buried animal deposits	59
	On the bones in the pottery of locus 130	65
Chapter 5	A first fruits offering rite	71
Chapter 6	The cemetery of Qumran	77
Chapter 7	Toilet facilities	95
Chapter 8	A Greek-style bath	103
Chapter 9	Methods of chronography	115

Part Two
Designation of the constructed parts and completed list of loci

Chapter 10	Designation of the architecture	123
Chapter 11	List of the constructed parts of the excavation	129
Chapter 12	List of loci	135

Part Three
The archaeology of Qumran – an attempted reassessment

Stratigraphic diagrams 154

First section: The eastern front and the annexes to the southeast

Chapter A	The workshop in the southeast quadrant	157
	Locus 153	165
	Locus 44	167
	Locus 61	173
	Locus 59	181
	Locus 60	185
	Loci 45a and b	191
	Locus 177 (45c)	202
	Loci 62 and 63	205
	Locus 80	213
	Locus 65	217
	Locus 84 and kiln 918 (Locus 64)	221
	An added locus: 145	229
Chapter B	The series of pools and the southeast workshops	237
	Loci 72 and 73	241
	Locus 68	251
	Locus 69	255
	Large reservoir Locus 71	259
	Locus 75	267
	The workshop of Loci 143–144	272

Section II: The south and west front

Chapter C   The surroundings of south reservoir 91 277
             A workshop: Locus 81 281
             Reservoir Locus 91 294
             Loci 83 and 85 299

Chapter D   Two locations with an installation of presentation shelves 305
             Locus 77: 311
             Locus 86 327

Chapter E   The south platform 359

Chapter F   The western boundary 369

Section III: The north enclosure

Locus 134 381
Loci 130–131 383
Locus 132 415
Locus 138 425
Locus 135 431
Loci 136 and 137) 434
Locus 172 (129 and 133) 438
Loci 140 and 141 444

Part four
Qumran Terracotta Oil Lamps

Typology And Catalogue Of Finds 447

Wheel-Made Lamps (031-037)
031. Folded-rim lamps 449
032. Deep bi-conical lamps with flat base and long ridged nozzle attached to lower body 451
033. Shallow lamps with body bi-conical or rounded in section and long ridged nozzle attached to upper body 454
Fragments attributed to 032-033. 459
034. Large and flat circular lamps 462
035. Ridged nozzle attached to the outer rim of flattened top of the lamp 466
035-Prime 467
036. Knife-pared ("Herodian", spatulate) lamps 467
Lamp fragments of Qumran Type 036 488
Base/wall fragments attributed to Type 036. 502
037. Unclassified wheel-made lamps 504

Mould-made lamps (041-048)
041. 506
042. Lamp with two side lugs and nozzle tapering to rounded end 507
043. Lamps with circular body and straight-sided convex-topped nozzle with rounded end 507
044. "Judean radial lamps" 510
045. Lamps with circular body on base ring and spatulate (splayed) nozzle;
     ring handle *(as a rule, provided with a longitudinal groove)* 511
Fragments attributed to 045. 514
046. Decorated shoulder framed on both sides by multiple fine ridges; large filling hole; lug handle 515
047. Two versions of Italian type lamps (Loeschcke type VIII), imported and local/regional respectively 515
048. "Candlestick" lamp type 518
Conclusions 519
Bibliographical References and Abbreviations: 523

Afterword to the English version 527

Index
Lists and bibliography

List of figures	533
List of plates	539
Bibliography	541

a) Qumran plateau attached to the cliff piedmont by a peduncle (to south-east)

b) The steep bank of the Wadi Qumran. On the left, in the background, the black mass of the *khirbeh*, and on the right, in the cut of the plateau, the promontories of the artificial caves.

fig. 2.　　The Qumran plateau

Introduction

The misuse of books is the death of sound learning.
People think they know what they have read,
and take no pains to learn.
In fact with observations of all kinds
it is not a matter of reading but of seeing.

Jean-Jacques Rousseau
Émile ou de l'Éducation
1762

Nothing offers a better expression of where we stand in relation to the archaeology of Qumran than these words of Rousseau's: we are to see, and after we have seen it is a good thing to take another look. The mistake would be to believe that the archaeological interpretation of a site is a closed file. The subject of Qumran is undergoing profound change, and it is in that spirit that we shall view it. There is a need for patience and for due time, while reason demands that you do the right thing and wisdom requires you not to insist on set intuitions. Chinese wisdom says that truth is an onion that one peels layer by layer. Qumran is an onion that de Vaux has picked, peeled and then planted. We have harvested it, peeled it and are replanting it so that others can peel it in their turn. The truth is still to come.

Publication of the archaeology of the site has been delayed for various reasons which have to do on the one hand with external circumstances and on the other with the nature of the archaeological files in the condition in which we received them. Qumran, the excavations and the study of them took place against the background of professional and political tensions. This was a Franco-Jordanian project with strong English participation, thanks to Lankester Harding, who was director of the Department of Antiquities of Jordan. De Vaux led a fifth campaign in February and March of 1956, and in October the Suez Crisis erupted, in which Jordan and France were not on the same side; the French missions in Jordan found themselves in a difficult situation. In the 1960s, Jordan authorized interventions at the site over which de Vaux had no control; when Jerusalem was taken in 1967, progress was hampered by a diplomatic injunction calling for the project to be suspended pending settlement of the political status of Jerusalem. De Vaux's premature death in 1971, at the age of 67, was a serious setback. There was a risk that Israeli excavations in the first decade of the new millennium, which opened up sites de Vaux had not touched, might produce contradictory information; as it turned out, they did not bring changes to the original plan.

De Vaux did not submit the final report of the works he directed, nor tell us what he was really thinking; we do not have his last word and we do not know what he would have decided. The fertility of his intellect leaves us in his debt, and it was a privilege to continue his task. Qumran seemed so much his legacy that it was difficult to make modifications. There can be no doubt that he intended to publish archaeology whose scope and shape was largely his own. Between 1958 and his passing, thirteen years elapsed, which saw the

fig. 3. Khirbet Qumran during the 1955 campaign

publication of the early part of the study of the caves, in parallel with that of the manuscripts. The Schweich Lectures, published in 1961, summarized the annual excavation reports with a few adjustments, and their posthumous re-edition in 1973 took account of the main criticisms he had received. De Vaux was well aware that his interpretation had raised questions that preoccupied him. He knew that the dossier had filled out and that some perspectives had opened up. Was he right to wait? Being familiar with his great scholarly honesty, we know that he was always willing to make radical revisions when such were warranted. It remains the case that the English revision of the Schweich Lectures left its mark on Qumran studies with the skilful combination of his intuitions, the excavation findings and his mastery of the sources. The lectures form an impressive historico-archaeological synthesis, but one whose coherence, though persuasive, is only apparent. Nonetheless, partly thanks to the English language, they have become his authoritative legacy. Can the interpretation be amended? Yes, and it will be useful and necessary to examine the basis for it.

The general outline of the archaeological dossier was known, well enough for research not to be interrupted. Thanks to the summaries de Vaux had given as the years and the excavations passed, some felt they had enough material to construct hypotheses, and not enough was known about them for criticisms to be raised. This does not change the fact that de Vaux is still the indispensable basis for constructions. His account offered the advantage of clarity, but the debate that followed was contradictory. Some readers of the manuscripts assure us that de Vaux is sufficient, and that the Essene Qumran of his archaeology is an exception that should not be touched. However, scholarly rigour demands that we move on. Those viewing the remains see Qumran as one site among others on the banks of the Dead Sea. The cool-headed might want it to be both: a Jewish site, as exceptional as Masada or Garizim, while at the same time clearly being one human settlement among others in Judea at the turn of the millennium. We shall try to avoid favouring either one; both need to be examined separately with the methods on which they each depend.

The *École Biblique* decided to resume publication of the archaeology at the point where de Vaux had left it. Initially, our goal was to present the available documentation in the project de Vaux had conceived, so as to present his results just as we found them. The ordering of the archives and the objects detained us for several years. It became increasingly clear that the dossier as a whole had aged, not only in the form and manner of the documentation but also in the way it was approached. Had de Vaux let himself be swayed by the bias of biblical archaeology, in which the written document is master of all and archaeology illustrates the text? Yet the site has its own internal coherence, its own evolution and chronology. What would the interpretation of the excavations have been if the sources had been silent with regard to Essenism, and if the manuscripts had not been discovered? There can be no doubt that in the 1950s, as today, it would have been seen as a special Jewish site, because the unusual number of inscriptions or graffiti were indications of a high cultural standard.

Research on the manuscripts is growing in precision and scope, and research into the site is no different in this respect. The manuscripts raise questions to which archaeology might have answers, at least in relation to issues of history. The caves are inscribed in a landscape, and in their materiality the parchments are an object of archaeology. It is doubtful, however, whether the archaeology of the site can solve all the questions. Qumran is a place and, at a precise moment in time, the group that used it and the group that possessed the manuscripts, who are not the same, knew or met each other. They maintained links and we may believe, though not confirm, that they were Essenes; unless and until the contrary is demonstrated, this is still the most probable scenario. Logic, then, dictates that the two groups should be studied separately, in terms of their archaeology and their history, while expecting to be able to merge them together. By combining the results we hope to be able to take things forward.

De Vaux's interpretation was a proposal. His arguments have since been weakened, because at the turn of the millennium the archaeology of Palestine benefited from some extensive projects. John Strugnell had confessed: "We began Qumran with simple ideas." There were manuscripts and sources, the site was seen in a new light, and the links between all these terms created a tapestry of evidence unspoilt by contradictions that might have arisen. The Qumran settlement was conceived of, without too much hesitation, as a religious community grouped around an exceptional library, saved at some point from the Roman threat. To start with literary and historical concepts to explain an almost silent archaeology was a parlous undertaking.

fig. 4.   Photogrammetric reconstruction of the environment of the Qumran site, (Lionel Mochamps)
         From the Jordan Air Force aerial photographs, 1953

However, on opening a file that was initially limpid but had become so complex, there were no great surprises. It is important to remember that de Vaux, the site archaeologist, was both the key figure in the collection of manuscripts and at the same time the director of their publication. He had a perfect grasp of their profound significance for scholarship. It was inevitable that he would have viewed the site as their envelope. The disproportion between the thousand manuscripts of a library which would have required a society with exceptional intellectual and religious dynamism – rare in Antiquity and especially in contemporary Judea – and the modesty of an archaeological site isolated in the steppe, should have alerted minds. Here was an irrational fact that was erased from view because of the special importance attached to the sources. The reading of the site by the pioneers of Qumran was then adopted without due critique and without taking account of the disproportionality. However, what the sources tell us of the way of life of religious societies, particularly in relation to customs and laws, was intended for the edification of the reader of the time; the ancient historian's record of it represents not a certified account of life in these societies but what people remembered of it or wanted to say about it. Reality should not be confused with reading. The theory of community life does not fit with the configuration of the remains and the "Essene community of Qumran", implicitly confused with community in the broader sense (yahad), has been overloaded with the leading role. The gap between the life of a group and the account of it that has come down to us is particularly sensitive in the case of Qumran. The account has conveyed the ideal life of a society, or evaluated it, at the moment when its history was close to completion. We cannot view Essenism, or potentially any other sect, as a static shot. The received account would be a frozen snapshot which does not take account of the unavoidable internal movement of a political and religious institution. It has to be accepted that in two centuries, this society, like all sects of this region and time, evolved in the context of a proliferating Hellenistic Judaism: the changing situation would have left traces which archaeology is able to perceive but which the account has not caught. What, ultimately, do we know of the lives led by those who frequented these places? Archaeology's priority is to present the shells of the triviality of the days in which intellectual and religious life slides along, leaving only a trace. The vision of Qumran as one village among others is possible, and some claim to have seen it. The number of craft facilities that invaded the settlement remains an enigma that needs solving. To investigate the priority of a religious structure here, as de Vaux did as a pioneer, followed by many, is a legitimate, arbitrary and certainly risky undertaking. The Essene scenario at Qumran is still no more than an educated guess. Nonetheless, Qumran remains a site where Jewish religious practices are in evidence. It is appropriate to venture beyond a strictly secular reading, and the archaeologist must bear in mind the ever-present background noise emitted by the manuscripts. It will be prudent to take the Judaic context as the most sensible key to the interpretation. We ourselves have tried to find this key. Our work is therefore presented in two parts. The first sets out the arguments that allow us to question de Vaux's interpretation. It is intended as a proposal. The second is a technical examination of the remains of the periphery of the site. In our view it was best to set them out separately and to advance with caution.

In our Volume I we decided to accompany the album of photographs of the site with a selection of the minutes of the excavation which de Vaux had been careful to edit himself when preparing the Schweich Lectures. We called this a Synthesis because it brings together what de Vaux himself deemed useful for his interpretation, and it shows the direction of his thinking. Our decision to match up the photographs taken on the fly with the description of the loci was tricky, given the baldness of the notes taken on site on a day-to-day basis. However, the Qumran excavations are now part of the history of Palestinian archaeology, and we are careful not to make judgments. The baldness of the notes reflects on the one had the excavation methods current at the time, and on the other the circumstances in which the works were conducted, under difficult economic conditions. At this point it should be remembered that de Vaux conducted excavations with a sense of urgency, to outwit looters. There was a lack of employed workers; for strategic reasons in the collection of manuscripts, at the time it seemed a good policy to hire the Taʿamres who bargained with them; the excavation method suffered as a result.

The excavation process would be different today, with increased resources and with logistics and technology that did not exist sixty years ago. We have no doubt that de Vaux's publication would have illustrated his clear and sober interpretation, presented without ado, in the image of his presentation of the caves and of Murabbaʿat in the DJD volumes. It would have been the one that we have decided not to make. First,

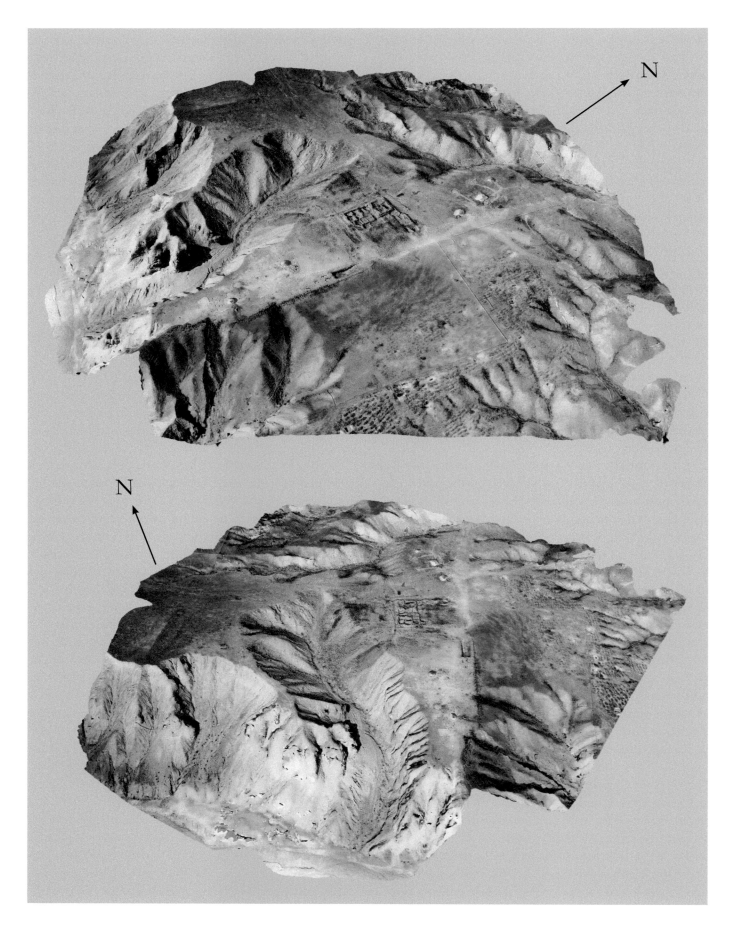

fig. 5.   Photogrammetric reconstruction, views towards the northwest and north, (Lionel Mochamps)
From the Jordan Air Force aerial photographs, 1953

excavations in the region relating to this very period have since developed considerably, and new documentation is available; criticisms of the archaeology of the site have become pressing and need to be taken into account. Further, publication methods have changed and much more is expected of an ancient excavation than it is able to give, with the precision and technical detail that are demanded today. Our assessment has been subject to numerous hesitations, and we are aware that it is sometimes in an awkward position, which is why we are publishing it as a site dossier.

We have deliberately opted to consider only the Qumran of Vaux, who was master of the work, to reopen the files the way one inspects the foundations when checking the safety of a building. We have not entered the debate on the archaeology of Qumran, which has since been amplified with some researchers – a healthy debate, but imaginative, involved and often contradictory. Aiming to confine ourselves to the origins, we needed to cover the whole of Qumran. The vestiges of the site have suffered the ill effects of erosion, successive restorations and cosmetic adjustments for the purposes of tourism, and the excavation is still there in its volume, its proportions and its environment. The portrait that the archaeologists drew of them is still there, too: an abundance of objects, classified and restored, catalogues which record and draw them; the archives are still there, a hand-written site log, edited on the spot, sometimes elliptical, too often patchy; a typed synthesis, a working sketch of the interpretation that was forming, preliminary reports which, in the course of the campaigns, fine-tune and correct, the Schweich Lectures which forged the Essene theory; simple line diagrams which imprinted the image of Qumran on memories; hundreds of photographs of the site, often mediocre, but taken on the fly by de Vaux, presenting the excavation in its freshness, and others taken by photographers for the Antiquities Service, which are professional but large in scale, capturing only general views.

The patiently assembled Qumran corpus deserved an autopsy. We checked through the available data to establish reference points and organize them. The written documents were compared, not simply to spot contradictions, hesitations and regrets, but to establish dependable archaeological facts. The plans, criticized for their combination of architectures, the few preparatory surveys and the rare sections or elevations provided elements of stratigraphy which, sadly, are isolated from each other and generally speaking impossible to link up. The reading of the Journal was the guide for recreating a sequence while following the scheme of works by careful examination of the photographs of the site. Recreated layers are the result of this and free-hand stratigraphic diagrams, never to scale, illustrate the attempts at them. The elevations recorded on the surveys, often unusable, indicate the tops of walls and rarely floors. The reestablished stratigraphy will remain artificial, and in the absence of a better alternative, it will be best to accept the approximations. Despite their imprecise location, the coins were helpful in correcting the chronology. De Vaux had granted them a key role, without due caution. Most of them give only an indication which is not particularly useful. Fortunately, some of them, duly stratified, set out the proposed chronology. We dismantled a mechanism, and we are obliged to rebuild it without any assurance that it works.

The work committed itself to presenting pottery whose abundance at Qumran is surprising, given the modesty of the site. Before getting to the heart of the matter, we thought the classification conceived by de Vaux would suffice. The task was more difficult than foreseen because of a methodological flaw: the norm when presenting items of pottery requires that they be classified in a sequence that follows the stratigraphy, leading on to the chronological table; but the relationship between stratigraphy and chronology is one of the major difficulties of the excavation conducted by de Vaux. The pottery was not ordered according to the succession of the layers in the levels. The typology of the pottery was fixed in accordance with a theoretical periodization. In general terms, de Vaux reversed the process by adopting periods of natural history which the reconsideration of archaeology now dictates should be abandoned. De Vaux constructed an artificial typology, continued by Paul Lapp, which was for a time authoritative.

We present the pottery by locus and in the framework of sequences that have been laboriously reconstructed. The lack of stratigraphic rigour during the excavation is reflected in the imprecision of the groupings that we propose. A selection has been made among some 4,000 sherds not retained by de Vaux but which he had kept after noting the locus and the date of the dig. Reference to the dates of the Journal made it possible to attribute them to one stratum or another. They then complete the typology of a particular deposit. Finally, the manner of description, succinct, is that adopted by de Vaux in his day. All the pottery has been redrawn in response to the publishing norms required nowadays.

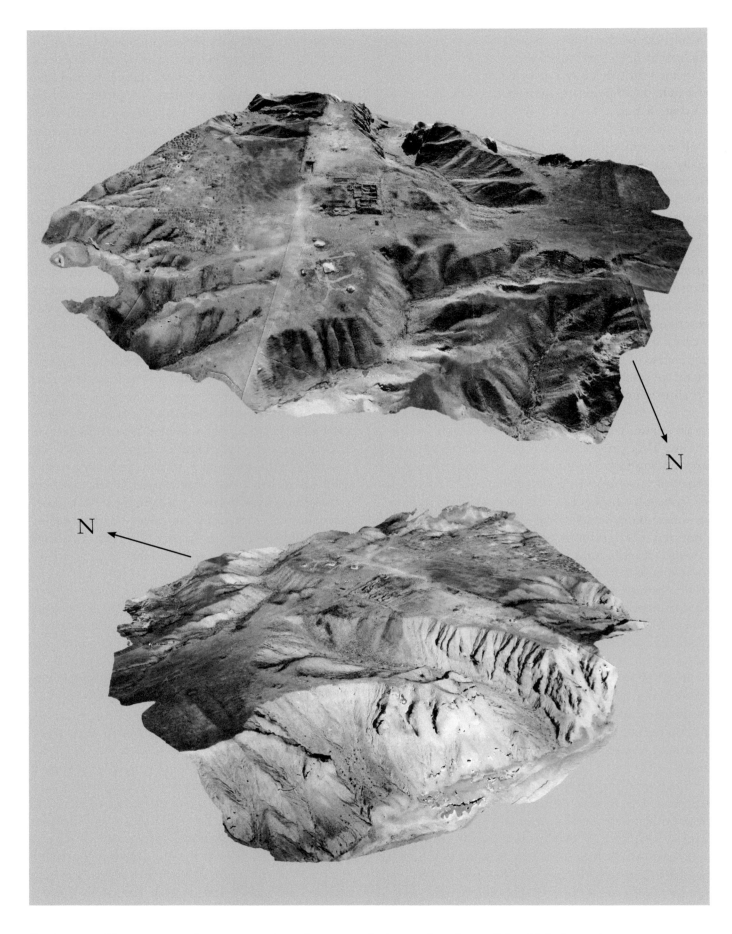

fig. 6. Photogrammetric reconstruction, views towards the south and east, (Lionel Mochamps)
From the Jordan Air Force aerial photographs, 1953

Finally, the pottery corpus is not commented upon, for lack of time. We thought it more urgent to present it to the scholarly community who will continue the research. The reinterpretation of the site was a prerequisite for us.

The distribution of tasks between authors is normally set out at the beginning of the project. Alain Chambon took responsibility for the preparation of the technical files and their follow-up: direction of the workshop drawing the pottery and the non-ceramic objects, management of the index files, realization of the plates and catalogues, monitoring of the plans and surveys, numbering of all the constructed elements of the site, together with preparation of final copies of the diagrams which will aid all researchers citing and describing Qumran in the future. The present author took on the archaeological investigation and the resulting review of the stratigraphy and chronology. He is therefore solely responsible for the analysis and proposals contained in the present volume.

The entirety of the site was studied. The present volume IIIA presents only the ring of installations surrounding the central building. As this is complete, it makes sense not to delay publication. It presents the coherence brought to it by the new layout of the refoundation by a sectarian group – Essene, if that is preferred – around an older core. We saw the latter as a redeveloped Hasmonaean settlement, containing a more complex stratification than the surrounding ring, and meriting a separate study of its own, which will appear in volume IIIB. For a summary presentation of the Hasmonaean site, we refer the reader to our publication of the archaeology of Qumran, volume II.

Study of the lamps found on the Qumran estate, the *khirbeh*, the caves and Aïn Feshkha, was a long and exacting task, as the documentation was scattered or in a precarious state. Certain lamps have disappeared, others are in a repository in a Belgian university, inaccessible to us, and some have been smashed and require restoration. Jolanta Młynarczyk, of the University of Warsaw, kindly took responsibility for these. The completed study of the lights is of such interest for observing regional exchange, defining the cultural field of the inhabitants of Qumran and establishing the chronology of the site that it would not have been sensible to put off the publication. That is why an attempted synthesis of the lamps forms our concluding chapter. It has a rightful place in a work presenting the essential features of the site's pottery.

Those who have contributed in one way or another to the project of publication are numerous, and it would be remiss of us not to acknowledge our indebtedness to them in this regard: Joséphine, Akram and Edward for drawing the pottery, and Hershel Shanks who contributed to the costs; Manon Saenko and Nathalie Hirshi for its restoration; Jean-Michel de Tarragon, Juhana Saukkonen for the photography and Bart Wagemakers for providing an unedited negative of locus 86; Mariusz Burdajewicz for the elegant representation of the lamps; Pierre-Marin Boucher for the preparation of files. The following have been valuable consultants: Bruno Callegher for issues of numismatics and Jonathan Adler for a better approach to religious and talmudic anthropology; Etienne Nodet, Mireille Bélis, Edith Parmentier and Rachel Bar-Nathan for their constructive criticisms. We are indebted to Marie-Hélène Thuillier for repeated rereadings of the texts and her persistent care in spotting editorial obscurities; and to Jean-Michel de Tarragon again, for ensuring typographically clean proofs. The work has been typeset entirely at the *École Biblique* and we are grateful to those who have patiently brought the work to fruition: Jocelyn Dorvault, Louis de Lisle, Benoît Rivron, and especially Kiyoshi Inoué, who spent long years developing and experimenting with the computer system for handling the images; Lionel Mochamps gave the whole thing a final polish to ensure its typographic and iconographic quality. We must commend the cordiality and the unfailing concern to help of both Alegre Sawariego and Hava Katz, conservators of the Rockefeller Museum, where the Qumran documentation is held. We would underline the quality of the fraternal welcome by the Dominican members of the IDEO who provided us with the necessary calm, at their convent in Cairo, for mastering a long and exacting subject; we would like to thank them warmly. Our gratitude goes to Bertrand Viriot for an exceptional donation which made possible the completion of the typesetting of the work. Our appreciation also goes to the Association des anciens et amis de l'*École Biblique* (Paris), and to its secretary Alain Saglio, who generously and unstintingly completed the annual budget.

None of this would have been possible without funding by the Direction Générale de la mondialisation of the Ministère des affaires étrangères. Its successive directors have, one after the other, met the challenge of such a publication, and encouraged its appearance in the French language for the original version. We are sincerely appreciative of their commitment and support.

Jean-Baptiste Humbert

Roland de Vaux archaeologist

To construct it is sometimes necessary to deconstruct. Our critical reading of the Qumran of Père Roland de Vaux does not in any way cloud our respect for his work, undertaken with intelligence and talent. R. de Vaux, who arrives in Jerusalem in 1933 aged 30, is a man of the texts. Biblical archaeology was enjoying its highest reputation. A stone's throw from the *École Biblique*, W.F. Albright, hero of this method, reigned over the archaeology of the Palestine Mandate from 1922 to 1936 as Director of the American School of Jerusalem. The young de Vaux had respect for him and was friendly with him. He entered archaeology in the 1930s, when the aristocracy of British Mandate Palestinian archaeology had taken root and planted its ensigns on the major sites of the Bronze and Iron Ages. At that time, biblical history was the noble path for archaeologists. He was the contemporary of K. Kenyon who, in the late 1930s, made an inventory of Samaria; while de Vaux is at Tell el-Fârʿah, Kenyon is excavating Jericho, and the links they maintain are constant. De Vaux did not begin his career on a biblical trajectory. In 1937, he cleared a mosaic at Mâʿin (Jordan) with R. Savignac, who, with M.G. Horsfield, had exhumed the Nabataean temple of er-Ramm. In 1944 he led a stratigraphic excavation on the medieval site of Abu Ghosh and in 1946 cleared the Byzantine site of ʿAïn Maʿamoudiyeh to the west of Hebron. Then, in 1946, de Vaux considers that the *École Biblique* is ready to take on a wide-ranging archaeological project, following the example of the great international institutions, and undertakes the excavations at Tell e-Fârʿah, which he conducted between 1946 and 1960. He commenced the excavations at Qumran in 1951 and managed the *tour de force* of alternating campaigns between Fârʿah and Qumran. Kenyon was interested in Jerusalem where, in 1961, she mounted a joint project with de Vaux, at the south of the esplanade of mosques, interrupted in 1963.

In his research, de Vaux prioritized the Old Testament and we can believe that his interest, rooted in this field, did not take him spontaneously to archaeology of the Hellenistic and Roman periods. His choice had been Tirça, the ancient capital of Samaria and on the contrary, Qumran for him was a parallel track, initially a life-saver, in which we have no doubt that he excelled. We would suggest that at Tell el-Fâʿrah he had made the motives of biblical archaeology that were in fashion at the time his own, and his choices in his interpretation would seem to confirm this. Would he have been torn between the two disciplines, biblical and intertestamental? In short, would he have prioritized the Text at Qumran, in the same way that he placed the biblical Tirça at the source of his interpretation of Iron-Age Fârʿah?

De Vaux liked to present himself as an archaeologist, an Old Testament exegete and a historian, and he mastered all three disciplines. However, man of texts that he was, the Dead Sea manuscripts and the historians of Antiquity would have held his interest more than the archaeology of the site. At Qumran, de Vaux showed himself as a historian first.

Part One

Review of the interpretation of the archaeology of Qumran

fig. 7.   Pool 48–49, broken by fault 2a of the earthquake

First chapter

Earthquake, fire and exile

The Land of Damascus

Qumran was hit by an earthquake. After some initial hesitation, de Vaux thought it right to date it to 31 BC and drew what he felt were the appropriate conclusions. This was not the best chronological option. Recent excavations have brought new data to light that tend not to support this choice. A careful reassessment of the remains themselves, followed by a careful rereading of the excavation reports and logs, have convinced us that the earthquake did not hit Qumran before its abandonment. A severe earthquake certainly caused damage at Qumran, but this was a deserted Qumran, and the damage, worse in some places than others, remains visible, never having been repaired. De Vaux pushed the earthquake back by a century, consequently assembling the components of the timeline in the wrong chronological order. An event that marked the end was placed at the beginning. Although de Vaux's account is consistent, it is negated by the archaeology.

Qumran bears the marks of obvious fractures, cracks and collapses. It is reasonable to see these as the effects of an earth tremor. The marks were attributed to the earthquake of 31 BC, famous from Josephus's record of it in *Bell.* I, 370 and *Ant.* XV, 121-122; but the arguments for this were not reexamined. The earthquake derives its importance entirely from the publicity given to it by Josephus, despite the fact that it was not equal in severity to the seismic jolts of the Byzantine era. De Vaux associated the fall of the roof of locus 86 with the earthquake, and as the objects inside it were sealed by a burnt roof he concluded that the earthquake had triggered the fire. It was just one step further to surmise that the fire pushed the community into exile. This set up the chronological scheme: foundation in the 2nd century (Period Ia), development, earthquake-fire, 31 BC (Period Ib), exile, return-restoration, destruction in AD 68 (Period II), reinstallation post-68, abandonment (Period III). The year 31 BC, between the foundation and the destruction, was the axis around which a chronology revolved. Two "biases", therefore, weaken the proposed partitioning of time.

The first bias was to subject archaeological fact to the yoke of history. The dubious practice of prioritizing history over archaeology is an old debate. History cannot correct the weaknesses of archaeology, and vice versa, because the two things are not inherently the same and it is dangerous to apply the methods of one to the methods of the other. It is significant that de Vaux slid from archaeology to history by resorting, in the excavation reports, to *Periods*. A period is defined as a specific length of time. But at Qumran, the concept of period has trumped the working out of a stratigraphy on which to base the chronology; de Vaux' notion of period, which in this case goes beyond the idea of duration, recalls history in the form of a series of events to which a precedence is attributed. The historian takes precedence over the archaeologist. Knowledge of the sources is a guide which, precious though it is, constrains and inhibits as it illuminates. De Vaux appreciated the weight of history; he accepted its yoke. This was his right, but it was a choice. It would have been better not to set aside the constraints of archaeology before assuming

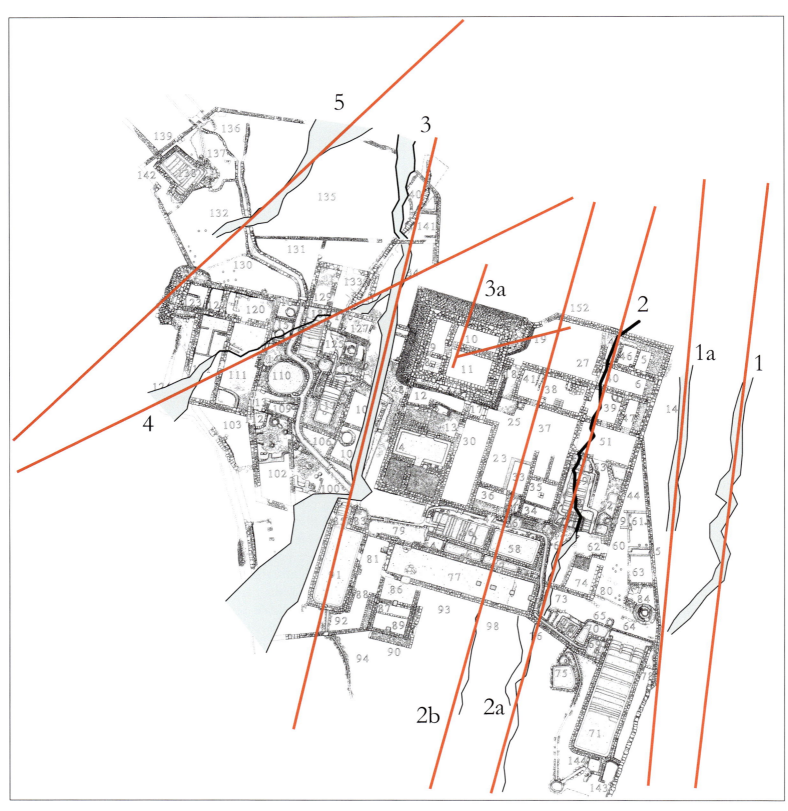

fig. 8. Illustration of the different faults of the earthquake

the history. After all, it is not always right to interpret archaeological facts on the basis of what the ancients tell us; we still need to take account of the motives and intentions of the author. As a method, this is risky. There was a need to maintain a certain distance, with a degree of caution. It is almost certain that none of the ancient authors who wrote about the Essenes ever visited Qumran. It is not at all certain that what was written about the Essenes related specifically to Qumran. De Vaux knew this and yet throughout the course of his interpretation, *the* Qumran community played the part of the Essenes, being required to speak and act on their behalf. The interpretation of Qumran is essentially an Essene story. Biblical archaeology conducts its research with an authoritative text as its starting-point, and de Vaux seems to have acquiesced to this. The archaeology of Qumran is imprinted upon the historical sources like a palimpsest.

The second bias results from an erroneous assessment of the stratigraphy as to its relationship to the evolution of the site. De Vaux adopted the division of time into periods and not into levels as is customary in land archaeology. He tackled a fragmentary stratigraphy which did not lead to a chronology because, instead of taking the evolution of architectural features horizontally, he sought it in depth. It should be remembered that de Vaux alternated campaigns at Qumran with those of Tell el-Farʿah, where he was faced with a complex stratigraphy spanning three millennia. There, he established a stratigraphy in levels. Qumran, however, is a site whose occupation was much shorter and where stratification is reduced, so it required a different way of dealing with stratigraphy. The stratification, though simple, were not understood according to its formal way. From the beginning of the excavations, Qumran was seen as a simple story: a community had come and settled. But there are two Qumrans, encased one within the other, with two separate architectural phases. The first is an ancient core, the large, square, one-storey house, marked in the ruin by a mass which made a blot on the aerial photographs taken before the work. The second phase offered a stratification with the reoccupation of the Hasmonaean core in two stages, in the middle of the 1st century BC and after 68. Around the ancient, massive core, a ring had opened up, recent and lower: the so-called "Essene" level which expanded in stages, but always on the same plane. Qumran displays two systems of occupation with interlinked and overlapping architectural features, where de Vaux saw only a single homogeneous tissue, not distinguishing the areas of contact. Something wasn't right. The recourse to history alleviated the difficulty, and the development of an Essene Qumran, the literary sources being compelled into transparency, conferred upon the site the meaning, vocation and unity that was then given to it.

The unique character of the discovery of such exceptional manuscripts gave permission for an extraordinary reading of the remains. Having affirmed that Qumran was the centre of the Qumran community, the abundant literature describing it seemed like an opportunity it would be silly to pass up. Manuscripts, ancient sources and the fully discovered site formed three "chambers" connected by a corridor allowing free passage from one to the other. De Vaux thought it possible to find in the ruins what he had read in the texts. The narrative of the Schweich Lectures, vouched for by legitimate archaeological observation, constructed the narrative of an Essene history. This is an impressive and intelligent historical reconstitution; hence its success. De Vaux missed the fact that Qumran also bears the stigmata of an unwritten history which has to be read from the stones. Furthermore, de Vaux's own input – a religious topography with medieval resonances, communitarian and anachronistic – clouded his view.

Let us go back to the earthquake, the exile that followed it and the way in which they were perceived and described. The rift valley of the Jordan and the Dead Sea is an area of high seismic intensity. Numerous earth tremors are recorded in the texts, and just listing them creates a rich chronography. They are liable to provide as many handy historical reference points as archaeologists care to use to secure their chronologies. Discerning the traces of an earthquake is not easy, however, because in many cases people have made skillful repairs to the damage. It is true that other earthquakes destroyed entire towns or large buildings; there are numerous archaeological witnesses to be found at sites that have never been abandoned. However, for the southern Levant, the eighth century was the century of repeated earthquakes which destroyed Romano-Byzantine urbanism, when the cities of the region did not stop being inhabited. In the majority of cases, the inhabitants reinstalled themselves in or on the ruins, with varying degrees of luxury and skill. De Vaux had the occupants return to Qumran thirty years after the supposed catastrophe. Paradoxically, the representation of *Plans* Ib and II shows that the site has not changed, and moreover that the stratification is virtually non-existent: ... *The floors of levels I and II are merged together or remain at very close levels* (RB 61, 1954, p. 211). Would the destruction have caused so little damage, and is there no trace of the abandonment during the exile? Then why leave the premises for an exile in Damascus? De Vaux had a suspicion that neither earthquake nor fire had caused the abandonment: *One might wonder whether the earthquake and the fire were exactly contemporaneous. At first I thought the earthquake had affected an already destroyed and abandoned building* (*L'archéologie*, p. 17). We now know that the time of the earthquake is deferred to after the desertion of the site; and that the fire, or simply a destruction, has nothing to do with an earthquake. The exile and the abandonment had been set in an imperfect context. When de Vaux had finished, nothing had been established.

The earthquake had been fixed as one of the key arguments for interpreting the evolution and history of the site, and we find references to this in the *Journal*.

- Locus 48 (19/4/53): *The descending staircase seems cracked along its entire length. The eastern part (and all the rest of the building to the east) has slipped by 30 to 40 cm. Impressive testimony to the earthquake of which we already saw traces in the tower, and which must separate periods I and II* (fig. 7).
- Locus 58 (22/2/54): *hypothesis: after the earthquake, cisterns 49 and 50 were abandoned*; and on 2/3/54: *the lining has a long fissure which cuts the cistern quite close to its eastern extremity, but this absolutely does not look like the cut from the earthquake in cistern 49.*
- Locus 72 (31/3/54): *Here we find the earthquake fault, breaking a bare floor such as the one in locus 73* and on 1/4/54: *an indication that the principal channel has been cut by the earthquake, which raises questions about many things.*
- Locus 73 (6/3/54): *We follow the earthquake fault, which has cut a lime floor, across the locus.*
- Locus 74 (9/3/54): *The line of the earthquake becomes clear to the west of 74 (and 66) and is also manifested in the thrust of the east-west wall, the eastern part of which has subsided.*
- Locus 102 (17/3/55): *It seems evident (...) that this collapse is due to the earthquake and continues that of locus 104* and on 21/3/55: *The explanation of this pit by the earthquake remains difficult (how were the walls remain standing?), but we can see no other solution.*
- Locus 111 (10/2/55): *The door to locus 103 is closed, the gutter is disused, the eastern wall is doubled to the interior of the locus, close to the middle of the room. One might then wonder whether this transformation could be a consequence of the earthquake, and the doubling of the eastern wall could be a repair (or a support to facilitate the covering). One might also propose a link with a possible destruction of the eastern part of the secondary building (the earthquake again?)* and on 14/2/55: *The clearance is completed: the floor has been split diagonally by an earthquake crack, continuing the one seen in locus 115* (9/2/55): *A crack has broken this floor; is this an effect of the earthquake?*
- Locus 134 (5/4/55): *Looking for the continuation of the ancient trench (...): the filling-in of the trench could be quite recent!*

Description of the earthquake (fig. 8)

An earthquake reduced Qumran to ruins and it was never restored. De Vaux struggled to pin the earthquake to 31 BC. Initially he was not really convinced by the arguments he adduced. In *Revue Biblique* 61, 1954, the report of the excavations of the 1953 campaign, details the effects of the earthquake: *In the tower, the east wall has cracked, the lintel of the door between loci 10A and 28 is broken, causing the collapse of the ceiling of L. 10A: on the south and east walls of this locus, the gutter is marked by two descending lines converging towards the south-east corner. The south-west block of the building seems to have suffered less damage at the bottom but we do not know what happened to the upper parts. The most serious damage seems to have occurred in the eastern area. From the entrance to pool 49 as far as the north of L. 51 runs a crack which has split the floor of the two interior pools and the base of L. 51, while at the same time the whole part to the east of this line dropped by around 50 cm. Consideration could be given to a sudden collapse of the ground but the indications found in the tower make it more likely that there was an earthquake* (RB 61, 1954, p. 210). In *L'archéologie* (p. 15-19), which he edited in 1960, in several dense pages de Vaux sets out his reasons for arriving at the sequence he worked out: earthquake – fire – abandonment. Shortly after this he repeats the description of the destruction given in the *Revue Biblique*, in the same terms. Commenting on what he discovered a year later, in 1954, he adds: *The tower was shaken, its eastern wall was cracked, the lintel and the ceiling of one of the lower rooms gave way (...). In the south area, the indications are less clear, except in the annex of the great hall, the back of which has collapsed, entombing the deposit of pottery ...* (*L'archéologie*, p. 16). This last comment is inaccurate; only the burnt ceiling fell in and the walls are intact. The ashes covering the vases would have given him the idea of a fire and he would have taken the blocks of stone containing the back of L. 86 as reinforcements of a building, none of which collapsed.

In the tower he noted a destruction – *cracked lintel, collapsed ceiling,* etc. – which he thought it right to attribute to the earthquake. The ruin and dislocation of masonry are trump cards which the archaeologist can lay on the table when arguments fall short of proof. The dilapidation observed in the tower, attributed to 31, seems to be confused with the damage from the sacking in 68: *The end of the period is marked by a violent destruction: in the main building, the northwest tower, with its slope of stones at its base, resisted better, but all the rooms of the southwest and northwest were overwhelmed by the collapse of the ceilings and superstructures* (*L'archéologie*, p. 28). The destruction–restoration–destruction sequence is difficult to see. The partial restoration of the buildings posed a problem for de Vaux: *... the buildings damaged by the fire and the earthquake were not immediately repaired* (*ibid.*, p. 18). It is rather difficult to reconcile all this.

The damaged tower is not the only witness which raises doubts. More obvious still is the architectural sequence proposed in the southeast quadrant of the central building. Pools 48-49 and 50, Period Ib, were split by the earthquake and never restored, and Coüasnon's *Plan* of Period II does not provide any further indication in support of this allocation; it is clearly improbable that the heart of the settlement would have remained an unorganized empty space, particularly during the century of Period II, the time of the greatest development of Qumran. The situating of their degradation in 31 BC derived from a poor reading of the stratigraphy. Here, there was a contradiction that needed to be resolved. Logic dictates that the pools in the southeast quadrant remained in good condition and in service up to 68 and their representation is missing in the *Plan* of Period II.

Fault "3", the most serious one, which split the site into two parts, was not interpreted as such. It split the western side of the settlement along its entire length, from north to south. Along its route, remains have disappeared, been destroyed, or have been swallowed up. Starting from the south, the corner of storeroom 97 has collapsed into the ravine; the southern half of L. 104 has been razed and the concretized mass of reservoir L. 91 has resisted; the break skirts it in a zigzag line, destroying the aqueduct at the point where it joins the pool at L. 83 (L. 79); in the large open space at L. 99, a "trench" runs as far as L. 128, the western portion of which has disappeared; main door 582 of the outbuildings has been dislocated, and there remains only a loosened fragment of the threshold; the dividing wall of L. 134 and 135 has been holed as well as wall 657 to the north of L. 135. The "trench" has been repaired in various places. Locus 99 had a mortar floor which was broken in two, and the two parts are no longer on the same level: *We find a plastered floor one level lower, like (...) the plastered floor of L. 105* (21/3/55, L. 99) and *the western half has subsided by 10 to 15 cm.* In the same L. 99 *we descend around one meter in spoil earth. It seems that we were emptying an ancient trench!* (23/3/55). The observation was right. In L. 105 *this floor has been burst open by a large flattened piece of mortar, which we remove* (22/3/55). In L. 107: *In the north we follow the trench to the east of L. 105, following the line of the broken plaster* (28/3/55). L. 128 was better observed: *The two plasters and the gravel stop on the same line, revealing a trench which continues in L. 105 and 107,* on 26/3/55: *we follow the ancient trench* on 29/3/55: *the two plastered floors and the gravel continue on each side. The earthquake hypothesis is improbable. A trench made by the Romans as a defense work? Difficult to accept* (30/3/55). L. 134 (31/3/55): *We open it to find traces of the entrance. We find only collapsed stones and nothing in place.* Further to the north in L. 134 (5/4/55): *Last, we look for the continuation of the ancient trench coming from the south. Indistinct here, it could be that it does not cut across the good floors here (...) The filling-in of the trench would be quite recent.* So the "trench" certainly is ancient and there can be little doubt that it is a good witness to the earthquake, because nothing has been repaired for the whole of its length. The aqueduct was also cut in L. 79, where it arrives at L. 83; large reservoir 71 from Period III could thus no longer be supplied: this confirms that the earthquake struck an abandoned site. The most surprising thing is that de Vaux himself notes that the aqueduct was broken at the place where the earthquake caused the widest fault, where masonry has been swallowed up, at L. 72: *We find the earthquake fault, breaking a bare floor such as the one in locus 73* (3/31/1954, L. 72) *and an indication that the principal channel was cut by the earthquake, which put everything's in the balance again* (1/4/54, L. 72). The decommissioning of the hydraulic system confirms definitively that the earthquake is subsequent to the abandonment. From the words used – that such an archaeological fact "raises many questions" – we may infer an implied admission that everything is called

fig. 9. Faults 1 and 1a of the earthquake in Locus 145. The upper layers of ash, the latest ones, have flowed into the crevice (2002)

into question again. Now, confronted with the evidence, de Vaux decided against reconstructing his chronology. Was he intending to do so in the ten remaining years of his life? We do not know.

We suppose so, as there was clearly too much imprecision. The excavations showed that the ruins bear the marks of numerous incidences of damage. There can be little doubt that the fall of the ceiling of L. 86, attributed to the earthquake of 31 BC, occurred in 68. There are not two separate collapses during this period, just one. The ceiling did not fall in twice. The internal structure of the tower collapsed in 68. Furthermore, Coüasnon's *Plan* still has the tower in active use in Period III, after 68. This is an illogical sequence. If there had been restorations after 68, then the collapse he describes would have been cleared. Even after sensing that the rupture of the aqueduct meant that the destruction occurred later, after Period II, he did not settle the matter. All these hesitations suggest that de Vaux himself had sensed that the argument of the earthquake of 31 BC had collapsed.

The rupture of the aqueduct was sufficient to negate the earthquake and all the consequences that ensued from it. The works conducted at Qumran by the Israeli army in the Territories in the first decade of the 21st century produced further evidence. The space excavated at the east of the establishment permitted us to see at a glance the east-west sections still in place in the eastern path (fig. 9). A stripping of the surface laid bare the virgin floor, burst open by the earthquake by two parallel faults, and over a long distance. In section, the blankets of ash on the surface had run to fill in the crevices. This was irrefutable proof that the earthquake was subsequent to the latest occupation of Qumran (see comments on L. 72 and L. 73). On the extensive paving which borders the settlement to the south, the published aerial photography[1] shows two lines of fracture in the paving: the one in the east corresponds to the crack which split L. 72 and L. 73 and L. 48 and L. 49. If the destructions that struck the site were caused by the earthquake, then we may even doubt that the site was destroyed in 68. It may just have been abandoned. And why not after the time when the Roman squad camped there? Our Level 4, Period III, could be pushed even further back.

In need of episodes and outstanding facts to fit out his account, de Vaux promoted the formula earthquake–fire–exile. He stifled his doubts and bet on probabilities. Was the earth tremor accompanied by a fire? *Seats of fires were ignited; it is not surprising that the earthquake set off a fire and no testimony from the archaeology contradicts this solution. (L'archéologie, p. 17 and 18). Nor does any testimony confirm it, however. (...) if I admit that the fire coincided with the earthquake of 31 BC, that is because this solution is the simplest one ... (ibid., p. 18).* How did hesitation turn into certainty? With the earthquake discounted, there remains the fire. Earthquake and fire would have caused the inhabitants to flee. The facts are blurred, we may repeat, when, without an earthquake but with a fire that it is difficult to situate in time, nothing points to an abandonment. De Vaux was not unaware of the weak points in his argument: *All this assumes an abandonment, for it is very unlikely, as has been proposed, that some of the inhabitants will have continued to live there (...) camping in the ruins (ibid., p. 19).* He is preoccupied once again with the reasons for the abandonment and with those for the return, which would probably need to be sought in external events.

The abandonment of the building between Periods I and II raises a more important and more difficult question. Why did the community wait for about thirty years to repair the building burnt out by the earthquake? There is only one answer: it is because they had no need of it (...). Only, it is difficult to believe that they left because of this earthquake: the latter could not forcibly exile people living in tents and huts or the cliff caves. The most likely scenario is that the community had already left in 31 BC and that the earthquake burned down an empty building. (...) Archaeology will no doubt never tell us why the community deserted the Qumran site for 30 or 40 years. But the texts that are dependent on it ... (RB 61, 1954, p. 234-235). Archaeology may tell us why the community, or rather the inhabitants, never left.

The only argument de Vaux could use in support of exile and abandonment rests on numismatics, on the inadequately small number of Herodian coins, just a dozen of them, suggesting that *this dating is only probable but if one accepts it [i.e., that the Herodian coins found at Qumran would not have been in circulation before the year 30], these coins no longer belong to Period Ib (L'archéologie, p. 18);* or *they may have been brought in at the time of the reoccupation* (the return) *(ibid., p. 19).*

De Vaux hesitated because, in his view, things were not immediately clear: *One might wonder whether the earthquake and the fire were exactly contemporaneous.*

---

1. Yitzhak MAGEN, Yuval PELEG, *Back to Qumran. Final Report (1993-2004)*, Jerusalem, 2018, JSP 18, p. 47, fig. 51.

At first I thought the earthquake had affected an already destroyed and abandoned building. I then abandoned this solution ... (*L'archéologie*, p. 17). The remark that the earthquake had affected *an already destroyed and abandoned building* was pertinent. We would salute the talent of the archaeologist, whose intuition was right, and regret that the historian took it away: the date 31 BC offered him a windfall prop for his interpretation, and he did not turn it down. This was the pivot for his chronology, fixing an abandonment with "before" and "after" levels. A kind of logic had led him to exploit the events that he had so intelligently reformulated. Finally, it gave him an opportunity to slip an exile into the narrative. For him the exile in Damascus, one of the main points, politically and religiously, in the account of the Essenes, had to have left its mark on the ruins.

At this point, with no earthquake and no fire, and no reason to leave Qumran, has the exile become a blockage in the interpretation that we are trying to reshape? It would be easy to say no more about it. We shall not, however, hide our concern to examine an argument that would better connect the Qumran site to the question of the Essenes. The exile in Damascus is a key moment in the Essene story, and now that we have reduced the archaeological and Qumranic reasons for an exile, the difficulty mounts. However, we believe a compromise is possible.

The exile occurred in Damascus, or more precisely *the land of Damascus*. The location of the *Damascus* in question has been the subject of various proposals: The Babylon candidate only had literary links in its favor; the Syrian metropolis was not really a credible candidate, separation from Judaea not necessitating such a distance, and the Essene way of life as sketched in the Damascus Document not seeming very compatible with urban life; furthermore, *Damascus* did not live in tents. An allegorical Damascus opened the field by scattering the topographic possibilities. But Damascus, a capital city, is Damascus, and the solution opened by historical geography is more promising. In a short but well-argued article, Robert North defends its legitimacy[2]. The logic of separation requires that *Damascus* should not be too far from Qumran. In itself, the meaning of this exile does not imply a destination to which one flees, but rather a displacement, a distancing, a separation. Here, we meet the movement that makes a sect, in the true sense of the word. The proposal, currently without adherents, that Damascus is simply Qumran was supported by some authors, and at least one point by de Vaux himself; a religious group "separated" from Jerusalem, and Qumran sufficed geographically to be Damascus, by a loose attachment of the north of the Dead Sea to the Nabataean Kingdom (fig. 10).

The geopolitical context of the period may help to pin this down. In 87 BC, Damascus had fallen to Nabataean attacks and its protection had been more or less tolerated by Rome. Damascus, Bostra, Petra and Hegra formed a kingdom, and the economic and political preeminence of Damascus over Petra may explain the fact that Transjordan, a crossroads for caravaneers, was included in the formula *land of Damascus* because it was dependent on Damascus. It was conceivable that the northern part of the Dead Sea would have been included in such a political entity. Those who supposed that it would have included Qumran in its territory relied on the fact that for a time this zone presented a *de facto* unity with Jericho, En-Gedi, Machaerus and Livias. The supposition relied on this argument to place Qumran within the ambit of Damascus and to favor the assimilation of Qumran with Damascus. It has not been adopted. What we take from this is that the small territory around Qumran is of sufficient size for the events that we suppose to have taken place there. Surely, one of the most suitable places to separate from Jerusalem or from Qumran would have been simply the eastern shores of the Dead Sea, which had the advantage of leaving the Holy Land without leaving it too far behind? Perhaps we should take *exile* this way; after all, doesn't going into exile mean first and foremost *to have left*? To go into exile you have at least to exit.

The opposite bank was just a stone's throw from Qumran. A few hours away, directly opposite, ez-Zara/Callirrhoe was a wharf, converted and embellished by Herod. Navigation on the Dead Sea, which is well attested, was the most common means of travel along the maritime basin, the land circulation of which was cut by the mountain peaks. The palm groves and gardens, which are still at ez-Zara today, were the eastern copy of the palm grove of Qumran, adapted to the agricultural vocation of the Essenes, and an area surrounded by *erubim* like at Qumran. No site is more like Qumran than ez-Zara. We would go as far as to say that they were twinned, two contexts of residence with palm grove mirrored east and west. The archaeological potential of ez-Zara revealed by the excavations is certainly Jewish, with furnishings identical to those

---

2. Robert NORTH, "The Damascus of Qumran Geography", *PEQ* 1955, p. 34-48.

of Jerusalem, ritual baths, Herodian coins, etc.[3] The Hasmonean fortress of Machaerus, rebuilt by Herod, was no more than three hours' march away. The sector was a Jewish base for Judaea in the orient. Graffiti by rebels from the Jewish War have been found in the ruins of Machaerus[4]. Beyond, at some distance on the Transjordanian plateau, there stretches the rich agricultural plain of Madaba, protected by the steppe. The region presented a refuge, close at hand, secure, and viable. The tents of the new alliance of the Damascus Document may be an echo of the camp of the exodus. The symbolic reference, "they live in camps according to the rule of the country ..." (CD VII, 6) may be based on the fact that Transjordan was precisely the land of the Saracens, hence the tents. And this is the meaning that Trajan was to retain in naming the *Provincia Arabia*, a meaning borrowed from the word *arab*: "nomad", or better, "somebody not living in permanent buildings". We might even dare to suggest that the "camp of tents" is a metaphorical phrase: The word "camp" may mean "those who joined have come together" in the country of tents, i.e. "on the eastern shore".

There at least we have the witness of archaeology. The question of chronology arises here. The Damascus Document has not been precisely dated, and it does not contain any reference that might link it firmly to the chronology. Discussions about situating the Document before or after 31 have no further relevance to the present issue. The abandonment confirmed its composition before 31, while a post-31 date of composition weakened the Essenism of Qumran. Without abandonment, the chronological field is open, and we are free to return to the idea that we would like to promote: namely, that the sectarian settlement at Qumran came about progressively, and not before the year 100; that Qumran is not to be confused with *the* Essene community; that the establishment was one of the founding sites, halfway between Jerusalem and Machaerus; and that the two banks of the Dead Sea had maintained tight and organic links between them. The Document cannot be held as constitutive of the history of the Qumran site and may have been composed without any reference to Qumran, at any moment in the course of the first century BC. In our present context, it is more correct to speak of the *place* of exile with a timeless value, than of exile in the sense of a definite *time*, transferred from the time in Babylon.

The link we would like to strengthen between the two shores, by the expediency of a place of exile in close proximity, would confirm the Essene choice of the Dead Sea and more particularly its northern basin. The place taken by Qumran in this scheme finds itself reinforced in the pairing of a Judaean Qumran with a diaspora on the Transjordanian shore. Pilgrimage for Passover and the cemetery of a diaspora on Judaean soil harmoniously reinforce the Essene character of the site.

---

3. Christa CLAMER, *Fouilles archéologiques de 'Aïn ez-Zâra - Callirrhoé : villégiature hérodienne*, Beyrouth, 1997, p. 63ff.

4. Haggai MISGAV, "The Ostraca", in Győző Vörös, *Machaerus I*, Milan 2013, p. 259ff.

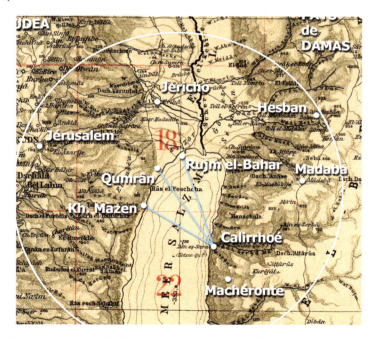

fig. 10. A possible Essene domain situated in the northern basin of the Dead Sea

fig. 11.   The long wall of the Qumran terrace viewed toward the south close to the *khirbeh*.

Chapter 2

The long walls of Qumran

Or the permanent limits of the camp of Deut 23.4 and CD I, 7-10; War II, 137

The different proposals for interpreting Qumran oblige us to choose between a secular reading and a religious reading. The secular reading, which is certainly legitimate, albeit possibly partisan, is in any case weak[5]. The sequence of arguments that lead us to opt for a society that is religious in character begins with the Jewish content of the manuscripts, which are linked to the Qumran site by the morphology of the jar and the palaeography of the graffiti found there[6]. The archaeological site offers facilities and systems that are not forbidden to link with religious customs in the absence of another compelling reason. The site needs to be viewed in the context of its immediate environment. It possesses a cemetery which has little point if the communitarian character of the establishment is impugned. The Qumran site is attached to long walls which remain inexplicable, unless one sees them as traces of the constitution of a closed domain, delimited by literal *erubim*, marking a town boundary. We shall see that some vestiges of the two sites around the Dead Sea, poorly explained by the excavators, may furnish us with useful comparisons.

Limits of a fictional town within its walls

In the sites of Qumran, Ain-Ghuweir and ez-Zara/Callirrhoe, the archaeologists have noted the existence of "long walls" for distances and a continuity that exceed the needs of agriculture. The most spectacular one is that which links Qumran with Ain-Feshkha, its construction extending to two and a half kilometers. The walls of Ain-Ghuweir and ez-Zara have been described. Some archaeologists' pronouncements about them have been more satisfactory than others. The different interpretations of these works have not produced agreement: such as to catch stones rolling down the mountain or to pen in cattle. They cannot have been land parcel divisions, and, without immediate neighbours, they certainly cannot mark territorial boundaries or cadastral properties. The comments de Vaux made about them are on the right track.

The long wall in the palm grove

The Hasmonaean residence of Qumran and the house of Ain-Feshkha, together with the palm grove, formed the same property. The house of Ain-Feshkha was a pavilion in the palm groves, on the bank of a perennial stream. It is true that its water is increasingly bitter, but it is still potable and it quenches the thirst if nothing else is available. Not long ago we saw herds of goats drinking there. To add to the pleasures of the water, Ain-Feshkha made it possible to take regular ablutions, unlimited and all-year-round. For Qumran,

---

5. Yizhar HIRSCHFELD, *Qumran in Context, Reassessing the Archaeological Evidence*, Peabody 2004; Y. MAGEN, Y. PELEG, JSP 18, p. [130-135]; *Idem* "The Qumran Excavations 1993-2004: Preliminary Report", in Y. MAGEN, *Judea and Samaria. Researches and Discoveries*, Jerusalem, 2008, JSP 6, p. [401-406]; Norman GOLB, "The Qumran-Essene Hypothesis: A Fiction of Scholarship", *Christian Century* 109, 1992, p. 1138-1143.

6. André LEMAIRE, "Inscriptions et graffiti", *Qumrân*, Vol. II, 6, p. 341-388.

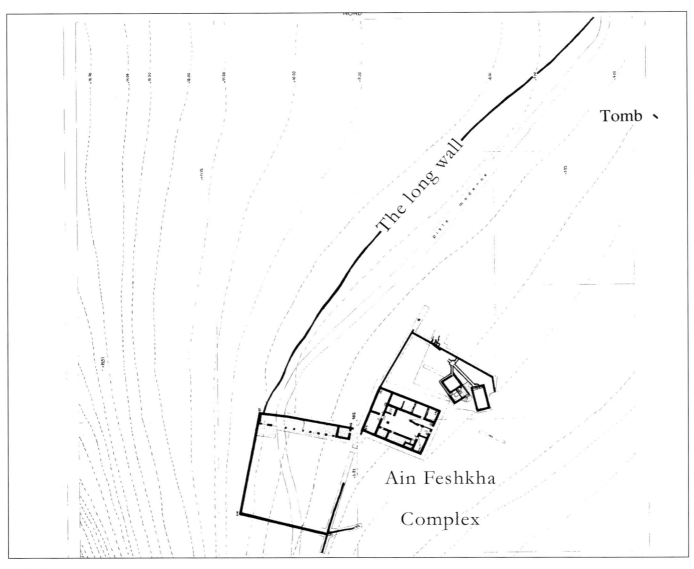

a) Coüasnon survey

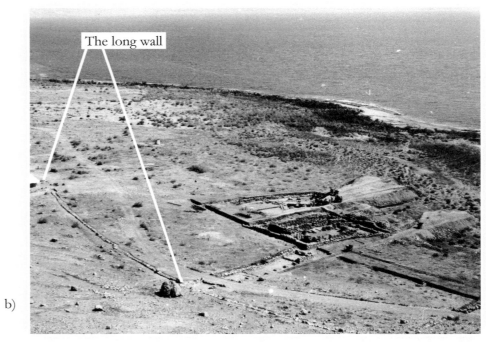

b)

fig. 12. Ain Feshkha with the long wall running towards the north

when water was scarce the spring will have been the best option. The journey on foot from Qumran to Ain-Feshkha takes little more than thirty minutes. Qumran has important cisterns when Ain-Feshkha has run out. The large capacity of the Qumran water tanks points to the needs of a society of considerable size; in a region where it rarely rains it is better to see these as storage facilities. Users in the past had to cope with cycles of drought. Some years the rains would have been insufficient to supply. At Qumran, water not stored in closed cisterns, poorly protected, will spoil in the long run. Ain-Feshkha, then, provided a constantly available supply. For all domestic needs and ritual baths, the spring would be indispensable at times. The two sites were therefore connected in terms of water consumption. As we see, they were linked by a long wall (fig. 12).

Five hundred metres away, de Vaux recognized a wall running in the coastal plain. He associated this with Ain-Feshkha, not connecting it with Qumran. He carefully describes the construction. It seems appropriate at this point to recall his notes:

The large wall is actually what is marked as canal on the English map, toward the south and to the east of the Ain-Feshkha road. It begins at around 300 m to the southwest of the khirbeh promontory and runs for about 500 m to the south, in a zigzag line with gaps.
We cleared it for 12 m, close to its northern extremity, at the point where to the east it backs on to an enclosure of 20 m from north to south and 8 m east to west. Here the wall is 50 m to the east of the Ain-Feshkha road. The stone is irregular, 0.90 by 1.10 m, placed on the gravel of the mountain, which is only about 25 cm below the present surface. On an adjusting course of small stones there is a course with two facings of large stones, generally set on edge on the western facing. It will not have been much higher as there are hardly any fallen stones in the vicinity. More to the south, the mode of construction is different: there is only one tier of very large stacked stones. It seems that the construction varies according to the elements of the zigzag. They can be interpreted as land boundaries or garden enclosures.
It is impossible to date and nothing points to its having been designed and constructed at one time. Some scattered sherds, very broken, belong to the Qumran phase. There is nothing else. Such a considerable work can only belong to a period of occupation of the region: Iron II or Qumran. But the construction of the Iron II walls at the khirbeh is different (thus the large north-south surrounding wall, if indeed it is Israelite). So this may indeed be a Qumran work (23/3/56)[7].

The wall is presented as a simple enclosure encircling orchards and gardens. De Vaux hesitated to attribute it to the Iron Age, an attribution which is untenable today anyway. He compared the mode of construction in large non-squared blocks with the enclosure walls or barriers attributed to the Iron Age in the Buqeia higher up then, significantly, along the wall of the Qumran promontory. The stonework of the Buqeia sites does not have a great deal in common with the walls we are dealing with, except for the utilization of large stones. On the other hand, the promontory wall leans from the *khirbeh* at a late angle, so it cannot go back to the Iron Age. De Vaux proposed not to extend the wall, in the palm grove as far as Ain-Feshkha, except at the time of the Essene occupation, for which no witness to the Iron Age has been collected. He concluded his note: *So this may indeed be a Qumran work*. He was right.

The wall in the palm grove is not homogeneous along its route. At a certain moment, masonry continues to have been erected between the two sites and by an economy of means, discontinuous elements will have been linked between them, which is revealed by the zigzag course. De Vaux suggested that the *canal* marked on an English map was the beginning of the wall downstream of *wadi* Qumran. Not much remains of these unprotected vestiges. Close to the *khirbeh*, the demands of modern life have eliminated all ancient vestiges; as for Ain-Feshkha, the asphalt main road has destroyed or buried the junction of the wall with the Feshkha building. From what we have observed, the structure has no rectilinear course, parallel to the shoreline; it will have bordered the palm grove. The masonry of the different segments is not always identical. Some parts are garden walls; in one location the structure in question may be the inner wall of a pool. We may have seen the "isolated" square building without recognizing it. At least once, we saw the masonry of large stones as bond stones like on the Qumran promontory, and which is to be found also at Ain-Feshkha, running in a northerly direction, uncovered for 48 m and attached to the northwest angle of the enclosing wall at L. 33. The long wall therefore constitutes a delimitation, isolating the cultivated parcels on

---

7. Roland de Vaux, *L'archéologie et les manuscrits de la Mer Morte*, Londres, 1961, p. 47-48; Jean-Baptiste Humbert, *Khirbet Qumrân et 'Aïn Feshkha*, vol. I, Fribourg, 1994, p. 367 and photo 531, p. 269.

a) Western ravine in 1951 (to the south)

b) Southern end of the long wall on the terrace, to the south

fig. 13. The ravine and the long wall of the terrace form a closed space the sea side. It has to be accepted that its construction testifies to efforts to associate them, to give them a topographic unity.

The masonry, in the same course of large blocks forming stacked bond stones, is not unique in the region. The best example, which has the advantage of proximity, is at ez-Zara, the ancient Callirrhoe of Herodian times, on the opposite bank of the Dead Sea. A semicircular wall extending for more than two kilometers follows the relief, inscribing the circle of greenery with its rest areas in the gardens and bordering the oasis on the mountain side. It is interrupted at points where torrents have carved out ravines; its function is neither defensive nor pastoral. It protects nothing, seeming indented at both ends, and both man and beast can breach it without effort. The wall was low, not higher than one meter, where it has not been destroyed. Here again, the construction is a surround. The scheme is repeated at Ain-Ghuweir, discovered by Ian Blake[8]. Ain-Ghuweir is the closest site of habitation, fifteen kilometers from Qumran. We found nothing of it, but the wall – not described – was identified for a length of 350 m, enough for a modest, scattered settlement[9]. Here again, the facilities extend between the wall and the sea. These walls have little other function than to isolate an inhabited zone from the shore.

The long wall of the promontory to the south of the khirbeh (fig. 11, fig. 13, and fig. 14)

With the façade of the buildings which it extends, the "long wall" of more than 100 m reveals a boundary of the site, bordering the eastern side of the promontory. It presents the specific mode of construction that we have described. Today, the wall has been broken down almost everywhere, except in the north, but the fallen blocks have not been plundered (non-inhabited sector). Here again, its height when reconstituted would not be more than a meter. It does not represent a defense; it is easily breached. We must accept that it is a delimitation.

---

8. Ian BLAKE, "Rivage occidental de la mer Morte", *RB* 73, 1966, p. 564-566.

9. Pesah BAR-ADON, "Another Settlement of the Judean Desert Sect at En el-Ghuweir, on the Shores of the Dead Sea", *ASOR* 227, 1997, p. 1-25.

At what point in time was it erected? The Hellenistic residence was extended to the east by a triangle formed by loci 44, 45, 61 and 84. It ends in the south, on the approaches to reservoir 71, exactly where the promontory wall extends it. The junction of the two constructions is not harmonious. The plan drawn up by Coüasnon would suggest that the eastern wall of the triangle meets up with an older promontory wall. Such is not the case: the point where one might see a connection between the two walls is in reality the underlying remains of an older corner. Coüasnon's *Plans* of Ib and II do not take this into account (fig. 54 and fig. 55). The direction of the wall that has disappeared is uncertain; it does not seem to correspond to the part of the loose stone paving (loci 93, 94, 98), the edging of which, with a drain, has been better cleared during recent excavations. The corner has been taken down to construct, or rather to extend, reservoir L. 71. The eastern triangle would be older than the reservoir, and the latter older than the promontory wall in question. The construction of the wall therefore belongs to the recent phases of the site. If its construction was part of a larger project, then such a project is late in the history of the site.

What was the reason for the construction of the long wall? The framework to the north of the *khirbeh* forms a bar, as if to block-off the promontory. The northern enclosure ends in a crater to the west. The precise functions of the wall and the enclosed space have not been formally demonstrated. We are sensitive to the fact that a piece of work like this, a barrier in an open field, "separates" or ensures a role of physical or moral protection which must on no account be confused with a defense. The establishment had subsided, folded in on itself as if to gather itself, and, with its massively reinforced tower, it may be thought to have been fortified. The promontory wall does not defend anything and depends on the *khirbeh*, which has joined up with the wall of the palm grove.

The long walls are extensions of Qumran. It is surprising that no thorough examination has been undertaken to understand the manner and reasons for the siting of the settlement in the immediate topographic context. The *khirbeh* occupies a position shifted toward the west, against the eastern ravine when, toward the east and the south, there was no lack of space. All the more so when Qumran was set up before the cemetery and the space it occupies to the east was still available. Then the site developed. Some scholars, including de Vaux, have tried to link

a) Long wall on the terrace, from the east

b) Long wall in its axis north-south, to the south

fig. 14.　　Long wall 951 bordering the terrace to the east

the transformation of the site to a sudden growth of "the community". The promontory that stretches to the south was an obvious place to augment community facilities, because of the topographic advantages it offered: an open field in a space of almost 4000 m² when the *khirbeh* takes up as much, finally defined by steep slopes or escarpments. The slope to the east, with bluffs to the west and south, gave it a natural unity. The wish to adapt the establishment to a numerous group would have led to first clearing the interior passageways and enlarging or multiplying the covered spaces. But, on the contrary, Qumran presents the paradox of a pointless concentration of development in a vast landscape, open and uninhabited. And the site stands to the west because the former Iron Age construction, probably an observation post, overlooked the eastern ravine. The promontory has not been developed: the "demographic push" is improbable and we need to look for another reason why the constructions were left aside. The occupation of the space has been maintained toward the west, and the additions that gradually modified the original site have joined the ravine. The northern enclosure is the connection between the settlement and the eastern ravine (see on L. 138).

From Qumran, access to the palm grove runs through the ravine. This is the most practical location path for leaving from Qumran to the palm grove and for coming back from Ain-Feshkha. The crossing of passageways is suggested by the situation of the ritual bath at L. 138 immediately at the entrance to the establishment (plate XI). The bath assumes repeated crossing by the ravine, starting close to door 702, positioned at the northwest of the constructions. The spot is at the intersection between the east-west pathway linking the Hyrcania with Qumran after crossing the cliff, and the north-south oriented road from Jericho to Ain-Feshkha. Door 702 was certainly one of Qumran's most used doors, at least in the last phase of the occupation, before 68. The objection might be raised that it looks like a service door, that it did not open internally onto a clearly defined space, that it is crossed by low walls and the water supply (L. 137, L. 132, L. 131), but the place has been modified in the course of the last occupations and has suffered from erosion more than elsewhere: the connection with the ravine has disappeared.

The gently sloping ravine separates the *khirbeh* from Caves 4Q, 5Q, and 10Q. The promontory, the settlement, the ravine, and the caves were connected, inhabited and frequented at the same time, and the whole complex was viewed as an entity. The two series of manuscript caves, 7Q to 9Q to the east and 4Q, 5Q and 10Q to the west, were not cavities isolated from one another, like those of the cliff; two millennia of erosion and probably repeated earthquakes have distorted the layout of underground galleries which were dug as shelters. Those who lived at Qumran used them as places of refuge or hiding places. The two shelters were part of the settlement, especially as the series in the east was only accessible by the *khirbeh*[10]. The whole thing was the top of a domain that was extended southwards, carefully delimited as far as the end of the palm grove. The different elements are linked without a break to create a continuous periphery. On the promontory, the long wall (1) is the first link in the chain of *erubim*, which is attached to the eastern front and the closed corner to the northeast of the establishment (2). In the east, the promontory wall clearly separates the cemetery off to the side, as the law demanded. The low wall of the north enclosure (3), L. 135 (wall 657), follows the edge up to the top of the ravine, the western slope of which (4), very steep, constitutes a natural line. The ravine falls into *wadi* Qumran, the bed (5) of which is flat at this point; either its thalweg was accepted as a natural boundary or an enclosure constructed on the south bank, carried away by later floods, rejoined the *canal* of the English map (6); the zigzag construction in the palm grove was attached to the corner of the workshops of Ain-Feshkha (7). The stream (8) from the source to the sea marked the southern boundary. The shoreline (9) closes the domain to the east, and the space is enclosed.

Enclosure segments of the settlement

At the risk of offending the secular theory, we must try to interpret the long walls of Qumran, Ain-Ghuweir and ez-Zara as enclosures, elements of a surrounding legal wall to meet religious obligations. Such surrounding walls have no defensive capability and cannot have been ramparts. They would have been ineffectual as cattle pens. Their purpose was not to retain stones rolling down the mountain as the stones do not roll to the Dead Sea more than elsewhere. It is noteworthy that the surrounding walls of Qumran, Ain-Ghuweir, and ez-Zara

---

10. J.-B. HUMBERT, "Cacher et se cacher à Qumrân: grottes et refuges", in Marcello FIDANZIO, *The Caves of Qumran*, Leiden, 2016, p. 34-63, see p. 58-61.

a) *Erubim* lining the Qumran complex. North extension opening onto the ravine lane

b) *Erubim* area separated from the cemeteries on the right by the long terrace wall (strong black line)

fig. 15.   The Qumran domain defined by the *erubim*

a) The ravine. In the background, the modern road has followed the contour of the old palm grove and the long wall towards Ain Feshkha.

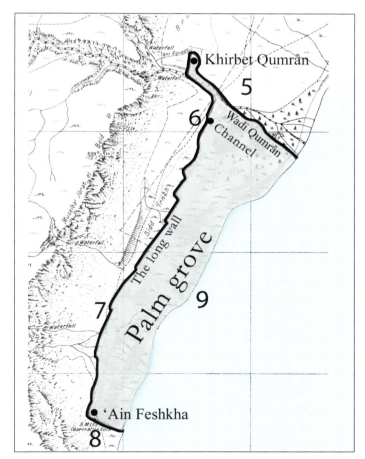

b) Extension of the erubim of the Qumran domain linked to Ain Feshkha.

fig. 16. The western ravine links Qumran to the palm grove to form the closed domain.

fig. 17. Plan and photographs of the long wall of ez-Zara, Transjordan bank
a) General plan of the palm grove of ez-Zara. *Archaeological excavations of Ain ez-Zara/Callirrhoe*, p. 9
b, c and d) Remains of the long wall in the eastern sector of the site
With the kind permission of C. Clamer

present an identical mode of masonry in large non-squared blocks as bond stones, and that their height, when preserved, does not exceed one metre; but later, the height of the walls of the talmudic *erubim* was fixed at ten *tefashim*, i.e. roughly one metre. One might object that Qumran Judaism is pre-talmudic and that the precepts of rabbinism are inadequate in the archaeological interpretation of the site. It remains the case, however, that rabbinic Judaism is not without its roots. And in the present context, if the proto-*erubim* were conceived at Qumran in the first century AD, it is difficult to see why the heights fixed for the walls would have noticeably changed one or two centuries later.

We propose surrounding Qumran with an extended enclosure, interpreting the long walls as a border wall connecting the sites to form a closed domain. The idea comes to us from present-day Jewish Jerusalem: a line stretched from post to post, marked by small suspended pennants, marks out visually the expansion of a fictional town within its walls. The Damascus Document allowed a thousand cubits' free movement inside a town during the Sabbath and festivals, whereas it was regulated outside the walls. It was obligatory for the area to be marked out. Qumran would have been considered as a town or rather as a camp, as the religious settlement had to be in a sanctified place. The whole complex, inhabitable and cultivated, formed a "domain" where one can find the camp of Deut 23:14 (cf. CD 10:7-10; *War* 2:137) with its internal coherence: "your camp must be holy" (Deut 23:15). The extended access to the Ain-Feshkha spring may have been the initial motive for its creation: inclusion of a running water source in the camp was probably a necessity in the last months of the dry season.

Do have we to accept to use the talmudic term *eruvim*? Should the Qumran enclosures be objected to because they would be anachronistic? Qumran predates the Talmud. But the facts are there. No example has been seen in Judea. The towns or other agglomerations stretched within boundaries that it was unnecessary to mark out or extend. We have proposed that others should be recognized. Masada constitutes a unit that is naturally defined by its steep relief, so it was unnecessary to mark its border. The long wall of Ain Ghuweir can scarcely have had another purpose than to indicate another domain. Ez-Zara is the most typical example with its semicircular precincts enclosing the palm grove and its rest areas next to the shoreline. There can be no doubt that its Herodian level was Jewish up to 68, the gardens of ez-Zara being the property of Machaerus (fig. 17).

The enclosed territories add consistency to the concept of the holy domain in reference to the camp of the Exodus, some examples of which are manifest in the Dead Sea basin (fig. 10). A unit of this kind is made credible by the *polis* mentioned by Dio Chrysostomos (see the note "cemetery"). This supports the idea that the Essenes were scattered along the banks, even if they were not the only ones living and cultivating the land there. And that, little by little, Qumran was able to become a community reference point, to which scattered cells would be attached around the Asphaltic Lake.

fig. 18.　　Locus 130, the block of ash in pool 173

Chapter 3

Ashes and traces of fire

Stratification and stratigraphy

The evolution of the Qumran site seems simple. As de Vaux has set it out, in broad terms, it forms a credible story which, fifty years later, deserves some adjustments. Reading the notes about the ashes and charcoal which he himself considered allows us to step back into the excavator's thought processes.

The witnesses to the fire randomly tap out the rhythm of time, presenting as many reference points to mark out the chronology:

1. Of the indistinct origins, there remains a stump from the Iron Age of the seventh century BC, without substance apart from a pottery oven which produced ashes.

2. Slight in substance, without trace of fire, in the last quarter of the second century BC, the Hasmonean occupation was a secondary residence, little used and then destroyed.

3. What we call Qumran is a re-founding, sectarian or otherwise, in the first century BC and most likely in the second half of that century. Activity there was noticeably intense and left traces of fire almost everywhere. It is probable that it came to an end in a destruction that took place in AD 68, possibly by fire.

4. A parlous restoration produced domestic ash.

The occupation of Qumran took place over a little more than a hundred years, between the middle of the century before and the middle of the century after the turn of the era. Layers of ash and carbon deposits are one of the archaeologists' keys to separating the levels and, where possible, matching them to history. De Vaux excavated them, recorded them in his notes, placed them in his chronology, and referred to them in his historical interpretation. It is appropriate to reexamine them without *a priori* attribution. The Qumran settlement was limited in duration, which is why the stratification there is quite scant *intra muros*: two levels only are preceded by an underlying occupation that it is difficult to distinguish. The ring of regular spoil outside the walls, on the other hand, has produced a stratified accumulation. Apart from the small trench at the northern foot of the tower, de Vaux did not have the time nor plans to probe the exterior of the ruins. He would have found a very useful sequence there. The argument for the earthquake of 31 BC as a reference point for the chronology has collapsed. With an earthquake that hit the site well after 68, we can abandon the destruction level of 31 BC, traces of a fire, and an abandonment. We needed to accept an occupation without jolts, as elsewhere, with only decelerations and accelerations of time. Finally, the fire of 68 is not proven either, which does not stop us supposing that the site was destroyed. It is just as easy to believe that it collapsed after having been deserted. We have dropped the periods of historical inspiration as de Vaux shaped them based on his reliance on inadequate argumentation.

All around the site, several more or less independent scatterings of ash were noted in the *Journal*. De Vaux interpreted them as ash produced by the cleaning of the burnt layers from the fire of 31 BC, when the

fig. 19. Examples of wood carbonized by slow combustion:
a) Locus 4, carbonized wood of the door
b) Tomb 17, carbonized wood of a coffin

fig. 20. Locus 35, fragments of a carbonized piece of furniture

a) Emptying the furnace against the foundation of staircase 223, Locus 13

b) Charred roof, slow combustion, Locus 51

fig. 21.   Ash deposit

exiles returned: ... *The same community that had left Khirbet Qumran came to resettle there. (...) they cleared up and made repairs (...) some rubble was taken to the north of the ruins on the slope of a ravine, where one of our A trenches found it. (...) other rubble was simply thrown outside the walls: it formed a pile at the foot of the north wall of the secondary building and the west wall of the same building. (...) however it was decided not to clear certain rooms which were under too much rubble ... L. 10 in the tower and L. 89 remains of 'the fire' of 31 BC in the 'small refectory* (L'*archéologie*, p. 19-20).

We shall pass over the fact that the earthquake did not take place. The excavator could have mentioned the evidence that the burning of light roofing could not have produced heaps of ash, and that the dumping of collapsed materials mixed with ash does not produce regular black and gray layers as we see them on the photographs (fig. 21b). Antiquity did not have much in the way of ecological concerns in the vicinity or surroundings of inhabited premises: there was an indoors, which was taken care of, and an outside, where one could throw things away. Ash was scattered as soon as one crossed the boundary walls. Ash thrown into the ravine in the west was washed away in the rains; it cannot have been in great quantities because the *khirbeh* lacked openings on this side. To the north, the presence of ash is complex; the rubble in trench A (north ravine) reveals layers of domestic refuse ash and daily broken pottery, nothing of which indicates the "clearing" of a ruin. Inside the walls, thick traces of repeated encampment have been found with a kitchen oven and scattered buried remains of meals. In front of the main entrance to the central building, ash deposits testify to the fact that the main gate area had become disused and people had repeatedly deposited other domestic ash waste there. To the east, there are multiple deposits of refuse: Iron Age potters had spread oven ash a short distance away; here too, settlement camps would plow-in meal left-overs; a quicklime oven, half-buried in the previous levels, left large quantities of black deposits, far enough away to be able to confirm that they had slid into the earthquake faults (fig. 24a). Finally, to the south, under the extensive gravelling and even under the buildings that were subsequently added, there are deposits of ash from Iron Age ovens; vestiges of leftovers from meals in the open air are also very numerous there.

What de Vaux calls "ash" (*cendre*) evidently relates to different materials or deposits. First, on his site, the archaeologist distinguishes ash that has been displaced from ash that had been preserved at the place in situ of the structure or the phenomenon which produced it. It is possible to distinguish ash that has been deposited from ash produced by an accident. The former results from flushings or spreadings, while the latter is found in hearths or burnt layers. The former is diffuse, the latter compact.

What he calls "charcoal" (*charbon*) is often confused with the result of slow combustion of organic material which has the appearance of charcoal without having been subjected to the effects of fire; a wooden frame that has collapsed without fire looks like charcoal in an excavation, a good example of this being the burnt rafters of L. 44 (fig. 22a and b). It is difficult to distinguish *a posteriori* between one and the other when the available archives are rudimentary, as nothing can substitute for observation *in situ*. The appearance of the collapse is more reliable when deciding between a fire and slow combustion following a collapse. A burning wooden frame fragments in a sudden fall; in an abandonment, the frame collapses in separate sections which are found in the position in which they fell. The minutes that we have inherited are thin in detail; the photographs can be a help.

The *Journal* notes the presence of several traces and vestiges of fire. L. 2 (26/11/51): *we reach a burnt layer*; L. 6 (12/12/51): *a fold in the east wall rests on a layer of ash (…), a transverse wall rests on a layer of ash from the lower level*; L. 8 (26/2/53) *ashes extend between the plaster and the west wall*; L. 13 (27/2/53) *we descend into a thick layer of ash* (fig. 21a); L. 14 (4/3/53): *spread on the lower level are dry and fine ashes*; L. 15 (18/3/53) *On the ground, ash, burnt wood (…). Many of the pots often burnt*; L. 17 (8/3/53): Black layer and ashes, and on 9/3 east of L. 17: *we descend to a level of ash*; L. 19 (8/3/53): *the socket filled with burnt wood*; L. 26 (14/3/53): *the walls of the locus are placed on a layer of ash*; L. 27 (14/3/53): *the fold of the north wall is placed on a thick layer of ash* and on 22/3/53: *the base of the ash level which is thicker here than anywhere else*; L. 30 (28/3/55): *the ash seems to run under the eastern wall* and on 30/3/55: *cleaning of the ash hole (…), the ash does not go deeper and penetrates only slightly under the wall.* – Comments: *beneath dump, burnt wood*; L. 32 (9/4/53): *the layer of destruction (…) has burned the stones of the west wall*; L. 38 (14/3/56): *beneath, ash and another floor (…), in these ashes, several Israelite sherds (and nothing else)*; L. 41 (14/3/56): *a new floor (…) with a layer of very hard ash*; L. 44 charred rafters, see fig. 22a and b; L. 51 (21/4/53): *there is a layer of burnt reeds* (fig. 23b, c et d; fig. 24c); L. 60 (25/2/54): *a burnt layer which roughly marks the ground* (L. 60.2); L. 61 (27/2/54): *all the walls (…) made of brick*

a) Locus 44

b) Locus 44

c) Locus 86

d) Locus 89

fig. 22. Fallen roofing

(...) rest on a layer of ash (L. 60.5); L. 62 (2/3/54): *under the floor which corresponds to the threshold of locus 43 (...) we reach an ash layer* (L. 62.3); L. 64 (1/3/54): *at the bottom, we reached a layer of ash and (3/3/54) a rectangular space, hollow, filled with ash* (phase 84.5); sub L. 66 (L. 178) (2/3/54): *this almost sterile layer rests on a level of ash*; L72 (4/3/54): *beneath [i.e., a wall with just one facing], a layer of ash*; L. 73 (4/3/54): *next to cistern 68 (...) stretches a layer of ash, 0.50 m thick* (fig. 23a); L. 77 (15/3/54): *two alignments of stones with ash: a hearth?*, on 16/3/54: *ash and burnt wood run underneath [the oven]* and on 23/3/54: *another coated floor deeper down, then ash. The layer of ash passes under wall 77*; L. 85 (23/3/54): *smashed pottery, mixed with ash and fire debris*; L. 86 (16/3/54): *a layer with a lot of ash*; (22/3/54) *remains of burnt joists* (fig. 22c and d); L. 101 (4/2/55): *the recess served (...) to accumulate the ash of a hearth (...) at the entrance to this recess, a base (...) covered by the ashes. On the base and above ashes* and on 6/2/55: *this tank (...), in the interior lie ashes*; L. 111 (12/2/55): *a semicircular partition (...) in the interior lie ashes*; L. 125 (24/2/55): *box room, the end of which was filled with ash. Yesterday's cinders do not seem the result of an ore*; L. 130 (26/2/55): *ashes and pottery appear*, on 28/2/55 *a thin layer of ashes and alluvium*, on 2/3/55: *all thrown away with the ashes*, on 3/3/55: *this ash rests on a bed of earth and pebbles (...), the pots of the sedimentary deposit seem to be from the same period as those of the ash*, on 13/3/55: *a little ash, some sherds* and on 26/3/55: *the hole with ash in the center of the plastered floor (...) pottery identical to that of the upper ash deposit*; L. 134 (13/3/55): *we continue to dig in the earth and ash*; L. 135 (7/3/55): *the ashy earth*, on 9/3/55: *brown and black ashes*, on 14/3/55: *in the ash where we find two coins* and on 15/3/55: *we complete the clearing in the ashes to the northeast and southeast*; L. 137 (9/3/55): *beneath [i.e., the wall] stretch ashes; at the north trench (5/4/55): layer of ash and spoil earth.*

Consequently, the layers and clumps of ash, at Qumran as well as elsewhere, have a variety of origins. The refuse from hearths or ovens, in regular or randomly scattered layers, has often been confused with the ash of a possible fire or the slow carbonization of fallen wood. De Vaux had attributed more or less scattered accumulations of ash to the layer of the fire following the earthquake of 31 BC. Ash and rubble outside the walls had been interpreted as thrown out during cleaning of the rooms on the return from exile. The argument is null and void, given proof that the earthquake was later than the abandonment of the site. First, it is not certain that an earthquake would cause a fire, especially in Antiquity. Conquerors set fire to a conquered town, but that is not an obligation, and an earthquake does not cause a fire other than in exceptional circumstances. Then we have to recognize that there is a lack of witnesses to a destruction of Qumran that de Vaux thought was more or less generalized, and the only firm witnesses are to a progressive collapse with, in some cases, a restoration. The alternation between construction, destruction, abandonment, and reconstruction is a chronological formula that is dear to archaeologists especially in the Middle East, and excavating at Qumran, de Vaux was keen to apply it to Tell el-Far'ah.

The deposits of ash to the east of the *khirbeh* are difficult to rank. Relationships between the layers are not always visible: organizing their sequence remains arbitrary in the absence of detailed observation. The stratigraphic position of the layers remains a guess: recent soundings show that the workers of the 1950s, clearing debris along the walls, and more precisely masonry sections 315 and 900, had broken the relationship of the layers with the construction (fig. 23b). The only option left to us is to restore them. The sondages soundings taken in the 2000s (Magen and Peleg), in the sections made in the east of the estate, exposed wide blankets of ash with charred lentils. This cannot have been the product of the evacuation of traces of the fire as de Vaux proposed, their repetitive spread representing a horizontal, thin, and ragged profile. The upper ash relates to the end of the occupation. The deep ash deposits associated with bone deposits mixed with pockets of ash that are difficult to match up with each other, precede the building of the east annexes. All these layers are divided here and there from the east wall of the settlement (W900), which has quite a low base and has interrupted them. In the absence of a stratigraphic section, one can only conjecture their position. The east and west deposits of deep ash, found here and there in wall 900, do not, at first sight, seem to be independent of each other. However, some observations lead us to distinguish between them. The clearing work conducted in 2000, precisely at the east of W900, exposed a stratification of the lowest levels[11], and the deep ash indicates the oldest occupation on the site: the bottom of the 2000 excavation corresponds to virgin soil. The oldest occupation antedates the Hasmonaean residence and we can assign it to the Iron Age.

We arrange the different series of ash in three elements, from bottom to top: 1) ash on the virgin soil, 2) ash associated with the burial of animal bones, 3) ash lying close to the surface.

---

11. View of the site during a courtesy visit.

a) Locus 73

b) Loci 62 and 153 (52-51)

c) Locus 35

d) Locus 35, detail

fig. 23. Spreading of ashes

1 – The deep ash is a result of spoil from the Iron Age, sherds from this period having been collected more in this sector[12]. The ash is spread towards the south and east. In L. 178 (sub-L. 66), two ovens arranged head-to-toe, an ancient arrangement, have in accordance with their morphology rightly been interpreted as pottery kilns. The layer of ash is revealed when we search the virgin soil of the marl terrace; so it is deep there, at the approach to the kilns, and it comes from them. In L. 73 (on 4/3/54), at a distance of less than three meters, *a layer of ash roughly 0.50 m thick (…) contains many Iron II sherds* allows us to it see as coming from kiln-cleaning. The mention *next to cistern 68* does not imply a pertinent association between spoil earth and cistern; the foundation trench for pool L. 68 was not identified. As the preference is for kilns to be installed outdoors, those that we call L. 317 and L. 318 are located under the residence and predate it. Only their base is preserved, the top part having been leveled during the construction of the large main building. In the open air, they belonged to an Iron Age settlement that is difficult to map out. The debris sealing the deep ash easily testifies to accumulation by erosion during five centuries of abandonment, before the year 100 BC, following the interruption of the occupation in the middle of the first millennium.

2 – The Journal mentions, in the eastern annexes, bone deposits in broken pots (fig. 18). They are identical to those of L. 130, L. 132, L. 135 and elsewhere in the site (L. 88, L. 93, L. 98) and their precise nature has given rise to polemic (see below footnotes number 14-18). In L. 130 they are described in a context of thick ash: they would have been buried where the fires prepared them. The association between "accumulation of bones" and "ash" constitutes a stratigraphic reference. In the eastern annexes: L. 65 (on 7/3/54): *many sheep (?) bones grouped with broken jars;* in L. 73 (on 4/3/54): *we uncover a group of animal bones in the pottery debris. Other animal bones in a jar under the Roman wall (...). Between loci 72 and 73;* in L. 80 (6/3/54): *many animal bones mixed with pottery.* In the contiguous L. 61, it is clearly noted with good reason, that the ash precedes the installation of the partitions: *All the walls are of brick on a bed of small pebbles. They are resting on a layer of ash* (27/2/54). We suspect that these ashes do not run under the walls but that they were cut when the walls were built. They still remain anterior. Finally, in L. 60 (27/2/54), de Vaux notes, usefully: *There must have been something there before the division into loci by the brick walls. An ancient level was encountered here.* The ash floor, like that of bivouacs, is placed before the restoration of the settlement, even in L. 143 (27/3/55): *Bones of a large animal mixed with sherds, but it is unclear whether this relates to an intentional burial.* The bones contained in the broken pottery are associated with lumps of ash which, in their entirety, are interspersed in stratigraphy and in the time between the spoil of the former kilns and the rejects from kilns L. 64 and L. 84.

The bone deposits are concentrated outside and at the foot of wall 315 which borders the central building and do not extend into L. 145 to the east of wall 900. In L. 73 a deposit skirts the southeast corner of the residence and drops under wall 852 of L. 77; the deposits extend toward the west as indications show in L. 92 (26/3/54). All the deposits predate the constructions which encircle the southeast corner where the bivouacs were established along the walls. We see the same arrangement in the deposits of L. 130, in the shade of north wall 401 of the western annexes. Here at least, the repeated burial of *"deposits"* took place in the early days of the reoccupation; the practice spread over time and it is impossible to say when it came to an end.

3 – At the end of the occupation of the site, two other kilns had been interpreted by de Vaux as pottery kilns, a large one (918, L. 64) for firing large pieces, and a small one (917, L. 84) for small pieces. Furnaces for pottery or the production of lime, as is common in the region, tended to be placed to the east of habitations, in the lee of the dominant west winds to avoid creating a nuisance. De Vaux notes that it was *impossible to find where failed firings were thrown* (L. 84 on 14/3/54). *Large kiln 918* is not a pottery kiln; elsewhere (see on L. 84 below) we explain that it needs to be viewed as a lime kiln; it has not been shown that the *small kiln* had been maintained on Level 4 (Period III). Some slag that de Vaux preserved without identifying it is added to that identified in the 2000 excavation to the east (L. 145), and it would be better to check that it is not all from the Iron Age (kiln 918). L. 84 produced two ash pockets in place and we hypothesize that the extended blankets of ash, close to the surface, are linked to kiln 918 which is assigned to the end of Level 3C. The scattering from these late kilns may be mixed with domestic waste from Level 4 (Period III). These are the "ashes" that slid into the earthquake faults. The accumulation of ashes in pool L. 72 provides an example of reverse stratigraphy. Drawn from the cleaning of the Iron Age kilns during the digging of pool L. 68, ash was thrown into disused L. 72. The

---

12. J.-B. HUMBERT, *Khirbet Qumrân et 'Aïn Feshkha*, vol. II, Fribourg, 2003, p. 468.

a) Earthquake fault, Locus 145

b) Ash deposit, Locus 20

c) Ash sealing the Locus 51

fig. 24. Evidence of ash or charcoal produced by slow combustion

accumulation in question should not be confused with a fire that would have put an end to Level 3C.

Two traces of probable fires were observed in L. 89 and L. . 44 (fig. 22). They may be the result of slow combustion. A layer of ash could seal the ruin of Level 3C. In L. 52, a black layer, never recorded or described, is visible on a photograph (fig. 23b). Relatively thick and spread regularly, the ash area would correspond to a fire or better to the slow combustion of plant material from the roof. Its extent is unknown. Having seen it, de Vaux did not take it into account; he might have considered and accepted it as subsequent to his earthquake of 31 BC as it interrupts occupation in the sector of the southeast quadrant of the residence during his Period Ib. We do take it into consideration: in our stratigraphic scheme, fire or no fire, it marks the destruction of the year 68 AD. The evidence to the end of Level 3C would be interspersed in the third group, so that we cannot decide between an end by fire and a simple abandonment. The signs of the final, brutal destruction are, now without any doubt, the effect of the post occupation earthquake.

fig. 25. Slaughtering of sheep at Qumran for the festive meal at the end of the excavation, 1956

Chapter 4

Buried animal deposits

Passover left-overs?

This subject seems very sensitive in Qumran studies, which is why we would like to avoid dealing superficially with a ritual which would require a thorough examination of the biblical texts and wider sources. One can accept this as a challenge, or one can forget about it. We appreciate the efforts of Y. Magen and Y. Peleg to release Qumran from its contradictions. However, they went ahead with the advantage of new excavations that they had conducted, which probably identified some loci whose investigation remained incomplete after 1956, but without adding anything to the archaeology of the whole and without responding to questions still pending. They left aside the religious character which the first interpretations considered essential. The imperative reinterpretation of Qumran as a commercial artisanal complex does not correspond to the poor economy of the site shown by the archaeology. One can of course ignore the manuscripts, which in one way or another constrain the site, and declare null and void its Judaic character, so that the questions no longer arise. John Strugnell repeated: "We started Qumran with simple ideas." De Vaux took care to advance, put out hypotheses and then refrained from going further. He was certainly on the right track. Magen and Peleg, trying to be helpful, came back to simple ideas. It is astonishing how they seduced or relieved a large number of researchers. The difficulties will return, as removing them does not solve them.

De Vaux collected all the data concerning the deposits. The synthesis of it he offered is valuable because he himself had supervised all the elements of the excavation[13]. The deposits were scattered in open areas around the covered buildings and, in most cases, around the perimeter of the residence and its outbuildings. One deposit was buried in L. 23 but outside, in the courtyard at the heart of the complex. Others collected *intra muros* had been interred on the periphery, i.e. under the walls of the residence in L. 73, L. 80, L. 90, and L. 92. They provide proof that the practice of burial preceded the addition of rooms that were not part of the original planning. A strong concentration was exhumed in the north enclosure L. 130, L. 131, L. 132, and L. 135. In fact, deposits were buried almost everywhere. The note published in *Revue Biblique* specifies: *A trench [...] of the large esplanade of the south encountered thirteen of these deposits and it seems certain that if we were to scour the esplanade we would find many more. [...] The excavation found animal bones deposited between the large shards of jars or pots, sometimes placed in intact pots or closed by their lids, and sometimes covered by a simple plate. In the majority of cases, the shards come from several jars or pots, to which fragments of one or several bowls, covers or plates were added* (translated from *RB* 63, 1956, p. 549) (figs. 26 and 27).

Initially the interpretation of the deposits seemed logical and simple. The identification of faunal remains was conducted by Professor F. Zeuner of London. De Vaux had acknowledged that the result was subject to a margin of uncertainty as Zeuner had assessed only 39 deposits. However, the whole renders an image that will not be too far from reality: Adult

---

13. R. de Vaux, "Fouilles de Khirbet Qumrân", *RB* 73, 1956, p. 548-549. Text repeated in *L'archéologie*, p. 10-11.

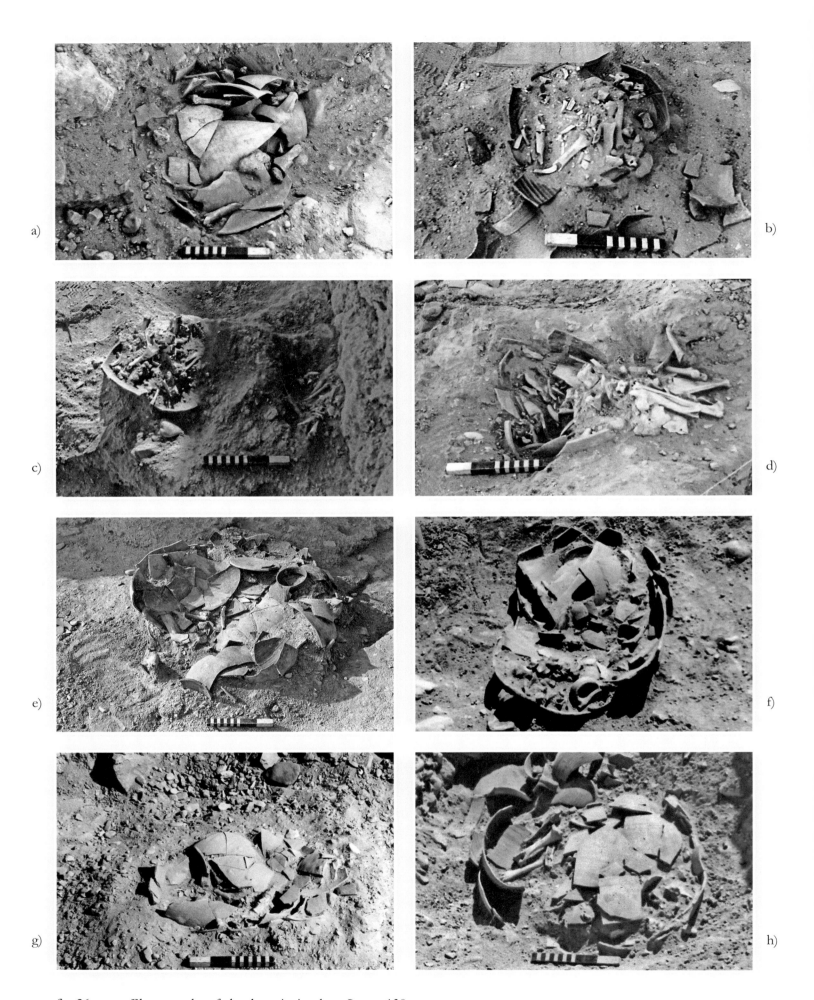

fig. 26. Photographs of the deposits in place, Locus 130

sheep 5, adult goats 5, sheep or goats without possible distinction 26, lambs or kids 10, cattle 6, cows or bulls 4, and one unidentified animal the size of a small cow (*L'archéologie*, p. 11). These can only be remains of meals. Since the Essene community of Qumran took meals *that had a religious character* (*L'archéologie*, p. 10), a degree of care was taken concerning waste : *the general principle of this custom is clear: this care with which the bones were set aside after the flesh had been cooked and eaten reveals a religious intent* (*L'archéologie*, p. 11). The animal evidence that emerged from the excavation was scattered and lost and we have to rely on the information from the preliminary reports: the ... *bones are clean and some are charred, which means that the meat was generally boiled and sometimes roasted. They represent only part of the waste collected in the refectory or the kitchen* (RB 63, 1956, p. 549). De Vaux accepts that, despite the important number of deposits which is well below the quantity of meal remains that two centuries of Essene settlement could have left. Meals that had a religious character would not have been everyday meals. For remnants that one would have liked not to despise, would it not have been better to throw them into a ditch close to the refectory rather than scattering the waste around the buildings and strewing them on the esplanade? The formula of the consecrated meal was simple, but he was unable to demonstrate it: *It is true that neither the Community Rule nor any other Qumran text alludes to this particular rite of bone deposits, and this lacuna is quite regrettable* (*L'archéologie*, p. 86). The question was adjourned and remained in abeyance.

Other proposals have been made. F. M. Cross thought the remains could be communion sacrifices[14], which de Vaux rejected as being not in compliance with Lev 7:17. E.-M. Laperrousaz, who took a keen interest in the question, reviewed some other opinions which de Vaux had again signaled and discarded. After attempting to understand how the meals were conducted, Laperrousaz proposed his own version of the facts: the deposits as a whole were the remains of a Pentecost meal that had been interrupted and hurriedly buried[15]. The proposal has not attracted support. The inclination to religious readings of the archaeology was an irritation, sometimes with a hint of annoyance: *The kind of absurdities scholars are forced into when faced with explaining perfectly straight-forward phenomena in the irrational terms of ritual*[16]. Magen and Peleg, among others, assume a decidedly lay interpretation of the archaeology of the site (*supra*, n. 13). The burial of the meal remains was intended only to protect the neighbourhood of Qumran from small predators and insects. One might wonder why the practice was not a habit elsewhere as well, and for the same reasons. Magen is right to recall that the sacrificial bones at Gerizim were "thrown over the wall" without fear of rats or flies, of which there would have been no lack[17]. Y. Hirschfeld, who excavated a rocky escarpment overhanging En-Gedi, saw huts there and thought it reasonable to accommodate some scattered Essenes there. He noted, pertinently, the remarkable absence of any bone remains, i.e. of "buried deposits" in the neighbourhood[18]. De Vaux did not note any in the Ain-Feshkha site. As Ain-Feshkha and Qumran were inhabited by the same society, like the En-Gedi escarpment possibly, the absence of deposits in the other sites questions the uniqueness of those of Qumran.

We proposed that the buried deposits were vestiges of the Passover celebrated by Jews (Essenes?) at Qumran and settled along the banks of the Dead Sea. We shall respond, if we may, to the objections that have been raised to this. That the bone deposits had a religious character has not been demonstrated; that they did not have such a character has not been demonstrated either. The fact itself is moot, and we need to take account of the unique context of Qumran. If the site was that of the Essenes, or of another Jewish sect, what would this tell us of the members who came to celebrate in such a remote spot? We know of a Jewish population around the Dead Sea on the eastern bank, particularly in the area of Machaerus. And why not, among them, people from Qumran? Now pious Jews had the habit at Passover of crossing River Jordan to the Holy Land in the west, as the eastern bank was not part of it. The ez-Zara excavations revealed patrician Herodian houses with Judean-style pottery. At a time when the Exodus was being remembered, Qumran would have been a chosen edge of the Promised Land at a convenient proximity to Jerusalem. The flesh of

---

14. Frank Moore Cross, *The Ancient Library of Qumrân and Modern Biblical Study,* 1958, p. 51-52, 76, cited by de Vaux in *L'archéologie*, p. 11.

15. Ernest-Marie Laperrousaz, *Qoumrân, l'établissement essénien des bords de la mer Morte. Histoire et archéologie du site,* Paris 1976, p. 218.

16. Y. Magen, Y. Peleg, "Back to Qumran. Ten Years of Excavations and Research, 1993-2004", in Katharina Galor, J.-B. Humbert and Jürgen Zangenberg, *The Site of the Dead Sea Scrolls, Archaeological Interpretations and Debates*, Leiden, 2006, p. 95.

17. Y. Magen, Y. Peleg, *Archaeological Interpretations,* p. 95-6; see also *Idem*, JSP 6, p. [396]; JSP 18, p. [127-129, 136].

18. Yizhar Hirschfeld, *Qumran in Context,* p. 238.

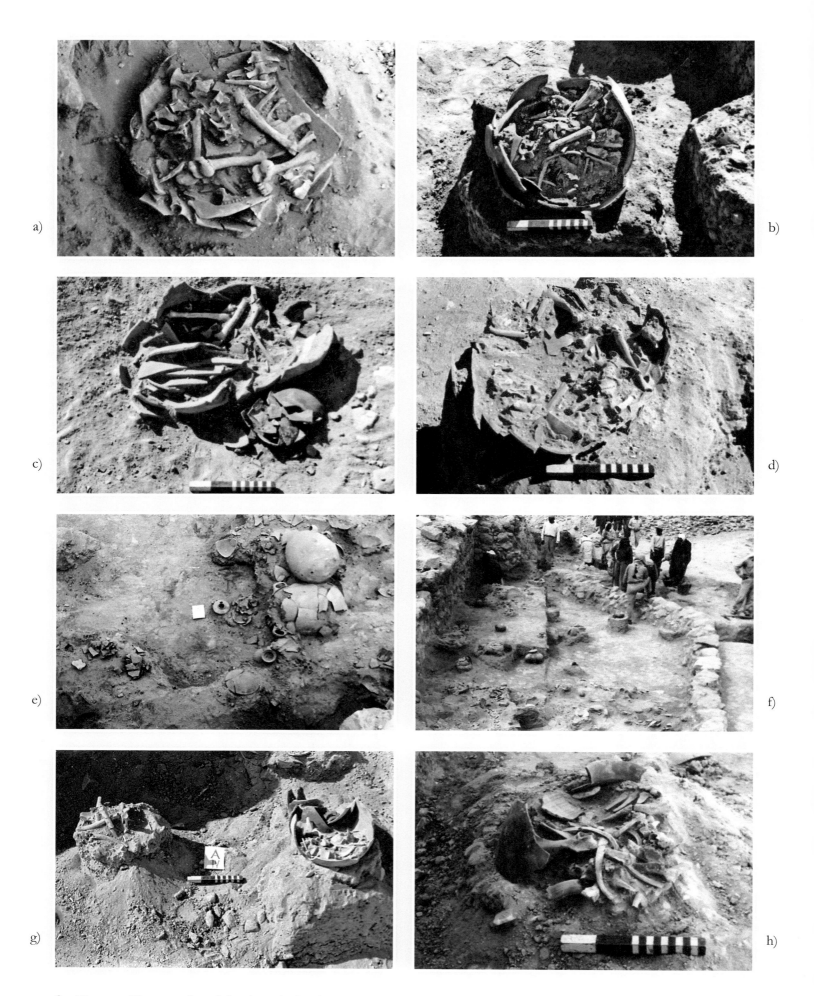

fig. 27. Photographs of the deposits in place, Locus 130

various animals, sometimes cooked, sometimes roasted, would surely, according to Zeuner, contradict the norm of a paschal lamb – was it the only meat tolerated? After the first and provisional identification of the fauna, we know that sheep and goat are certainly the majority in the deposits, but they are accompanied by livestock. We shall regard the data as indications of a religious anthropology diversified over time and according to region.

Arguments for and against the Passover hypothesis, and difficulties they raise.

The buried remains are identical in L. 130, L. 131, L. 132 and L. 135, and contemporary with numerous others revealed to the east and south of the *khirbeh*. A meal took place here repeatedly, and the remains are those of a meal in the open air. The oil lamps lying close to the deposits – at least seven of them in L. 130 – recall the paschal rite prescribed at dusk. Locus 130, among others, gains real coherence from this. Passover had to be eaten "in one house and you shall not take any of the flesh outside the house" (Ex 12:46); "you shall not leave any of it over until morning (Ex 12:10); "they shall not leave any of it over until morning" (Num 9:12). The concentration of deposits could be complying with the command not to scatter the remains, and to the need to bury them on site, at night, before sunrise. In the collection of pottery, the excavators selected whole pots or in a complete form, and characteristic shards. Numerous shards were not kept, churned up again and scattered by the repeated digging of new pits; they result from the numerous disturbed deposits that were not considered to be such. We identify jars that go with the equipment of a varied kitchen: plates, dishes, goblets, bowls, jugs and of course numerous pots and even saucepans or frying pans, two handles of which are recorded. In 2Chr 35:13, Passover is served "in pots, cauldrons, and pans" And in the same quotation, we read clearly that the offerings are "sacred." The custom of burying would comply with Deut 16:4.

The Passover of Exodus (Ex 12:5), the foundation text, defined precise standards: "You may take it from the sheep or from the goats", and "do not eat any of it raw, or boiled in any way with water, but roasted – head, legs, and entrails – over the fire" (v. 9). Why roasted? It is not impossible that the purpose of the requirement to roast the lamb was, in the exceptional circumstances of Passover, to give it a meaning of holocaust. Other biblical passages diverge, tolerating livestock and possibly another manner of cooking. The Passover of the Deuteronomic code says: "You shall slaughter the Passover sacrifice from the flock and the herd" (Deut 16:2). The royal Passover of Josiah's reform unambiguously included small livestock – lambs, kids – and large livestock, cattle (2Chr 35:7). Passover was therefore celebrated, at least in some cases, with both small and large livestock. This leads us to conclude that the presence of some bovine bones in L. 130 does not militate against the validity of the Passover hypothesis.

The deposits were buried in yellow sediment, mixed with clumps of ash, and in the vicinity of the ash pile of L. 130.2. The ash is everywhere, and yet the *Journal* does not say that the bones, scattered or contained in pots, were burned. Zeuner, however, noted some burnt bones. Would it have contravened the prescription of Ex 12:9 if the meat of animals was prepared by any other means than roasting? Would this be an impediment to recognizing the meal as Passover? The alternative rests on a supple or a strict approach to the verb used, *bashal*, meaning simply "cook" in its literal meaning. In the passages Ex 12:9 and 2Chr 35:13, the order for Passover cooking, *ba-esh* would unequivocally mean "roast over the fire." On the other hand, the Passover of Deut 16:7 uses the verb *bashal* without further precision, and that of 2Kgs 23:21 refers back to Deut 16:7. We may infer that they presume another manner of cooking. The Brown-Driver-Briggs dictionary gives: n° 1, "boil", and the equivalent meaning: "cook," with reference to the Akkadian, "bashâlu". Explicitly: 1 – *boil*, (transitive)…, *of offering*, 2Chr 35:13, adding: 2 – cook (general) and for 2Chr 35:13 (*ba-esh*). The meaning "cook" is the only acceptable one.

The prescriptions stipulate that the bones must not be broken: "They shall not break a bone of it" (Num 9:12); "nor shall you break a bone of it" (Ex 12:46). De Vaux observed: *Mainly vertebrae, ribs and long bones, but several times jaws and fragments of skulls* (L. 130, 6/3/55). Skull fragments would be in line with Ex 12:9 which requires that the lamb be kept whole together with its head. Why, then, did the excavation find skull fragments? It is to be regretted that the collected remains of fauna are lost; those found by the excavation of 1993–2002 promise a precise examination, useful to complete the superficial observations made at the time. The few photographs of the unscattered deposits are the only resource for determining whether the bones were broken or not. First, it would not seem customary, in the past as today, to break the bones while consuming the meat, at least of small livestock. The commandment not to break the bones is linked to that which stipulates that they be buried, which of course relates to the remnants of the meal and not the way the meal itself was eaten. The photos show some incomplete bones but there is nothing to demonstrate that they were not fragmented after they had been buried, over time. The whole thing has the character of meat remnants collected in a vase, after the meal.

The assumption that Passover was celebrated at Qumran cannot be dismissed out of hand. Although it requires further precision, it at least has the advantage of pursuing in a reasonable way the answer to the buried deposits at the point where de Vaux had left it in the air. The stratigraphic incoherence of the deposits observed in L. 130 would logically indicate that the depositions were repeated in the same place over a long time. Here we would have an indication of the periodicity of Passover in the form of a pilgrimage. Passover recalled the entry into the Holy Land after crossing the Jordan. The return to the Holy Land from the eastern bank would have taken on the meaning of pilgrimage.

The objections raised by the quotations from the Old Testament reflect the contradictions of a Judaism without real unity and whose customs varied in space and time. The uniqueness of Essenism allows us to suspect variants in relation to the law and in practice.

fig. 28.   Buried deposit, Locus 130, large cooking pot KhQ. 2342 (Grid A4)

Appendix

On the bones in the pottery of locus 130

An attempted interpretation of a "buried deposit" according to a photographic document

Hervé Monchot

The subject of "buried deposits," which has not been given a definitive explanation, is sensitive and controversial. The phenomenon is repeated in a significant way: it may well contribute to the archaeological interpretation of the site. A thorough examination of the animal remains is needed, but those found in the course of the excavations have not been preserved[19]. Y. Magen, who directed the work at Qumran in the 2000s, exposed other deposits. Their preservation is an opportunity and their anticipated presentation will be of great interest. In our introduction we made an attempt at a methodological approach in line with the photographs of the site taken between 1951 and 1956.

Report

First, for the high period of the Near East, it is rare to find bones in the archaeological context that have been conserved in the pottery. Usually, available animal remains are found in the form of a more or less consistent mass comprising several types, and correspond to rejected waste from meals in the deposit zones of villages[20], i.e. thrown into disused rooms or cisterns[21], behind walls, or simply abandoned in pits or ravines[22]. Rarely, there may have been refuse pits[23] dug for the purpose, but the chalky nature of the region hardly allows such systems for a burial. We should also recall that the waste in principle takes account of the last occupation of the site. The bones are most often fragmented and seldom complete. Fractures are the result of several overlapping processes: (1) butchery techniques (quartering, dismemberment, defleshing, manner of cooking), then (2) post-deposition phenomena (compaction associated with the weight of sediments, trampling, climate-related alteration – weathering)[24] that started after the bones were thrown away, not to mention (3) excavation techniques which can cause numerous breakages.

---

19. "Animal bones are one of the most frequent finds during archaeological excavations. In earlier excavations they were usually discarded as archaeologists had little use for them, but in the last thirty years examination of animal bones has become a sophisticated science revealing significant information about the ways the ancient Israelites and their neighbors utilized domesticated animals" (MacDonald, 2008: 30)

20. for example Monchot 2013; Reich et al. 2015

21. Reese 1981; Monchot and Béarez, in press

22. Bar-Oz et al., 2007.

23. *Favissae*, ritual pits situated in the enclosure of temples of various ancient civilizations of the Mediterranean basin, can produce numerous cultic objects and animal bones, especially from the Bronze Age.

24. For more information on the taphonomic processes acting on the constitution of a faunal collection, the reader may refer to, among others, Lyman (1994) or Méniel (2008).

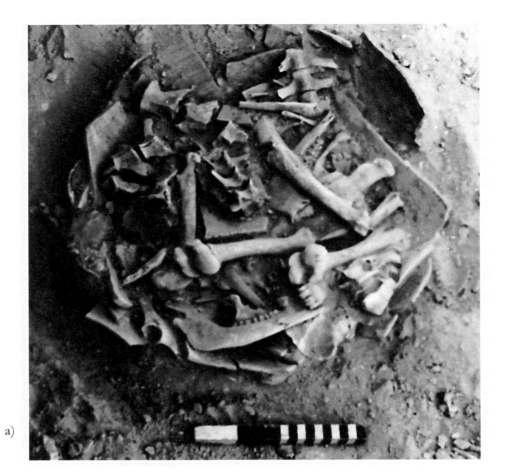

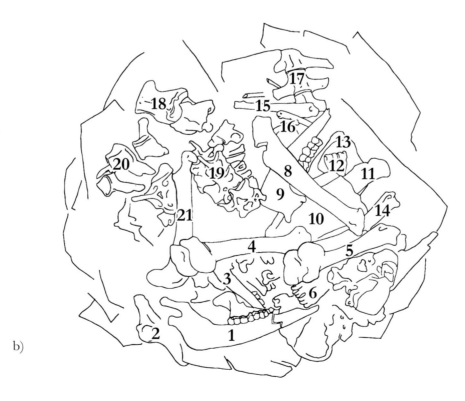

fig. 29.   a) Photograph of a buried deposit of Locus 130
         b) Identification of fauna

Bones still in natural conjunction are rarely found in an archaeological site and most often represent individuals which died naturally in situ, such as carnivores (cats, dogs et.) or animals left behind by humans when a site was abandoned, not consumed on account of illness or old age. However, entire animal skeletons can be found deposited in tombs (sacrificial activities) and exhumed during excavations, and be perfectly connected. We may take as an example the graves of dromedaries in the Emirates[25] or again the *favissae* of Bronze Age dog skeletons in Palestine (Tell Dor, Lachish, el-Yabneh etc.)[26].

Analysis of the photographs

The photographs clearly show a voluntary breakage of pots either resulting from post-deposition factors such as trampling, or compaction associated with the weight of sediments. The alterations seemed to have affected the container more than the contents. Several items of osteological information may be drawn from the analysis of the photographs. The photograph (fig. 29a) is without question the one which provides the most information; several bones are recognizable in it.

All the bones belong to individuals of the size of caprines (sheep/goat)[27]. Thus we may distinguish:

(1) a complete mandible presenting a post-deposition fracture at the level of the diastema;

(2) the acetabular cavity of a hip-bone (certainly complete);

(3) a mandible;

(4) a complete humerus, the proximal epiphysis of which is not united, of an individual aged less than 30-40 months[28];

(5) an entire humerus;

(6) a united distal extremity of a metapod, an individual aged at least 30–36 months;

(7) various skull fragments;

(8) a complete and epiphyzed adult left radio-ulna;

(9) an entire mandible;

(10) a certainly complete scapula;

(11) a proximal tibia, certainly epiphyzed;

(12) a distal extremity of a cohesive metapod (individual aged at least 30–36 months);

(13) the axillary border of a scapula;

(14) a proximal extremity metatarsal;

(15) fragment of a tibia;

(16) a rib;

(17) three sub-complete lumbar vertebrae;

(18) an axis, first cervical vertebra followed by the section of cervicals C3 to C7, 19 and 20 – three sub-complete lumbar vertebrae;

(21) a complete femur.

The data suggest the presence of a minimum of two adult caprines (2 to 3 years old). The presence of the skull, mandibles, vertebral sections and of all the long anterior and posterior bones suggests that the remnants of the animals were deposited in the pots whole. Nonetheless, it is not possible from the photo to know whether the latter were deposited whole in the pot, in connection after consumption of the flesh, as a dislocation of the main bone regions has occurred with the disappearance of organic matter (ligaments), or whether the animal was deposited whole but in main quarters (head, trunk and limbs linked to the appropriate girdles). The modest size of the jars (fig. 158b) suggests that the individuals were not deposited whole without primary butchering in advance. Only a detailed examination of the surface of the bones in search of butchery marks or traces of cutting linked to the preparation of the carcass or at the time of the meal, can plead in favour of one of the two hypotheses. It is still probable that the pots

---

25. Mashkour 1997.

26. Ackerman-Liberman and Zalashik 2013.

27. Even with complete sets of bones, the sheep/goat distinction is not easy: In his study Zeuner was able to identify only 10 individuals (5 sheep and 5 goats) out of a total of 46 caprines.

28. For the average age of joints of long bones among caprines: Barone 1986: 70.

were broken and the animal quarters deposited whole on the large shards at the bottom of a hole, then covered by other shards, and finally covered with soil. The excavation journal says nothing about this and the photos show only deposits separated from their covers. Meal remnants had filled numerous pots, some of which are intact. The link with boiled cookery is clearly indicated.

Other bones may be recognized in other deposits of L. 130

A caprine mandible, a right astragal are very clearly recognizable on photo 26c. Several long bones are present but it is not possible to narrow down the nature of them.

Several bone deposits of the size of a caprine are recognizable in the photo (fig. 26d): a complete epiphyzed right (adult) humerus; a complete right radio-ulna; a whole right scapula; a left femur, the bone fixed in sediment seems intact; a left talus (astragalus). The right front paw seems complete.

On photo fig. 26h as well as photo fig. 26d, one notes the presence of a right caprine humerus, with missing proximal epiphysis (age less than 30–40 months) and a distal extremity of a cohesive metapod of a caprine, the bone appearing complete.

Several long bones, more or less complete, are discernible on the photographs (fig. 27b, c, d, and g). In (b) one can also observe the presence of ribs and vertebrae.

Finally, several bovid bones (caprine and indeed calf) recognizable on fig. 27h: a complete hip-bone; a left radius which seems complete; several (at least 5) sub-complete ribs; a train of thoracic vertebrae (3–4).

A rapid examination of some available photographs confirms Zeuner's preliminary results (1960–1961), namely that the pottery contained several bones of one, two, or even three individuals, essentially caprines (lambs and kids) deposited whole. Zeuner wonders about the fact that certain items of pottery offer few bones by individual, but we should not forget that they have suffered the horrors of wind and weather, which caused the breaking of the pottery and the dispersion of increasingly fragile bones. If photo fig. 158b shows relatively well-preserved pots, photos fig. 26c and d show a rupture of the pottery with displacement (expulsion) of the contents, which is then no longer "protected." All this supposes that the bones could have been placed in the receptacle without too much difficulty, although the diameter of the opening barely exceeds around 7–10 cm for jars etc., 15–20 cm for large pots.

Roasted meat, boiled meat – Treatment by fire induces a change of colour of the bone by modification of its internal structure. Bones thus showing traces of charring[29] underline the fact that they had been in contact with a flame, without the cause being indicated (i.e. mode of preparation of the food). In archaeological sites, charred bones are most frequently the result of cleaning of "discharges" by fire, more than of roasting.

The preparation of food on the basis of boiled and simmered meat, like stew or ragoût, is the most common form of preparation and most frequently mentioned by the biblical texts[30]. Several considerations may be made for this manner of cooking: (1) a whole animal is never used, the parts without flesh (head and sole of paws) of the animal are generally left aside before boiling; (2) there is a preference for using regions rich in bones (rib dish, shoulder etc.) by deboning the animal and then breaking the bones to put it into the pan. Finally (3), the marrow or grease issuing from the break of the bone becomes part of the composition of the stew. Moreover, braised meat was considered a quality dish[31]. We should remember that the meat of domestic animals was considered a luxury dish, rare and onerous, only served on special

---

29. In his note, Zeuner mentions the presence of traces of charring on several bones but gives no further details.

30. "Put the cauldron [on the fire], put it on, and then pour water into it. Collect in it the pieces [of meat], every choice piece, thigh and shoulder; fill it with the best cuts – take the best of the flock. Also pile the cuts under it; get it boiling briskly, and cook the cuts in it" (Ezekiel 24: 2-5).

31. "So Gideon went in and prepared a kid, and [baked] unleavened bread from an ephah of flour. He put the meat in a basket and poured the broth into a pot, and he brought them out to Him under the terebinth. As he presented them, the angel of God said to him, 'Take the meat and the unleavened bread, put them on yonder rock, and spill out the broth'." (Judges 6: 19-20).

occasions such as religious ceremonies[32]. Bones involved in this type of preparation are never in contact with fire, unlike roast meat where the extremities of limbs can be in contact with flame. With the exception of the paschal lamb, the roasting of meal is not one of the most widespread practices in this period. Finally, we should note that for long-term storage, meat could be smoked, dried or salted, always in accordance with the textual indications[33].

In conclusion, the fact that the bones were protected in pots and then quickly buried is exceptional and betrays a ritual, and it may indeed suggest the burning of the paschal lamb. Unlike in western Europe or Greece from Antiquity to the Middle Ages, remnants of ritual meals are practically unattested in Near Eastern archaeology for this period. At the very most, bones left from banquets or festive meals, i.e. of animals consumed during a festival of breaking a fast or the celebration of sacrifice among Muslims[34], or again during banquets in the Nabatean triclinia, were never separated but simply mixed with other kitchen waste.

---

32. Numerous passages in the Old Testament texts underline the fact that among Semites domestic animal sacrifice is not a common act in nutrition, and that the latter is, rather, reserved for special occasions or cases of famine. Numerous references and citations in MACDONALD, 2008.

33. BOROWSKI 2003; MACDONALD 2008: 32-34

34. CHAIX and SIDI MAAMAR 1992.

Bibliography

ACKERMAN-LIEBERMAN P., ZALASHIK R., 2013. *A Jew's Best Friend? The Image of the Dog Throughout Jewish History*. Brighton.

BAR-OZ G., BOUCHNICK R., WEISS E., WEISSBROD L., LERNAU O., BAR-YOSEF MAYER D. E., REICH R., 2007. "Holy Garbage. A Quantitative Study of the City-Dump of Early Roman Period Jerusalem". *Levant*, 39: p. 1-12.

BARONE R. 1986. *Anatomie comparée des mammifères domestiques. Tome 1 Ostéologie*. Paris.

BOROWKI O. 2003. *Daily Life in Biblical Times*. Atlanta.

CHAIX L., SIDI MAAMAR H., 1992. "Voir et comparer la découpe des animaux en contexte rituel: Limites et perspectives d'une ethnoarchéozoologie," in: *Ethnoarchéologie: Justification, problèmes, limites. XIIe Rencontres Internationales d'archéologie et d'histoire d'Antibes*. Juan-Les-Pins: p. 269-291.

CHARLOUX G., BOUCHAUD C., DURAND C., MONCHOT H., THOMAS A. 2016, "Banqueting in a Northern Arabian Oasis: A Nabataean Triclinium at Dûmat al-Jandal, Saudi Arabia". *BASOR* 375, p. 13-34.

LYMAN R.L., 1994. *Vertebrate Taphonomy*. Cambridge.

MACDONALD N., 2008. *What Did the Ancient Israelites Eat? Diet in Biblical Times*. Grand Rapids.

MASHKOUR M., 1997. "The Funeral Rites at Mleiha (Sharja-U.A.E.). The Camelid Graves". *Anthropozoologica* 25-26: p. 725-736.

MÉNIEL P., 2008. *Manuel d'archéozoologie funéraire et sacrificielle. Age du Fer*. Gollion (CH).

MONCHOT H., 2013. "Quid novum ad mensam hodie. Food habits in a Roman mansio (Khirbet es-Samra, Jordan)", XIe Meeting de l'ASWA: "Archaeozoology of Southwestern Asia and Adjacent Areas" (Bones & Identity. Reconstructing social and cultural landscapes in the Archaeozoology of Southwest Asia), Université d'Haïfa, Israël

MONCHOT H., 2015. Food Waste or Banquet Leftovers? Archaeozoology of Bone Remains from the Qasr al-Bint and the Obodas Chapel, Petra. Workshop "Offerings to gods, offerings to men. Archaeology of rituals in the Nabataean world", organized by C. Durand and L. Tholbecq, under the High Patronage of the Department of Antiquities of Jordan, IFPO Amman

MONCHOT H., BÉAREZ P., 2016. « Des ossements dans les citernes. Les exemples de Dharih (Jordanie) et de Qalhât (Oman) ». *Syria*, p. 339-352.

REICH R., BILLIG Y., HAKKER-ORION D., LERNAU O., 2015. "Faunal Remains from the 1994-1996 Excavations at the Temple Mount, Jerusalem". *'Atiqot* 80: p. 19-34.

REESE D.S., 1981. "Faunal Remains from Three Cisterns (1977.1, 1977.2, 1977.3)," in: HUMPHREY J.H. (ed.), *Excavations at Carthage 1977*, Kelsey Museum, University of Michigan, Ann Arbor: p. 191-258.

ZEUNER F. E. (1960-1961) "Notes on Qumran", *PEQ* 92: 27-30.

fig. 30. Arrangement of the display stand of Locus 77, viewed towards the east

Chapter 5

A first fruits offering rite

Proposal

Locus 86, divided and then sealed with its accumulation of pottery and systems of truncated pillars, identical in L. 86 and L. 77, raise a number of questions of whose importance de Vaux was unaware. He saw them as refectories, with a scullery where the crockery was stored; the idea followed from the Byzantine or medieval cenobitic image that asserted itself. The proposal is still often accepted because it strengthens a communitarian theory that since then has become obsolete. Magen and Peleg, rightly rejecting the idea of refectories, located the storage of a pottery workshop there[35]. Our two authors adopted a stance of radical antagonism to de Vaux, but with the same arbitrariness. Their prejudice in favour of secularism was a method for them, and their conclusions are tenuous. The arguments in favour of refectories are faulty. De Vaux put out the hypothesis that the two *loci* may have been meeting rooms, and we accept the principle of this. Magness and Pfann, proponents of the communitarian theory, maintained the function of dining room.

J. Magness opted for a refectory established upstairs above the hall after the earthquake, the pillars supporting the shaken structure of the building[36]. The distribution of spaces needs to be taken into account if one envisages walking around. The kitchen proposed by de Vaux, L. 38, is at the opposite side, in the north of the settlement, and there is no evidence that it was used as a kitchen. No room in the south could pass for a kitchen. Besides the fact that the earthquake did not take place, and that nothing in the construction proves the existence of an upper level, the idea of a communitarian dining room upstairs does not fit with ancient practice: collective agape meals took place on the ground floor – simply as a matter of convenience. Can one imagine the repeated circulation of a group in narrow stairwells? The *triclinia* always opened on the same level, the upper floors being reserved for the apartment. We might add that it would be neither logical nor practical to store crockery on the ground floor if the refectory were upstairs.

For his part, S. Pfann, having happily abandoned the hypothesis of pillars and opted from the existence of tables, unfortunately transposes the modern concept of a refectory with high tables onto an eastern and ancient arrangement. As he does not renounce the communitarian theory, he needs a refectory, and cannot see it in any other way. He proposed that the "pillars" were the feet of tables, the wooden top of which had disappeared[37]. This configuration is anachronistic. Study of the table in Antiquity goes beyond the compass of our proposal. However, we may recall that tables on which meals are eaten were not customary, at least before Late Antiquity. In the *triclinium* the tables were always sideboards to put plates, and the representations of banquets, funerary or otherwise, do not show guests seated "at table". The iconographic and literary documents that have come down to us report only the festive or funerary testimony of a

---

35. Y. MAGEN, Y. PELEG, JSP 18, p. [130-135]; JSP 6, p. [401-6]

36. Jodi MAGNESS, *The Archaeology of Qumran and the Dead Sea Scrolls,* Grand Rapids, 2002, p. 122.

37. Stephen PFANN, "A Table prepared in the Wilderness", *Archaeological Interpretations,* p. 167ff.

fig. 31. Display stand 872 of Locus 86.
a) At the time of its discovery, its top in the indentation of partition wall 873;
b) Locus 86 during the excavation, state of display stand 872 (photo Leo Boer, with the kind permission of the Leo Boer Archive, *Archaeology in the Land of Tells and Ruins*, Oxford 2014, p. 158)

minority aristocracy which it is inappropriate to introduce to Qumran. The *triclinium* is neither popular nor in daily use: it is used only for banquets. Suffice it to remember that in Antiquity the daily meal was always taken quickly and without ceremony, seated with one's back to the wall. The custom has been maintained to the present day in the traditional east, where the table is an unfamiliar piece of furniture. The dining room table requires more chairs, for which there is no reference. The beds or benches of *triclinia* are hardly common in an environment of agriculturalists or artisans, and above all, none of the facilities at Qumran suggests them. Finally, to believe that the adepts took their meals standing would confer on the latter a ritual aspect to which nothing points. It is possible that de Vaux thought they were such as a result of his communitarian interpretation, with a more or less liturgical course, evoked on the basis of late rites. That the Essene meal had a religious basis is not in doubt, and we can conceive of it without a particular rite. The rite can be expressed soberly and without expense.

At the axis of the length of L. 77 and L. 86, masonries were discovered and described as "pillars" supporting a roof that had supposedly been weakened by the earthquake of 31 BC (fig. 30). Their irregular position was an embarrassment to de Vaux and his comments are not persuasive. In *Archaeology*, he writes in relation to L. 77: *The western end remained uncovered, and the reason for not continuing the series of pillars throughout the whole length of the room appears to have been in order that the majority of those assembled might be able to see the president when he took his stand on this platform.* The explanation *to see the president* is without foundation. It is appropriate to verify that the two series of masonry did not have the function of support. The material of the bricks is not sufficiently compact. See his remarks on L. 77: *we can discern the traces of implantation of a rectangular brick pillar, plastered* (10/3/54) or on L. 86: *against the south wall (...) a pillar of plastered bricks* (16/3/54). The bricks contain a strong sandy temper (degreasant), without sufficient resistance to support a heavy superstructure. The masonry of the square section, well proportioned, with a carefully applied fine mortar, was put in place without foundation, directly on the ground. The hypotheses triggered the minds of the excavators: the interpretation of pillars entailed the hypothesis of an upper floor which no longer exists. It was still necessary to suppose that the whole length of the room had not merited supported, which is hardly logical. But without an upper floor the pillars are pointless. Setting aside the idea of a separate storey, as the width of L. 77 and L. 86 is no greater than that of most of the other *loci* of the site, the covering alone has no further need of such supports. The restoration of a roof would be simpler than the building of pillars cluttering the rooms.

As it is not a question of pillars, we are left with two series of full parallelepipeds, unconnected and isolated. Those of L. 77 had been leveled, but in L. 86 they had, we believe, conserved their original height at the moment of their discovery. It is to be regretted that they were restored almost immediately, but the photographs of the site provide valuable information as to their morphology. The pillars are of the same height and their top parts seem regular, flat, coated with mortar. We do not see why their upper part would have been removed when L. 89 was sealed (see Plate VIII). Between the two segments of wall 873 the top of the parallelepiped was laid bare. The photograph (fig. 31a) attests to the fact that the workers pulled up stones to examine the flat top of the pillar. It seems even flat, by the evidence it was sealed in that state when partition wall 873 was erected. We think parallelepiped 872 was intact, or rather complete (fig. 31). According to the available indications of altitude it is necessary to recreate a height of 90 cm.

The parallelepipeds occupy the space in accordance with an identical arrangement in L. 86 and 77 (see figs. of L. 86). In both cases, the one backing onto the far wall is opposite the entrance door. The other parallelepipeds were set in place in the axial line of the rooms. In both cases, a person would aim for what he was entering for. In both cases, a small wall saves the space that contains the back-to-back parallelepiped, and in L. 86 it contains the pile of pottery. Two aspects distinguish them, their dimensions and their orientation: L. 77 is oriented to the east and the smaller L. 86 to the south. The parallelepiped backing on to the far end of L. 86 had a top partly torn off; 872, at the centre of the locus, 90 cm high, offered a shelf just in hand reach, it is better to interpret it not as a table but as a cradle, a display shelf. We also note that L. 77 provided fragments of two pottery stands (tubular supports of fired earth, in fragments). They are common in the east from the earliest Antiquity for the presentation of offerings (see pottery plate at L. 77).

The arrangement as a whole leads one to surmise a particular function of the places, for which no explanation can be definitive. Having no parallel, it cannot

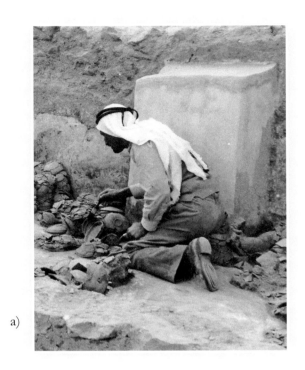

fig. 32. Display stands 871 and 872 in Locus 86, after restoration

be compared, and the archaeologist is reduced to conjecture. However, it is not prohibited to start some tracks. It is true that the interpretation of Qumran from a religious angle is the easy way. Between the entirely secular and the entirely religious there may be a middle term and the best thing is to accept that the two things were inseparable; in the societies of Antiquity, the religious was not yet extracted from secular life. Qumran suffers or profits, as it may be, from the shadow thrown by the manuscripts hidden nearby, and nothing can affirm that the site has nothing to do with the caves. The large manuscript pots in question, again entirely unparalleled, found in the caves and on the site, link them. Essene or not, Qumran is a place where religious people lived.

The fact that a paschal rite took place around the Qumran settlement does not grant it only a religious character intrinsic to the settlement. Its religious value applied not to the walls but to the pious activities conducted periodically. If we accept that the buried deposits are traces of a Passover pilgrimage, we may infer that one rite calls for another that the place should associate. Offerings had a predominant place in Jewish rites; sects obeyed the biblical prescriptions concerning first fruits and other offerings, even if it meant giving greater precision to the rubrics by making them more restrictive. The Essenes near Jerusalem "send votive offerings to the temple, but perform their own sacrifices" (Josephus, *Ant.* XVIII, 19). That the Qumran manuscripts codified offering sacrifices certainly reminds us that the rites were scrupulously observed[38]. We may legitimately hope to find some links to them.

Since the function of the parallelepipeds is in question, and so open to interpretation, we may conjecture a step, something organized, like the echo of a procedure around what looks more like display shelves than tables. It is not unreasonable either to reconstruct a gesture of offering. Some arguments permit us to place there a first fruits rite, even if we do not know how it would have been carried out around the display shelves. The circumstances are first favourable, as we have said, in the prolongation of the celebration of Passover in a designated place (Deut 16:11), in the context of a pilgrimage commemorating the entrance into the Promised Land (Ex 12:25) and the first consumption of its fruits (Lev 23:10). The rite brings the celebration of Passover to a conclusion with the offerings and possible sacrifices (Lev 23:12)[39]. Another element in favour of first fruits is the accumulation of pottery in L. 89. This cannot be refectory crockery. The composition of the range could suggest this with the hundreds of dishes, goblets, small plates, large bowls, jugs and storage pots, although the disparity in the number of each type hardly fits – we may note the surfeit of dishes compared with the rarity of goblets, although drinking was one of the constants of any meal. The small size of the plates does not make them items of table crockery either.

We recall that the refectory concept is anachronistic and that of a community *intra muros* on a Byzantine model is as well. The crockery of L. 89 may fit with a different use. The Qumran site, without being communitarian, was still a busy place, chosen by the riverside population to compensate for the absence of the temple (Deut 12:14) and to pursue the prescribed offerings "to establish His name" there (Deut 26:2). The occasion is the festival at the end of the harvest; the small plates presented grains of wheat, barley in the grain or threshed, baked loaves and flour mixed with oil (Lev 23:10-13), possibly leaven, salt, grains of incense; the dishes contained fruits of the earth, olives, dates, figs; and the goblets offered wine, malt, honey, oil, etc.; finally the bowls and the jars served as decanters and for storage.

If the rite of first fruits were recognized, it would complete the practices, celebration of Passover, diaspora cemetery which, reading between the lines, define a place of pilgrimage and assembly.

---

38. Robert A. KUGLER, "Rewriting Rubrics: Sacrifice and the Religion of Qumran," in *Religion in the Dead Sea Scrolls*, ed. John J. Collins and Robert A. Kugler, Grand Rapids 2000, p. 90–112.

39. See É. NODET for a discussion of this point: "Passover at Gilgal. From Joshua to Qumran and Jesus", *Orion Conference*, Jerusalem 2004.

a) Aerial view of the site and ruins of Qumran, looking west

b) The site is its cemetery

fig. 33.   The Qumran cemetery, aerial views
            (Jordan Air Force, Amman)

Chapter 6

The cemetery of Qumran

Of the community or of the sect?

Qumran is one of the rare Palestinian sites that have conserved a cemetery intact (fig. 35). It was unavoidable that de Vaux, champion of the community theory, should make it the domain of the dead of the sect that lived there. Because of their isolation in a thinly populated region, the site and the graves give the effect of a tightly gathered whole: without stepping back it was rational to attribute the cemetery to those who lived in the settlement. The excavators expected graves which, as far as possible, would recreate an anthropological resource. The portrait of the Qumranite was expected to be found in the cemetery. Funerary archaeology provides a wealth of information on the people when the sites have lost their lifeblood, and opening a grave was, in 1873, the reflex action of Clermont-Ganneau, the first explorer of Qumran. He was struck by the simplicity of the sepulchre.

Since then, the fifty or so buried graves have confirmed the repetition of the manner of interment and the bare character of the human remains. The rather disappointing result, less glorious than anticipated, did not impede investigation in various directions. It was thought it would be possible to draw indications from them on the purpose of the site, on its chronology and its establishment or on the numbers of the community. The morphology of the loculi seemed specific to Qumran society, understood as Essene. Today, costly analyses have set themselves the goal of establishing the DNA identity of the Qumranite, in the discreet hope of verifying a genetic link with one contemporary population or another. Given the elementary material of what was collected or observed, it seems the results have been over-estimated or over-exploited. Forcing the argument weakens the demonstration of it.

Even if he did not describe it in great detail, de Vaux had grasped the importance of the cemetery for strengthening the Essene character of the site[40]. The *Journal* (fig. 37) gives a brief technical description of each grave. His reading of the ruins translated his Essene version and the main cemetery was the funerary replica of it. The coherence he ascribed to the whole was such that he saw no reason to abandon it.

And yet the subject was far from exhausted. A recent western obstruction for the question of gender took over and caused a commotion. The scholars concerned by the subject thronged to the media. The serious academic was then embroiled in a crossfire of Anglo-Saxon erudition where quibbles and refinement no longer count; the subject remained without an object as the premise was false. That there were graves of men and women does not interfere in the Essene character of Qumran, and if there was debate, it needs to be shown that this was a false debate. De Vaux had opened the dossier in his day: he was surprised that a few remains of women should thwart the presupposition of a male cemetery. Women were there, an almost incontrovertible fact, first of all, and it is known that he hesitated, preferring ultimately to retrench behind the authority of the textual sources which, to tell the truth, made little mention of women.

---

40. *Qumrân Vol. I*, p. 346–352.

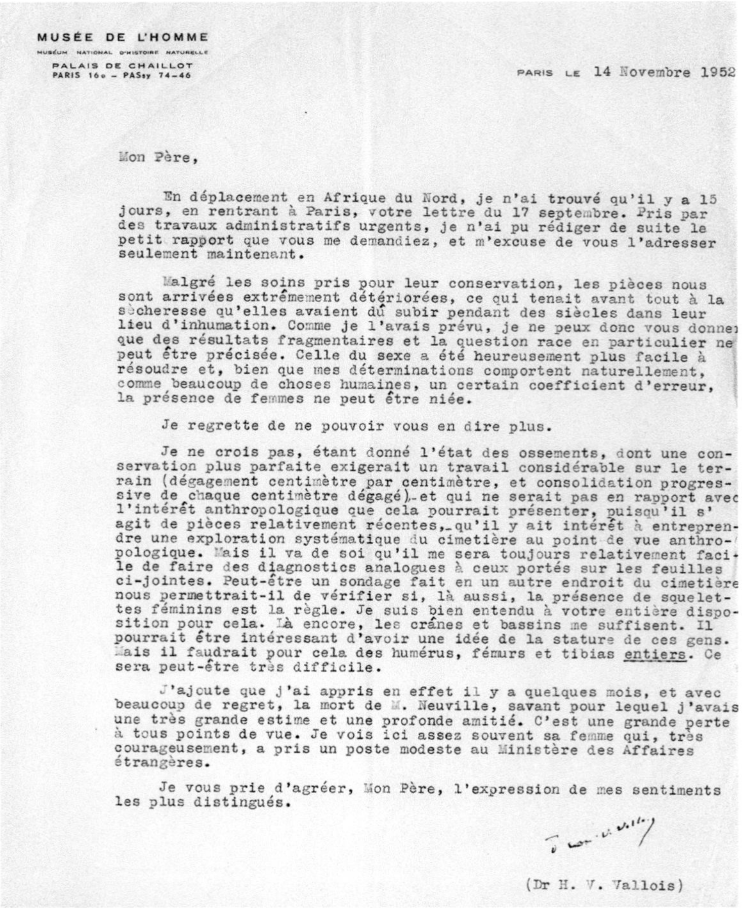

MUSÉE DE L'HOMME
MUSÉUM NATIONAL D'HISTOIRE NATURELLE
PALAIS DE CHAILLOT
PARIS 16e – PASsy 74-46

PARIS LE 14 Novembre 1952

Mon Père,

En déplacement en Afrique du Nord, je n'ai trouvé qu'il y a 15 jours, en rentrant à Paris, votre lettre du 17 septembre. Pris par des travaux administratifs urgents, je n'ai pu rédiger de suite le petit rapport que vous me demandiez, et m'excuse de vous l'adresser seulement maintenant.

Malgré les soins pris pour leur conservation, les pièces nous sont arrivées extrêmement détériorées, ce qui tenait avant tout à la sècheresse qu'elles avaient dû subir pendant des siècles dans leur lieu d'inhumation. Comme je l'avais prévu, je ne peux donc vous donner que des résultats fragmentaires et la question race en particulier ne peut être précisée. Celle du sexe a été heureusement plus facile à résoudre et, bien que mes déterminations comportent naturellement, comme beaucoup de choses humaines, un certain coefficient d'erreur, la présence de femmes ne peut être niée.

Je regrette de ne pouvoir vous en dire plus.

Je ne crois pas, étant donné l'état des ossements, dont une conservation plus parfaite exigerait un travail considérable sur le terrain (dégagement centimètre par centimètre, et consolidation progressive de chaque centimètre dégagé), et qui ne serait pas en rapport avec l'intérêt anthropologique que cela pourrait présenter, puisqu'il s'agit de pièces relativement récentes, qu'il y ait intérêt à entreprendre une exploration systématique du cimetière au point de vue anthropologique. Mais il va de soi qu'il me sera toujours relativement facile de faire des diagnostics analogues à ceux portés sur les feuilles ci-jointes. Peut-être un sondage fait en un autre endroit du cimetière nous permettrait-il de vérifier si, là aussi, la présence de squelettes féminins est la règle. Je suis bien entendu à votre entière disposition pour cela. Là encore, les crânes et bassins me suffisent. Il pourrait être intéressant d'avoir une idée de la stature de ces gens. Mais il faudrait pour cela des humérus, fémurs et tibias <u>entiers</u>. Ce sera peut-être très difficile.

J'ajoute que j'ai appris en effet il y a quelques mois, et avec beaucoup de regret, la mort de M. Neuville, savant pour lequel j'avais une très grande estime et une profonde amitié. C'est une grande perte à tous points de vue. Je vois ici assez souvent sa femme qui, très courageusement, a pris un poste modeste au Ministère des Affaires étrangères.

Je vous prie d'agréer, Mon Père, l'expression de mes sentiments les plus distingués.

(Dr H. V. Vallois)

a) Letter from H.V. Vallois

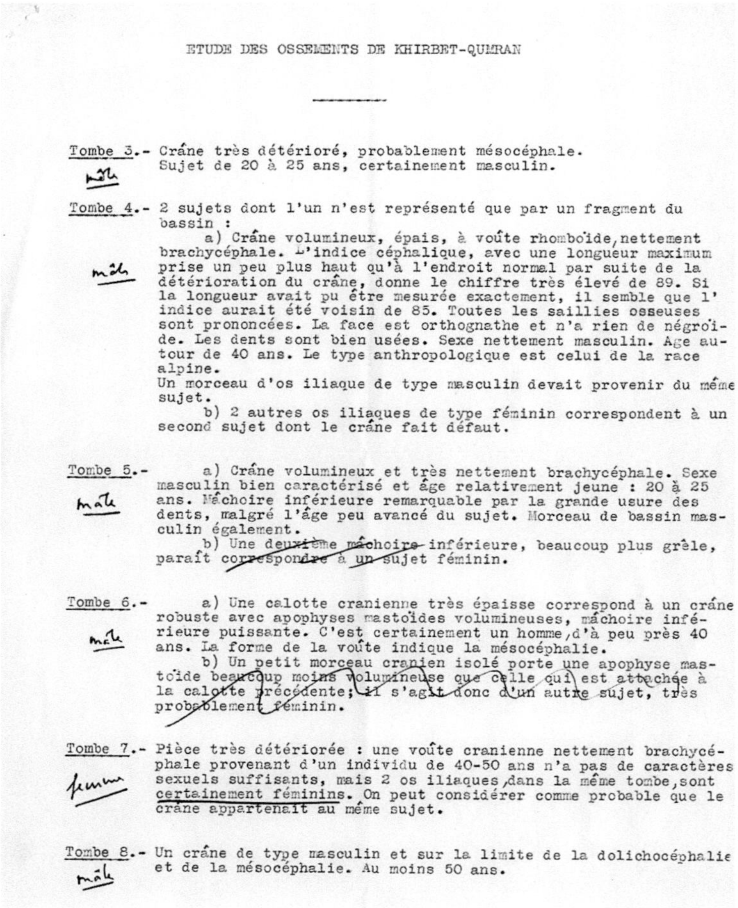

ETUDE DES OSSEMENTS DE KHIRBET-QUMRAN

Tombe 3.- Crâne très détérioré, probablement mésocéphale. Sujet de 20 à 25 ans, certainement masculin.

Tombe 4.- 2 sujets dont l'un n'est représenté que par un fragment du bassin :
a) Crâne volumineux, épais, à voûte rhomboïde, nettement brachycéphale. L'indice céphalique, avec une longueur maximum prise un peu plus haut qu'à l'endroit normal par suite de la détérioration du crâne, donne le chiffre très élevé de 89. Si la longueur avait pu être mesurée exactement, il semble que l'indice aurait été voisin de 85. Toutes les saillies osseuses sont prononcées. La face est orthognathe et n'a rien de négroïde. Les dents sont bien usées. Sexe nettement masculin. Age autour de 40 ans. Le type anthropologique est celui de la race alpine.
Un morceau d'os iliaque de type masculin devait provenir du même sujet.
b) 2 autres os iliaques de type féminin correspondent à un second sujet dont le crâne fait défaut.

Tombe 5.- a) Crâne volumineux et très nettement brachycéphale. Sexe masculin bien caractérisé et âge relativement jeune : 20 à 25 ans. Mâchoire inférieure remarquable par la grande usure des dents, malgré l'âge peu avancé du sujet. Morceau de bassin masculin également.
b) Une deuxième mâchoire inférieure, beaucoup plus grêle, paraît correspondre à un sujet féminin.

Tombe 6.- a) Une calotte cranienne très épaisse correspond à un crâne robuste avec apophyses mastoïdes volumineuses, mâchoire inférieure puissante. C'est certainement un homme, d'à peu près 40 ans. La forme de la voûte indique la mésocéphalie.
b) Un petit morceau cranien isolé porte une apophyse mastoïde beaucoup moins volumineuse que celle qui est attachée à la calotte précédente; il s'agit donc d'un autre sujet, très probablement féminin.

Tombe 7.- Pièce très détériorée : une voûte cranienne nettement brachycéphale provenant d'un individu de 40-50 ans n'a pas de caractères sexuels suffisants, mais 2 os iliaques, dans la même tombe, sont certainement féminins. On peut considérer comme probable que le crâne appartenait au même sujet.

Tombe 8.- Un crâne de type masculin et sur la limite de la dolichocéphalie et de la mésocéphalie. Au moins 50 ans.

fig. 34. Report of Henri V. Vallois, 14 November 1952. Musée de L'Homme, Paris.

b) Report by Professor Henri V. Vallois, 14 November 1952 Musée de L'Homme, Paris.

— 2 —

<u>Tombe 9</u>.- Débris très fragmentaires; on a cependant l'impression qu'il doit s'agir d'une femme (?).

femme ?

<u>Tombe 10</u>.- a) Crâne cérébral à peu près en bon état (le seul vraiment utilisable de toute la série). Sujet masculin de 40 ans à peu près, avec une voûte brachycéphale (indice céphalique : 82,1), une face large, un menton bien accusé. Le type est celui des brachycéphales arménoïdes.

mâle

b) A côté de la mandibule presque intacte du sujet précédent, une autre mâchoire inférieure très détériorée semble de type féminin, diagnostic que confirme l'existence d'un os iliaque de sexe féminin certain.

?

<u>Tombe 11</u>.- Une calotte cranienne, mésocéphale ou brachycéphale, et provenant d'un sujet de plus de 50 ans. Le sexe ne peut être précisé avec une certitude suffisante, mais il semble qu'on ait là un homme (?).

mâle ?

Conclusions

Les restes osseux examinés correspondent à 13 sujets, 7 hommes et 6 femmes, dont la répartition est la suivante :

Tombe 3 (Un homme, de 20 à 25 ans.

Tombe 4 (Un homme, autour de 40 ans.
(~~Une femme.~~

Tombe 5 (Un homme, de 20 à 25 ans.
(~~Une femme.~~

Tombe 6 (Un homme, autour de 40 ans.
(~~Une femme.~~

Tombe 7 (Une femme, de 40 à 50 ans.

Tombe 8 (Un homme, d'au moins 50 ans.

Tombe 9 (Une femme. ?

Tombe 10 (Un homme, de 40 ans.
(~~Une femme.~~

Tombe 11 (Un homme (?), de plus de 50 ans.

On notera à propos du tableau précédent :

1°- Qu'il ne paraît pas y avoir d'enfants. Cette absence ne peut cependant être certifiée. Les conditions de conservation des squelettes étaient très mauvaises et seuls les plus robustes ont résisté. C'est ainsi que, dans toutes les tombes, les squelettes féminins sont représentés

— 3 —

par des os plus fragmentaires et moins nombreux que les squelettes masculins. Il ne serait pas étonnant que les squelettes d'enfants, qui sont particulièrement fragiles, aient été totalement détruits. Il y a lieu toutefois de noter qu'aucune dent d'enfant n'a été trouvée. Or, les dents, dans l'ensemble, résistent à la destruction.

2°- Que l'âge relativement élevé (pour l'époque) de beaucoup des sujets et le nombre à peu près égal de sujets des deux sexes sont deux arguments qui parlent en faveur d'une population sédentaire et de vie telle que les hommes n'étaient pas exposés à mourir hors de chez eux (comme c'est le cas des populations guerrières par exemple).

3°- Que dans les tombes qui contiennent deux sujets, ceux-ci sont de sexe différent, les tombes isolées contenant indifféremment un homme ou une femme.

4°- Que le type physique, pour autant qu'il peut être estimé en raison du très petit nombre de crânes apportant des renseignements à ce point de vue, paraît être celui d'une population à tête large : 4 ou 5 sujets sont brachycéphales, 2 mésocéphales, 1 seul pourrait peut-être être légèrement dolichocéphale. On a là des représentants soit du type alpin, soit plutôt du type arménoïde, type qui, aujourd'hui encore, représente l'élément dominant de la population de Palestine et est très différent du type nettement dolichocéphale que l'on trouve à l'Est de la Mer Morte et dans le désert de Syrie. Les sujets inhumés à Khirbet-Qumran devaient être des Palestiniens. S'ils n'en étaient pas, du moins provenaient-ils d'un pays ayant la même composition anthropologique (comme les zones montagneuses du Liban et de la Syrie, ou l'Anatolie).

5°- Un dernier détail est la remarquable usure des dents, même chez les sujets d'âge peu avancé : ce phénomène, fréquent chez les populations anciennes ou primitives, est généralement attribué à l'usage de viandes mal cuites ou encore à l'habitude de broyer les céréales avec des meules grossières dont les grains siliceux se mélangent à la farine et attaquent l'ivoire dentaire.

c) Second page of the report

d) Third page of the report

For him, the Essene character of Qumran was not negotiable and his arguments had to confirm it. The complaint is repeated by all writers that de Vaux did not publish his definitive conclusions. What was one entitled to expect? What support is there for believing that he would have denied or added something? Should we expect him to change his mind only to strengthen an interpretation that prevailed and which contradicted his own? This would completely mistake who de Vaux was: we are convinced that he would not have modified the grounds for his interpretation.

Even if it is still true that an Essene Qumran has not been demonstrated, its Essenism is still an intuition which moves into a conviction that we would consider probable as long as the opposite has not been proven.

The Essenism of Qumran was confused by the question of gender. Discussion revolved around the number and exact placement of the women's graves and their orientation, and above all the fussy anthropological examination of the rare pelvises and skulls recovered. De Vaux did not think it appropriate to question the expertise made hurriedly by G. Kurth whose study supports the annual report, by which all the individuals of the main cemetery are men (*RB* 1956, p. 569-570). In *L'archéologie*, 1961, p. 38 and in *Archaeology*, 1973, p. 47, de Vaux wrote without hesitation: *Apart from a few cases which the poor state of the bones makes uncertain, all the skeletons of the well-ordered part of the cemetery are male, and equally those of the graves under a circle of stones at the western boundary of the cemetery.* He had sought the expertise of the best French anthropologist of the period, Henri Vallois of the Musée de l'Homme. The illustrious professor had hesitated in some cases as to the attribution "male" or "female." De Vaux forced the choice that fitted his interpretation: on Vallois's report, he crossed out "woman" several times in pen. We reproduce the document in fig. 34.

J. Norton, who furthermore remains mobilized by the question of gender, summarized the reasoning to which de Vaux held to save his Essene theory: *The Main Cemetery contained only males, the "peripheral cemeteries" (virtually) only women and children. The comparative orderliness of the Main Cemetery and the general disorder of the "peripheral cemeteries" demonstrated the low status of women amongst the Essene inhabitants of Qumran. By marginalizing the importance of the sections of the cemetery de Vaux felt that he was able still to present the evidence of the Main Cemetery as an argument for his text-based theory*[41]. From *L'archéologie*, 1961, p. 38, we learn that without further denying the presence of women, de Vaux still argues in favour of an Essene Qumran as the objections cannot be decisive: *In the main cemetery and the secondary cemeteries, we located more than 1200 graves; we opened 43 of them and the number is quite insufficient to establish a reliable statistic (...) This may also mean that the discipline evolved: the rule of celibacy would have been relaxed and marriage would have become permitted, which would explain why the feminine graves are found in what seem to be expansions of the main cemetery. This may mean, finally, that there were different groups in the community: the main group rejecting marriage (central cemetery) (...) and one or several groups which accepted it (the adjoining cemeteries) (...). The women's graves clearly do not prove that the community was connected with the Essenes, but they are not absolutely opposed to that* (p. 96-97). The formula was taken for granted and it is probable that de Vaux considered the file closed.

One day the subject took a polemical turn with an article issued from an American context[42]. The blow came like a cannonball which continues to roll with a certain movement. The author, L. Benett Elder, claimed to be doing nothing but reintroducing women into a file where there was no woman, or barely any. Essenism itself was of no interest to her. The examination of human remains conducted at the time of the excavations had been the fruit of preliminary observations, flexible enough to be reversed. The subject of gender suddenly gained an enlarged audience who had not yet visited Qumran. The bones had come out of the shadows where they had been thought to be hidden. Expertise and counter-expertise: erudite commentaries burst forward with greater or lesser objectivity, with the implied goal of counting the women. It was necessary to show that the anthropological examination of the bones had so far been approximate or erroneous, that women had indeed been buried at Qumran, and that it was necessary to draw appropriate consequences. The dilemma was clear: either the presence of women in the cemetery was an accident and the Essene thesis was safe, or Qumran had had its gynaeceum, and Qumran had not been Essene. We may conclude that statistical credit can be taken by the Essene side, and that it can just as well be taken by the opposite. Joseph Zias

---

41. Jonathan NORTON, "Reassessment of the Controversial Studies on the Cemetery", *Qumrân Vol. II*, p. 108ff.

42. Linda BENNETT ELDER, "The Woman Question and Female Ascetics among Essenes", *Biblical Archaeologist* 57, no. 4, 1994.

nuanced the debate with the hypothesis that the women's graves at Qumran were late, bedouin tombs[43]. Bedouins, nomads by definition, do not have a centralized cemetery; they bury their loved ones where they die. This is an appropriate consideration because cemeteries abandoned by the society that conceived them were reused by those who frequented the region later: graves attract other graves. J. Zias does not stray from the question of gender and from a traditional Essene interpretation of the site. Though possibly right, the hypothesis is not sufficient. Because of the weakness of the arguments, the knot is not cut. The best thing is to accept the women's tombs, and their number changes nothing. The answer lies elsewhere.

Let us hypothesize that the cemetery is *not* that of the people who lived at the site but that of a community, preferably Essene, an established diaspora in the region. Essenism is first of all a composite religious movement where currents could in turn be complementary or dissident. We may rely on Dio Chrysostom, who calls it a "polis" in the sense of a political and religious group, and situates it rather to the south of the Dead Sea[44], even if one should not give too much credit to the topographic precision of those describing the Asphalt Lake from Rome or Byzantium.

Quoting Dio on the Essenes from the angle of Synesius is simple, as the sentence is short:

Ἔτι καὶ τοὺς Ἐσσηνοὺς ἐπαινεῖ που πόλιν ὅλην εὐδαίμονα τὴν παρὰ τὸ νεκρὸν ὕδωρ ἐν τῇ μεσογείᾳ τῆς Παλαιστίνης κειμένην παρ'αὐτά που τὰ Σόδομα[45].

"(Dio) speaks highly of the Essenes, an entire polis, happy, established on the fringes of the Dead Sea, in mid-Palestine, somewhere on the side of Sodom" (our translation from Synesius, *Dio* 3:2).

We may infer that the exile of the *Damascus Document* was situated on the eastern bank (see above, on the earthquake). Accepting that the Essenes had installed themselves around the Dead Sea would defuse the controversy on Pliny's note which obliges us to confine *the* community to north of En-Gedi. In his account, Pliny will have repeated what he was told in Judea, and he would have described and "localized" the closest influential community, the one the people of Jerusalem will have pointed to. The historians of Antiquity spoke of a sect which had prospered in Judea, settled on the western bank of the Dead Sea. It would not be surprising if, on this point, the ancient historians had all depended, with varying degrees of freedom, on a single popular and apologetic source that was widely available at the time.

The quotation from Dio Chrysostom has not been given the respect it deserves. It provides information which we consider decisive regarding the concept of the Essene *community*. It certainly has neither the literary dimension nor the ideological force of that of Pliny, it is only a short sentence, and second hand thanks to Synesius, a polemicist converted to Christianity towards the end of the fourth century and author of a biography of Dio Chrysostom. We would be wrong to doubt the faithfulness of Synesius's transmission in relation to content more than form. There is good reason to suppose that he had read Dio, as he is one of the best commentators.

We may consider Dio to be a good reference in terms of chronology: he was born around 30–40 and died in 117 AD, making him a contemporary of Plutarch and Pliny, and a witness to the Roman seizure of Palestine. A native of Asia Minor, he spent the best part of his time in Rome, interrupted by three years as an envoy to Byzantium. There were plentiful archives in the two cities and we may regard him as well informed. He may have travelled to the orient. As a young man he was a contemporary of the end of Qumran, and in Rome the sect of the Essenes was at least known as a philosophical curiosity: he does not hide his admiration for wisdom. He does not present himself as a historian but as a philosopher.

It would be wrong to translate "the Essenes in a happy city, close to Sodom." The only possible city close to Sodom would be En-Gedi, as there is no other. The translation suggests that the Essenes were at En-Gedi, and distracts from Pliny's note. To prefer Pliny, one would need to abandon the passage from Dio on a geographical technicality. Wrongly so.

---

43. Joseph Zias, "The Cemeteries of Qumrân, and Celibacy: Confusion Laid to Rest?", *Dead Sea Discoveries* 7/2, p. 220ff.

44. H. Lamar Crosby, in *Dio Chrysostom*, vol. V, Cambridge MA and London, 1951, p. 379.

45. Geza Vermes and Martin D. Goodman, *The Essenes, according to the Classical Sources*, Sheffield, 1989, p. 58-59.

a) Toward south

b) Toward east

c) Tomb 5

d) Tomb 8

fig. 35.   The main cemetery in 1952

The geographical position of the Essenes is vague here and it is precisely because of that that it comes close to the truth we are trying to take hold of. According to Dio, the Essenes live on the fringes of the Dead Sea, but in Palestine and on the western side of the sea. Dio diverges from Pliny in mentioning Sodom, already with the advantage of freeing the sect from the strict region of Qumran. The reference is surprising because Sodom is not a place. Sodom has never been seriously identified with any archaeological site: the toponym is applied to an indefinite region and was able to become established, more or less, as a locality, without ancient support. Arab tradition placed it southwest of the Dead Sea, without further precision. Sodom, which has an unequivocally mythological character, certainly corresponds to a legendary tradition with a diffuse localization more than a precise topography. Sodom is mentioned for its sulphurous reputation, and not as a geographical reference which Roman readers, at least, would not be able to appreciate. Sodom does not feature in Roman geographical literature. C.P. Jones is right to suppose that the mention of Sodom is from the hand of Synesius, because it suggests a religious Christian context which Dio did not have[46]. So Synesius's intention cannot be held to be accidental. As a good commentator, he took up Dio's polemic against the cities where corruption was weakening morals. He would not have resisted approaching Essenes/Sodom with a good/bad rhetorical metaphor: to show the proximity of the Essene and the city of Sodom in a discourse in which the Essene model of virtue was contrasted with urban decadence. However, the city in question is not Sodom, as the word *polis* in Dio (Synesius) relates to the Essenes. So we should not translate *polis* by city but by *society*, or better, *community*. The primary, classical, meaning of *polis* clearly defines people; the *polis* was first and foremost the body of citizens or the urban community, or possibly the state. Its *raison d'être* was citizenship, cultural kinship or religious membership. Among the Greek authors, the best-attested meaning is "assembly of citizens". Chantraine favours the meaning "political and religious community". We conclude from this that Dio said, and Synesius passed it on, that the Essenes are not localized in one place but on the contrary represent a group in a large sense, dispersed on the side of the Dead Sea and Judea.

The society of the Essenes was distributed in different "communities" in Judea as far as the Dead Sea. This is why, if there were Essenes at Qumran, there ought also to have been there communities in the villages along the coast, Ain-Ghuweir, Ain-Turabi, En-Gedi, Masada, Ain Umm el Baghaq (En-Boqeq), Zoara etc. The ancient sources repeatedly mention the western banks of the Dead Sea as the Essenes' place of choice. There is no reason why other Essene communities would not have chosen to settle too on the eastern bank, and we accept that the "Land of Damascus" should be situated there. The Essenes prospered on the fringes because the region, while remaining close to Jerusalem and the agglomerations of Judea, was not easy to access and favoured communitarianism. At any rate, it is this society as a whole that constituted the *community* and Qumran would be just one example.

Although Essenism was accepted as a community in the sense of a sect, the *yahad*, it has often in contemporary discussion been reduced to *the* community of Qumran. The part has been taken as the whole. The shift in meaning has to be due to the weight of the manuscripts discovered on the periphery. De Vaux had accepted that the large quantity of scrolls constituted the settlement's library. The site would have been an intellectual and religious centre of the first order: *The Khirbet and the cemetery are merely the assembly centre for the living and the rest for the dead of a community which lived dispersed in the surrounding area, but which had an organization witnessed to by the ordering of the cemetery, particular funerary rites* (RB 60, 1953, p. 104). The prestige of the manuscripts came to the ruins, *The manuscripts found in the caves, whether they were written on site or came from elsewhere, were owned by the community and read by its members; they formed the library (L'archéologie, p. 81)*. Further on: *Cave 4 had received more than 400 manuscripts and it is situated very close to Khirbet Qumran: it was there that the communal library was hidden in haste, at the moment of abandonment (ibid., p. 82)*. Because of the convergence of notable real or imagined facts, Qumran was from then on accepted as a unique place, an exception. Throughout the chapter "The ruins and the text" (*L'archéologie*, p. 71–104), the reader finds it difficult to tell whether the word "community" means that of Qumran or of the sect as a whole. The equivocation was not intended but implicit. De Vaux has surreptitiously superimposed Qumran on the Essene *yahad*.

---

46. Christopher Prestige JONES, *The Roman World of Dio Chrysostom*, Cambridge MA and London 1978, p. 56, 64.

a) Tomb 36, loculus cover made of stones laid obliquely, on edge and wedged with pebbles

b) Tomb 29, the loculus cover, after removal of the cobble block

c) Tomb 28, the cover of the loculus is made of mud, square bricks.

fig. 36.   Covering of the loculi in the graves

The Qumran community is called into question. There are some who are afraid that if it were absent, the site would lose its meaning – as Essene, of course. The idea of community requires a number: What is the minimum number to make it credible? It was necessary to calculate and draw from the archaeology the facts which seemed consonant and which combined in favour of the number, and we must reconsider the communitarian character.

De Vaux set the number of Qumran inhabitants at between 150 and 200. What were the arguments required to decide on this figure? Certain features recognized at Qumran but uncommon at other Palestinian sites urged him towards this number. The shelter may be construed in the quantity of caves in the area, supplemented by a canvas encampment and huts erected at the foot of the cliff; the 1200 graves bear witness to a populated settlement; the volume of water storage facilities seemed to exceed the needs of an only limited group; the copious collection of manuscripts, taken to be the place's library, betrayed a rich, knowledgeable and complex society. None of these arguments is decisive.

If there was a scattered community, we have to suppose that they frequented the settlement, at least in order to perform their ritual ablutions. De Vaux placed the refectories (L. 77 and L. 86) where he imagined religious and therefore communal meals, but despite their respectable size, these loci cannot accommodate a large gathering of people, unless we suppose that there was a hierarchical selection at the heart of the group. On the contrary, the settlement was a space locked in itself. The archaeologist can easily see that the arrangement of the internal facilities, the laborious zigzagging internal traffic, the cluttered passageways, the small number of entrances and their narrowness, do not make this a populated place nor one visited by large numbers of people. Nothing points to a residence or frequenting of a group. The cluttered state of the places that are credibly habitable does not allow the accommodation of more than 15 to 20 individuals at one time. So there is a real contradiction with regard to the supposed numbers of the community. De Vaux, buoyed up by a set of glorious finds, initially thought big: *Population numbers here are rather difficult to assess. Considering the area in which they were distributed* [i.e., the spacing between the caves] (...) *we may imagine it would accommodate several hundred members, though one would hesitate to admit that it was as many as a thousand* (RB, 1953, p. 559). Reverting to more modest proportions, he estimated the group at 200 members, then settled on around 150, convinced that the *cramped dimensions of the central building could not cater for their needs (...), the number of graves in the cemetery is too great in relation to the possibilities of habitation in the buildings* (L'archéologie, p. 39). The surroundings compensated for the drawbacks: *We saw that some caves (...) were capable of functioning as accommodation, but that others had been merely storerooms or hiding places and that part of the community lived under canvas or in huts* (ibid.). In our view, de Vaux has here clearly transposed the cenobitic model of the great monastery of Mar Saba from the 6th c., to neighboring Qumran. Hagiography reports that there were a thousand monks at Mar Saba, including numerous hermits in the caves dug into the cliffs around the monastery. The proximity of the two sites and their common topographic context lent themselves to this.

We have revisited the surroundings of Qumran and have verified the inhospitability of the caves for habitation. As de Vaux reports, the cliff face is hollowed out with a thousand cavities, shelters, pockets of detachment, crevices or simple cracks. Only ten or so could provide a simple and precarious shelter where archaeology can recognize "inhabited caves". They were frequented at different periods: Chalcolithic, Bronze and Iron Age and also in the time of Qumran in a sporadic manner and in a limited period at the turn of the era. Their reduced space, nearly always caused by a low ceiling, does not make for practical shelter; no furnishing has been observed which would have been the least of things when, in the long or middle term, people would have been living in such uncomfortable places. The furniture discovered in the caverns is very minimal and indicates quick visits. Caves inhabited for more than a century would have left visible traces: in front of the entrances there would have been a dump area of debris formed by what was thrown out. Nothing like this is visible anywhere. The approaches to the main caves have produced only very few pottery shards: people in hiding are careful not to signal their presence. The caves harboured only fugitives in times of threat and crisis and we can imagine rebels there in moments of trouble and insecurity during Jewish revolts. And it is precisely because they were not habitations that they were hiding places, in a mountain area that no one would frequent. The ash and charcoal observed there are the remnants of camp fires of ancient and modern shepherds[47].

---

47. J.-B. HUMBERT, Cacher et se cacher à Qumrân, p. 41.

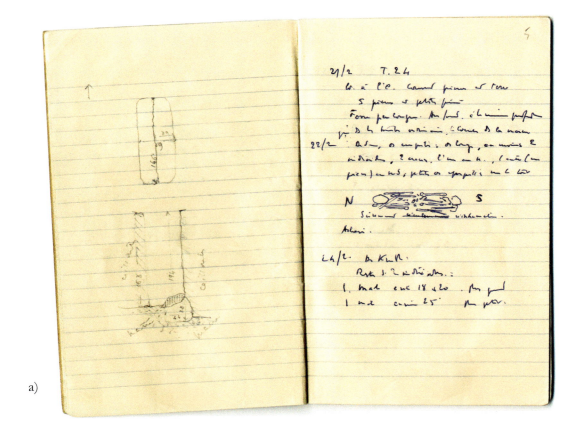

a)

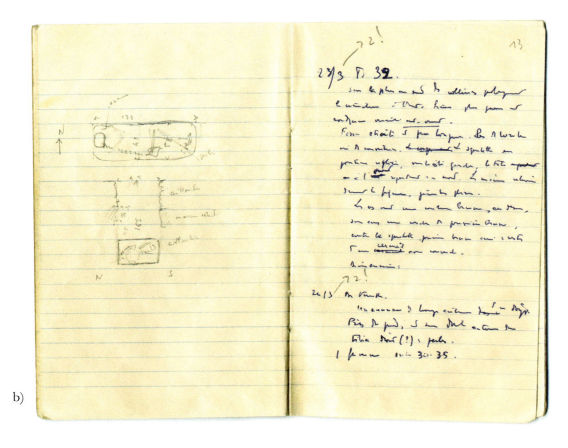

b)

fig. 37. *Journal* of the excavation of graves 24 and 32, in 1956

De Vaux also thought he could accommodate his Essenes "in tents or huts". The idea came to him from the tents mentioned in the *Damascus Document (CD)*. But what tents, when it is hardly likely that a canvas camp would have been set up before the walls of "Damascus"? The improbable image has been applied to Qumran where a similar canvas camp surrounded the settlement permanently. If one proposes to shelter men for a century and a half in tents at the foot of a cliff, is it credible that they would not have at least tried to build houses for such a long period, when stone buildings surrounded them on all sides? The Qumran settlement itself testifies that they knew how to build, and massively. Experience on the borders of the Dead Sea also shows that a tent is no protection from the torrid air, stifling in the long hot season. To the very present, semi-nomadic bedouin are retreating far into the mountains for the summer. Furthermore, for the archaeologist, even the temporary erection of a bedouin tent leaves a clear imprint on the ground for decades. Under-canvas accommodation for a century and a half would have left traces of layouts on the foothills. Everyday life, even of the utmost simplicity, produces quantities of debris which would accumulate where they are spread, and which an archaeologist is able to find: no such thing has been found either. The foot of the cliff is incontrovertibly sterile, and no one has ever camped there.

De Vaux saw his idea about the number of inhabitants also supported by the observation of a developed hydraulic system: *The most striking feature of this layout is the number and importance of the cisterns. The extension of the buildings and the growth in the number of inhabitants had the effect of requiring a more abundant and more stable provision of water in Period Ib* (*L'archéologie*, p. 6). The number and size of the large basins with steps made an impression on him. Were these large basins ritual baths? De Vaux was cautious here: *We must not jump to conclusions, as similar cisterns, with broad descending staircases and sometimes partitions on the steps are found (...) especially in the neighbourhood of Jerusalem to which a ritual use cannot be attributed with any certainty. It is even dubious that they were 'baths' for a pagan purpose. They were probably simple cisterns* (*RB* 1956, p. 539-540). Not all commentators followed his caution, and the dimension of the basins seemed to them to correspond to a function which, for many, meets the religious demands registered in the texts. Several studies have examined the morphology of the basins and sought to assess their total volume, the idea behind it being to provide an answer to the possibility of a bath[48]. The presence of steps is not exclusively typical of ritual baths. De Vaux proposes that only two tanks had been baths, loci 138 and 68. The substantial volume of the whole, which we estimate at 1000 m^3, is not excessive. The volume is a function of the capacity, which depends on consumption. Now, it is not easy to give credit to evaluations which were liable to distortion by variable factors. The basins were not designed to be filled up to the top. Not all of them were intended to be reservoirs for domestic water, a better protected basin would have been reserved for drinking water, etc. The most sensible factor is random provision, depending on rainfall levels. Qumran, on the boundaries of the steppe, receives less than 100 mm a year, and even extended drainage of rain collected from the foothills would not have sufficed for an accumulation of 1000 m^3 each year. Independent of these provisions that were thought necessary to accumulate for a large group of people, waters from the upper wadi Qumran were also caught. The latter is an episodic torrent which does not run regularly; there are dry years. It was necessary to plan ahead for times of drought and shortage. In short: The basins are normal reserves of water in a dry land and the hydraulic system cannot serve as indication of the number of Qumran's inhabitants.

Finally, can the cemetery help? Is it possible to draw a credible result on the basis of counting the 1200 tombs? Several factors that have a bearing have to be combined, and each of them cannot be defined with certitude. First, the duration of a community's occupation can vary by twice as much, depending on the changeableness of the population, slack or abundant periods, the mortality rate in Antiquity in general and in this precise region, the average age of the peasant sectarian, etc. Scruples have led to taking into consideration of those dying in combat, which would have lowered the average age of mortality, not counting dead brought from far away in wooden coffins and possibly the transport to Qumran of *remnants of members of this community who had died in Damascus*[49]. The attempted estimates lead nowhere - except that Laperrousaz was right, but only in the sense he himself gave to these numbers (see below).

---

48. See the bibliography compiled by Katharina GALOR, *Qumrân,* Vol. II, p. 319.

49. E.-M. LAPERROUSAZ, *Qoumran*, p. 101.

a) Grave 8, the 'bench' to the right of the loculus

b) Tomb 21. The mortar filling of the mud-brick loculus cover is still linked to the "bench".

c) Tomb 10, north cemetery

d) Tomb 7, outside the western boundary of the cemetery, in a vertical pit and without loculus

fig. 38.   Excavation of the graves and the state of the human remains

It has not been possible to confirm any of the arguments advanced in favour of any proposed number. We are not entitled to see the cemetery in the condition the inhabitants of the place. It does not correspond to the capacity of the population of the nearby settlement. It is more correct not to speak of *the* cemetery of Qumran, but to say that there is *a* cemetery at Qumran. We do not deny that it was communitarian, nor that it belonged to the community *of* Qumran but, on the contrary, we propose that it was used by a community, in the broader sense of a sect, living along the banks of the Dead Sea. That is what we would now like to tackle.

The spatial arrangement of the cemetery, estimated at 1200 graves, is nothing short of astonishing. Two arrangements are notable: the main cemetery is divided into three quarters separated by two alleys and each quarter is formed of successive ranks of around 20 tombs. One would look in vain, in the region in this period, for a cemetery that is reminiscent of modern planning in this respect. In Antiquity a necropolis was adapted to local topography. The arrangement of the tombs followed the landscape, divided between favourable places and less noble angles. Classical necropolises aligned cenotaphs to be seen by travellers as they exited cities. Byzantine cemeteries are organized only by the east-west orientation of graves, without a pre-established grid, even on flat terrain, favourable for managing space.

At Qumran, the original ordering of the cemetery is striking; the aerial photographs recreate the arrangement (fig. 4, fig. 15b and fig. 33). De Vaux, following Clermont-Ganneau, also noted the rigorous organization: *The graves (...) are arranged close together in regular ranks, distributed in three quarters separated by alleyways; this beautiful arrangement contrasts with the usual disorder of the ancient cemeteries of Palestine* (*L'archéologie*, p. 37). Clermont-Ganneau, reassured by the absence of furniture in the grave he had opened, had proposed seeing it as a late, pre-Islamic site, because of the non-standard, almost "medieval," orientation of the graves. Having verified already during the first campaign in 1951 that the ruins were Roman without later occupation, de Vaux was easily convinced that the cemetery was contemporary with them: *The date of the cemetery is more difficult to determine. It seems certain that it was used at the same time as the main building* (*RB* 60, 1953, p. 104). On the narrow prolongations in the east, the regularity of orientation of the graves seems less rigorous, perhaps because of the limitations of available space. The intuition of N. Golb was good, to cut the link between the site and the graves, as the cemetery does not present an image that corresponds to that of the site[50]. The military cemetery he proposes, the interment of the victims of the Roman assault on the fortress of Qumran, remains an idea without equivalent in Antiquity and which does not take into account the women's graves. The regularity of the graves, their position and morphology, is skewed by the diffracted image of the modern military cemeteries. Such a careful interment of victims after a battle makes no sense: in a battle circumstances the interment would have been conducted in a hurry. As there was a programme for the burial of bodies, the organization of the burial field has spread over time, so a "private" cemetery is a better fit.

The morphology of the graves at first seemed typical of the place, but it has been found elsewhere. The deep burial pits with their set-off *loculus* seemed specific to Qumran because this was the first time any had been discovered. The *loculus* is closed by a row of crude adobe bricks or flat stones (fig. 36), which may or may not be lined by a narrow seat. It represents a compromise between a traditional interment in open ground and an interment where the emptiness of a cave is deemed more respectful to the remains and which delays the disintegration of the body (fig. 38). This model of graves has since been discovered at Jerusalem (Beit Safafa) and in large numbers on the banks of the Dead Sea, at Ain-Ghuweir and Khirbet Qazone. The similarity gives credence to assume that the sect lived spread out along the Dead Sea; but as the attribution to the Essenes has not conclusively been demonstrated, we would at least point out the coincidence.

The cemetery was in use for quite a long time and we think that the initial tomb was dug at the northwest corner, at the prescribed distance from the *khirbeh*. It extended in a first row to the east as far as the slope, then a second row was installed south of the first in accordance with a grid which presupposes planning. The practice of interment would be followed as long as the sect lived close-by, i.e. more than a century, at least as long as Qumran played a communitarian role. Around 50 graves have been excavated, and the number is sufficient to gather enough indications in

---

50. N. Golb, "Khirbet Qumran and the Manuscript Finds of the Judean Wilderness", *Methods of Investigation of the Dead Sea Scrolls and the Khirbet Qumran Site*, New York 1994, p. 69–70.

fig. 39. Excavation of the graves and the state of the human remains

favour of an evolution. Looking more closely, the graves are not always identical. Beside the graves with a *loculus*, set off to the side at the bottom of the shaft (the most common type), some simple pits have produced stacks of bones, and we may deduce that the *loculus* was then no longer necessary to protect a body that had already lost its flesh. Some graves were marked by piles of oblong stones or by circles on the surface; some contained coffins made of cypress wood. The modes of interment imply different customs or procedures. We may note: T11 represents a re-interment: *The bones lie under two large paving stones, in a pile, head to the south but facing the ground. The remains of a hand were collected and the long bones arranged in bundles at the continuation of the skull.* However, we find no trace of the pelvis, vertebrae and jaws (*Journal*, T11) (fig. 40 a and b). *The deferred interment took place in haste and without care. Two of them were irregular pits, where the bones of an individual had been re-interred; in two others, a brown dust attested to the fact that the body had been deposited in a wooden coffin* (*L'archéologie*, p. 38). In tomb 16, two bodies were deposited at the same time: *The first body is at the bottom of the pit (...). The second has been placed next to it to the east in a sort of loculus (not deep enough), the latter seems to have been lightly compressed to leave room for the previous one* (*Journal*, T16). We must understand that two bodies were brought the same day, that the pit was ready and that there was insufficient time to dig another. Tomb 17 presupposes an animated scene: *In the interior of this row of stones which line the pit, a wooden coffin appears very worm-eaten. (…) The body has been completely turned over after the interment, following landslips (…). The spinal column, the ribs and the skull are in a tangle above the pelvis* (*Journal*, T17) (fig. 40d). The collapses are not there for nothing: rather, it seems that the coffin has been lifted into a vertical position in transit and the body has crumpled down into the shaft[51]. Tombs 23, 29 and 37 show the same picture, but this time the body must have been carried by two people in a sheet or a bag. It seems, furthermore, that the skeleton has slipped southwards: *The spinal column is folded into an S under the head and the shoulders have been lifted up* (*Journal*, T23). *The skeleton has slipped to the south: shoulder lifted up, spinal column dislocated and twisted* (*Journal*, T29). *The thorax, the pelvis and the femurs seem to be connected but the head which is not in place was found broken, under femurs with the bones of legs and feet* (*Journal*, T37); the body had apparently been transported folded. In tomb 18, *the body rests on a quite well preserved wooden coffin without traces of a lid* (*Journal*, T18). Tombs 19 and 33 each contained a wooden coffin. Tomb 24 clearly betrays a secondary burial: *In the loculus the bones had been stacked up: long bones of two individuals, two skulls, one to the north and the other (in pieces) to the south; the small bones were scattered about everywhere* (*Journal*, T24) (fig. 40c). Most of the bodies were buried with care, but the examples just cited attest to a laborious transfer. Everything leads us to believe that the majority of the deceased were not from Qumran, but had died elsewhere.

One will no longer be surprised to find graves of women and children. Even if Judaism was more the practice of men than women, women were not excluded and their status did not stop them from being able to enjoy the same privileges as men. Since Qumran was a heavily frequented place, probably during pilgrimages, we should not discount the possibility either that women or children who died during the occasion, would have been buried on site.

We can now loosen the isolation to which Qumran has been confined. The collected data indicate that, after death, bodies were transported as soon as possible and interred after a short delay. The dislocated bodies were transported from the general vicinity in cloths; others were carried from quite far away in coffins (fig. 40d and e), and the piled-up bones of the secondary graves came from even further away. One can recreate funerary journeys by navigation from almost all points around the Dead Sea within 24 or 48 hours. The modes of interment were adapted to the distances to be covered. The cemetery was common to several societies settled in the palm groves of the shores. There is no need to suppose that all the Essenes of the Dead Sea were buried at Qumran. Some of them will have been buried there and we do not know by whom nor for whom the choice was made. None of the cemeteries of the areas around the Dead Sea was exclusively Essene; the populations were mixed. Any attempt to calculate their number is doomed to failure. The societies of the period piously buried women like men. Why should it be surprising to find women and even children at Qumran? The inhabitants were not limited to a small group of reclusive celibates at the end of the world.

Let us hypothesize that the Jews settled on the eastern bank wished to be buried in Holy Land. Y. Yadin suggested that the cemetery of Qumran had been

---

51. The body of a child was found in a twisted position, crammed into the bottom of a large amphora from Cyprus, a sign that the body had been transported in the pot in a vertical position. Excavations by the *École Biblique* at Blakhiya, Gaza.

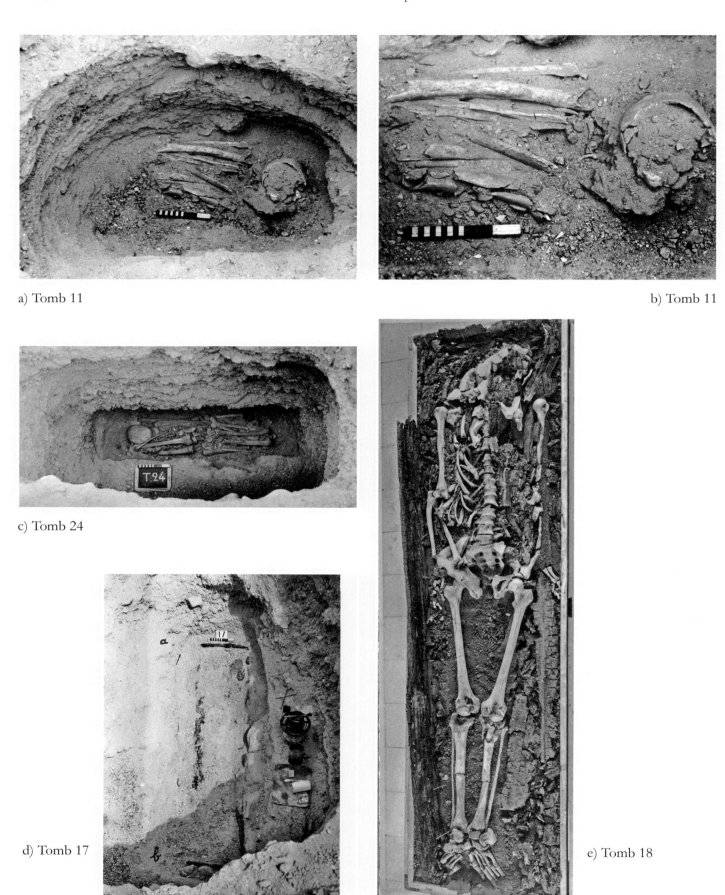

a) Tomb 11

b) Tomb 11

c) Tomb 24

d) Tomb 17

e) Tomb 18

fig. 40. Examples of delayed burial: secondary interments (a, b, c); in wooden coffins (d, e)

open to others, citing Ain-Feshka. Did he not know that Ain-Feshka was only a house? In saying "Ain-Feshka" did he mean the whole palm grove[52]? He took the idea from P. Bar-Adon who had identified and excavated some graves of the same type at Ain-Ghuweir, but the three sites had few inhabitants, even Ain-Ghuweir[53]. These authors cited settlements near to Qumran because they conceived of them as simple extensions of that site. They deserve praise for being the first to open up Qumran. However, we shall see that the sites of the western bank had their own cemetery.

Yadin mentions the useful reflection of Bar-Adon who, surprised that the graves of Ain-Ghuweir had contained broken pottery, proposed to see them as impure vessels from the house of death, therefore thrown into the pit with the body (*The Temple Scroll*, p. 324). The idea is right and suggests that most of the objects in the graves which have often been taken as offerings are not that. Further, we would like to explain that the graves at Qumran have not produced any furnishings because the bodies had been carried but without domestic pots in jars; and that the small cemetery of Ain-Ghuweir, which is not in the diaspora, was clearly used on the spot by the inhabitants.

The custom of diaspora Jews to be buried in the Holy Land is well attested. And we must insist on the importance of the practice. There are reasons to believe that this custom is pre-70 and began before the destruction of the temple as the central sacred place of the Holy Land. Some ossuary inscriptions in the form of writing reminiscent of Mesopotamian Aramaic from Jerusalem date to the first century AD and indicate secondary interments even before the First Revolt[54]. So the practice would be attested when Qumran is not yet deserted. The fact that the custom now only appears in texts from after 70, does not exclude the possibility to affirm that it was not customary before, and the cemetery of Qumran would be another example. The organized nature of the cemetery and the evidence of the repatriation of the bodies, sometimes from far away, point in this direction and, at least for now, we have no proof of the contrary.

The bodies were sometimes repatriated from far away. Beth She'arim in Galilee is the best example. The necropolis was that of the inhabitants of the place, Besara in Galilee, but the catacombs also welcomed the mortal remains of Jews from Phoenicia and Syria. We know this thanks to inscriptions which mention their origins. One catacomb which must be dated to the third to fourth century even sheltered notable Himyarites. Another funerary inscription in Aramaic, very probably originally from Zoara south of the Dead Sea, also mentions a Himyarite who died at Zafar (?) in Yemen and was interred in the Holy Land. It is dated palaeographically to the third or the fourth century. We offer a free translation[55]:

MAY THE SOUL OF YOSA BEN OFI (?) REST DIED IN THE CITY OF THE HIMYARITES / INTERRED FRIDAY 29TH OF THE MONTH OF TAMUZ / FIRST YEAR OF FALLOW / THAT IS, THE (ERASED) YEAR / OF THE DESTRUCTION OF THE TEMPLE / MAY HE REST IN PEACE.

The necropolis of Zoara is relevant because it is situated on the southern end of the Dead Sea. It was established by Jewish communities living between the eastern and west side of the thalweg which, in this place, marks the border of the Holy Land.

A second anomaly is striking: the modesty of the graves. In their overwhelming majority they are deliberately sparse: no real care into their constitution, and the bodies were deposited without affectation; there is no offering. For a society which is rightly held to be highly literate it would be astonishing, finally, if there was nothing to identify the graves, or if no name was mentioned. S. Steckoll claimed to have found, in contact with entombed bodies, remains of inscriptions on stones[56]. The information, like a wrong track, has not been taken up. It is true that the names of the deceased may have been written on perishable materials, but such a practice is not logical when the normal identification is outside the grave and not on the inside. We should take it that the dead wished to be left in anonymity.

---

52. Yigael YADIN, *The Temple Scroll*, Jerusalem 1983, p. 324.
53. P. BAR-ADON, *Eretz-Israel 10*, 1971, p. 88 (Heb.).
54. Emile PUECH, "Ossuaires inscrits d'une tombe du Mont des Oliviers", *Liber Annuus XXXII*, 1982, p. 367ff.
55. Joseph NAVEH, "Seven New Epitaphs from Zoar", *Tarbiz 1999-2000*, p. 619-635. I would like to thank Christian Robin very much for drawing my attention to this publication. I am grateful to Caroline Carlier for the translation. Although it came from the antiquities market, Zoara is the likely provenance.
56. Salomon H. STECKOLL, "Preliminary Excavations Report in the Qumran Cemetery", *RQ* 6. 3, p. 323-324.

a) Locus 112 to the southwest

b) Locus 112 to the south

c) Remains of the original paving and drainage

d) The "window" 809

fig. 41.　　The state of Locus 112 in 2014

Chapter 7

Toilet facilities

Locus 112

The question of the presence of lavatories in the Qumran precincts was the object of a debate that is now redundant. De Vaux had identified an installation in L. 51 which he saw as a toilet: *a terracotta pipe associated with a rammed conical bell (...) On the interior are a series of thin layers of dirty soil. There can be no doubt that this is a toilet, a cesspit* (L. 51, 21/4/53). People have not been slow to criticize the grounds for this interpretation, with good reason. The prescription that the call of nature should be answered outside the camp (Deut 23:13-14) opened a line of research for those who take things literally, whereas it is not clear that one should apply a theological text to an archaeological fact. De Vaux thought it possible to associate the pickaxe found in Cave 11Q with the levitical prescription that requires "carrying a pick to cover up your excrement" (Deut 23:13). The idea breaks down in that a single pickaxe recovered, or indeed several, would not have sufficed for the community imagined at Qumran. Whatever the number of residents of the settlement, it is not realistic to rule out a toilet *intra muros*. The custom of not going beyond the walls at night is almost universal, for reasons of security and comfort. The L. 51 facilities provided a stopgap. Three photographs here illustrate the installation in L. 51, but it is really difficult to recognize an adequate layout (fig. 42). On the other hand, a toilet is easily detectable on the Qumran precincts, and we would like to show that L. 112 presents convincing aspects of it.

Locus 112 did not attract much attention from the excavators and has not since prompted particular interest. On the *Plans* it is marked by a wall 759 in a quarter-circle, erected without care in the northern corner of L. 101: It does not figure on the *Plan* of Period Ib, only *Plan* II, nor is it documented on any photograph. It could pass for a late addition as is often encountered in buildings that are in decline. However, it remains intriguing. The excavators must have thought it was only a convenient shortcut, placed between two loci, L. 113 (L. 110) towards L. 103, via door 806 and a passageway between L. 112 and L. 113, wrongly restored on the Coüasnon *Plan* of Period II. Now L. 103 is a peripheral space to compensate for the steep slope of the western ravine, an uninhabited location without exit, and there is no need to facilitate access to it. Locus 112 is not a passageway.

Locus 103 is crossed by two covered drains, 523 and 787 (figs. 44b and c) which run into the ravine through a kind of "window" 809, well-constructed but low and directly above the chasm. The opening presents a recess which probably held a door panel of wood (fig. 44b and c). Under the support sill of the window, a quite large conduit has been carefully built in where the two drains came together. The surveys pay barely any attention to this: We understand that, for the excavators, isolated L. 103 was too peripheral to have been a significant feature in a settlement, and that "window" 809 was only an overflow.

96 Review of the interpretation

fig. 42.   Installation of Locus 51 as cesspool

The excavation of L. 112 was laborious and disappointing. The excavators dug in search of the continuation of the drain which crosses L. 103. The threshold between L. 103 and L. 112 was uncovered but nothing clear was found. The drain seems to have completely disappeared in L. 112 (L. 112 on 21/3/55). De Vaux expected the drain to serve as overflow from the cistern L. 110. Loci 109 and 113 were excavated in vain. Nothing upstream of drain 523 was found in the intermediate space between L. 112 and L. 110: *No trace of the drain. The search is abandoned* (L. 113 on 24/3/55). The supposed function of drain 787 no longer made sense.

The drawing of drain 523 is almost complete. Receiving the used water from the container around cistern 110, it runs west through door 528 in L. 111, then south by door 808 in L. 103 before flowing into window 809. Drain 787 was not reported on the *Plans* – neither Ib nor II. Its absence shows that L. 112 did not attract attention. Fortunately, in the boxes we found Coüasnon's 1955 survey of all the outbuildings of the residence: prepared with care, precise despite the 1:100 scale, it provides details which permit the interpretation of the locus.

Drain 787, correctly drawn, exits directly from L. 112 into L. 103 and runs towards bay 809. It is in fact interrupted in L. 112 and there is no reason to extend it under wall 543 in the direction of cistern L. 110. Drain 787 was meant to evacuate the used water from the place itself. Locus 112 is a small room, roughly triangular, accessed from L. 103 via door 806. This is a closed location, so the Coüasnon *Plan*, which situates a door in wall 543, is wrong. The space was never open. First, *Plan* Ib records masonry later blocking an open door (*Plan* II), but it is illogical to rebuild the stones of a wall that disappeared at the time of the excavation. It might just be necessary to reverse the sequence and place on *Plan* Ib a door which would have been blocked on *Plan* II. We reject the existence of the door; and supporting wall 543 stands as a continuous unit as far as the corner where it meets wall 507. The adoption of a passage between L. 112 and L. 113 had the benefit of avoiding drawing a cul-de-sac room which was difficult to interpret; it was reinforced by the illusion that *Plan* II creates of a corner marked by wall 544, built later and which, towards the north, divided L. 113 and L. 109. So Locus 112 is a dead end.

Locus 112 was reached from L. 113, by crossing L. 111 and L. 103, an open space; the toilet L. 112 does not communicate with the outside. There is, however, nothing left of the installation itself. Our understanding is that, at the behest of the excavators, the workers dug deep in vain in search of the continuation of drain 787. We suspect that the shape and materials of the pan were not cut blocs and paving stones. A few rare indications might not have been noted and the tight location should have been demolished without care. Coüasnon's 1955 survey made up for the lack of documentation; fortunately, he sketched, along the whole length and at the base of the walls, whatever had remained of a rather scant paving or the stony bed of a mortar floor that had disappeared over time. Today the place is recognizable despite the erosion and the restorations. We have photographed it because no picture was taken when the excavations were underway (fig. 41). It may be supposed that the floor was made of large pebbles and that a cross-section of it can be seen in the torn-up floor. The pan exit is still marked by a hollow.

Drain 787 passing under the northern jamb of door 806 is interrupted in the closed northwest corner, where the pan must have been situated. As the toilet was private, a wooden panel (leaf) has to be restored at door 806, the hinge of which needs to be attached to the northern jamb to facilitate passage in the concave face of partition wall 759.

For ventilation of the room, it is not certain that L. 112 was completely covered. An awning would have been able to protect only the pan part, guarding it at least from the inconveniences of bad weather and sun.

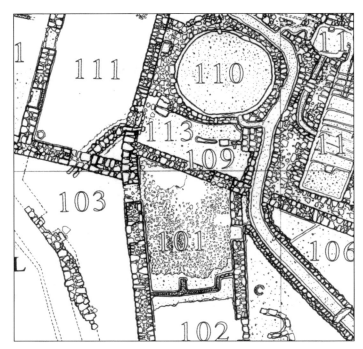

a) Coüasnon survey, Period 1b

b) Coüasnon survey, Period 2

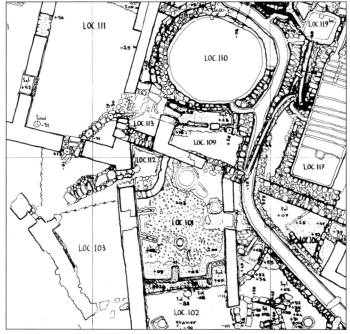

c) Coüasnon survey, 1955

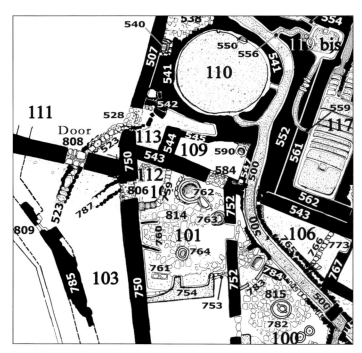

d) Designation of the architectural elements

fig. 43. Surveys and plans of the sector around Locus 112 and designation of the constructed elements

Toilet facilities

a) Drain 787 with exit through a wall opening

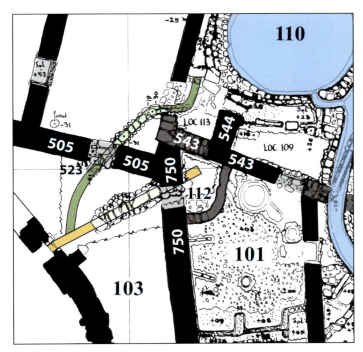

b) Layout of drainage drains to the southwest of cistern 110

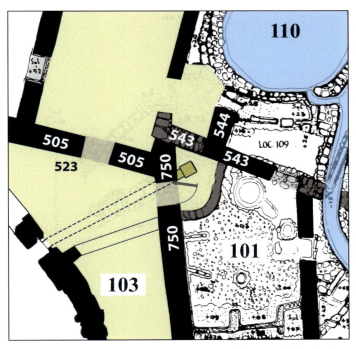

c) Reconstruction of the distribution of loci and circulation around L. 112

fig. 44.   Locus 112, discharge of the toilet

100 Review of the interpretation

Section

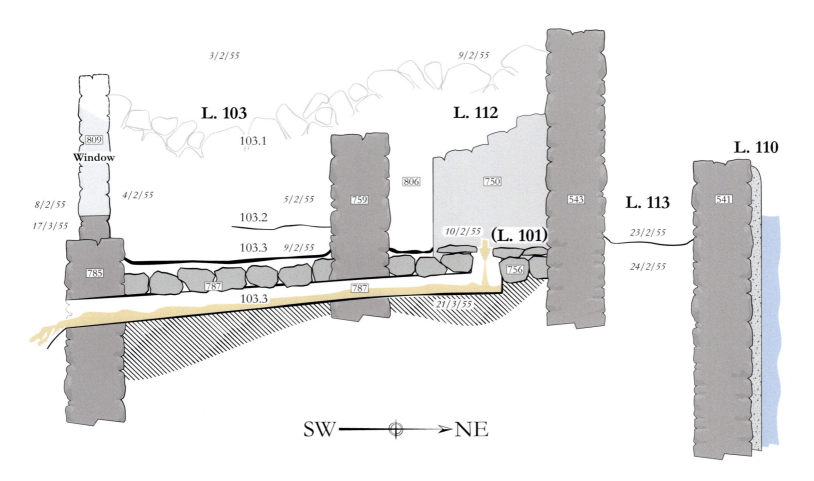

Restored elements	level	Definition	Journal dates	Coins	Position	No.	Chronology
103.1	Post 3C	Abandonment collapse	3/2/55				
103.2	3C	floor not identified	4, 5, 8/2/55	KhQ 2016 2006 2083 2009.1 to 33	upper level upper level deep against the ramparts	1 1 1 34	Proc. under Tiberius Agrippa Ist Agrippa Ist First Revolt, 66/69
103.3 112.2	3BC	sanitary installation	15-17/3/55 20/2/55 21/3/55				
L101	2–3A	Workshop					

Stratigraphic table of Locus 112 (for the chart of symbols, see page 155)

Plate 1

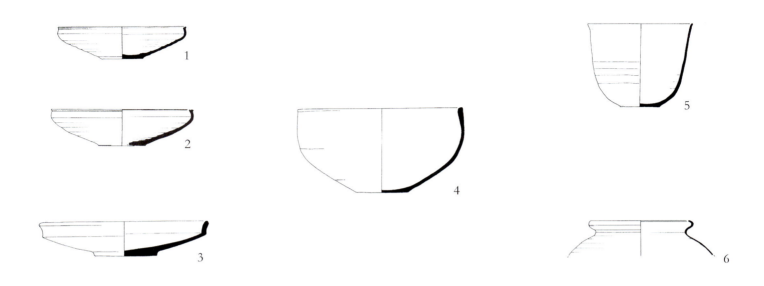

N°	N° Catal.	Position	Comments (archives)	Date	Description	Clay	Exterior
1	2058	103.2	-	08/02/55	plate	red earth	red wash
2	4092	103.2	-	05/02/55	small dish	red paste	beige
3	2071	103.2	-	09/02/55	plate	red earth	white wash
4	2059	103.2	-	08/02/55	large bowl	red earth	white wash
5	2086	103.2	-	09/02/55	goblet	red earth	white wash
6	4093	103.2	-	08/02/55	cooking pot	red paste	brown

Pottery catalogue of Locus 103

Locus 103, catalogue and pottery, scale ¼

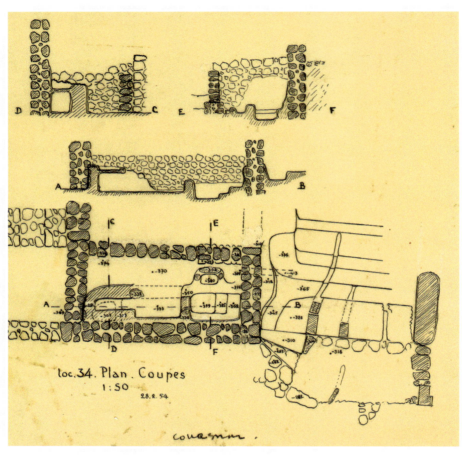

fig. 45. Survey plan and elevation of the installation of baths, Locus 34 (Coüasnon 1954)

Chapter 8

A Greek-style bath

Loci 34 and 35

Locus 34 was excavated from 25/3/53 to 31/3/53, then from 22/2/54 to 28/2/54. Locus 35 was excavated from 25/3/53 to 11/4/53 and on 13/3/56. Comments on them are poor and they have not been interpreted. We see them as a domestic bath of primitive construction, which has been maintained throughout all the different occupations and should be attributed to Level 2, as we hope to show. In L. 34 and L. 35, L. 42 and L. 48, southwest of the main building, the masonry is muddled like nowhere else on the site. Successive restorations and modifications have remodeled the constructions to comply with the distribution requirements of the watercourses that intersect there. In each quadrant of this southeast sector, there were water installations which, toward the end of the occupation, were in service at the same time: baths of L. 34 in the northwest, pool L. 48-L. 49 in the northeast, pool L. 58 in the southwest and in the southeast the series of small pools, L. 73-L. 69. The general feed at 346 supplied the whole arrangement, secondary drains were modified, and there were evacuations.

Locus 34 fills the southwest corner of the square courtyard of the residence (16 x 16.50 m). When south wall 293 of the locus was the southern side of the original courtyard, L. 34 and L. 35 stood as an isolated tower. The courtyard was reduced in stages - first by L. 30, a neat construction which did not encroach on the courtyard before the reoccupation of Level 3. The rest of the courtyard was divided in the last phases of the occupation. The Coüasnon *Plans* allocate ten or so *loci* arbitrarily between Periods I, II and III. Locus 33, a late addition in rough brick, stands out here, leaning against an all-stone building. A final partition closed the northwest of the courtyard with L. 24 and L. 25. They are closed to the east by wall 310, of exceptional thickness, for which there seems to be no reason. What remains of the courtyard in the northeast was in the open. The final constructions were rightly assigned to Level 4 (Period III).

In time, L. 32, L. 33, L. 34, L. 35 and L. 36 formed a knot of masonry so tight that the surveys had to simplify the overlapping (fig. 45). Sabre cuts were not noted, the partition walls were repositioned several times, the doors alternately opened and condemned. No architectural interpretation of the sector was carried out and the commentary is not satisfactory. Locus 35 is distinguished by the depth of its foundation: *Several soundings at the southeast corner of locus 35: the wall between loci 35 and 48 (292) and between 35 and 34 (306) descends lower than the cleared floor. Walls perhaps Israelite* (L. 35, 13/3/56). They belong to the Hasmonaean building. De Vaux affirmed the antiquity of wall 306, separating L. 34 and L. 35, which we accept. The elevation of wall 306 as it appears does not have the good workmanship of the Hasmonaean house (fig. 47c) but the place was reworked at a late stage and several times. A protruding line of stones can be discerned in the photograph, in which we checked the perpendicularity of the former facing. Photograph fig. 47c witnesses to its narrowness, a simple partition wall perhaps to be attributed to Level 4.

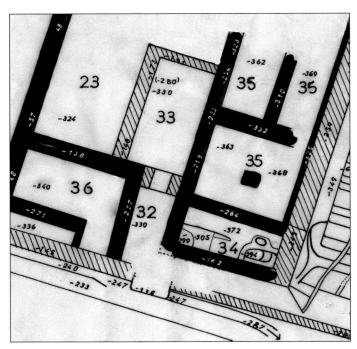

a) Original survey of the central building, 1953

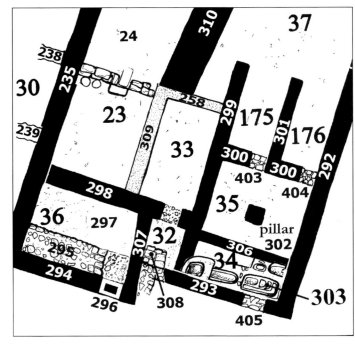

b) Designation of the architectural elements, Loci 34 and 35

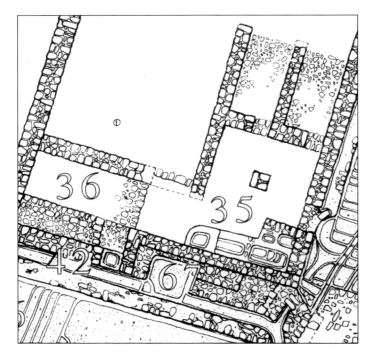

c) Loci 34 and 35, Coüasnon survey Period Ib

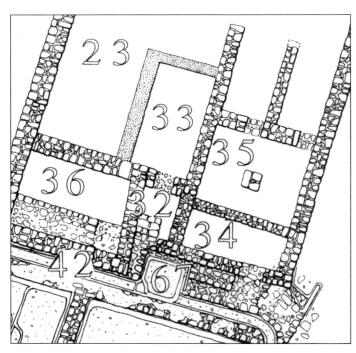

d) Loci 34 and 35, Coüasnon survey Period II

fig. 46.   Plans and surveys of Loci 34 and 35

The former compartment, L. 35 in the southeast corner of the courtyard, is in harmony with the original layout of the house and with the standards of its construction. It measures 4 x 4 m in its interior dimensions, a square module which structures the layout of the former house[57]. A square pillar 0.75 x 0.75 m occupies its centre; it is evident that L. 35 is the original stairwell leading upstairs, as often in aristocratic houses at the end of the Hellenistic period. To the extent that one can trust the stone-by-stone survey of the Coüasnon *Plan* (Periods Ib, II), we think the northwest corner of the locus was sharp. On the north side, wall 301 was not yet leaning on wall 300 and the stairwell stood free in the courtyard. Walls 293 and 306, ancient and contemporary, frame a narrow space of 1.80 m when, logically, stairwell L. 35 occupied the corner of the courtyard. The narrow space is precisely L. 34, which contains the bathtubs and, as the wet room is connected with the staircase, there is every reason to believe that it was planned in the initial layout of the space.

Having made the proposal, it is appropriate to set out the reasons for it. The difficulty for a proper understanding of the wet room lies in the brevity of the *Journal*'s notes on it, and the summary character of the surveys. The photographs help to mitigate the inconvenience. De Vaux was right to surmise that the installation of the baths, whose prime function he did not understand, was ancient (Period Ib). The installation no longer figures in the *Plan* of Period II. With Coüasnon, he worked hard to mark out the small room and we have to look again at each wall, its connections and its modifications.

On the *Plan* of Period Ib, north wall 306, poorly cleared in 1953, is sketched with a southern facing pulled down on the already cleared part (fig. 46c). We do not understand why the incomplete survey of 1953 was reproduced after 1956 on a plan drawn up after the excavation had been finished. Does this reflect reservations about deciding between two separate loci, 34 and 35, and a single locus comprising 34 and 35? It is possible to hypothesize that L. 34 and L. 35 form a whole, and to accept that the baths were freely accessible at the foot of the staircase, with the advantage of avoiding the narrowness of L. 34. It is also possible to reconstruct the former partition in two *loci*. In 1954, wall 306 was completely cleared and is presented on the *Plan* of Period II with the regular facings but without a door. This arrangement does not make sense when the *Plans* do not propose any means of access. A difference in the rendering of the stones suggests a passage in the block of wall 293, to the east: reconstruction is difficult because the threshold would stand more than 1.30 m above the floor of L. 34 and the access would drop into the baths. We have admitted that the full wall 306 is a restoration and that the leveling at its base (fig. 47b) would have preserved the alignment of a previous state where one could place a door opening onto the staircase at L. 35. If not, access to L. 34 must be envisaged in the west wall.

In the west, was wall 299 of the small room a full wall or was there a gap in it? The *Journal* does not mention any opening, even in passing: *We remove the wall between loci 32 and 34, which is secondary* (L. 34, 27/2/54). It is likely that at Level 4 (Period III), the location, ruined in 68, was condemned by poor masonry. When de Vaux notes that the wall *is secondary*, we have to understand that the masonry was of poor quality, not tied to the other walls it abuts, and that it seals a space which perhaps was not closed. So it would be necessary to explain that the wet room, on this side, had remained open to the small room of L. 32 or to the courtyard. During the excavation a more careful observation of the facing of wall 293 in L. 34 should have marked the tearing out or the first section of a chaining. Despite everything, the *Journal* reconstructs for us the trace of the closure *We finish clearing the wall between 34 and 32. We find the plastering at the back of the southwest pool, its junction with the south wall of L. 32, then it disappears* (L. 34, 28/2/54). Wall 299 has to be *secondary* because its support was hiding the plastering of wall 293. *The junction with the south wall of L. 32* means that the plastering of wall 293 continued towards the west; *then it disappears* signals the point where the disappeared wall was linked. Nothing is said about the length of the preserved plastering. Unexpectedly, the sketches (fig. 46a and d) represent an extension of wall 299 to the south which has nothing secondary about it and we do not know why: was this a conventional representation? Photograph fig. 47c shows its starting point, unless it could be a late closure still in place. Despite the hesitations, logic demands a closure and there is nothing to preclude the wall having been opened by a door.

Most excavators of Greek-style baths have occasionally found hearths for water heating nearby. In L. 32 the *Journal* reports: *We open the blocked door between loci 32 and 33 (...), no north wall but a passage towards the*

---

57. *Qumrân Vol. II*, fig. 1, p. 439.

fig. 47.   Locus 34 in the stages of excavation
a) Terracotta pipe 621 of workshop L. 34
b) The long bath, original lining remoulded, covering of mortar supporting part of a small tank
c) The bath viewed towards the east; to the left the thin dividing wall 306
d) The small seated bath

main courtyard (L. 37), (...) then phase II. (...) The passage is closed by two pilasters which frame a door; the layer of ash from the destruction (i.e., of phase I) runs under the threshold and under the pilasters, but has burned the stones of the west wall (L. 32, 9/4/53). The traces of ash recorded may witness to a destruction, but one not found elsewhere in the neighbourhood. The ash would indicate the position of a possible furnace in L. 32, and the north wall of L. 32 would have had a gap for a blocked door after the bath was converted into a workshop.

The abandoned bath was transformed and de Vaux considered L. 34 only as functioning as a workshop. The morphology of the two pools, however, could leave little doubt as to its original nature. Documentation on baths from the Hellenistic period was not abundant in 1955, but it was available. At the time of the Qumran excavations, some examples had been published: Gezer from 1912, Beth-Zur in 1931, Khirbet el-Kerak (Beth-Yerah) in 1944 and again in 1949. De Vaux, who was thinking this was an Essene site from its foundation, may not have been convinced by a wet room in a complex where elsewhere he had identified ritual baths. But bath L. 34 is older than the Essene settlement and belonged to the Hasmonaean residence. The excavator saw it as an unusual installation but of no particular interest: *The small pools installed in the south of the courtyard of the main building, loc. 34, and which served an undetermined use* (*L'archéologie*, p. 12). The annual reports do not mention it. Paradoxically, a number of photographs were taken at different stages of the clearing work: the discovery in the eastern pool of painted and inscribed pottery had attracted attention.

Examination of the drawings and photographs and then the morphology of the pools leave no room for doubt that these are baths reassigned for a use that remains "undetermined". We now need to describe them.

The configuration was preserved in this state because it was sealed by the resettlement after 68. The baths were damaged and were repaired. Photographs fig. 47c show that the height of the tub with a seat is not original and that the edges have been plastered in the incomplete state in which it was found. Part of the larger bathtub edge is missing and we cannot determine whether the wall was preserved or not, even collapsed, at the time of the excavation, which was quick. The western part, not destroyed, seems covered on the photo (fig. 47b). The excavation workers will have emptied it straight away, out of curiosity, as it appears in the photo. It is possible that the bath was filled in and clad with a thick mortar to serve as a workbench. It is also arguable, on the other hand, that the bath was not filled in: in fact, on the photograph showing it in elevation, a thickening in the south part of the pool, with a very pronounced corner, supports the cover only where it is still preserved; this leads us to suppose that the receptacle was empty: there is no point to a cover in a filled-in pool.

The eastern pool had been filled, as the pot was held upright by the earth and covered by a stone lid. Thick fragments of wood with varying degrees of charring lay, in one case, close to the buried pottery and, in the other, set in mortar at the head of the large bath, inserted under the partition wall of a small pool in a higher position. There was a wooden frame on top of the arrangement. The small pool, although not hard to discern on the photographs where it seems incomplete, has been poorly drawn on the sketches and its rounded shape has been reconstructed (fig. 47b). It can be accepted as such. Its elevated position, however, makes little sense unless it is intended to collect water. *The pools of locus 34 were fed by the cistern that interrupts conduit 42* (L. 67). *The opening in locus 34 seems to be in the west wall, extending from the pool which occupies the southwest corner* (L. 34, 22/2/54). The proximity of the small tank L. 67 would have provided L. 34 with water, provided that there was a conduit crossing wall 293 which separates them: de Vaux looked in vain for this conduit, which will now be hidden by the restorations. The bottom of pool L. 67, one meter deep, corresponds in elevation to the level of the small reception pool of L. 34, but there is no visible conduit to connect them. We may hypothesize that wall 293, rebuilt or restored in Level 4 after 68, destroyed or covered the supposed conduit.

On guided tours of the site, de Vaux spoke of a dyeing facility, though without great conviction. Dyeing textiles by soaking them in the pools would have fitted the picture, but the configuration of the installation contradicts this option, because the pools were put to new use, one filled-in, the other partly dismantled, and both poorly adapted to holding liquids. The pot, together with its stone lid, was an empty container, placed there as a cesspit. It is not a jar as de Vaux describes it in the reports and the catalogues, but a kind of large pipe with symmetrical openings at top and bottom, and the two openings present the same profile (fig. 49). The pipes are generally fashioned with two asymmetrical

fig. 48. Examples of African baths.
a) Associated tub and seated bath, Tabiet el-Ramleh (Aboukir, Egypt) (photo Paolo Gallo, by author's permission)
b and c) Seated Hellenistic baths of Kerkouane (Tunisia), partly restored (photos Humbert 2011)

openings to allow coupling. Elsewhere, the system was not capable of emptying large quantities of liquid, unless the small flat-bottomed vat was equipped with a run-off, which was not noted; known examples of these flat-bottomed vats do not have them. That the pipe bears the name Yohanan inscribed on one side and the surface of the other is dabbed with fingermarks, is a surprise. We do not see this as a symbolic act of writing a name on a pot that is destined to be buried, but as a result of the playfulness of an artisan constructing the sump. His hand soaked in red ochre, it seems he traced his name on one side with his fingertip and wiped the other several times with the same hand. The action was not significant as the pot was going to be buried.

The cesspool arrangement here remains unexplained, its function unknown since dyeing process needs several wide vats which are missing here. We note that it is not isolated and would associate it with the other buried pottery, with or without a missing bottom - like in L. 2, L. 60, L. 61, L. 81 and L. 51, the latter having been mistakenly interpreted as a latrine. The repetition of such a system for collecting liquids indicates a practice or a habit of not spilling any of it; the subject merits further study.

Locus 34 is a domestic bath in the late Hellenistic tradition. It is not unique in Palestine, we may compare it with the baths in Gezer[58] and Kh. et-Tubeiqa (Beth Zur)[59]. Locus 34 is an elongated narrow space, 4 m long by only 1.80 m wide. The 1 m width between the baths and wall 306 would leave a clearance of only 0.80 m, which is not much but adequate, as often in domestic Hellenistic water rooms. We may recall the hypothesis of a bathroom fitted on the same level as the staircase, an arrangement we think unlikely. We may also recall the possibility that L. 32 was in communication so as to have access to a furnace for heating water; any communication of this sort has been destroyed. The floor of the water room was a high-quality mortar cladding, as it was preserved right up to the time of the excavation: the photograph (fig. 47b) attests to this. It may have been restored when the space was converted into a workshop.

The bath is composed of four elements, integral to the construction, with functional arrangement 303 is rational: in association with we find a long tub, a second, shorter one with a bottom, a foot-washing pan and a drain. The small bath occupying the southeast corner of the space may have originally been the only pool, the long bath being added subsequently: they have a shared partition wall widthwise and the juxtaposition of the coats of plaster suggests this. The arrangement corresponds exactly with a bath, with two coupled baths, known in the Near East in the Hellenistic period and even, in slightly different forms, with other Mediterranean pool installations. The large tub is a little over two meters in length, its size permits users to recline or immerse themselves for a ritual bath. The low tub is the seated type and corresponds to a bath in which one showers with the aid of a bowl. It is furnished with an arm rest in the corner of the wall, which is also found elsewhere. The funnel-shaped hollow adjoining it may have served as a foot-bath for use before (getting into) entering the small bath tub. At that time, the large and small baths were sometimes separated, even in a very tight space. The baths in question were domestic Hellenistic baths, found in agricultural complexes. The two different pools correspond to two ways of bathing: the seated bath provides a hygienic service and the recumbent one is for therapeutic purposes. None of the three pools has a drain and this situation, which is common, has been noted in pre-Roman period baths. The best examples have been discovered in Egypt[60]. The resemblances between the domestic bath of Qumran and that of Tabiet el-Ramleh (Aboukir peninsula) confirm the function and date of our installation in the first century BC[61]. In the numerous baths of Kerkouane in Tunisia, the two baths are often coupled, but the short seated pool is the more common type[62] (fig. 48).

If baths are usually without a drain, the waste pipe of L. 34, which carries waste water from the locus rather than the baths for more than twelve meters shows the care taken in the construction. In the northwest corner

---

58. R.A.S. MACALISTER, *The Excavation of Gezer 1902-1905 and 1907-1909*, London, 1912.

59. Ovid R. SELLERS and William F. ALBRIGHT, "The First Campaign of Excavation at Beth-Zur", *BASOR* 43, 1931, p. 2-13.

60. Marie-Françoise BOUSSAC, Thibaud FOURNET, and Bérangère REDON, *Le bain collectif en Égypte*, Études urbaines 7, IFAO, Cairo 2009. We would like to thank T. Fournet for drawing our attention to the appropriate references.

61. Paolo GALLO, "Un bain à la grecque dans l'île de Nelson", *Le bain collectif*, op. cit., fig. 9, p. 72.

62. Mohammed H. FANTAR, *Kerkouane, Cité punique au pays berbère de Tamezrat*, Tunis 2007, p. 53. Pierre CINTAS, "Une ville punique au Cap Bon en Tunisie", *CRAI* 1953, p. 256-260.

fig. 49. The cesspool pipe of the workshop of Locus 34

of the locus, a rectangular collector was wide and deep enough to take a bucket of water without overflowing. The eastern wall 292 of L. 34 is crossed by a terracotta pipe: *Draining towards the northeast, first a rectangular channel of stones, then a terracotta conduit which runs under one of the steps of cistern 49. It must end outside the buildings and be rejoined on its trajectory by the waste pipe from locus 52* (L. 34, 22/2/54). It is doubtful that workshop L. 52 was contemporary with bath L. 34, but in the workshop the system's drainage was maintained even after the baths were put to a different use. The terracotta pipe, quite deeply buried, headed east, crossing the east wing of the residence (earth platform of L. 48 and L. 52 then L. 60 and L. 61). The run-off outside the walls had taken the form of a drain 910 at right angles to the building; this channel will have been covered and extended with the establishment of the annexes in the southwest (see the Triangle).

The whole installation, including the floor, was coated with mortar. Cracks in the partition walls attest to repairs of the coating and the manner of masonry. The seated pool does not seem to be in its original state; its edge is irregular in heigh, the coating results from an inept restoration which may go back to the decline of Level 2. In fact, the pool in the workshop was filled in and a terracotta pipe placed there. We can clearly distinguish the difference between the two mortars: The one from the interior of the large bath is thicker and less smooth than the fill of the seated pool (fig. 47). The sharp northwest corner of the pool is covered with mortar where the sharp northeast corner of the large pool should rest. When the corner of the seated pool was restored, the corner of the tub was destroyed. The fact remains that the dividing wall of the large bath, torn up at the floor, has not been restored. What was left of this rim at the time of the workshop, more fragile, may have been removed during the excavation. The exposure shows the inside of the dividing wall of the long tub as large bricks of mortar, covered by a lime wash connected with the ground. On the photograph (fig. 47c) one can easily make out in the indentation of the edge of the pool, a brick of the old dividing wall in a fallen position, unless the dividing wall was cast as a single block between two wooden walls forms. The heavy screed that covers it would not be original but an old restoration and a restructuring to support the covering of the later configuration. The foot tub, roughly shaped with the help of four stones joined together with mortar, is integral to the seated tub, which must also be brick-built. The foot tub, which is rarely seen in comparable rooms, may be a later addition or even belong to the workshop; however, a semi-circular vat, attached to a large Gezer bath may have the same function[63].

The question of water supply to the bath in its original state must now be addressed. De Vaux did not resolve this question (see below). A water supply to the workshop may have been concealed, but it is impossible that there would have been a water supply for the baths of Level 2, since pool L. 67 of L. 42 drains and aqueduct post-dating them were constructed in the ruins of the west wing of the residence. By chance, the baths have been preserved under an odd installation. None of the baths comparable to Qumran's benefited from a direct water supply. Despite the sometimes considerable capacity of the baths – that of L. 34 is close to 250 liters – they were filled up by hand. It is highly likely that the only water supply point for the Hellenistic residence of Qumran was the round cistern L. 110, situated in the outbuildings to the west. It is astonishing that the baths were so far away from the cistern. We may imagine that use of the large baths was not a frequent habit, unlike the seated bath, whose tank was not designed to be filled to the brim, but served more as a receptacle. In Hellenistic houses, the *wet room* was installed near the entrance rather than in a remoter wing some distance off[64]. It is true that the large dimensions of the Qumran mansion provide an insight into a special way of life. We have accepted that Hasmonaean Qumran was endowed with an upper floor, access to which was by a stairwell (L. 35). At this time, the upper floor was the apartment of the family and women. So we may take it that the bath had not been installed to the side of the entrance door of large house, but as close as possible to the apartments at the foot of the staircase, since the installation of a wet room upstairs would have posed challenging technical problems.

The domestic bath of Qumran L. 34 fits harmoniously into the context of a residence of the late Hellenistic period. It should be assigned to Level 2, i.e. to the first century BC, probably the first half of the century. When the site was reoccupied towards the middle of the first century BC (Level 3), the area changed its function. The ritual baths were then installed elsewhere to replace the tubs. We see there was a radical change of culture and mentality between two successive societies.

---

63. Cf. *Excavation Gezer, op. cit.*, fig. 112.

64. The very well-preserved water room of Blakhiya (Gaza) is to the left of the exit from the entrance corridor. Cf J.-B. Humbert and T. Fournet, *Balnea* (forthcoming).

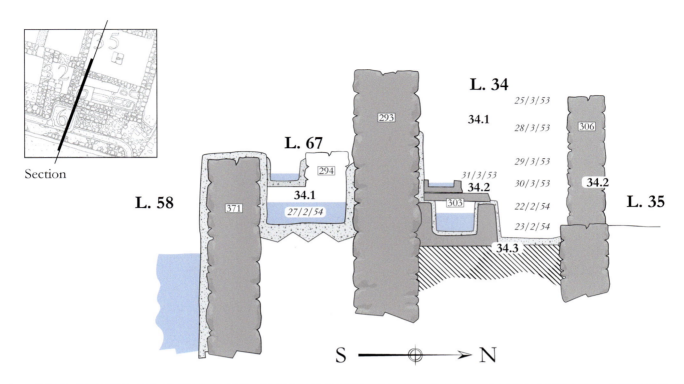

Restored elements	Level	Definition	Journal dates	Coins	Position	Nb.	Chronology
34.1	4	Undefined space, post-68	25/3/53 28-29/3/53	KhQ. 590 605	upper level L. 34 upper level L. 34	1 1	Ashkalon, end of 1st cent. AD. Theodotion, 4th cent. AD.
34.2	3B/C	Workshop	30/3/53 31/3/53	662		1	Proc./Claudius, AD 54
34.3	2A	Greek-style bath	30-31/3/53				

Stratigraphic table of Locus 34 (for the chart of symbols, see page 155)

N°	N° Catal.	Position	Comments (archives)	Date	Description	Clay	Exterior
1	672	34.2	lower (catalogue)	30/03/53	bowl	° grey earth, fine, well-fired	mauve wash
2	673	34.2	lower (catalogue)	30/03/53	bowl	° burnt earth	
3	623	34.1	2 upper (catalogue)	29/03/53	small jug	° red earth	white wash
4	3421	34.1 inf.	(catalogue)	29/03/53	jug	red paste	beige-red
5	3425	34.1 inf.	(catalogue)	29/03/53	jug	grey paste	beige
6	3422	34.1 inf.	(catalogue)	29/03/53	jug	white wash	off-white
7	683	34.2	lower (catalogue)	30/03/53	flask	° pink earth, fine	
8	3424	34.1 inf.	(catalogue)	29/03/53	kettle	red paste	red
9a	682	34.1	upper	28/03/53	neck of jar with graffiti	red brick paste	
10	3423	34.1 inf.	(catalogue)	29/03/53	cooking bowl	red paste	brown-red
11	954	34.1 inf.	(catalogue)	29/03/53	cookinng pot	° red earth	
12	3426	34.1 inf.	(catalogue)	29/03/53	pierced sherd of jar	red paste	beige
13	619	34.1	upper (catalogue)	29/03/53	lamp	° buff earth	
14	675	34.2	lower (catalogue)	31/03/53	goblet	° grey earth	white wash
15	3419	34.2	(catalogue)	31/03/53	Nabataean plate	red paste	brown-red
16	660	34.2	below in covered reservoir 303 (catalogue)	31/03/53	small jug	light buff earth	
17	661	34.2	lower (catalogue)	31/03/53	lamp	° buff earth	
18	622	34.2	lower (catalogue)	31/03/53	stopper of jar no. 19	limestone	
19	621	34.2	lower (catalogue)	31/03/53	wide pipe with inscription	red earth, well fired	

Catalogue of pottery Locus 34,   *° According to de Vaux*

Plate 2

Locus 34, pottery, scale ¼

De Vaux' interpretation			Reconsidered interpretation		Chronology	
Dates	History	Periods	Archaeology	History	Levels	Dates
- 800 ?	2 Chron. 26, 10	Israelite fort Iron II	Wall elements, ash slick (pottery)	Iron Age II fort	Level 1	- 700 ?
- 580	Gap		Gap			- 580 ?
- 135	John Hyrcanus	Period Ia				
- 104	Alexander Jannaeus	Period Ib	Large house on the Hellenistic model	An aristocratic Hasmonean residence	Level 2 Phase A	- 104
- 63	Pompey at Jerusalem		Destruction			- 63
- 56	Gabinius destroyed Hyrcania		Abandonment ? Reinforcements on the periphery of the main building	Episodic attendance of a new group, beginning of the pilgrimage	Level 2 Phase B	- 56
- 40	Parthian raid					
- 34	Antony hands over the Dead Sea to Cleopatra					
	Herod captured the Dead Sea and the second destruction of the Hyrcania		Beginning of the development of inhabited areas	Development of the pilgrimage Beginning of the cemetery deposits of buried bones	Level 3 Phase A	
- 31	Earthquake and fire					- 31
- 30 à - 10	Gap Exile		Loci 77, 86, 135, establishment of inner hydraulic system, development of workshops	Development of the settlement	Level 3 Phase B	- 30
1 to 67	Relocation, development and build up	Period II	Decline of the pilgrimage, complements to the hydraulic system	Climax of the installation corresponding to the sources	Level 3 Phase C	1 to 50
			Hiding of manuscripts, Use of refuges (artificial caves)			c. 60
68	Destruction (?) and dispersal						68
132-135	Roman outpost Presence of rebels ?	Period III	Roman post (?) then civil occupation (?)	Reduction of the dwelling to the restored central building	Level 4 (5 ?)	132-135
			The damaged establishment	Earthquake	Gap	IVe c. ? VIe c. ?

Chronological table

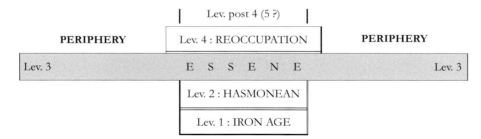

Diagram showing the variation in the extent of occupation of the khirbeh

fig. 50.   Proposal for a new chronology

Chapter 9

Methods of chronography

Attempt at an absolute chronology

The establishment of Qumran's chronology combined data from the written sources with the archaeological data available at the time. The seeds of the site's chronology were sown already before excavations began, because the chronology was rooted in a long debate on the Essene question, reinvigorated by the discovery of the scrolls. De Vaux then progressively structured the theory without abandoning the Essene story. The details, then, had to come from archaeology. De Vaux certainly proceeded methodically by articulating details of the architecture, pottery and numismatics, to which he devoted constant and sustained interest: *These pieces of information provided by the architecture, ceramics and coins permit the proposal of a history* (RB 61, 1954, p. 231). De Vaux' reconstruction joined the pre-established data. In spite of himself, his chronology is a storyline taken from history, or a duplication of it. A site chronology, however, always depends on adopting a stratigraphy, which lies in an embryonic state in archaeological data, not history. Did it seem impossible for de Vaux to establish a stratigraphy, or superfluous? In any case: de Vaux did the archaeology of a documented and coherent Essene history. The "Essene theory" had acquired an authority which was hardly open to negotiation. He did not diverge from it. De Vaux's chronology matches an "Essene history" so perfectly that it has been applied subsequently to the history of the caves and the scrolls. In the plan to focus on Qumran as a whole, it seemed logical that the scrolls belonged to the site, or at any rate that they had close ties to it. That the manuscripts were Qumran's library was initially accepted as an unquestionable fact. The internal chronology of the library of Qumran, however, posed serious questions that were not apparent in the early days. The quality of the Essene sources, the supposed isolation of the archaeological site and the unique and homogeneous collection of the manuscripts considered as a sealed deposit led to a locked internal chronology.

However, advances in the archaeology of the region at the turn of the era opened Qumran up to an external chronology. So when the weakness of the interpretation became apparent, there was discussion of the choices to be made.

The de Vaux chronology is undergoing reconsideration at present and needs revision – but can we do this when the stratigraphy, which we can only recreate, is a datum we are unable to confirm? Let us first recall de Vaux's chronology in 1954 (RB 61, 1954, p. 234).

Period I
Ia – Construction under John Hyrcanus, 135–104 BC.
Ib – Completion of the construction of the settlement Earthquake, spring of 31 BC.
    Exile

Period II
Restoration under Herod Archelaeus, AD 4 –6.
Destruction in June AD 68.

Period III
Military occupation from 68 to the end of the first century
    Abandonment
Occupation during the Second Revolt, 132–135

Questions of stratigraphy - The archaeological site of Qumran had a stratification that de Vaux observed. He repeatedly assigned "upper level" and "lower level", sometimes noting the succession of one masonry after another, attributing them without hesitation according to a pre-established system of Periods. Such a chronology did not fit with the archaeological data. The archaeologist orders the succession of constructions in accordance with a floor-wall-floor sequence articulated by the wall tying and foundation trenches. The concept of foundation trench, however, is absent from the *Journal*. The alternation of ash lenses of ash and ashy floors or masonry burned or associated with ash constitute in themselves stratigraphic 'signatures' or "links" that have been correctly noted. Often isolated, they are independent of one another, and the stratigraphy prompts us to associate or distinguish them. The stratigraphic "links" referred to the expected synchronisms, as long as they were identical in composition. For example, floor-ash-floor or ash-floor-ash sections are repeated in a certain number of loci. The respective locations in the stratification sometimes fit into sequences that seem identical when they are not, distorting the synchronism. The error was to conceive Qumran as an archaeological site whose entire extent followed a single, general and regular sedimentation. In fact, however, the stratification of the older central building differs from the surrounding ring of more recent constructions. The stratification of the central building has four successive occupations:

Iron Age (Level 1),
the Hellenistic house (Level 2),
the sectarian settlement (Level 3),
the post-68 restoration (Level 4).

The occupation of the outer ring, viewed together as a single "period", postdates the foundation of the site and was abandoned before its final occupation (Level 4). The stratification in the central building is four times thicker than in the peripheric ring. The stratigraphic articulation between the ring and the central building needs to be clearly distinguished. The two sequences, central building and ring, are not identical and their interpretations are different. That of the central building is compressed and that of the ring dilated: the central building has been restructured to adapt it to the ring, and the latter has benefited from an architectural evolution unbroken for more than a century. The correspondences are often difficult to establish. The gaps are not always detectable.

The idea of a communitarian settlement, considerably extended before 31 BC, suggested itself to de Vaux at a very early stage, as if the organization of the spaces had been conceived as a whole from the foundation. De Vaux was wise: *It is difficult to determine the time when this settlement was made* (L'*archéologie*, p. 4). He did not imagine how the ring and central building, so radically different, were linked. He was thinking of a formal foundation by the group that had detached itself from Jerusalem and re-settled, following a plan of organization, on the Iron Age remains. The presentation in Coüasnon's Plan Ia is of a site under construction, the size of which implied a larger project. However, Plan Ia, which lacks coherence,

displays no organized structure. The Ia establishment, however, is what remained of the large Hasmonaean house, which he must have known; the only things missing are the corner pillars on the north side.

Successful adaptation to the desired function is evident in the strong coherence of the Plan of Period Ib, maintained up to 68. It is true that during the excavations, the archaeologist works hard to understand the organization of the site he is working on before drafting any plan of it. At his site, de Vaux imagined himself as a user of the premises, and he seems to have concentrated on the last state of the occupation that he had cleared. He also relied on Coüasnon, who, being an architect, was careful to present things in a logical order. When Plan Ib was drafted, de Vaux and Coüasnon failed to grasp the overlaps of successive architectures, focused as they were on the idea that the site was founded by and for a community. The link between the successive phases of masonry was, however, to be identifed. Two mistakes skewed the interpretation: Qumran is dominated not by one, but by two different and combined construction programmes; the organization of the remains during both phases does not reflect a static occupation but corresponds to the specific evolution of the two groups that lived there for a hundred fifty years. Any appreciation of a chronology requires checking the means of the chronology – a chronology embedded, but not locked up by a historical framework. The archaeological site keeps its internal logic. The modifications of the architecture punctuate the passage of time. Rather than positing a preceding Essene programme, it is better to assume that Qumran was founded quietly, with diffuse beginnings and with little connection to an earlier, unrelated base. The evolution was fixed on the basis of two dates: 31 BC seemed like a firm pivot, and 68 AD presented itself as the necessary end-point, corresponding to a known point in history. The absolute chronology, anchored on these two milestones which appeared so solid, has hitherto been almost unanimously accepted. The destruction in 68, a historical datum confirmed by numismatics, is not open to question. However, in our view the timeline breaks down. We were told that the earthquake took place after the abandonment of the site and no longer related to the chronology of the first century BC: the date 31 is not linked to any of the remains. The thread of the pre-68 chronology is stretched to breaking point. We were asked to postulate an occupation without a fire, without an exile and without an interruption. The origins of the sectarian establishment are hidden in a past without another reference than the reoccupation of a disused Hasmonaean residence in the middle of the first century

BC. The transition of de Vaux's Period Ia to Period Ib is a matter of convenience, and has no consistency at all. Without an earthquake and without an abandonment, the distinction between Periods Ib and II falls. From its sectarian foundation up to 68, Qumran witnessed continuous occupation which we could not link with any historical event.

The absolute chronology – Next comes the issue of absolute chronology. De Vaux reinforced the succession of his Periods by means of numismatics. When working out his chronology, he attributed a role to the coins which is cautious yet decisive. At some points he took account of the fact that the reading of coins on their own was insufficient for dating the layers or loci that contained them. For more than a hundred years, the Qumran site had been restructured or restored in ways that mixed the archaeological sediments and churned up the floors. Therefore the collection of the majority of coins is erratic in provenance. Apart from a few rare cases where coins were precisely stratified, they were collected in the process of rapid excavation and their stratigraphic position was not recorded with precision. This is all the more true when floors close together could diverge by as much as a hundred years. In Volume I, as an appendix to the notes of the *Journal*, we published de Vaux's list of the coins collected in each locus. The list rarely presents a homogeneous collection, and in most cases it is risky to connect finds with a stratified element. As the position of some coins is in fact assured, their attribution is a useful indication. It remains the case that by applying the imperative principle that links stratigraphy to chronology, the most recent find dates the archaeological unit. We have been obliged to cite only those coins in the stratigraphic tables for each locus that offer a probable correspondence; most of them have lost their usefulness as reference points. Only coins in groups sufficient enough to form a collection were considered, and only if the groups were still associated with an element whose stratification was credible.

We must also criticize the attribution of coins to Periods. Fortunately, the catalogues sometimes mention a precise location *near the floor* or *on the floor*, and in this case they provide a precise datum – but one which still needs to be interpreted. We may take as an example the small pool located in L. 83 which, among others cases, yielded 25 coins from the First Revolt, years II and III; for each coin, the index cards mention *near the floor*. And de Vaux comments: *These coins were mixed with the debris and the sherds thrown (in 68) into this pool and were recovered by the new occupants of Period III when they cleared part of the ruins in preparation for settling there* (*L'archéologie*, p. 29). The excavation workers clearing the pool, found the coins in the debris near the ground. De Vaux attributed them to Period III. But the 25 coins found at the bottom of the pool constitute a hoard thrown before abandonment of the site. If the workers removed the coins with the fill without care, it should have been impossible for de Vaux to note that the coins were close the bottom of the pool. The hoard was hidden in the pool before it was filled in, as the *debris and the sherds* correspond precisely to typical deposits at the bottom of cisterns and water pools. Here, the short gap between Periods II and III hardly modifies his chronology.

The chronological benefit provided by the buried treasure is not convincing. The find of 561 coins distributed between three hidden pots, in close proximity, prompted de Vaux to make a clever calculation to date their burial to between 8 BC and 1 AD (*L'archéologie*, p. 27), relying on the expertise of Henri Seyrig. De Vaux considered the stratigraphic position of the three pots as certain: *These three pots were buried under the floor[65] of Period II and above the floor of Period Ib; the analysis of the treasure can therefore provide an element to distinguish the two periods chronologically* (ibid., p. 27). Taking his reasoning further, he wrote: *Or perhaps it was hidden in the ruins when the site was abandoned between Periods Ib and II, or it was put in a safe place at the beginning of Period II* (ibid., p. 28). From this, he concluded that the return from exile must have occurred between 9/8 BC and 1 BC/AD. Confident, de Vaux accepted the argument put forward by Seyrig: the striking of tetradrachms presented a regular, dated series finishing in 118 of the Tyre era. *The burial must therefore have occurred around 126 (of Tyre) at the latest*, i.e. in AD 1 (ibid., p. 27 n. 2). *But this date only gives a terminus post quem for the burial* (ibid., p. 27). His necessary caution does not, however, preclude a burial just after AD 1; but the burial cannot be dated at all. The fact that the interruption in habitation between Periods I and II was not caused by an earthquake was not something that was ever part of his reasoning. The position of the hoard between floors Periods Ib and II was used to give chronological precision to the transition from Period Ib to Period II. The demonstration would have had weight if de Vaux had noted that floor of his Period II was duly sealed: the dated sealing would have provided the *terminus ante quem*, but unfortunately such is not the case. There is nothing to suggest that the owner of the hoard had been an inhabitant of Period II. The argument weakens further when we know that hoards are generally buried deep; consequently, the treasure could have been interred all

---

65. Volume I, Locus 83, p. 318.

though Period II, for example in the turmoil of the year 68, and even later still. The hoard was assembled for its weight in silver. It is quite clear that it originated after AD 1, its *terminus post quem*, and that it circulated for a long time only because of the value of its weight. It was completed with the last coin of the hoard, minted (struck) after 8 BC.

The interpretation of the distribution of the coins in loci 185 and 89 (L. 86) may have serious consequences regarding the chronology (see also on L. 86-L. 89). Locus 89 contains the thousand pots that constitute a homogeneous deposit. De Vaux assigned L. 89 to the end of Period Ib and L. 86 north (L. 185) to Period II, while Loci 86, 87, 89 were re-occupied in Period II, *but at a slightly higher level* (L. 86, 18/3/54). Locus 89 from Period Ib would have been ruined by the earthquake and fire of 31 BC and then put to new use on the return from exile in the Land of Damascus. At a time when Qumran pottery typology was not well documented, de Vaux's assignment of the abandonment of the pottery accumulation in L. 89 to the precise date of 31 BC, by deduction, provided a normative reference point. L. 86 also is problematic. It is divided into two parts: one evidently containing the pottery of 31 BC and the other an assemblage abandoned in 68 AD. The *Journal* contains a misunderstanding in the identification of the two floors: the so-called "upper" floor which is not the "upper level", should have been the floor of the second storey fallen during the earthquake. Eleven coins collected in L. 185, north of L. 86, are from the reign of Agrippa Ist (40–44) and of the procurators under Nero (54–68). They constitute a homogeneous hoard without any intrusive coins. They are all explicitly attributed in the de Vaux' Synthesis to the (upper level), second storey (*Qumran I*, p. 319); according to the *Journal*: *The upper level is the fallen second storey (upper floor,). Removal of the upper layer of 86: this is not a floor but the collapsed upper storey (...). The floor of this period is the plastered floor visible under the Roman conduit. The wall which closed the locus on two sides of the central pillar is built directly on the plastered floor* (L. 86, on 22/3/54). The other side to the south of wall 873 raises questions; called L. 87, it is shared by the wall of L. 89, in turn simply separated from the latter by a poor partition wall (874). *A plate found on the plaster just at the foot of the wall between L. 87 and 86 proves that the floor (stayed) remained the same after the construction of the wall* (L. 87, on 22/3/54). The floor of locus 87 also produced a coin with a *terminus post quem* after Agrippa Ist (KhQ.1436 in file cards and *Qumrân I*, p. 319). The sealing of the back of L. 86 (L. 89) must be placed at the end of Period II (our level 3C). Loci 89 and 185 (86 north) are therefore practically contemporary, and the pile of pottery stored in L. 89 must be associated with the coins of the procurators under Nero and Agrippa Ist.

The numismatic argument also suffers from an another weakness, as the duration of the coins' circulation must be taken into account. For reasons of internal economy, the circulation of coins issued by rulers extended beyond the end of their reigns so that the date stamped on the coinage only gives a *terminus ad quem* which can only be an indication. The numismatic arguments put forward by de Vaux are therefore fragile: one single coin of John Hyrcanus made it possible to envisage the beginning of his Period Ib between 135 and 104 BC: *It is possible that (the buildings) were already constructed under John Hyrcanus: one could argue from the (twelve) Seleucid coins that continued to be legal tender under his reign (...). In any case, the small number of Seleucid bronzes makes it very difficult to have Period Ib start before John Hyrcanus* (*L'archéologie*, p. 15). More than one hundred coins of Alexander Jannaeus (103–75 BC) have been collected. If one disregards the hoard of 561 coins from Tyre, which merits only a single entry in the statistics, the minting under Alexander Jannaeus by far accounts for the majority of the coins at Qumran. Nevertheless, de Vaux used Jannaeus's coins to argue that the settlement developed and prospered before the end of his reign, i.e. 75 BC. Nothing is less sure. In the framework of our chronology, the coinage of Alexander is not significant because of its extended circulation, maintained up to the first century of our era. We have proposed that the architectural heart of Qumran was a large, aristocratic Hasmonaean house[66]. De Vaux considers it legitimate to rely on eleven Seleucid coins from the second century as attesting to the beginnings of his Period Ib. With regard to the six silver coins, he himself notes: *We have to remember that the silver coins stay in circulation for a long time and are not very useful for dating an archaeological level other than as a rough terminus post quem* (*L'archéologie*, p. 15). For the rare bronze coins, de Vaux rightly notes that the coinage of Antiochus III, IV and VII remained in circulation long after the end of their reigns, waiting until Jewish coins were minted at the end of the second century under John Hyrcanus (ibid., p. 15). The number of Seleucid coins is so meagre and their circulation so extended in time that they cannot provide precise evidence for an occupation before the beginning of the first century BC. There is no viable settlement at Qumrân before the reign of Alexander Jannaeus. John Hyrcanus had built the Hyrcanion around 120 BC, which was the earliest moment when the palm grove of Ain-Feshkha would

---

66. *Volume II*, p. 467-481.

have come under his protection. Alexander Jannaeus did not pacify the Jordan Valley until the very beginning of the first century BC. Although geopolitical circumstances were favourable to the region of Jericho, the renovation of the Hasmonaean palace of Tulul Abu al-'Alayiq (Jericho) probably would not have happened before the reign of Salome Alexandra (75–67 BC). Alexander Jannaeus issued abundant small-denomination coinage to promote the popular and domestic economy, which was in circulation up to the end of the first century BC. The region was ravaged by war: Gabinius destroyed the Hyrcanion in 57 BC, and Jericho was the theatre of internecine struggles between Antigonos II and Herod. When we propose that a Hasmonaean residence was built at Qumran in the first half of the century shortly before these conflicts, we have to note that while the pottery of this period is thinly attested, the coins of Alexander Jannaeus are well represented. The rarity of the pottery suggests that this aristocratic house was a seasonal residence. If we accept that the residence was ruined or abandoned in the turbulent history of the mid-first century BC, in addition to the fact that it was a temporary habitation, we can understand why its pottery and furniture are rare. Setting aside the Alexander Jannaeus collection, the greatest number of coins belongs to the 1st century AD, before AD 68, probably to the mid-thirties of that century, from the procurators and Agrippa Ist to the First Revolt. If we accept that the Jannaeus coinage remained in use well into the first century AD, then we infer that the site of Qumrân was most inhabited in the last period, until 68. By a process of deduction, we propose that most of the Qumran pottery must be assigned to Level 3B-C, the end of de Vaux Period II.

Reconsideration of the stratigraphy – On the basis of a reexamination of some significant points of the interpretation worked out by de Vaux, and taking into account a better assessment of the stratigraphy and the numismatics, we propose an adjusted chronological chart of the archaeological site. To preserve the nomenclature adopted by de Vaux with modifications would have given rise to confusion. We have abandoned the formula of Periods I, II and III in favour of Levels 1 to 4, in Arabic numerals. In the diagrammatic table that we present, we have placed our proposal synoptically alongside de Vaux's chart. The reader is invited to assess the proposed changes at a glance.

While there is no reason to object to the Iron Age settlement (Level 1), we insist on the difficulties raised by the succession of the three Periods (it). The weakness of the archaeological facts does not confirm them. Instead a civil settlement preceded the habitation of a probably sectarian group which resettled the site. The earthquake did not take place, nor did abandonment for the sake of exile. Only the end point, the sacking of Qumran in 68, is almost assured, the destruction could be mainly assigned to the later earthquake. The division into the three de Vaux Periods has been dropped in favour of three successive occupations that cover the same architectural evolution according to another interpretive grid and another stratigraphic reassessment. De Vaux drew the three Periods and their justification from a unique sectarian phenomenon, tapped out to the rhythm of a Judaean historical background: the settlement of a Jewish dissident group, interrupted for a time of exile, and finally dispersed during the First Revolt. We propose to replace de Vaux's Periods with three occupation levels, slightly diverging from the previously accepted chronology, and reflecting the distinct functions of three independent groups that followed different ways of life.

1 – The first occupation (Level 2A) was an aristocratic, seasonal residence of short duration in the first part of the first century BC, with the site left in ruins. The hastily restored remains were reoccupied but were not extended; they perhaps served as an entrenched camp (Level 2B).

2 – The second occupation was continuous, without interruption, from the second half of the first century BC to the dispersion of 68. This was a Jewish group that one can safely suppose to have been religious and that adapted the place to a specific way of life (Level 3A). The settlement then developed progressively according to need (Level 3B). In the first century it reached its fullest development, establishing a domain encompassing the palm grove of Ain-Feshkha and finally diversifying its artisanal activities (Level 3C).

3 – After 68 and a possible occupational gap, the short duration of which is difficult to assess with any accuracy, squatters or another group restored only the core of the settlement. A civil presence may have succeeded it, and we cannot exclude or prove the possibility that some Qumran survivors will have returned (Level 4). This settlement was limited, but possibly extended into the second century according to the numismatics and an undefinable Level 5 attested by a few walls postdating the earthquake and some rare Byzantine coins. At that time, Qumran may have been a modest outpost of the monastery of Khirbet Mard, installed at Hyrcanion.

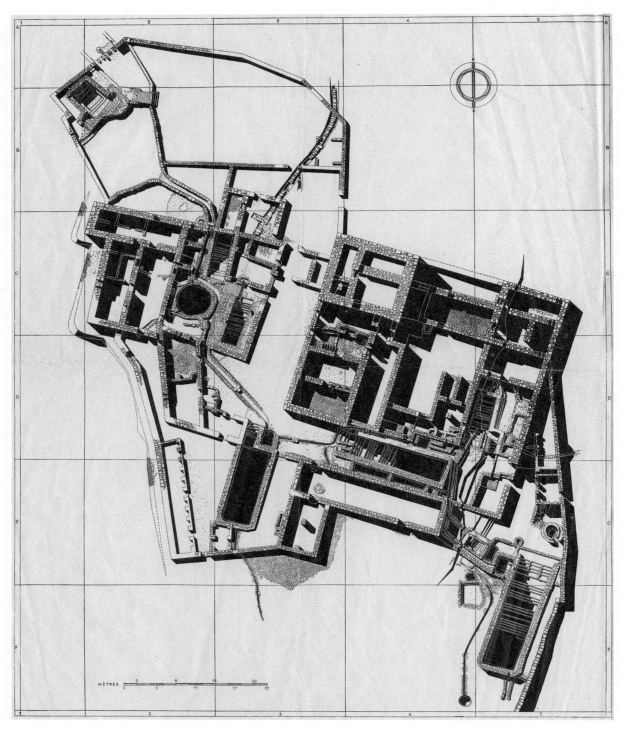

fig. 51. Coüasnon Plan, Period Ib, shaded

Part Two

Designation of the constructed parts and completed list of loci

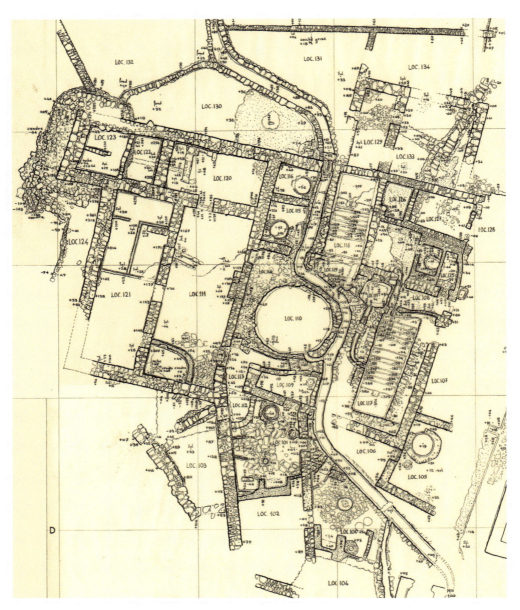

fig. 52. Western annexes of the residence, C.H. Coüasnon, 1956

Chapter 10

Designation of the architecture

Identification of the constructed parts

The three *Plans* of Qumran published by de Vaux are well known; they have been repeatedly reproduced and are engraved on the memories of those who are familiar with the archaeological site. They constitute the reference point, the topographic standard despite the Israeli army's ten seasons on the site – they did not modify them. The *Plans* set out a scheme in Periods; it is not, however, one that stands up to new analysis. The plans are the work of Charles (Hyacinte) Coüasnon (1904–1976), a French architect of historical monuments, a Dominican from the *École Biblique*, who assisted Fr. de Vaux at Tell el-Far'ah and at Qumran. Before C.H. Coüasnon took charge of documenting the topography of the site, surveys had been made by two Dominicans from the *École Biblique*, Michel du Buit and Jourdain-Marie Rousée. The collection of remains that emerged from the earth in separate sectors was not properly managed, and work on them lacked precision (fig. 53). Reports on the surveys can be found in *RB* 1953, p. 90, loci 1: 1 to 4, the part which was the object of a sondage, and a plan of the visible walls over the entirety of the ruin (EBAF archives), and in two fold-out inserts in *RB* 1954, p. 232: the main building (1) lower level, pl. V, and (2) upper level, III, pl. VI.

Armed with the competencies of a master of his art, Coüasnon managed to set out the complete plan of the settlement and then that of Ain Feshkha. A note in *RB* 1956, p. 535, announces: "The plan has been drawn up by Fr. Coüasnon, on the basis of surveys made by himself and by Olivier Unwin, Fr. Du Buit and Fr. de Vaux". In *RB* 1956, we find for consultation (at p. 576) the first folded insert with a complete outline plan of the site, numbering the loci on transparent paper: it can be superimposed on a second folded insert presenting the survey of the remains, stone by stone, in axonometric form. This shows the general plan of the constructions on a 20 x 20 m grid, oriented to the north. There are some indications that Coüasnon completed his plans in the year following the excavations. The "Plan" of Qumran, deemed finished, then became the prototype for multiple variations, a tool to propose an evolution of the architecture, leading on from that to a chronology. It is highly likely that the archaeologist was attentive to the different comments on sequences which the architect set out. They worked in tandem. Some aberrations can be explained by resistance on Coüasnon's part on one point or another – he had a lively character. In 1960, while working on the Schweich Lectures, Coüasnon was able to propose five grids in line with a chronology to which de Vaux must have agreed. It is clear that de Vaux was thinking of correcting it. The illustration in *L'archéologie* presents them on five plates: Pl. III, Plan of the Israelite building; pl. IV, Plan of Period Ia; pl. VI, Plan of Period Ib; pl. XVII, Plan of Period II; pl. XXII, Plan of Period III. The same arrangement appears without change in the English version, *Archaeology and the Dead Sea Scrolls*, London, 1973.

An architect of the old school, Coüasnon was fond of pen-and-ink surveys. In his hand and the flair of his pen-strokes it is not difficult to recognize a distinctive flourish, almost like an engraving (fig. 52).

His *prototype plan* of Qumran was produced in three Periods, and has been reprinted many times. It has become a fixe image, an untouchable reference. It displays undeniable aesthetic qualities. The three plans are strikingly assured in presentation, with a marked elegance and cohesion. One might say that those qualities forged an image that it would be difficult to criticize, or which one would hesitate to dismantle: it is viewed as a final result, following a lengthy period of maturing.

However, it will be useful to understand how the plans were prepared and designed. Investigation of the architecture requires us to know what is sure and what needs to be revised or criticized. The archives conserved at the *École Biblique* gather together the plans and dozens of designs and surveys that come from three or four hands. Unskilled hands are easily identifiable by the lack of smoothness in their pencil work or their heavy inks, and Coüasnon's hand can be spotted right away. So in this collection it is astonishing to note the absence of the surveys themselves. There is no reason why they should have been lost.

It is probable that initially only a survey to situate the general settlement was undertaken, realized *on a plane table*, using measurements of angles and distances. The overall plan realized is precise and reliable. It was completed with some detailed drawings of better-preserved configurations, which had attracted attention. The preparatory drawings with final inking are rare, achieved by collating different parts on the full line-drawing canvas. The question is: How much credibility can we attach to the stone-by-stone representation, which gives the overall plan an attractive, finished look? Coüasnon, the architect, sketched at 1:100, a scale which avoids detail, to the advantage of the arrangement of the constructions in relation to each other. Coüasnon viewed details as unhelpful or even a nuisance. Fortunately, wall-ties and sabre cuts are often noted, but continuations in the masonry are not identified, except at door locations, where there are signs of doorposts. At some points it is striking that long segments of walls display conventional stone-by-stone rendering. The ease of returning to the premises to verify details was valuable despite the substantial restorations to which the site had been subjected. For example, the east wall of large pool 71 was, the evidence suggests, built in two parts: the northeast section, constructed of large blocks as bond stones, and the different south section, which the plan does not show.

We have insisted enough on correcting de Vaux's interpretation, which has weaknesses at two points. First, the three periods he posited are artificial, articulated in line with arguments which have lost their point: the argument of the earthquake which supposedly struck Qumran in 31 BC must be abandoned. Then, rather than an Essene Qumran installed on a ruined Iron Age site, a foundation on a Hasmonaean core is to be preferred. Finally, the chronology has to be shortened: given the brevity of its inhabitation – a little over a century and a half – its duration is not manifest in a stratification of the floors, with very few exceptions here and there in the older central building. De Vaux's interpretation has arbitrarily cut through layers when it is evident that the site, which evolved in space by progressive extension, did not pile up vertically but extended outwards. Guided by de Vaux, Coüasnon worked on the plans with dogged adherence to the three Periods, which today still constitute an authority that it is difficult to dislodge. But the proposed sequence is not justified. The *plan of the Israelite building* (*L'archéologie…*, Pl. III) has no basis. The *plan of Period Ia* (*ibid.*, pl. IV) is implausible. The *plan of Period Ib* (*ibid.*, pl. VI), of the supposed destroyed level, presents a site formed by arbitrarily associating all the sectors, which were added in stages. For no good reason, the *plan of Period II* restores an exact copy of Period Ib, without structural modification.

The study we present in this volume has not been concluded. Examination of all the constructed units may help identify a line of development. Stages of occupation by the same social group will follow a logical evolution, which needs to be properly understood. We deconstruct the organization of the plans; but having filled-in the gaps, we have to admit it is difficult, for the time being at least, to piece together the continuous sequence of the remains.

It is customary in archaeological publications to present the succession of levels and to lay out a superposition: applying himself to this discipline, de Vaux invented *Periods*. Some will think that the present volume lacks such a presentation. We decided against this because a succession of this sort cannot be established when the archaeological evolution of Qumran is continuous, preceded by a brief Hasmonaean settlement, and followed by a precarious reconstruction after 68. Our Hasmonaean level 2 has an internal coherence. Our level 3 brings together Periods Ia, Ib and II. The site developed and grew in a constant and perhaps regular progression up to 68 which cannot be neatly split up into separate *phases*. Our level 3 may stand out, in both time and quality, as the main occupation of the premises.

We would caution the reader not to look below for any stratigraphic or chronological association in the line drawings naming the walls, the masonry and the doors. The only purpose of the way they are arranged is to identify the constructed units that facilitate the description of the remains and the commentary on it.

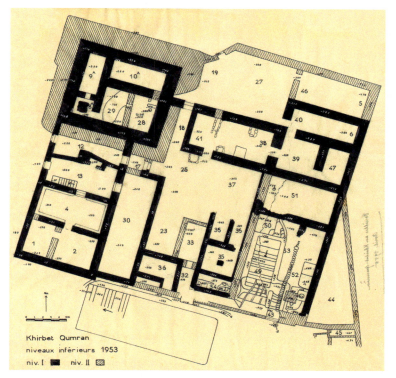

a)

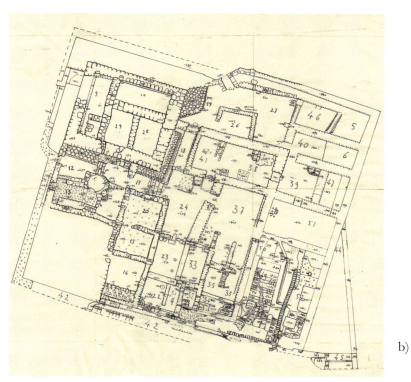

b)

fig. 53. Examples of types of survey in the course of the excavations
a) The central building, Du Buit and Rousée, 1953
b) The central building, details of the constructions, Du Buit and Rousée, 1953

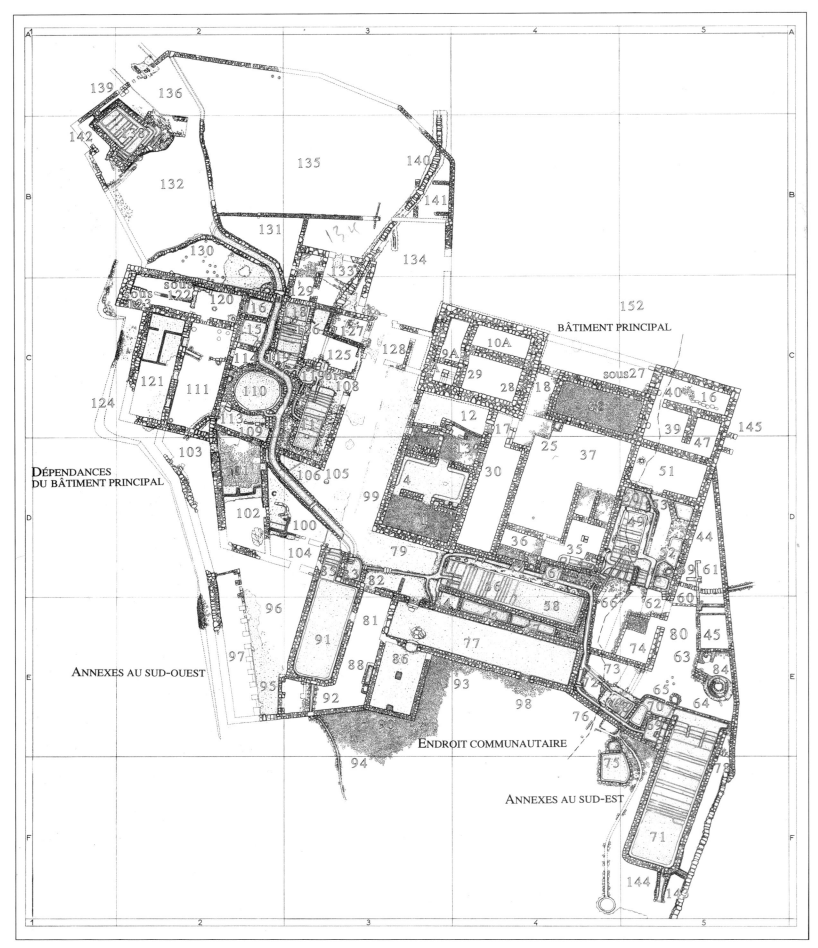

fig. 54. Plan Period Ib, Coüasnon 1956

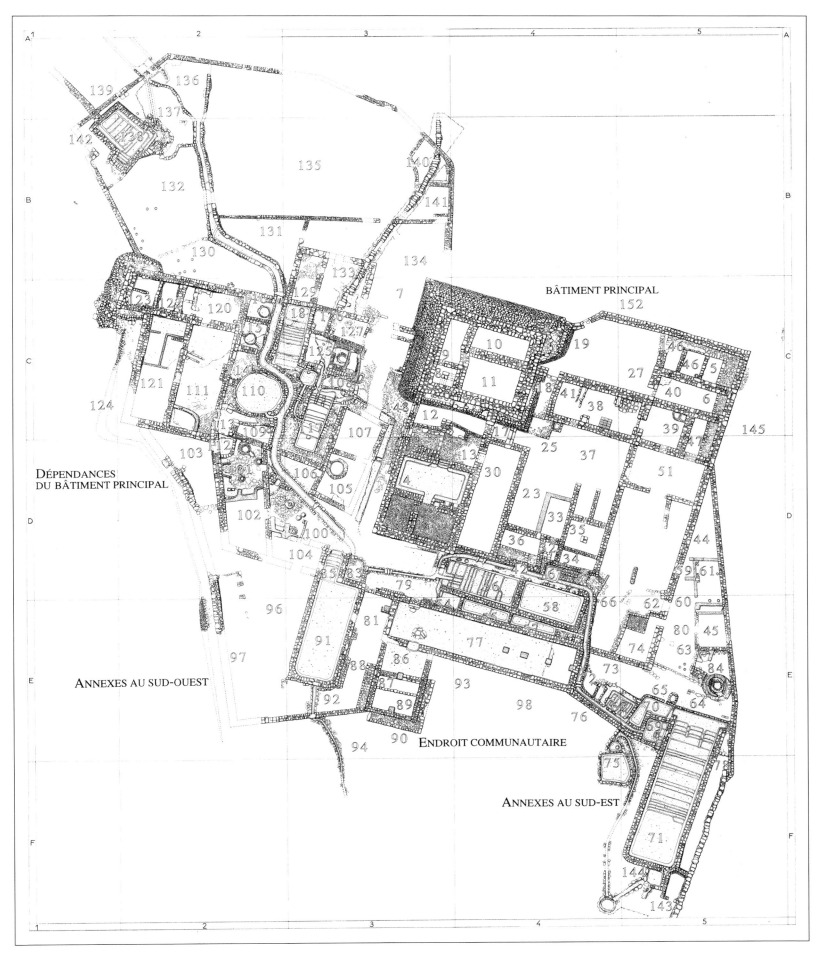

fig. 55.   Plan Period II, Coüasnon 1956

fig. 56. Plan Period III, Coüasnon 1956

Chapter 11

List of the constructed parts of the excavation

Masonry, floors, drains, doors etc.

The coordinates refer to plates I to XII

N°	Coord.	Plate	Definition
200	(D3)	II	south wall of L. 1-2
201	(D3)	II	north wall of L. 1-2
202	(C/D3)	II	west wall of L. 1, 4, 12, 13, 150
203	(D4)	II	east wall of L. 1, 2, 4, 12, 13
204	(D3)	II	bench-seat against wall 201, L. 1
205	(D3)	II	niche in wall 201, L. 1
206	(D3)	II	wall between L. 1/2
207	(D3)	II	rework of wall 201, L. 1/150-149
208	(D3/4)	II	wall between L. 4/13
209	(D3/4)	II	bench-seat east of . L. 4
210	(D3)	II	bench-seat west of L. 4
211	(D3)	II	niche in wall 201, L. 4
212	(D4)	II	niche in wall 201, L. 4
213	(D4)	II	niche in wall 208, L. 4
214	(D3)	II	three-step staircase between L. 4/13, sealed by floor 415
215	(D3/4)	II	rework of wall 208 between L. 14/150, 149
216	(D3/4)	II	partition between L. 149/150
217	(D3)	II	pile of stones west of L. 150
218	(D4)	II	rework of wall 203 (L. 14, 15, 20 and 149)
219	(C3)	II	west partition between L. 12/13
220	(C3/4)	II	west partition between L. 12/13
221	(C4)	II	niche against partition 220, L. 13
222	(C3)	II	west raising of floor, L. 13
223	(D3)	II	ascending staircase, L. 13
224	(D3)	II	rework of staircase 223, L. 13
225	(C3)	II	rework of the partition 219, L. 13
226	(C3/4)	II	kiln, L. 14
227	(C/D4)	II	staircase threshold to the east of the kiln 226, L. 14
228	(C4)	II	south buttress of the tower, L. 14
229	(C4)	II	three-step staircase, L. 14
230	(C4)	II	niche made in buttress 228, L. 14
231	(C4)	II	niche made in buttress 228, L. 14
232	(C/D4)	II	wall between L. 17/25
233	(C/D4)	II	staircase of L. 17
234	(D4)	II	wall between L. 17/20
235	(D4)	II	wall between L. 30/22, 23, 24
236	(D4)	II	south wall of L. 30 and 21
237	(D4)	II	blockage between L. 17/30
238	(D4)	II	wall between L. 15/20
239	(D4)	II	wall between L. 15/16
240	(D4)	II	block of stones, south of L. 21
241	(D3)	V	foundation of wall 202 or top of an older wall, L. 148
242	(C3/4)	I	south wall of the tower
243	(C4)	I	north wall of the tower
244	(C3)	I	west wall of the tower
245	(C4)	I	east wall of the tower
246	(C4)	I	partition between L. 8-9/10-11
247	(C3/4)	I	partition between L. 8/9
248	(C3)	I	pillar of the staircase 386, L. 8
249	(C4)	I	wall between L. 10/11
250	(C4)	I	mortar bench, L. 10A
251	(C4)	I	partition between L. 28/29
252	(C4)	I	clay box, L. 28
253	(C3)	I	west glacis of the tower
254	(C3/4)	I	north and east glacis of the tower
255	(C4)	I	east buttress of the tower
256	(C3)	I	front of door 582, L. 7-134/128
257	(C3)	I	internal doubling of the front of door 256
258	(D4)	II	brick wall L. 33/25-37
259	(C3)	I	south wall of L. 128
260	(C4)	I	north wall of L. 18

Designation of the constructed parts

N°	Coord.	Plate	Definition
261	(C4/5)	I	north wall, L. 38
262	(C4/5)	I	wall between L. 38/37(courtyard)
263	(C4)	I	wall between L. 18/41
264	(D5)	I	wall between L. 39-47/51
265	(C5)	I	wall between L. 39-47/40-6
266	(C5)	I	wall between L. 40-6/46-5
267	(C5)	I	wall between L. 38/39
268	(C/D5)	I	wall between L. 39/47
269	(C/D5)	I	east wall of the residence
270 A	(C4/5)	I	north wall, L. 27
270 B	(C4/5)	I	north wall, L. 46/5-16
271	(C5)	I	east wall, L. 5-16
272	(C5)	I	east buttress, L. 5
273	(C5)	I	wall between L. 146/27
274	(C5)	I	partition between L. 46/146
275	(C5)	I	staircase threshold between L. 5/46
276	(C5)	I	resumption of wall 273, L. 27
277	(C4/5)	I	interior buttress of wall 270
278	(C5)	I	resumption of wall 273, L. 27/146
279	(C5)	I	fragment of wall placed on wall 274, L. 146
280	(C5)	I	partition between L. 5/46
281	(C4)	I	west wall of L. 26
282	(C4)	I	north wall of L. 26
283	(C4)	I	east wall of L. 26
284	(C/D5)	I	interior buttress of wall 269, L. 47
285	(C5)	I	interior buttress of wall 269, L. 6
286	(C4)	I	rough brick installation, L. 38
287	(C4)	I	small north pool of stones and mortar, L. 38
288	(C4)	I	small south pool of stones and mortar, L. 38
289	(C4)	I	two north-south parallel lines of stones, L. 38
290	(C5)	I	double silo, stones and pisé, L. 39
291	(D5)	II	wall between L. 51/37(courtyard)
292	(D4)	II	with 291, east side of the courtyard, L. 37
293	(D4)	II	south wall of the courtyard, L. 37
294	(D4)	II	wall between L. 36/42, at right angles to 307
295	(D4)	II	south reinforcement, L. 36
296	(D4)	II	pool in wall 294, L. 36/42
297	(D4)	II	block of stones north of L. 36
298	(D4)	II	wall between L. 22/23
299	(D4)	II	wall between L. 35/33
300	(D4)	II	wall between L. 35/175-176
301	(D4)	II	wall between L. 175/176
302	(D4)	II	central pillar, L. 35
303	(D4)	II	bath installation in the southeast corner, L. 35
304	(C4)	II	small pool, stones and mortar, L. 25
305	(C4)	II	stone-lined platform in the northwest corner, L. 25
306	(D4)	II	wall between L. 34/35
307	(D4)	II	wall between L. 32/36
308	(D4)	II	stone-lined step, L. 32
309	(D4)	II	brick partition between L. 23/33
310	(D4)	II	large stone wall between L. 37/24-25
311	(D4)	II	wall between L. 23/24
312	(D4)	II	brick partition between L. 22/31
313	(D4)	II	brick wall between L. 22/42
314	(D5)	IV	wall between L. 50/51
315	(D/E5)	IV	east wall of the residence
316	(E4/5)	IV	wall between L. 74/72-73
317	(E4/5)	IV	pottery kiln, mouth to the north, L. 178 (below L. 66)
318	(D/E5)	IV	pottery kiln, mouth to the south, L. 178 (below L. 66)
319	(D5)	IV	pool, northeast corner, L. 53
320	(D5)	IV	west wall of pool 319, L. 53
321	(D5)	IV	mortar pool at the centre of L. 52
322	(D5)	IV	reinforcement against 315, L. 52-53
323	(D5)	IV	step threshold of 322, L. 52-53
324	(D5)	IV	mortar pool at the centre of L. 52
325	(D5)	IV	draining of pools 321 and 324 towards pool 179, L. 52
326	(E/5)	IX	three steps ascending from L. 65 to pool L. 73
327	(D5)	IV	stone tank in block 322, L. 52
328	(D5)	IV	mortar tank in block 322, L. 52
329	(D/E 4/5)	IV	stone-lined platform, floor of L. 66
330	(E5)	IV	step threshold between L. 66/74
331	(D5)	IV	east rim of cistern L. 48-49
332	(D5)	IV	north rim of cistern L. 48-49
333	(D4)	IV	west rim of cistern L. 48-49
334	(D5)	IV	north rim of cistern ledge L. 179
335	(D5)	IV	east rim of cistern ledge L. 179
336	(D5)	IV	edge of partition between pool L. 179/48-49
338	(D5)	IV	rim of pool L. 50
339	(D5)	IV	supply from L. 50 into L. 52-53
340	(D5)	IV	resumption of wall 314
341	(D5)	IV	north-south dividing partition, L. 53, defining L. 191
342	(D5)	IV	late step threshold between L. 43/191
343	(D5)	IV	threshold of the large door between L. 43/191
344	(D5)	IV	large stone pillar, southeast of L. 191, above L. 52
345	(D5)	IV	evacuation to the south, covered and passing under threshold 343, L. 43
346	(E4)	IV	eastern section of the aqueduct, downstream from L. 83
347	(E3/4)	III	south side of the residence
349	(D3)	III	wall cutting L. 79 to define L. 151
350	(D/E3)	III	leveling bed underlying 347 (older wall?) L. 82
351	(E3)	III	rough brick partition, dividing L. 82
352	(D3)	III	support of channel 346 to the west of L. 56
353	(D3)	III	vestige of a wall under wall 200
354	(D3)	III	vestige of east-west wall, L. 151
356	(D/E3)	III	diversion of channel 346 towards L. 77 and L. 79
357	(E4)	III	partition between L. 54/55
358	(E3)	III	bedding of foundation of wall 347, or older wall, below L. 54
359	(E3)	III	west rim of pool L. 54
360	(E4)	III	partition between L. 55/57
361	(E4)	III	high mortar bottom, L. 55
362	(E4)	III	low mortar bottom, L. 55
363	(E4)	III	east partition of L. 57
364	(E4)	III	high mortar bottom, L. 57
365	(E4)	III	low mortar bottom, L. 57

List of the constructed parts of the excavation

N°	Coord.	Plate	Definition
366	(E4)	III	vestige of wall, perhaps southern extremity of 292
367	(E4)	III	block of stones reinforcing the corner of L. 58
368	(E4)	III	overflow of pool L. 57
369	(E4)	III	east rim of cistern L. 56-58
370	(E4)	III	south rim of cistern L. 56-58
371	(D4)	III	north rim of cistern L. 56-58
372	(D3)	III	mortar projection insulating 346 of pool L. 56
373	(D/E4)	III	division between pools L. 56/58
374	(D/E4)	III	division of pool L58 into two L. 153-154
375	(D4)	III	stone reinforcement to the south of courtyard L.37 (L. 34)
376	(D4)	III	block of stones on block 375, south of L. 34
377	(D4)	III	diversion of aqueduct 346 towards pool L. 48-49
378	(E4)	III	support of channel 377
380	(C3)	II	north door between L. 12/99
381	(C3)	II	north door between L. 12/99
382	(C5)	I	blocked door, east of 261, between L. 27/38
383	(C3)	II	niche in wall 219, L. 12
384	(E5)	IX	door between L. 74/80
385	(C4)	I/II	entrance to the tower, from the south, in L. 29
387	(C/D4)	II	door between L. 17/25
388	(C4)	II	door between L. 12/17
389	(D4)	II	door between L. 13/30
390	(D4)	II	door between L. 2/16
391	(D4)	II	narrow part of door 389
392	(C4)	II	door between L. 25/38
393	(C4)	I	door between L. 19/38
394	(C5)	I	door between L. 38/39
395	(C5)	I	door between L. 27/40
396	(C5)	I	vestige of Iron Age wall, projecting to the east of the site
397	(D5)	I	vestige of Iron Age wall, projecting to the east of the site
398	(D5)	I	vestige of Iron Age wall, projecting to the east of the site
399	(C4)	I	small exterior door in the north front, L. 19
400	(C4)	I	western extension of wall 262, fitted under the tower, L. 18
401	(D5)	I	door between L. 39/51
402	(D5)	I	door between L. 47/51
403	(D4)	II	door between L. 35/175
404	(D4)	II	door between L. 35/176
405	(D4)	II	door between L. 34/42
406	(D4)	IV	door between L. 35/48
407	(D5)	IV	door between L. 51/53
408	(D/E5)	IV	vestige of wall attached to block 342, L. 191
409	(D4)	II	door between L. 25/37
410	(C4)	I	door between L. 10A/28
412	(C3)	I	passage between L. 8/9
413	(C4)	I	door between L. 9A/ 11-29
414	(C4)	I	door between L. 10A/11-29
415	(D3)	II	floor of beaten earth, in the door between L. 4/13
416	(E5)	IX	vestige of wall projecting from 316, L. 65
417	(D3)	III	mortar-coated niche in wall 349, L. 151
418	(D3)	III	restored passage in wall 349 between L. 99/3-151
500	(B2)	XI	section of the upstream half of the aqueduct, entirely restored post-68: extended by downstream turn 805
501	(B/C2)	XI	north wall of the western annexes, L. 130/168
502	(C2)	VII	wall between L. 168/111-121
503	(B/C2)	VII	west wall of L. 123
504	(C2)	VII	west wall of L. 121/124
505	(C2)	VII	south wall of the western annexes, L. 111-121/103
506	(C2)	VII	wall between L. 111/121
507	(C2)	VII	east wall of the outbuildings of the residence, L. 111/113-114
508	(C2)	VII	wall between L. 171/169-170
509	(C2)	VII	partition of L.168 into L. 169 and 170
510	(C2)	VII	partition pierced by three vertical openings between L. 120/122
511	(C2)	VII	partition of the western part of the loci 169/170 into L. 123 and 167
512	(C2)	VII	restoration of the northern front of the annexes of the residence, between L. 122/130
513	(C2)	VII	niche made in wall 503, L. 120
514	(C2)	VII	south partition (pisé) of silo L. 161 (partition of L. 121)
515	(C2)	VII	south partition (pisé) of silos L.162-163 (partition of L. 121)
516	(C2)	VII	partition (pisé) separating silos L. 162-163 (partition of L. 121)
517	(C2)	VII	vestige of wall in L. 121
518	(C2)	VII	blocked door in wall 506, converted into a reinforcement, L. 172
519	(C2)	VII	door between L. 111/121
520	(C2)	VII	blocked door in wall 506, converted into a reinforcement, L. 111
521	(C2)	VII	vestige of a transverse channel L. 111
522	(C2)	VII	vestige of a transverse channel L. 111
523	(C2)	VII	evacuation drain cutting the southwest corner of L. 111
524	(C2)	VII	reinforcement or support against wall 507, L. 111
525	(C2)	VII	pisé partition of silo L164 (in L. 111)
526	(C2)	VII	buttress at the crest of the ravine to support L. 103
527	(C2)	VII	niche in wall 506, L. 111
528	(C2)	VI	blocked door between L. 111/113, converted into a cupboard, L. 111
529	(C2)	VII	vestige of a bench, south of L. 111, in L. 164
530	(C2)	XI	sluice in wall 412 of channel 673, south enclosure north
531	(C3)	VI/XI	wall south of L. 172 and north of the annexes
532	(C2)	VI	wall between L. 115/116
533	(C2)	VI	wall between L. 114/115
534	(C2)	VI	edge of drain 500 against L. 115-116
535	(C2)	VI	silo of pisé, L. 116
536	(C2)	VI	silo of pisé, L. 115
537	(C2)	VII	door between L. 111/114, converted into a cupboard, L. 114
538	(C2)	VI	stone-lining floor of L. 114
539	(C2)	VI	vestige of south wall of L. 114
540	(C2)	VI	cesspool, L. 110, vestige of abandoned conduit 521 (L. 111)

Designation of the constructed parts

N°	Coord.	Plate	Definition
541	(C2)	VI	coping of cistern L. 110
542	(C2)	VI	access steps to coping 541
543	(C/D 2-3)	VI	south wall of the annexes of the residence, L. 109/112 and 117/106
544	(C2)	VI	wall between L. 109/113
545	(C2)	VI	north step threshold between L. 109/113
546	(C2)	VI	mortar projection on the floor of L. 113
547	(C2)	VI	partition between L. 109 and drain 500
548	(C2)	VI	west rim of cistern L. 118
549	(C2)	VI	channel between pool 173 and cistern L. 110, underground to L. 115-116
550	(C2)	VI	overflow from L. 119 towards L. 110
551	(C2-3)	VI	border of the basin of the high ledge between . L. 118/119
552	(C3)	VI	east edge of aqueduct 500 between L. 110/117
553	(C2)	VI	wall L. 115/114, under wall 533
554	(C3)	VI	south wall of L. 125/117
555	(C/D3)	V	east wall of the annexes, L. 117/107
556	(C3)	VI	channel linking aqueduct 500 with pool L. 119bis
557	(D2)	X	beginning of wall L. 192, dividing L. 103, attached to wall 785
558	(C3)	VI	channel linking pool L. 119bis and pool L. 117
559	(C3)	VI	lower channel, not in use, linking pool L. 119bis and pool L. 117
560	(C2-3)	VI	tributary lower channel from 558, out of use, to drain 500
561	(C/D3)	VI	west rim of cistern L. 117
562	(D3)	VI	south rim of cistern L. 117
563	(B/C3)	VI	east rim of cistern L. 117
564	(B/C3)	VI	buried overflow channel from L. 117 towards the ravine north of the site
565	(C3)	VI	disused feed from L. 117 from the western façade of the residence
566	(C3)	VI	disused feed from the west of the residence towards L. 117
567	(C3)	VI	descending step threshold of the entrance of pool L. 117 (L. 108)
568	(C3)	VI	east wall of cistern L.118/125
569	(C3)	VI	wall between L. 125-166/127
570	(C3)	VI	wall between L. 126/127
571	(C3)	VI	threshold of reservoir L. 126/125
572	(C3)	VI	border of kiln 577 platform, L. 166
573	(C3)	VI	south border around kiln 577, L. 166
574	(C3)	VI	north border around kiln 577, L. 166
575	(C3)	VI	small wall between L. 108/165
576	(C3)	VI	front of kiln 577, L. 166
577	(C3)	VI	kiln or furnace, L. 166
578	(C3)	VI	pisé partition blocking the opening of L. 165 onto L. 148
579	(C3)	VI	small pool against partition 578, L. 148
580	(C3)	VI	wall between L. 127/128
581	(C/D3)	V	remains of stone-lined floor between the residence and its annexes, L. 128-148
582	(C3)	V	main door of the entrance in the annexes of the residence, between L. 134/128
583	(C3)	V	wall between L. 125/128
584	(D2)	VIII	door between L. 109/101
585	(C3)	VI	door between L. 127/128
586	(C3)	V	door between L. 108/99-148
588	(C3)	VI	connection between L. 119/119bis
590	(C2)	VI	kiln? L. 109
591	(C3)	V	separation between L. 128/155
592	(C3)	V	drain with sealed diverticula, put out of use by ramp 252 east of the tower
593	(C3)	VI	projection dividing the upper steps of L. 117
594	(C3)	VI	projection dividing the upper steps of L. 117
596	(C3)	VI	door between L. 108/165
597	(C2)	VII	door between L. 111/120
598	(BC1-2)	XI	reinforcement block at the western extremity of L. 168
599	(A2, B2)	XI	beginning of dismantled wall, L. 132/135
600	(A2)	XI	sharp bend articulating walls 655 and 657, L. 135, northern extremity of wall 599
649	(B3)	XI	mortar floor, L. 133
650	(A2)	XI	mortar upstream of sluice 658
651	(A2)	XI	northeast edge of aqueduct 650, L. 139
652	(A2)	XI	southeast edge of aqueduct 650, L. 139
653	(A2)	XI	separating projection of sluice 658 between the old and new sluices, L. 139
654	(A1)	XI	southwest wall of L. 139
655	(A1-2)	XI	wall between L. 138-136/139
656	(B1)	XI	southwest wall, L. 138-132
657	(A2-3)	XI	long north wall of the north enclosure (L. 135)
658	(A2)	XI	transition sluice at the entrance to the site, L. 136
660	(B3)	XI	east wall of L. 134-135
661	(A/B2)	XI	northeast edge of L. 138
662	(A1)	XI	northwest edge of L. 138
663	(B1)	XI	southwest edge of L. 138
664	(B2)	XI	north seat, L. 138
665	(B1)	XI	south seat, L. 138
666	(B2)	XI	southeast wall of L. 138
667	(B2)	XI	buttress of the eastern corner of L. 138
668	(B2)	XI	vestige of a block fixed under buttress 666
669	(B2)	XI	overflow of bath 138
670	(B1-2)	XI	evacuation drain of overflow 669
671	(B2)	XI	east edge of aqueduct 500
672	(B2)	XI	edge of aqueduct 500 in L. 130: it seals a former stretch of mortar masonry 698
673	(B2)	XI	state of the drain in front of aqueduct 500
674	(B3)	XI	beginning of wall against wall 657, L. 140
675	(B2)	XI	vestige of an extension of buttress 667?
676	(C2)	XI	tank or masonry kiln of crude earth in the southeast corner of L. 173
677	(B2)	XI	diversionary sluice of aqueduct 673 towards evacuation of 706, L. 130-132
678	(B2-3)	XI	long south wall of L. 135/130-131-134
679	(B/C3)	XI	disused evacuation drain at an angle in L. 129-133, links up with evacuation 564
680	(B/C3)	XI	wall between L. 129/131
681	(B3)	XI	north wall between L. 129-133/134
682	(B/C3)	XI	east wall between L. 129-133/134
683	(C3)	XI	wall between L. 129/133
684	(B3)	XI	wall between L. 131/134
685	(B3)	XI	line of stones, vestige sealed by wall 678, L. 134-135
686	(B3)	XI	vestige of a disused drain in front of 564, L. 134
687	(B3)	XI	west wall between L. 141/135

List of the constructed parts of the excavation

N°	Coord.	Plate	Definition
688	(B3)	XI	north wall between L. 141/135
689	(B3)	XI	crosswall? L. 141
690	(B3)	XI	enclosure wall between L. 140/135
691	(B3)	XI	brick partition between L. 156/157-158-159
692	(B3)	XI	brick partition closing compartment L. 156
693	(B3)	XI	brick partition between compartments L. 157/158
694	(B3)	XI	brick partition between compartments L. 158/159
695	(B3)	XI	narrow seat in the eastern corner of L. 140
696	(B3)	XI	Buttress against 657
697	(B/C2)	XI	dismantled west rim of pool L. 173
698	(B/C2)	XI	vestige of masonry from the north edge of L. 173, sealed by aqueduct 500
699	(A2)	XI	north edge of collector 707, L. 136
700	(A2)	XI	restoration of collector parallel to 707, L. 136
701	(A2)	XI	low east wall of the original collector before parcelling of the enclosure, L. 136
702	(A2)	XI	door between L. 136/139
703	(B3)	XI	passage between L. 134/135
704	(B3)	XI	passage from L. 134 to the exterior
705	(C3)	V	restoration of door 582, L. 134/128
706	(B2)	XI	disused diversion of aqueduct 673 to the west ravine, interrupted by reinforcement 592, L. 130-132
707	(A2)	XI	first collector of aqueduct 673, L. 136
708	(A2)	XI	west branch of overflow 707
709	(B3)	XI	passage between L. 134/131
710	(C/D3)	V	"old trench" = earthquake fault 3
749	(D2)	X	poor wall between L. 96 and 103
750	(D2)	X	wall between L. 101-102/103
751	(D2)	X	south wall of L. 102-104
752	(D2)	VIII	wall between L. 101-102/100-104
753	(D2)	VIII	pisé partition between L. 101/102
754	(D2)	VIII	arched niche wall 753, L. 101
755	(D2)	VIII	arched niche in wall 753, L. 101
756	(D2)	VIII	vestige of floor of large coated pebbles, L. 112
757	(D2)	VIII	restoration of wall 753 between L. 101/102
758	(D2)	VIII	converted door as inset in wall 752, L. 102
759	(D2)	VIII	wall between L. 101-112
760	(D2)	VIII	box against wall 750, L. 101
761	(D2)	VIII	late partition in front of niche 754, L. 101
762	(D2)	VIII	large kiln, L. 101
763	(D2)	VIII	kiln, L. 101
764	(D2)	VIII	fixed wooden cylinder, unknown function, L. 101
765	(D3)	VIII	wall reinforcing the N-E rim of conduit 500, L. 106
766	(D3)	VIII	line of stone, L. 106, unknown function
767	(D3)	VIII	wall between L. 105/106
768	(C3)	VIII	north wall, L. 107
769	(C/D3)	VIII	east wall, L. 105-107
770	(D3)	VIII	south wall of L. 105
771	(D3)	VIII	wall between L. 105/107
772	(D3)	VIII	large kiln, L. 105
773	(D3)	VIII	cupboard in wall 769, L. 106
774	(D3)	V	disused drain coming from west of the residence, in the direction of L. 110?
775	(D3)	VIII	pisé wall between L. 100/104
776	(D2)	VIII	cupboard in wall 775, L. 104
777	(D3)	VIII	cupboard in wall 775, L. 100
778	(D2)	VIII	cupboard in wall 775, L. 100
779	(D2)	VIII	pisé box, southwest corner of L. 100
780	(D2)	VIII	semi-circular installation, L. 100
781	(D3)	VIII	stone partition, L. 100
782	(D3)	VIII	mill, L. 100
783	(D2)	VIII	partition, L. 100
784	(D2-3)	VIII	vestige of wall made obsolete by installation of aqueduct 500, L. 100
785	(D/E2)	X	long wall closing the site to the west
786	(E2-3)	X	southwest closure of the khirbeh
787	(D2)	X	drain below L. 112 evacuating towards opening 809, L. 103
788	(D2)	X	north wall of L. 97
789	(D/E2)	X	eastern portico between L. 97/96, pillars a, b, c
790	(D3)	VIII	wall between L. 85/104
791	(D3)	X	wall between L. 83/85
792	(D3)	X	wall between L. 83/79
793	(D3)	X	wall between L. 83/91
794	(D/E3)	X	west wall of cistern L. 91
795	(D/E3)	X	east wall of cistern L. 91
796	(E3)	X	south wall of cistern L. 91
797	(E2)	X	wall between L. 95/189
798	(E3)	X	north wall of L. 189, supported on edge 796 of L. 91
799	(E3)	X	overflow channel of cistern L. 91, L. 92-94
800	(E3)	X	wall doubling edge 795 of L. 91, possibly to cover L. 81-88
801	(E3)	X	reinforcement of wall 851, L. 81-88
802	(E3)	X	mortar tank, L. 81-88
803	(E3)	X	mortar tank, L. 81-88
804	(E3)	X	mortar tank, L. 81, northeast corner
805	(D3)	VIII	diversion channel of aqueduct 500
806	(D2)	X	door between L. 101/103
807	(E2)	X	door between L. 95 and the exterior
808	(C2)	X	door between L. 111/103
809	(D2)	X	window from L. 103 onto the exterior
810	(C/D3)	V	vestige of mortar floor between the annexes and the residence, L. 99
811	(C3)	V	reinforcement, continuation of 810 to the north
813	(D3)	X	door between L. 81/79-82
814	(D2)	VIII	paving of L. 101
815	(D2-3)	VIII	paving of L. 100
816	(E3-4)	VIII	stone-lining on terrace L. 94 to the south of the settlement
850	(E3)	VIII	wall between L. 77/81
851	(E3)	VIII	wall between L. 86/88
852	(E4)	VIII	wall between L. 77/72
853	(E3-4)	VIII	wall between L. 77/93-98
854	(E3)	VIII	steps between L. 79/77
855	(E3)	VIII	circular stone paving, L. 77
856	(E3)	VIII	door between L. 77/86
857	(E4)	VIII	stand leaning on wall 852, L. 77
858	(E4)	VIII	second stand, L. 77
859	(E4)	VIII	third stand, L. 77

N°	Coord.	Plate	Definition
860	(E4)	VIII	fourth stand, L. 77
861	(E4)	VIII	partition insulating the far end of L. 77 towards the east
862	(E3)	VIII	narrow housing in the northwest corner of L. 77
863	(E3)	VIII	hearth (?) against wall 850, west of L. 77
864	(E3)	VIII	stone and brick blockage of door 856, L. 77
865	(E4)	VIII	collapsed kiln, late phase, L. 77
866	(E3)	VIII	mouth of channel 356 crossing wall 347 and overflowing into L. 77
867	(E3)	VIII	wall between L. 86/93
868	(E3)	VIII	wall between L. 86-89/90
869	(E3)	VIII	reinforcement of wall 868, L. 90
870	(E3)	VIII	reinforcement of wall 867, L. 93
871	(E3)	VIII	stand leaning on wall 868, L. 86
872	(E3)	VIII	stand, middle of L. 86
873	(E3)	VIII	blocking wall of back of L. 86, including 872
874	(E3)	VIII	low partition screen isolating the accumulation of pottery of L. 89, between L. 89/87
875	(E3)	VIII	unlikely opening in a tearing of wall 868, L. 86-89
876	(E4)	VIII	door between L. 77/98
878	(E3)	X	collector drain of paving 816, L. 90/98
900	(D/E5)	IX	wall closing the site to the east
901	(D5)	IX	brick wall, L. 44 south
902	(D/E5)	IX	west wall of L. 61 (brick or cob)
903	(D5)	IX	south wall of L. 59 (brick and cob)
904	(E5)	IX	south wall of L. 61 (brick and cob)
905	(D5)	IX	cupboard in wall 902, L. 61
906	(E5)	IX	low wall L. 45a/45b (brick and cob)
907	(E5)	IX	south wall of L. 45b
908	(E5)	IX	wall between L. 45b/80, in four pillars A, B, C and D at intervals, later blocked
909	(E5)	IX	proposed door in wall 901, L. 45b
910	(D5)	IX	covered channel under L. 60/61
911	(E5)	IX	south step threshold of L. 60
912	(E5)	IX	east wall of L. 80
913	(E5)	IX	step threshold or foundation south of L. 80
914	(E5)	IX	north-south alignment of stones, L. 80
915	(E5)	IX	north-south alignment of stones, L. 80
916	(E4)	IX	descending staircase, L. 84
917	(E5)	IX	potter's kiln, L. 84
918	(E5)	IX	lime kiln, L. 84 = L64
919	(E5)	IX	cesspit, L. 65
920	(E5)	IX	north border, L. 70 and L. 71
921	(E4-5)	IX	south wall L. 72-68-69
922	(E4)	IX	border of channel 346, south of L. 72/73
923	(E4)	IX	feeding drain of L. 68 (L. 72/73)
924	(E4)	IX	west wall of pool L. 68
925	(E5)	IX	north wall of pool L. 68
926	(E5)	IX	east wall of pool L. 68
927	(E4-5)	IX	border of channel 346, south of L. 68
928	(E4)	IX	east wall of L. 180
929	(E4)	IX	north wall of L. 180
930	(E4)	IX	pile in north corner of L. 182
931	(E5)	IX	north wall of L. 69
932	(E5)	IX	west wall of L. 69
933	(E5)	IX	south wall of L. 69
934	(E5)	IX	south passage to L. 69
935	(E/F4-5)	IX	drain towards cesspit 936, L. 183, restoration of 966
936	(F4)	IX	cesspit, south of L. 183
937	(E4)	IX	tank connected to drain 935, L. 75
938	(E4)	IX	stone-lined floor, L. 183
939	(E4)	IX	west drain diverted from drain 935
940	(F5)	IX	west wall of pool L. 71
941	(F5)	IX	east wall of pool L. 71
942	(F5)	IX	south wall of pool L. 71
943	(E5)	IX	pipe L. 69/71
944	(F5)	IX	overflow of pool L. 71
945	(F5)	IX	east border of L. 144 (rework of 944)
946	(F5)	IX	west border of L. 144
947	(F5)	IX	south border of L. 144
948	(F4-5)	IX	drain from L. 144 towards 936
950	(E5)	IX	blockage between walls 967/900, L. 78
951a	G/H/I 4-5	XII	east closure of the south promontory of Qumran, in three segments: from north to south: a) 49 m, b) 13 m, c) 8 m
951b	(J3)	XII	east closure of promontory, isolated south segment: 22 m
952	(F5)	IX	wall closing L. 78 to the south
953	(F5)	IX	overflow of L. 144
954	(E5)	IX	bed of stone on brick wall 904
955	(D5)	IX	vestige of wall 901 (brick and cob), L. 44/61
957	(F5)	IX	south wall of pool L. 143
958	(E5)	IX	north wall of L. 181
959	(E5)	IX	north border (brick and cob) of L. 177
960	(E5)	IX	west border (brick and cob) of L. 177
961	(E5)	IX	projection to the north of L. 71
962	(E5)	IX	projection to the north of L. 71
963	(E5)	IX	south buttress of kiln 918, L. 65
964	(F5)	IX	return to the west of wall 900, in L. 78
965	(D5)	IX	door between L. 59 and 60
966	(E/F4-5)	IX	lower drain, L. 183
967	(E5)	IX	east wall of L. 187 (extending 941)
968	(E5)	IX	bend junction between 900 a and b, L. 64/65
969	(E5)	IX	overflow from drain 346 into drain 935, L. 183
971	(E4)	IX	north wall L. 186
972	(E4)	IX	east wall L. 186
973	(E5)	IX	west wall of L.187 (extending 940)
974	(E5)	IX	wall L. 182/181
975	(E4)	IX	west wall of L. 182
976	(F4)	IX	upper tank of L. 75

Chapter 12

List of loci

Definition and location

The coordinates refer to plates I to XII, the numbers of the walls limiting the loci are indicated between two *

Locus	Coord.	Definition
1	(D3)	Room, *200, 201, 202, 203*; afterwards divided into L. 2/189
2	(D3)	Room east partition of L. 1, *200, 203, 206, 207*
3	(D3)	Open space south of L. 1, *200, 349, 348*
4	(D3)	Room, *201, 202, 208, 203*; below L. 149/150
5	(C5)	Oblong room, *266, 273, 270, 271*; above L. 146, 46, 190
6	(C5)	Oblong room, *265, 266, 267, 269*
7	(C3)	West exterior of the tower, formed by the angle *253/256*
8	(C3)	Stairwell of the tower, *242, 244, 246, 247, pillar of staircase 386, door 412*
9	(C3/4)	Ground-floor room of the tower, *244, 243, 246, 247, door 412*
10	(C4)	Ground-floor room of the tower, *243, 245, 246, 249, doors 414, 410*
11	(C4)	Ground-floor room of the tower, *242, 245, 246, 249, doors 410, 413, 414*
12	(C3)	Room to the west of the residence, *202, 203, 208, 242, doors 380, 381, 388, 389, 415*
13	(D3-4)	Partition south of L. 12, *202, 203, 208, 219, 220, doors 381, 389, 415*
14	(D4)	Partition east of L. 13, * 215, 218, 227*
15	(D4)	Room above L. 30, *218, 235, 238, 239*
16	(D4)	Room above L. 30, *235, 239, 218, 238*
17	(C4)	Corridor with steps between L. 14/23, *234, 232, door 387, passage 232*
18	(C4)	Corridor between L. 25 and L. 19, *235, 263*
19	(C4)	Open air space, east of the tower, *254, 261, 267, 273, 277*, shared by L. 26
20	(D4)	Room above L. 30, *218, 234, 235, 238*
21	(D4)	Massive reinforcement to the south of L. 16, against *236*
22	(D4)	Room at level 4, south of the courtyard of the residence, *235, 298, 307, 313*
23	(D4)	Room in the middle of the courtyard of the residence, *235, 311, 309, 298*
24	(D4)	South part of locus *25, 311, 235, 310*
25	(C/D4)	Open air space in the courtyard of the residence, *311, 235, 262, 310, passages 322, 409*
26	(C4)	Room in the open air space, L. 19/27, *261, 281, 282, 283*
27	(C4/5)	Open air space with L. 19, above L. 147, *261, 254, 277, 273, 267, door 399*
28	(C4)	Room, partition of L. 11, *242, 251, 249, 245*
29	(C4)	Room, partition of L. 11, * 242, 246, 249, 251, door 385*
30	(D4)	Long room added in the western part of the courtyard of the residence, *203, 242, 232, 234, 235, 236*
31	(D4)	Box room, partition of L. 22, *313, 312, 298, 307*
32	(D4)	Passage in the south of the courtyard between L. 22/33

Locus	Coord.	Definition
33	(D4)	Room in the middle of the courtyard of the residence, *298, 309, 258, 299*
34	(D4)	Room in the southeast of the courtyard of the residence, with pools, *293, 299, 306, 292*
35	(D4)	Square room in the southeast of the courtyard of the residence, pillar 302, staircase?, *306, 299, 300, 292*
36	(D4)	Room at the southwest corner of the courtyard of the residence, *294, 235, 298, 307*
37	(D4)	Residual space in the courtyard of the residence, *310, 262, 291, opens onto L. 175, 176*
38	(C4/5)	Room to the north of the courtyard, lobby of the residence, *261, 267, 262, 263, doors, 392, 393, 382, 394*
39	(C/D5)	Square room northeast of the residence, *267, 265, 268, 264, doors 394, 401*
40	(C5)	Oblong room, northeast of the residence, west part of L. 6, *267, 266, 269, 265, door 395*
41	(C4)	Western end of locus L. 38, * 262, 263, 261*
42	(D4)	Excavated sector along the south wall of the residence, *200, 236, 294, 293*, L. 79, 56-58
43	(D/E5)	Entrance area of the resettlement, Level 4, *292, 315, block 342, drain 345, door 343*
44	(D5)	Triangular space, north of the southeast annexes, *315, 900, 901*
45	(E5)	Room with pillars, centre of the southeast annexes, entry lobby (?) L. 45b, *907, 908, 906, 900, door 909*; L. 45a, accommodation with vessels, *906, 900, 904*
46	(C5)	Compartment under L. 5, *266, 274, 272, 275*
47	(C/D5)	Oblong room, northeast of the residence, *264, 268, 265, 269, door 402*
48–49	(D5)	Pools installed in the eastern part of the residence: *331, 332, 333, 292*, L. 50-52-53
50	(D5)	Pool to the north of L. 48-49, *292, 314, 332, edge of 338*, fed by disused drain 337
51	(D5)	Room in the eastern sector of the residence, *291, 264, 315, 314, door 337, 407, 401, 402*
52	(D5)	Workshop with pools, *335, 331, 314, 315, 408, door 407*
53	(D5)	Passage crossing L. 52, towards L. 51
54	(D/E3-4)	Small pool west of series L. 54-57, *370, 347, 357, 359*
55	(E4)	Second small pool of series L. 54-57, *370, 360, 347, 357*
56	(D4)	Pool with steps to the south of the residence, linked to L. 58, *371, 373, 370, 372*
57	(E4)	Third small pool east of series L. 54-57, *370, 366, 347, 360*
58	(D/E4)	Deep pool contiguous with L. 56, *371, 369, 370, 373*
59	(D5)	Passage between L. 60/44, *315, 901, 902, 903*
60	(D/E5)	North part of courtyard L. 80, *315, 903, 902, 908, 913*
61	(D5)	Room in the northern part of the southwest annexes, *900, 901, 902, 904, drain 910*
62	(D5)	Undefined space as a surface above the southwest corner of the residence, east limit 914
63	(E5)	Undefined space as a surface above the southeast corner of the residence, west limit 914
64	(E5)	Lime kiln included in L. 84, against 900
65	(E5)	Open air space between L. 71 and kiln L. 64, *900, 918, 913, 316, 925, 920*
66	(E4/5)	Undefined space between pool L. 48-49 and L. 72-73, *369* - L. 48, *315, 316*
67	(D4)	Small relay pool onto channel *346*, crossing L. 42
68	(E4/5)	Small stepped bath, series of small pools, annexes to the southeast, * 921, 924, 925, 926*
69	(E5)	Small stepped bath, series of small pools, annexes to the southeast, * 931, 932, 933, 973*
70	(E5)	Small pool at right angles and as cesspit, tributary to reservoir L. 71, *920, 926, 932, 931, 973*
71	(E/F5)	Large reservoir in the southeast, (973, 967), *940, 941, 942*
72	(E4)	Enlarged pool in L. 73, *928, 929, 852, 941*
73	(E4)	Open air space separated from L. 65 by staircase 326, *316, 852, 921, 924, 925*
74	(E5)	Open air space in the southeast corner of the residence, *316, 315, door 324*
75	(F4)	Press tank at L. 183
76	(E4)	Open air space to the south of the series of small pools, south of 921
77	(E3-4)	Long east-west room, four bases in the axis, *852, 847, 850, 853, doors 854, 856, 876*
78	(E-F5)	Lost space, long and narrow, between reservoir L. 71 and long wall *951 and 900, 941, 952*
79	(D3)	Open air space access by the west of pools L. 56-58, *200, 372, 347*, crossed by drain 346
80	(E5)	Open air space in the southeast annexes, *315, 902, 908, 912, 913*
81	(E3)	Open air space between L. 86/91, passage via L. 189 towards the south exterior, L. 94, *795, 348, 850, 851, door 813*
82	(D3)	Passage contiguous with L. 79 to access L. 81, *348, 792, door 813*
83	(D3)	Diversion pool feeding pools L. 91 and L. 56-58, *791, 792, 793, drain 346*
84	(E5)	Boxed-in open air space, southeast annexes, serving kilns 917 and 918, *900, 907, 912, staircase 916*
85	(D3)	Stepped passage towards reservoir L. 91, *790, 791*
86	(E3)	Room with two bases in north-south axis, *856, 867, 868, 851*
87	(E3)	Partition of L. 86, *874, 851, 856, 867*
88	(E3)	Median part of L. 81, connected to L. 92, (800, 801), *795, 851*
89	(E3)	Partition of L. 86, including the south of L. 87, *873, 851, 868, 867*

List of loci

Locus	Coord.	Definition
90	(E3)	Large exterior south front of the khirbeh, stone-lined, *786, 868, 867, 853, 921*, including L. 94, 93, 98
91	(E3)	Large reservoir in the southwest of the khirbeh, * 790, 794, 795, 793*
92	(E3)	South part of L. 81, opening onto L. 189,* 796, 786, 851, 777*
93	(E3-4)	Median sector of L. 90
94	(E/F3)	West sector of L. 90
95	(D/E2-3)	South part of the large courtyard southwest of the khirbeh, *789, 786, 797, 794*
96	(E2)	North part of the large courtyard southwest of the khirbeh, *789, 751, 797, 794*
97	(D/E2)	Long porticoed shelter, southwest corner of the khirbeh, *786, 785, 788, 789*
98	(E4)	East sector of L. 90
99	(D3)	Large open air space between the residence and services, *555, 202, 244, 256, door 582*
100	(D2-3)	Open air space in the southwest corner of the annexes, mill, crossed by aqueduct *500, 752, 543, 767, 770, 775*
101	(D2)	Workshop, covered? *543, 752, 750, 753*
102	(D2)	Open space previously connected with L. 101, *753, 752, 751, 750*
103	(D2)	Lost space recovered as terracing, *750, 505, 785, 788*, connected to L. 96
104	(D2/3)	Intermediate locus between L. 100 and L. 102, *775, 790, 751, 752*
105	(D3)	Later workshop built on the space of L. 99, *770, 767, 771, 769*
106	(D3)	Residual space after the foundation of the aqueduct, *543, 765, 767*
107	(C/D3)	Late workshop built on the space of L. 99, *768, 769, 771, 555*
108	(C3)	Access landing to cistern L. 117, *554*, pool L. 119bis, *587, 555, door 586*
109	(C2)	Box room contiguous with L. 113, *543, 545, 547, 544, door 584*
110	(C2)	Large circular cistern at the centre of the annexes, coping 541
111	(C2)	Room with long side, *502, 507, 505, 506, doors 808, 518, 519, 520, 597*
112	(D2)	Lavatories, *750, 543, 759, door 806*
113	(C2)	Box room serving cistern L. 110, *544, 543, 507, steps 542*
114	(C2)	Lost space against cistern L. 110 after closing of door *519, 507, 533, 500, paving 538*
115	(C2)	Small workshop in the annexes, *507, 532, 533, 500, kiln 536*
116	(C2)	Small workshop in the annexes, *507, 501, 500, 532, kiln 535*
117	(C3)	Stepped pool in the annexes, *554, 555, 543, 552, rims 561, 562, 563*
118	(C3)	Stepped pool in the annexes *531, 548, 568*, including L. 119
119	(C2-3)	Distribution pool from pool L. 118, *548, 554, 557*
119 bis	(C3)	Distribution pool from pools L. 117 and L. 118, *554, 552, 561*
120	(C2)	Room after partition of L. 168, *501, 502, 510, 507*
121	(C2)	Room with long side in the western annexes, *504, 502, 506, 505, doors 518, 519, 520*
122	(C2)	Partition of L. 168, *501, 502, 510, 511*
123	(C2)	Partition of L. 168, *502, 503, 509, 511*
124	(C1/2)	Lost space as terrace at the crest of the ravine, *504, 502, reinforcements 598, 526*
125	(C3)	Workshop of the annexes with a furnace, *554, 568, 571, 569, 578*, crossed by drain 564
126	(C3)	Rectangular pool adjoining L. 125, *531, 570, 571, 568*
127	(C3)	Entrance gatehouse in the annexes, *569, 570, 531, 580, door 585*
128	(C3)	North entrance vestibule in the annexes, *256, 244, 259, 555, door 582*
129	(B/C3)	Partition of L. 172, *680, 681, 683, 531*, crossed by drain 679
130	(B2)	Open air space in the north enclosure, containing buried deposits, *531, 672 (500), drain 706*, containing pool L. 173
131	(B2)	Open air space, partition of the north enclosure, *671, (500), 678, 684, 680*
132	(B2)	Open air space in the north enclosure, *656, L. 138, 706, 500*
133	(B/C3)	Partition of L. 172, *683, 681, 682, 531*, crossed by drain 564
134	(B3)	Space to the southeast of the north enclosure, *678, 660, 253, 531, 682, 684, doors 582, 704, 685*
135	(B2/3)	Large open air space, to the north of the north enclosure, *657, 660, 678, (599), door 703*
136	(A2)	Original receptacle at the arrival of aqueduct 650, *northwest of 655*
137	(A/B2)	Space serving L. 138, *655, 661, drain 500*
138	(B1-2)	Stepped pool, ritual bath, *661, 662, 663, 666, reinforcement 667*
139	(A1)	Exterior space, walls worn away by erosion, *654, 655, aqueduct 650*
140	(B3)	Open air space taken from L. 135, crossed by drain 564, *690, 657, 688*
141	(B3)	Small square room, taken from L. 135, *688, 657, 689, 687*
142	(B1)	Lost space west of the north enclosure, exit from bath L. 138, *655, 656, 663*
143	(F5)	Lean-to south of reservoir L. 71, *951, 952, 956, 957*
144	(F5)	Small pool with run-offs, south of reservoir 71, *942, 945, 946, 947*

Loci attributed after the excavation for purposes of publication

Locus	Coord.	Definition
146	(C5)	Partition of L. 5, *272, 273, 266, 274*
147	(C4-5)	Undefined space below L. 27, could go back to Iron Age
148	(C3)	Circulation residence/annexes, *ramp 252, 202, 786/811, 578, paving 581, doors 380, 381*
149	(D3/4)	East partition of L. 4, *218, 215, 216, 207*
150	(D3)	West partition of L. 4, *207, 216, 202 (212), 215*
151	(D3)	Locus established above loci 79, 82, *200, 349, 855*
152	(C4-5)	Exterior space of the khirbeh, north of wall *270*
153	(D5)	Surface level above L. 44, 45, 61, 62
154	(D/E4)	Open air space above pools L. 56-58, post-68
155	(C3)	Partition of L. 128, *256, 244, 259, 591*
156	(B3)	Partition of L. 141, *691, 692, 689, 660*
157	(B3)	Partition of L. 141, *691, 693, 688, 660*
158	(B3)	Partition of L. 141, *691, 693, 694, 688*
159	(B3)	Partition of L. 141, *691, 694, 688, 687*, crossed by drain 564
160	(B3)	Partition of L. 141, * 691, 692, 678*
161	(C2)	Partition of L. 121, *502, 504, 506, 514*
162	(C2)	Partition of L. 121, *504, 514, 515, 516*
163	(C2)	Partition of L. 121, *506, 515, 514, 516*
164	(C2)	Compartment installed in L. 111, *525, 506, 505*
165	(C3)	Low part serving furnace of L. 125, * 576, 574, 575, 578*
166	(C3)	Part containing furnace of L. 125, * 572, 573, 574, 576*
167	(C2)	Partition of L. 123, *502, 503, 509, 511*
168	(C2)	Large long-sided room before partitions, * 501, 502, 503, 507, door 597*
169	(C2)	Partition of L. 168, *501, 503, 508, 509*
170	(C2)	Partition of L. 168, *502, 503, 509, 508*
171	(C2)	Partition of L. 168, * 502, 507, 508, 501, door 597*
172	(B/C3)	Rectangular room before partition, in the north enclosure, *531, 683, 681, 682*
173	(B/C2)	Pool with mortar floor, disused, in L. 130, *697, 672, 698, 512, 531*
174	(C/D3)	Restored space serving cistern L. 110 before the digging of L117, *507, 543, 555, 554*
175	(D4)	Partition of L. 37, undefined space, *299, 300, 301*
176	(D4)	Partition of L. 37, *292, 300, 301*
177	(E5)	Partition of L. 80, compartment called L. 45c by de Vaux, *960, 959, 908*
178	(E4/5)	Formerly "under 66": non-delimited space with kilns 317 and 318
179	(D5)	Entrance landing in pool L. 48, *334, 335, 336*
180	(E4)	Later lean-to on L. 72, *921, 852, 928, 929*
181	(E5)	Small later post-68 room, on L. 69, *921, 973, 974, 958*
182	(E4/5)	Small later post-68 room, on L. 68, *921, 925, 974, 975*
183	(F-4/5)	Open air workshop adjoining the stone-paving of L. 99, *921, 940, 942, 951*
184	(D5)	Space, deemed empty on the plans, above L. 48, 49, 50, 52, 53, *316, 314, 315, 292*
185	(E3)	Later partition of L. 86, to the east, *851, 867, 853, 873*
186	(E4)	Lean-to above L. 72/73, *971, 972, 852, 821*
187	(E5)	Dismantled locus, marked by walls of different thicknesses *973, 967*
188	(E5)	Open space, previous L. 65, *913, 900a, 852, 316, and L. 187, 70, 69, 68, 72*
189	(E3)	Lobby after door 807 (esplanade, L. 94), *777, 786, 797, 798*
190	(C5)	Partition below the northeast corner of L. 5, *266, 271, 272, 270, 275*
191	(D3)	Later partition of L. 1, *200, 202, 207, 206*
192	(D2)	Restored room between L. 96 and 103, *785, 749, 750, 557*

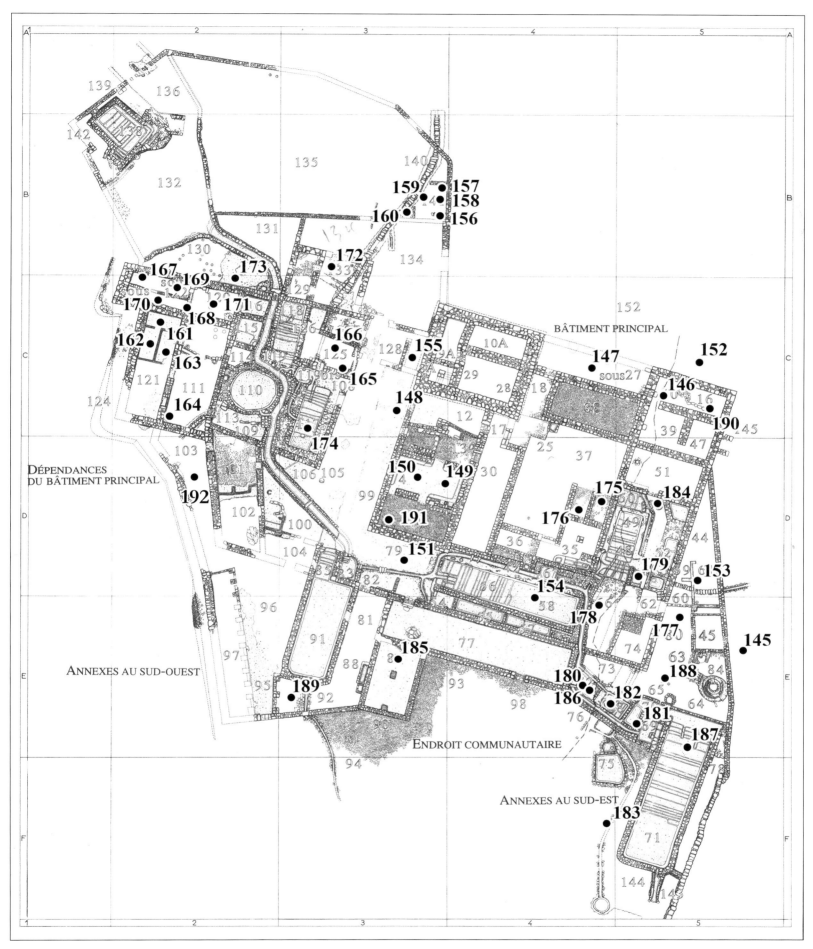
fig. 57. Location of loci added for publication purposes

PLATE I

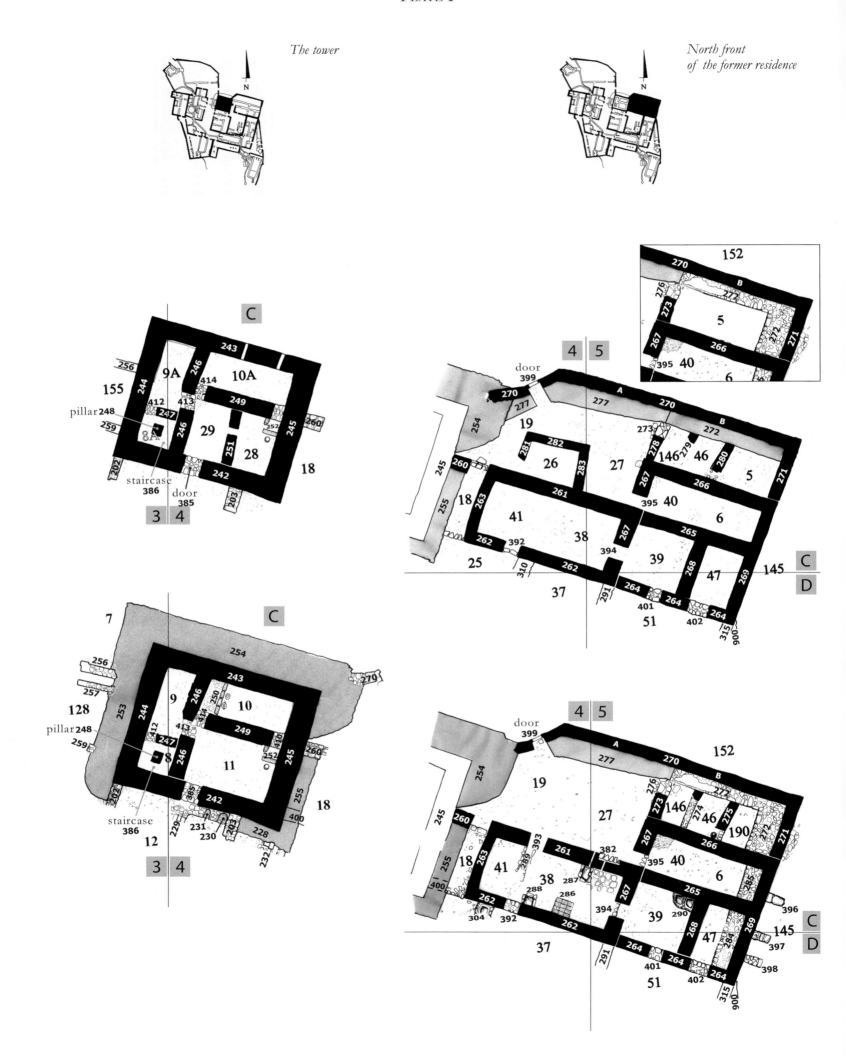

Plate II

East wing and courtyard of the former residence

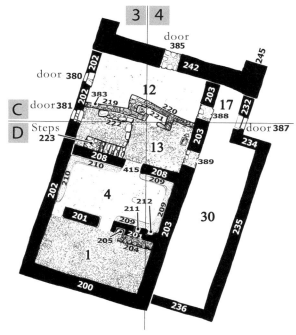

Western aisle

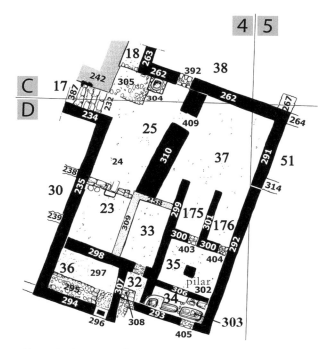

Above the former residence

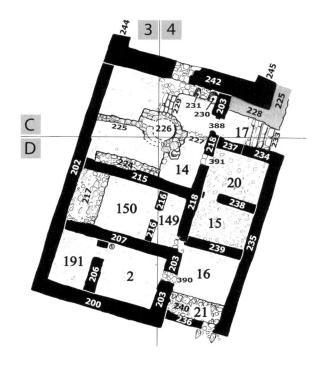

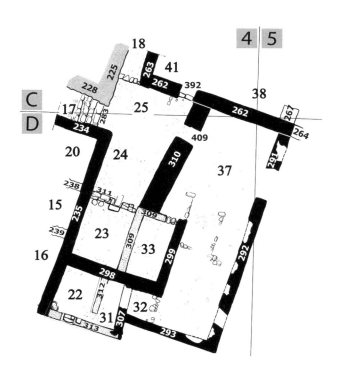

Plate III

South wing of the former residence

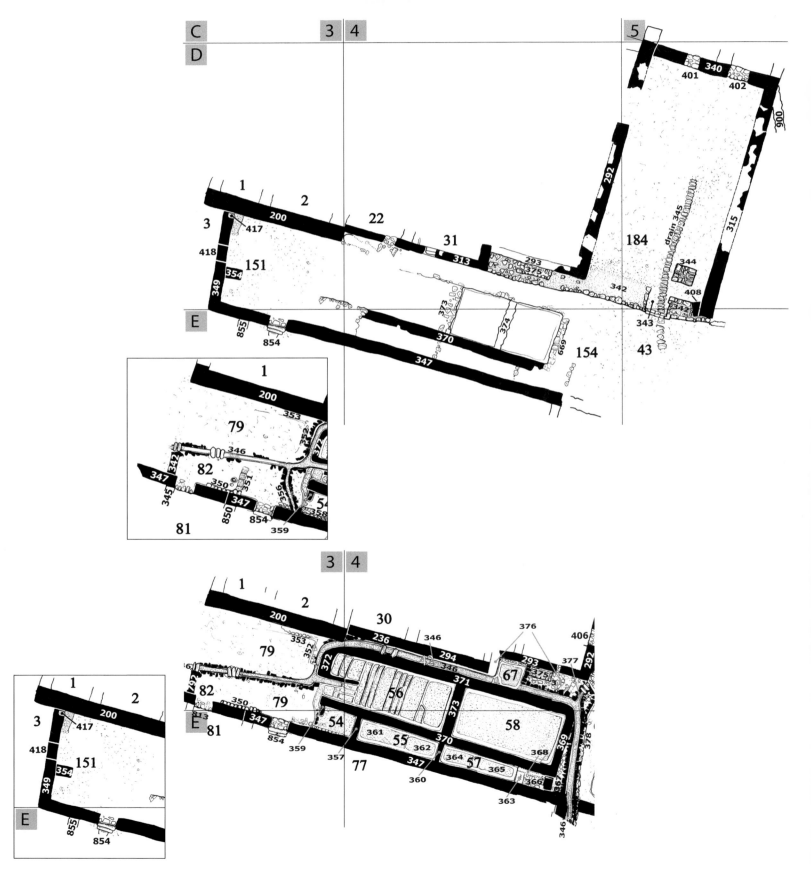

Plate IV

East wing of the former residence

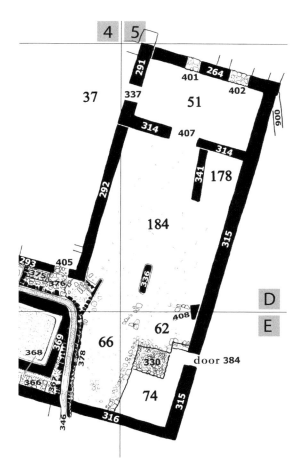

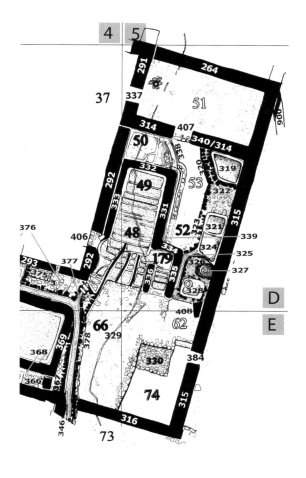

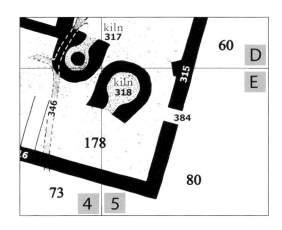

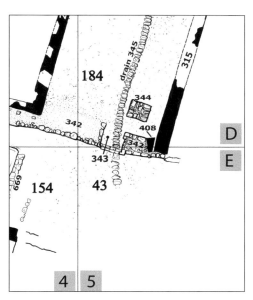

PLATE V

Space between the former residence and its annexes

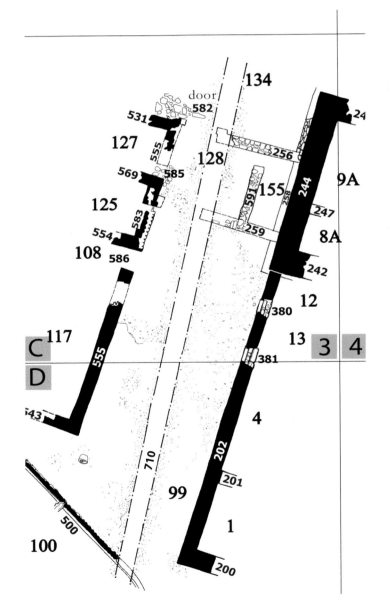
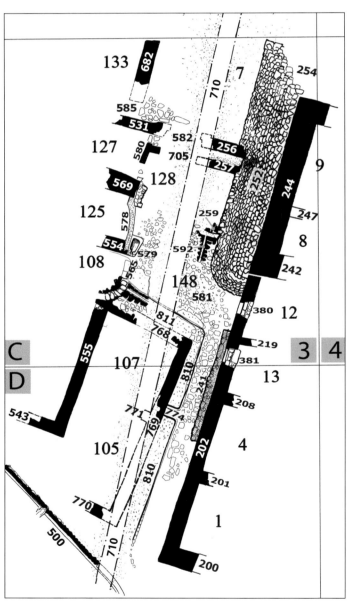

Plate VI

Services of the former residence

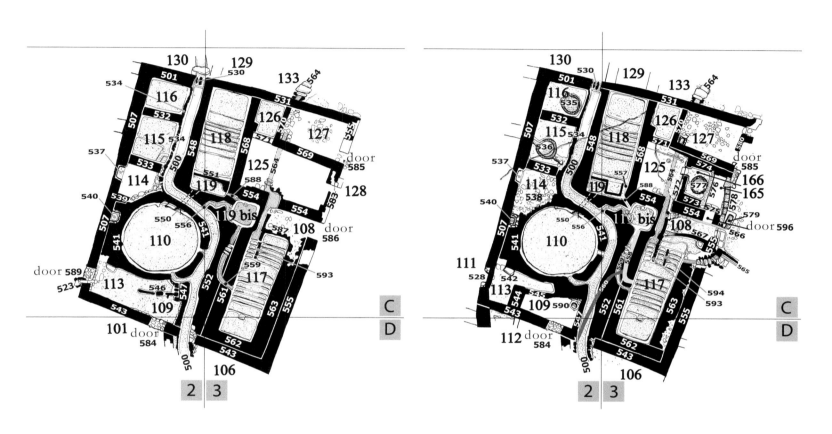

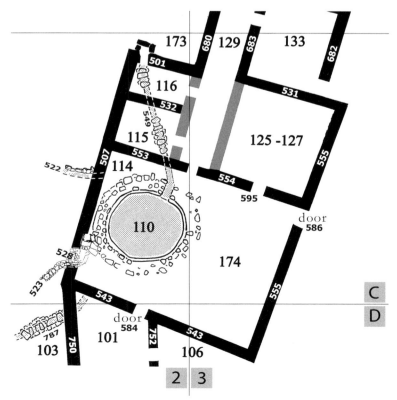

Plate VII

Body of the building to the west of the annexes

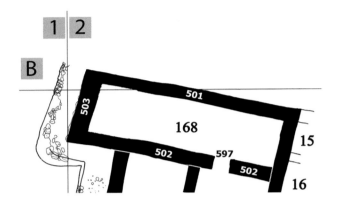

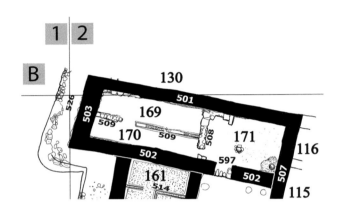

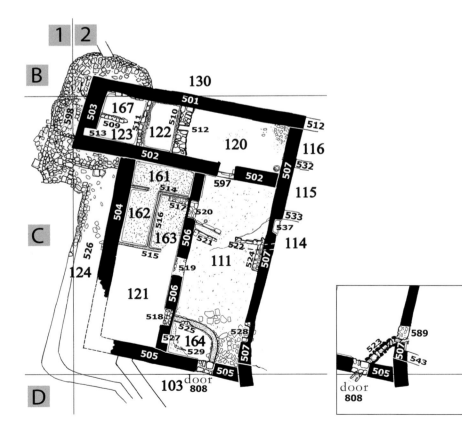

Plate VIII

The southwest workshops

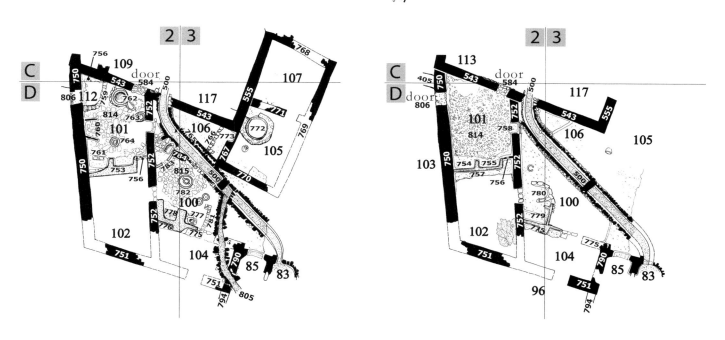

Body of the building to the south of the residence

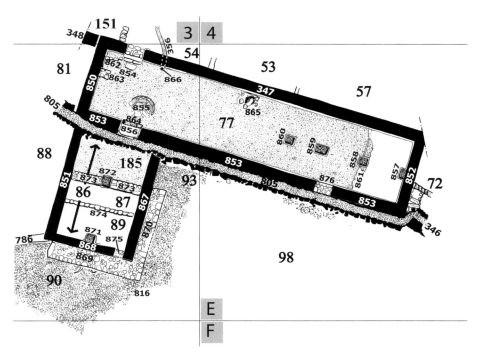

PLATE IX

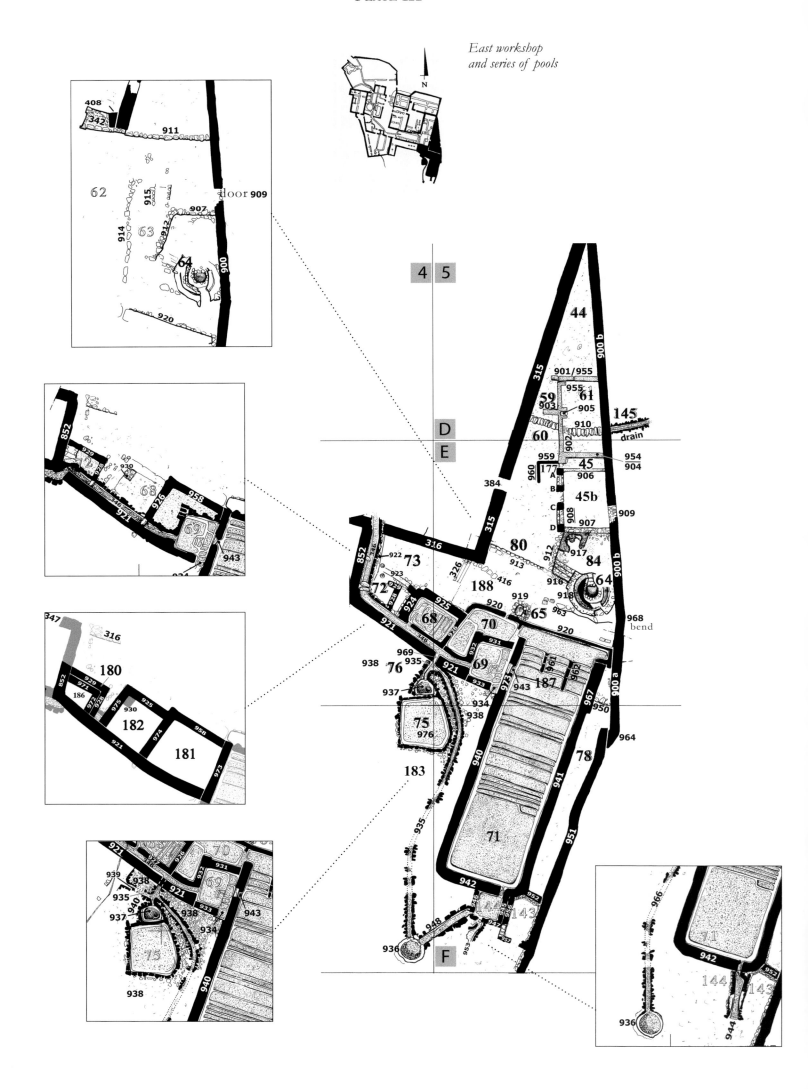

East workshop and series of pools

PLATE X

Southwest annexes

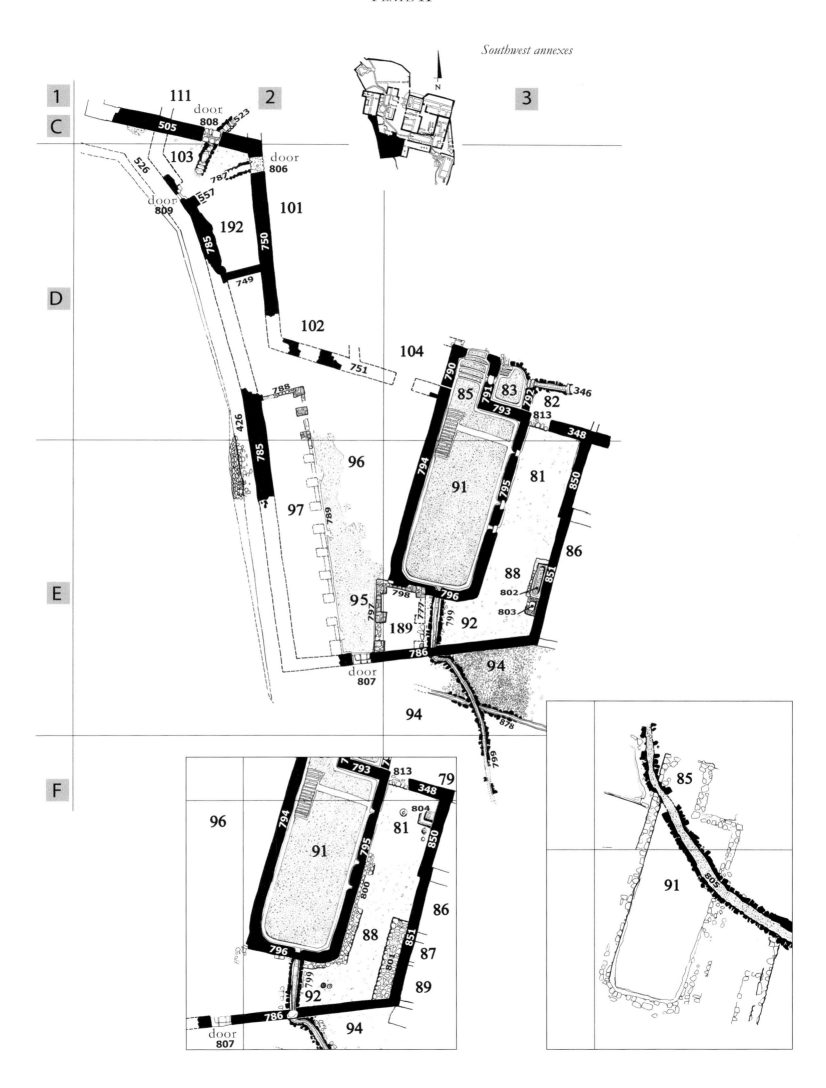

Plate XI

The north enclosure

PLATE XII

The long wall on the terrace

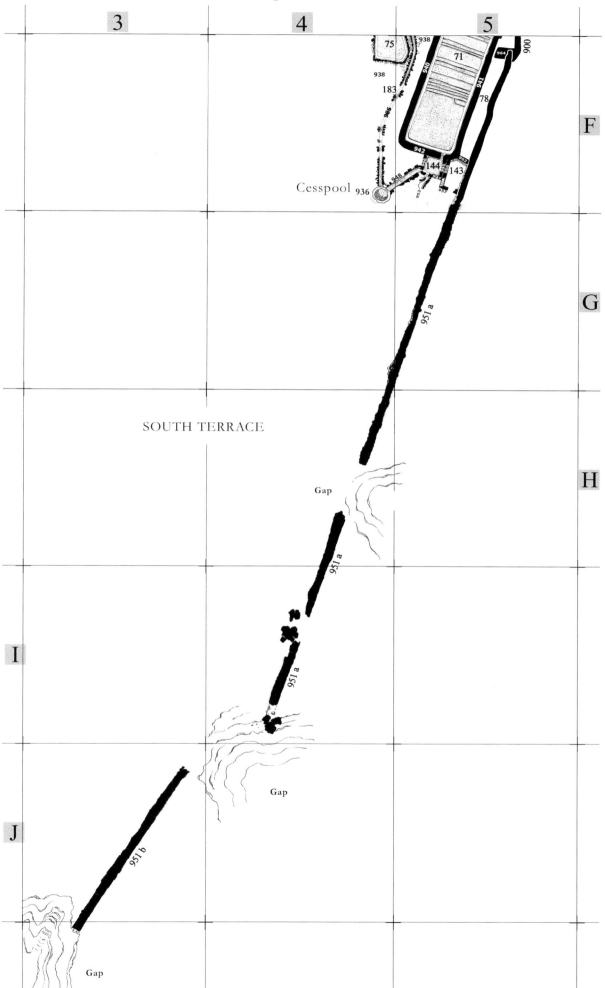

fig. 58. The sun dial KhQ 1229 from the upper layers of Locus 45 (sub 84)
Publication: Paul Tavardon, *Le disque de Qumrân*, Pendé 2010

Part Three

The archaeology of Qumran – an attempted reassessment

*Investigation of the archives –
Reports, excavation journals, surveys, plans and photographs*

Stratigraphic diagrams

The revised chronology and history of the site is a provisional framework that must now allow to check the stratigraphy. The stratigraphy which organises time distributes the pottery. De Vaux proposed a succession of three Periods, which we have modified in favour of four levels. The pottery had to be arranged in the order of restored levels. An inventory was made of each L. to situate the identifiable elements of the archaeological sediment. Hand-drawn diagrams, originally working documents, were a help to us in reproducing a stratification. It then seemed useful to tidy them up and present them despite their unrefined appearance. To show that we recognized sequences in the sediment mass, a sketch is better than an explanation. The diagrams reduce distances and do not reflect exact elevations. Their intention is simply to facilitate reading.

The diagrams have been provided with three-figure numbers identifying the walls and partitions. The thickness of the restored layers is arbitrary. Starting with the upper parts, the numbered layers illustrate careful reading of the *Journal* of the excavations combined with examination of the plans and photographs; for example, for L. 130, the upper layers appear with the designation 130.1, then 130.2, 130.3 etc., as the depth increases. Our task consisted in establishing coherent successions. We know they are fragile: approximations in the site minutes, the scarcity of elevation sections and the absence of notes on foundation trenches prohibit greater precision.

The layers were divided according to levels 1 to 4 instead of the de Vaux' three Periods. The layers have been redistributed and renamed according to a new nomenclature of levels 1, 2, 3 and 4 to distinguish them from *Periods*; the piecing together of which was not without difficulty. The succession of the layers guided the attributions, but account was not taken of considerations drawn a priori from the typology of the pottery established by de Vaux. We almost failed to recognize collections of pottery stratified in the deep layers. The main part of Qumran's corpus of pottery would belong to the final phase. The chronological distribution of the pottery is indicated in the catalogue of plates by the number of the layers to which vessels have been attributed.

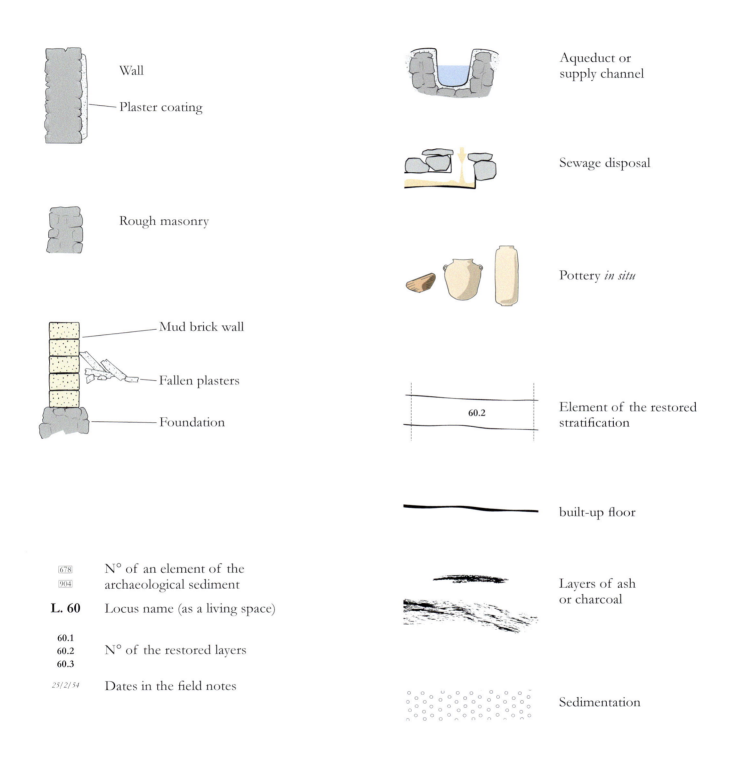

fig. 59. Chart of the symbols used in the illustration of the stratigraphic diagrams

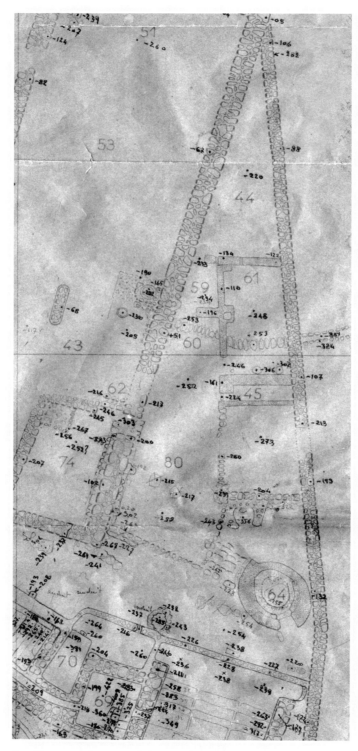

fig. 60. Survey of the southeast triangle with elevations, 1953

First section

The eastern front and the annexes to the southeast

Chapter A

The workshop in the southeast quadrant

Loci: (153), 44, 62-63, 80 (177), 45a and b, (145) 59, 60, 61, 65, 64-84

Study of the southeast annexes brings three sectors together:

1 – The triangular extension, the area as a whole defined by de Vaux in the course of the excavation, initially under the heading L. 44. It comprises L. 44, 45a and b, 59, 60, 61, 62-63, 64, 65, 80 (to which we have added L. 153). Below, we have adopted the term the triangle.

2 – The series of pools comprises L. 72-73, 68, 69, 71 and adjacent installations 70, 75, 143, 144 (to which we have added L. 180, 181, 182, 183, 186, 187 and 188). L. 145, outside the annexes to the east, is dealt with at the same time as the triangle, as it flanks it externally.

3 – To the study of the southeast annexes we have added that of the quadrant, L. 74, 66, 48-49, 50, 52, 53, called the east workshop, in the southeast of the main building, as on Level 3 the three sectors communicating with each other form a rather extensive work unit.

General settlement and evolution of the development

The southeast corner of the quadrant of the residence was rearranged when the series of pools L. 72, 68, 69, 70, 71 was constructed. It is not impossible that the stones pulled from one were used in the construction of another. At a given moment in its history, the settlement was open on this side and the opening required that it was closed further away. We shall attempt to discern the successive advances.

We reconsider the sector in accordance with a reestablished Level 3. We have rejected the early date of the earthquake; the first consequence demands that we reject the idea that the sector of pools L. 48-49, 50 and 52 remained disused as the Plan of Period II suggests. We must shift the whole arrangement of L. 48-49, 50-52 of the Plan's Period Ib to Period II. The whole sector will have remained in active use at least up to the end of Level 3C.

158 The archaeology of Qumran – an attempted reassessment

fig. 61. Overview of the southeast workshops (from Coüasnon Plan of IIb and III)

The southeast sector of Qumran preserved half the quantity of stored water. Either the water capacity was increased in response to developing activities, or the quantity of water available had attracted workshops. It is likely that a combination of both factors lies behind the extension to the east. We would insist on the fact that the whole thing constitutes one work unit. The link between the east workshop, the triangle and the series of pools was assured by L. 74-66, which functioned as a crossroads. L. 74-66 may have facilitated traffic, yet access routes towards the workshops seem barricaded. To a degree, the group of southeast annexes would have been isolated.

The long north-south wall and large pool 71 configured the eastern façade of the settlement. An understanding of their development produces some pointers that are of interest for the chronology of the architectural modifications.

The eastern half of the southeast annexes ended up occupying the whole triangle. The triangle was formed to the east on the area of land separating the *khirbeh* from the cemetery. The boundary of the constructions is clearly marked by wall 900 up to the point where, via L. 71, it rejoins the series of pools L. 72, 68, 70 and 69. However, wall 900 did not always mark the boundary of the annexes, and we have to visualize a series of restorations shaping the whole sector over time.

The building of wall 900, sloping and 40 m long, did not occur at one time, and we are able to situate its place in the evolution of the construction (fig. 60 and 61). The location was initially an *extra muros* spot where bone deposits in broken pots, *buried deposits*, were scattered in different places, interpreted in L. 130 and 132 as remains of bivouacs in the shadow of the residence (see p. 59). Then the series of pools L. 73, 68, 69 and 187 was created in stages, slanting towards the southeast, following the slope. It is difficult to believe that the tanks were constructed outside the walls, and elbow 968, which articulates wall 900 into two segments (900a to the south and 900b to the north) leads us to suppose there was an intermediate enclosure in the only south portion of the triangle.

In terms of the logical use of space, the placement of large pool 71 seems shifted to the east in relation to the ruin as a whole; it looks like an addition and must be the most recent element of the successive additions to the water system. It is the mouth of the main drain, and its shifted position towards the southeast follows the slope of the plateau. It should be noted that it was installed towards the south rather than the east. Placing it further to the east would have aggravated the spread of the inhabited space and would have brought it too close to the cemetery. As it was being built, it will have sealed older constructions which can be surmised from anomalies in the masonry. The obliterated construction may have been a room or a pool (L. 187?) enlarged at a later stage to become L. 71 (see on L. 71).

At a final stage, the triangle was created by closing wall 900b and divided by crude earth partitions; one might wonder why. Recent surveys by the Israeli army completed a dig which de Vaux left interrupted. Drain 910, which crosses L. 60 and 61, was known, as it appears in the Coüasnon *Plans*. However, with adjoining levels evacuated, the infrastructure of the brick walls was exposed and we are therefore able to see what de Vaux did not see. He had interpreted a bed of small stones as a bed for the brick partition walls. It now seems that the bed of pebbles is a leveling bed, correcting the line of underlying stone masonry. Either the rough brick walls witness to the repair of a previous arrangement, or this is a mode of construction using rough brick on a stone bed. We would hesitate to infer the presence of a previous level as the site's evolution indicates that the triangle is a late addition. Here we have an indication of repeated restorations, sometimes over a long period, sometimes sporadic, as elsewhere. Crude earth constructions require constant maintenance. However, L. 45 witnesses to a former state, where we have tried to place an access point (see on L. 45).

The problem of access to the annexes and to the east workshop

Given that access to the workshops was impeded, and that little space was available for circulation between them, the workers there cannot have been numerous. According to the Coüasnon *Plans*, the annexes together form a cul-de-sac, furthest away from the doors recognized in L. 136, 128 and 18. The access points are not immediately discernible. On the Coüasnon *Plan* of Period Ib (fig. 54) it can be seen that traffic is clogged everywhere and movement is impeded.

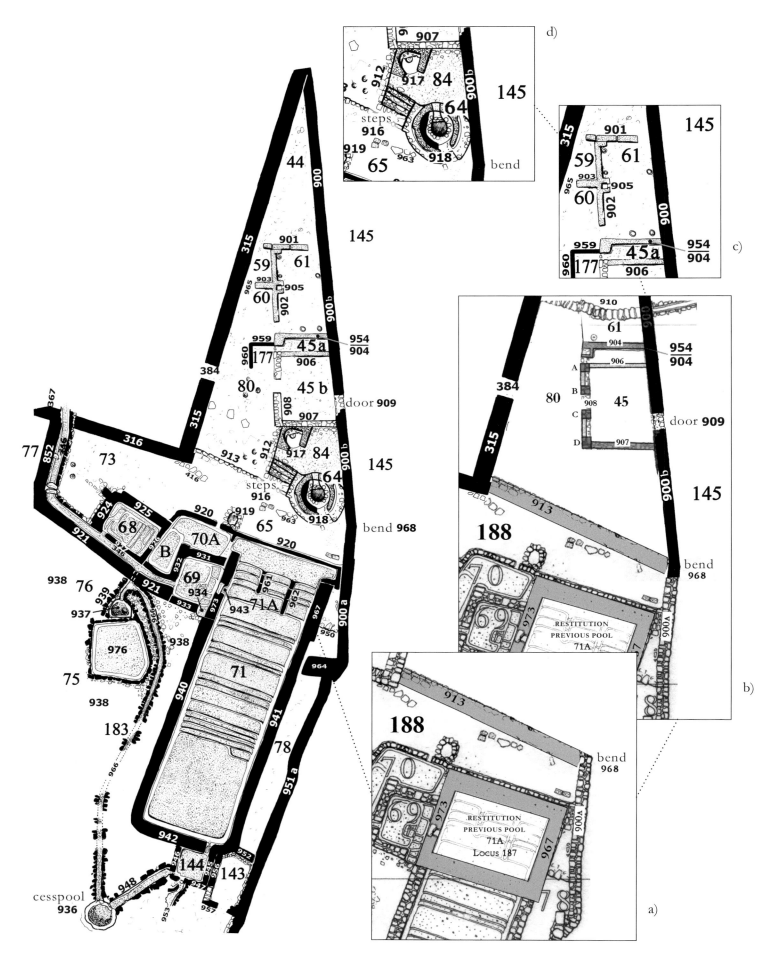

fig. 62.   Southeast annexes, designation of the constructed elements

To the north, from the interior of the settlement, L. 52-53, the system of tanks and pool 48-49 block the passage. The system made it necessary to cross drains and pools: passage was possible but not organized. To the south, the series of small pools makes a barrier, turning away from the south esplanade. We shall see that an exit (pre-L. 69) to the terrace (L. 183) may have opened the workshops towards the south during an early phase of the annexes, but that an exit is not an entrance; it would at least have had the advantage of clearing the alleyways and approaches there. To the west, L. 42 is open but not practicable, except in an emergency, as it would have been necessary to walk on edge 371 of pool 56-58, and then cross the upper threshold of wall 369 backing onto conduit 378.

Access from the east, though doubtful, should also be considered; it would resolve some of the difficulties we have in estimating the number of people visiting the premises. The formula has its advantages but runs counter to the idea of a settlement turning its back on the outside world. The southeast workshops would have been accessible from the outside, L. 145, by a door 909 cut into wall 900, providing communication between L. 45 and 145. The survey of wall 900 sketches a gap with collapsed ties but no upright or threshold (fig. 63). Is the gap an old one? Some arguments favour a passage, while others do not. Different plans and surveys opted for this (Period Ib; fig. 63a), indicating, with two larger blocks at an angle, almost aligned in the masonry, a north upright and half of a south upright. Using shading, Coüasnon's *Plans* (Ib and II) cautiously indicate an interruption at the height of L. 45, and another preparatory survey (fig. 63b) sketches a door with two uprights marked. Is this an over-interpretation by the drawer? We should note that the plan of presentation of the loci in 1954 confirms the opening (fig. 63d). It is probable that, at the heart of the settlement, people had to exit in order to reach pool L. 71 by way of the courtyard, L. 80.

On the other hand, the logic of the enclosed settlement demands a blind eastern façade. There must be a good reason for the existence of a passage via the east. Was L. 45, which produced an abundance of objects, a store? A store is not a passage, and L. 45 was not a store; free access to the outside may make sense. The quantity of pots thrown outside the wall at this spot and the abundance of layers of ash in L. 145, outside the walls, form a refuse area, a relatively busy one. The excavated earth in L. 145, partly excavated by de Vaux and then in the 2000s, shows that the open space between the buildings and the cemetery had been a zone of activity; this would support the idea of a communication point. The rejected pottery in L. 145 may perhaps have passed through L. 45. Might it be suggested that in the absence of a door, the pots would have been thrown over wall 900? The action is unlikely. Finally, it is possible that the gap noted in wall 900 was simply a breach opened later after 68, Level 4, to create an exit towards the countryside. The hypothesis would not take account of the fact that the crockery was thrown away in the course of the previous level. Paradoxically, Coüasnon's *Plan* of Period III closes wall 900. We shall see below that door 909 of L. 45 may be significant.

How was the east workshop had been first a passageway?

In L. 52, vats and tanks 319, 321, 324, 326, 328 form a working system whereby the required water came from pool 48-49. De Vaux proposed seeing this as a laundry room – an anachronistic view, retrojecting the modern concept of the washhouse. Washing was an art that was practised much less frequently than today, and there was no need for such an elaborate arrangement. The space is cluttered and it is not surprising that there was no marked way through if the space could be crossed with care.

Workshop L. 52-53 was served by L. 51 in the north, from the central courtyard (L. 37) which always had the function of a space in the internal layout. The passageway, in fact, rules out the lavatory in L. 51. On the contrary, pool 48-49 was accessible from the south, from a poorly defined space, labelled L. 66. The east workshop was the end-point of two north-south axes of circulation, from opposite directions: workshop 52-53 from the central courtyard, and pool 48-49 from L. 80-74. So how were the southeast annexes accessed? Management of the inhabitable space stops where the circulation clogs up. So, we have to believe that before it became clogged, L. 52 could be easily crossed, even if its use was neither intense nor regular.

We have a solution to propose, but we shall not insist on it. The east workshop of L. 48-49, 50 and 52-53, did not come about at one time and the passage was gradually impeded as vats and tanks were extended. We shall see below that drain 339 (L. 52)

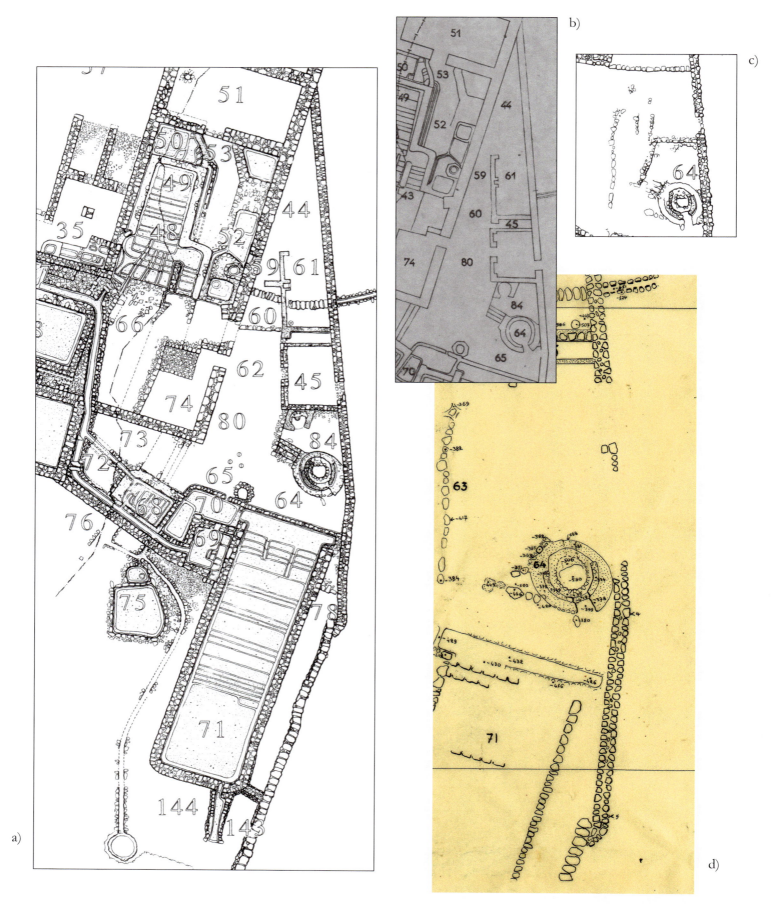

fig. 63. a) Overview of the southeast workshops (from Coüasnon plan of Ib)
b and c) Surveys with the option of the passage between L. 45 and 145, 1953
d) Preparatory survey of the south segment of wall 900

which fed pool L. 50, was abandoned in favour of an outlet from pool 48-49, L. 179. The surface of L. 179 fits exactly in the framework which crosses the workshop on its axis and the alleyway can be recreated. As drawn on the *Plan*, the evidence for the passageway is transparent. In this case, the central alleyway of L. 52, cleared of all obstacles, constituted the ordinary access to all the annexes.

The passageway option does not put an end to the clutter. It is the product of accumulation, and the accumulation betrays increasing activity up to the end of Level 3C. This observation applies to the settlement as a whole, which was never more active than at the point when it was deserted: we leave it to others to explain why Qumran was never as heavily populated as close to its end.

A resettlement, Period III which is our Level 4, took place at Qumran after the year 68. The presentation of it, being too short, lacks consistency[67] and the Coüasnon *Plan* of Period III fails to accommodate it in a ruined environment. The *Plan* rightly proposes a resettlement in the former residence, bordering on pool 71, fed by an adjusted aqueduct. Its water supply, reduced to L. 69 and 71, was then detached from the accommodation. As proposed to us, the *Plan* fails to fit the southeast quadrant, apart from a drain which goes nowhere and comes from nowhere, at the side of a heavy pillar which is attached to nothing. Without a planned layout, the rooms have no assigned purpose. The *Plan* of Period III does not display any rational organization.

The resettlement period is called into question. The Roman army was able to use the deserted site, at least up to 73, the fall of Masada; the repair of some breaches would be sufficient for an encampment. However, the return was not simply an episodic occupation, as the aqueduct was restored and diverted to feed the biggest of the pools, *i.e.* a maintained L. 71. Partitions were added to modify spaces and the uniformly poor quality of the restorations shows they are later. *Plan* III rightly encloses the settlement in a former Hasmonaean residence, excluding the south part, abandoned across its entire width where pools 56-58 were filled-in. We recall that the Hellenistic annexes of the outbuildings to the west and all other peripheral additions were only low constructions, confined to ground floor level. The resettlement of the accommodation probably withdrew to the dominant core of a site where the curtains of the former residence, continuous and higher, had, despite the ruin, retained the advantages not of defence but of protection in time of need. The new occupants had reconstituted an enclosed space. The threshold of L. 43 was suitable for its entrance: *a large door opening (the largest of the khirbeh) with two leaves* (L. 43, 14/4/53), under which an elaborate evacuation runs.

In volume II, we proposed an evolution of the Qumran settlement in several successive phases in which our Level 2B is a transition stage between the ruin of the Hellenistic residence and the settlement of an organized society, sectarian or otherwise[68]. Level 2B is an abandonment which followed the repurposing of the Hasmonaean residence of Level 2. The main building would have had the appearance of an entrenchment with substantial heaps of stones leaning against the interior side of the walls, to reinforce its perimeter without enclosing the covered parts to the south of the central courtyard. Arguments for assigning the entrenchment to the middle of the first century BC are not compelling. The heaps of stones are located only in the enclosure of the residence where the stratification is fuller because it was laid over time. They did not affect the deepest floors, being added after the original site had come to an end; the excavation archives, the diary and the surveys, never mention the sequence of constructed units nor the presence of foundation trenches. The result is that the position of the heaps of stones is not fixed in the stratigraphy, nor in the chronology either: the entrenchment could just as easily be that of the Roman army after 68. In the reconstruction of the west wing of the residence, three rooms, L. 15, 16 and 20, are among the best-preserved remains of the post-68 levels, Level 4 or 5 or Level 4/5. L. 21 is not a room but a stone heap, numbered 240, and de Vaux was keen to state: *It is only a fill-in contained to the north by a wall, to diminish the length of L. 16 and facilitate its covering at the time of the reoccupation.* (L. 21, 8/3/53). He is wrong: heap 240 (= L. 21) did not have the function of helping to cover L. 16; in a rectangular room, in order to cover it, the beams are laid in width and not in length. The base of heap 240 seems associated more or less with the stucco fragments of L. 30, which collapsed at the end of Level 3C. Heap 240 is very probably posterior to the collapse of L. 30 and so more recent than the year 68, Level 4. If it is accepted that heap 240 is one of the elements of the reinforcements as a whole, then the entrenchment

---

67. R. de Vaux, *L'archéologie*, p. 34.

68. *Qumrân* Vol. II, p. 435, An entrenched camp

must be attributed to Level 4. Finally, the principle of coherence leads us not to prefer an entrenchment in the middle of the first century of our era.

We have verified that Level 4 (Period III) precedes the earthquake, and that late and modest constructions are posterior to the earthquake: the latter show traces of a Level 5, the last incarnation of an occupation which disappeared and became extinct. Level 5 was self-evident when intact masonry sealed the fracture caused by the earthquake. The latter affected only certain parts of the site and it is not possible to attribute the restorations, beyond the faultline, to Level 4 or 5. Further, we are unable to assign a date to Level 5 and to identify who would have frequented it. If its existence is tenuous, that of Level 4 is less so, and with one thing and another, it is difficult to define the stages of Qumran's post-68 posterity, and their content.

Who lived at Qumran after 68? Probably a military squad first, while a siege was in progress? A handful of those who had fled and now returned? Another group tempted by the solitude of the premises? People involved in the 135 revolt, for the duration of a war? Some anachoretes who had come down from Hyrcanium? And why not each of the groups in succession, in a discontinued habitation? The pottery does not help us with identification of one group or another, or with their possible distinction as to whether before or after 68. The sherds are missing. It is probable that de Vaux did not preserve the fragmentary pottery of eroded surface levels, which have little substance, and his excavation method immediately opted to wait for sealed pre-68 strata, as they presented the advantage of cross-referencing the cave manuscripts. At any rate, the sequence of the pottery does not vary within too narrow a chronology, and the pre-68 pottery is the same as that which came after 68. Nothing has appeared which might have been the crockery of the Roman army. The only thing is that the metal evidence has provided proof of a military outpost. The pottery is lacking to testify to temporary use by second-century rebels. It is also lacking for attestation to a Byzantine retreat.

Would the coins be helpful? Those collected on the site are too few to mark out a reliable post-68 chronology, in the four centuries that followed. At best, they offer indications. The collection contains six coins minted between 68 and 73; seven coins in the middle of the second century; ten are from various points in the third and fourth centuries. The fact that coins were lost in each century shows that Qumran had at least maintained its role as a staging post on the route from Jerusalem to the gardens of Callirhoe, Macherous, and from there towards southern Transjordan. Travelers always passed through there.

fig. 64.   Locus 44 towards the south, open towards Locus 61 (left) and towards Locus 59 (right)

Locus 153
A restored L. from an imprecise and late occupation

In April 1953, de Vaux extended the excavation to the east of the residence. He notes: *New L. to the east: triangular addition* (L. 44, 15/4/53). So, we must understand that under the heading *L. 44*, the triangle was stripped down in a single operation in the course of several days: surface works which de Vaux considered not necessary to share. The identification of distinct new loci was made *a posteriori* as gradually more clearly delimited partitions appeared. At the time of a limited sondage, an underlying floor was hit and labeled *L. 44*. However, the whole sector excavated one year later, in 1954, was to keep the same label L. 44 (fig. 65).

In 1954, a note in the *Journal* reads: *L. 44 is divided into new L. 59, 60, 61* (L. 44, 23/2/1954). The surface excavation extends to the entire triangle and relates in fact to L. 44, 45, 59, 60, 61, 63, 64 and 84 and *up to the east of L. 78* (*Journal*, L. 45, *list of finds*) The finds from the upper levels over a large area bear the number 44, again, on the lower level, as well as what came from the only northern point of the triangle. The provenance of all the sherds, from the surface to the deep floor with its sealed objects, is given as *L. 44*. As far as possible, we have tried to reattribute the objects of L. 44 and 45. Brief comments on objects in the *Catalogue* affect the attributions. The indication *south of 44* (*sud de 44*) does not mean the *south part of L. 44*, nor does it correspond to L. 45, which is in the south as the plan indicates; rather, it relates to the surface layers sealing L. 59, 60 and 61.

Consequently, a L. 153 with arbitrary boundaries has been created to collect the erratic pottery of the upper layers. The *Journal* and the *Catalogue of objects* mention *ancient spoil to the east of L. 44, objects to the exterior of L. 44, to the south of 44*. The *Catalogue* underlines: *L. 44 south (...) Upper Level* for the two potteries KhQ 1021 and 1022 recorded on 23/2/54, a day in the course of which, however, the excavated surface was divided up into 59, 60 and 61. On L. 44, 25/2/54, de Vaux notes, under the heading *L. 44 south*, the exposure of a heap of stones 954), more than 5 m from L. 44, on rough brick wall 904 separating L. 61 and 45; the archaeologist decided that day that it is necessary to attribute heap of stones 954 to Period III, i.e. to the final occupation of the site. On 23/2/54, he divided his L. 44 into 59, 60 and 61, although the new division was not operational. For example, it does not stop him still attributing on 24/2/54 the placing of L. 63 at *L. 44 south*. In the *Journal*, for the allocation of the objects of L. 59, he refers to *L. 44 south*; the same on 23 and 24/4/54 for the objects of L. 60; on 25-27/2/54, he again refers to *L. 44 south*. Despite the new distinction of L. 59, 60 and 61, he continued to use 44 as the excavation progressed.

L. 153 brings together the product of the surface layers sealing the northern part of the triangle formed by L. 44, 45, 59 and 61 and including the upper part of L. 64 and 84. The layers situated under the surface of the south part were excavated one week after the bottom of L. 44 was reached; they were the goal of the works under code L. 62/63.

Sparse, poorly preserved construction units, just below the surface, are noted on certain surveys, but they cannot be ordered: it will be appropriate to attribute them to the final occupation of the site (Level 4). The rather inconsistent reallocation of the pottery collected under the heading *south of L. 44 – upper level above loci 59, 60, 61* (*Journal* L. 44) and *Objects 1954 of L. 45 – including the future L. 84 and the upper part of L. 64* (*Journal* L. 45) is presented on Plate 3. We have taken account of the *Catalogue* notes.

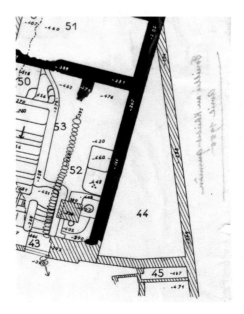

fig. 65.   Locus 44 on the 1953 survey

Plate 3

Restored elements	Level	Definition	Journal dates
153.1	3–4	Surface layers, outside stratigraphy	L. 44 = 19-22/2/54 L. 45? L. 64 = 1-3/4/53 L. 78?

Stratigraphic diagram of Locus 153

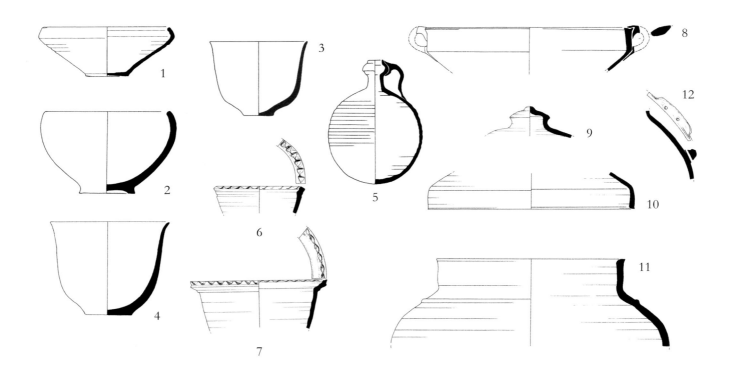

N° Pl.	N° Catal.	Position	Comments (archives)	Date	Description	Clay	Exterior
1	1021	153.1	\= 44 south \= 153	23/02/54	flared bowl	° red earth	red wash
2	804	153.1	\= 44 south or 44.1	14/04/53	bowl	° burnt earth, swollen	
3	1115	153.1	\= 61 south 61-1\= 153	27/02/54	goblet	° red earth, burnt	white wash
4	1134	153.1	\= 66 upper	27/02/54	goblet		white wash
5	1033	153.1	\= 44 S-E \= 61.1	24/02/54	small globular jug	° grey earth	pink wash
6	3186	153.1	\= 44.1	14/04/53	jug white ware	off-white paste	off-white
7	3056	153.1	\= 44 south	18/02/54	bowl	light brown paste	dark brown
8	3055	153.1	\= 44 south	18/02/54	saucepan	orange paste	brown-red
9	3999	153.1	\= 44.1	14/03/53	knob of jar lid	brown-red paste	beige
10	3054	153.1	\= 44 south	18/02/54	jar lid	dark brown paste	beige
11	3057	153.1	\= 44 south	18/02/54	neck of jar	light brown paste	beige
12	4001	153.1	\= 44.1	14/04/53	shoulder and handle type scroll jar	red paste with grey core	beige-red

° *According to de Vaux*

Locus 153, pottery and catalogue scale ¼

Locus 44

L. 44 appears in the *Journal* only on 15/4/1953, when pottery was recorded in the *Catalogue* under this number from 7/4/53. It emerges that the observations were not recorded in the *Journal* until one week after work had begun. The *Journal* does not give an exact account of the course of the excavation. In the *Journal*, notes under code L. 44 extend beyond the location labeled 44 in the Coüasnon *Plans*, so limited to the north point of the triangle of the southeast annexes (fig. 65). But the whole triangle was first named 44, then the first step was taken without defined limits (see on L. 153 above). While the workers dug the site from 18/2/54, it is only on 23/2/54 that it is divided into 59, 60, 61, the number *44 middle* (24/2/54) having been reserved for the north point of the triangle. When he compiles the list of objects of L. 44, de Vaux operates a reallocation of objects in line with a designation of the loci *a posteriori*. We have taken his list as a guide. We have tried to redefine the final L. 44 as the archaeologist tried to do. We note that the excavation of L. 44 deep was conducted in two days separated by one year: 15 April 53 (sondage) and 24 February 54, final excavation. We have attributed to L. 44 deep the objects which de Vaux assigned to it after reallocation.

The result of our analysis is clear: The final L. 44 is a dead-end, with access narrowed by the two successive passages of corridor L. 59. At first sight it could serve only as a storeroom. However, the north space of the triangle was not always as isolated as it appears: the photograph (fig. 64) shows a partition 901 of rough brick which joins neither wall 900 to the east nor wall 315 to the west. Furthermore, two openings have been made at a height of roughly one metre. It is notable that the western opening was obliterated by the elbowed north end of wall 902. The space to the south of 901 was a single entity before division into L. 59, 60 and 61. We have to infer that partition 902 came to lean against partition 901 and not the other way round as the Coüasnon *Plans* of Periods Ib and II show it. L. 44 is a space whose function escapes us and which, after restructuring, remained connected to L. 61.

The 1953 sondage had hit the *floor of L. 44* (15/4/53). The *Journal* specifies *at a depth of 1.50 m* without mentioning the presence of complete pots, recorded at the same date, one of which is pot KhQ 917, even though it has an exceptional shape. Attention turned to a floor, *the mouth of a conduit with its cap*, and the excavators looked in vain for a conduit or cistern. The photograph (fig. 64) does not enable us to situate the cap with any certainty; perhaps we should see that it rests with its lid in the only right angle of the room, to the southeast?

The systematic excavation was resumed one year later, on 18 February 1954, and the sondage was widened to the entire space of the L.; at the same time and with the same code an inventory was made of the exterior of wall 900 and, to the south, a vast unidentified sector. On 23/2/54, L. 44 was finally divided into L. 59, 60 and 61. The only room which kept the name L. 44 after work was completed is the north of the triangle. We understand that L. 44 was emptied in one day, 24/2/54, since in 1953 the investigation was limited to a sondage.

The accumulation covering the finally identified remains was called 44.1. On 24/2/54 we read of L. 44 that what was cleared were *three beams of palm trunks, parallel east-west, remains of a collapse (44.2)*. It is regrettable that no survey provided a situation for them. Fortunately, photographs were taken *in situ* (fig. 66a), where carbonized wood is visible. They enable verification that the rafters are indeed perpendicular to wall 900, and their regular spacing, estimated at 60 cm, reveals an ordinary framework. The photo (fig. 66b) shows in the cross-section thick layers of black ash which reveal an extension of the framework with the imprint of less well-preserved rafters.

As far as it is possible to judge from a photograph, it appears that the preserved rafters show signs of rapid carbonization: the charcoal has burst open and split. These look more like indications of destruction by fire. The fact that the charred remains do not lie directly on the floor of the room but on a blanket of earth (44.3) indicates a violent fall of the roof. Destruction by fire can hardly relate to anything else than the ruin of 68 which brought an end to Level 3C. The objects exhumed in 1953 or 1954 must rest onto a floor (44.4) not mentioned. De Vaux separated from it part of the heterogeneous collection of pottery and other finds scattered around L. 44. The finds constitute a sample appropriately *dated to 68*, sealed by the destruction. And with close connections in the space, it confirms the same stratigraphic position (our Level 3C) as the pottery collected in L. 45, 59, 60 and 61.

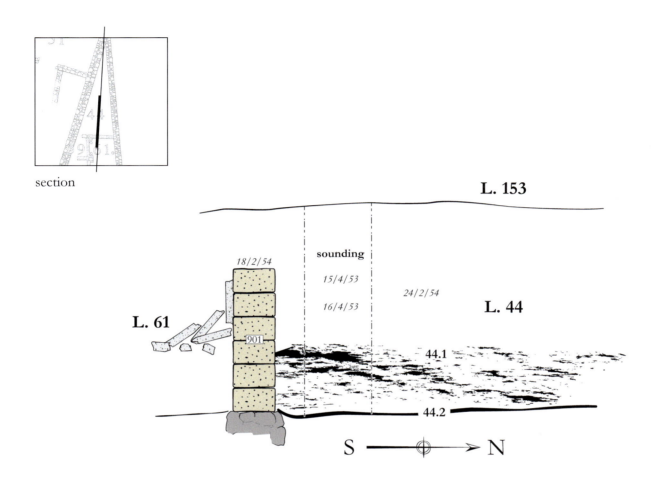

Restored elements	Level	Definition	Journal dates	Coins	Position	N°	Chronology
44.0 = 153.1	Post 4?	Low walls without stratigraphic connection	14-16/4/53	KhQ. 984	upper level	1	Turkish (?)
44.1	Post 3C?	Filling-in of L44	24/2/54				
44.2	3C	Roofing of L44	24/2/54				
44.3	3C	Collapse of L44	24/2/54				
44.4	3C	floor of L44	24/2/54	KhQ. 1069 1030	on the ground southeast, lower level	1 1	Proc. under Tiberius Agrippa I[st]

Schema and stratigraphic diagram of Loci 153 and 44

Other stone objects from this location, a cul-de-sac, were recorded: KhQ 822, 823, 824, 825, 826 in 1953 and KhQ 1082, 1240 in 1954: flagstones, discs and tiles. The evidence suggests this was a deposit of fragments awaiting re-use. They provide no indication as to the function of the premises. Floor 44.3 constituted the bottom of the excavation, but there is nothing to show it was the deepest.

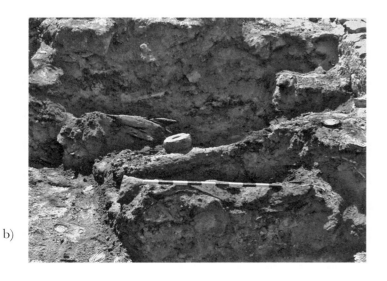

fig. 66.   Locus 44
        a) Burnt layer, towards the northwest
        b) Rafters of the collapsed roofing, towards the south
        c) The mouth of the channel and its cover

N° Pl.	N° Catal.	Position	Comments (archives)	Date	Description	Clay	Exterior
1	1084	44.2	on the ground	24/02/54	bowl	° grey earth	white wash, burnt
2	1083	44.2	on the ground	24/02/54	bowl	° grey earth	burnt
3	1097	44.2	on the ground	24/02/54	bowl	° red earth	burnt
4	1034	44.2	ground, middle	24/02/54	small ovoid jug	° red earth	white wash
5	1636	44.2	lower level	07/02/54	pot	° grey earth	
6	3186	44.2	-	14/04/53	cream ware jug	off-white paste	off-white
7	3088	44.2	-	16/02/53	jug handle	red paste	beige
8	1246	44.2	on the ground	24/02/54	cooking pot		
9	1086	44.2	on the ground	24/02/54	jar lid	° red earth	white wash, burnt
10	1035	44.2	ground, middle	24/02/54	jar lid	° red earth	white wash
11	917	44.2	-	15/04/53	jar	° pink earth	white wash, fine
12	1239	44.2	on the ground	24/02/54	jar		
13	1066	44.2	on the ground	24/02/54	jar support	° pink earth	pink wash
14	3038	44.2	-	24/02/54	funnel	° red earth	grey wash
15	1096	44.2	on the ground	24/02/54	lamp	° fine buff earth	burnt

Catalogue of pottery Locus 44   ° *According to de Vaux*

Plate 4

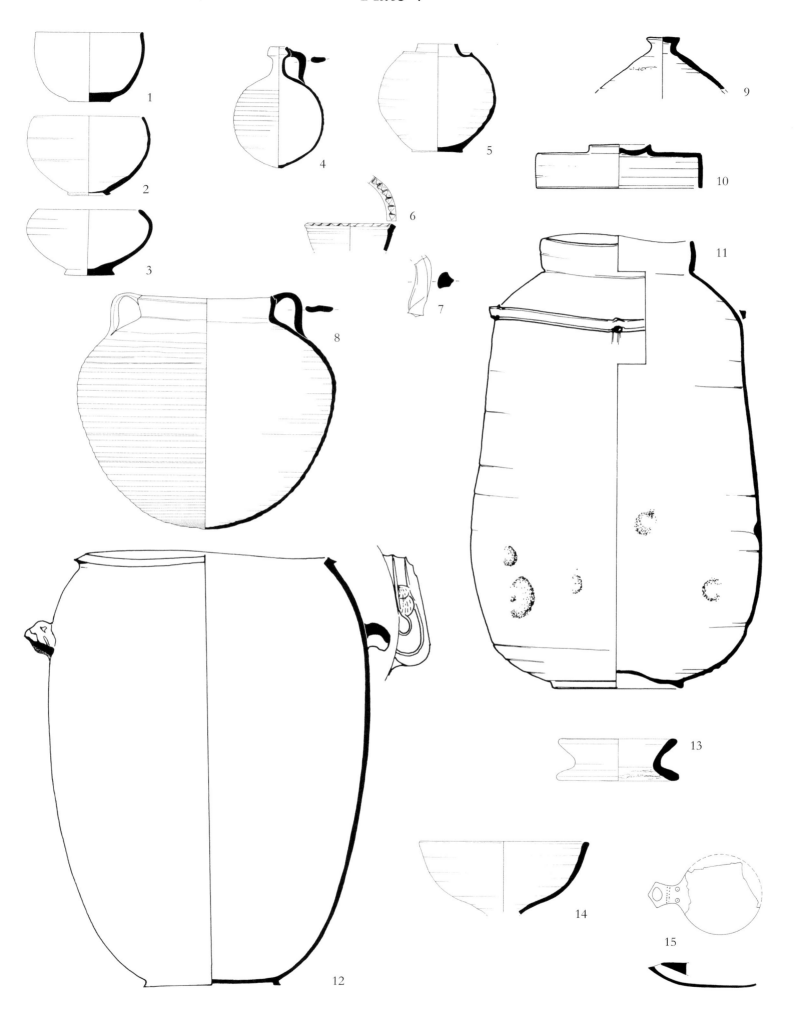

Locus 44, pottery, scale ¼

Plate 5

Plate 4, 8

Plate 4, 11

Plate 4, 12

Locus 44, photographs and pottery

Locus 61

L. 61, partitioned in rough brick, backs onto oblique wall 900, with stone masonry. It was excavated as such from 25/2/54 onwards. It is difficult to establish the stratigraphy for the upper part, because the upper strata of L. 44 and 153 were not distinguished (see above). The top of the brick partitions was recognized on 24/2/54 (L. 44 south).

The walls constructed entirely of rough brick, 901, 902 and 904, do not rest *on a bed of pebbles* (27/2/54); see above on L. 60. At Qumran, rough brick is used mainly to partition premises and to prepare workshops at a more advanced stage of occupation. The facing of the walls was coated with a roughcast of beaten earth, lime-washed many times; when de Vaux mentions the coating (25/2/54) we understand this to mean a layer of mortar added on top of the beaten earth. There are two coatings, one applied on top of the other, which is an indication of the care taken with the presentation. The fallen layers of coating accumulated like plates slabs at the base of the walls; the fall in form of *sheets* assumes a long exposure to the elements, a progressive weathering of the remains, and not a sudden, violent collapse of the partition walls. We may deduce that this part of the site had remained standing, in disuse for quite a long time before collapsing: the leveling resulted from erosion. It may be accepted that the triangle was abandoned during the reoccupation of Level 4, as proposed in Coüasnon's *Plan* of Period III.

The dig recorded only one floor, 61.3, associated with some non-standard installations. We have attempted to restore, for L. 60, a stratigraphy close to the passage between L. 60 and 61, and have suggested that it would apply to L. 61. It is possible that the rough brick partition wall 904, resting on a thick bed of pebbles, would have had a foundation trench. However, examination of the photographs does not provide confirmation that the stratification, which includes the layer of ash, is repeated in an identical fashion in L. 61. For L. 61, de Vaux made only one summary description of the installations, which, by the way, the *Plans* divide between Periods Ib and II, which we are unable to verify.

A well-preserved niche 905, against west wall 902, was part of a configuration towards the middle of the room. Today the niche has deteriorated; it would have been helpful to know the mode of covering, of which the *Journal* says nothing. Nor does it describe the interior cavity; Coüasnon's *Plan II* restores a square section of it. The installation has not survived intact: in its façade, protuberances of mortar attest to the fact that the niche was preceded by another compartment as far as the base of the opening. The photographs (fig. 68) reveal the dividing wall of what remains of a kind of tank coated with mortar, destroyed before 68. The niche opening presents some sharp edges which suggest a wooden framework, which has disappeared: the niche was closed by a shutter. The configuration recalls niche 221, which is similar in L. 13. On the photograph (fig. 68a) low to the right of the opening one can see a buried jar, the opening of which was protected by pebbles. It was extracted (fig. 67a). The pool and the buried jar were related, but their function eludes us. Pools coated with mortar indicate handling of liquids.

Three jars buried in the ground were divided along the west wall 902 and south wall 904 and their opening was protected by a border of pebbles *forming a mouth* (27/2/54). Another backed onto the east wall 900 (fig. 69).

Two cylindrical holes are mentioned as silos against partition wall 904, *the largest openings which follow on from the jar interred in the southwest corner, along the south wall* (L. 61,18/3/54). There is nothing to indicate that the holes would have contained the extracted jars from in Antiquity. De Vaux called them *silos* and their internal coating, mortar of rammed earth or lime, may have provided an indication of this; but he says nothing about it.

The configuration interred against wall 900 merits comment. Two pots were buried one on top of the other (fig. 67c and d). The upper jar is cylindrical in type, slightly ovoid, with small horizontal ear-shaped handles (KhQ 1474, Plate 8). It is positioned in a shifted position on a lower pot, a kind of *cylinder of crude earth* (18/3/54), to judge by its appearance, only slightly hardened by fire. De Vaux calls it a *silo* but does not describe it, and we do not know whether there was a bottom to it. The word *cylinder* would tend to indicate that it is without a bottom, which the photograph does not show (fig. 67d). The cylinder has a large opening, as if a jar was to be fitted into it. It is now lost and does not appear in the *Catalogue* of recorded objects. The photograph indicates that it

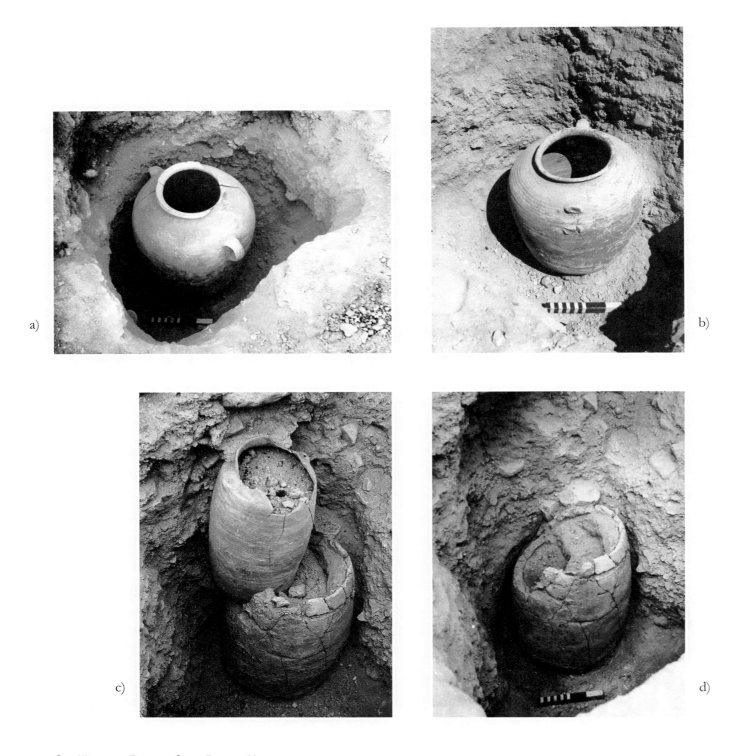

fig. 67.   Pottery from Locus 61:
   a) Buried jar to the north of pool 905, a slab of mortar from which can be made out in the left lower corner.
   b) Buried jar in the northwest corner.
   c) Jar KhQ 1474 fitted into a cylinder of crude earth
   d) The crude earth cylinder against the east wall

was cracked: it could not have been extracted intact, and the excavators did not think it useful to restore it or preserve a fragment of it. We are tempted to see it as a kind of cesspit. According to the photograph (fig. 67d), the lower cylinder is filled with a fine material, like a ribbon affixed to the rim, and its density suggests decanted clay. Would this have been a filter for receptacles placed on top? However, jar KhQ 1474 has a complete bottom which could not have emptied. The absence of stratigraphy makes it difficult to accept that this was an installation that was restored when a level was undergoing renovation. The rough and ready piling of the two pots, however, looks like the result of a poor repair. In the first phase, time would have been taken to set up a cylinder for the purpose; in the second, a rejected jar would have been used. It would be helpful to know what material filled the upper jar.

It is appropriate to include this configuration in the series of pots that were interred at Qumran within the boundaries of the settlement, along walls or close to passageways. We would link it with that of L. 51, where de Vaux had supposed there was a sanitary installation, functioning as a cesspit.

This whole collection, according to the *Plans*, was used in the course of Periods Ib and II, not synchronized, and this is astonishing. The installation of the stacked jar and cylinder is assigned to Period Ib. It is placed in the southwest corner of L. 61, to the right before you go through the door towards L. 60. The other jars interred along the walls and the two *silos* were attributed to Period II, as if they had replaced the cylinder installation, which is not proven. Niche 905 appears, since the *Plan* of Period Ib, without the buried jar against the north partition of wall 902, and the passage between L. 60 and 61 is closed, for which there is no justification. It is better, for the sake of consistency, to keep the collection together, the more so if the distinction between Periods Ib and II seems obsolete, the architectural evolution having been continuous and unbroken. However, we have not managed to give an interpretation of these installations as a whole.

fig. 68.   Niche 905, Locus 61:
a) towards the northwest
b) towards the west

176 The archaeology of Qumran – an attempted reassessment

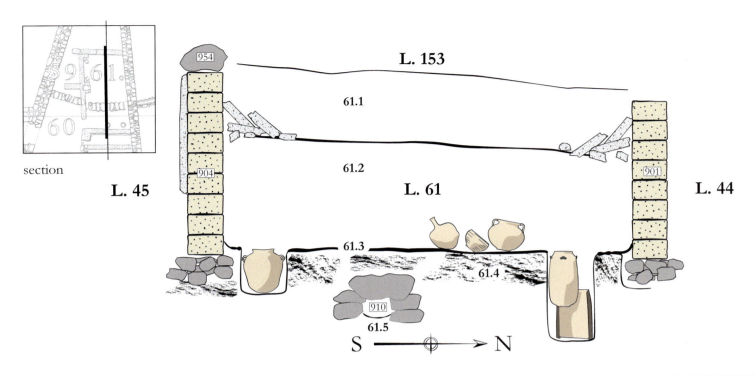

Restored elements	Level	Definition	Journal dates	Coins	Position	N°	Chronology
153.1		Inconsistent	23-24/2/54				
61.1	4?	Inconsistent	25/2/54				
61.2	3C	Collapse	27/2/54				
61.3	3B/C	floor of L61	27/2/54	KhQ. 1088 1089	on the ground	1 1	Proc. under Nero Proc. under Claudius
61.4	3A/B	Buried deposits	27/2/54	1305	In the drain	1	Herod Archelaeus
61.5	2A-3A	Evacuation of L34	27/2/54	1304	In the drain, to the east	1	Agrippa I[st]

Schema and stratigraphic diagram of Locus 61 (for the chart of symbols, see page 155)

fig. 69.   Passage from locus 60 to Locus 61; the silos and the location of the buried jar.

Plate 6

Plate 8, 27

Plate 87, 15

Plate 8, 25

Plate 8, 16

Plate 8, 26

Locus 61, photographs and pottery

N° Pl.	N° Catal.	Position	Date	Description	Clay	Exterior
1	1105	61.2	25/02/54	bowl	° pink earth	white wash
2	1129	61.3	27/02/54	plate	° grey earth	white wash
3	1130	61.3	27/02/54	plate	° grey earth	white wash
4	1118	61.3	27/02/54	plate	° red earth	pink wash, burnt
5	1111	61.3	27/02/54	plate	° grey earth	white wash
6	1079	61.3	24/02/54	dish	° red earth	pink wash, glossy
7	1080	61.3	25/02/54	dish	° red earth	pink wash, glossy
8	1389	61.3	15/03/54	plate	° grey earth	white wash
9	1113	61.3	26/06/54	bowl	° grey earth	white wash
10	1475	61.3	18/03/54	bowl, close to jar N° 30	° grey earth	white wash
11	1125	61.3	27/02/54	bowl	° grey earth	white wash
12	1112	61.3	27/02/54	bowl	° red earth, fine	scraped with a knife
13	1124	61.3	27/02/54	bowl	° red earth	burnt
14	1128	61.3	27/02/54	bowl	° grey earth, very fine	white wash
15	1110	61.3	27/02/54	plate, pierced	° red earth	red wash, painted inscription
16	1122	61.3	27/02/54	bowl	° red earth	white wash
17	1121	61.3	27/02/54	bowl	° red earth	traces of white wash
18	1117	61.3	27/02/54	goblet	° grey earth	white wash
19	1120	61.3	27/02/54	goblet	° red earth	white wash
20	1108	61.3	27/02/54	globular pot	° grey earth	white wash
21	1131	61.3	27/02/54	globular pot	° grey earth	white wash
22	1132	61.3	27/02/54	asymmetrical flask	° grey earth	white wash
23	1107	61.3	27/02/54	cylindrical vessel	° red earth	white wash
24	1109	61.3	27/02/54	jar lid	° grey earth	white wash, burnt
25	1404	61.3	15/03/54	jar	° grey earth, fine	white wash, burnt
26	1403	61.3	15/03/54	jar with a sign engraved on the shoulder	° grey earth	white wash
27	1106	61.3	27/02/54	jar support	° red earth	
28	1133	61.3	27/02/54	jar support	° red earth	
29	1474	61.3	18/03/53	cylindrical jar with four hooks	° red earth with grey section	red wash
30	1303	61.5	09/03/54	unguentarium	° red earth	pink wash

Catalogue of pottery Locus 61   ° *According to de Vaux*

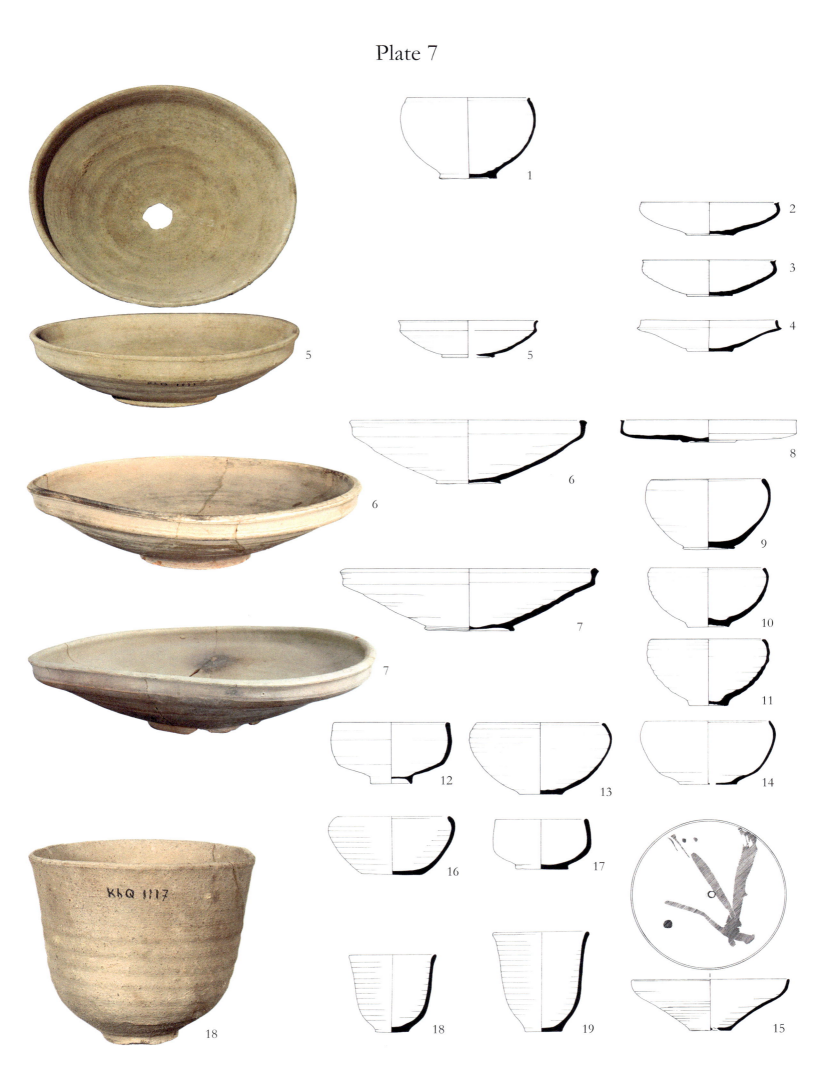

Locus 61, pottery, scale ¼

Plate 8

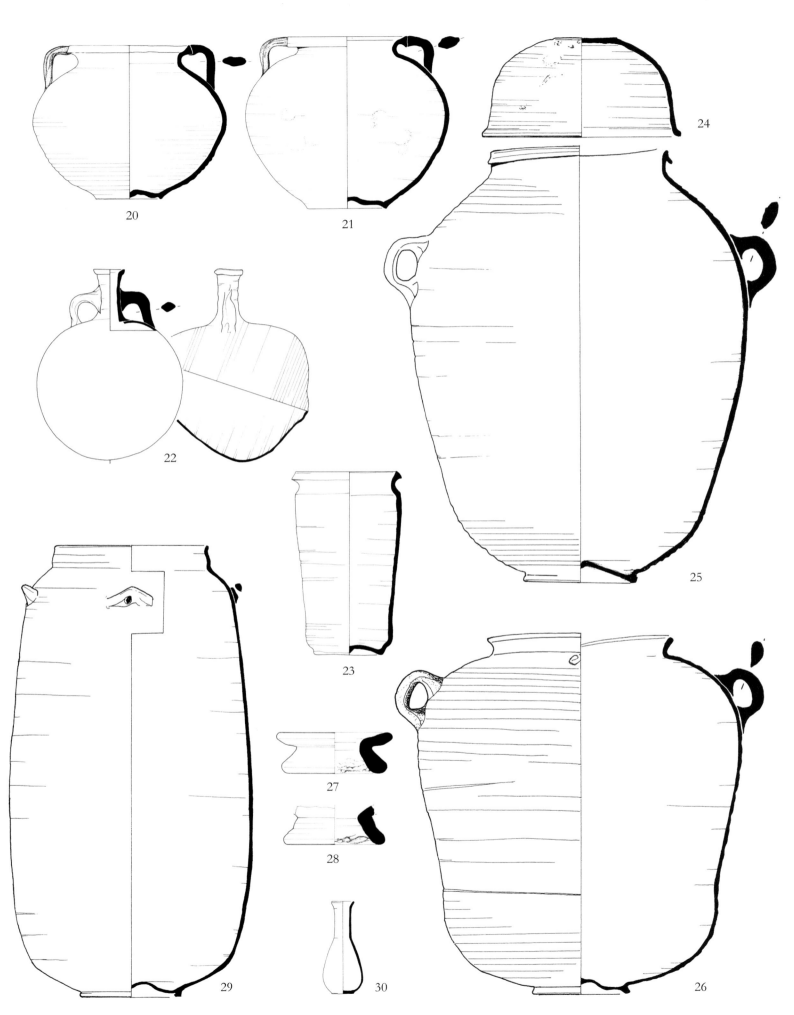

Locus 61, pottery, scale ¼

Locus 59

L. 59 is not a room; it is best to think of it as the passageway between L. 80 and 44, but a closed passageway, secured by a lock. Two lots of nails KhQ 1043 and 1081 suggest that L. 59 may have been closed by a wooden door, either to L. 60 or to L. 44, or perhaps both; the passageway between L. 59 and 44, however, which is very narrow, had no need of a door leaf. The collection of nails now restores it.

As the uprights of the passageways do not show a groove of any kind, the leaves would have been held by a simple wooden frame, not built-in flush. We need to link this with the *many iron nails* (24/2/54) found with part of a lock, KhQ 1042, collected in L. 44. The location of the two collections of nails, close together or separated, is not specified.

The small area L. 59 is lost space, used for storage. A pile of pots was found there, and a bronze cauldron which the photograph (fig.70) shows sitting upside-down on top of the pots. The vessels, most of them broken, are embedded inside each other and arranged in an east-west alignment. Their position and their arrangement indicate that they fell from a set of shelves placed against partition wall 903. One of the collections of nails may have belonged to the furniture. The pots are not broken on the ground but held in the layer of the collapsed roofing or the upper portion of the partitions. The pile signals a violent fall and the place has been subjected to a moment of destruction which is attributed to that of Level 3C, in 68.

The *Journal* specifies that the pottery was lying *1.20 m from the surface* (on 23/2/54); the pile is therefore placed at the same depth as the group of vessels, which come from L. 44 at 1.50 m (L. 44, 15/4/53), 45, 61 and 80.

a) Bronze cauldron KhQ. 1040

b) The bronze cauldron above piles of pottery

c) The pottery that fell in good order at the foot of the wall 902

fig. 70.   Locus 59

fig. 71. Locus 59 towards the northeast. Wall 902, from the front, on which wall 901 rests.

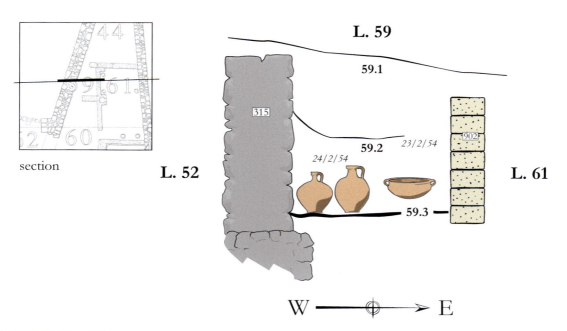

Restored elements	Level	Definition	Journal dates	Coins	Position	N°	Chronology
153.1	3-4	Inconsistent	February 1954				
59.1	Post 3C	Destruction and accumulation					
59.2	3C	Objects seals in 68	23-24/4/54				
59.3	3B/C	floor of L59 restored		KhQ. 1038	on the ground	1	Agrippa Ist

Schema and stratigraphic diagram of Locus 59 (for the chart of symbols, see page 155)

Plate 9

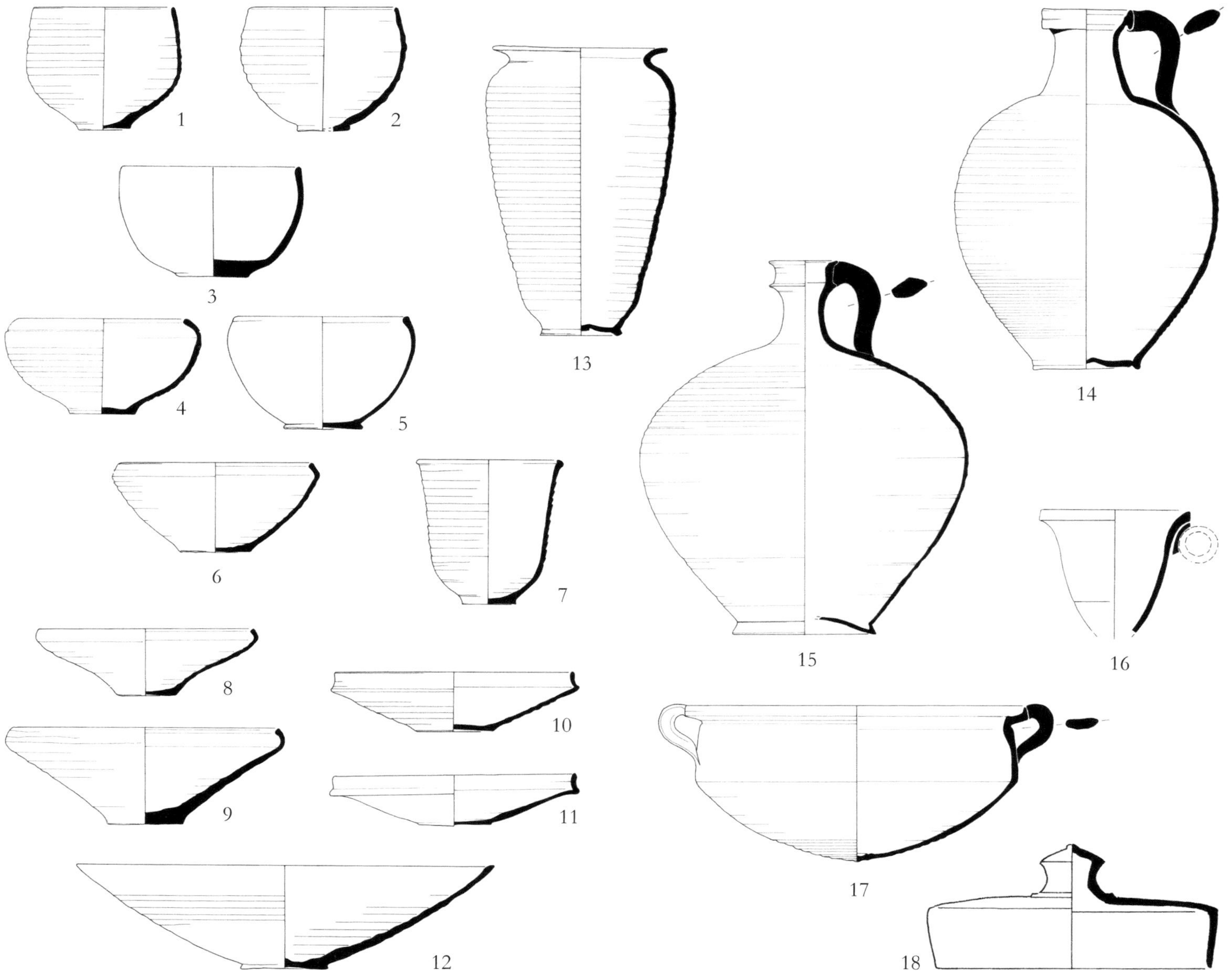

N° Pl.	N° Catal.	Position	Comments (archives)	Date	Description	Clay	Exterior
1	1048	59.3	on the ground	24/02/54	bowl	° red earth	white wash, burnt
2	1057	59.3	on the ground	24/02/54	goblet	° grey earth	grey wash
3	1047	59.3	on the ground	24/02/54	bowl	° red earth	white wash
4	1046	59.3	on the ground	24/02/54	bowl	° red earth	white wash
5	1058	59.3	on the ground	24/02/54	bowl	° pink earth	pink wash
6	1056	59.3	on the ground	24/02/54	bowl	° grey earth	pink wash, burnt
7	1055	59.3	on the ground	24/02/54	goblet	° red earth, coarse	pink wash
8	1051	59.3	on the ground	24/02/54	plate	° grey earth, coarse	white wash
9	1053	59.3	on the ground	24/02/54	plate	° pink earth	pink wash
10	1049	59.3	on the ground	24/02/54	plate	° red earth	pink wash, burnt
11	1059	59.3	on the ground	24/02/54	plate	° pink earth	pink wash, burnt
12	1052	59.3	on the ground	24/02/54	large plate	° red earth	pink wash
13	1060	59.3	on the ground	24/02/54	flared cylindrical pot	° grey-pink earth	pink wash
14	1045	59.3	on the ground	24/02/54	jug	° red earth	white wash
15	1237	59.3	on the ground	24/02/54	jug		
16	1065	59.3	on the ground	24/02/54	cup?	° grey earth in section	red and grey
17	1076	59.3	on the ground	24/02/54	cooking pot	° red earth	
18	1054	59.3	on the ground	24/02/54	jar lid	° red earth	white wash, burnt

° *According to de Vaux*

Locus 59, pottery and catalogue scale ¼

fig. 72. Locus 60
a) Top of the stack of pottery of Level 3C
b) Buried jar KhQ 1679 surrounded by a circle of stones (according to the catalogue: actually Locus 61?)
c and d) Jar KhQ 1630 buried in front of the door of Locus 61

Locus 60

L. 60 is simply the northern part of L. 80, excavated the following week. We know from the *Journal* that L. 60 and 61 were excavated on Thursday 25th and Saturday 27th February 1954; they were contiguous and were inventorized at the same time. Coüasnon's *Plan* of Period Ib shows the deep drain 910, from which we deduce that the work progressed without any record of it being made. Clearance of the upper layers of accumulation (60.1) began on 25/2/54.

An initial comment in the *Journal* illustrates the first day of the dig *We uncover a bowl and an element of terracotta pipe on a burned layer which more or less marks the floor* (L. 60, 25/2/54): The photograph (fig. 72a) does not show ash – which, it is true, could extend outside the field of view of the photograph. It is not confirmed that what was seen and described by de Vaux was a floor: a layer of ash is not a floor; however, as a precaution, we call this level 60.2. The two vessels belong, rather, to the top of the underlying heap of pottery which the excavator uncovered later but did not record. The layer of pottery 60.3 is sealed by 60.1/2. The depth of the two pots, 60.2, can be assessed at 80 cm below the top of the brick partitions, and the presence of ash at this depth, though approximate, may indicate a layer from burning of the roofing 44.2. The pottery collected below therefore belongs to Level 3C, destroyed in 68. It had accumulated on a floor which is neither acknowledged nor correctly photographed: floor 60.4 in our hypothesis.

On 27/2/54 the *Journal* reports: *Under the bowl (...) we find the foundations of the west wall.* The *foundation*, which is not to be confused with the *base of the wall*, is the leveling bed of 315, as it appeared in L. 80 (fig. 80a). The workers were not stopped clearing the facing of the wall, to the detriment of the connection with the floors. We are able to verify that the thick surface of occupation at the approach to wall 315a was correctly stripped: this is floor 80.5, dug with a pick, against the masonry, and there is a good chance that this may be that of the residence, Level 2AB, as it covers just the leveling of the wall.

From this we have deduced that floor 60.4, on which pottery heap 60.3 rests, may be confused with the occupation of the loci of crude earth, unlike the deeper level 60.5 of *buried deposits* attested in continuity in L. 80 (80.4). On 27/2/54 the *Journal* states: *There must have been something there before the division into loci by the brick walls. And already, something still lower.* We shall suppose a correspondence between level 60.5 of the *buried deposits*, i.e., *the something before the division of the loci* and the level of the residence 60.6, i.e., the *something still lower.*

The minutes of the 1954 *Journal* on L. 60 are brief and do not lead to a clear interpretation. For 1/4/54 we read: *Under the bowl and yesterday's matching pottery (northeast corner) we find a plate which ought to be the lid of a jar, which is found below, inserted to the rim*, and the sentence which follows: *We start a perpendicular trench to the large north-south wall near the Level of the foundations. A few cm under the ground where we stopped: a jar in place with its lid, just in front of the door to 61; and a floor approx. 15 cm lower. There must have been something there before the partitioning by brick walls. And something else below? with the small silo of the corner of 61.* These are floors 60.5 and 60.5.

To which floor should jar KhQ 1630 interred with its lid KhQ 1631 then be attributed? 60.4 or 60.5? In the case of other jars buried at Qumran, the floor to which the jar belongs does not cover it, the mouth of it remaining open almost to the brim, with or without a lid. We would have noted that the position of KhQ 1630 is specified to be *in front of the door of L. 61*. However, to bury a jar in a passage is at odds with logic, which would expect it to be buried before the rough brick partition of L. 60 and 61, flush with the level of the lower floor, 60.5. But an examination of the photographs (fig. 72c and d) shows, rather, the opposite and prompts us to attribute it to floor 60.4, despite its odd position in the passage. What the documents show suggest it is better to distinguish the elements of stratification in the approach to the passage between L. 60 and 61.

Following the photograph (fig. 72c), we note:

— that *the bed of small pebbles* (L. 61, 27/2/54), the bed of the brick partition wall 954, is a real foundation of small stones which can be made out at a height of more than 50 cm, and

— that the cross-section shows a possible foundation trench for brick wall 902. De Vaux is therefore right to note: *There must have been something there before the division of the loci by brick walls* (L.60, 27/2/54). The foundation of 902

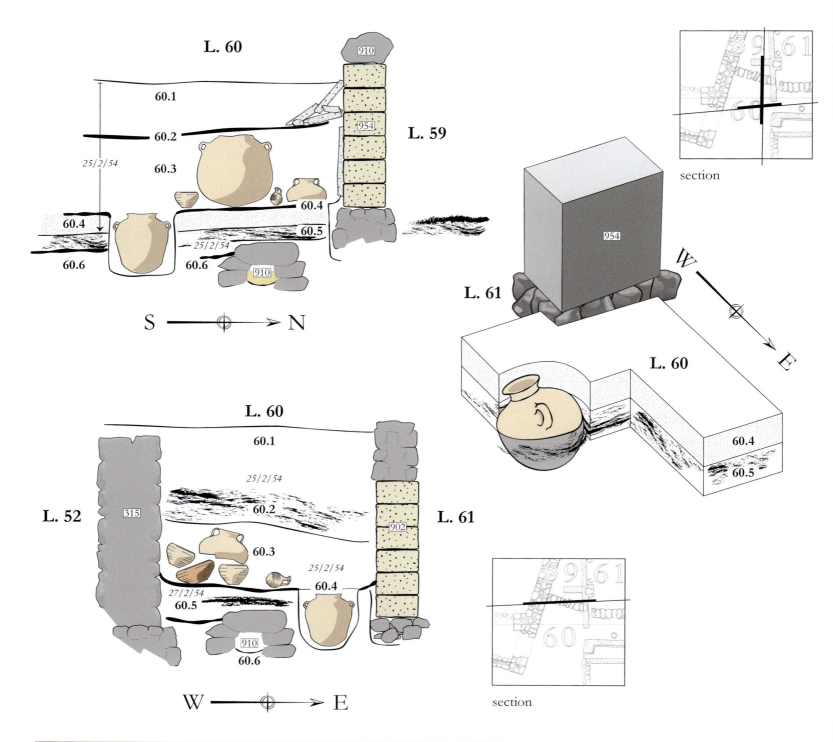

Restored elements	Level	Definition	Journal dates	Coins	Position	N°	Chronology
153.1	4?	Inconsistent	see L. 62/63				
60.1	Post 3C	Destruction and accumulation	25/2/54				
60.2	Post 3C	Traces of ruin of 68	25/2/54				
60.3	3C	Objects sealed in 68	27/2/54	KhQ. 1071	60cm above floor	1	Agrippa I[st]
60.4	3B/C	floor of L60	27/2/54	1072	on floor	1	Aretas IV
60.5	3A/B	ash floor?	27/2/54				
60.6	2A	Drain evacuation of L34					

Schema and stratigraphic diagram of Locus 60 (for the chart of symbols, see page 155)

seems indeed to have cut through the lower floor 60.5.

Following the photograph (fig. 72c), our interpretation would be:

— that the hollowed relief in the south wall of L. 61 was the trace of the frame of a door, the threshold of which, now gone, may have been cut in a timber. One can make out the hanging of the upright in its horizontal hold and recreate the level of the threshold which corresponds exactly to floor 60.4;

— noting that the stratification in L. 60 is visibly in place, the floor 60.4 overhanging to the right should rejoin the opening of the jar with its lid, and the jar must be associated with this floor, 60.4; floor 60.5, lower down to the left, would be of ash, as far as one can tell from a photo, and the jar would have crossed it; the darker ring around the jar could correspond to the pit which contains it;

— and that, contrary to what the *Journal* affirms — *All the brick walls (...) rest on a layer of ash* (L. 61, 27/2/54) — the ash of 60.5 would not run under wall 954. None of the brick walls having been dismantled, it could not be shown nor demonstrated that the ash ran under the walls. No matter. In section, the ash floors precede the brick partitioning.

If these observations are correct, the interred jar KhQ 1530 is contemporary with that buried in L. 80. Floors 80.2 and 60.4 are the north and south parts of the same occupation, and are in continuity.

The excavation continued: drain 910 crosses the annexes on the *Plans* of Periods Ib and II, although the *Journal* does not mention it at L. 60. The presence and depth of the channel are, nonetheless, indicated in the *Journal* at L. 61 (on 27/2/54): *Just below the floor, the room is crossed from west to east by a drain*, and this is floor 61.4 at Level 3B/C. Although drain 910 is not deep, it still shows two phases. The western section 910a, in L. 60, is contemporary with wall 315, which it crosses perpendicularly, in a drain to the exterior. During the building of rooms of rough earth, drain 910b was extended beyond wall 900, which it also crosses perpendicularly. Walls 315 and 900 not being parallel, the point where the two phases meet is marked by an elbow, sealed by wall 902; the first segment of 910 in L. 60 depends on wall 315, and the second, in L. 61, depends on wall 902; the first segment is early and the second is only a necessary extension of it at the time when the annexes were constructed. It may be that the drain was the overflow for cistern 49 and we may suspect that it was originally the evacuation for bathroom L. 34. The drain would therefore go back to Level 2A.

The photograph album lists the photo EBAF 12117, Qm, Loc. 60 with the note: *L. 60, jar in the northeast corner*. The photograph shows a jar, the upper part of which has been removed and the shoulder of which is cracked everywhere; it is surrounded by a box made of stone (fig.72b). The *Journal* does not mention it, and it does not figure in the Coüasnon *Plans* either.

Floor 60.6, *Already, something even lower* (L. 60, 27/2/54), at least attests to the fact that the virgin ground was not reached. The *lower* floor, 60.6, would find its counterpart in L. 61. A regular stratification appears in the hole enlarged to remove the jar in the southwest corner of L. 61, and a deeper floor 61.6 is evident in cross-section, as well as a clearer ribbon (fig. 72c and d). It could go back to Level 2. The work was not resumed in the triangle and the verifications of 2002 brought it to an end[69].

---

69. Y. Magen, Y. Peleg. JSP 6, p. 364.

Plate 10

Plate 11, 17

Plate 11, 15

Plate 11, 18

N° Pl.	N° Catal.	Position	Comments (archives)	Date	Description	Clay	Exterior
1	1063	60.2/3	on the ground	25/02/54	bowl	° grey earth	pink wash
2	1100	60.2/3	on the ground	25/02/54	bowl	° grey earth	pink wash
3	1101	60.2/3	on the ground	25/02/54	bowl	° grey earth	white wash
4	3024	60.2/3	-	01/04/54	plate	brownish-red paste	beige engobe
5	1102	60.2/3	on the ground	25/02/54	plate	° red earth	white wash, burnt
6	1104	60.2/3	near the ground	24/02/54	plate	° grey earth, fine	pink wash
7	1078	60.2/3	on the ground	25/02/54	plate	° pink earth	pink wash
8	3025	60.2/3	-	01/04/54	plate	light brown paste	brownish-red
9	3020	60.2/3	-	01/04/54	bowl		
10	1603	60.2/3	lower level	01/04/54	pot	° red earth	white wash
11	1077	60.2/3	on the ground	25/02/54	small globular jug	° pink earth, fine	pink wash
12	3017	60.2/3	-	03/04/54	flask	grey paste	greyish-beige
13	3016	60.2/3	-	03/04/54	cooking pot	brown paste	brown
14	3021	60.2/3	-	03/04/54	cooking pot	brown-red paste	brown
15	1064	60.2/3	on the ground	25/02/54	pipe	° red earth	white wash
16	1631	60.2/3	lower level	06/04/54	limestone cap of N° 1630		
17	1630	60.2/3	lower level	06/04/54	ovoid jar	° red earth	pink wash
18	1679	60.2/3	N-E corner	25/02/54	spherical jar	° red earth	
19	3022	60.2/3	-	01/04/54	jar support	grey paste	grey
20	1103	60.2/3	on the ground	25/02/54	jar support	° red earth	

° *According to de Vaux*

Locus 60, catalogue of pots and photographs

Plate 11

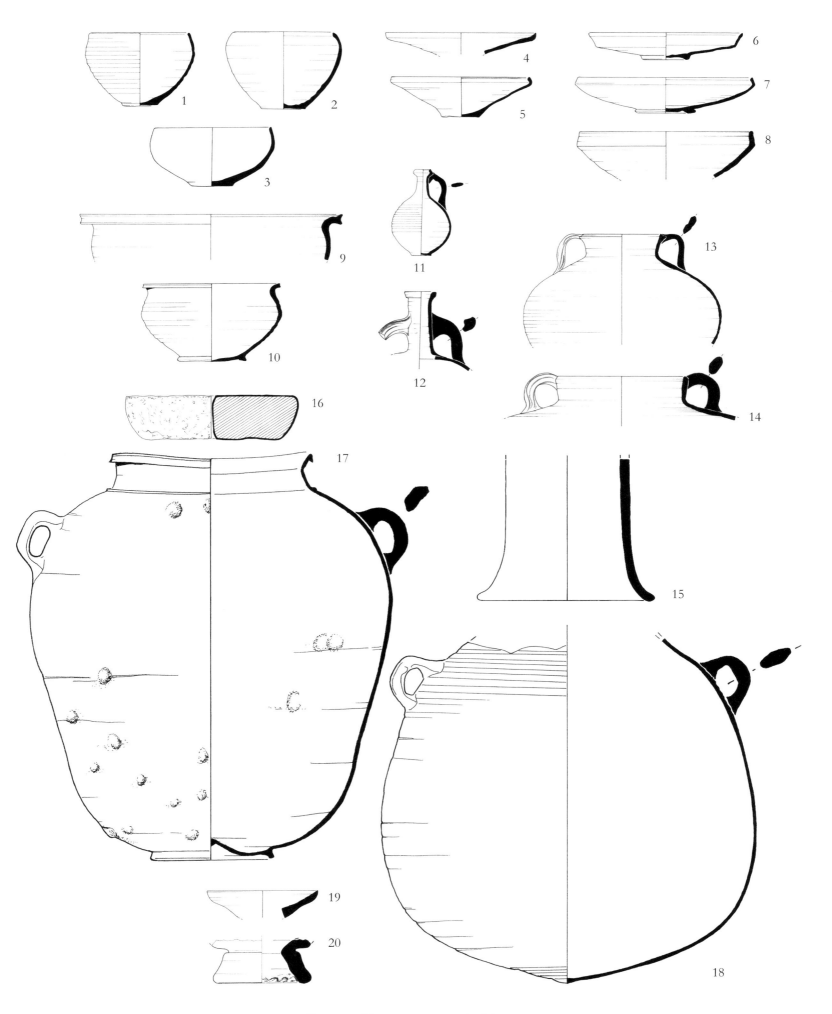

Locus 60, pottery, scale ¼

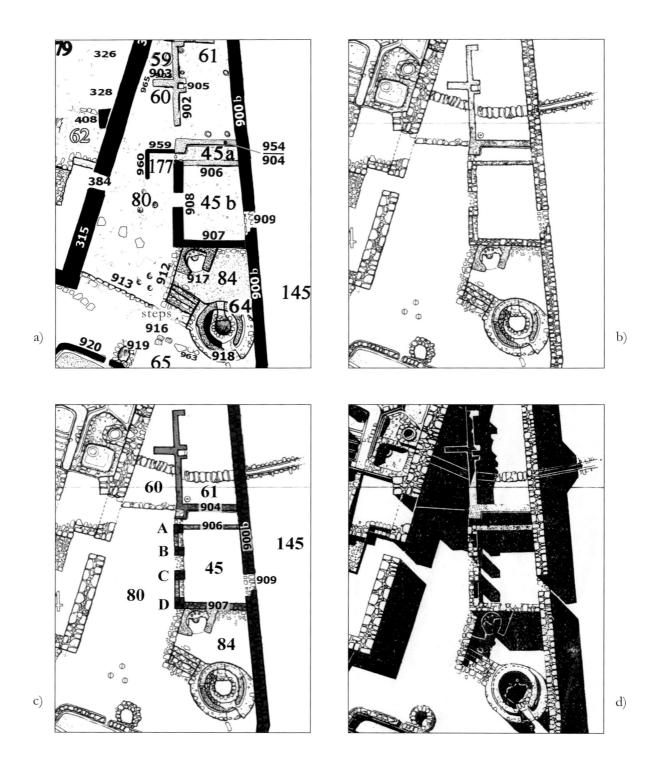

fig. 73. Locus 45
a) Designation of the constructed elements, (b) of Coüasnon's survey, (c and d) of the restoration

Loci 45a and b

The masonry of L. 45, the openings and a door, the gap for which is not proven, and the important objects that it has produced, make the interpretation and the function of the room difficult. The excavation of L. 45 hesitated in several directions. We know that de Vaux often did not actively supervise loci himself, but that it was the workers digging at a particular place who oversaw the coherence of the dig. Furthermore, reading the *Journals* of the excavation makes it clear that the notes and the denomination of the loci were recorded after the fact. In April 1953, the dig was not conducted in one go (see L. 153). Progression of work on the site meant that the south of L. 44, being too extensive, was named 45 so as to explore the surface layers as far as directly below L. 64, i.e. for almost ten metres. Under the label "45", the dig reached L. 62/80 to the west; under *45 south* the deep layers of L. 84 were reached to the south. The term L. 45 first designated the narrow tank containing complete pots, where a jar said to be a *manuscript* jar attracted attention. The excavation was conducted in two days, 15th and 16th April 1953. The place was *rich in pottery* and we can follow the progression of the dig: *To the south of L. 45a, a small room 45b, very rich in pottery (...) To the west of the latter, another small L. 45c* (L. 45,16/4/53). One year later, in 1954, the excavation was resumed: *Prolongation of L. 45c* (L. 45, 4/3/54). It is not possible to decide whether the prolongation was in depth or in horizontal extent. In both cases, the deep layers of L. 80, those of the *buried deposits*, were able to be reached.

The work was guided by the collection of pottery, at the cost of their location. The jars were extracted in tank 45a; to the south of the tank lay an important heap of vessels of all sizes. The heap of pottery was stacked in L. 45, which is a well-defined space, opened by one or two doors, the tank labeled 45a constituting only the northern part. De Vaux distinguished tank 45a from the room itself, 45b. However, the collection of pottery drew the workers into L. 80, west of L. 45, where large jars had emerged. Although outside L. 45, the place was designated as 45c. Outside L. 45, sealing the layers of L. 80, we have called L. 177 45c, and have dealt with it separately. The sherds emerging from *45 south* were reintegrated into the objects of L. 84.

The precise stratigraphic allocation of the movable objects remains approximate. Nothing is said of the deposits that covered the different hoards of pottery. Their rapid exposure suggests that the deposits were not far below the surface and that they were not damaged by the late occupation (Level 4/5). The stratification of the southeast annexes was completed with the abandonment of the site in 68. Logic prompts us to attribute the good preservation of the vessels to the level destroyed in 68. De Vaux, assessing the difficulty in his *Journal*, had attempted a topographic reallocation of the pottery collected under codes 45a, b and c. We have paid regard to this. The pottery listing (L. 45) use indications like *under the brick wall, a, b, c, above (sup.), floor* and *below (inf.)* (catalogue). The indications above and *brick wall* relate the movables to the upper strata, but it is not possible to link them to Level 4 with any certainty. The indications *below* and *floor* prompt us to associate the vessels in question with Level 3C. It remains the case that the major part of the pottery was recorded under the simple rubric of L. 45. The diary of L. 45 begins only on 15/4/53 and the pots we show grouped together were recorded before this date without specification of their location. However, the complete pots must have been uncovered from the top of the heap of vessels later attributed to L. 45b. They are shown separately in Plate 13, under 45.2. Pots from an upper level (Level 4) may have been mixed with it. We especially regret the lack of precision because the sundial KhQ 1229 (fig. 58), otherwise called *stone disc*, is not located in this collection.

Examination of L. 45 provides an opportunity to interpret the southeast annexes as an entity built from the beginning of Level 3, a resettlement to be situated towards the middle of the first century BC. We have already suggested that the annexes are a secondary addition, installed in stages. The eastern part of the triangle was subsequent to the series of small pools L. 72-59 enclosed by a wall 913 which joined elbow 968 marked in wall 900. The triangle itself has been subject to unsynchronized rearrangements. L. 45 occupies a central position in the southeast annexes and it may initially have been the only one. Today, the former pieces of masonry are difficult to recognize under recent reconstructions. It seems that the added L. 61, entirely of rough brick, redivided the northern sector of the triangle. L. 45 is built of stone. The Coüasnon *Plan* of Period Ib quite clearly presents original masonry: the eastern wall 908 features four pillars (fig. 73b, c and d) blocked off from each other by thinner partition walls of rough earth. We do not know whether they were original or what their height

192   The archaeology of Qumran – an attempted reassessment

a) Mortar plaster on the south face of wall 904

fig. 74.   Locus 45a and b

b) Jar KhQ. 799 in situ in the Locus 45a

c) Pottery in situ in the Locus 45a and b

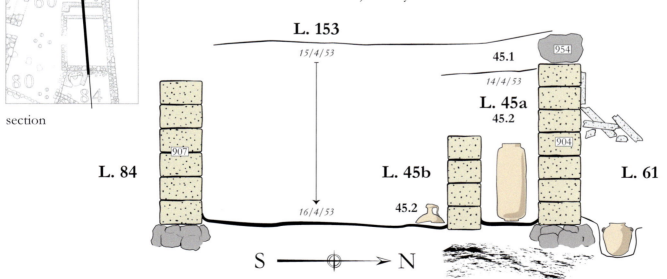

Restored elements	Level	Definition	Journal dates	Coins	Position	N°	Chronology
45.1	3C	Accommodation of jars	15/3/53	KhQ. 1144	upper level	1	Proc. under Nero
45.2	3C	floor of 45b	16/3/53	1233	lower level	1	First Revolt, year 11

Schema and stratigraphic diagram of Locus 45 (for the chart of symbols, see page 155)

was. L. 45 may have been only a kind of porch or open pavilion. The storage of numerous pots may lead us to conclude that the place was later closed and that the location had a different function. A door 909 to the exterior was thought likely. If one accepts it, pavilion 45 may have been the lobby of an entrance to the settlement, subsequently obsolete. The treatment of the walls is more carefully done than elsewhere. What remains of a smooth coating on a pisé mortar armed with sherds testifies to the care given to this room (fig.74a). The triangle would then have once been a forecourt, and door 384, inserted in wall 315 directly in line with the exit from L. 45, reinforces the likelihood that this was the circulation plan: door 384 does not feature in the Level 2 plan of the residence, and the opening must have been made during the construction of the triangle. Finally, as the series of small pools preceded the erection of the triangle, courtyard L. 80 would also have left free access to the ritual baths L. 68 or 69. Kiln 918 (L. 64) then broke up the original configuration.

The hypothesis that L. 45 was open to the exterior was considered above (p. 161).

fig. 75.   Locus 45a, towards the west

Plate 12

Plate 13, 18   Plate 13, 22

N° Pl.	N° Catal.	Position	Comments (archives)	Date	Description	Clay	Exterior
1	793	45.2		14/04/53	plate	° red earth	burnt
2	1256	45.2	-	06/03/54	plate with pourer lip	grey paste	grey
3	782	45.2	-	14/04/53	plate	° coarse grey earth	white wash
4	781	45.2	-	14/04/53	plate	° grey earth	pink wash, burnt
5	1375	45.2	-	13/03/54	carinated dish	° red earth	white wash
6	792	45.2	-	14/04/53	carinated plate	° red earth	
7	795	45.2	-	14/04/53	plate	° fine red earth	pink wash
8	789	45.2	-	14/04/53	bowl	° grey earth	white wash
9	788	45.2	-	14/04/53	bowl	° red earth	white wash
10	790	45.2	-	14/04/53	bowl	° red earth	white wash, burnt
11	1263	45.2	-	06/03/54	bowl	red earth with grey section	white wash
12	791	45.2	-	14/04/53	goblet	° grey earth	white wash
13	1258	45.2	-	06/03/54	goblet	grey earth	white wash
14	787	45.2	-	14/04/53	goblet	° pink earth	pink wash
15	786	45.2	-	14/04/53	goblet	° red earth	exterior grey wash
16	3398	45.2	-	03/03/54	kettle	brownish-red paste	grey and pink
17	1281	45.2	-	06/03/54	jug	° grey earth	white wash
18	938	45.2	-	23/04/53	large bowl	° red earth	quite fine, quite well fired
19	778	45.2	-	14/04/53	cooking pot	° red earth	
20	779	45.2	-	14/04/53	cooking pot	° red earth	
21	780	45.2	-	14/04/53	cooking pot	° grey earth	white wash
22	1282	45.2	-	06/03/54	jar	° grey earth	white wash

° According to de Vaux

Locus 45, catalogue of pots, recorded before 15/3/54 and photographs

Plate 13

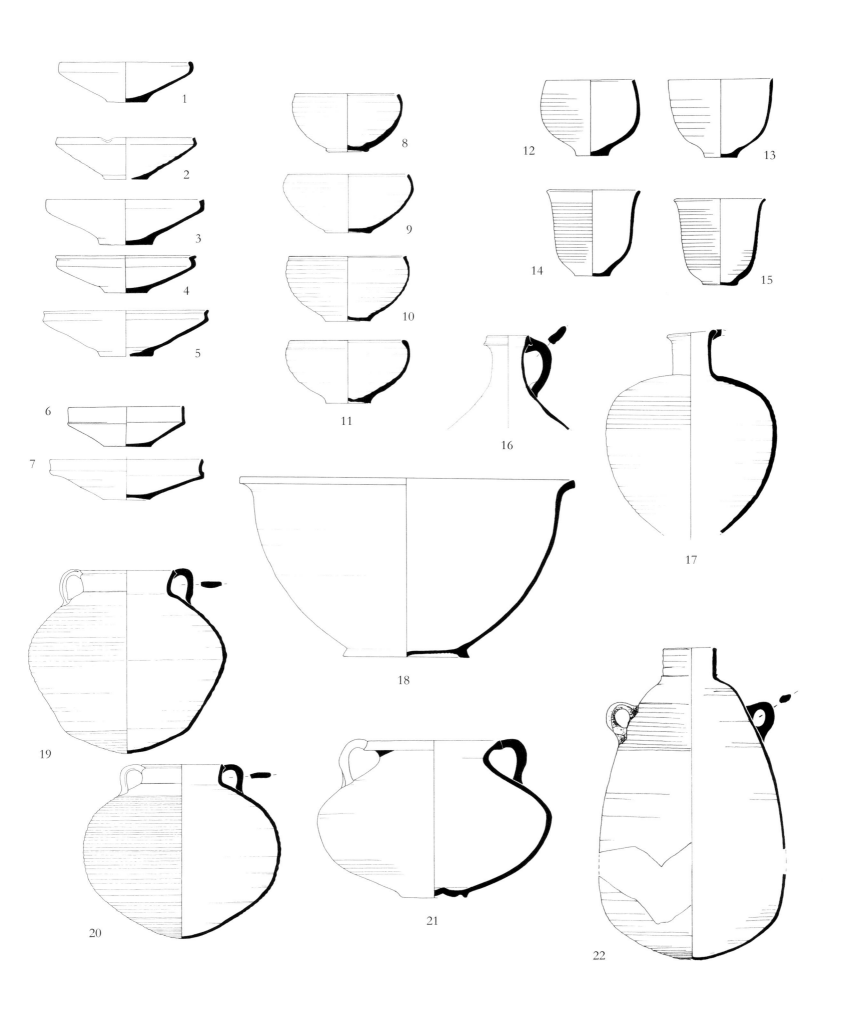

Locus 45, pottery, recorded before 15/3/54, scale. ¼

Plate 14

N° Pl.	N° Catal.	Position	Comments (archives)	Date	Description	Clay	Exterior
1	3401	45.2	45a	01/03/54	goblet	grey paste	grey
2	796	45.2	45a	14/04/53	bowl	° red earth, fine	pink wash
3	797	45.2	45a	14/04/53	bowl	° grey earth	pink wash
4	798	45.2	45a	14/04/53	bowl	° grey earth	pink wash
5	3403	45.2	45a	01/03/54	saucepan	brown paste	burnt
6	3400	45.2	45a	01/03/54	large pot	red paste	red
7	3397	45.2	45a	01/03/54	small ovoid jug	brownish-grey paste	brown
8	3399	45.2	45a	03/03/54	piédouche	brownish-red paste	brownish-red
9	916	45.2	45a	13/04/49	jar	° greyish-pink earth, quite fine, well fired	
10	3404	45.2	45a	01/03/54	neck of jar	brown paste	brownish-red
11	912	45.2	45a	13/04/49	jar	° pink earth, quite fine, well fired	white wash
12	799	45.2	45a	13/04/49	jar	° red earth	grey and pink
13	800	45.2	45a	13/04/49	filter jar	° red earth with grey section	exterior white wash

° *According to de Vaux*

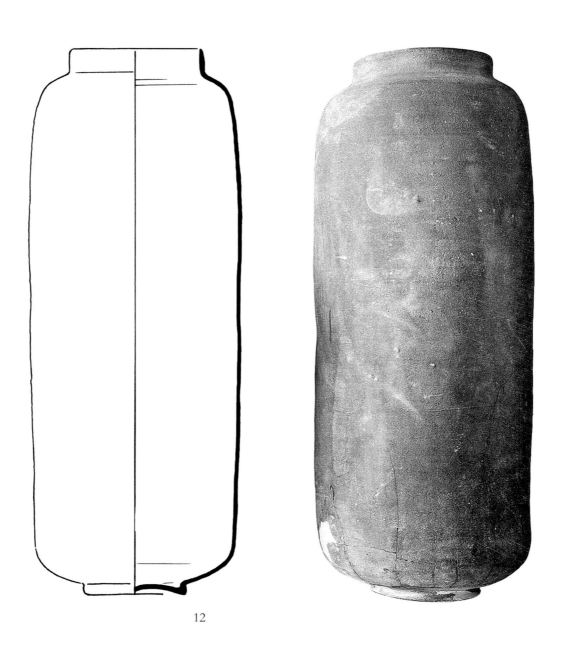

12

Locus 45a, pottery and catalogue scale ¼

Plate 15

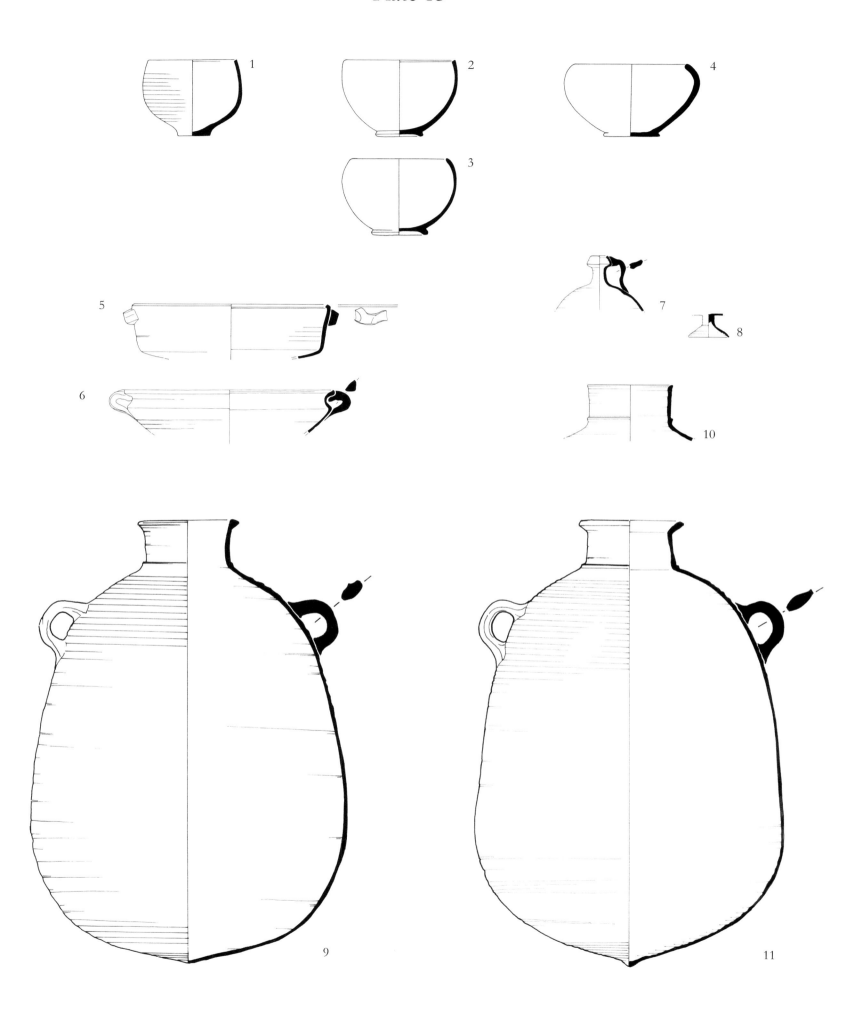

Locus 45a, pottery, scale ¼

Plate 16

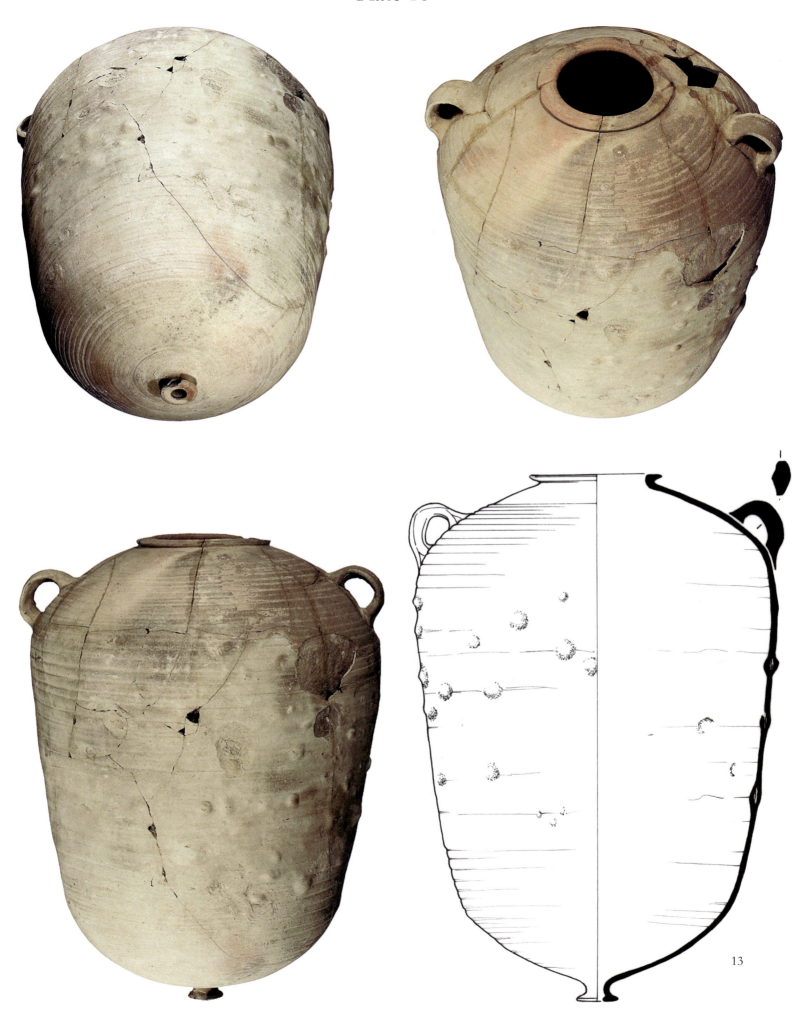

Locus 45a, pottery, scale ¼

Plate 17

Plate 19, 16

Plate 19, 17

Plate 19, 15

Plate 15, 9

Plate 15, 11

Locus 45a and 45b, photographs of pottery

Plate 18

Plate 19, 7

Plate 19, 1

Plate 19, 12

N° Pl.	N° Catal.	Position	Comments (archives)	Date	Description	Clay	Exterior
1	813	45.2	45b	15/04/53	plate	orange paste	light brown
2	1244	45.2	45b	04/03/54	plate, pierced	brownish-red paste	beige
3	817	45.2	45b	15/04/53	carinated plate	orange paste	light brown
4	815	45.2	45b	15/04/53	carinated plate	orange paste	beige wash
5	1271	45.2	45b	06/03/54	carinated plate	° red earth	burnt, red wash
6	812	45.2	45b	15/04/53	goblet	° red earth	red wash
7	820	45.2	45b	15/04/53	bowl	° grey earth	white wash
8	819	45.2	45b	15/04/53	bowl	° grey earth	white wash
9	1245	45.2	45b	04/03/54	bowl	° red earth	white wash, burnt
10	1231	45.2	45b	04/03/54	small globular jug	° red earth	pink wash
11	810	45.2	45b	15/04/53	goblet, lid of jug N° 809	° grey earth	white wash
12	809	45.2	45b	15/04/53	jug	° red earth	
13	808	45.2	45b	15/04/53	goblet, lid of jug N° 807	° grey earth	white wash
14	807	45.2	45b	15/04/53	jug	° red earth	
15	1242	45.2	45b	04/03/54	two-handled pot		
16	834	45.2	45b	15/04/53	two-handled pot	orange paste	beige wash
17	1241	45.2	45b	04/03/54	cooking pot		
18	851	45.2	45b	15/04/53	kettle	° red earth	grey interior

° *According to de Vaux*

Locus 45b, catalogue of pots and photographs

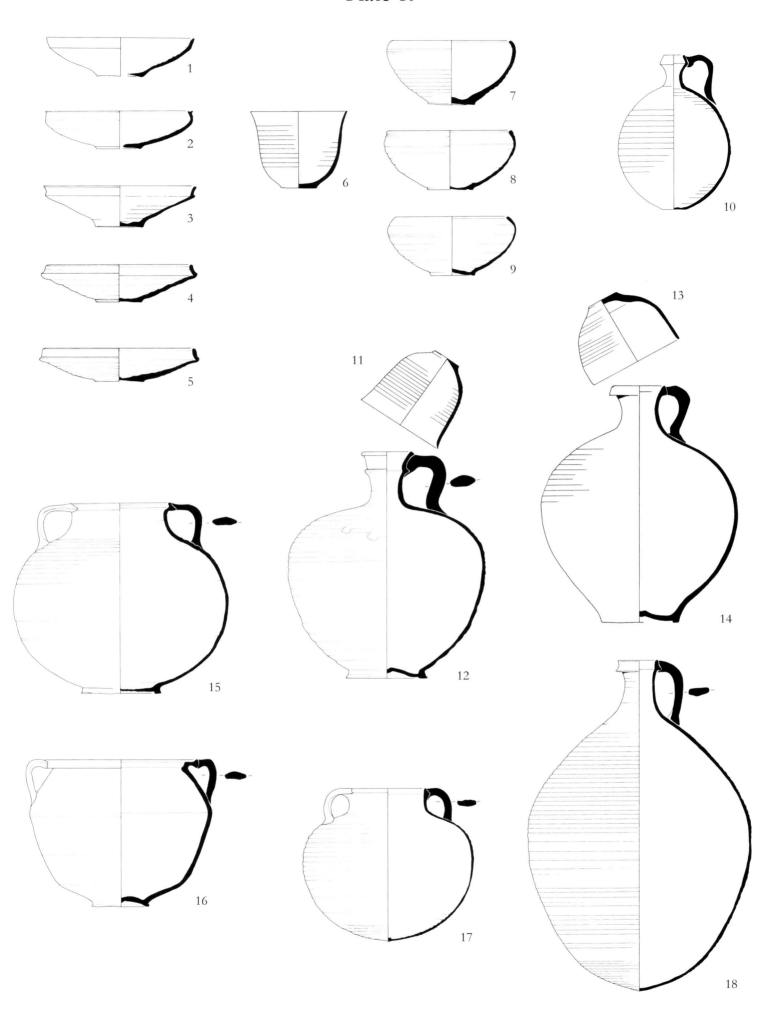

Plate 19

Locus 45b, pottery, scale ¼

Locus 177 (45c)

In the architecture sequence, L. 177 was later to encroach upon L. 80. It was identified at the time of the 1953 campaign and it appears, simply sketched, on the preparatory plans (fig. 76a). It must be viewed as an extension of L. 45. In L. 177 and 45, the deposits of pots uncovered form a whole which was sealed by the destruction of the year 68. L. 177 was not represented on the Coüasnon *Plans* of Period Ib and II; however, L. 177 is recorded under 45c in the the *Journal* on 16/4/53. A diagrammatic survey of 1953, not published but found in the archives (fig. 76b), proves that it captivated attention. We have to see it as a kind of caisson adjoining L. 45. Encroaching on the space of L. 80, it seals the level of *deposits* 80.4. The caisson of crude earth has not been preserved.

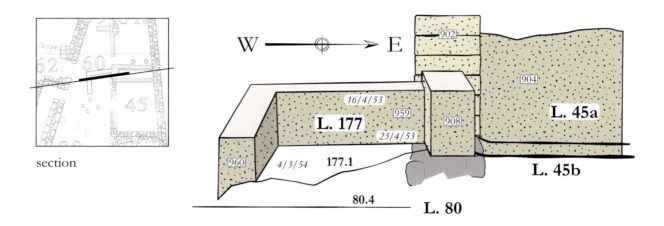

Restored elements	Level	Definition	Journal dates
177.1	3C	Accommodation of pottery	16/4/53 4/3/54

Stratigraphic diagram of Locus 177 (for the chart of symbols, see page 155)

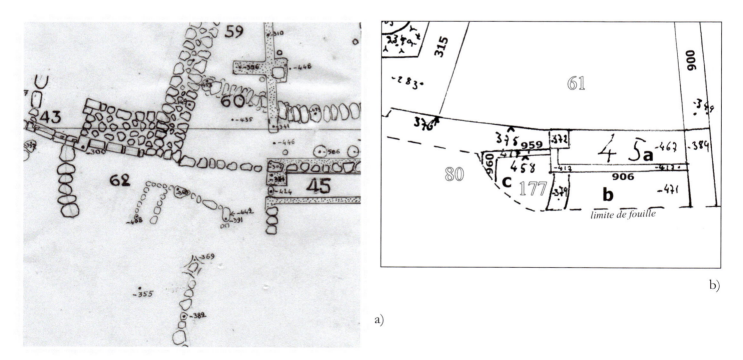

fig. 76. a) Locus 45 a, b, c, Coüasnon survey at 1:100, 1953
  b) Hand-drawn sketch on the preparatory survey of 1954. Locus 177 was wrongly positioned by Coüasnon. The elevations correspond to different zero references.

Plate 20

Plate 21, 9

Plate 21, 10

Plate 21, 11

Plate 21, 1

N° Pl.	N° Catal.	Position	Comments (archives)	Date	Description	Clay	Exterior
1	838	177.1	45c	16/04/53	plate	° grey earth	white wash, burnt
2	840	177.1	45c	16/04/53	plate	° red earth	
3	839	177.1	45c	16/04/53	bowl	° grey earth	pink, white wash
4	837	177.1	45c	16/04/53	small globular jug	° red earth	burnt
5	836	177.1	45c	16/04/53	small globular jug	° grey earth	white wash
6	835	177.1	45c	16/04/53	small globular jug	° grey earth	white wash
7	3389	177.1	45c	16/04/53	kettle	brown paste	beige
8	3388	177.1	45c	16/04/53	kettle	red paste	beige
9	846	177.1	45c	16/04/53	jar	° pink earth, grey section	red
10	920	177.1	45c	23/04/53	jar	° red earth	grey on exterior, traces of quite fine and well-fired white wash
11	908	177.1	45c	23/04/53	jar	° grey earth	white wash

° *According to de Vaux*

Locus 177 (45c), catalogue of pots and photographs

Plate 21

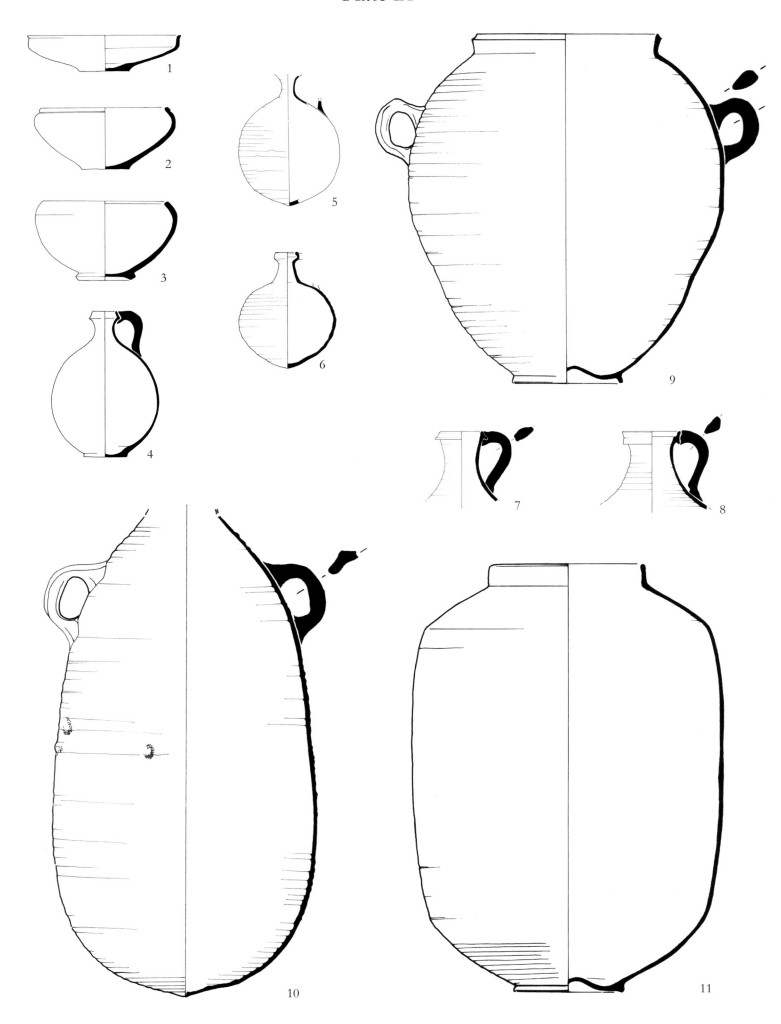

Locus 177 (45c), pottery, scale ¼

Loci 62 and 63
A poorly located surface level

Naming L. 62 a space without topographical markers is difficult to locate a posteriori. De Vaux seeks to prolong wall 315, which encloses the site to the east, to the south. He thinks he can recognize the southeast corner of the central building which was heavily reworked. The corner of the main building will have been identified later to the southeast of L. 74. He extends the clearance starting from L. 60, and the space called 62 (1/3/54) includes the later named L. 63, on 4/3/54, when the imprecise line of stones 914 appears. A complementary error made the reading of the place more difficult: in the Coüasnon *Plans* (published in *Fouilles de Khirbet Qumrân et de 'Aïn Feshkha*, vol. I, p.17-18 and vol. II, p. xxiii-xxiv), L. 63 was wrongly placed in L. 45b. It is appropriate to correct this.

Loci 62 and 63 are contiguous, and since they belong to the same field, we consider them as a unit. The excavation was conducted quickly and its confused results are not very reliable. De Vaux descended below L. 43, of his Period III, anticipating reaching the destruction of the year 68, Period IIb. He collects pots without recording their context. The *Catalogue* recorded only one bowl at L. 63: KhQ 1259, **joined to the shelf of pottery of** L. 62. L. 62 seals L. 80 and L. 52, and further to the east L. 63 seals L. 84. The removal on 4/3/54 of the bad low wall 914 which separates them will have redefined L. 80 to the east and 74 to the west (fig. 78 and 79). L. 80 extended as far as wall 315, while L. 74 designed the deeper space to the west of this wall.

At L. 62, a *surface clearing* is effectuated (1/3/54) without defined limits; exposed, on 2/3/54, is the layer which *descends below the floor corresponding to the threshold of L. 43* and which we may situate more or less directly above L. 52. L. 62 designated the excavation as far as the west of wall 315, as L. 74 is placed *south of 62* (L. 74 on 6/3/54); however, it is indicated elsewhere (L. 62, 1/3/54) that excavated surface 62 extends also *to the south* of L. 60 and *around the southeast corner of the large building*. The investigation therefore progresses slice by slice, and at this point towards the south. De Vaux removed the surface layers without much hesitation, as long as the walls did not appear. The only stratigraphic element recorded – *We reach an ash layer (...) under the threshold of L. 43* (L. 62, 2/3/54) – is not easy to situate. The levels below the surface should be those of L. 43 and adjoining loci (Level 4) and should help us to decide in favour of, or against, an occupation of the triangle after the year 68.

By chance, the photographs show detail of the stratification of the spot. Wall 315, underlying L. 62, appears partly cleared on the left of the enlarged photograph (fig. 77a). The mound on the second plan shows the surface of the site before the dig, and in the section of the excavation, to the left, one can clearly make out the stratification of L. 62 (west of wall 315): two blocks separated by a layer of ash (62.2) estimated to be 10 to 25 cm in thickness. The ash appears again in the top left-hand corner of the photos. The photo (fig. 77a) shows a large plan of it overhanging wall 314, one stone of which bears the cipher L. 52, repeated on the floor; the section thus faces the west.

One must suppose that the ash of 62.2 was not cut by wall 315 but that it rested on it. The eastern wall 315 of the residence had remained upright at Level 4 (Period III). Here again, the horizontal plan of wall 315, in a site which has not been plundered, indicates that the superstructure was of rough brick. The *Journal* of L. 52 does not note any important heap of ash to the west of 315, which would have been an extension of 62.2 to the west. The block of earth under 62.2 would have accumulated by the erosion of upper parts of crude earth after the year 68 and the ash of 62.2 must belong to Level 4. De Vaux was concerned about the ash elements, to which he devoted special stratigraphic attention: an extension of 62.2 to the west would not have passed unnoticed. Nothing is known of the layers that sealed L. 52: the investigation of L. 52 below did not start until 21/4/54 (L. 52)). The layer of ash 62.2 had been spread in the area of kiln 918, but without a stratigraphic connection with the latter. This may have been the result of the spreading of the ash in a northerly direction to avoid spoiling the approach to pool 71 when there was still water in it. This would provide the argument that the layout of the triangle was abandoned to the benefit of a work space around kiln 918, i.e., *extra muros*. The lime kiln would have been in active use for a long time and de Vaux had his reasons for keeping it in his Period III (see on L. 84).

fig. 77. a) Layers of ash in Loci 52 and 62, from the photo PAM 40427
b) Two upper layers above wall 315 are separated by ash 62.2
c) Loci 52 and 53 and Locus 43 in the background.

However, the connection between the coat of ash 62.2 and kiln 918 has not been established, and the maintenance of the kiln's active use after the year 68 has not been shown. The occupants of Level 4 confined in the former residence were able to throw their ash outside, only a short distance from door 343 of L. 43. The spreading of Level 4 would have covered the collapse of Level 3. In this case, the abandonment of kiln 918 after the destruction of 68 would be consistent, given that the majority of the pools, coated walls and mortar floors of the large rooms were no longer in use. Lime production would no longer have been so necessary.

In its extent to the east of 315, the ash 62.2 separates two blocks. The upper block 62.1, Level post-4/5, is the product of erosion after abandonment. The ash of 62.2, the result of domestic waste, must be associated with Level 4/5. Lower block 62.4, clearer, would correspond to the collapse of Level 3C or its leveling after 68.

Threshold 343 of L. 43 (Level 4, post-68) appears at the centre of the photograph (fig. 77c) like a narrow rectangle, horizontal, bathed in sunlight, discernible to the right of heavy pillar 342. Its level seems lower, by 50 cm or more, than the ash of 62.2; after evacuation of the destruction of Level 3C, the floors *intra muros* of Level 4, would be thinly buried. On the second day of work in L. 62, the *Journal* (2/3/54) notes: *we descend below the floor corresponding to the threshold of L. 43*. Large door 343 of L. 43 is distinguished on 14/4/53 then cleared on 14 and 15/4/55 (on L. 43) without a floor appearing. The *floor corresponding to the threshold of L. 43*, which we labeled as a hypothetical 62.3, will have extended in front of the door lower than the threshold. Instead of the predicted floor, the same day (2/3/54) he *reaches a layer of ash*, 62.5 which cannot be confused with the other ash of 62.2, too high in the section. The excavation of L. 62 was carried out more quickly than in L. 63, and it is highly likely that the exposure of the line of stones 914, which will require L. 63, is posterior to the excavation of ash layer 62.5. The ash of 62.5 is not deep enough to be confused with 80.3 (Level 3A/B). Since the excavation of L. 62 did not end within the horizon of low wall 914, an attempt is made to link it to another layer of ash. Ash 62.5 could correspond to a pocket of ash in L. 52 visible at the base of the trace left to the lower left of the central heavy pillar 344 (fig. 77a). In a coherent stratigraphic sequence, this ash, lying lower than the threshold of L. 43, would identify 62.5 and would show the destruction of Level 3C.

We must attribute to layer 62.5 the pots whose position is (unhelpfully) specified as *upper level (Niv. sup.)* in the *Catalogue*. The qualification *upper (supérieur)* presupposes the function of a known, deeper level; the *upper level* in the *Catalogue* can only refer to L. 43, but this produced no pots. One might, however, hesitate in relation to jar KhQ 1158 (Plate 24,3), the form of which is unique in the corpus of Qumran pottery, with its considerably widened lip and its thin lining. Despite the lack of evidence attesting to a continuity of the ash, 62.5 seems to have produced jar KhQ 885 (Plate 24,4), lying under the threshold of L. 43 (22/4/53). Its neck is missing but the shape of the body and the thinness of the lining would encourage attributing to it the same type as that of KhQ 1158.

L. 63 is not sufficiently documented to help us recreate the stratification. Our guess would be that it is identical to that of L. 62. The *Journal*, very brief, is interrupted on 5/3/54 without having described anything, and the excavation might have been completed on 6/3/54 since sherds were not recorded on that day. The only complete form, bowl KhQ 1259, has an entry in the *Catalogue*.

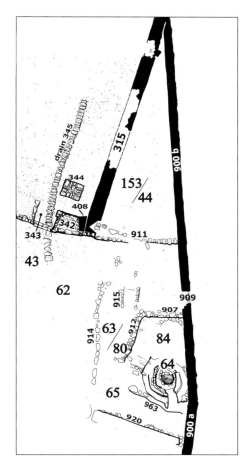

fig. 78.   Numbering of constructed elements (late levels) of the triangle

208 The archaeology of Qumran – an attempted reassessment

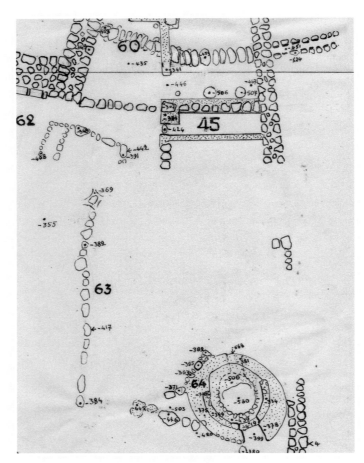

fig. 79. Initial location of Loci 62 and 63

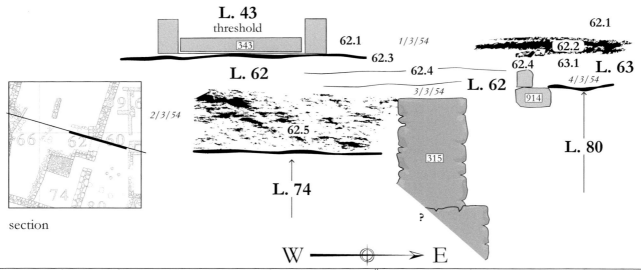

Restored elements	Level	Definition	Journal dates	Coins	Position	N°	Chronology
62.1	Post 4–5	Surface layers	1/3/54				
62.2	4	Ash, domestic waste or from kiln 918 Jar KhQ 1158	2/3/54				
62.3	(4)	floor exterior L43 (restored)	2/3/54				
62.4	Post 3C	Collapse of crude earth	2/3/54				
62.5	3C	Ash, destruction of 3C	2/3/54	KhQ. 1135, 1156	upper level	2	Herod Archelaeus

Schema and stratigraphic diagram of Loci 62 and 63 (for the chart of symbols, see page 155)

Plate 22

No. Pl.	No. Catal.	Position	Comments (archives)	Date	Description	Clay	Exterior
1	1259	63.1	-	3/5/1954	bowl	° grey earth	white wash
2	4072	63.1	-	3/3/1954	large goblet	red earth	brown
3	4066	63.1	-	3/5/1954	jar lid	dark grey paste	grey and beige
4	3015	63.1	-	3/5/1954	jar	grey brown paste	light grey
5	4086	63.1	-	3/5/1954	jar stand	grey paste	grey
6	1264	63.1	-	3/5/1954	inscribed shard		

° *According to de Vaux*

Locus 63, pottery and catalogue

Plate 23

Plate 24, 13

Plate 24, 16

Plate 24, 1

Plate 24, 2

Plate 24, 3

N° Pl.	N° Catal.	Position	Comments (archives)	Date	Description	Clay	Exterior
1	1171	62.3	\= 62 upper	03/03/54	plate	° red earth	pink wash
2	1228	62.3	\= 62 upper	03/03/54	plate	° red earth	white wash
3	1158	62.3	\= 62 upper	02/03/54	jar	° red earth	pink wash
4	885	62.1	\= 43	22/04/53	jar	° red earth	white wash
5	1154	62.3	\= 62 upper	02/03/54	lid or plate	° grey earth	white wash
6	1227	62.5	-	04/03/54	lid or plate	° red earth	white wash
7	1153	62.3	\= 62 upper	02/03/54	jar support	° red earth	
8	1226	62.4	-	03/03/54	goblet	° grey earth, fine	
9	4063	62.4	-	03/03/54	large goblet	dark grey paste	grey
10	3001	62.4	-	03/03/54	large dish	red paste	beige engobe
11	2993	62.4	-	03/03/54	painted plate	red paste	light brown, red painting
12	3003	62.4	-	03/03/54	neck of filter vessel	off-white paste	off-white
13	3012	62.4	-	03/03/54	scroll type jar	grey paste	beige
14	4065	62.4	-	03/03/54	jar support	dark grey paste	grey
15	3002	62.4	-	03/03/54	pipe?	dark brown paste	beige engobe
16	2996	62.4	-	03/03/54	large jar	brown paste	beige engobe
17	3011	62.5	-	03/03/54	plate	red paste	beige engobe
18	1250	62.5	\= 62 inf.	03/03/54	bowl	° red earth	red wash
19	1247	62.5	\= 62 inf.	03/03/54	bowl	° red earth	white wash
20	3007	62.5	-	04/03/54	jug	red paste	beige engobe
21	3010	62.5	-	04/03/54	jar support	red paste	grey-brown

° *According to de Vaux*

Locus 62, catalogue of pots and photographs

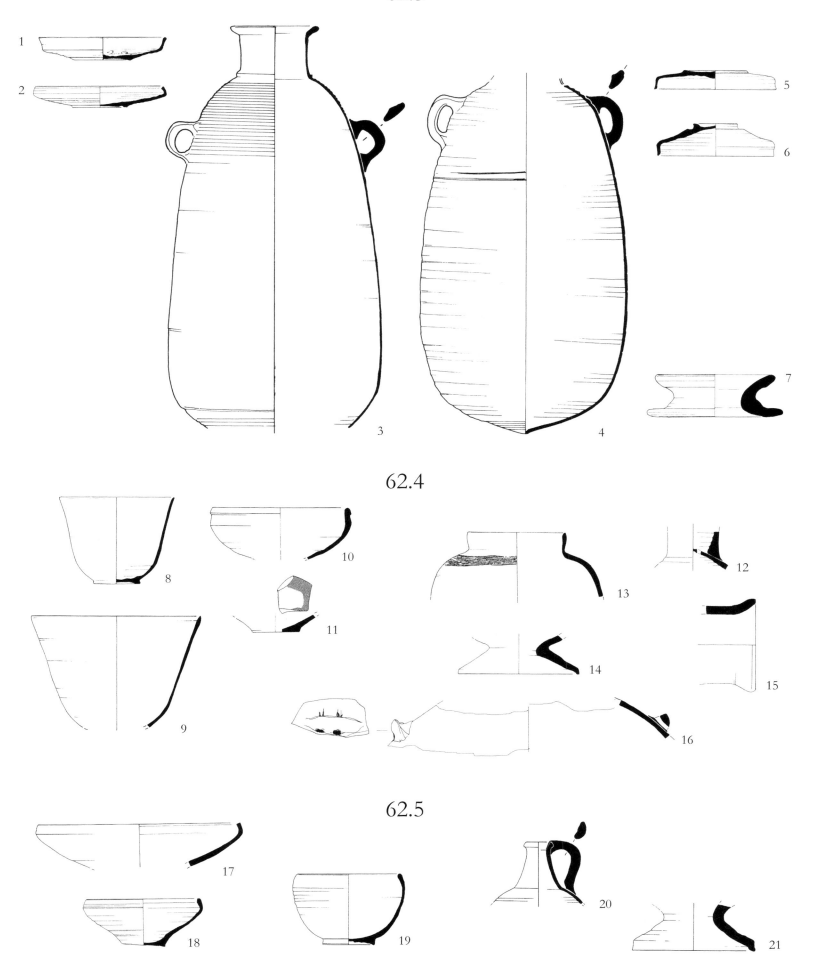

Locus 62, pottery, scale ¼

a) Floor 80.5 cut along the wall 315

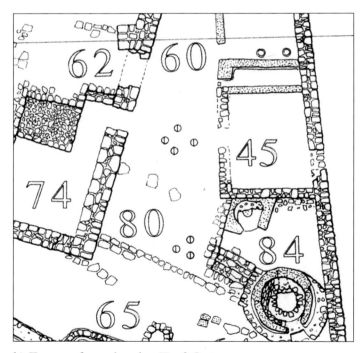

b) Excerpt from the plan II of Coüasnon

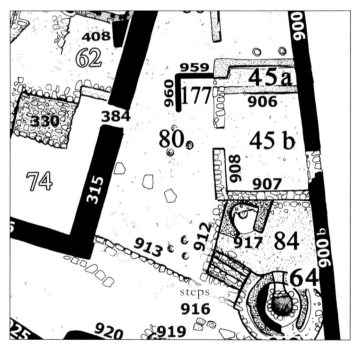

c) L. 80, designation of constructed elements

fig. 80.   Locus 80

Locus 80

According to the *Journal*, L. 80 only begins with lower layers *in part to the south of loci 62 and 63* (6/3/54). On the first day of the work, the *Journal* notes: *Many animal bones mixed with pottery* (6/3/54), not saying that they are *buried deposits*. The sketch (fig. 81) specifies *Ash – Sherds* and the *deposit* becomes probable. The tiny circle, a symbol adopted by Coüasnon for *buried deposit*, is repeated seven times on his *Plan* of Period II. One might attempt to link this deposit to a lower level.

The depth indications are missing but we know that the bones were lying quite low down. The upper layers were cleared under the heading L. 62. Reached on the first day was *An uncertain floor with an east-west alignment of stones* (6/3/54): it is staircase threshold 913.

The sketch (fig. 81) shows the eastern face of wall 315. The two hatched facets cut low wall 913. From the terminology of the 1954 excavation, *Floor 3 – Yellow Earth – Sherds*, we need to understand: *layer of yellow earth on a bed of sherds*. The yellow earth must be 80.1, the fallen rough brick superstructure, and with the argument of the sherds, we would restore a floor 80.2 even though the *Journal* does not record it. *Floor 2* of the sketch is called 80.3 without further indication in the *Journal*; was it perhaps confused with the separation of the beds? Finally, the sketch specifies the position of layer 80.4, *Ash Sherds – Floor 1*, abutting the base of low wall 913. The quick drawing shows that low wall 913 rests *on* 80.4 and that *ash and sherds* lie rather to the south of 913. The second hypothesis is preferable if *Ash Sherds, Floor 1* is a recognized *deposit*: the *deposit* were buried before the construction of the annexes, and 913 is a staircase threshold, necessary but more recent, to the layout between L. 65 and 80, – or better still 913 would have been able to mark the restored northern enclosure of L. 188 before the digging of large pool 71.

Installed to the north of L. 80, the partitions of L. 61 and 45 *rest on a layer of ash*, 61.4 (L. 61, 27/2/54). Without any further argument, we cannot decide whether to link or to separate the ash of 61.4 under L. 61-45 and the *deposits* of 80.4. However, the note of L. 80 says that the bones were mixed with the pottery, not specifying *deposits*, and one could see them as refuse from an ordinary kitchen. But the sketch indicating the ash (fig. 81) does not contradict the look of a *buried deposit*, perhaps a less typical one, parallel to those of L. 130, 131 and 132. We propose to associate the ash of 80.4 and 61.4 with that which extends under L. 61-45: their stratigraphic synchronization is not certain, given the lack of a connection or height indications. The association of bones/sherds/ash of 80.4 with other similar traces in L. 65 is corroborated by the observations of the *Journal* on L. 65 on 7/3/54. *Many sheep bones grouped together with the broken jars (...) to be compared with the bones found in 80 and those of 130, 132.*

On the Coüasnon *Plan*, the *east-west alignment of stones* 913 is assigned to Period III. It is, however, quite deep, as the photo shows (fig. 80a). From the front, 913 has only two beds and seems to be without a foundation. Finally, it rests on what could be assimilated to the floor, which we have called 80.5, cut by the workers to uncover the leveling of 315. We restore it as a former floor, external, to the east of the residence. Low wall 913 does not rest directly on 80.4 and would correspond to more recent floors 80.2 or 80.3.

There was some hesitation over the levels underlying 80.3: de Vaux records, *under the floor (80.3) a small jar inserted up to the neck* (11/3/54, and photograph fig. 82). KhQ 1465 and its lid KhQ 1466 are initially associated without hesitation to one level: *We clear this level 'Period II?'*, 80.4 (13/3/54). Seeing it interred, de Vaux had attributed it to floor 80.4, which seemed to contain it. Two days later, *0.15 cm lower we reach another level* [80.5], *but which is not the deepest* (80.6) (13/3/54). On 14/3/54 de Vaux makes the correction: *The interred jar corresponds to the new floor*. The text is elliptical and does not allow us to decide if the new *floor* designates *another level* or *the deepest* level. We find it difficult to believe that an intact pot with its lid in place would have remained upright at the time of the collapse between 80.5 and 80.4. The jar was buried and it is more consistent to attribute it, without much risk of error, to 80.4. Its association with the older floor 80.5, which must be that of the Hasmonaean occupation, is improbable: the form of KhQ 1465 has more recent parallels on the site and 80.4 fits it better; so it could be associated with the *buried deposits*.

Would it be justified to assign floor 80.5 to the residence (Level 2A) and *the deeper* 80.6 to Level 1?

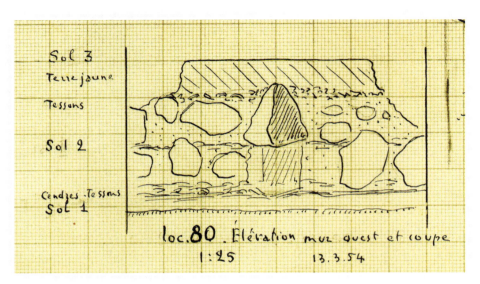

fig. 81.   Locus 80: elevation of west wall 913 and section

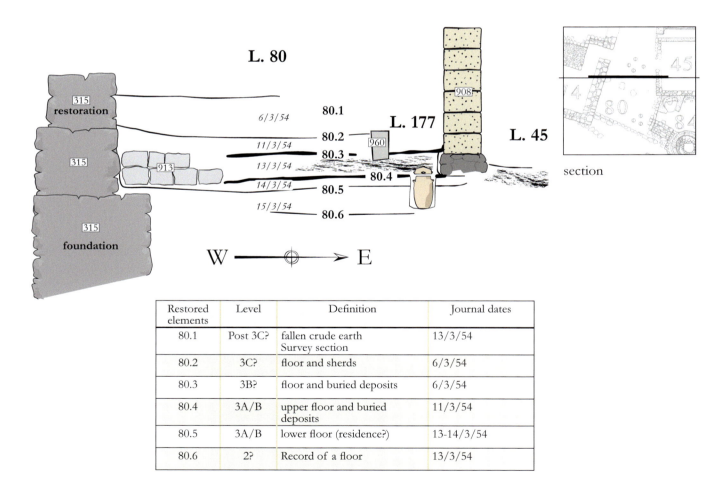

Restored elements	Level	Definition	Journal dates
80.1	Post 3C?	fallen crude earth Survey section	13/3/54
80.2	3C?	floor and sherds	6/3/54
80.3	3B?	floor and buried deposits	6/3/54
80.4	3A/B	upper floor and buried deposits	11/3/54
80.5	3A/B	lower floor (residence?)	13-14/3/54
80.6	2?	Record of a floor	13/3/54

Schema and stratigraphic diagram of Locus 80
(for the chart of symbols, see page 155)

Plate 25

fig. 82. Locus 80: small jar KhQ 1465 and its lid KhQ 1466

Plate 26, 10 and 11

Plate 26, 9

Plate 26, 12

N° Pl.	N° Catal.	Position	Comments (archives)	Date	Description	Clay	Exterior
1	4383	80.5	-	13/03/54	lid of jar	brownish-grey paste	beige
2	1370	80.5	\= 80 inf.	13/03/54	jar		
3	4391	80.5	-	13/03/54	neck of jar	beige paste	beige
4	1372	80.5	\= 80 inf. (in jar 1370)	13/03/54	bowl	° grey earth, poorly fired	white wash, chipped
5	1371	80.5	\= 80 inf. (in jar 1370)	13/03/54	bowl	° greey earth	white wash
6	1373	80.5	\= 80 inf.	13/02/54	large bowl	° grey earth	white wash, burnt
7	1374	80.5	\= 80 inf.	13/03/54	lid of jar KhQ 1369	grey earth	pink wash
8	4373	80.5	-	13/03/54	neck of jar	red paste	beige engobe
9	1369	80.5	\= 80 inf.	13/03/54	jar		
10	1466	80.4/5	\= 80 inf.	17/03/54	lid of jar KhQ 1465	° red earth	pink wash
11	1465	80.4/5	\= 80 inf.	17/03/54	jar	° red earth	red wash
12	1349	80.5	-	11/03/54	bowl	° grey earth	white wash
13	1410	80.6	\= 80 inf.	15/03/54	plate	° red earth	red wash

° *According to de Vaux*

Locus 80, catalogue of pots and photographs

Plate 26

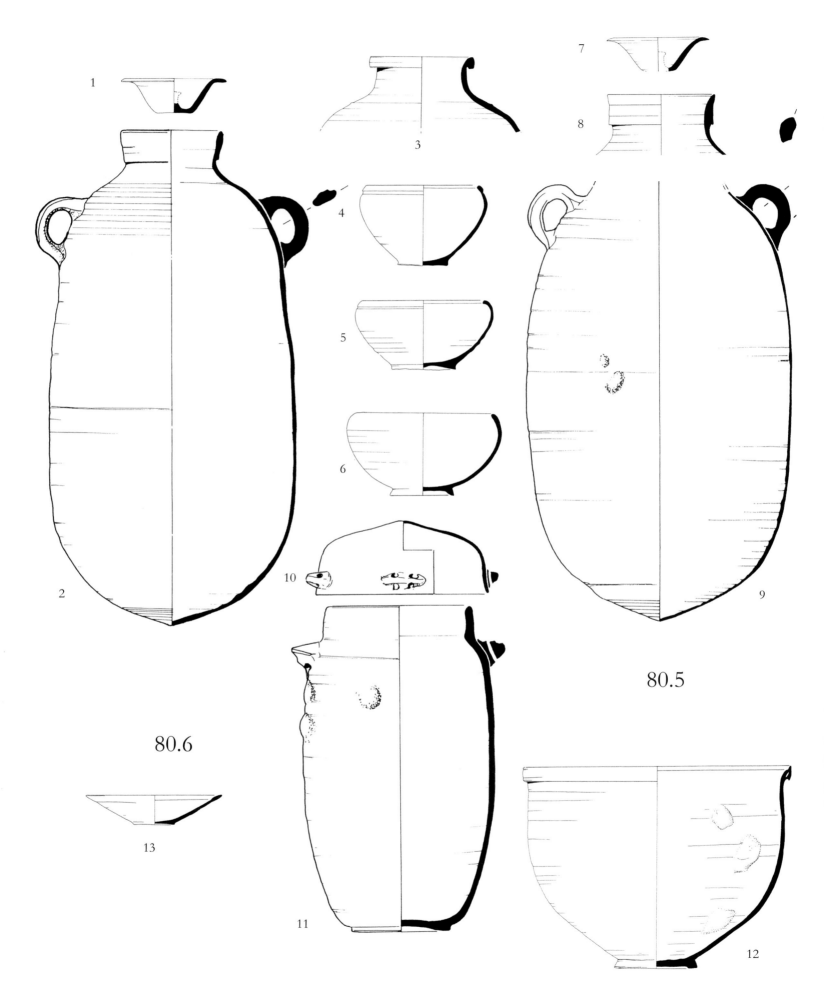

80.5

80.6

Locus 80, pottery, scale ¼

Locus 65

Adjoining kiln 64, L. 65, over its east-west width, is the area of access to pool L. 71. The speedy excavation was conducted on the fringes of the clearance of pool L. 71, in a single day: 7th March was a Sunday and de Vaux was absent from the site in Jerusalem on 7, 8 and 9 March, leaving a few workers hard at work on clarifying the limits of pool 71, a task without much associated risk. Supervision was relaxed, and the *Journal* records: *between 64 and 71, many sheep bones against the walls with broken jars and bowls with oblique lining (...) 9 March: return at midday* (L. 65, 7/3/54). The deposits recall those of L. 130, to which they show some resemblance. The *listing* of finds (L. 65) records only five objects, probably preserved because they were complete. Ten sherds were kept as samples.

L. 65 would not have continued to hold our attention without the *buried deposits*. Their presence may be regarded as surprising in a narrow space where they would have impeded access to the water. But they are deeper than the most recent floor of access to L. 71, and we are convinced that they preceded the layout of the triangle and the construction of pool 71. The *deposits* were not buried in a constructed zone.

The excavation cleared away the surface of the south zone of L. 153, vestiges of Period III, Level 4. The restoration of the floors is only a matter of conjecture as the *Journal* does not mention them. The most recent floor, which was repaired, 65.2, must be linked to pool 71, Level 4, post-68. The excavation respected its foundation, called 963, in the form of a buttress sketched by a line of stones on the *Plan* of Period II, and which can be discerned on the enlarged photograph (fig. 83) in front of the worker who is digging. Although they are not separated by much in time, this floor 65.2 of access to water could not be confused with that of the last use of kiln 918, even if the kiln was abandoned.

The use of the kiln is indicated, in the upper left of the section diagram of L. 64, proposed by de Vaux (fig. 84b) with the alternate hatching symbol, which means *rock*, wrongly used. The kiln is set deep, and its foundation trench is sealed by the upper masonry, the low part having been installed as an earthwork. Floor 65.3 of access to pool 71 on Level 3B/C could be confused with that of Level 4, 65.2. Circulation to the south of the kiln dominates higher up (fig. 84b) as it seems rational to see it on the drawing, at the level of the base of the aeration opening. It will be remembered that circulation around the kiln belongs to L. 84 (see on this L.): in the south it occurred directly above L. 65. The complete recovered pottery of the *deposits*, noted in association with the sheep bones (7/3/54), must be associated with a circulation floor, 65.4, which precedes the digging of pool 71.

The *Catalogue* of objects presents a list of pots. The sherds recorded on 6 March come from the upper layer (L. 153.1) as they were collected previous to the L. 65 entry in the *Journal*. The *Catalogue* notes several pots found *on the ground,* without further indication. We would hypothesize that this is the circulation ground 65.4, contemporary with the *deposits* and which, holed by the foundation of kiln 918, would correspond, without much need for hesitation, to floor 80.3 of L. 80. The *deposits* alone had produced sufficient sherds to enable the reassembly of complete forms. Jar KhQ. 1289 was pierced to be used for filtering water (pl.27:10).

The speed of the excavation certainly caused mixing of the pottery from the three floors later restored. Recorded on 7 March, the pottery should come from lower stratum 65.4, and certain forms have parallels in the deposits of L. 130. However, there is no way of correcting the mix-ups.

fig. 83.   The buttress of Locus 65 containing kiln 918

KhQ 1289 Plate 27, 10

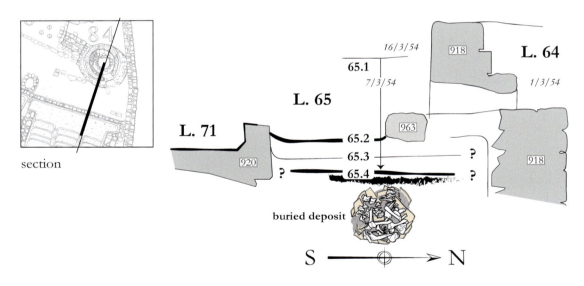

Restored elements	Level	Definition	Journal dates
153.1	Inconsistent	surface	(6/3/54 Catal.)
65.1	4?	Collapse of 4	(6/3/54 Catal.)
65.2	4	floor of L65	7/3/54
65.3	3C	L65 before L64	7/3/54
65.4	3A/B	Unallocated space	7/3/54

Schema and stratigraphic diagram of Locus 65 (for the chart of symbols, see page 155)

Plate 27

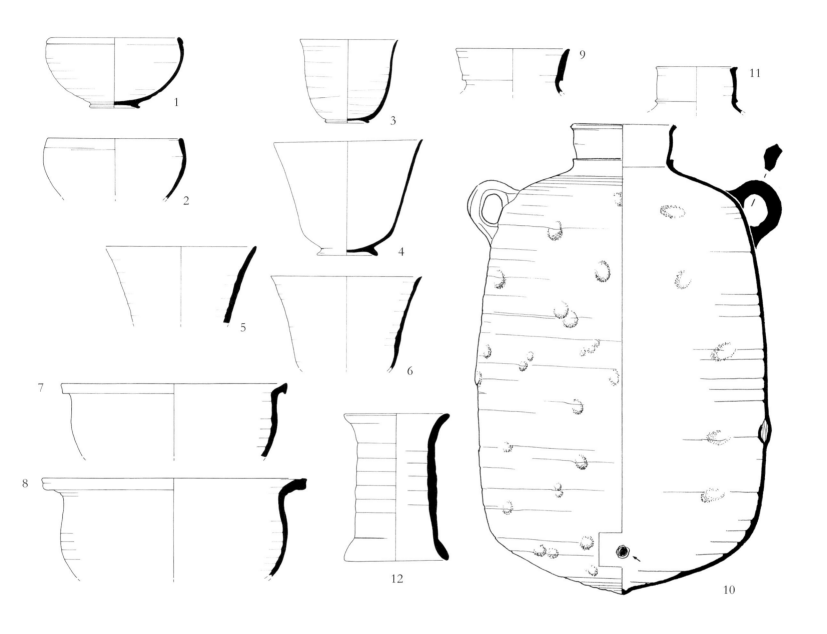

N° Pl.	N° Catal.	Position	Comments (archives)	Date	Description	Clay	Exterior
1	1280	65.2 ?	on the ground	06/03/54	bowl	° pink earth	pink wash
2	3034	65.2 ?	on the ground	06/03/54	bowl	beige clay	beige
3	1286	65.2/3	on the ground	07/03/54	goblet	° red earth	pink wash
4	1270	65 ?	on the ground	06/03/54	large goblet	° pink earth, grey in section	red wash
5	3035	65 ?	-	06/03/54	large goblet	red paste	red engobe
6	3031	65.2/3	-	07/03/54	large goblet	brownish-red paste	light brown
7	3032	65.2/3	-	07/03/54	bowl	light brown paste	beige engobe
8	3036	65.2/3	-	07/03/54	bowl	grey paste	beige
9	5163	65.2/3	-	07/03/54	neck of jar		
10	1289	65.4	lower floor	07/03/54	jar		
11	3030	65 ?	-	06/03/54	neck of jar	dark brown paste	brown, beige engobe
12	1287	65.3/4	on the ground	07/03/54	pipe	° red earth	

° *According to de Vaux*

Locus 65, pottery and catalogue scale ¼

a)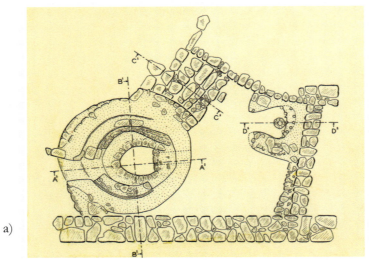

b)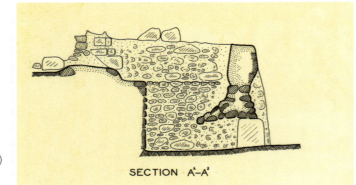

c)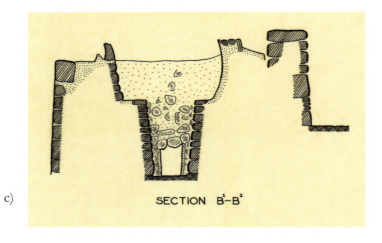

fig. 84.   Section of Locus 64, north-south (de Vaux, 1954)

Locus 84 and kiln 918 (Locus 64)

On 14/3/54 (L. 84), the *Journal* notes: *this name [84] is given to the space between kiln 64 and L. 45*. However, the place had already been excavated, as on 3/3/54 de Vaux had reached deep ash, under the heading of L. 45 south: *We finish emptying the ash hole, against the lime hole: Many sherds, no complete forms. It is a pile of detritus. We reach a bottom of large pebbles, which is lower than the floors of loc. 59, 60, 45. The north face of the lime hole appears, then; at its base one enters by a door which was subsequently filled-in. Two states in this construction. What was its original purpose?* The pottery emerging from this sondage, recorded in L. 56, was classified in L. 84.

It will be appropriate, first of all, to clarify the denominations relating to L. 64 and 84. According to the method applied by de Vaux, the L. designates a place of limited habitation, or a place outside the constructed zone. Kiln 918 was unnecessarily numbered *L. 64*, when it is only an installation in L. 84. So, in our study we dispense with the term *L. 64*: kiln 918 is found in L. 84. It seems that L. 84 served the two kilns 917 and 918.

The large circular kiln 918 was excavated in one day, 1/3/54 (L. 84). We use the name 84.1 for its filled-in state, about which nothing is said. In the notes on L. 64, the *Journal* includes a description of L. 84, although the latter is not the subject of a new comment until 14/3/54, laconically noting the flight of steps from L. 65 to the supply of kilns 917 and 918: *this name is given to the space between lime hole 64 and L. 45 (14/3/54)*.

While 917 is a pottery kiln, 918 must be a lime kiln, the duration of use of which is not fixed. The presence of a lime kiln would be unsurprising on a site where a number of floors and stretches of masonry were roughcast with mortar. How and why would a large kiln have been constructed in this location? Unlike the southeast portion of the triangle, being entirely made of rough brick, L. 84 is built of stone. It is inserted into the right-angled layout of the settlement, positioned parallel to the southeast corner of the residence and, widthwise, into the extension of pool 71; this width also defines L. 65. A square of the grid seems, at this point, to have been supported on the underlying structure of L. 187 and 188 (see on L. 71). It is difficult to tell whether the stone construction preceded that of brick: the building of each betrays space management which respects the grid of the overall set-up while nonetheless being supported on long enclosure wall 900. It is likely that they were built at the same time, and wall 907 (north of L. 84), at an angle, creates the partition between L. 84 and 45. The arrangement of the constructions reveals an explicit desire to place the kilns *intra muros*, which was not really a necessity in a location where there was no lack of space outside the walls. Here it was not a matter of protecting a kiln, but of exerting strict control over its use. We see this as a feature added to those which document the wish to enclose the inhabited space at Qumran. The kilns are linked and their mouths face each other. It seems, however, that pottery kiln 917 was destroyed while lime kiln 918 may have been maintained.

Observations on kilns 917 and 918

Kiln 917, half of which is preserved, presents the characteristics of pottery kilns, but its modest dimensions are striking. Internally, the fireplace measures roughly one metre across, under 0.50 m of the arch of a bed plate supported by a central pillar. The bed plate is pierced by tight flues to heat the room above, although it is true that no trace of that has been preserved. We need to recreate it. The dome of the kiln must have been of fire-resistant earth which the workers will not have identified in the debris. The small size of the kiln is surprising; and the poor capacity for a batch does not betray a permanent pottery installation, because of the lack of space and the absence of rejects or failed firings. We have to suppose it had a particular function, intermittent at best, and which it is difficult to surmise; it is not proven that this is a kiln designed to produce ordinary pottery and to be in regular use.

On L. 84, we learn (14/3/54) that de Vaux confesses his surprise at not finding any firing wasters: *But it is impossible to find where failed firings were thrown*, and the remark applies to both kilns which, in de Vaux's final option, had been designed for firing pottery. After some hesitation, in relation to kiln 918 de Vaux moved from the interpretation of a lime kiln to that of a pottery kiln designed for *large pieces: they were put in the kiln through an upper opening and arranged on a shelf*[70]. The pottery function is not convincing, and we have to query it and return to de Vaux' initial intuition.

---

70. R. de Vaux, *L'archéologie*, p. 13.

222 The archaeology of Qumran – an attempted reassessment

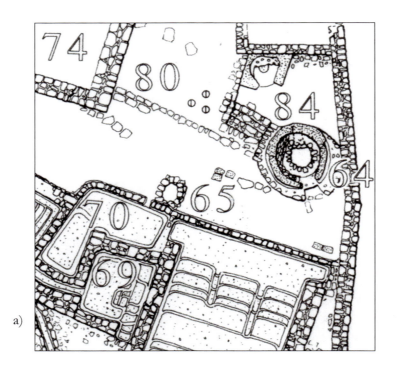

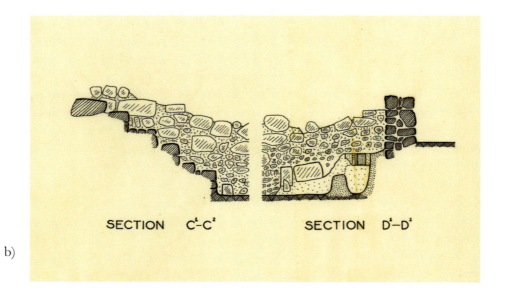

fig. 85. a) Survey of Loci 64 and 84, from Coüasnon Plan (Period II)
b) Diagram section from the pottery kiln 917, L. 84 (1954 survey)

Kiln 918 (L. 64) does not conform to the morphology of the ancient pottery kiln. De Vaux seems to believe that the jars were inserted into the kiln from the top. Insertion of the jars from the top supposes that the kiln cover was closed after the kiln had been filled, which is not easy from a technical point of view, as without the aid of a support, the cover would rest on the vessels to be fired. The opening made in the partition from L. 65 is not large enough for a man to pass through it. Now we should not confuse the elaborate morphology of a large kiln such as 918 with the rudimentary technique of firing pottery *in a pit*, where the light cover is placed right on top of the batch of vessels. The shelf (*banquette*), or circular stage which de Vaux describes and draws, is narrow and would only have allowed a few pots to be placed there in poor equilibrium and in a batch whose size would have been barely worth the effort. Finally, such an arrangement does not separate the kiln room from the furnace by a bed plate, necessary for the distribution of the temperature and the fire. In this kiln, there is no trace of the fixings for a bed plate that supposedly disappeared. So, the kiln may have been a *rod* pottery kiln (with shelves, in medieval style), which would be anachronistic in the present case. We have to accept that the kiln was open at the top, and therefore drop the idea of a pottery kiln.

De Vaux had, however, hesitated to interpret the *circular construction* of L. 64. The presence of lime 84.3 at the bottom of the hole was explicit. In the preliminary reports, he had described kilns 64 and 84 as pottery kilns[71]. In the *Journal*, he was less affirmative after noting the presence of lime in the kiln: *a smaller hole,*

---

71. R. de Vaux, "Fouilles de Khirbet Qumrân", *RB* 1956, p. 543.

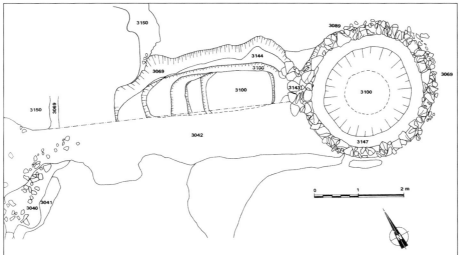

fig. 86.   French Gallo-Roman lime kiln
Arnaud Coutelas, *Le Mortier de chaux*,
Edition Errance, Paris 2009, p. 43

in the interior of which there was much lime (L. 64, 1/3/54), *the north face of the lime hole then appears* (3/3/54); finally, adopting a middle term: *The kiln subsequently served as a lime store* (14/3/54). The morphology of the kiln is better suited to the production of lime. The intuition of the archaeologist was correct, witness the legend of the Album of photographs of the site: a snapshot, 12083, page 340, confirms it: *L. 64: lime kiln; towards the southeast*. De Vaux later changed his mind: the lime, which has to be taken into account, would have been thrown into a converted pottery kiln: but to throw lime into such a kiln is a curious step, to say the least. The evidence suggests that the option of a kiln for firing scroll jars was more useful for his Essene interpretation of the site, linked to the cave scrollls.

If kiln 918 was a lime kiln, there is a need to explain why lime was found in the furnace. We have to take it as residual lime. In fact, the process of lime production entails burning blocks of limestone, and grinding them after cooling, sprinkling them with water to reduce them to lime, and finally filtering the dried product. The sequence of operations is thus completed not in the kiln but in a vat. We have to believe that the kiln was abandoned while it still contained previously heated blocks, which is our hypothesis. The process of conversion to lime is only possible when the limestone has been kept at high temperature for several days, and to do this the intake of air has to be interrupted by a small orifice in the mouth to keep the flame at high temperature for as long as necessary. The *Journal* correctly notes its sealing (L. 64 on 3/3/54): *the (lower) opening was filled-in*. The kiln was clearly abandoned with its batch. In the long run, infiltrations of rain will have set in motion the physicochemical process of conversion from limestone to lime which had fallen into the hearth of the furnace. Under the lime, by all logic, lies the ash of 84.4, a vestige of the fireplace: *At the bottom, we reach a layer of ash* (L. 64, 1/3/54).

We can reconstruct the morphology of the lime kiln without pushing the available data too hard. In Antiquity, lime kilns are often in pits, the mouth of the kiln being accessed by a few steps. The kiln is thus semi-interred. Its lining was thickened to aid thermal insulation. Kiln 918 displays exactly these features.

The low part (fig. 84c) is the fireplace (1), the mouth (2) of which opens to the north in L. 84; the upper part is the firing chamber (3), where the blocks of limestone are stacked, supported on the corbelling in an arched structure. Another less sophisticated formula is attested in which the fuel fills the heating chamber and the chinks between the blocks of limestone. The fire must be intense and be controlled for at least three days and three nights. The buried kiln permits great economy of fuel. The deep space in front of the mouth serves as an ash pit.

The lining of the firing chamber was coated with a thick covering of crude clay to stop the walls being baked. To concentrate the heat effect, the lid, lost after each batch, rested on the piled blocks. It was lifted off to recover the blocks after cooling.

The stratigraphy in front of the mouth in L. 84 is one of the least detailed: *a hollow space, filled with ash (...) many sherds (...) we reach a bottom of large pebbles lower than loci 59, 60, 61 and 45* (L. 45 *south*, 3/3/54), or two days before that, on 1/3/54: *At the bottom, we reach a layer of ash which corresponds to the floor of small rooms 45, 59, 60 and 61* (3/3/54). We have no hesitation in attributing the production of ash to the clearing of the kiln, any association with the ash of the loci mentioned in the area being unconvincing.

In fact, nothing shows that kiln 918 is as old as the floors of the loci mentioned. The Coüasnon *Plans* place it in the three Periods Ib, II and III, while small kiln 917 only appears on *Plans* Ib and II. This does not seem consistent, as kiln 918, thought to produce *large pieces* (meaning *manuscript jars*), was useless after 68, Period III. On the other hand, the disappearance of a pottery kiln on the *Plan* of Period III would have confirmed this logic if it had produced pots, which is probably not the case, because of the contradiction between small kiln and large pots.

De Vaux decided in favour of the antiquity of kiln 918, on the basis of the argument that to reach the mouth, it was necessary to descend five steps cut into the surrounding layers (fig. 84a and 85) which he thought had accumulated over time. Here we have an example of imprecise understanding of the prevailing evolution of the site: this was understood as an accumulation in thickness over time, whereas the site developed by lateral extension. In the triangle, the occupation floors are a long way down and without much thickness while the upper strata are only collapses. The lime kiln was probably designed to be semi-buried from the beginning, in a kiln pit. Floor 84.7 at a higher level than L. 65 corresponds exactly to circulation in the workshops.

The ash of 84.5, as much at the bottom of the hollow L. 84 as in kiln 84.4, was independent of the nearby coverings. Moreover, de Vaux noted the difference of the levels, L. 64 (3/3/54): *We reach a bottom (L. 84) of large pebbles, which is lower than the floors of loci 59, 60, 61 and 45*. In the *large pebbles* of 84.6 one can see in front of the mouth of kiln 918 either an area of poor paving or the abandonment of stones for burning.

Question of stratigraphy: Level 3C or 4?

Kiln 918 is assigned to Level 3 and probably quite late, after the southeast annexes were laid out. When did they stop being used? The collapses of the walls at Qumran seal the vestiges of Level 3C. However, despite its brevity, post-68 Level 4, to which kiln 918 may be attributed, must have also left traces which are difficult to distinguish from earlier ones. The stratigraphic position of the scattered ash could have helped us to establish connections with other features, but we do not know enough about it to make a decision. In the complementary sondages of 1994–2004 to the east of the *khirbeh* (L. 145), important coverings of ash were discovered which, in the square section, had filled by trickling the eastern fracture from the recently discovered earthquake (excavations of 2000[72]). The ash lay quite close to the surface, and because of this it is better to attribute it to the last decades of the occupation of Qumran. The ashes indicated at L. 62/63, but in an uncertain position, belong to the same spread (see on L. 62/63, fig. 77a and b): the best option is to assign them to Level 4, too. It is better to link the late ash to refuse from the post-68 occupants.

Kiln 918 (L. 64) may have been maintained after 68. Nearby, after the ruin of Level 3C, there are architectural restorations which de Vaux attributed, rightly, to Level 4 (Period III). The series of small pools L. 72–68 would have remained filled-in. Be that as it may, pool 71, which adjoins L. 84, had remained in use with its restored supply. The pottery collected at L. 84, in the pocket of ash of 84.5, indicates to us the point when use of the kiln ceased. Jar KhQ 1401 would invite us to place the objects of L. 84 in Level 4 by dint of the inscription it bears. Certainly, the jar is not of a common type with its handle formed of a horizontal band, but it is local: a test of provenance sets it in a Palestinian paste. A. Lemaire has proposed reading the Roman numeral LXI, *sixty-one*, painted on its shoulder[73], which he is still entitled to verify. This large pot certainly comes from a level *in situ*, i.e., the ash debris of 84.5 which lies scattered in front of the mouth of the kiln. If the Latin reading is confirmed, the jar would be an indication, but no more than an indication, that L. 84 remained in use at Level 4, post-68, as the jar was abandoned in front of the kiln. If the document is Latin, and could thereby linked to the Roman army, it is difficult to see it as compatible with a Jewish context. But the jar is local. We are referred back to the question, long debated, of the identity of those who lived at Qumran after 68. The actual archaeological substance of the resumption of habitation after 68 is not perceptible in the eastern sector of the ruins; kiln 918 would be an exception. We might be surprised by the manufacture of lime at a temporary Roman camp. There are other indications of a Roman presence, however, and Roman objects have been identified: pieces of military equipment, surgical instruments, a stamp of the Xth Legion, etc. Logically, they belong to Level 4. So, a piece of Latin graffito would not be out of place. Similar military material has been identified at Masada without more useful precision than the first century AD. On the contrary, without ruling out an intermittent military presence, it is surely not irrational to suggest that at a particular moment, Level 4 will have sheltered a Jewish occupation – and why not a sectarian one? The jar with Latin writing would have been thrown into hole 84.

---

72. Y. Magen, Y. Peleg, JSP 6, p. 362.

73. A. Lemaire, *Qumrân*, Vol. II, p. 355.

fig. 87.   Locus 64 and Locus 71 in the background

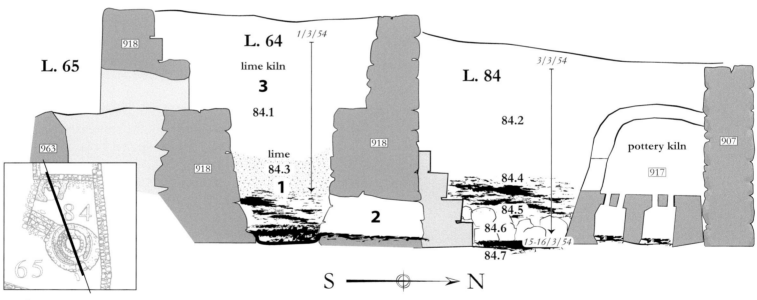

Restored elements	Level	Definition	Journal dates	Coins	Position	N°	Chronology
84.1 (=L. 64)	Post 4	Collapse and erosion	1/3/54				
84.2	Post 4	Collapse and erosion	3/3/54				
84.3 (= 64)	3C/4?	Lime mass	1/3/54				
84.4 (= 64)	3C/4?	Ash from the fireplace	1/3/54				
84.5	3C/4?	Ash waste	3/3/54	KhQ. 1161	In the ash	1	Proc. under Claudius
84.6	3C/4?	Lime stones	14-15/3/54				
84.7 (= 65)	3C	floor, serving the kiln	7/3/54				

Schema and stratigraphic diagram of Loci 64 and 84 (for the chart of symbols, see page 155)

Plate 28

Plate 29, 20

Plate 29, 21

Plate 29, 22

N° Pl.	N° Catal.	Position	Comments (archives)	Date	Description	Clay	Exterior
1	3391	84.1	45 south	01/03/54	plate	red paste	beige
2	4408	84.4	84	14/03/54	small dish	brown paste	grey-beige
3	4407	84.4	84	15/03/54	plate	red paste with grey core	red
4	4412	84.2	84	14/03/54	small globular jug	light brown paste	beige
5	1408	84.4	84	14/03/54	jug	° red earth	
6	4413	84.4	84	14/03/54	jug	dark red paste	beige
7	4410	84.4	84	14/03/54	neck of jug	dark brown paste	brownish-red
8	3394	84.2	45 south	02/03/54	filter jug	red paste	red
9	1167	84.4	45 south in the ash	02/03/54	miniature pot with a handle	° red earth	pink wash
10	1160	84.2	45 south	02/03/54	small vessel without a handle	° red earth	white wash
11	3396	84.2	45 south	02/03/54	saucepan	brown paste	brown
12	3392	84.2	45 south	02/03/54	cooking pot	red paste	brown-red
13	4409	84.4	84 east	15/03/54	cooking pot	red paste	brown
14	3393	84.2	45 south	02/03/54	cooking jug	light brown paste	brown-red
15	3390	84.1	45 south	16/04/53	kettle	red paste	beige
16	4411	84.2	84	14/03/54	kettle	orange paste	red
17	1169	84.4	45 south in the ash	02/03/54	lamp	dark brown	beige
18	1141	84.1	45 upper	01/03/54	lamp	° red earth	
19	3395	84.1	45 south	02/03/54	funnel	grey paste	red
20	1385	84.4	84 inf.	14/03/54	jar support	° red earth	
21	4406	84.2	84	14/03/54	neck of jar	brownish-grey paste	beige engobe
22	1401	84.4	lower level	14/03/54	jar inscribed with three painted letters		

° *According to de Vaux*

Locus 84, catalogue of pots and photographs

Plate 29

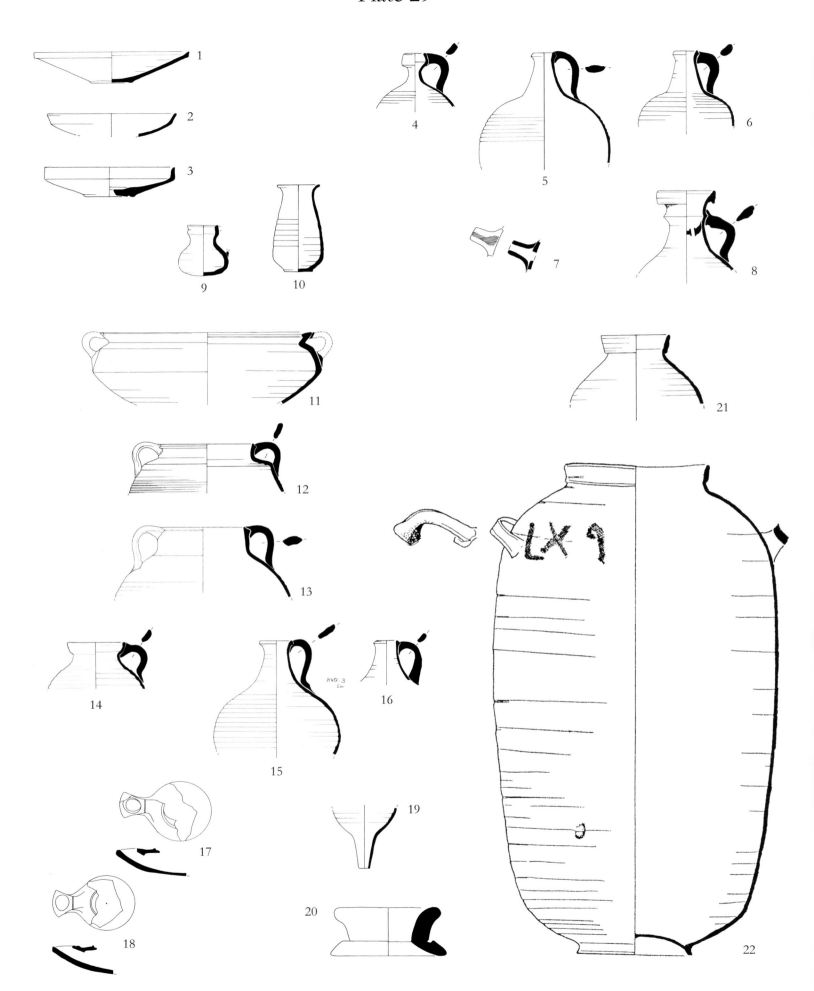

Locus 84, pottery, scale ¼

An added locus: 145
The eastern space on the outside of the settlement

In the *Qumran I*, we already gave the name L. 145 to the whole of the eastern exterior of the settlement which had so far not received a name of its own. In the course of the 1954 campaign, as the clearance progressed towards the east, the place was excavated under the rubric L. 44. The removal of surface layers was extended towards the east under code 45, to the *east of L. 45* or *east trench*, then under number 44 outside the constructions and quite a long way to the south. It is probable that code 44 was instead linked to a team of workers whose work was carried out at a space that was not yet apportioned.

L. 145 is our *a posteriori* term for better clarification of the spread of the pottery of the loci *extra muros*. It brings together different hoards taken from the listing of finds. The note *east of 44* does not designate the eastern part of L. 44: these are *the ancient remains* (L. 44, 22/2/54) outside the *khirbeh*. In the *Journal*, we also meet *exterior of 44*, which we must take as *outside of*, i.e. to the *east of 44*. In the *Catalogue* of objects, the formula *east trench* must be understood as the trench to the east of the ruin, dug to clear enclosure wall 900. In fact, de Vaux strips the east wall of the settlement to complete the plans of the architecture and focuses his efforts on the framework to the detriment of the stratification of the exterior spaces. His efforts are concentrated on the building itself. He does not undertake to open to the east of wall 900, although this would have given him, in section, a history of occupation outside the settlement. The clearing of 2002 revealed, in section, the 1954 trench: it had barely crossed, at the top of the archaeological bed, the latest layers of ash which had run into the crevasse created by the earthquake and revealed by the Israeli army excavations of 2002. The notes *east of 84* and *east of 45–78*, written on some sherds in ink, attest to the fact that a fairly deep inspection of the masonry was pushed as far as the length of pool 71, 25 m further to the south. To L. 145 we have added the sherds named *to the east of 46–6*, *i.e.* more than 15 m to the north, and what has been kept relates only to the Iron Age.

At the time of the daily recording of finds, de Vaux felt the need to recall the origin of the pottery. That is why, in the *Fichier*, the *Catalogue* and the *Journal*, he specified their provenance with the notes *to the south* and *to the east*. We have had to recompose the distribution of the objects in line with the notes as to origin. We have taken account of the evident fragility of the record.

L. 145 presents the material that came from the east of the ruin, excavated in sporadic fashion and by restricted sondages, at a distance from each other. Their presentation does not presuppose any organization, neither topographic nor stratigraphic. We may distinguish three lots:

1 – Scattered finds without consistent provenance. The Iron Age sherds testify to a level from the end of the seventh century, which de Vaux had rightly noted and which will be presented separately[74].

2 – Material belonging to a deposit collected at the level of L. 61–45 is linked to the occupation identified in 2002 in the stretch of land between the *khirbeh* and the cemetery. The pottery preserved presents forms which are complete but small in size – dishes, plates, etc. – and large fragments, including fragments of jars. The complete forms would be linked to this occupation.

3 – The exterior of the complex was much used. The 2002 excavation hit a refuse layer which can be seen as discarded pots, in numerous fragments. The boundaries of this external occupation were not defined. Consultation of the plates presenting the pottery easily convinces us that the objects collected in L. 145, most of them small, open forms, are table objects. That regular visitors or workers would have taken their meals outside is not impossible.

De Vaux did not separate lots 1, 2 and 3.

---

74. Mariusz BURDAJEWICZ, "History of the Qumran Caves in the iron Age in the Light of the Pottery Evidence", in M. FIDANZIO, *The Caves of Qumran*, Leiden, 2016, p. 253.

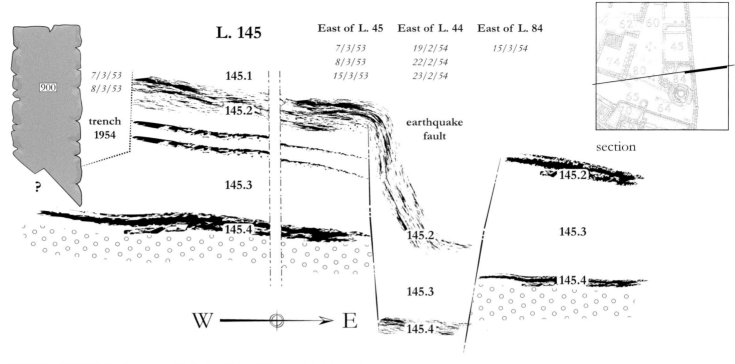

Restored elements	Level	Definition	Journal dates	Coins	Position	N°	Chronology
145.0	Post 4	Earthquake fault	?				
145.1	3C-4	surface of east trench?	7-8/3/53	KhQ. 1144 (L45)	Outside stratigraphy	1	Proc. under Nero
145.2	3A/B/C	Spreading of Ash East trench?	?	1232 (L45) 1016 (L44) 1536 (east of 71)	Outside stratigraphy Outside stratigraphy Outside stratigraphy	1 1 1	Proc. under Claudius Agrippa Ist Herod
145.3	2?	accumulation	?	1253 (east of L78)	Outside stratigraphy	1	Alexander Jannaeus
145.4	1 (Iron Age)?	Spreading of Ash East trench?	?				

Schema and stratigraphic diagram of Locus 145 (for the chart of symbols, see page 155)

N° Pl.	N° Catal.	Position	Comments (archives)	Date	Description	Clay	Exterior
1	2989	-	44 east	no date	tubular jar		
2	3027	-	44 east	no date	tubular jar	grey paste	grey
3	3080	-	44 east	21/02/54	neck of jar	dark brown paste	beige
4	4798	-	east trench	no date	neck of jar	brown paste	beige
5	3078	-	44 east	21/02/54	neck of jar	dark brown paste	beige
6	4719	-	east of 45-78	07/03/54	jar support	dark grey paste	beige engobe
7	1302	-	east of 45-78	08/03/54	jar support	grey earth	
8	4731	-	east of 45-78	07/03/54	neck of jar	red paste	beige
9	3076	-	44 east	21/02/54	neck of jar	grey paste	beige
10	4805	-	east trench	no date	neck of jar	light beige paste	light beige
11	4834	-	east trench	no date	neck of jar	red with grey core	beige engobe
12	3079	-	44 east	21/02/54	neck of jar	dark grey paste	beige
13	1015	-	44 east, ancient spoil	23/02/54	lamp	buff earth	partly burnt
14	3067	-	44 east	22/02/54	jar	red paste	beige
15	4818	-	east trench	no date	jar sherd, painted band	orange paste	beige
16	4797	-	east trench	no date	jar with horizontal hooks	light brown paste	beige engobe
17	4804	-	east trench	no date	cooking pot ?	orange paste	beige

Catalogue of pottery Locus 145

Plate 30

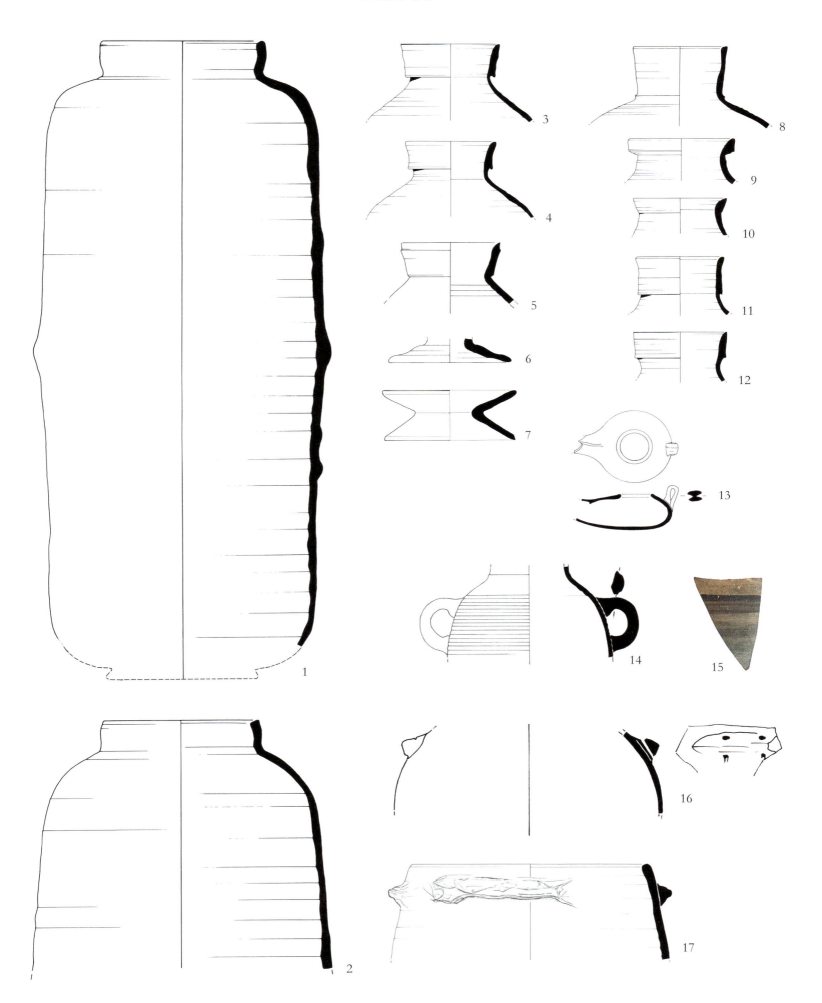

Locus 145, pottery, scale ¼

N° Pl.	N° Catal.	Position	Comments (archives)	Date	Description	Clay	Exterior
1	3064	-145	44 east	22/02/54	bowl	light brown paste	beige
2	1654	-145	45 Tr. east	no date	bowl	red earth with grey section	white wash
3	1292	-145	east of 45-78	07/03/54	bowl	° red earth	white wash
4	4817	-145	east trench	no date	bowl	orange paste	beige-red
5	3066	-145	44 east	22/02/54	bowl	brown paste	beige
6	1622	-145	44 east	06/04/54	bowl	red earth	white wash
7	1000	-145	44 east / spoil	21/02/54	bowl	red paste	pink earth
8	4836	-145	east trench	no date	bowl	red paste	beige, burnt
9	4860	-145	east trench	no date	bowl	red paste	beige
10	3071	-145	44 east	21/02/54	goblet	orange paste	red
11	4832	-145	east trench	no date	small dish	orange paste	red
12	4831	-145	east trench	no date	small dish	brown paste	beige
13	1007	-145	44 east / ancient spoil	22/02/54	plate	° grey earth	pink wash
14	3059	-145	44 east	22/02/54	plate	red paste	beige
15	3069	-145	44 east	21/02/54	plate	light brown paste	red
16	4816	-145	east trench	no date	small dish	orange paste	beige
17	4819	-145	east trench	no date	saucepan	brown paste	brown, burnt
18	1629	-145	east trench	06/04/54	plate	° red earth	well fired
19	1006	-145	44 east / ancient spoil	22/02/54	plate	° red earth	chipped
20	3062	-145	44 east	22/02/54	plate	dark grey paste	grey
21	4829	-145	east trench	no date	edge of deep plate	red paste	beige engobe
22	1637	-145	east trench, to the east of 61	07/04/54	plate	° red earth, porous	
23	3068	-145	44 east	27/02/54	plate	brownish-red paste	brownish-beige
24	4723	-145	east of 45-78	07/03/54	plate decorated with black paint	light brown paste	light brown
25	4801	-145	east trench	no date	bowl	orange paste	beige-red
26	4837	-145	east trench	no date	bowl	dark brown paste	beige engobe
27	3070	-	44 east	22/02/54	bowl	brown paste	beige
28	4721	-	east of 45-78	07/03/54	bowl	beige-yellow paste	light brown engobe
29	4812	-	east trench	no date	bowl	brown-red paste	grey
30	4810	-	east trench	no date	jug base	greyish-brown paste	reddish-brown
31	4800	-	east trench	no date	bowl	red paste with grey core	grey
32	1413	-	east of 84	15/03/54	plate	° red-grey earth, well-fired, pink core	
33	1002	-	44 east / spoil	21/02/54	plate	° red earth, fine	pink wash
34	1312	-	east of 61, in drain 910	09/03/54	carinated plate	° red earth	white wash
35	1293	-	east of 45-78	07/03/54	plate	° red earth	white wash
36	1411	-	east of 84	15/03/54	plate	° red earth	pink wash
37	4830	-	east trench	no date	carinated plate	orange paste	brown and red

Catalogue of pottery Locus 145 ° *According to de Vaux*

Plate 31

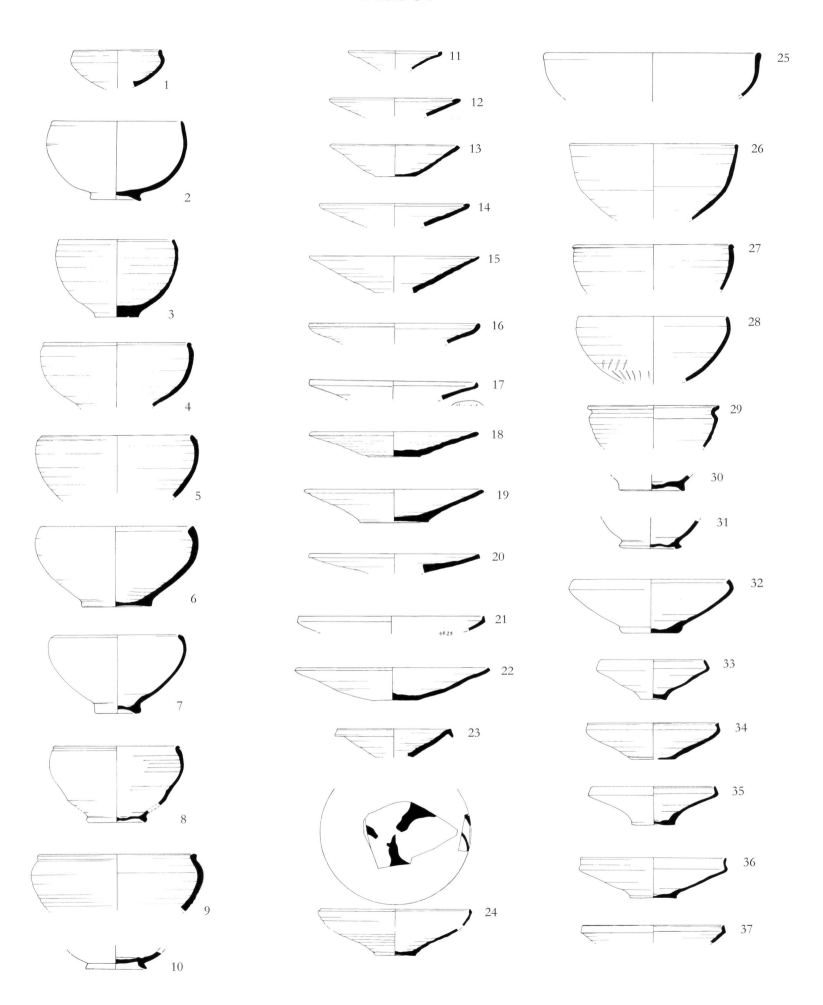

Locus 145, pottery, scale ¼

N° Pl.	N° Catal.	Position	Comments (archives)	Date	Description	Clay	Exterior
1	1652	-	trench east of 45	08/04/54	large goblet	° red earth	white wash
2	4838	-	east trench	no date	large goblet	red paste	red-beige
3	4790	-	east trench	no date	large goblet	brown paste	brown-red
4	3063	-	44 east	22/02/54	goblet	dark grey	dark grey
5	4807	-	east trench	no date	goblet	grey paste	grey
6	4772	-	east-west trench	02/04/55	bowl	brown paste	brown and red
7	3061	-	44 east	22/02/54	bowl	light brown paste	beige
8	1651	-	east trench	07/04/54	bowl (fragment)	red earth	pink wash
9	1390	-	east of 45	07/03/54	bowl	° red earth	
10	4803	-	east trench	no date	small jug	brownish-grey paste	beige engobe
11	3065	-	44 east	22/02/54	jug	red paste	red
12	4727	-	east of 45-78	07/03/54	jug	brown paste	beige-brown
13	3058	-	44 east	22/02/54	flask handle	red paste	beige
14	4720	-	east of 45-78	07/03/54	jug, decoration incised before firing	yellowish paste	yellowish
15	1638	-	trench east of 45	07/04/54	small vessel	° buff earth	
16	4806	-	east trench	no date	jug base	orange paste	beige-red
17	1283	-	east of 45	07/03/54	miniature vessel	° red earth	pink wash
18	4726	-	east of 45-78	07/03/54	bowl	red paste	reddish-beige
19	4799	-	east trench	no date	crater	orange paste	brownish-red
20	4724	-	east of 45-78	07/03/54	crater	red paste with grey core	red
21	4809	-	east trench	no date	crater	grey paste with red core	grey
22	4835	-	east trench	no date	crater	red paste and surface	
23	4728	-	east of 45-78	07/03/54	cooking pot	brown paste	brownish-red
24	3074	-	44 east	21/02/54	cooking pot	orange paste	red
25	4813	-	east trench	no date	cooking pot	red paste with grey core	red-brown
26	4824	-	east trench	no date	cooking jug	red paste	brown

Catalogue of pottery Locus 145   ° *According to de Vaux*

Plate 32

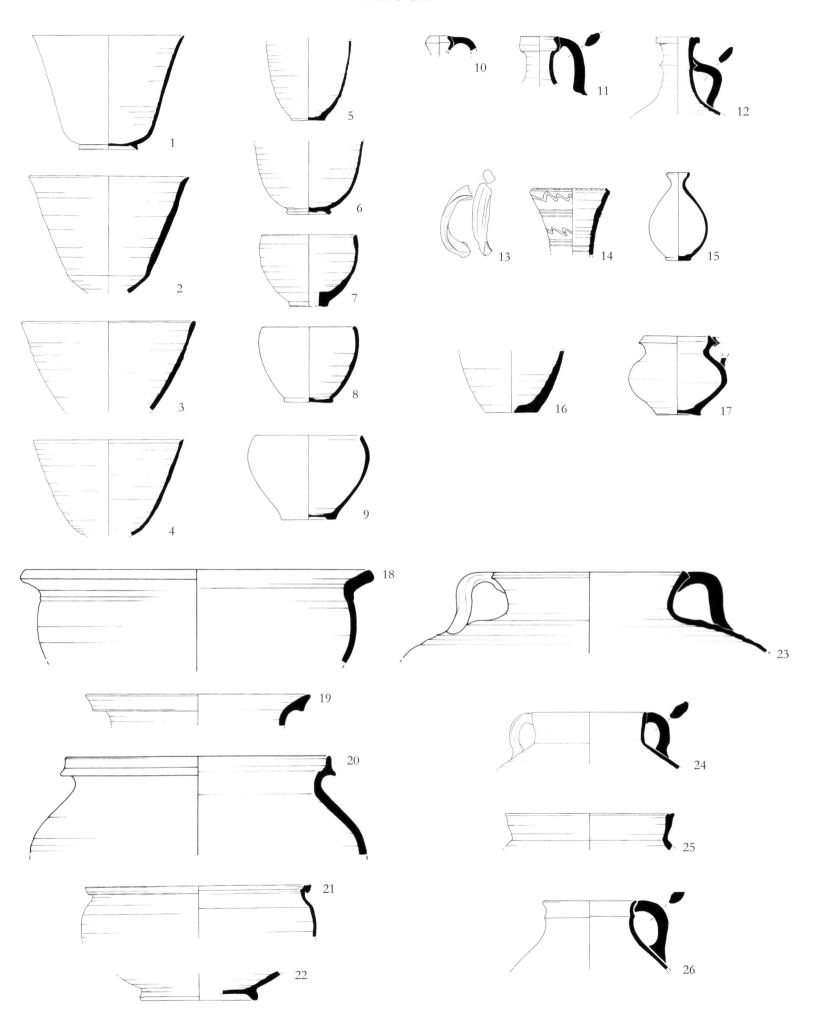

Locus 145, pottery, scale ¼

Plate 33

Plate 31, 22

Plate 31, 32

Plate 31, 18

Plate 30, 1 et 2

Plate 30, 14

Plate 30, 5

Plate 30, 3

Locus 145, photographs and pottery

Chapter B

The series of pools
and the southeast workshops

Loci: 72, 73 (180, 186), 68, 69 (181, 182), 71 (183), 144, 143, 75, 70

Presentation

The southern sector of the southeast annexes coheres in its circulation and its use of water. If it is accepted that the hydraulic system was extended in stages following the logic of the best angle of inclination, the south-east sector looks like an outgrowth on the main building, corresponding at some point in time with a growth in storage. It may be imagined that such growth had become a necessity for a population that had grown in number; it may also be an indication – and this seems more likely – that even without an increase in the number of inhabitants, the level of stored water no longer met needs.

The series of pools of the southeast annexes constitutes the outlet and the final phase of the hydraulic system, and examination of the available documentation reveals that it was subjected to important modifications. From the general configuration of the installations, following the stages that led to the complete system, we may deduce that L. 71 is the latest because it is the most remote, and that its position brought about the closure of the triangle by wall 900 and not vice versa. However, the pool that can be seen today in its full extension was probably not the original construction, but a reworking with the upper part modified. Wall 900 enclosed the sector where a certain quantity of water was necessary in the tanks and baths, and the top of 71 was initially a pool or a workshop. The crude earth constructions of the triangle represent its final phase of arrangement. Coüasnon's *Plan* of Ib places it early in the evolution of the site: nothing demonstrates that he was right.

We shall try to imagine the reasons for the complex. At one time, large pools 56-58, dug inside the residence in response to a wish to concentrate space, constituted the end-point of the hydraulic system. Later, the arrangement of small pools necessitated diverting the main water supply following the contours of the constructions in place. Pool 72 was put out of use to the benefit of the construction of ritual bath 68. The trace of the earthquake that affected L. 72 provides means for the chronology which, when corrected, will allow us to reconsider the sequence of the restorations. L. 69 was subjected to radical modifications and we shall see that it was probably not always a pool. Pool 70, angled and in two stages, is not an overflow but a sink, dependent on large *birkeh* 71.

The excavation notes state that the main channel, at the height of L. 72, bears traces of the earthquake. In the *Journal*, de Vaux notes (L. 72, on 1/4/54): *Indication that the main channel was cut by the earthquake, which raises many questions.* From 1954 he had suspected that the sequence of Periods, organized according to *before* and *after* 31 BC, was in tatters but, against all expectations, he pressed on regardless, keeping to a high chronology. The date of the earthquake now being uncertain, the connection between stratigraphy and chronology needs to be revisited – better knowledge of the sequences may afford complementary arguments, despite the scarce documentation of elevations.

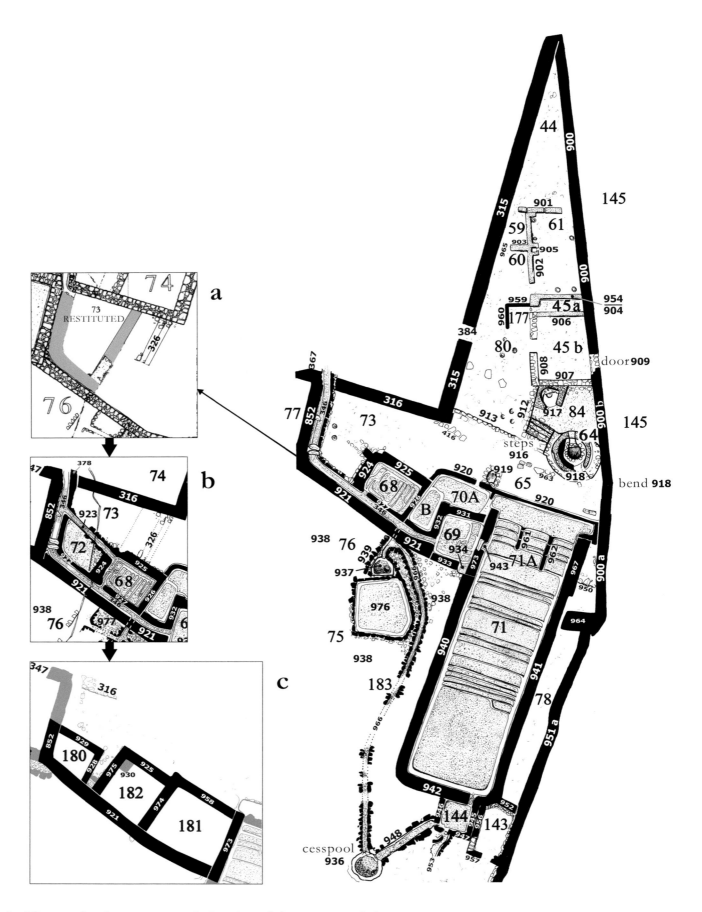

fig. 88. Southeast annexes, designation of the constructed elements

The series of pools and the southeast workshops

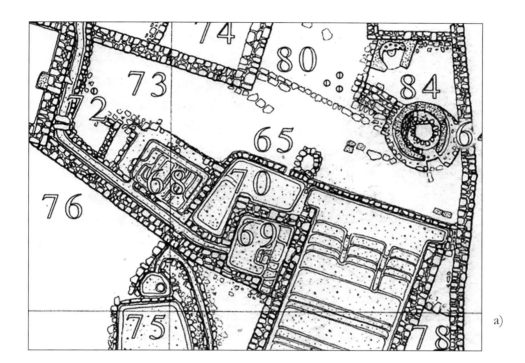

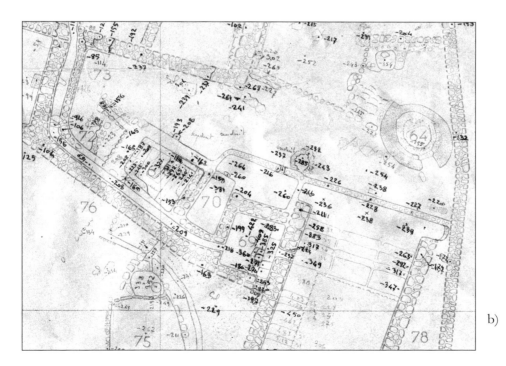

fig. 89. Series of pools:
a) Coüasnon Plan (Period II)
b) From survey of work with elevations

a) Locus 86 nested in the corner of the feeder and the edge of the bath L. 68 (drain 346 has been cleared)

b) General view of Loci 68, 72, 73 to the east (L. 186 has been removed)

c) Locus 72, bottom and south wall plastered with mortar

fig. 90.   Loci 72 and 73, stratification

Loci 72 and 73

Surface remains

Lacking a convincing layout, Coüasnon's *Plan* (Period III) does not take account of all the constructed units recorded. We shall attempt to reconstruct them and set them in order. The excavation was rapid, in an environment heavily affected by the earthquake and repeated restorations. L. 72, excavated in three days, 4/3/54, then 31/3/54 and finished on 1/4/54, warranted three brief notes in the *Journal*. L. 73 excavated in a single day, the same 4/3/54, is graced with two brief notes on 4 and 6/3/54. Sherds were recorded on 6/3/54, but there is no record of further observation. The connection between the *Journal* and the surveys is poorly coordinated.

On 4/3/54, the *Journal* tells us: *A first level, very close to the surface, is bordered by a wall with a single facing, without a discernible floor that might have been associated with it.* This wall, the only one mentioned in the text, the only one preserved on the *Plan* of Period III and the first uncovered below the surface, must be the one we call 928. It needs to be connected at right angles to wall 929 (L. 180) at a slightly open angle (fig. 91). The diagrams show it with a single facing. The photographs barely attest to these walls (fig. 92). According to the accessible documentation, these are the only stretches of masonry without any sign of breaks caused by the earthquake in this location; they have to be taken into consideration as they are intact and obliterate the aqueduct 346 in both westerly and southerly directions; they therefore postdate the earthquake. The diagram shows it (fig. 91b and c), and the note confirms it (L. 72 on 4/3/54): *the Roman wall (?) which spans the channel between the L. (L. 73)*. The fact will have an impact on the chronology and the moment where the earthquake is best situated.

Two diagrammatic surveys preserve the tracks of two other *walls*, 924 and 923, which would form a third square (L. 72, fig. 91a, b, c and d). Here we distinguish first two arrays of stones set edgewise, parallel to the preceding square. They were taken into account during the preparation of the neat versions of the *Plans* for Periods Ib and II. Drawn with a single facing, they would have been better understood later, one as the south rim of supply 923 of bath 68 (fig. 91e), and the other as the backrest, to the west, of seat 924 of the bath.

The diagrams show two more walls, 971 and 972, forming the other square (L. 186), parallel to the two others, fixed in the previous one, but deeper. It was surveyed without due care and no note says anything about it: the diagrams (fig. 91d and e) present it roughly, in freehand. The survey (fig. 91d) shows fault 971 spanning aqueduct 346 to the west, where there is no western part, carried away by the earthquake. The photographs expose the overlapping of the constructions. L. 186, earlier than L. 180, must be an outhouse from the final occupation of the site, Level 4/5.

Corner 928-929 guides us in recreating a room from the final occupation which may have been a box room, L. 180 (6 m^2 restored), abutting enclosure wall 921, sealing the elbow of the main disused channel. We may link it with surface masonry, although no floors are associated with it. Box room L. 180, in walls 928 and 928, seals L. 186, confined by walls 971 and 972, which are older and even less spacious (4 m^2 restored). The Coüasnon *Plan* attributes to Period III, without naming them, L. 180, 181 and 182. We are unable to show this. At a stretch, L. 180 may also have been a hut, somewhat later than Level 4, but in any case posterior to the earthquake as it is unscathed. We may regard it as a Qumran equivalent to the reworkings that affected Ain Feshkha for a long time after the abandonment. When Khirbet Mard (Hyrcanium) was a monastery, what remained of the palm grove of Qumran-Feshkha a two hours' walk away, was a vegetable garden and an orchard, irrigable and fertile. Two erratic coins, weak indications collected in the area, testify to the fact that Qumran was visited after Level 4: the one found in L. 68 is Roman, from the 4th century, and the second, Arab (?), is listed at L. 72.

The stratigraphic sequence at the approach to the earthquake fault

We read in de Vaux's own hand on L. 72: *the channel was cut by the earthquake which put everything in the balance again* (L. 71, 1/4/54). The consequences of the earthquake are easy to read on the photographs (fig. 90b and fig. 92 a and b) where a fracture that can be seen to have been filled-in after having broken the pool into two parts, and the eastern part (elevation at -223 cm) is 45 cm lower than the western part

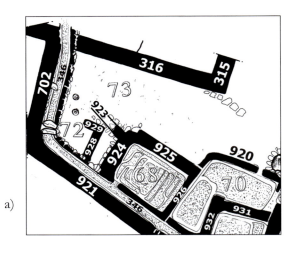
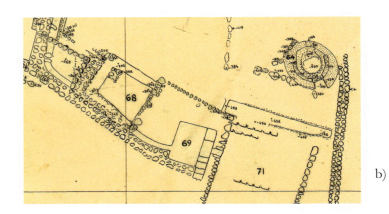
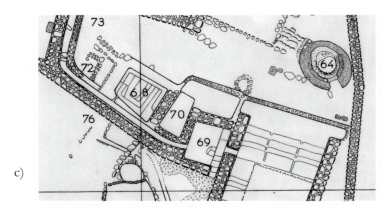
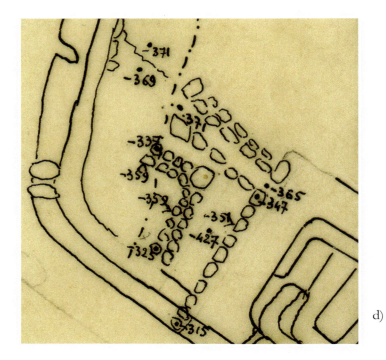
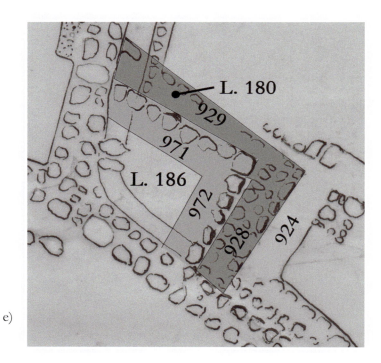
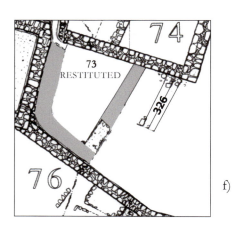

fig. 91. a) Designation of the constructed elements
b, c, d) Concise surveys of late remains to the south of the southeast annexes
e) Reconstruction of Loci 180-186 according to the 1954 surveys
f) Reconstitution of original pool 72/73

(elevation at -178 cm) in a vertical thrust, identical to that of cistern L. 48-49. No document shows the ruptured drain, and de Vaux affirms that the south partition of the drain had also have given way, and that a thrust was seen in the masonry at the back in wall 921. The photograph (fig. 92b) is supposed to show the fracture from the earthquake, but it is barely visible in the south face of wall 921; the aerial photographs of the 2000s attest to breaks on track 2a (see fig. 8).

Below the intact walls of L. 180 and in the immediate area, the walls, the mortars of floors and partitions are articulated by several accumulations of ash, so that it is difficult to see how the whole thing coheres: walls, mortars, floors were dislocated in extent and broken in depth. The western slab remained in place while the eastern part has subsided. We have developed a rereading of the earthquake in the relevant note (see note on earthquake, p. 25).

The overlapping of accumulations of ash

A first layer of ash, 72.5 (=73.3) is identified (L. 72, 4/3/54): *Below (the wall with a single facing, 923) a layer of ash*. Neither the depth nor the horizontal extent is noted. L. 72 and 73 are contiguous; they were excavated at the same time, on the same day, and we may assume the distinction between the two loci was made *a posteriori*. Another unrecorded accumulation of ash, which does not look any different from the previous one, is, however, present on the photographs (fig. 90b). It can be surmised in the foreground, in the stump left by the excavators, and spreads mainly to the left as far as a clear break in a mortar floor, which break was seen and noted (L. 73, 6/3/54). *Across the L. one follows the earthquake fault which cut a lime floor*. The preserved border of this mortar extends the break which has broken up the bottom of pool L. 72. The vestiges of mortar in the two loci belong to the same slab which has subsided, and must have constituted the bottom 72.7 (=73.3) of a larger pool which we should describe.

The photograph (fig. 90b) shows that the ash runs under drain 923 and curves into L. 73 as far as where it meets 73.2, *the lime floor* (of mortar). The accumulation of ash, then, will keep the designation 72.5 in the two loci. Drain 923 sinks into this ash which preceded it. The plans and photographs show that 923 was shifted more to the west, and was never restored. The earthquake has mixed up the western portion of L. 72 and 73, all the way along main channel 346. The diagrams (fig. 91b, c and d) rightly indicate the start of 923 on the main channel.

Locus 73 and the Iron Age spoil

L. 73 provides us with supplementary information. An accumulation of ash was noteworthy enough to have captured the attention of the excavators. The *Journal* specifies (L. 73, 4/3/54): *Against cistern 68 and no doubt more to the west (against L. 72), a layer of ash spreads, about 0.50 m in thickness at this point, less thick elsewhere; it contains many Iron II sherds, always incomplete forms. This is clearly spoil. We collect an ostracon with two lines of some letters in palaeo-Hebrew, Samarian type*. Further, the pile of ash 72.5 was photographed (fig. 94d) and a diagrammatic section follows its extension under L. 72. Among the rare stratigraphic sections drawn, the diagrammatic section with the legend *loc 68 – loc 72* (fig. 94d) does not directly relate to L. 68-72 but junction 72-73, and restores the elevation of the layers to the east of the two pools. The masonry sketched is that of the lining of the pools at the back of the section.

From the photograph (fig. 94c) we can deduce that the accumulation of ash 72.5 was poured from west to east, in several regular and homogeneous motions, ruling out a layer from a fire. De Vaux concludes in the *Journal* (L. 73, 4/3/54): *This is clearly spoil*. The concentration of Iron Age pottery in this location was not underlined enough: among the selected sherds from L. 72, 73 and 80, one hundred and fifty are from this period. De Vaux does not say that this was an Iron Age deposit, but he thinks so. He is right because in turn the digging of pools 72 and 68 breached the Iron Age level at the appropriate place. Given the proximity of the pottery kilns of L. 178 (*under 66*), we have proposed that ash 72.5 was the displaced result of the flushing of the furnaces.

The accumulations of ash layer 72.5 are thin and intermingled, but they have the same origin. Iron Age ash 73.4 is appropriate position, lying horizontally. Ash 72.5 of L. 72 is set in the stratigraphy between the disuse of pool 72 and the construction of bath 68, as the ash runs under drain 923 (bath 68) and spills over into L. 73. We would hypothesize that ash 72.5, which fills pool 72, is the product of the digging of

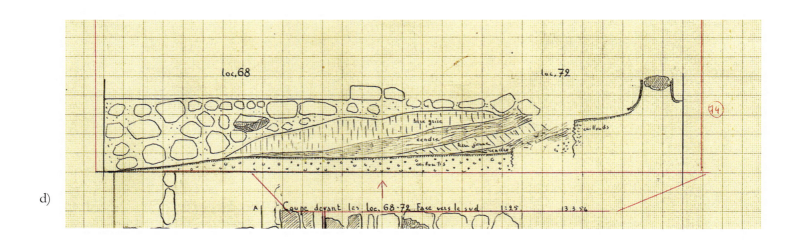

fig. 92. a) Locus 72 fractured by the earthquake
b) South face of wall 921 (L. 76)
c) and d) Photo and survey of the ash under Loci 72 and 68

bath 68 which follows it. The photographs (fig. 92a and c) attest to the fact that the Iron Age debris had accumulated under the bath.

Fortunately, analysis of the section (fig. 92d) clearly establishes the earthquake fissure; the sequence of ash layers is interrupted close to the fracture, and even ash swept into the fault is sketched there. Line of stones 923 which rings the debris layers is interrupted, to the right, by an ashlar block leaning towards the fault. The diagram extends to the west in what the photograph is showing the aqueduct in section. The fracture was produced between the aqueduct and what remains of drain 923. The trench has been filled in, in disorder.

Reconstruction of a primitive pool 72/73

Since Antiquity this place has been the object of a upheaval which, as is rightly inferred, is due to the earthquake. Pool 72 may be reconstituted by following the mortars of the linings and the floor, although neither the freehand sketches nor the plans show them complete. Surveys and photos reveal the removal of masonry 923 from the supply drain in the northwest corner. The earthquake has separated the bottom of the pool into two parts, but after being taken out of use, then filled-in and evened-out to establish access to bath 68. The southwest corner is open and rounded to meet up with the curve of the aqueduct which at this point resumes the easterly direction (fig. 93), probably after pool 71 was constructed. The small pools were fed upstream by the aqueduct which ended at the height of L. 77. To the west and south, the linings of L. 72 were carefully coated with a mortar; the coating of the south partition extends to the east under the north wall of bath 68 (fig. 90c and fig. 92a). It is highly likely that its eastern end is wall 924, resumed later to contain L. 68 to the west, but enlarged at the top to seat and lean the bath; the photograph (fig. 94c) shows that the thickening of wall 924 (L. 68) rests on the fill 72.4 of the original pool (L. 72). We could place the northern partition under drain 923, but there are several indications to show that the restored pool should be enlarged to the whole northern part of L. 73. Several observations allow us to reconstruct a pool 72-73 extended as far as wall 316.

1 – We have seen that the bottom of pool 72 extends, at the same level, into L. 73, which is also broken by the earthquake in line with the north-south fracture (fig. 90b); the slab of mortar seems to end, toward the east, in the extension of wall 924.

2 – Wall 316, north of L. 73, is destroyed quite low, as far as its southeast corner; its hanging that supports the aqueduct, however, has preserved several beds. On the photographs (fig. 94a and b) we can distinguish a rectangular slab of mortar attached to the south lining of this wall. It corresponds to the level of the aqueduct and must be the shallow remains of an abandoned diversion of channel 346, as its bottom is clearly drawn in a horizontal line where it is not difficult to discern the toothing; below, the bed is still in place with rounded pebbles, two of which, pulled up, have left a clear negative image in the cement. One can see what remains of the supply to the original pool after its junction with the aqueduct was closed. The disused junction remains indicated by the curve of the aqueduct at this precise point (fig. 93). Further downstream of the drain, the photograph shows a stone placed across and set in its fixing coating. Without blocking the width of the conduit, it could slow the flow without interrupting it. It served as a sluice, needed for supplying the restored pool.

3 – Coüasnon *Plan* of Period Ib (fig. 88b and fig. 96a) features dotted lines, to which we shall return. Fixed to the north corner of bath 68 is a vestige of a disappeared stretch of masonry, which fortunately a dotted line continues in the axis of the eastern face of wall 924; it may have constituted, to the east, the edge of a pool closing off the whole width of L. 72-73. The *Plan* of Period Ib testifies to a concern, during preparation of the final copy, not to omit three other dotted lines which, again towards the east, reconstruct ascending steps 326, preceding the disappeared pool.

The area, though ravaged by the earthquake, gains in coherence with a single restored 72-73 pool, then taken out of use in order to settle bath 68. The sloping space between 73 and 65 reveals a rational constructed transition, which was missing. The proposal of a restored pool is confirmed by the observation that drain 923 which feeds L. 68 is without foundation. No wall ever limited L. 72 to its southern portion. The Coüasnon *Plan* creates the illusion that the drain closed pool 72 to the north.

fig. 93. First part of the elbow for condemned feed to pool 72-73. Towards the west.

"Locus 73:
A buried deposit of bones
a witness to an earlier level"

Buried *deposits* 73.3 are indicated in this area (L. 73, 4/3/54): *We uncover a group of animal bones in the pottery debris. Other animal bones in a jar under the Roman wall (?) which spans the channel between loci 73 and 72.* There is only one stretch of masonry, line of stones 929, which *spans* the aqueduct at the junction of L. 72 and 73. The *Journal* calls it *Roman* (L. 73, 4/3/54) because, being close to the surface and spanning the aqueduct, it must be assigned to Period III (Level 4) and seen in context of the supposed occupation by the Roman army. We do not know at what depth the jar was found. De Vaux's note *under the Roman wall* does not mean underneath the wall but lower down, directly in line with the wall, without any further indication of depth. The progress of the dig was so speedy at this location that the first observation noted relates to the bones in the pottery debris.

A small circle, symbol for *buried deposit*, marks the two deposits on Coüasnon's *Plan* of Period II, at the preserved junction of the two loci against the aqueduct beyond the western edge of the fault (fig. 91a). No floor is recorded, and it may be admitted that observation of the deposit was impeded by the disruption caused by the earthquake. In our view, the burials 73.3 are to be associated in terms of stratigraphy with those of L. 65 and L. 80, and they preceded the series of pools. Logically, ash accumulation 73.4 representing refuse from the Iron Age kilns that had remained in place, must extend below *buried deposits* 73.3. It seems that the excavation was not pursued in this area, as the base of the marl terrace is not mentioned.

Stratification

L. 180, not affected by the earthquake, was assigned to a short-lived, late occupation. L. 186, barely any deeper, preceded L. 180, and seems posterior to bath 68, despite the fact that both rest on ash accumulation 72.5 which condemns pool L. 72. A mass of earth 72.4 supports drain 923 of bath 68, after the filling-in of pool 72.7. The *buried deposits* at 73.3 represent the deepest witness reached, and therefore the earliest.

The stratigraphic sequence may be reconstructed as follows, from the earliest to the most recent:

1. The Iron Age ash accumulation 73.4

2. Two *buried deposits* 73.3

3. Pool 72.7 in its original state 72-73 extends to the north

4. Disused, the bottom of L. 72 is partly filled with earth 72.6

5. Pool 72 was then filled-in by ash 72.5 rejected during the digging of bath L. 68

6. Bath 68 seals ash accumulation 72.5

7. L. 186 could be attributed to Level 4

8. L. 180 betrays the final installation before the abandonment of Level 4

The earthquake disrupts the 1 to 7 sequence.

a) Reconstruction of the eastern wall of the restored basin 73

b) To the right of aqueduct 346, a remnant of the plaster of basin 73 removed. To the east.

c) Ash pile 72.3 in L. 72 (middle) and 73 (left)

d) Remnant of ash heap 73.3 against the foundation of bath L. 68

fig. 94.   Earthquake fracture in Loci 72 and 73

The series of pools and the southeast workshops

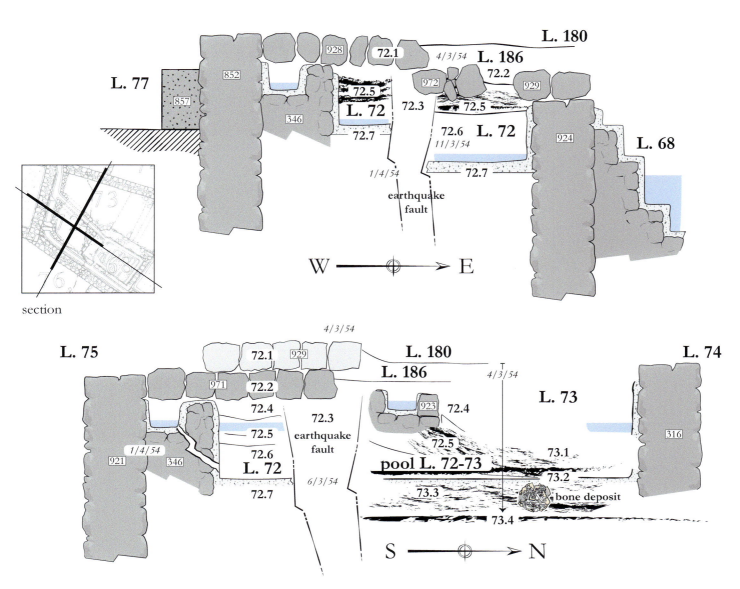

Schema of Locus 72 (for the chart of symbols, see page 155)

Restored elements	Level	Definition	Journal dates	Coins	Position	N°	Chronology
72.1	5 – Post 4	L. 180	4/3/54	KhQ. 1254	?	1	Arab (?)
72.2	4	L. 186	?				
72.3	Post 3C	Earthquake fault	6 and 31/3/54				
72.4	3C	drain of L. 68					
72.5/73.1	3C	ash	4/3/54				
72.6	3C	filling-in	4/3/54?				
72.7	3B/C	Pool L. 72-73	31/3/54				
73.3	3A	Buried deposit	4/3/54				
73.4	1 (Iron Age)	Ash reject	4/3/54				

Stratigraphic diagram of Loci 72 and 73 (for the chart of symbols, see page 155)

Plate 34

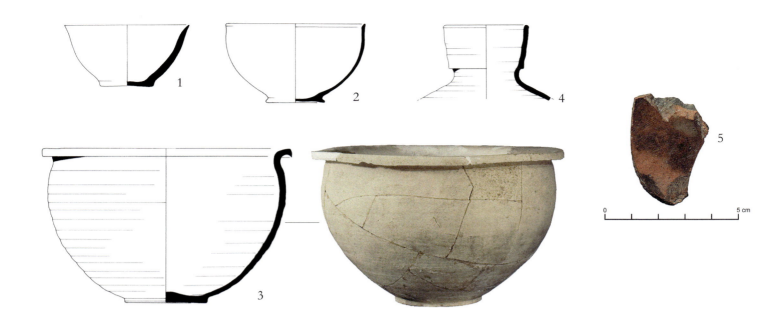

Catalogue of pottery Locus 72

N° Pl.	N° Catal.	Position	Comments (archives)	Date	Description	Clay	Exterior
1	1598	72.4	-	01/04/54	bowl	° red earth	
2	1269	72.3	-	06/03/54	bowl	° pink earth	white wash
3	1243	72.1	upper level	04/03/54	bowl		
4	4069	72.3	-	06/03/54	neck of jar	red paste with grey core	light brown
5	4697	?	-	no date	dish, black paint decoration, Nabataean?	grey paste with red core	brown

° According to de Vaux

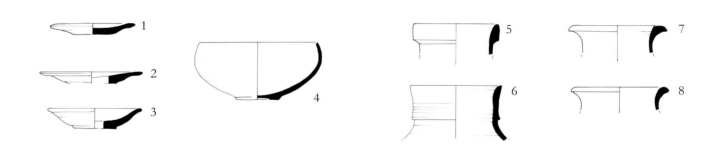

Catalogue of pottery Locus 72

N° Pl.	N° Catal.	Position	Comments (archives)	Date	Description	Clay	Exterior
1	4956	?	-	no date	lid of jug or jar	brown paste	beige
2	4955	?	-	no date	small dish or lid	red paste with grey core	beige-red
3	4954	?	-	no date	jar lid	red paste	beige
4	1260	72.3	-	06/03/54	bowl, exterior S-E corner of L. 74	° red earth	pink wash
5	4745	?	-	no date	neck of jar	orange paste	beige-red
6	4076	?	-	08/03/54	neck of jar	brown paste	beige
7	4746	?	-	no date	neck of jar	dark red paste	light red
8	4747	?	-	no date	neck of jar	brown paste	light brown

° According to de Vaux

Loci 72 and 73, pottery and catalogues, scale ¼

Locus 68
A ritual bath

Description of the ritual bath

L. 68 was excavated in three days, 2nd, 3rd and 4th March 1954, before the investigation of L. 72 and 73 began. Nothing is said of the nature of the fill of the pool and only a few morphological features of its feed are recorded (L. 68, 3/3/54): *We descend in the cistern: some steps appear. The main channel borders it to the south;* then (L. .68, 4/3/54) *a small bath with several steps, fed by a diverticulum from the main channel.*

Contrary to what is said here, we would observe that it is not customary for a bath to have two feeds which would have been in unlikely competition. However, it is indeed customary that the ritual bath, which keeps the idea of running water in its conception, possesses an entrance, a feed and an outlet as an overflow. We would put bath L. 68 parallel to L. 138, the only pool that is certainly a ritual bath, with its steps and its upstream feed 700; downstream, it is equipped with an overflow crossing the south seat 666.

De Vaux was right to see L. 68 as a stepped bath (fig. 95). The depth of the water reaches 1.65 m, which is suitable for the immersion of a man. The western and northern rims are wide enough for circulation and their top, preserved at the time of discovery in the northwest corner and well preserved on the west seat, was coated with a smooth mortar which is clearly visible to the right of the photo (fig. 96b). We deduce from this that the bath was not covered, at least not with a hard cover; the larger stones in the southwest corner and the middle of wall 924 may have supported wooden posts for a vegetable wooden cover or of palm leaves. Often at Qumran, access to the water installations was not facilitated and, in some cases such as this, a reconstruction of the circulation remains uncertain. The construction of bath L. 68 followed the filling-in of pool L. 72-73, and entrance to it will have been made after leveling to the west; two high descending steps led into submersion, and the northern rim, coated, functioned as a handrail up to the four steps when emerging; to leave before the northwest corner required descending only to 50 cm.

The earthquake and the sequence of masonry

Examination of the *Plans* and the photographs helps better understand the function of the pool surrounded to the north and south by two drains, the south aqueduct and a feed to the north. De Vaux seems to have distinguished them in the *Journal*: *The main channel borders it to the south (...) and (...) fed by a diverticulum of the main channel* (L. 68, 3/3/54), but it is not said that the diverticulum replaced the main channel. Now, it is in this location that de Vaux observed the rupture of the aqueduct, which put his chronology in question (L. 72, 1/3/54). The examination allows us to affirm that the *main channel* 346 and the *diverticulum* 923 (fig. 96a) carried water at the same time, but alternately. The elbow of the aqueduct was obstructed; it is appropriate to verify whether the condemnation was, or was not, a poor restoration following the earthquake, and we think not. We shall admit in a first approach that the diversion by drain 923, entailing the disuse of the elbow, had corrected the rupture of the aqueduct at the height of bath 68; and it was perhaps due to the choice that had to be made for the restoration that de Vaux maintained the early chronology of the earthquake. In relation to L. 72, the archaeologist had noted on 4/3/54: *Small L. to the west of 68 (...) The main channel borders the L., skirting it to the east.* If the shortcut by the drain had corrected the interruption of the aqueduct, it is not clear why all this work was done when it would have been easier and quicker simply to plug the leak.

However, not all aspects provided by the terrain had been taken into account. We shall attempt to show that the earthquake postdates the blockage of the aqueduct. First of all, it was logical to keep aqueduct 346 in use to provision reservoir L. 71, since the fold 805 to feed it is beyond doubt for after the year 68 (Level 4, Period III). We must not confuse two interruptions of flow at more or less the same spot downstream from the diversion to drain 923: a sluice, and the condemnation of the aqueduct. A sealed mortar stone across the conduit functioned as a sluice, it was fortunately spared by the workers: Coüasnon's *Plans* of Periods Ib and II keep a record of it, and the photograph (fig. 93) shows it still set in place. The stone would hold the wooden sluice in

a)

b)

fig. 95. Bath L. 68, towards the east

place or the bung of rags to force the water into diverticulum 923. At least a metre downstream from this sluice, the foundation of L. 186 blocking the channel with low wall 971 indicates the disuse of the aqueduct. A second symmetrical blockage is due to the foundation of low wall 972 of the same L. 186 and confirms that the aqueduct was no longer in operation (fig. 90a). The three quarry stones of the far end of 928, of L. 180 across the channel were preserved by the workers in the extension to the south of the back of seat 924; the surveys (fig. 91d and e) show low walls 928 and 929 intact.

There is no specification in the records as to the exact location where the aqueduct was broken. The fault traced on Coüasnon's *Plan* of Period Ib is approximate. Blockage 928 downstream was not dismantled and de Vaux saw the unrepaired break in the mortar. So, the survey rightly placed the fault downstream from low wall 928, and we must accept it. De Vaux should have noted that the earthquake broke an abandoned aqueduct and that this confirmed the need to revise the early date of the earthquake, but he did not take this into account. We should add that, on *Plan* Ib, the line of the fault to the east of the aqueduct has been inked-in without proof. That the fault crosses feed 923 without breaking it had no impact because in any case, in 1954 as in 1960, the earthquake was considered to be much earlier. Now, drain 923 is clearly broken by the earthquake but a little further to the west, where all the *Plans* show a collapse.

The earthquake, which interrupted the supply to bath L. 68, never repaired, is consequently posterior to the abandonment of the site. Three chronological observations are also called for: First, L. 180, which stops the aqueduct, is in fact posterior to Level 4 (Period III) as it condemns its biggest installation pool L. 71 and its supply. The series of three rooms L. 180, L. 181 and L. 182 cannot be assigned to Level 4, but is posterior to it. Further, the fact that the two low walls 928 and 929 are intact directly above the earthquake fault proves that L. 180 is posterior to the earthquake to be placed after Level 4 and before the erection of the three rooms. Finally, at least the two rooms L. 181 and L. 182 are indications of a Level 5, to which my attention was never drawn. The occupation that de Vaux placed here disappears in the chronology.

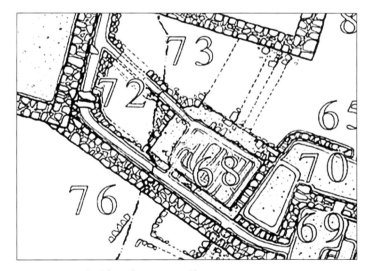

a) Loci 72-73, Plan Coüasnon Ib extract

b) L. 182 above the filling of L. 68

fig. 96.   Locus 68

Plate 35

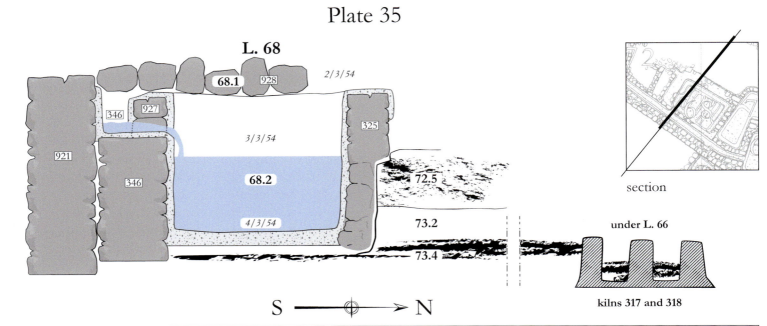

Restored elements	Level	Definition	Journal dates	Coins	Position	N°	Chronology
68.1	Post 4–5	Precarious accommodation, L182	2/3/54	KhQ. 1147	Drain 923 (?)	1	Roman, 4th cent.
68.2	3B/C	Ritual bath L68	3-4/3/54				
73.3	1	Ash waste restored	L73 – 4/3/54				

Schema and stratigraphic diagram of Locus 68 (for the chart of symbols, see page 155)

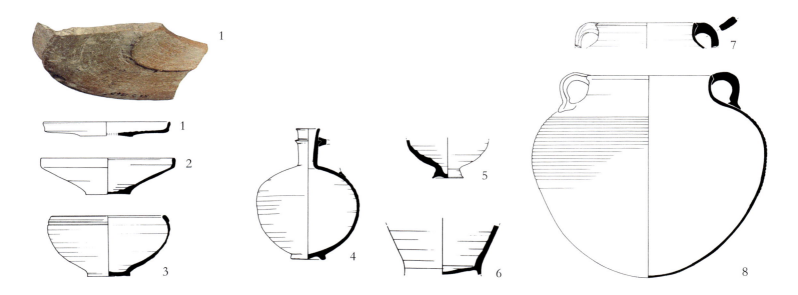

N° Pl.	N° Catal.	Position	Comments (archives)	Date	Description	Clay	Exterior
1	1248	68.2	lower level	03/03/54	plate	° red earth	
2	1152	68.1	upper level	02/03/54	plate, lid of KhQ 1151	° grey earth	white wash
3	1168	68.1	upper level	02/03/54	bowl, in cooking pot KhQ 1151	° red earth	white wash
4	1262	68.2	In 923	06/03/54	small jug, in channel 346	° red earth with grey section	red wash, glossy
5	4062	68.1	-	01/03/54	small jug	red paste	pink
6	4058	68.1	-	02/03/54	jug, white paste	beige paste	brown engobe
7	4074	68.2	-	06/03/54	cooking pot sherd	red paste	red
8	1151	68.1	upper level	02/3/54	cooking pot	° red earth	

° *According to de Vaux*

Locus 68, pottery and catalogue, scale ¼

Locus 69
Decantation pool or ritual bath?

Pool 72-73 is contained to the west and south by aqueduct 346, and the two were contemporary. Pool 72-73 was thus not a terminus of the hydraulic system, and installations existed downstream. The aqueduct then ends at pools 69 and 71, linked together, the reworking of the masonry in each case displaying an evolution. Examination of the documents, however, does not allow an assured reconstruction of the original installations. We shall confine ourselves to a few suggestions.

The excavation of L. 69 was conducted jointly with that of L. 68, L. 72 and L. 73 on 3rd, 4th and 6th March 1953, the 5th being a public holiday. The whole sector of small pools was the object of an extensive and rapid excavation. The notes in the *Journal* are at best brief (L. 69, 3/3/54): *another cistern feeding the main channel (...) we find at last the passage of the water towards large cistern 71.*

The rudimentary remains of Level 5 (post-Period III), Loci 181 and 182

The upper level, which we have called L. 181 (fig. 98b, c and d), was not given any comment and, being attributed to the post-68 level, it appears only on the *Plan* of Period III. No photograph testifies to it. North wall 958 is drawn with two facings on the surveys while west wall 974 exists only with the reproduction of the bad beds that surmount thickened wall 926 (fig. 98c and d). The quick neat copy (fig. 98c) gives it with two facings which may be a restoration. Finally, Coüasnon's *Plan* of Period III has straightened up walls with two facings (fig. 98d). L. 181 assumes a filled pool 69. Indications of its inhabitation are weak, as no floor is associated with it. It is adjacent to L. 182 which sealed bath 68, with scarcely any further existence in the *Journal* (L. 68, 2/3/54): *used in its upper part as a habitation in Period III, because of a large pot in place.* Added to this is what was understood as the socket of a door in the northwest corner (L. 68, fig. 88c and fig. 96). The elevations compared confirm that the two upper loci are founded in the leveling of Level 3C. The only thing that matters is that L. 181 and L. 182 may be linked together with Level 5 by their association with L. 180.

The evolution of the masonry in L. 69 and L. 71, upper part (fig. 98) and proposals for a rearrangement.

Certain reworkings on architectural features are noted on the plans and surveys by sabre-cuts and in the walls by differences in thickness. The north

fig. 97.   Locus 69 towards the southeast.

segment of wall 967, thicker than south segment 941 is the vestige of an earlier construction, modified at the time when large pool L. 71 was installed. It will have joined pool L. 69, and the north segment 973 of wall 940 may have been its opposite wall; 973 is less thick than 940 which leans on it. The two walls 931 and 933 of pool L. 69 lean against 973 and, remarkably enough, they are not tied to wall 932 to the west either.

Parallel walls 967 and 973 do not form an identifiable unit. Walls 931 and 933 are blockages, and setting those aside, a freed L. 69 would seem to be the missing passage from the southeast annexes to the large south terrace. It could have doubled L. 189 which, designed as a lock chamber, facilitated circulation between the western sector of the settlement and the terrace. The possible passage in L. 69, serving the southeast annexes, would have benefited from the proximity of bath L. 68 in the same way as passage 650 enjoyed the proximity of ritual bath L. 138.

Such a supposition would lead us to reformulate the previous function of the series of small pools: L. 70 is a late addition which did not impede the passage. Before reservoir L. 71 was built, the terminus of the aqueduct may at one time have been bath 68 with an evacuation 969 towards L. 75 (fig. 99).

Pool L. 69 was then planned. There would have been a need, becoming a habit, to go via pool L. 69 which could be crossed, and which would at the same time have served as a bath. Two ritual baths would have been next to each other, L. 68 inside and L. 69 on the way back from L. 75 and L. 183. The depth in L. 69 is consistent with 1.80 m depth of water. From the terrace, one descended into pool L. 69 by narrow entrance 934 opening onto a flight of eight steps, which would not be necessary if L. 69 was a decantation pit upstream of reservoir L. 71. Exiting was enabled by the marked landing – 283 then by spanning wall 931, as a sill 40 cm high, descending into L. 65 before pool L. 70 was built.

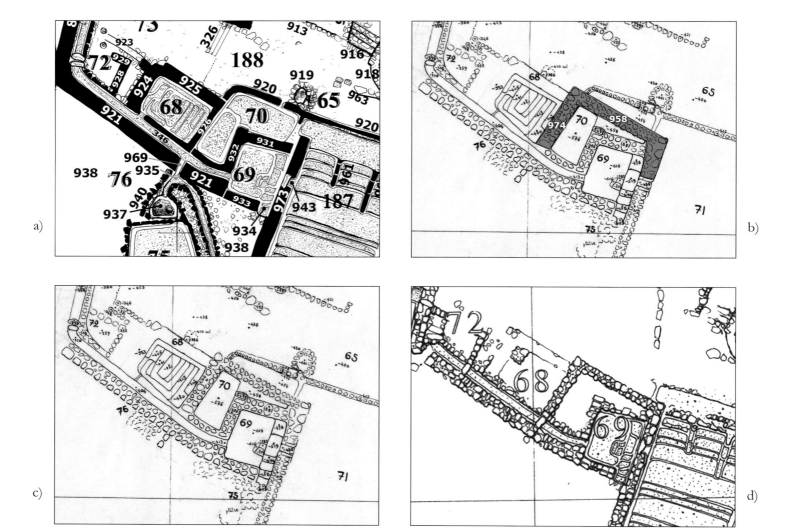

fig. 98. Final constructions in the southeast annexes: Locus 180 Level 4/5?

The series of pools and the southeast workshops 257

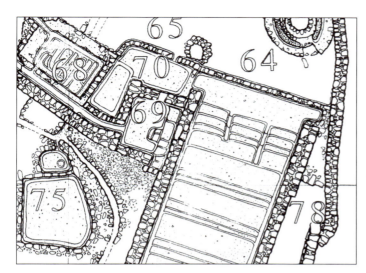

fig. 99. Loci 69 and 71, from plan Ib

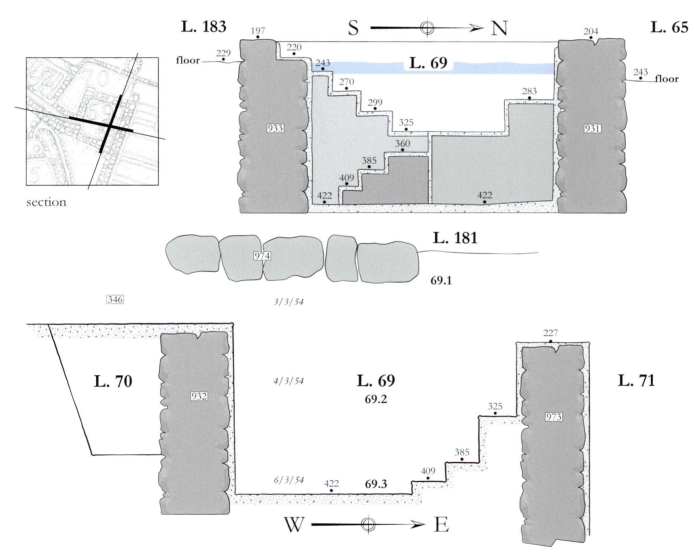

Restored elements	Level	Definition	Journal dates	Coins	Position	N°	Chronology
69.1	Post 4–5	L. 181	3/3/54				
69.2	Post 3C	filling-in	4/3/54	KhQ. 1177	Filling-in	1	Agrippa Ist
69.3	3B (?) C	pool 69	6/3/54 (bottom)				

Schema and stratigraphic diagram of Locus 69 (for the chart of symbols, see page 155)

Plate 36

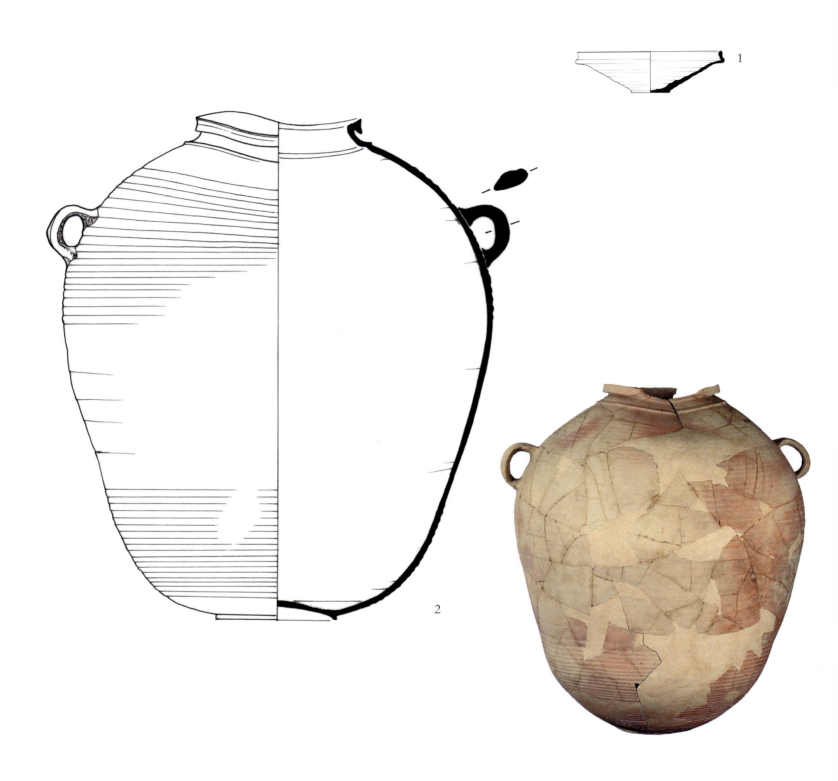

N° Pl.	N° Catal.	Position	Comments (archives)	Date	Description	Clay	Exterior
1	1294	69.3	bottom	07/03/54	plate	° red earth	
2	1290	69.3	bottom	07/03/54	jar		

° *According to de Vaux*

Locus 69, pottery and catalogue, scale ¼

Large reservoir Locus 71
End of the hydraulic system

Reservoir L. . 71 is the most substantial construction of the *khirbeh* and constitutes the end-point of the hydraulic system in its final phase. The excavation was not complete: a trench a little more than a metre wide was made along west wall 940 with the objective of straightening out the elevation: *We clear only along the west wall to complete the drawing of the staircase and establish its depth* (L. 71, 7/3/54). We have no other description, it is true, of a fill accumulated by erosion and the collapse of upper parts. The bottom of the pool, however, would have been covered by the decantation silt which would have produced some sherds. Only two Hasmonaean coins were collected, too worn to be of use. Work was completed quickly in three days between March 7 and 10, 1954. As nothing is noted on the 8th, the *Journal* indicates that from the 7th to midday on the 9th de Vaux was in Jerusalem, and the assumption must be that work was not interrupted. On 9/3/54, the note on L. 71 relates to L. 78, where the investigation was completed only on 29/3/55. The spoil earth soil dump was accumulated on the reserved part. No pot nor sherd was selected.

The Coüasnon *Plans* of Period Ib and II display two anomalies in the arrangement of the masonry, which call for a reinterpretation of the sequence of the constructions. They suggest that the space was subjected to reallocation in successive stages. If wall 900 was constructed to join pool L. 71, it would logically have adjoined its east wall 941. But it extends to the south eight metres further than the corner of the pool before starting an elbow 964 to the west. Coüasnon's *Plans* take little account of this and lead us to believe that 900 is supported on 951, the *long wall* of the terrace, which is not accurate. A preliminary survey shows that 951 crosses 964 (fig. 100a). A quick examination of the locations confirms that the foundation of 964 passes under the *long wall* 951, which therefore postdates it.

Elbow 964 was clipped by an architectural restoration. Wall 941 needs dividing into two parts: the north segment, now called 967, is wider than south segment 941. Observation of the site confirms the differences in the masonry, not taken into account by the Coüasnon surveys. North segment 967 is formed by large blocks of stone, more or less square, and placed as headers (fig. 100b). The south segment is still 941 and, with its small stones, constitutes an extension of segment 967. Bearing in mind that the thickness of wall 964 is the broadening of the foundation for a sharp angle, a disappeared stretch of masonry may be restored to it that would have joined the wall, now 973, the north part, narrower than its southern extension 940. Pool L. 71 in its final form is therefore not original; preceding it, under its northern part, will have been another pool: L. 187. Its restoration prompts another, L. 188 to the north of pool L. 71, kiln 918 of L. 64 not yet having been built. The location displays some reworking.

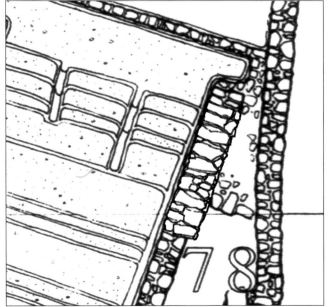

fig. 100. a) Survey 1, 1954
b) Correction of wall 967

a) The pools area before the excavation

b) The blocks are laid in regular courses in the southwest corner

c) Masonry of the southeast corner

fig. 101.   Reservoir L. 71 before the excavation work

Two restored L. 187 and 188

In support of the restoration, we propose four sequences of masonry, from the earliest to the most recent:

– 967 and 973 = L. 187

– 968 and 900a + (913 restored) = L. 188

– 940 and 941 = L. 71 and 900b

– 951

Walls 967 (to the east) and 973 (to the west), extended by walls 940 and 941 respectively, probably belonged to an earlier construction ending to the south at one of the projections of the staircase and to the north at the space of the upper landing. L. 187 may have been a room, or more likely a pool, enlarged to create large L. 71. Elbow 968 marks a reworking in the constructions and presents as an abutment to what remains of wall 913, with its noticeable slope in relation to the surrounding right angles. The same slope affects the installation of kiln 918 (L. 64) with its staircase 916. All this suggests that wall 913, nothing of which remains except for the north facing, would have been a former enclosure embracing the outgrowth to the east of the small pools. The space thus enclosed restores a L. 188 (fig. 103). L. 64 and 84 will have been added later.

Description of reservoir L. 71 (fig. 101)

The reservoir, measuring 17.50 x 4.50 m with 5 m maximum depth, registers a capacity of 300 m³. Its shifted position towards the east remains intriguing, as there was no lack of space and slope to dig it more to the west in L. 98 without extending the aqueduct. We presume it was added to the series of small pools when water consumption increased. It is the most recent pool in the series. Its large capacity made it a water reserve which, exceeding the needs of the southeast annexes, would have been meant for the settlement as a whole. But it has to be repeated that access to it was not facilitated. Two thirds of the bottom of the pool form a staircase with irregular steps, spaced by tiers. The ancient Near East dug underground reservoirs accessible only by an intlet and they should be called cisterns; the other reservoirs which one could enter to access the water were pools or basins. Several commentators have suggested that the steps facilitated access to saddled animals that carried water, or allowed quicker flushing of the low parts. However, it is reasonable to bear in mind that animal urine and excrement would contaminate the water. Besides this, the configuration of traffic inside the settlement does not permit any planned passageway for donkeys or mules.

The entrance landing of L. 71 forms the most elevated part of the basin where the water was contained by rim 920. The landing and its watertight rim, coated with the same cement, have poor communication with the final tank L. 70A/B; a gully furnished with a low projection would be able to start the flow from the high landing of L. 71 towards L. 70, but it is rather unlikely that the latter would have served as an overflow for large pool L. 71 as its capacity is too small and there is already an overflow to the south. Tank 70A is, as it were, deprived of a feed and will have served as a vat. Handling of the water on the landing may have required draining used water without letting it fall back into the pool. So L. 70 suggests some kind of work linked to the water which the environment does not allow us to identify. Upper tank L. 70A was furnished with an overflow towards L. 65; one might deduce that, when it overflowed, pit 919 later mitigated the nuisance of inundations. Lower part L. 70B, curiously installed as a basement, did not necessarily function as a cesspit: *the north-south branch is an incompletely plastered pit (...) filled-in with this yellow clay* (L. 70, 8/3/54).

Interpretation of the pottery workshop

De Vaux proposed these installations as the facilities of a pottery workshop[75]. We shall see that there is no indication that pool L. 75 served to store or decant clay. The clay found accumulated in the deep part of L. 70 is not necessarily the product of decantation but rather that of erosion by heavy downpours. Arguments for interpreting the location as pottery workshop are not compelling. Pit 919, where de Vaux saw the potter's wheel, only makes sense if there was another drain within reach of L. 71 and L. 65. The lower part of the pit is not wide enough to contain an inertia wheel. When frequent water is handled in a place as organized as this, the drainage has to be well. Pit 919 rather presents the morphology of a cesspit.

---

75. R. de Vaux, *L'archéologie*, p. 34.

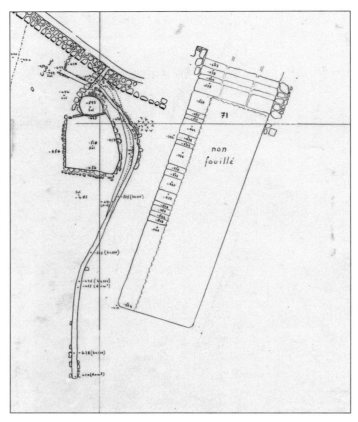

a) Survey Coüasnon 2, 1954

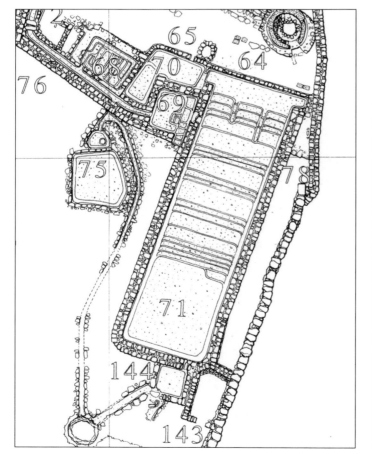

b) Plan Coüasnon Period Ib

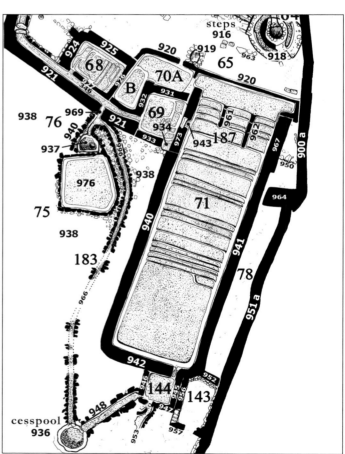

c) Numbering of built elements

fig. 102.   Coüasnon surveys and plan of the L. 71 sector

Considerations as to the construction and function of L. 71

The total capacity of water stored at Qumran is just under 1000 m³. Reservoir L. 71 received almost a third of it. Reservoir L. 91 managed a capacity of 250 m³. Their combined capacities provided more than half of the reserve, and providing for them required both engineering skill and time: engineering, given the dam in the gorge at the foot of the cliff, which decanted floods; and time, as the gorge is not filled with water every year. The capacity of the pools will have mitigated precipitation risks and it is quite likely that the erection of the dam and the digging of the large pools, at any rate L. 71, were conducted in the context of work on the project.

Following de Vaux and contrary to the opinion of most scholars, reservoir L. 71 needed to be covered. To prevent spoiling of the accumulated water, especially in the case of long-term storage, protection against sunlight is common practice. The east-west width does not come to more than 4.50 m, which is a standard for vernacular architecture in the region, corresponding to the standard length of available wood. The exploitation of the type of palm tree indigenous to the Dead Sea area, attested on the nearby shore and on the site, provided the kind of quality required for timber. The height below the ceiling has to be restored at the approach to the pool, in accordance with the height of a person. The photographs impressively show the even leveling of the load-bearing walls, which corresponds broadly to the original masonry; one would think that two beds of stone (0.75 m high), projecting above the circulation floors, protected the base of the walls from erosion, and we suggest that the superstructure was of rough brick. If the height of the approach is estimated at 1.80 m, the height of the crude earth could barely exceed 1.20 m. To this were added the timber and the covering of palms or reeds, then rammed beaten earth. The approach from the north avoided subjecting the mass of water to the effects of the sun. The configuration of the entrance shows that it was mainly open for its whole width, and L. 65 served it.

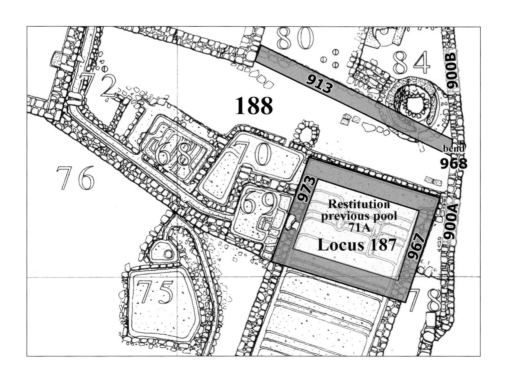

fig. 103.   Proposed reconstruction of Loci 187 and 188

a) Before the excavations

b) After completion of the exploratory trench

c) After the end of the excavations

fig. 104.   Reservoir L. 71

The series of pools and the southeast workshops 265

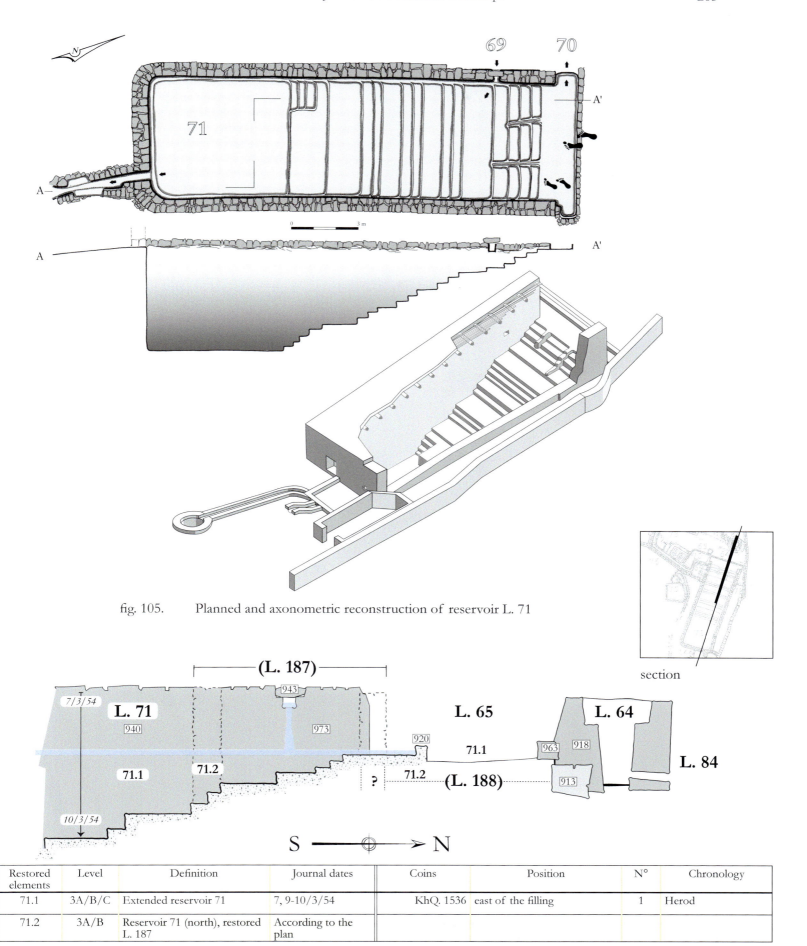

fig. 105. Planned and axonometric reconstruction of reservoir L. 71

Restored elements	Level	Definition	Journal dates	Coins	Position	N°	Chronology
71.1	3A/B/C	Extended reservoir 71	7, 9-10/3/54	KhQ. 1536	east of the filling	1	Herod
71.2	3A/B	Reservoir 71 (north), restored L. 187	According to the plan				

Schema and stratigraphic diagram of Loci 71, 187, and 188 (for the chart of symbols, see page 155)

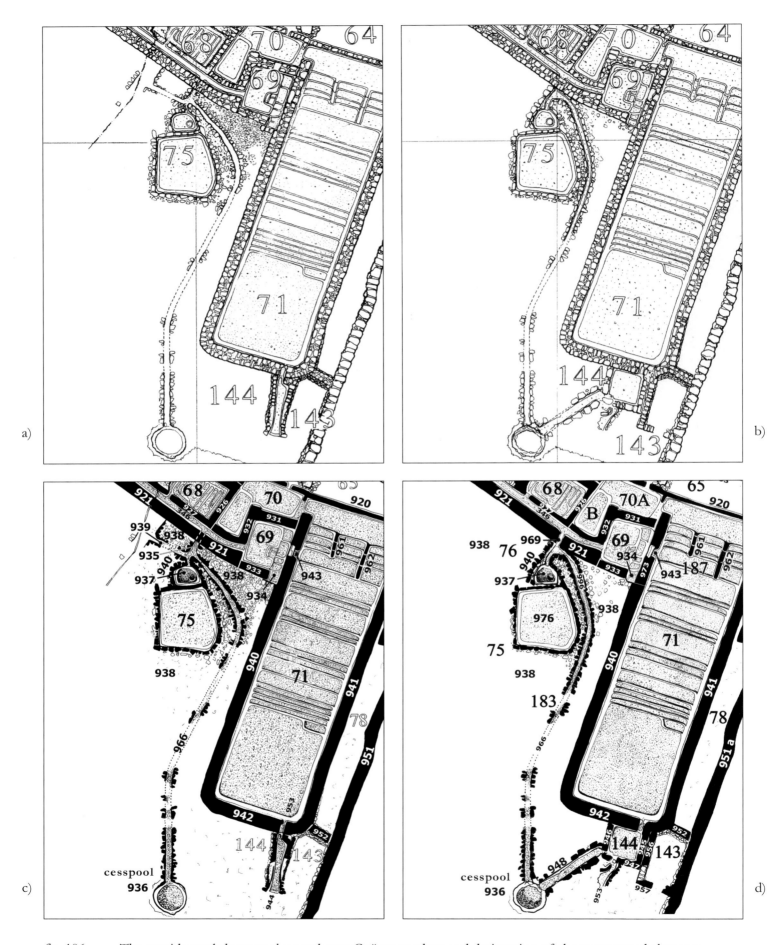

fig. 106. The outside workshops to the southeast, Coüasnon plans and designation of the constructed elements
a) First installation
b) Late installation
c and d) Designated walls

Locus 75
The outside workshops,
southeast annexes, locus 183

L. 75 was cleared with care in four days, 9/3/54 and then 1, 3 and 4/4/54. Here we see a workshop with an arrangement of tanks, a feed and evacuation drains. On the day of the excavation, de Vaux immediately interpreted the L. as an outbuilding of the pottery workshop, although he expressed some caution: *Hypothesis: this may be where the potter decanted the glaze before putting it into pit 70 which was intended to serve as a reserve on the other side of the main channel* (L. 75, 3/4/54). Two weeks before, he had the intuition that kilns 917 and 918 (L. 64 and L. 84) were pottery kilns: in the Schweich Lectures, the intuition had become a certainty, and he confirmed the interpretation by assuming a potter's wheel in 919 at L. 65 - which was however missing.

The presence of what he calls *clay*, by the way, confirms such over-interpretation. *The quadrangular pit contains clay, more or less pure* (L. 75, 3/5/54). *We dig in yellow, compact earth* (L. 70, 4/3/54). *The (...) pit incompletely plastered (...) filled with this yellow clay* (L. 70, 8/3/54). The works of the 2000s were an opportunity to return to and develop the hypothesis of the potter's workshop. The bottom of pool 71 contained decanted material, judged to be appropriate for the production of ceramics[76]. The proposal to see in pool L. 71 a decantation pit for clays is surprising. A stepped pool 20 m in length is anything but a potter's decantation vat. If there was clay in pool L. 71 and pits L. 70 and L. 75, we note that it apparently was not retrieved. Because of its recessed position, L. 70 is hardly likely to catch enough natural run-off to generate such a deposit, and it is true that its function remains a mystery. We may link these deposits of *yellow clay* with what de Vaux had interpreted as alluviums in L. 137 and L. 132 or clay in L. 130 washed in as a sudden flood (see L. 130). In L. 132, however, it was not *brought in*. We accept that the yellow matter is the product of floods. The natural runoff in the area would indeed have produced this fine, beige-yellow silt. More or less everywhere, the same silt will have filled the holes left gaping *after* the abandonment.

Finally, if the clay deposit was allowed in when washed up, it would be better to attribute it to the production of *pisé*, a large quantity of which was needed for maintaining roughcast and covers. We recall that the majority of the walls of the added wings around the residence possessed a superstructure of rough earth.

Critique of the "potter's workshop" at Qumran: Was L. 75 a wine-press?

We challenged the idea of a potter's workshop while verifying the viability of its arrangement. We insisted on the peripheral enclosure of the settlement, and we have to state that L. 75 is *extra muros*, while L. 70, the supposed L. 64 kilns and the potter's wheel are *intra muros*. They are separated by the enclosure, without provision for communication, and it is not obvious that a potter would split up work between different places without regard for the operational sequence. It is true that we have suggested a passage through L. 69 before its conversion to a bath or a pool: there can be no question of that here, as the presumed passage was discontinued when the clay deposits were sealed by the abandonment of the site at the end of Level 3C. If small kiln 917 was intended for pottery, it may, for example, have furnished objects of small dimensions such as lamps. The small amount of clay needed could have been drawn occasionally from L. 70; however, among the functions of Qumran, one cannot accept that of a massive and regular production of pots. The facility is not suitable for a craft industry of that kind. For anyone who visited traditional potteries, L. 75 is nothing like the pit where paste was decanted or prepared. Pit 937 is too slender for feasible decantation.

The arrangement of L. 75 is much more like that of a wine-press, and the palm grove may have accommodated vines. S. Pfann[77] has proposed a date press, and the idea has been picked up by Y. Magen.

---

76. Y. Magen, Y. Peleg *Archaeological Interpretation*, p. 66; *Idem*, JSP 6, p. 365; JSP, 18 p. 90, 92-3

77. Stephen Pfann, in J.-B. Humbert, "L'espace sacré à Qumrân" *RB* 55, appendix, p. 212ff.

a) Basin 75 to the north-east

b) Basin 75 to the south

fig. 107. Locus 75

How can we imagine that dates can have been crushed or trampled when the viscosity of the crushed mass does not have sufficient fluidity to run into the reservoir, and when the separation of the stones from the pulp cannot be achieved there? We have observed the production of date purée which is made, patiently, with the help of a stoning tool. Vat 976, on the other hand, is quite suitable for trampling grapes with its border of small flat stones placed on edge, the juice being collected in tank 937, lower than 0.75 m, through an opening visible against the light (fig. 108). At the bottom, the latter has a concave cupola suitable for pressing liquids. Stone paving 937, in the reentrant of the aqueduct and pool 71, surrounds a working area which was flushed with water.

A drainage network circles L. 75. An outlet 969 releases the stream of water from aqueduct 346 which immediately divides into three opposing directions. It pours *recto tramite* into pit 937, enters as an overflow into drain 966/935 and turns towards the west via channel 939 towards another tank, nothing of which remains; it might have been destroyed by the earthquake fault. Long evacuation 935, which ends at cesspit 936, restored and continued in 966, attests to the interest and care given to activities on the premises.

fig. 108.   Locus 75, towards the south. Note the back-lit flap in the partition wall of the pool.

270 The archaeology of Qumran – an attempted reassessment

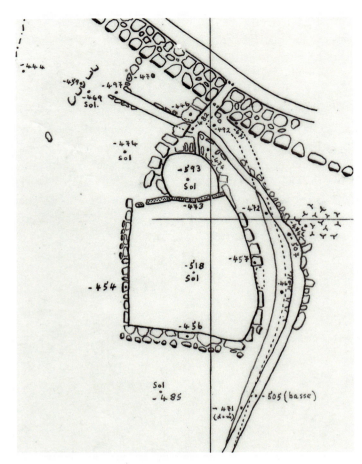

fig. 109.   Locus 183, surveyed in 1954

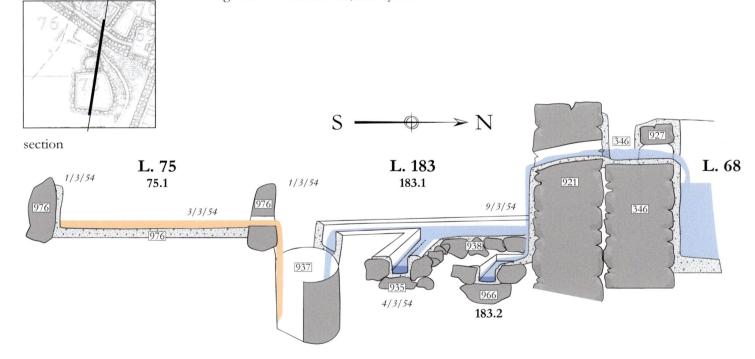

Restored elements	Level	Definition	Journal dates	Coins	Position	N°	Chronology
183.1 75.1	3B/C	wine-press, drain 938	1-4/4/54	KhQ. 1607		1	Herod
183.2	3B/C	outlet 966	4/4/54?				

Schema and stratigraphic diagram of Loci 75 and 183 (for the chart of symbols, see page 155)

Plate 37

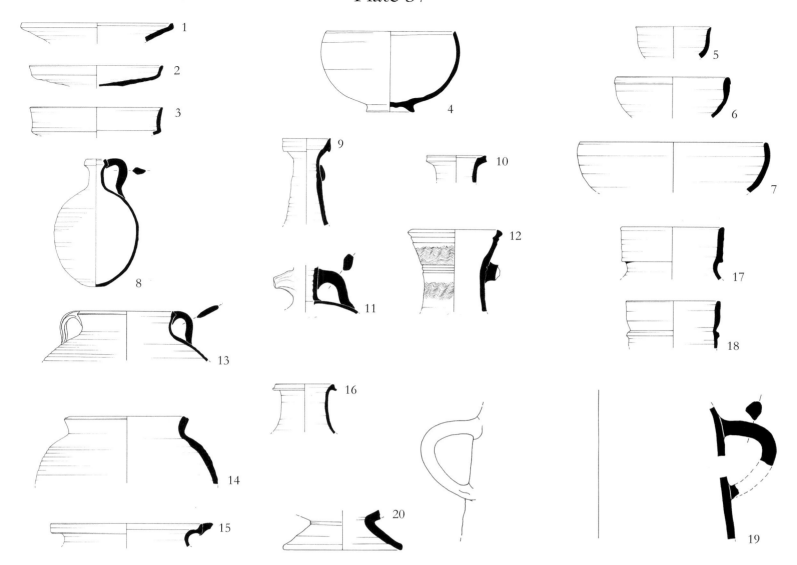

N° Pl.	N° Catal.	Position	Comments (archives)	Date	Description	Clay	Exterior
1	4319	183.2	-	05/04/54	dish	red paste	beige
2	4312	183.1	L. 75	03/04/54	small dish	brownish-red paste	grey
3	4316	183.1	L. 75	03/04/54	dish	reddish-brown paste	beige
4	1643	183.2	L. 75 south	08/04/54	bowl	° grey earth	
5	4297	183.2	-	05/04/54	edge of small bowl	red paste	brown
6	4308	183.1	-	04/04/54	edge of bowl	orange paste	beige
7	4293	183.2	L. 75 south	10/04/54	large bowl	brownish-grey paste	beige engobe
8	1606	183.2	-	05/04/54	small jug	° grey earth	pink wash
9	4320	183.2	L. 75 south	10/04/54	neck of jug	light brown paste	beige
10	4309	183.1	-	04/04/54	neck of jug	orange paste	light red
11	4305	183.2	-	05/04/54	flask neck and handle	light red paste	beige
12	4292	183.2	-	08/04/54	neck of jug	white paste	off-white
13	4294	183.1	L. 75	03/04/54	neck of cooking pot	orange paste	reddish-beige
14	4306	183.2	-	05/04/54	neck of cooking pot	red paste with grey core	red-beige
15	4311	183.2	-	05/04/54	neck of cooking pot	red paste with grey core	beige
16	4313	183.2	-	06/04/54	kettle	red paste	light brown
17	4302	183.2	L. 75 south	10/04/54	neck of jar	orange paste	beige engobe
18	4314	183.1	-	04/04/54	neck of jar	brown paste	grey
19	4318	183.1	-	04/04/54	jar, white paste?	beige paste	beige
20	4298	183.2	-	05/04/54	jar support	brown paste	beige

° *According to de Vaux*

Locus 75, pottery and catalogue, scale ¼

The workshop of Loci 143–144

To the southeast of the settlement, the reentrant angle formed by the series of small pools (L. 68, L. 69, L. 70) and large reservoir L. 71 had attracted open-air activities. The reentrant contains L. 183 associated with L. 75. To the south of L. 71, a modest working area L. 143-144 benefited from the overflow of L. 71. The two workshops needed water and we note that they are the only installations outside the walls. Exploration of the area took place in 1955, one year later than the partial emptying of pool L. 71. The existence of press-like installation L. 75, excavated in 1954, allowed to hope for other installations around L. 71, and L. 143 and L. 144 were uncovered, the most southerly of the whole settlement. The fact that L. 144, very modest in size, was the object of the excavators' careful attention for five days attests to the fact that investigation methods had become more precise by 1955. L. 143 was cleared in two days, at the same time as the adjoining L. 144.

On the general plans, the isolated position of installation L. 143-144 is striking. The excavators found it of rather less interest. Soberly described in the *Journal*, it was not taken into account in the interpretation of the site. It attracted some attention, however, for having produced a bowl with an inscription.

The description of the location is brief and it is difficult to follow its layout. A stratigraphic comment specifies that a corner of L. 143 seals rendering of L. 144. It is possible to believe that one succeeds the other, that one was joined to the other at a later date: *the southwest corner of L. 143 was constructed on the plaster associated with L. 144. Unfortunately, the corner of L. 144 was skipped so as to follow the channel better* (L. 144, 28/3/55). The telegraphic style of the *Journal* suffers from gaps and some imprecision. Coüasnon *Plan* Ib, the first period, features an overflow 944 of reservoir L. 71, but nothing is said of it in the notes, and *Plan* Period II shows two other drainage channels, 953 and 948. One hesitates to identify the channel mentioned in the *Journal* on 28/3/55 with any of these features. It is evident that 956, the narrow west wall of L. 143, is exactly superposed on the eastern edge of overflow 944; southeast corner 947 of L. 144 has been attached *to follow the channel*, without further specification; this can only be 944. So, there is a good chance that overflow 944 was sealed by tank 144 and is earlier. *Plan* Ib is right to consider it earlier.

Overflow 944, exiting from the south side of reservoir L. 71, is carefully constructed, 3.50 m long and drained excess water. Its unusual length was intended to avoid too much spread water spoiling the wall of reservoir L. 71 and its coating. The precaution does not apply to long wall 951, the foundation of which, quite shallow, could be damaged. It may be inferred that the long wall of the esplanade was built later and that cesspit 936 was dug separately for sanitation of the area. Vat L. 144 then served as intermediary for the overflow of reservoir L. 71, and the flood guided by channel 948 fell into cesspit 936. The release from vat L. 144 also worked by means of small pipe 953.

From this we take it that vat L. 144 is contemporary with box room L. 143, and they together condemned overflow 944 to create a small workshop. The storage of water in 144 implies that it was drawn from L. 71. The question of the covering of L. 71 is raised once again. Either the reservoir was open to the sky and water was drawn from it while leaning on the coping, or the reservoir was covered and an opening for drawing would have been made in south wall 942.

L. 143, closed by a door, accommodated objects useful for activities carried out in L. 144 and perhaps also in L. 183. This deserves comment. In vat L. 144 tasks of purification were probably undertaken outside the bounds of the settlement. Among the pots collected in storeroom 143, comments were made on *a jar, half-buried, a bowl inscribed twice with the same word: mem, gimel, 'ain*. A. Lemaire expressed the hypothesis *that this may be a hophal passive participle of the verb ng', 'touch', 'contract', with the nuance 'render impure'*[78]. Lemaire rightly hesitates to identify an improbable name, and the inscription with charcoal better indicates a utilitarian measure than a mark of possession. L. 143 will have contained a bowl or pots that did not comply with purity standards. That L. 143 may have been an isolated location accused of impurity sends us back to the idea that the enclosure surrounding the settlement responded more to a topographic pure/impure limit than to purposes of protection. The interpretation of L. 69 as a passage to return inside the walls at the same time as being a ritual bath, gains support from this.

---

78. A. Lemaire, *Qumrân*, Vol. II, p. 370.

Another comment on L. 143 comes to us from the *Journal*: *Bones of a large animal (vertebrae) mixed with sherds but with no clarity as to whether it had to do with an intentional burial* (27/3/55), then a cautious addition: *It is not sure that the bones were related to the sherds* (L. 143, 29/3/55). It is possible that the conjunction of animal bones and sherds may indicate a *buried deposit*. Too far from the former residence where the *deposits* were thought to be concentrated, this vestige is, however, evident in a series of burials which extend to the south like those of L. 80 and L. 65. Elsewhere, the excavations conducted in the 2000s uncovered other deposits during the clearing of stone paving 815 (L. 90, L. 93, L. 94, L. 98), also to the south of the workshop 143-144. The *buried deposit* is possible but we cannot confirm it, and de Vaux was careful not to do so.

On the other hand, one might hypothesize that this small workshop was the butchery for the inhabitants of Qumran, where animals were slaughtered: its location outside the walls, the remains of animal bones, the small vat of L. 144, the downstream end of the hydraulic system linked to the cesspit for blood to run and to wash meat, the proximity of ritual bath L. 69, the lean-to for hanging the implements and the inscription which may refer to purity rules: all these elements are supporting arguments.

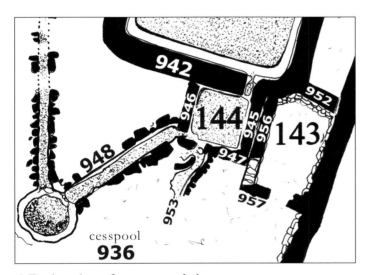

a) Designation of constructed elements

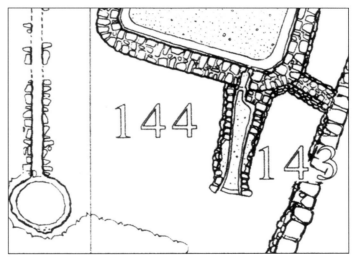

b) From the Plan Coüasnon, Period Ib

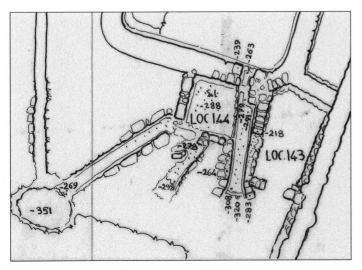

c) From the survey by Coüasnon 1954

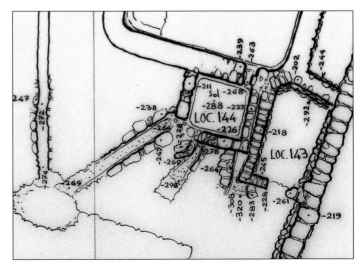

d) Final survey by Coüsanon

fig. 110.   Surveys of Loci 143 and 144

fig. 111.   The southwest corner of L. 143, dismantled to clear drain 944

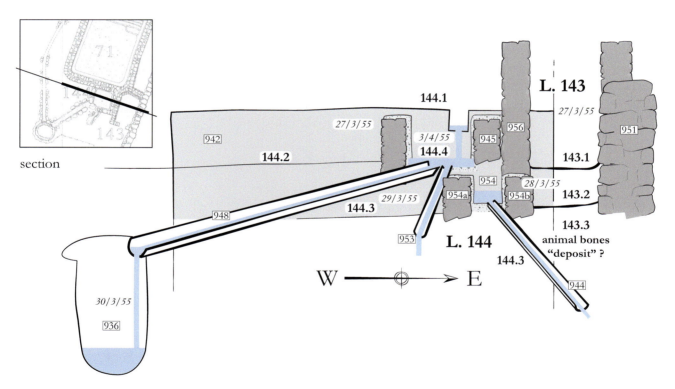

Restored elements	Level	Definition	Journal dates
144.1	Post 3C–4	Abandonment	27/3/55
144.2 143.1 143.2	3C	Tank L144 Cesspit 936 Storeroom L143	28-30/3/55 3/4/55
144.3	3B/C	Overflow 954 of reservoir 71	27 and 29/3/55
143.3	3A?	Level of buried deposits?	27-29/3/55

Schema and stratigraphic diagram of Loci 143-144 (for the chart of symbols, see page 155)

Plate 38

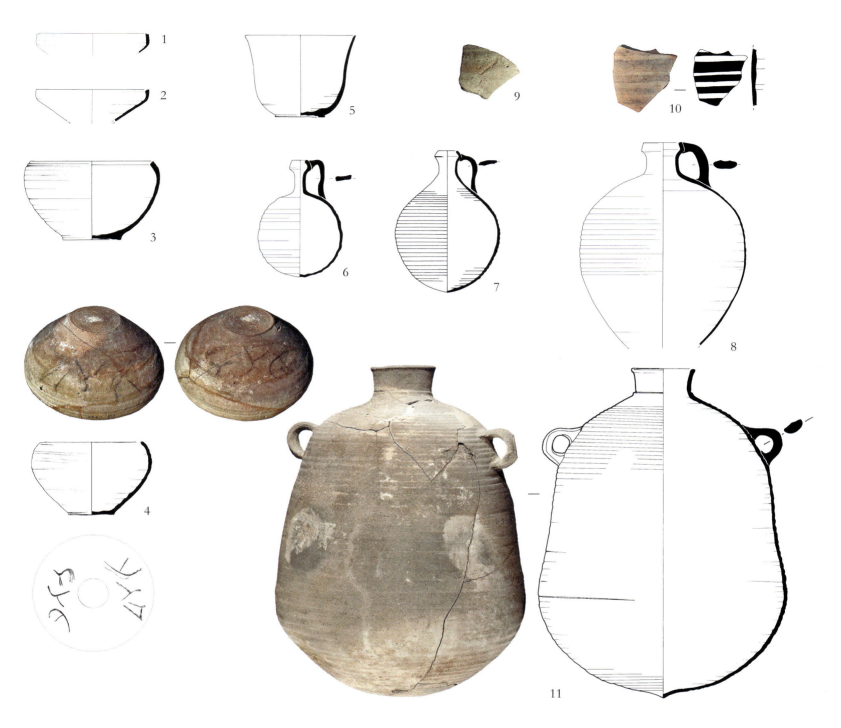

N° Pl.	N° Catal.	Position	Comments (archives)	Date	Description	Clay	Exterior
1	4282	143.1/2	-	27/03/55	short dish	orange paste	dark red engobe
2	4281	143.1/2	-	27/03/55	short dish	red paste	beige and red
3	2599	143.1/2	-	27/03/55	bowl	° buff earth	white wash
4	2587	143.1/2	-	27/03/55	bowl (inscription in charcoal)	° grey earth	white and pink wash
5	2564	143.1/2	-	27/03/55	goblet	° grey earth	white wash
6	2563	143.1/2	-	27/03/55	small jug	° pink earth	beige
7	2562	143.1/2	-	27/03/55	kettle	° buff earth	beige
8	2565	143.1/2	-	27/03/55	jug	° buff earth	beige
9	4280	143.1/2	-	27/03/55	sherd of jar	grey paste	beige engobe
10	4283	143.1/2	-	27/03/55	painted sherd of jar	grey paste	grey-beige
11	2661 F	143.1/2	-	27/03/55	jar	° grey earth	remains of pink wash

° *According to de Vaux*

Locus 143, pottery and catalogue, scale ¼

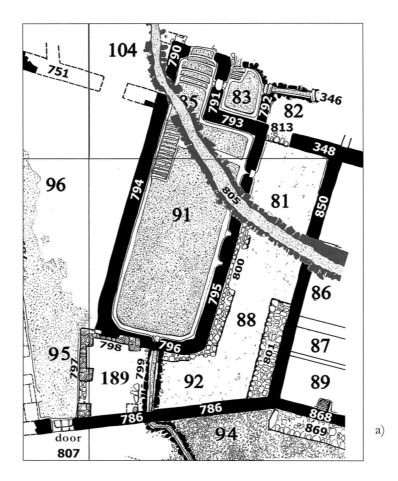

fig. 112. Locus 81
 a) Wall 800 and aqueduct 805, levels 3 and 4
 b) and on the photograph, projecting to the left of reservoir 91

Section II

The south and west front

Chapter C

The surroundings of south reservoir 91

Loci 81, 88, 92, 91 and 83

Topographic definition

The uncovering of the diversion of aqueduct 805, which is clearly from the latest period (de Vaux, Period III), had been the argument for separating the space into L. 81 and 88. A square extension to the west had prompted the excavator to call it L. 92. There is no reason to keep L. 88 and 92. They are unhelpful divisions of the same well-defined space for which we choose to keep the term L. 81.

The excavation, conducted in the course of the 1954 campaign, extended the site to the west of L. 77. De Vaux gave the label L. 81 to the space between L. 77, which he saw as a refectory, and pool L. 91, recognized but not yet excavated. The space, which has a square layout, served as a planned clearing between L. 77 and pool L. 91, towards the south exit to the terrace (by way of L. 189). The boundaries of the L. need to be redefined. The excavation meeting late channel 805 suggested a provisional boundary. The surface layer in this confined space was not isolated and layer 81.2 did not produce anything useful. It is appropriate to join the fruit of the next two stages of the excavation, L. 88 and 92 to L. 81. The only objective of L. 88 was to dig south of channel 805. L. 88 and 92 are the extension of L. 81. We shall deal with L. 88, 92 and 81 under the term L. 81.

L. 92 had no clear boundary to the west. The narrow passageway was not given a name and was partially restored under the term L. 189. The junction between L. 189 and L. 92 was not defined and the excavation of the two loci did not distinguish any separation. They were excavated in superposition. From L. 189, a single goblet was preserved which may belong to L. 189 or L. 92. The arrangement presents as a lock chamber between two doors, suggesting a concern for protection, although there is no hint as to its use in this area. The reconstruction of the L., on de Vaux's plan of Period Ib, is not convincing. West partition wall 797 is assured. The east partition wall was restored by symmetry from a pillar which the survey shows engaged in the lining of pool 91, no trace of which is found today. The supposed east partition wall does not join up well with the overflow of pool 91. It is better to see the space ending with partition 797. L. 81 was installed as a square. L. 189 has to be viewed as the entrance lobby to the settlement from the south esplanade.

Stratigraphic data

The *Journal* is sparing with data. The progression of the work in the area can be followed only in broad strokes.

a) Late channel 805 represented the most recent witness. It obliterates pool L. 91 and crosses L. 81. The installation of the drain implies that the area had been abandoned with the filling-in of pool 91. The builders tracked its course in a ruin.

b) At L. 81 on 16/3/54, the excavator distinguishes three levels, a, b and c, in a synthetic approach. Level c) designates the diversion of final channel 805. A diagrammatic survey indicates a wall 800 which doubles east wall 795 of pool 91, hugging its southeast corner. The *Journal* took no account of this. It has every chance of being late. An elevation allows us to restore its level to the same height as the wall of 91. It was entirely removed and it seems not to have had a foundation. Is it a reinforcement? Is it contemporary with the installation of 81.3? If so, it would have crossed out the overflows laid in wall 795.

c) The *Journal* states that what we collected in L. 81.3 was discovered from 11/3/54 onwards. The *Journal* stops on the 16th but the jars were not uncovered until 20/3/54 and some pots were still being recorded on the 24th. The work will have lasted at least until this date, but it prompted no notes. The *Journal* is just as laconic in relation to L. 88, which in fact represents the central part of L. 81. L. 92 prompts no description at all except the record, on 26/3/54, of the remains of sheep (?) bones, and there is no indication of depth. The complete pots recorded during the excavation and the eleven sherds preserved are given the date 18/3/54. The four other pots associated with a deposit of animal bones are indicated and we must presume they are in place. The work will have been conducted at this location at least until the 7/4/54, but no account of it is given.

d) De Vaux thought that the oldest installation in L. 81 was represented by the four jars against the east and west walls (fig. 117). The next one comprised the layout of mortar tanks 802 and 804, against east wall 851. The installations of mortar, 804, are given three elevation marks. The floors are not described and are poorly marked.

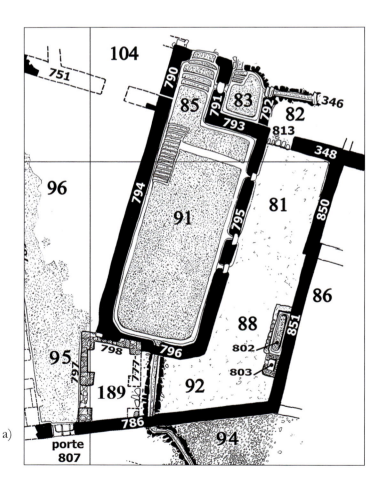 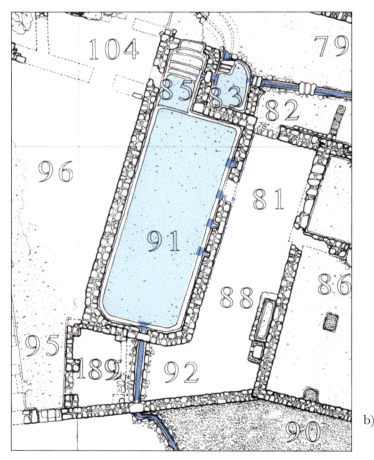

fig. 113. a) Locus 91, numbering of the walls and surroundings
b) On the Coüasnon plan with supply outlets

e) The overall plans, drawn up by periods, attest to the fact that reinforcement 801 of wall 851 (L. 86) was removed to clear tanks 802 and 803. It can be seen complete on the photo (fig. 112b), then we see what is left. It was taken down to uncover the tanks. The reinforcement sealed the tanks. It is described in the *Journal* at L. 92, on 18 and 25/3/54: *It seems to have been made in two goes*. This may have been the wall and its foundation. Discussion of the reinforcement of L. 86 is deferred to the description of L. 93.

f) Witnesses to an older occupation are available The photographs testify to the fact that the sondage in L. 81 hit virgin soil at roughly one metre below the preserved top of the walls. The poorly executed layers sections however do not permit us to discern the intermediate floor and show only one fairly extensive layer of ash with deposits estimated at 10 cm in thickness (fig. 115a). On the plan, a deep floor 81.6 has clearly been dug to instal jars KhQ 1486 and 1492, and it is impossible to say whether it is of beaten earth or mortar. Its depth is estimated from the base of jar 1486, the size of which amounts to 58 cm. Elsewhere the photo (fig. 116b) shows the layer of gravel which de Vaux describes as virgin soil. So we may estimate the thickness of the excavated sediment at 0.70-0.75 m. There are indeed three layers which it would be appropriate to define differently starting with the most recent.

Reconstruction of the stratigraphy:

– 81.1 The diversion of the aqueduct in the inhabited area is set in

– 81.2 a layer of abandonment on the ruin; it covers

– 81.3 a workshop with mortar tanks and interred jars

– 81.4 having had a possible episode preceding 81.3.

– 81.5 Backfill on 81.6 containing superior jars.

– 81.6 A floor dug by the burial of inferior jars, possibly associated with 81.7.

– 81.7 An exterior strewn with ash with deposits of animal bones.

– 81.8 Use of the house in the first half of the first century BC.

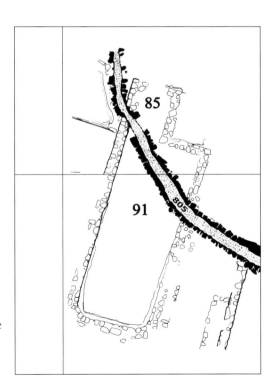

fig. 114. Locus 91 fill-in, crossed by late drain 805, 81.1

fig. 115. Buried jars in Locus 81
a) Clearing of the buried jars
b) Jars deprived of the Level that contained them

A workshop: Locus 81
(Loci 81, 88 and 92)

A workshop: 81.3 – The series of jars and mortar tanks are contemporary and form installation 81.3. The workshop is part of the extension of the settlement during the sectarian period and will have been destroyed in the First Revolt, ca. AD 70. There was no reoccupation other than the diversion of late aqueduct 805. The surveys suggest that the location was then in ruins. Clearance of the surface (81.2) will have begun on 16/3/54 to the south of channel 805, i.e. under the rubric of L. 88. The stratification was mixed up on the surface. Recorded at this date are complete pots which can only belong to the underlying layer 81.3. The next day, 17/3/54, the *Journal* mentions the excavation of an *upper level*. The day after that (L. 81, 18/3/54) did not produce any pottery and we may deduce from this that the excavation was deeper than 81.3. Consequently, the main part of the pottery assigned by de Vaux to L. 88 belongs to installation 81.3.

It is highly likely that two of the three jars were buried as far as the base of their lids. They are intact, and a mixing-up, even in stages, would not have left them undamaged. Further, still with their stone lids, they recall other identical arrangements in which jars were buried (L. 2 and 61) and sealed. We restore the floor where the jars were used, 81.3, at the base of tanks 802 and 804. On one photograph (fig. 116a) we can discern the remains of a slab of smooth coating of wall 348. The low part of the slab curves vertically and forms a horizontal line which restores contact with floor 81.3. The photograph confirms that the threshold separating L. 81 and 82 is raised as far as the base of the slab of smooth coating, which corresponds more or less to the height of the necks of the jars. Here we take it as certain that the floor of L. 81 was therefore cleared for more than half a metre.

The smaller tubular jar, KhQ 1498, was placed deeper and its top cannot appear under floor 81.3. It may have been placed lower for burial without the possibility of opening. It may also testify to an earlier arrangement which was recovered by leveling ballast up to the necks of the three other higher jars. If that is the case, we propose the episode of a possible floor 81.4.

The function of the workshop and the mortar tanks is not known. The photograph (fig. 116b) shows tank 802 (L. 88) roughly stripped. The front lining has disappeared and the tank seems surrounded by a band of mortar where one can recreate a similar channel to the one which is well preserved in the neighbouring tank 804. The string course may also be testimony to the floor with a mortar border: the *Journal* does not note any floor on this plane and the photographs do not give any hint of one. If it is accepted that circulation was established at the height of the necks of the buried jars, the tanks were low, without depth. Their lining could have been taken off, but the photographs rather show the intact rims. The northern limit of tank 804 is not known. The bottom slopes to the north and the channel on at least two of the three sides may have collected a liquid. On its southern side, the photograph shows the well-preserved corner of another tank that has disappeared. The vestige may possibly also be that of the floor and of the smooth plaster covering of the wall. The elevation corresponds to the floor of workshop 81.3. Tank 802, longer, may have the same layout as that of tank 804 with its channel. Tank 803 is only attested with the general plan and is represented directly above tank 802; it may be a repair.

Worthy of note are the three openings made in east wall 795 of *birkeh* L. 91. One might think they served to draw water from the pool 91. But they are more suitable as overflows: The openings, widening at the top, are wide openings of 25, 20 and 10 cm respectively; they were not large enough, however, for a pail to be passed through them. In the reconstruction of the elevation of the constructed elements in the L. 81, the overflows join floor 81.3 of the workshop. Clean water would have been poured on it. The openings would, rather, have collected rainwater, and the workshop would have been open to the sky.

It remains the case that the proximity of pool 91, access to the inspection holes which make it available, the installation of the tanks, and finally the presence of three or four terracotta funnels (pl. 40), suggest that workshop 81's activities would have handled water. The interred jars may have had the function of sinks. Jar KhQ 1490, pierced by a run-off at the bottom of the bulge, was placed immediately to the right of the entrance from L. 82.

fig. 116. a) Slabs of wall coating in Locus 81 and the raised passage towards Locus 79
b) Installation 802 seals the older levels: ash 81.7 (Level 3A)

Layer of ash 81.7 – The layer of ash results from repeated spreading, from a fire or a domestic oven. It shows that at that time the area was an exterior. The layer lies at the same level as the bed of gravel and reveals the earliest activity at this location. One cannot hypothesize a fire: the space is outside the house and destruction by fire would have left a thick consumed mass, which is not the case here. The sondage did not confirm the possible link between the ash and wall 348/793, which, in our view, constitutes the south wall of the Hellenistic house. It is possible that the wall and the ash are linked, and that the ashes were emitted at the time of the house and spread by the rains. However, the ash rather seems to come from periodic encampment which one would place after the abandonment of the house than in the early period of the sectarian establishment which began the practice of burying meal left-overs. In fact, at the extreme end of L. 92, the excavation *Journal* notes on L. 92, 26/3/54 *sheep (?) bones interred under a plate, in a hole in the gravel of the mountain.* Associated with this are a bowl and the bottom of a jar still in place, KhQ 1488. A short distance away, other buried deposits were sealed under L. 77 and 92 (26/3/54), associated with others under the paving which rejoins the terrace (oral communication by P. Rousée, present at the excavation). The first deposit like others show that at the time of the burials, the sector was not built. Floor 81.6, if it is of beaten earth, could be associated with the interred deposits.

The bottom of jar KhQ 1488, belonging to the series of pots interred whole in the northern part of L. 81, should rather be assigned to 81.7. The jar is not complete and de Vaux thought it had been topped by the founding of channel 805. It may have belonged to the deeper level. The shape of the bottom recalls jars KhQ 1632 and 1633, associated with the buried deposit, topped in the same way. So we attributed KhQ 1488 to layer 81.7 with due care for stratigraphic and typological consistency.

Under the term L. 92 – The space was not delimited. The collected material is not situated in the space nor in its depth, except, though without a record of elevation, for the three items of pottery linked to the deposit of *sheep bones* in the L.'s turn to the west. Twelve sherds with complete forms were collected on the same day, 18/3/54. The *Journal* does not specify the depth reached on this date. It would have been noted that the whole of the upper part of L. 81 was excavated on 18/3/54. The separation into three L., 81, 88 and 92 is artificial and such definitions may have been brought in *a posteriori*: the whole sector was worked on at one time. So there is a considerable likelihood that the complete pots recorded under the label *L. 92* on 18/3/54 belong to installation 81.3. We have therefore grouped them together.

The recording of the three vessels of the sheep bones deposit is accompanied by the note *under lower level*. There can be little doubt that they belong to the deepest ash layer 81.7, close to the virgin ground.

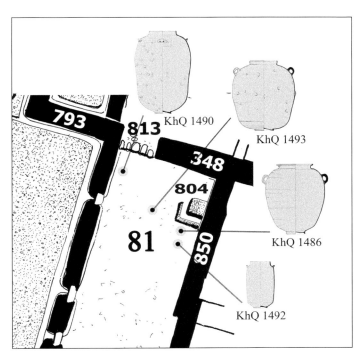

fig. 117. Arrangement of the buried jars of Locus 81

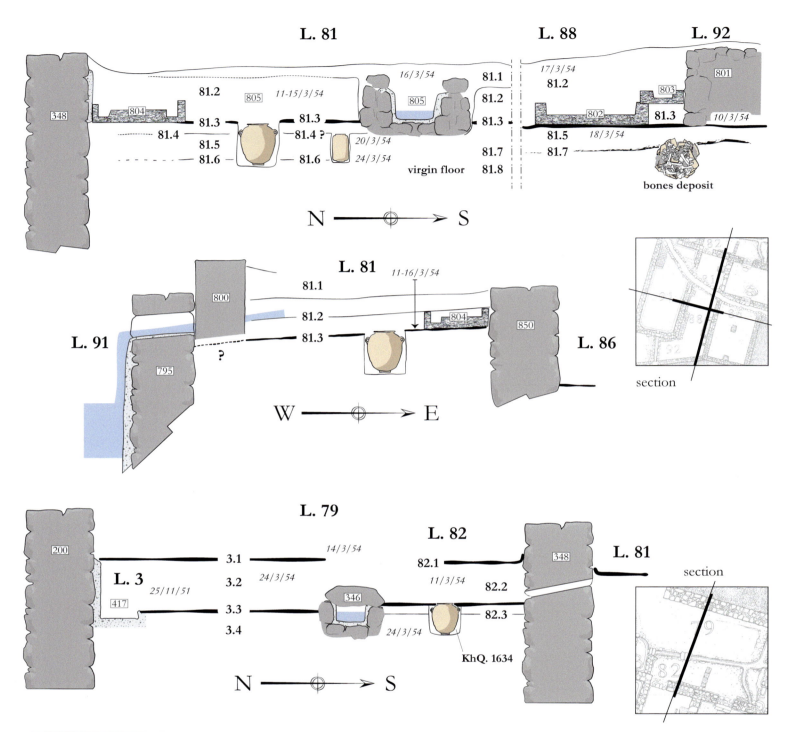

Schema and stratigraphic diagram of the Locus 81 (for the chart of symbols, see page 155)

Plate 39

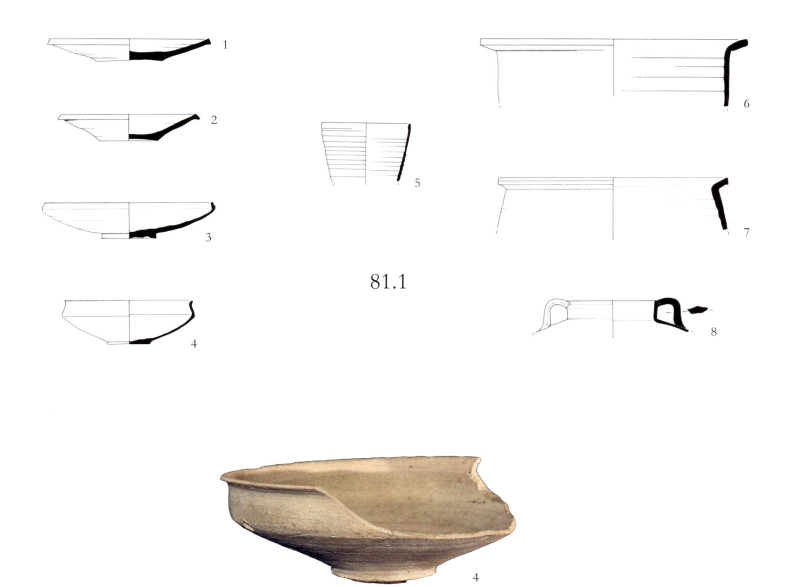

81.1

N° Pl.	N° Catal.	Position	Comments (archives)	Date	Description	Clay	Exterior
1	1447	88.1	L. 92	16/03/54	plate	° red earth	beige-red
2	1446	88.1	-	16/03/54	plate	° red earth	beige-red
3	1448	88.1	-	16/03/54	dish	° red earth	white
4	1442	88.1	-	16/03/54	bowl	° red earth	pink
5	4427	88.1	-	16/03/54	goblet	orange	red-beige
6	4424	88.1	-	16/03/54	bowl	red with grey core	beige-red
7	4433	88.1	-	17/03/54	bowl	brown-grey paste	beige
8	4431	88.1	-	16/03/54	cooking pot	red with greyish-red core	brownish-red

° *According to de Vaux*

Locus 81-1, pottery and catalogue, scale ¼

Plate 40

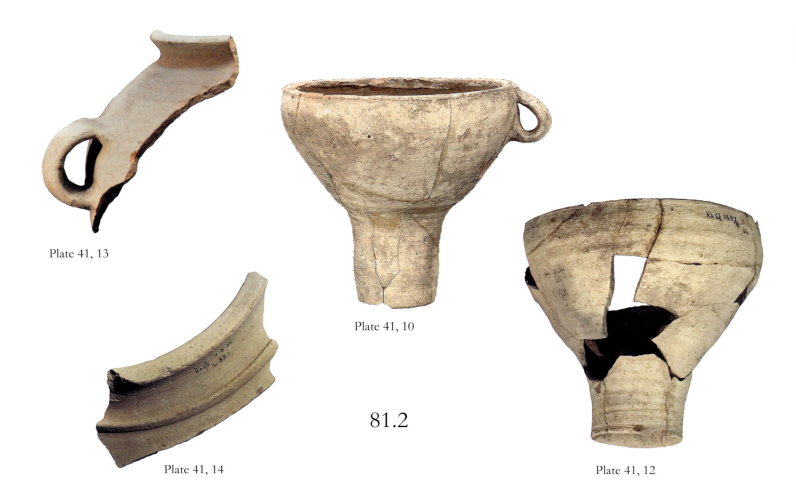

Plate 41, 13

Plate 41, 10

81.2

Plate 41, 14

Plate 41, 12

N° Pl.	N° Catal.	Position	Comments (archives)	Date	Description	Clay	Exterior
1	4430	81.2	L. 88	17/03/54	plate	red paste	reddish-beige
2	1578	81.2	L. 189	29/03/54	goblet	° red paste	white
3	4428	81.2	L. 88	17/03/54	jug	orange paste	beige
4	3587	81.2	L. 92	18/03/54	jug	red paste with grey core	grey beige engobe
5	3582	81.2	L. 92	18/03/54	bowl	red paste	beige
6	4425	81.2	L. 88	20/03/54	dish	orange paste	beige
7	3588	81.2	L. 92	18/03/54	cooking pot	red paste	brown-red
8	3589	81.2	L. 92	18/03/54	cooking pot	dark grey paste	dark grey
9	1409	81.2	L. 81	15/03/54	lamp	° red earth	beige
10	1477	81.2	L. 88	17/03/54	funnel	° red earth	white wash, burnt
11	3580	81.2	L. 92	18/03/54	funnel	light brown paste	beige
12	1497	81.2	L. 92	18/03/54	funnel	° red earth	white
13	3583	81.2	L. 92	18/03/54	jar	light red paste	beige
14	4429	81.2	L. 88	17/03/54	jar	dark grey paste	greyish-beige
15	3584	81.2	L. 92	18/03/54	jar	dark brown paste	beige engobe
16	3581	81.2	L. 92	18/03/54	lid	red paste	beige
17	4432	81.2	L. 88	17/03/54	lid	brown paste	beige
18	1496	81.2	L. 92	18/03/54	lid	° pink earth	white
19	3585	81.2	L. 92	18/03/54	jar	red paste	red

° *According to de Vaux*

Locus 81-2, catalogue of pots and photographs

Plate 41

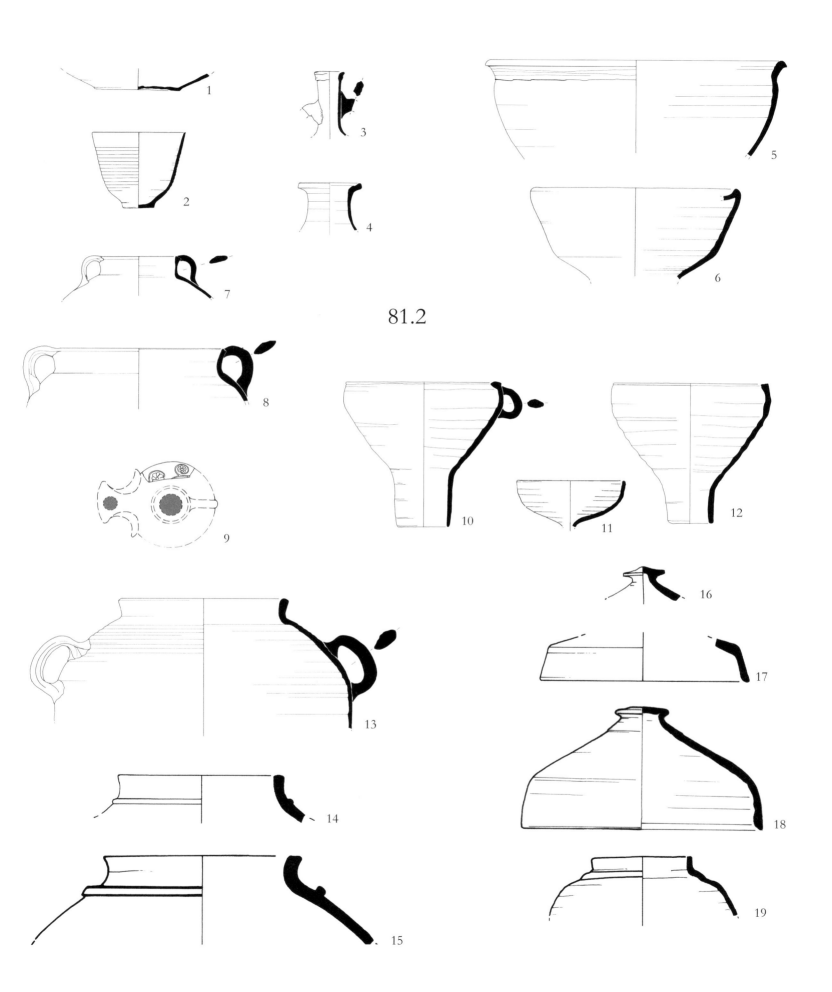

Locus 81-2, pottery, scale ¼

Plate 42

(charcoal graffiti)

N° Pl.	N° Catal.	Position	Comments (archives)	Date	Description	Clay	Exterior
1	1498	81.3	-	20/03/54	plate, closes 1492	° red earth	white
2	1492	81.3	-	20/03/54	scroll type jar	° red earth	white
3	1407	81.3	-	16/03/54	bowl	° red earth	brownish-red
4	1391	81.3	-	20/03/54	lamp	° red earth	pink
5	1486	81.3	-	20/03/54	jar	° red earth	white
6	1493	81.3	-	20/03/54	jar	° red earth	white
7	1488	81.3	-	20/03/54	jar	° red-brown earth	white
8	1490	81.3	-	20/03/54	jar	° red earth	pink

° *According to de Vaux*

Locus 83-3, pottery and catalogue, scale ¼

Plate 43

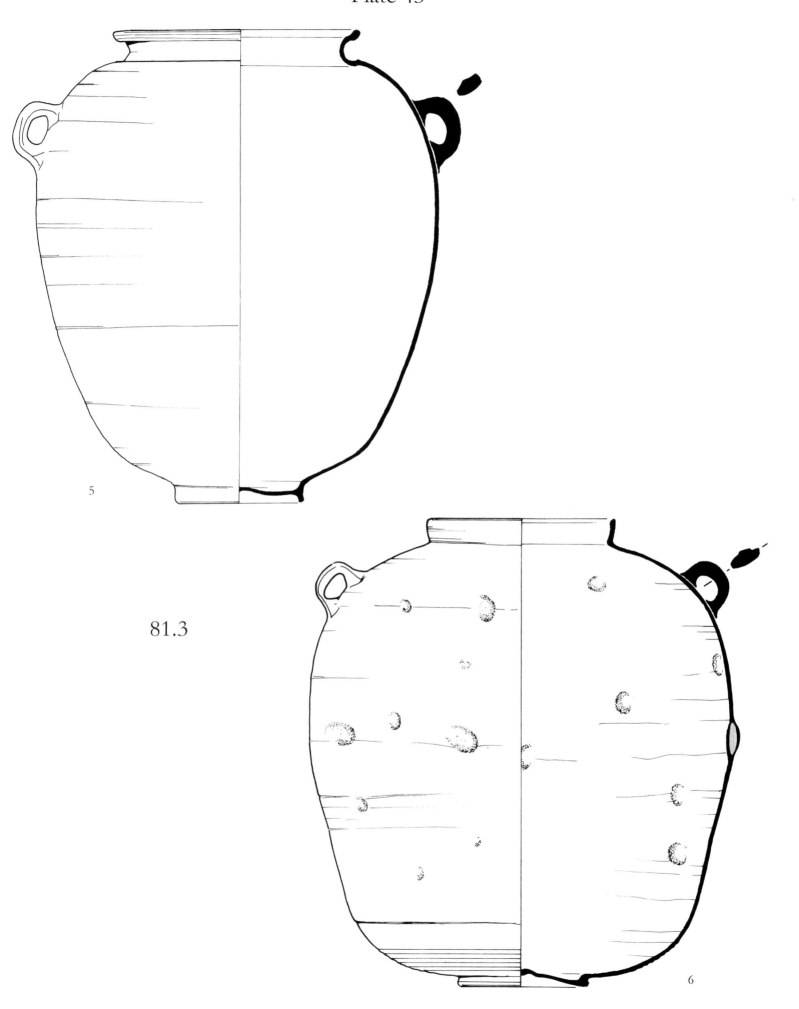

81.3

Locus 81-3, pottery, scale ¼

Plate 44

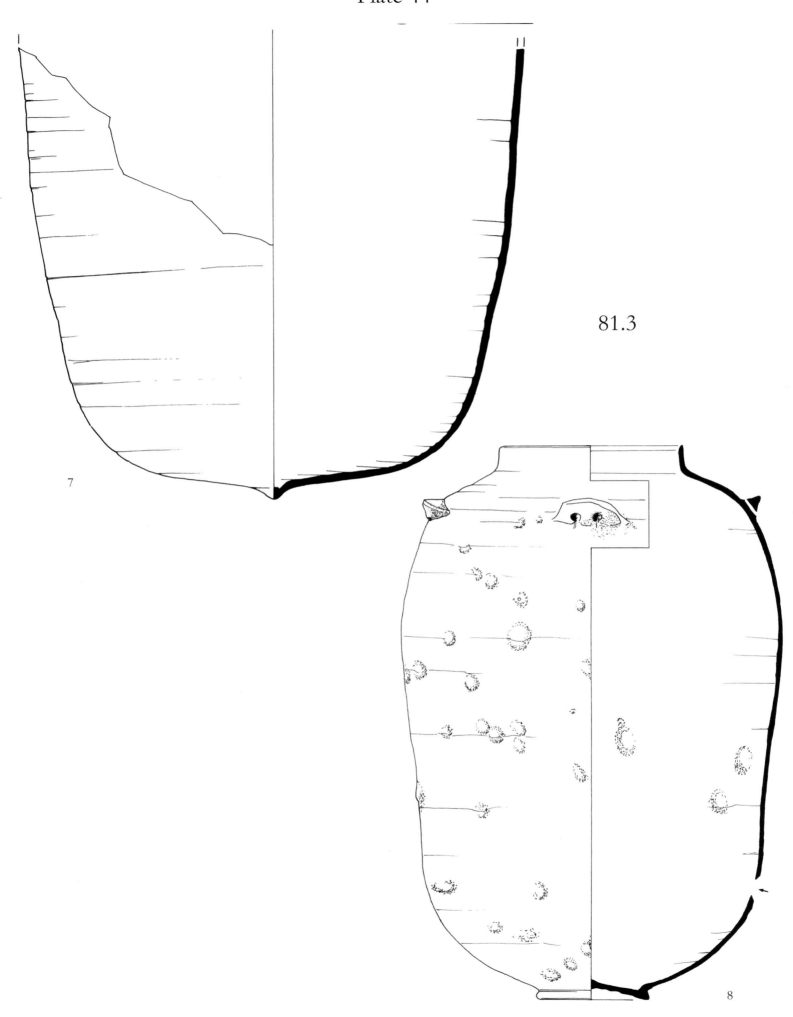

Locus 81-3, pottery, scale ¼

Plate 45

Plate 43, 5

Plate 43, 6

Plate 44, 7

Plate 44, 8

Locus 83 -3, photographs of pots

Plate 46

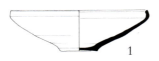
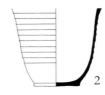

81.4

N° Pl.	N° Catal.	Position	Comments (archives)	Date	Description	Clay	Exterior
1	1533	81.4	L. 81	06/04/54	plate	° red earth	white
2	1499	81.4	L. 88	16/03/54	goblet	° grey earth	pink

Catalogue of pottery Locus 81-4   ° *According to de Vaux*

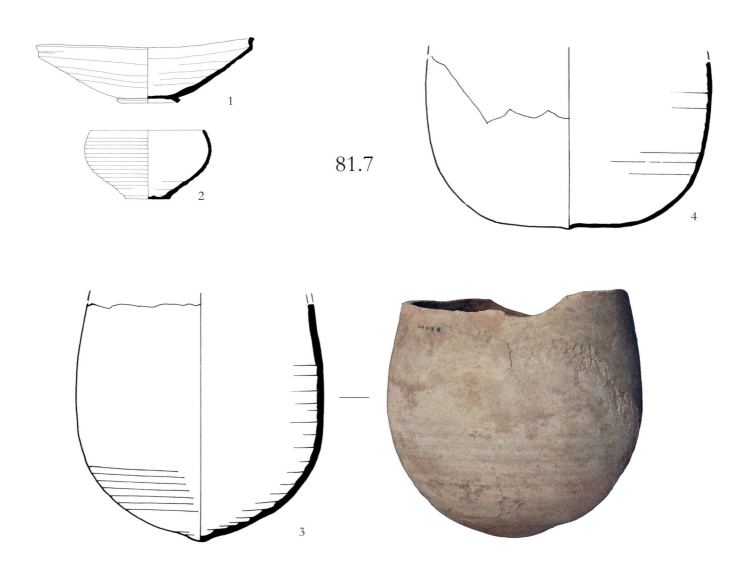

N° Pl.	N° Catal.	Position	Comments (archives)	Date	Description	Clay	Exterior
1	1624	81.7	L. 92	06/04/54	plate	° red earth	white
2	1623	81.7	L. 92	06/04/54	bowl	° grey earth	
3	1632	81.7	L. 92	06/04/54	jar	° red earth	
4	1633	81.7	L. 92	06/04/54	jar	not seen	

Catalogue of pottery Locus 81-7   ° *According to de Vaux*

Locus 81-4, pottery and catalogue, scale ¼

Plate 47

fig. 118.   Locus 82, jar KhQ 1634

N° Pl.	N° Catal.	Position	Comments (archives)	Date	Description	Clay	Exterior
1	1644	82.2/3	L82 niv. inf.	8/04/54	small dish	° red earth	
2	1634	82.2/3	L82 niv. sup.	7/04/54	jar	° red earth	
3	1649	82.2/3	L82 niv. sup.	07/04/54	limestone lid of jar 1634	stone	

° *According to de Vaux*

Locus 82, pottery and catalogue, scale ¼

Reservoir Locus 91

Pool L. 91 is a deep reservoir, the only one of this type at Qumran besides pool L. 58. An access corridor of six steps, L. 85, leads from L. 79-99 to a perpendicular drop of 3.50 m. The dimensions 12.6 x 4.6 x 5 m in depth gave it a capacity of almost 250 m^3. Its volume and its position precisely in the axis of the east wall of the residence are evidence of a well-planned project. It was placed encroaching on the half of the southwest corner of the residence which disappeared at the time of the restoration, because it was ruined, and because access to pools 56-58 required a clearance. The earthquake destroyed the water supply system. In L. 79, the inlet of the previous aqueduct 500 has completely disappeared, the late channel 805 has been pulled out in L. 104. The aqueduct which, upstream, crosses the building of the annexes (L. 110), starts a sharp turn to reach it. There is a good chance that 91 was for some time the culmination of the hydraulic system, marking a significant stage in the settlement's development. The culmination of a hydraulic system always includes a general overflow to avoid spills. L. 91 has its own 799, which crosses L. 92 and seems, on the Coüasnon *Plan*, to lose itself in L. 94; however, the clearance work of the 2000s has shown that the drain borders paving 816 of L. 90–93, and flows into cesspit 936 in L. 183, south of large pool 71. Cesspit 936 seems to be unsuitably distant from L. 91, but it had the advantage of not muddying the edges of the paving. It is appropriate at this point to indicate that when large pool 71 was the culmination of the hydraulic system, it possessed its own overflow, linked to the older cesspool 936.

We can see an evolution in the northern part of the reservoir, limited to the deep pool. In fact, if we accept that pools 56–58 form a later extension of the water system, L. 83 functioned as a redistribution pit necessary for supply by an alternative sluice with L. 91 on one side and L. 56–58 on the other. In the residual space the encroachment of L. 83 created corridor L. 85, the access to reservoir L. 91.

The relationship between L. 91 and L. 81 was discussed in our description of the latter and it is not easy to explain. What sort water do the three or four inspection openings collect that drop into L. 91? Is it rainwater? We cannot really see any other possibility. If it is true that the openings have the advantage of evacuating rainwater in an open space, it was simpler to direct the runoff via L. 88 towards the exterior, L. 94.

L. 91 is relatively early in the development of the hydraulic system, but it was disused after 68. Channel 500 crossing the outbuildings of the residence was doubled by channel 805, made of massive, rough-and-ready construction, which condemns L. 86 and seals L. 91. To do this, the reservoir was filled-in, and in Antiquity filling was heavy work: more than 250 m^3 of material had to be found and transported. It is to be regretted that de Vaux did not make any notes on the nature of the fill. He supposed that, after the revolt, a group of men reoccupying a ruined site only restored part of it. The central building, better constructed, will have been chosen and cleared as a priority, followed by the derelict surroundings, which will have provided the volume of debris needed for the fill. So the fill cannot be expected to have a stratification, even a disorderly one, that we might have been able to interpret. The reservoir was filled from different sides and materials were thrown in haphazardly. De Vaux needed seventeen days to empty a little over half of the basin, i.e., at least 150 m^3, which represents an extensive task. The uncompleted work was to prevent the collapse of channel 805 which the intention was to preserve.

The stratification of pool 91 is very simple. The backfill in a single block is 91.1 and what was collected at the bottom is 91.4. The excavation *Journal* fortunately notes that he recognized the layer at the bottom of L. 91: *We clear the bottom in the south part* (L. 91, 30/3/54), and *In section, we see the deposit of the cistern still in service then above it, discarded spoil* (L. 91, 1/4/54). We can accept that the pottery recorded on those two days, dropped into the pool before the year 68 should be assigned to the label 91.4. The other complete pots, or sherds preserved as samples, are the product of the large mixture we call 91.1, though homogeneously from pre-68 occupation.

The surroundings of south reservoir 91

fig. 119. Reservoir 91 looking towards the east with the staircase discovered in 2000 (photo 2015, Lionel Mochamps)

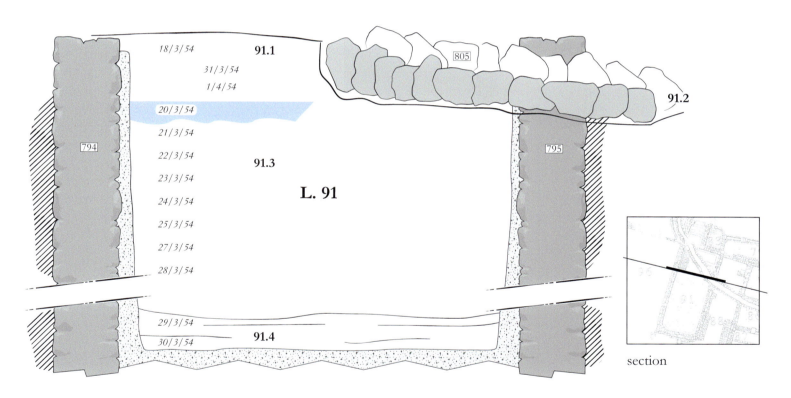

Restored elements	Level	Definition	Journal dates	Coins	Position	N°	Chronology
91.1	Post 4	Abandonment level	29/3/54		(no stratigraphic significance)		
				KhQ. 1504	upper level, north	1	First Revolt
91.2	4	Drain 805	See on L86	1506	upper level	1	Agrippa
				1521	in the backfill to the east	1	Proc. under Augustus
91.3	Post 3C	Filling-in of the reservoir	29-31/3/54	1563		1	Agrippa Ist
			1/4/54	1581-1582	near the ground	2	Agrippa Ist
91.4	3A/B/C	Construction of the reservoir		1583	near the ground	1	3rd cent.

Schema and stratigraphic diagram of Locus 91 (for the chart of symbols, see page 155)

N° Pl.	N° Catal.	Position	Comments (archives)	Date	Description	Clay	Exterior
1	1511	91.1	-	22/03/54	plate	° red earth	
2	4503	91.4	-	30/03/54	plate	red paste with grey core	red
3	4501	91.2	-	23/03/54	bowl	brown paste	red
4	1567	91.2	-	27/03/54	plate	° pink earth	pink
5	4510	91.2	-	22/03/54	small dish	orange paste	beige
6	4496	91.2	-	23/03/54	bowl	light brown paste, radiant shaped decoration	grey
7	4486	91.2	-	23/03/54	bowl	orange paste	beige engobe
8	1600	91.1	-	31/03/54	bowl	° red earth	
9	4494	91.2	-	23/03/54	bowl	orange paste	beige
10	1597	91.1	-	31/03/54	goblet	° grey earth	traces of white wash
11	4491	91.2	-	22/03/54	jug	red paste	light red
12	4492	91.2	-	22/03/54	jug	dark brown paste	beige
13	4485	91.1	-	31/03/54	jug	orange paste	beige-red
14	4497	91.2	-	27/03/97	jar	grey-brown paste	beige
15	4490	91.2	-	23/03/54	bowl	red paste	beige engobe
16	1605	91.1	L91	4/04/54	jug	° grey earth in section	pink wash
17	1627	91.1	L91	03/04/54	vessel	° red earth	
18	4507	91.4	-	29/03/54	jar	orange paste	red
19	1595	91.4	L91	30/03/54	two-handled pot	° red earth	white
20	4480	91.1	-	03/04/54	cooking pot	orange paste	brown
21	4495	91.2	-	28/04/54	cooking pot	dark brown paste	red
22	1593	91.4	L91	30/03/54	pipe	° pink earth	pink
23	4493	91.2	-	23/03/54	jar	brownish-red paste	brownish-red
24	4488	91.2	-	23/03/54	crater	orange paste	beige
25	4508	91.2	-	23/03/54	jar	red paste with grey core	beige-red
26	4511	91.2	-	27/03/54	lid	brownish-red paste	beige
27	4482	91.2	-	23/03/54	jar	dark brown paste	beige engobe
28	4484	91.2	-	23/03/54	jar	red paste with grey core	reddish-beige
29	4483	91.2	-	23/03/54	jar	dark brown paste	light brown
30	4505	91.2	-	23/03/54	goblet	brown paste	beige-red
31	4500	91.2	-	27/03/54	bowl	red paste	beige engobe
32	4489	91.2	-	22/03/54	crater	dark brown paste	beige engobe
33	4487	91.2	-	23/03/54	crater	dark brown paste	beige, burnt
34	4498	91.2	-	27/03/54	jar	red paste with grey core	beige-red
35	4499	91.2	-	27/03/54	jar	red paste	red
36	4509	91.2	-	27/03/54	jar	orange paste	beige

Catalogue of pottery Locus 91   ° *According to de Vaux*

Plate 48

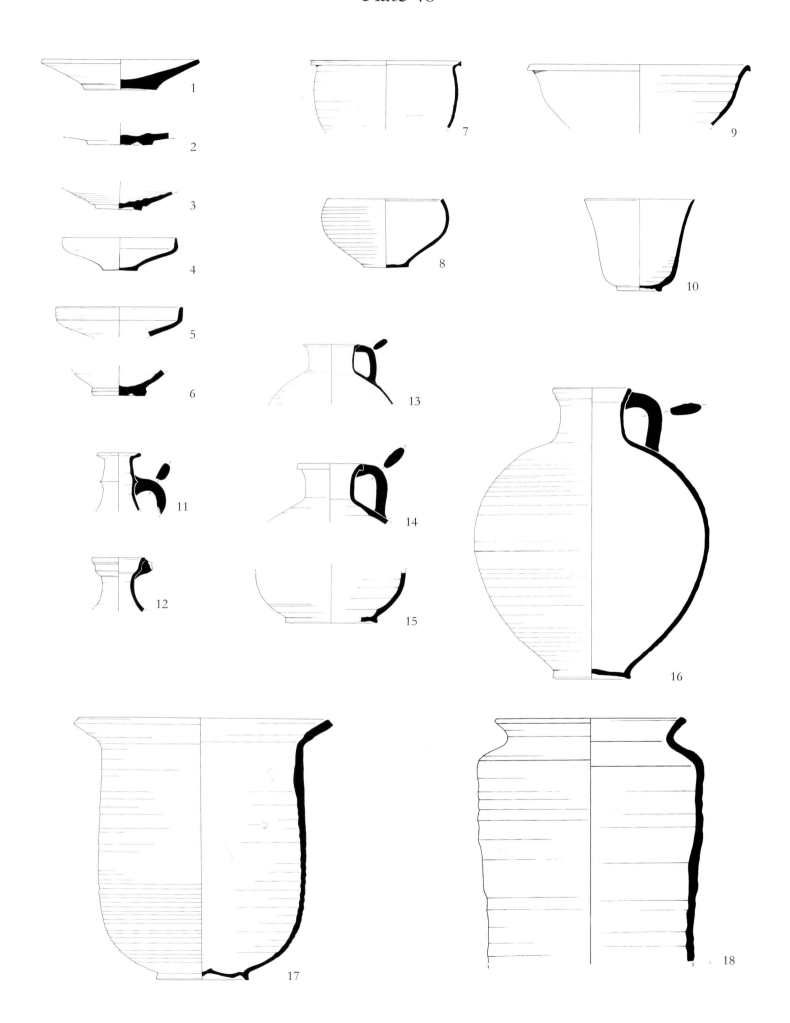

Locus 91, pottery, scale ¼

Plate 49

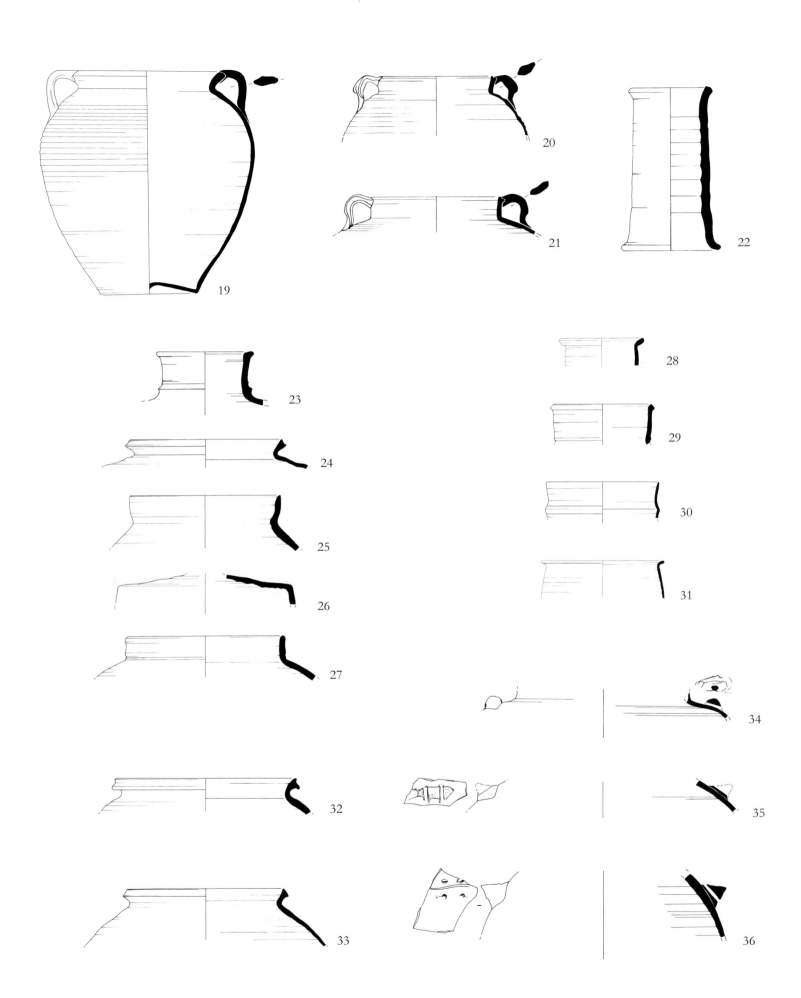

Locus 91, pottery, scale ¼

Loci 83 and 85

L. 83 is a pool for supply and distribution. L. 85 is a stepped access point for reservoir L. 91. L. 83, 85 and 91 form a coherent whole, constructed in two goes; they were filled at the same time; the late diversion of channel 805 seals L. 91 and condemns L. 85. The collection of masonry of the three loci reveals an evolution in the canalization. The location was radically reworked because, at the site of L. 83, the demolished corner to the southwest of the main Hasmonaean building has to be restored. The space was reallocated to simplify the water distribution. Reservoir L. 91 was the culmination of the aqueduct, and channel 500 overflowed into it without further extension. The addition of L. 83 had become necessary when pools 56–58 were established: L. 83 was designed to direct the flow downstream, towards pools 56–58, which then became dependent on reservoir 91.

Locus 83

L. 83 was excavated in three days, or rather in two days, 11 and 13/3/54, Friday 12th being a day off, and 29/3/54 being devoted to finishing work and clearance of the diversion outlets (L. 83, 14/3/54). The emptying of its 5 m³ capacity was quick: here again we can verify the speed of the excavation conducted at Qumran, an echo of which is found in the conciseness of the *Journal*. About the opening on the first day, we read: *To the west of L. 82 a small cistern opens. We find eighteen bronze coins and a silver Neronian coin* (L. 83, 11/3/54). We learn from the entries in the *Catalogue* that coins were lying on the ground, so the meaning must be: *at the bottom of the pool. Several more coins of the First Revolt come out* (L. 83, 13/3/54). They obviously come from a hoard and are not scattered coins.

If we only read the *Journal*, which reports that coins were found on the 11th, the first day of the excavation of the pool, we would have had to believe that the pieces were rather close *to the surface*, and then that those collected on the 13th were scattered at different depths. The preliminary report of the 1954 season is more descriptive: *In L. 83 (...) they were mixed with spoil and sherds, (...) they were thrown there by the new occupants of Period III when they were cleaning the large building*[79]. The filling of the pool was not caused by a roof having collapsed nor by the collapse of upper parts of the masonry as the installation was not covered, there being no need. The pool was intentionally filled and the coins would have been buried by those who filled it, not noticing them (*they were thrown*) while clearing a location elsewhere where they had originally been buried; this is what *mixed with spoil* seems to mean. The details fortunately given on the record cards assure us that each coin was found *on the ground*, so we know that they were lying on the floor of the pool reached on the first day. On the second day, the pool's full clearance was completed. In the *Revue Biblique* 1956 report (p. 566) we read that the coins were *mixed (...) with sherds* and we can believe this: the workers took care of the bottom of a pool, where fragments of vessels dropped into the water are commonly found. The coins really are *at the bottom*, their abandonment preceding the filling-in of L. 83 and not vice versa.

The hoard in 83.2 was hidden before 68, i.e. at the very end of level 3C. The abandonment of Qumran, following complex events, makes sense of this burial, while de Vaux's proposal that the deposition was an inadvertent act is without significance. It remains the case that the bottom of a pool is not really a suitable place to preserve an amount of money whose value was known. L. 83 is a distribution pool which did not conserve water because of strong evaporation. Either the coins were thrown into a bottom of dirty water which concealed them, with the hope of recovering them after a short delay; or the pool was not cleaned

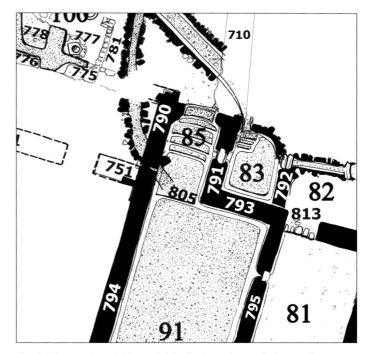

fig. 120. Loci 83 and 85, designation of the walls

---

79. De Vaux, *RB* 1956, p. 567.

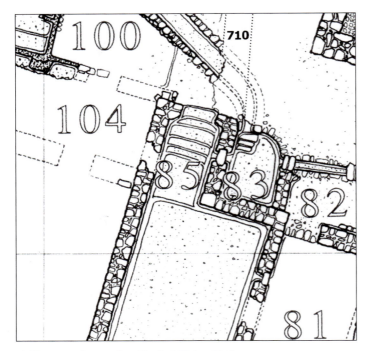

a) Excerpt from plan Period II by Coüsanon

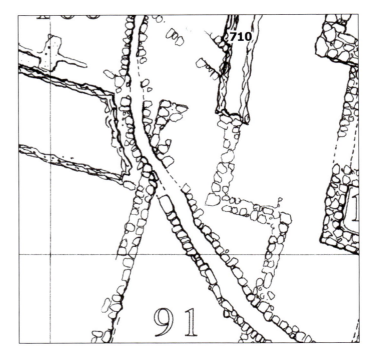

b) Excerpt from plan Period III by Coüsanon

fig. 121.   Loci 83 and 85, plans

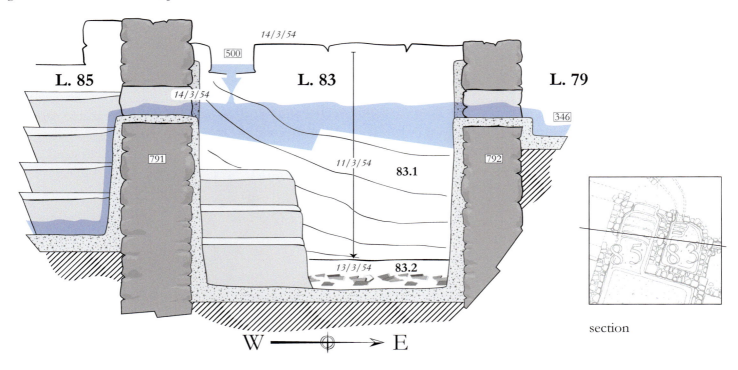

section

Restored elements	Level	Definition	Journal dates	Coins	Position	N°	Chronology
83.1	Post 3C	Filling-in	11-13/3/54	KhQ. 1327-1344, 1356-1363	near the floor	25	First Revolt
				1364 and 1395	near the floor	2	Agrippa I[st]
				1345	near the floor	1	Proc. under Nero
				1365-1366	near the floor	2	Proc. under Claude/ Tiberius
83.2	3C	Vessel from the bottom of the pool	13/3/54				

Schema and stratigraphic diagram of Locus 83 (for the chart of symbols, see page 155)

out, and the hoard was buried in the deposit of silt, moist or dry, which hid the bottom of the pool. In either case, everything points to an action performed in haste.

Locus 85

L. 85 was condemned with L. 91, by the restorers of the habitation of Level 4. The late diversion of drain 805 was installed on the top of the backfill. The filling-in of the two loci, coming close to 250 m³, results from the clearance of the ruin; it presents a disordered stratification and nothing that comes from it can be regarded as stratified. De Vaux was right to retain only ten or so pots from the enormous block of L. 91. L. 85 was leveled but the backfill had sealed, on the steps descending into the reservoir, the remains of ash and pottery crushed in their correct stratigraphic position. They testify to the ruin in 68 and signal the end of Level 3C. De Vaux notes the destruction by fire: *ash and fire debris* (L. 85, 23/3/54). The fire is not obvious and we may see this as the result of slow combustion. The stratigraphic sequence, reservoir – fall of roofing with ash – filling-in – laying of drain 805, is in place here; the ash is the remains of the vegetable roofing and we infer from this that the reservoir and its lobby were covered, which no restoration shows. It would be astonishing if only L. 85 had been under cover. The indication of the pottery is notable: *We clear the steps on which there were remains of at least three jars and a goblet* (L. 85, 29/3/54). The latter is catalogued for L. 85 (29/3/54). De Vaux did not record the rest of the jars.

By chance, some sherds were preserved and we have been able to retrieve them. We can state without hesitation that they belong to the end of Level 3C. We present them in association with element 91.2, as they were sealed by backfill 91.1 (fig. 122). The excavator had preserved only necks of jars with a large opening. There are enough to assign them a function and the collection cannot be accidental: the jars with a large opening are water jars and they are accompanied by a goblet. Placed in the lobby of the reservoir, jars and goblet here were intended to quench the thirst of the inhabitants of the premises. May we add that a single goblet would indicate that the inhabitants in question could not have been numerous? Reservoir L. 91, therefore, was reserved for drinking water. De Vaux decided not to excavate it completely, so as to preserve the diversion of aqueduct 805 from Level 4 which partly covers it. Full excavation was done by the Israeli in the 2000s. They discovered a staircase in excellent condition which goes all the way to the bottom. So the staircase does not appear on the Coüasnon *Plans*. We have restored it for a better understanding of the water supply system (fig. 119, 123a). It is appropriate to indicate that the morphology of the pool is unique at Qumran, and yet identical to reservoirs of ancient and modern Palestine, with a landing to draw water vertically with pails, and a narrow staircase starting from the north to reach the low level of the water or to clean the bottom. The other pools at Qumran have steps across their whole width, an arrangement which helped identify them as ritual baths. It is probable that reservoir 91 is the earliest of the series and that the type with steps right across was adopted subsequently.

Finally, it should be noted that the excavation did not uncover the outlet of channel 500 in distribution pool L. 83: *The water came via the north and the channel-pool junction is very much destroyed* (L. 83, 14/3/54). The Coüasnon *Plan* of Period III, post-68, has taken account of a break in the masonry of channel 805 of Level 4. The *Plan* of Period II has left an important blank at the point where drain 500 joins L. 83. The break of 805 and the interruption of 500 are connected, confirming the impossibility of the supply of water, and also of habitation. This gap in the *Plans* corresponds precisely with the southern origin of de Vaux's *ancient* trench (L. 99, 22/3/55; L. 128, 29/3/55; L. 134, 5/4/55), where we see earthquake fault 3 (710) (fig. 121). We take from this supplementary proof that the earthquake was posterior to Level 4, i.e. post-68.

Plate 50

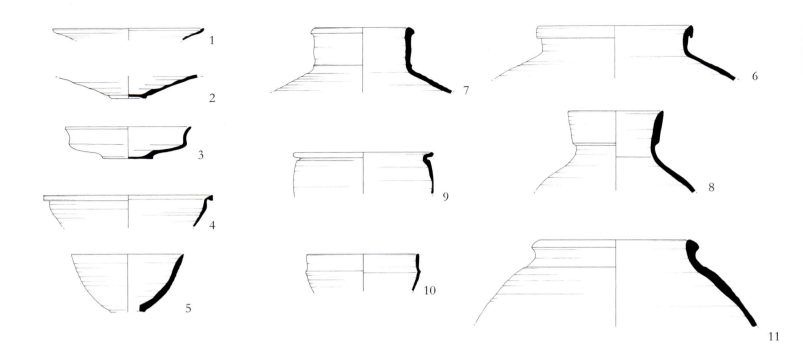

N° Pl.	N° Catal.	Position	Comments (archives)	Date	Description	Clay	Exterior
1	4402	83.2	-	13/03/54	plate	orange paste	light red
2	4405	83.2	-	13/03/54	plate	brown paste	beige-grey
3	1379	83.2	-	13/03/54	plate	° red earth	white
4	4396	83.2	-	13/03/54	bowl	orange paste	beige
5	4401	83.2	-	13/03/54	bowl	red paste with grey core	beige-red
6	4395	83.2	-	13/03/54	crater	red paste	beige engobe
7	4399	83.2	-	13/03/54	jar	red paste with grey core	light brown
8	4400	83.2	-	13/03/54	jar	red paste with grey core	beige engobe
9	4397	83.2	-	13/03/54	bowl	red paste with grey core	beige-red
10	4403	83.2	-	13/03/54	goblet	orange paste	beige-red
11	4394	83.2	-	13/03/54	jar	dark grey paste	beige and red

° *According to de Vaux*

KhQ. 4399, 7   KhQ. 4400, 8

Locus 83, pottery, catalogue and photographs, scale ¼

Plate 51

fig. 122. Smashed jars at the foot of the steps of Locus 85

L. 85

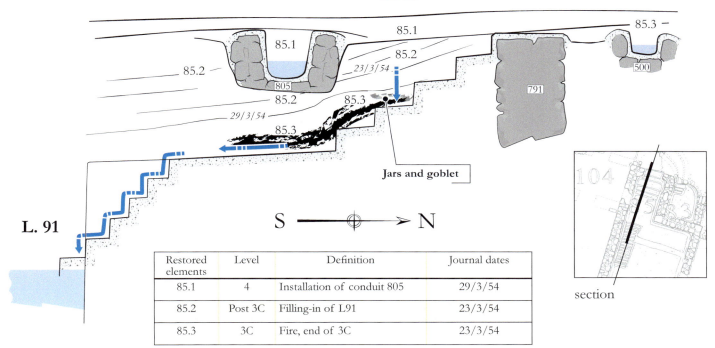

Restored elements	Level	Definition	Journal dates
85.1	4	Installation of conduit 805	29/3/54
85.2	Post 3C	Filling-in of L91	23/3/54
85.3	3C	Fire, end of 3C	23/3/54

Schema and stratigraphic diagram of Locus 85
(for the chart of symbols, see page 155)

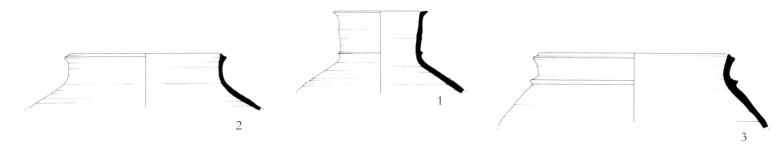

N° Pl.	N° Catal.	Position	Comments (archives)	Date	Description	Clay	Exterior
1	4360	85.3	-	23/03/54	jar	red paste with grey core	beige engobe
2	4358	85.3	-	23/03/54	jar	orange paste	beige engobe
3	4359	85.3	-	23/03/54	jar	brown-red paste	beige-pink

Locus 85, pottery and catalogue, scale ¼

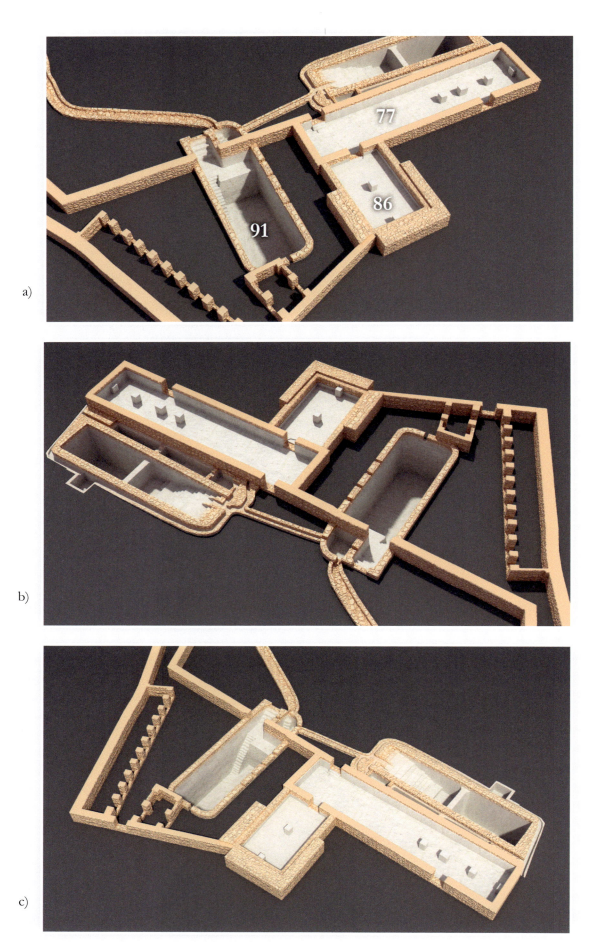

fig. 123. Axonometries of Loci 77, 86, 91 (Lionel Mochamps)

Chapter D

Two locations with an installation of presentation shelves

Locus 77, and locus 86 with divisions loci into 87, 89 and 185

Loci 86 (87 and 89) and 93 (90, 94 and 98) border the settlement to the south on one side, opening onto the terrace on the other. In Volume I, we called this space *the communitarian area* as, for reasons of internal consistency, it was more important that the composition of the photograph album of the excavation of the first volume should respect the archaeological formula defined by de Vaux: the excavation *Journal* commented on the *Album*. The communitarian structure of the site being without convincing support, however, the location loses this label which needs to be made more specific, and to be analysed and described in other ways.

Interpreting the area in the framework of cultural practice, as we propose, does not mean refusing a debate, but we try to argue for an intuition which opened another track when the hitherto convenient interpretation seemed no longer appropriate. We propose to follow it, but we do not insist on it. De Vaux had seen the large L. 86 and 77 as refectories or community rooms. The location does indeed betray a certain number of original features regarding position, construction, distribution, layout and function. There is in fact nothing comparable in Near Eastern archaeology to help us understand it, so caution is appropriate in view of the uniqueness of its function. Furthermore, the repeated restorations and the architectural modifications that affected it, among the most significant of the site, insert the area in a chronological framework; the place has a history, a reduction of spaces in stages, which presupposes a particular function. Still, the weakness of the archaeological arguments does not facilitate its interpretation.

The minutes of the excavation *Journal*, more detailed than elsewhere in relation to the work in L. 86 and 77, show the excavators' interest in the two long rooms explored from the 9th to the 31st March, i.e. during less than twenty working days. The evacuation of the upper layers was rapid as the *Journal* notes laconically on 15/3/54: *L. 77 finished*. An upper floor was recognized; then, in L. 77, a mortar floor was reached on the first day. Reading the *Journal* on L. 77 and 86, we note the excavator's assimilation of *period* and *level*, equivalent terms for him, but which lead to confusion. Two periods I and II then two floors I and II are recorded (15 and 28/3/54) and the conventions of data recording lead the reader to expect that *floor 1* is higher, more recent, the first to be cleared. But, on the contrary, de Vaux associates *floor II* with *period II* and *floor I* with *period I*. *Floor II* is thus more recent than *floor I*. We shall see below that the pillars in L. 77 were part of the initial project and we draw from this the conclusions reinforced by the similarity of the respective layouts in L. 77 and L. 86.

The stratification and the problem of chronology

As the stratification is not too churned up and the levels have been described, we still need to attempt an interpretation to examine very carefully the sequence of transformations of L. 86 because the general chronology of the site depends on it. The destruction of L. 89 by fire attributed to the earthquake of 31 BC

306 The archaeology of Qumran – an attempted reassessment

a) Upper floor 879

b) Lower floor 880

fig. 124.   Locus 77

was, for de Vaux, the pivot on which the chronology of Qumran rested. In his restoration, he had fixed the sequence in a logical and simple way. The two refectories had formed a unit which was broken in 31 BC with the blocking of L. 89 and its thousand pots. The destruction of 68 would hardly have affected L. 185. In de Vaux' Period III the diversion of the aqueduct had condemned the doors in the south wall of L. 77 to rehabilitate the elongated room. However, the sequence of the different constructed elements, so simple at first sight, needs to be substantially re-situated in time. If one takes account of the contrast between the poor quality of the masonry of the aqueduct and the care devoted to sealing the passage between L. 86/185 and L. 77, it seems doubtful that this would have been parts of the same building programme. The blocking of the doors was not necessarily subsequent to the new layout of the drain of Level 4. With the earthquake now rejected, the presence of coins from the mid-first century AD in close contact with the layer of ash prompts to shorten the chronological range of the century between 31 BC and AD 68. The succession of architectural modifications in L. 86, modified in L. 89-87 and L. 185, took place, on the contrary, in a much shorter space of time, namely just before 68 (blockage of L. 89) up to the re-installation in L. 77. The set of coins found in L. 86 and L. 185 proves that the partition of L. 86 into L. 89/185 cannot be much earlier than 68, i.e. the end of Level C. The mass of ash covering L. 89-87 and also L. 185 very likely points to the destruction of 68; at least to an accidental fire in the very last years before 68. If the ash of L. 89 is from the year 68, L. 185 above the ash would then be posterior to 68, and should be placed in Level 4. The question then arises as to when and who, after 68, blocked the door between L. 185 and L. 77 and restored the plastered wall of L. 77, and who at what time restored drain 805. We have to accept that the occupation in L. 185 was short in duration; it would witness to an intermediate occupation between the destruction of 68 and the re-installation in L. 77, as L. 185 was put to new use by the construction of drain 805 during Level 4. We know that its installation was precarious and that the pottery cannot be decisive for dating, as before and after 68 it had no reason to be different.

The remaining alternative is to give up this fragile chronological arrangement and to accept the interpretation which we had previously adopted without considering the numismatic argument, taking it that the layer of ash in L. 86 and L. 89 antedates the year 68. The successive condemnations of spaces may be conceived of as more spread out in time. It may have been produced by a fire, but we find it hard to believe that such a confined fire would have led to cutting off the bottom of L. 86. The elements of rafters lying carbonized on the level of the plastered floor and the mass of ash may have resulted from the slow combustion of the roofing and of a thick layer of vegetation protecting the stack of pots. In L. 89 the ash covers the stacked vessels, while in the northern part of L. 86, under L. 185, the rafters have fallen to the floor. In this case, L. 185 would be pre-68 and it would be very surprising if the destruction of 68 that supposedly affected it left no traces. The blocking of the door between L. 185 and L. 77 would also be pre-68 along with the repairs to its plastering. Consequently, during the re-installation, post-68 L. 77 will have been inhabited but separated from the reduced complex of the buildings of Level 4, and downgraded.

308 The archaeology of Qumran – an attempted reassessment

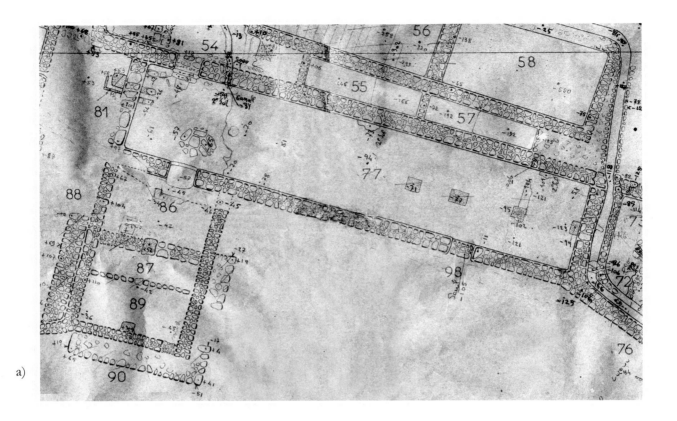

a)

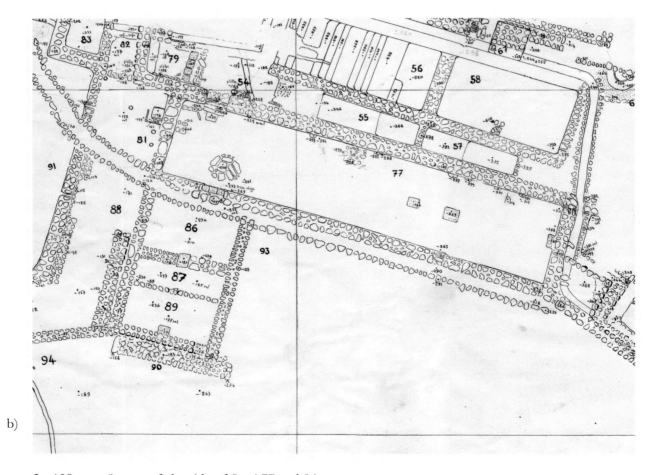

b)

fig. 125. Survey of the side of Loci 77 and 86
 a) survey 1 south sector
 b) survey 2 - 1954

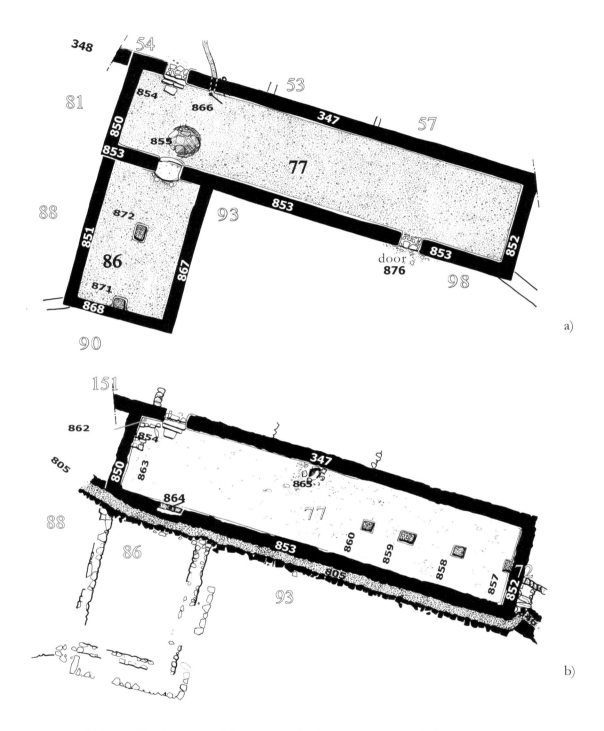

fig. 126. Designation of the walls and of some constructed elements (L. 77 and 86)

fig. 127.   South front of the settlement: Locus 79 to the foreground and 77 then 86 to the rear

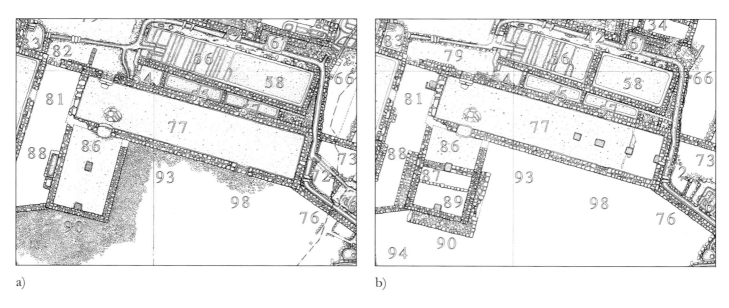

fig. 128.   a) Periods Ib and b) II (Coüasnon 1954)

Locus 77:
The longest locus of the settlement

Description of the remains

1 – The building

The original building of the residence, the homogeneous line of which has been preserved, was partly masked by late and composite stretches of masonry; the Coüasnon *Plan* of Period III groups them, rightly, in an occupation phase posterior to 68, i.e. our Level 4. One cannot separate L. 77 from them in a way that makes it difficult to place L. 77 within the stratigraphy, since the final floors have either not been preserved or remained undetected by the excavators. Some poorly described elements may be traces of them, but they cannot serve as reference point for anything, nor even barely so.

On the other hand, the underlying layers in well preserved L. 77 and 86 form an architectural block adjoining the south wall of the main building. It is not clear if this block was designed in one go and there is no proof that the two loci, though elaborated in the same layout, are strictly contemporary. The preservation of the stretches of masonry attracts attention because of the evenness of their surfaces, unlike the former residence which they abut, the ruinous relief which follows the height of the walls, the fall of which had preserved the low parts. On the contrary, L. 77 and L. 86, collapsed on themselves, lay on an evenly flattened mass, which the aerial photograph confirms (fig. 133). The site had not suffered any pillaging; the ruin was intact at the time of the excavations. The rough earth superstructure will have melted onto the preserved beds of stone. It follows that the locations concerned did not support a floor and that the meagre amount of fallen material is testimony to this. Everything points to the fact that the stone masonry has remained intact and that it was only the collapse of the rough brick superstructures that show the regular and tabular profile that we see (fig. 124a and 140a). We could have imagined the two rooms as open-air courtyards, no cover being necessary given the occasional use we are proposing to attribute to them. However, the accumulation of vessels immersed in a mass of ash and the remains of burnt timber in L. 89, and the care devoted to blocking L. 87 and L. 185 convince us that these rooms were covered.

Wall 850 which closes L. 77 to the west, is one of the few in the whole settlement to present an ashlar of large blocks laid as headers. We do not know the reasons for this: only long wall 951, which closes the southern terrace, is comparable to it. Such an anomaly should have been noted. The sabre-cuts would testify to a condemned passageway, unless originally the L. was mainly open to the west via an earth platform predating L. 81 for which there is no evidence. We shall see below that other points of access served the premises and that its circulation was modified.

2 – The floors

The two floors recognized during the excavation, tied to the installations in L. 77, allow us to confidently restore two levels. We have said that late floors may have eroded and that the profile of the end of occupation might have faded away. Fig. 126a sketches a plan where some elements have elevation marks; we list these with reference to the *Journal*: 865 ... *against the north wall, perhaps debris from a kiln?* (13/3/54); 863 ... *in the northwest corner [...] two alignments of stones with the ash: a hearth?* (15/3/54); ... *a circle paved with large stones* ... (15/3/54); 857 ... *against the east wall [...] a rectangular brick pilaster* (10/3/54). Then, three pillars are mentioned in succession: from east to west 858, 859 and 860; finally two floors of coated mortar: the upper one 879 with elevations - 257 m, -261 m and -267 m, and the lower one 880 with elevations -291 m, -299 m and -301 m. They are separated by a thick fill, estimated at 30 cm. Upper floor 879 was a radical restoration while lower floor 880 was defective: *The plaster of the lower level is poorly preserved, but better than that of the upper level* (L. 77, 25/3/54). The solidity of the mortar walls depends on the density of their support or on the resistance of their coverings and we conclude from this that at both stages the work lacked quality. On the photograph (fig. 129b), a correct bed of river pebbles, which levels a bed of regularly placed small stones, fills the space between the two floors: the care given to the construction of floor 879 confirms that this was not a simple surface repair but a full-scale restoration.

It needs to be shown that the pillars belong to the initial layout of L. 77. The fact that upper floor 879 was a restoration of the premises does not confirm de Vaux's proposal according to which the installation of the pillars

a) Connection of the central piedestal with the 883 floor of Locus 86

b) Remains of two successive floors 879 and 880

c) The preserved plaster coating in the northwest corner of the Locus 77

d) Trace of pillars in the ground 879 (photo enlarged)

e) The plasterwork preserved against wall 852 (to the east)

fig. 129.   Floors and mortars of the walls, Loci 77 and 86

was the work of restorers of a site reoccupied after an abandonment. At first sight, his demonstration may have been persuasive: *The three pillars and the pilaster of the east wall are (...) founded directly on the plaster of period I. They are from period II (28/3/54).* But why are they then founded on inferior mortar? According to de Vaux, the builders were shoring up roofing or a floor weakened by the earthquake: *the collapsed upper floor: there was a first floor* (L. 86, 22/3/54). The earthquake separates periods I and II. The hypothesis is open to question as the transition between the two periods was smooth (see on L. 72) without any earthquake or abandonment. The unique layout of the pillars of L. 77 also occupies L. 86, unaffected by any restoration, while here too the repairs would have been necessary after the earthquake. In L. 86, pillar and pilaster rest on a single mortar floor without any underlying level; the photographs attest to their good preservation and finishing (fig. 129a); it is clear that no restoration took place with them. The pillars are indeed associated with lower floor 880.

3 – The mortar coatings

The continuation of the investigation leads us to examine the coating on the walls. It is to be regretted that the mortars were not the object of any comment during the excavation. An observation on the better condition of their preservation would have helped refine our opinion. We may add that their fragile state and a rather rough excavation technique – pickaxe strokes cut into the coatings – hamper good observation of the photograph. To what extent can one associate the walls coating with any levels or a particular stage of occupation? The coating sealing the blocked doors in L. 77 testifies to a restoration post-68 (c'/d). The photographs (fig. 127 and 129e) show damaged coatings. However, despite their condition, they seem to clad the walls following three horizontal bands, the evenness of which is striking and can hardly be accidental. Two bands of white coating frame an inserted strip of what could be the pisé of a support. On the lower band we see a strip of lime mortar linked to the original floor 880 (a/a') which was quite well preserved reaching to a height of 50 cm (fig. 124b). One can see in it the upper border of the coating with its marked fold, extending to the east against the wall visible to the left of the photo (fig. 129e); photograph fig. 129d suggests a similar one band was applied to wall 852 at the east wall of L. 77.

The low part of coating would have protected the foot of the walls when cleaning with large amounts of water: according to de Vaux, sluice gate 866 piercing wall 347 served to flood or purify the premises. The system of floor washing foreseen in the original phase and linked to floor 880, was also modified. Supply was cut when main aqueduct 346 was extended in L. 79, downgrading diversion 356 towards L. 77 (fig. 131); the sluice gate was sealed by a more or less square stone (fig. 131d). No drainage collector was identified in L. 77. We do not know if it existed or if it was dismantled. The consequence is that the interruption of the washing confirms the change of function of the premises at the time of the post-68 restoration.

The inserted band of pisé would be a crude coating on top of the mortar of the plinth. It is right to think that the whole roughcast was of mortar and that its support on the wall gave way on a string course, the only element to have been badly prepared. The northwest corner of L. 77 indeed displays a complete roughcast (fig. 129c). It is manifest, moreover, that the lower edge of the intermediate pisé corresponds to floor 879 of the restoration.

L. 86, however, once contemporary with L. 77 and built to the same model, was better preserved at the time of the excavations thanks to having been blocked; the original state of the walls had been maintained (fig. 140c). The mortar plinth is intact here, with a well-marked upper edge, and the coating continues upwards in crude pisé. In this case, the lower coatings would protect the bottom of the walls when washed with large amounts of water.

This proposal still leaves the reason for the upper band of mortar open. Its horizontal bottom edge is so straight that one hesitates to think it was accidental (c'/d). It testifies to the last, significant restoration in L. 77 which blocked the doors. Would a mortar re-covering the top of the walls after blocking L. 86 have whitewashed only the former strip of pisé? *The fill (...) is (...) finished with a coating of pisé and a layer of lime* (L. 86, 18/3/54). We accept that the presence of mortar of the upper band militates in favour of a rehabilitation of L. 77 after 68. The lower edge of the upper band may correspond to the unidentified floor of L. 77 on Level 4 after 68. The string course of inserted pisé, on the other hand, would be a witness to the layer of destruction/abandonment under a Level 4 floor. The most recent mortar coating blocked door 856 in south wall 853 and is attached lower down: it confirms that the last restoration, posterior to the blockage, implies that L. 77 would have been maintained over a long period. De Vaux proposed a re-occupation after 68.

a) The condemned door 856

b) The condemned door 876

c) The external blocking of the door 876 (to Loc. 98)

d) The mudbrick blocking of the door 856 (from Loc. 86)

e) The earliest passage in door 856 (to Loc. 86)

f) The blocking of the door 856 (from Loc. 77)

fig. 130.　　The blocked doors of Locus 77

The archaeologist had attributed a restored L. 77 to the post-68 period. That the building was used after 68 is likely, but in what condition? At a late stage a number of walls redesigned the space between the main building and L. 77 when the site was re-occupied. To the northwest, we have called this *intermediate space L. 151*, closed to the west by wall 349 (see pl. III). De Vaux's Period III shows it as an undefined area, certainly an exterior. We accept the covered perimeter of the re-installation as presented on Coüasnon *Plan* III, in the former residence without L. 151 and with L. 77 separated from the building complex. We do not, however, understand the function of L. 77 outside an inhabited perimeter, restored with the blocking of doors and coatings of lime-washed walls. Would the blocking of doors and the new coating be from before 68? This raises the question of the establishment, quality and organization of Level 4 (i.e, de Vaux's period III).

*The layouts
in the transformation of the premises*

1 – Installations with pedestals

In L. 77 and 86, the presence of preserved pillars in a regular shape and in a somewhat illogical position did not hold the attention of the excavators, nor that of commentators. Their place in the architectural fabric requires comment.

The excavation *Journal* remains inconclusive regarding the link between pillars and floors I (800) or II (879), but decides to attribute the pillars to a precise phase: they are from period II (L. 77, 28/3/54). But the role of support pillar needs to be dropped; we shall return to this (see on L. 86). Reading Coüasnon's *Plans* of Ib, II and III, the pillars or pedestals do not seem to always have the same function in L. 77 and L. 86. According to the Coüasnon plans, in Period Ib L. 86 has pillars and L. 77 does not; in Period II, L. 77 has pillars. Should we accept the implicit conclusions the *Plans* draw about them, namely that L. 86 was cluttered with props before L. 77 that their function was necessary in L. 86 and not in L. 77 If we accept the hypothesis of simple pedestals, or of another layout not for support, are we to believe that their function was abandoned in L. 86 only to be maintained in L. 77? It seems not; we must, on the contrary, take it that L. 86 was an addition to L. 77; the discontinuity of the function in the two locations is no longer an issue. For period Ib, Coüasnon's *Plan* omits the pillars in L. 77 – we shall show that they are original – while, paradoxically, he includes them in L. 86 (fig. 128). In Period II, he introduces them in L. 77, while he rejects them in L. 86. In Period III, they are kept in L. 77, while L. 86 is shown in ruins. Their presentation seems to be without a logical train of thought.

The pedestals are associated with deep floor 880 and are original to L. 77. In a location where a specific arrangement is foreseen, the normal work sequence is first to construct the floor as a whole in the whole available space between the walls, then to create the layout on the hardened floor. So it is normal that the pedestals, standing directly on the freshly finished floor, should be associated with it without a foundation (fig. 129a). They relate to two successive points in a same process of construction. De Vaux's hypothesis has reversed the procedure: the pillars were initially constructed on a former floor – then the backfill was brought in – and associated with upper floor 879.

The pedestals of L. 77 are therefore linked to lower floor 880, and it is probable that they were not preserved during the restoration and the laying of floor 879. From the reminder that (...) *they were then encased by the gravel and plastered floor* (L. 77, 28/3/54, 29/3/54)[80], we must understand that on upper *floor II* (879) (the *Journal* not specifying which), the surface of the pedestals was marked; de Vaux evidently thought they were pointed. We have highlighted them on the photograph by enhancing the contrast (fig. 129d). Upper floor 879 was finished after leveling-off the pillar-pedestals. That L. 77 was deprived of pillar-pedestals after restoration reinforces our decision on the architectural evolution of the premises, and drops the support function of pillars as, without further explanation, they are no longer necessary supports after restoration.

2 – The Doors: Wandering and re-allocation of the space

At a given moment, circulation in L. 77 was radically modified. The Coüasnon *Plans* prioritize the circulation in periods Ib, II and III from the interior of the settlement and the access to L. 77 via L. 79 (and not L. 54, as erroneously stated in the *Journal*). Main access 854 is a *beautiful door (...) We collect curved plastered elements*

---

80. Erratum: correct 28 and 29 of *Qumrân*, Vol. I

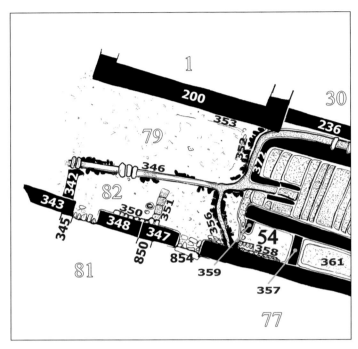
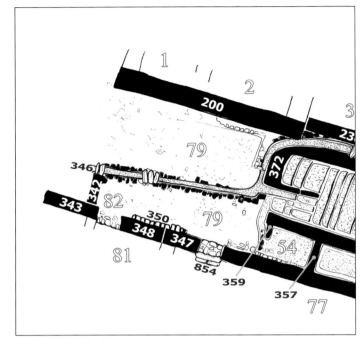

a) The channel 356 is linked to channel 346

b) Drain decommissioning 356

c) Loc. 54: the edge of the channel 346 (middle) cancels the pipe 356, and the outlet 866 (Loc. 77)

d) The exit of outlet 866 is closed by a stone (Loc. 77)

fig. 131. Construction and condemnation of supply 356 of Locus 77

which may come from the corners (L. 77, 9/3/54). The break in level is at 75 cm when *we clear the staircase which descends into the room from L. 54 [sic] [= L. 79]: we count five steps* (15/3/54, fig. 129c). The incline corrects the natural slope. It should be noted that main entrance 854 was perhaps originally only a service door, an internal, secondary passage. It was able to become the sole access only after the closure or conversion of the other two doors; it provides access to L. 77, then door 856 leads to L. 86. It seems indeed paradoxical that to reach 77–86 one had to walk through a cluttered layout which required crossing the projection of the aqueduct, when the dimensions of L. 77 show that it was intended for the use by large numbers of people.

The paved south terrace was not always an enclosed space and protected inside the settlement precincts, as long wall 951 closed off an open space and divided L. 77 in a southerly direction. The whole of L. 77-86, which opened to the esplanade, would have corresponded to the paving laid as a reception area. So we propose that the most logical original access to L. 77 from the exterior would have been via L. 93-98, with no need to cross the settlement. It looks as if the people using L. 77 were visitors, not residents.

Door 876 enters L. 77 from L. 93/98. It was blocked during the restoration of L. 77 (fig. 130b). The inside blockage was botched, the stacked pebbles, without a bed, are masked by a coat of mortar. On the contrary, the outside blockage, better built with sized stones, leads us to understand that at one point it was cleared as a façade before the late aqueduct 805 bordered it (fig. 130c). The door does not fit in the axis of the layout of pedestals, which are positioned in harmony along the east-west arrangement of the room. Bumping into pedestals as one entered would have undermined the layout of the spaces; comings and goings would have been confused. Door 876 is better thought of as an exit for a visitor having accomplished what he came for. In this case, we may go so far as to propose that door 856, which communicates with L. 86, was logically the original entrance of L. 77. The circle of stones (fig. 132b) seems indeed to confirm the priority of the passageway, marking the individual's position directly in front of the entrance. And door 876 to L. 93 would have been consonant with the logical purpose of the exit.

Proposing the original entry via door 856 into a space re-organized in this way, requires that L. 86 was not yet built up. The fact that doors 876 and 856 were carefully blocked obliges us to review the evolution of the circulation. Nothing proves that L. 86 was designed at the same time as L. 77: that it leans on it makes it more recent, even if only by a little. The repair of aqueduct 805 after the ruin of 68 cut the junction of walls 851 and 867 with the south wall of L. 77: the mode of support of L. 86 on L. 77 is no longer verifiable. However, it can be taken as an argument in favour of L. 86 being built as a support. Wall 853 of L. 77 has preserved its rectilinear facing where wall 867 would have been connected; we cannot verify it to the west where its edge is chipped by aqueduct 805. Finally, L. 86 erection in this corner position would have been favoured by an already established access 856.

Passageway 856 does not guarantee that L. 77 and 86 are contemporary. The floor of L. 86 is some 30 cm higher than the former floor 880 of L. 77. We note that the repair of L. 77 then aligns floor 879, more or less, with the level of L. 86, although the equivalence between the elevations could be by chance. The blocking of the door by the bed of aqueduct 805 did not completely destroy the layout of the passage, without which it is no longer possible to verify the presence of a potential original threshold, because the location is now destroyed. De Vaux cleared the mortar linking the two loci without taking deeper sondages. In any case, the good condition in which threshold is seen before being blocked (fig. 130e) does not allow us to restore to it sockets for two door leaves anchored in symmetrical cavities: ... *on the north side where the siting of a piece of wood is hollowed in negative. We can even see the trace of two pins which, towards the middle, fixed the piece of wood* (L. 86, 18/3/54). It is best to see this as the recess for two wooden posts of a doorjamb. Furnished with a single door leaf, the passage was not free.

The condemnation of door 856, unlike that of door 876, had been made with more care (fig. 130f.). Coüasnon's *Plan* of Period III, according to de Vaux, establishes it as a modification rendered necessary by the diversion of the aqueduct restored after 68: *The passage was blocked up in the course of period III, at the time of the construction of the late channel* (L. 86, 16/3/54). Photograph fig. 132a underlines the coarse constitution of the northern edge of the aqueduct, ignoring the blockage when it crosses L. 86: *The room has been cut by the bad channel which runs along L. 77 (...) and (...) a bad channel, which clips the southeast corner of L. 77, cuts room 86* (L. 86, 16/3/54). On the other hand, the

fig. 132. a) Aqueduct 805 crossing Locus 185 (86)
b) Stone circle 855 in front of threshold 856 and reduced sondage.
c) Debris from kiln 865 in L. 77

inside facing of door blocage inside L. 77 is a partition fitted with rough bricks (fig. 130f), recessed to accept a thick roughcast, coated in turn with a lime mortar. The coating seems associated with the upper string course (fig. 130a)). Bearing in mind that the blocking of 856 seals L. 86 with its movable objects intact, one can see the coating as the disguising of the wall.

Chronology

1 – Evolution of the installations

What was the relation between L. 77 and L. 86? In the hypothesis by which L. 86 is an addition, at what point in time can one situate its construction? The different modifications which affected L. 77 and L. 86 give us information on the displacement or interruption of their respective use. They were the object of re-workings in the course of an identifiable evolution, and we are unable to decide between a radical reorganization or one that took place in stages: sensitive lifting of the floor in L. 77, condemnation of the two doors 856 and 876, and finally new plastering of the walls of L. 77 to seal their blocking-up. After the erection of L. 77 with its pedestals, two modes of juxtaposition in the space are possible : either L. 77 and L. 86 were in use at the same time, and then the function of L. 86 was maintained at the expense of that of L. 77. Or the interruption of the activities in L. 77 and L. 86 was synchronized. We may set out the two scenarios.

- a) First scenario. The two loci functioned together and their construction may have been contemporaneous. However, it is more likely that L. 86 (b) was added to L. 77 (a) at an early point to double its function. L. 77 was then put to new use (c), its pedestals knocked down, the floor (879) lifted to serve as an area for walking or as a lobby whereas in L. 86 the function would have been extended (c). At a third stage, L. 86 was condemned (d), door 856 blocked, and L. 77, with repaired wall coatings, would have remained a large room without its original installations, for indeterminate use.

- a) Second scenario. The stages can be simplified. After the erection of L. 77 (a') and then L. 86 (b'), the function of the two loci was interrupted at the same time. L. 86 went out of use, the doors were blocked up, dismantling the pedestals in L. 77 was accompanied by lifting floor 879 and the wall coatings were remade (c').

2 – The architectural sequence of L. 77 (and 86)

77.1 – On the surface, layers of abandonment-erosion without great consistency: natural collapse of the constructions.

77.2 – An occupation separated from the body of the dwellings, Level 4 and/or 5?

Under collapse accumulation 77.1 de Vaux suggests a rather unconvincing level which he implicitly attributes to his Period III. Without reference to any floor, he notes: *the construction of two stone alignments (...), like the kiln against the north wall, seems posterior to the destruction of the building* (L. 77, 15/3/54). Stones and kiln are above a block 77.3, not very thick, resulting from the fall of earth roofing after the ruin of 68. The level is manifested only by two installations: *against the north wall, perhaps the debris of a kiln* (L. 77, 13/3/54), which is called 865. Then under the term 863, the *two alignments of stones with ash: a hearth?* (15/3/54). Further to the west, the two ranks of stones 863 are not commented upon; they also contained ash and form a likely hearth.

Kiln 865 appears on the photograph (fig. 132c). It was made of refractory earth and *we note elements of two corners and a curved part. Was this a pottery kiln (...) two or three firing rejects were found close by?* (16/3/54). There is nothing to permit a decision as to whether this was a pottery kiln. The proposal lacks evidence despite the two firing rejects collected near a heterogeneous abandonment layer; one would have expected greater quantities of ash to have been produced from the repeated firings of pottery. The material, the arrangement of the fallen slabs and the dimensions of the whole room are more suggestive of a plain kitchen oven, the use of which continues in the countryside today. A bread oven (*tabun*) would have been semi-interred, which has not been verified. It was not the object of a precise survey, and only the barely legible freehand sketch indicates two lines of agglomerations of burnt earth forming a square which one estimates at just under a metre on each side; its limits drawn on the survey are those that the worker cut to keep the slabs in place. The restored form could also be that of a silo or an earthen vat fired at low temperature.

Kiln 865 is later than the ruin/abandonment of the L.: *ash and burnt wood run underneath as far as the plastered coating of the wall.* (16/3/54); *it is certain that it is posterior to the destruction of the room* (16/3/54), and *this construction, (...) seems later than the destruction of the building*. The top of the fireproof earth was preserved up to the 225 cm mark; its foundation reached 255 cm, when upper mortar floor 879 was confirmed around 270 cm. Restored layer 77.2 has no other significance than to mark the end of the occupation.

Kiln 865 and hearth 863 are linked to occupation Level 4 after 68. Their rather high position in the stratification places them at the end of the sequence. The presence of hearths suggests that the location was then in the open air or without door leafs to have accommodated fires, that it not a completed rehabilitation: *the spoil in the eastern part (of L. 77) reaches 0.70 m in thickness and was not removed* (L. 86, 18/3/54). So it is a kind of shed where fire places, or storehouse separated from the living quarters by a courtyard on the site of the filled-in pools L. 56-58. Finally, keeping the pillars, as proposed in Coüasnon's *Plan* of Period III, should be dropped. At this time, they had been leveled.

> 77.4 and 5 – The restoration of the floors – Mortar floor 879 (77.4) extends under the thin layer 77.3 and rests on a well-made floor 77.5, almost 30 cm thick, which raised the lower floor 77.6 to provide a better bed since *the plaster of the lower level is poorly preserved* (25/3/54). The establishment of floor 77.4, leveling the pillar-pedestals, confirms the change of use for which L. 77 was designed. It is not impossible that the intention was to put L. 77 and 86 on the same level, as L. 86 dominates the original L. 77.

> 77.6 – The erection of L. 77 – The building leans on wall 347, the south side of the large sqare Hasmonaean residence which precedes it. L. 77 is the largest room of the settlement: it measures 24.90 x 6.30 m externally and 22.90 x 4.90 m internally, i.e. 113 m². The mass of walls 852 and 853 attests to the builders' care to build solidly; they reach 0.80 m in thickness and the western wall, less thick, is partly formed from heavy, carefully set bond stones. Sondages of the foundations were not undertaken. Original floor 880, taken down in the middle part where the pedestals of the L. stand, is preserved in the western part. The photograph (fig. 124b) shows

that it has no contact with the pedestals, and it is not clear how de Vaux saw them as placed on the lower floor; as he states that their base was simply deeper than the upper floor, did he take it to be a foundation? It must be acknowledged that lower floor 880 and the pedestals are contemporary (see above).

In its recent phase (879), the floor of the L. 77 undergoes towards the east at a lower level, a descending step estimated at 25 cm, separates the space into two distinct parts. It is difficult to account for the anomaly which could be the result of a rush to conduct the dig. It is improbable that the upper floor 879 was not extended to the far end, towards the east. On the other hand, the hypothesis may be formed that low wall 861, which bars the room widthwise at the height of pedestal 858, was a partition blocking the western end of L. 77, assuming it rested on lower floor 880. The observation was not made and it is no longer possible to verify today. In this case, upper floor 879 would have leaned against low wall 861, and lower floor 880 behind it would have remained in previous state. The proposal to imagine the far ends of both L. 77 and 86 condemned in the same way makes sense. On the other hand, that pedestal 857 lowered against wall 852 like three others, does not confirm the supposed sealing.

> 77.7 – An underlying phase that was not excavated? – The circle of flat stones 855 excited the curiosity of the archaeologist; the first cut of floor 880, *a sondage around the circle of stones* (L. 77, 23/3/54), was to confirm its thickness and possibly reveal what it might hide or cover. It was soon apparent that the circle covered nothing and was merely a marker on the floor. On the other hand, the first cut cleared a small portion of an older floor (fig. 132b): *under the plaster there is another deeper coated floor* (L. 77, 23/3/54). The *Journal* notes are in telegram style: in the comings and goings as the clearance progressed, one might hesitate and think that the deeper floor was 880. De Vaux had clearly distinguished the two floors *I* and *II* a week earlier, and he would not have confused them. Furthermore, photographs (fig. 132b and 134) help us organize the elements better in relation to each other: the sondage spreads out in a crescent around the circle, towards the east; the circle of stones belongs to the original phase and lies at the same level as floor 880 on the top left and as threshold L. 86 on the top right; a

deeper floor is seen in the indentation as a smooth surface sloping towards the east. It cannot be a matter of an arbitrary halt under the worker's trowel; the excavation techniques applied in the course of the seasons were not so sophisticated, and the deeper floor is a real coated floor, which the *Journal* confirms. Here we have the only evidence of an early occupation called 77.7. Neither the photograph nor the *Journal* shows or says whether it is associated with wall 853, cut by it, or passes underneath, and nothing further can be proposed.

- 77.8 – An Iron Age layer – Lower still than floor 77.7: *ash and finally, virgin soil* (L. 77, 23/3/54) indicates the very first occupation. Two arguments situate it in the chronology: *In the ash we collect only a few Iron II sherds. The layer of ash passes under the south wall of 77* (23/3/54). All along the fringe of the *khirbeh*, deep layers of ash were identified. If they came primarily from pottery kilns on the eastern side, here they would correspond better to a discharge zone by the Iron II installation.

Eight coins were collected.

- KhQ 1307 – Demetrius II (145 – 125 BC), KhQ 1308 – Antiochus VII (138 – 129 BC), KhQ 1318 – Judas Aristobulus (104 – 103 BC), KhQ 1396 – Alexander Jannaeus (103 – 76 BC), although found *on the floor to the west*, they are all fortuitous finds, lost from Level II.

- KhQ 1381 – **Hyrcanus II (c. 60 BC)**; also a chance discovery despite being found *on the upper floor*. This coin motivated de Vaux to push back the date of the installations.

- Three other coins, without a precise stratigraphic position, correspond to Level 3.

fig. 133. Appearance of Loci 77 and 86 before the dig, 1953, aerial photograph, Jordan Air Force (JAF 6)

fig. 134.   Locus 77 after the dig

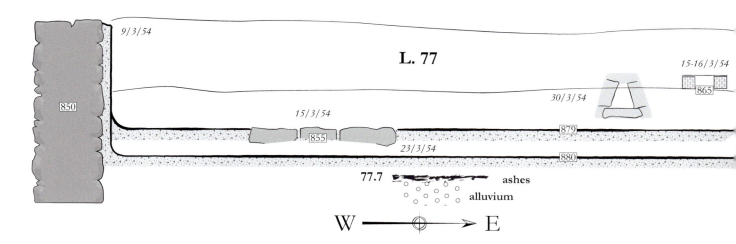

Two locations with an installation of presentation shelves 323

Restored elements	Level	Definition	Journal dates	Coins	Position	N°	Chronology
77.1	Post 4	Abandonment	9/3/54				
77.2	4	Silo/kiln?	10, 16/3/54				
77.3	Post 3C	Collapse	10, 11, 13/3/54				
77.4	3B/C	floor 879	14-15/3/54	KhQ. 1317 1585 1586	upper level	1 1 1	Agrippa I[st] Agrippa I[st] Proc. under Augustus
77.5	3B/C	Bed of 879	24, 25, 28/3/54				
77.6	3B/C	floor 880	30-31/3/54				
77.7	2B? / 3A?	floor 77.7	23/3/54				
77.8	1	Ash	23/3/54				

Schemas and stratigraphic diagram of Locus 77 (for the chart of symbols, see page 155)

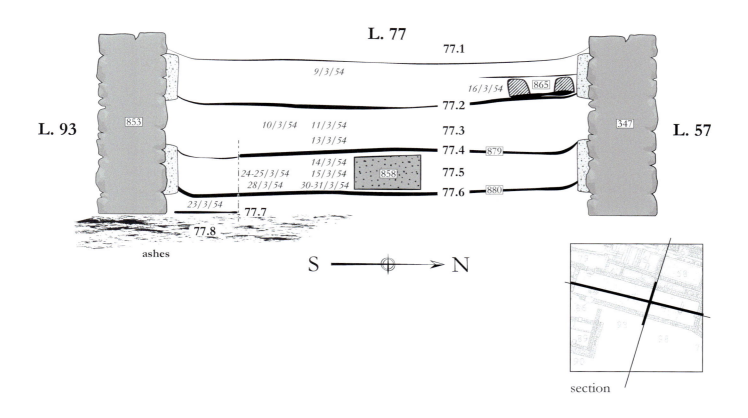

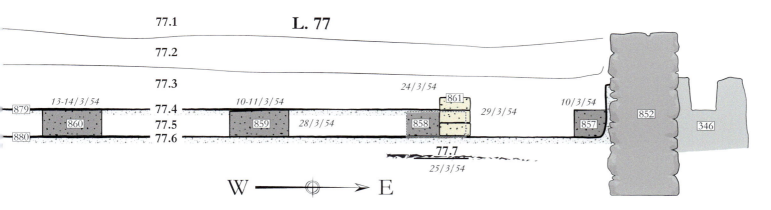

Plate 52

Plate 53, 12

Plate 53, 14

Plate 53, 13

N° Pl.	N° Catal.	Position	Comments (archives)	Date	Description	Clay	Exterior
1	1323	77.3	west, upper level.	10/03/54	plate	° grey earth	white wash
2	1322	77.3	middle, upper level	10/03/54	carinated plate	° red earth	red wash
3	1350	77.3	south-west, upper.	11/03/54	bowl	° red earth	white wash
4	1352	77.3	south-west, upper.	11/03/54	bowl	° red earth	pink wash
5	1388	77.4/5	west, upper.	14/03/54	bowl	° red earth	pink wash
6	1393	77.5	west, upper.	15/03/54	bowl	° pink earth	pink wash
7	1325	77.3	west, upper.	10/03/54	bowl	° grey earth	red wash
8	1377	77.3	south-west, upper.	11/03/54	goblet	° red earth, fine	white wash
9	1326	77.3	west, upper.	10/03/54	goblet	° grey earth	pink wash, burnt
10	4339	77.3/4	lower level	29/03/54	jar	red paste	beige
11	1392	77.5	west, upper.	15/03/54	small spherical jug	° grey earth	
12	1568	77.5	upper level	28/03/54	plate/lid	° red earth	
13	4345	77.5	west	14/03/54	jar	grey paste	beige engobe
14	4244	77.5	-	14/03/54	jar	red paste with grey core	beige
15	4347	77.3	west	13/03/54	jar	orange paste	beige
16	4348	77.5	-	14/03/54	support	beige paste	beige
17	1348	77.2	upper level	09/03/54	support	° red earth, chipped	
18	4324	77.3	-	10/03/54	jar support	brown paste	burnt
19	1383	77.4/5	on the ground	14/03/54	jar support	° red earth	
20	1347	77.3	on the ground	10/03/54	jar support	° red earth	
21	1382	77.4/5	on the ground	14/03/54	jar support	° red earth	
22	1320	77.3	on the ground	10/03/54	jar support	° red earth	
23	4333	77.3	-	10/03/54	jar support	brown paste	burnt
24	1384	77.4/5	on the ground	14/03/54	jar support	° red earth	
25	4341	77.3/4	lower level	29/03/54	cooking pot	red paste	beige
26	4340	77.3/4	lower level	29/03/54	cooking pot, Iron Age?	red paste with grey core	beige engobe

° *According to de Vaux*

Locus 77, catalogue of pots

Plate 53

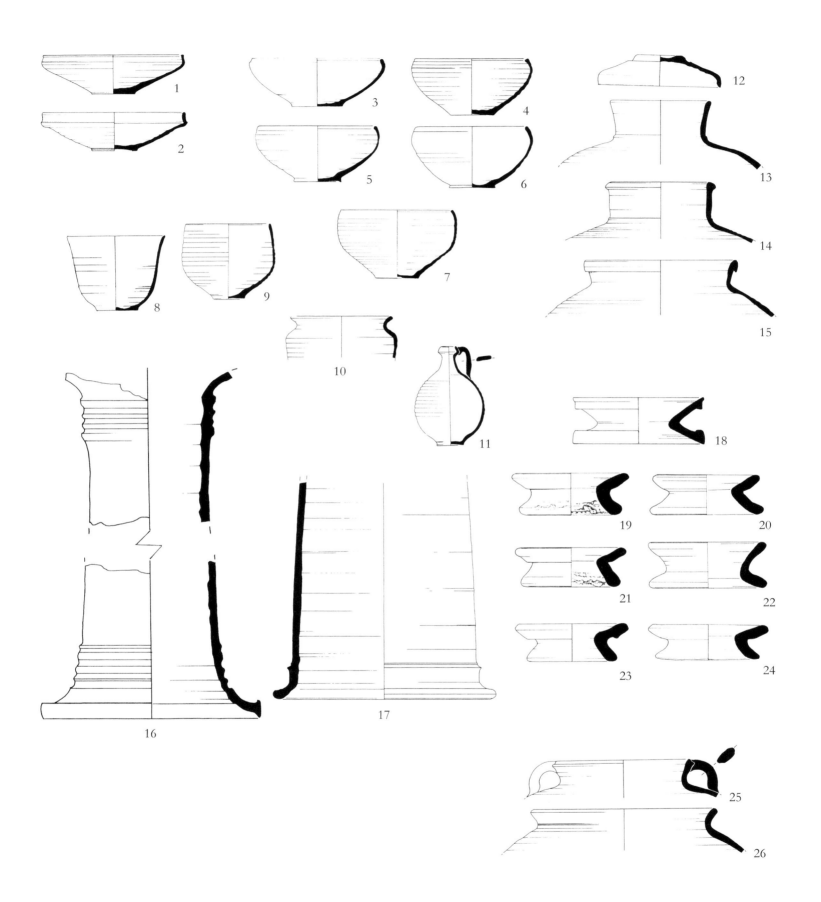

Locus 77, pottery, scale ¼

fig. 135. Arrangement of the display stands of Locus 86, looking south

Locus 86
(87, 89, 185)

Identification of the different stages of occupation and the questions it poses

L. 86 is a complex archaeological subject in its own right, meriting special attention inasmuch as its purpose has provoked debate ever since de Vaux interpreted it as a secondary refectory; this, however, is no longer convincing. The three L. 86, 87 and 89 together constitute one of the richest parts of the *khirbeh*. The exceptional accumulation of pottery, stacked and divided up with care (fig. 144), has attracted attention. A careful reading of the various archives relating to it convinces us that the initial space was subjected to repeated transformations, for reasons which are unclear. Nevertheless, the documentation is poor: rudimentary notes, plans and drawings with elevations are rare. Fortunately, good photographic cover offers a bountiful, last resort.

Situating L. 86 in the series of evolving constructions causes some hesitation, especially as the successive partitions and later disuse to which L. 86 has been subjected deeply anchor it in the history of the site. The first occupation of the L., sealed by a layer of ash covering the movable objects, is a key reference point in stratigraphy and chronology of the whole site. Should we see this layer as result of a destruction by fire in 68, which would inevitably trigger speculation on the history of the site, or was it caused by a *simple* fire? In either case, whether the premises were not cleaned or were badly reconditioned, this remains a question we must try to answer, and the answer will favour a late date. Beforehand, it is imperative to distinguish all elements of this site in order to set them out clearly (see on chapter D).

Some errors of judgment weaken the interpretation which de Vaux proposes to coordinate the different misfortunes that struck the premises. Foundation, occupation, transformations, fire, and cancellation of spaces caused a series of reactions which punctuate the sequence. De Vaux and Coüasnon's *Plans* place the construction of L. 86 in Period Ib which, in their view, comes to an end in 31 BC with the earthquake. Their Period II after the catastrophe recommences with a clearance and a restoration; the pillars erected in L. 86 and L. 77 are thought to remedy the fragility of a damaged upper floor. But erroneously, pillar 872 in L. 86 appears already in *Plan* Ib, before the earthquake took place. We have already pointed to the paradox (p. 315) that, in L. 77 on the same *Plan* Ib, the so-called supports are missing, logically because they were not needed before the earthquake. Then, the thick layer of ash 86.3 and of wood burnt by the fire of the earthquake is according to *Plan* Ib, later than the pillar

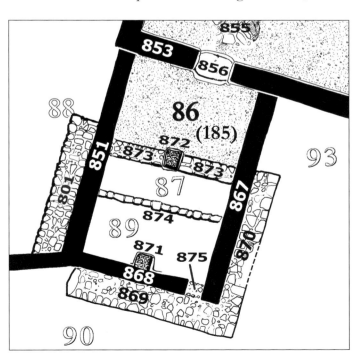

fig. 136. Loci 86, 87, 89, then 185, designation of the elements

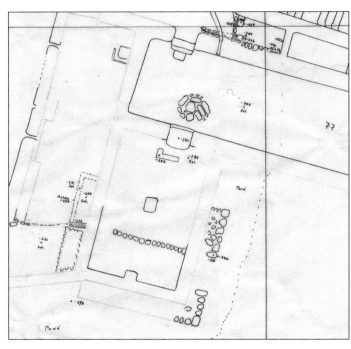
a) First draft of Locus 86 (1954)

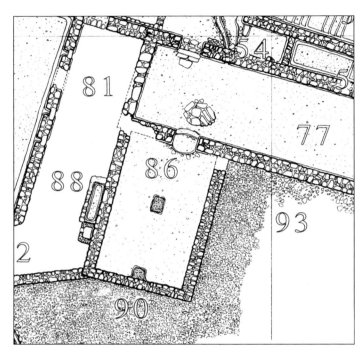
b) Locus 86: Plan Period Ib (Coüasnon)

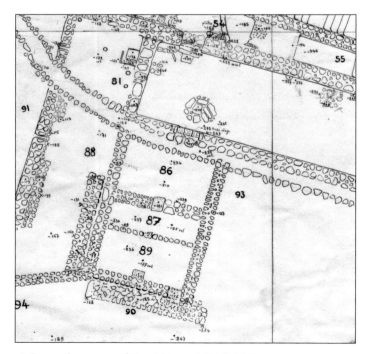
c) Second survey of Loci 86 and 89 (1954)

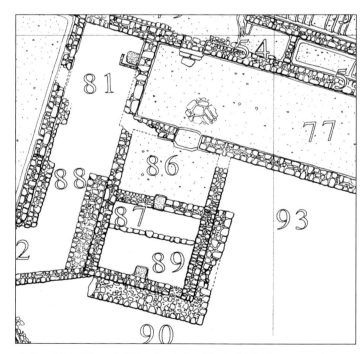
d) Loci 86, 89 and 185 after Plan Period II (Coüasnon)

fig. 137.   Locus 86

thought to repair the damage. The absence of the earthquake in the chronology of Qumran solves these contradictions: L. 86 evolved smoothly up to the fire, then the events that affected it succeeded one another in a short span of time.

Since the earthquake did not take place, there is nothing pointing to 31 BC, and ash layer 89.3 as testimony to a violent destruction or fire drops out of the arbitrary chronology which so far had fixed it down. The ash layer in L. 89 cannot have been the result of the 31 BC earthquake; further, L. 89 cannot have been left in a state of abandonment for a century, up to the moment when the settlement was extended. The ash must be linked with the destruction of AD 68 as well as be its consequence (see on L. 77).

Finally to respect the logic of the chronology in L. 86 (89), de Vaux felt constrained to identify a trace of his Period II and insert it somewhere: *Loci 86 – 87 – 89 were used in period II, but at a slightly higher level* (L. 86, 18/3/54). The sentence betrays more an idea than an observation. Did he need a prominent element subsequent to destruction layer 89.3 in L. 89? He assigns it to *a floor to which a door corresponds* (L. 89, 18/3/54). Now, floor 89.2 which he suggests can hardly exist, since it did not produce any objects; it would have been accessible by 875, not a door but at best a simple breach made in the south wall (868), with no outside steps to reach it from L. 90. The practice is not normal given the prosperity of the site. Such an *upper* level is nowhere illustrated; its substance is so weak that Coüasnon's *Plan* of Period II shows nothing of it, except, discreetly, door-opening 875 in wall 868. The succession of occupations in de Vaux's Period Ib–Period II therefore does not seem justified. On the other hand, the *Plan* of period II showed partitions L. 89 and L. 87, and on this point it is correct.

Description and definition of L. 86, 89 and 185

L. 86 was built on bare ground: a reduced sondage, under its mortar floor 881, hit the Iron Age spread of ash 86.2: *A sondage under the plastered floor (...). Immediately below lies ashy earth with some Iron II sherds, then the virgin soil* (L. 89, 30/3/54). The ash 86.2 extends the layer 77.8 below L. 77. L. 86 was built with blocks partly recovered in the ruin of the Hasmonaean residence (Level 2). At least one block attests to this, recovered in the southeast corner with walls 867 and 868, cut in the fine style of worked blocks of the *khirbeh* and characteristic of the beautiful herodian constructions of Rujm al-Bahr and Kh. Mazen among others nearby. The block is engraved with a mason's mark, a Greek letter *chi* (fig. 139b), adding to the other *alphas* and *deltas* already listed[81].

L. 86 is linked organically to large room 77, to which it may have formed an extension or for which it was substituted (cf. on L. 77). It became a feature of the history of the site at quite an early stage, although it is difficult to be precise as to when; it was closed down in stages, went definitively sealed, and finally ruined, while after 68 L. 77 was granted a final and precarious restoration, 77.2. The extension of the occupied surface surrounding pool L. 91 postdates it, as wall 786 (south of L. 88-92) which encloses it to the south, rejoins L. 86 and leans on it at an angle. The foundation of L. 86-77 must precede the decisive stage which converted the open settlement into an inward-looking settlement which it had become before collapsing in 68. L. 86, whether joined to L. 77 or not, certainly seems to be added and, having fallen out of use, was closed down before the destruction of the site. In a way, it manifests the moment of the largest extension of Qumran, and therefore merits our full attention.

The building measures 8.50 x 6.40 m externally. The internal surface, inside the walls, amounts to 40 m². At two points in time which cannot be specified, it was divided up into three defined spaces. De Vaux did not opt for a logical division of the spaces in line with the sequence of partitioning. How was the original L. called 86 laid out? It clearly seems to be a single item: *86, 87, 89 (...) forming a single room* (L. 86, 16/3/54). Initially, poor partition wall 874 separated L. 86 into *L. 89 to the south and 87 to the north, L. 89 new L. to the south of 87* (L. 89, 16/3/54). During the excavation, L. 87 related only to the box room between poor partition 874 and blind wall 873, whereas L. 89 designated the space between poor partition 874 and the south wall of the L., 868. Now, poor partition 874 had split L. 86 in two: L. 89 to the south. However, because blind wall 873 is not yet built at this point, we extend L. 87 as far as the door in wall 853 of L. 77. At a second point in time, blind wall 873 cut L. 87 in two, and the new space created to the north, which remained open towards L. 77, wrongly continued to be excavated under the label L. 86. With the

---

81. *Qumrân*, Vol. II, p. 446-7

fig. 138. a) Locus 86 east, set in which is Locus 185
b) The two stands, at the time of the dig, are flat-topped

appearance of blind wall 873, the new space to the north should have been labeled; this we have done, calling it L. 185. Since it is closed off to L. 77, the succession of loci was established smoothly, in four stages:

– The complete L. 86.

– The complete L. 86, a low wall under poor partition 874 is only an internal arrangement to simply mark a limit, which does not divide the room as a whole.

– Later, partition 873 separating L. 86 into two new loci: to the south the one which is sealed and is given the name L. 89; and L. 89 was divided by the low wall 874 creating L. 87 which no longer makes sense as a define space. The only space available from the north becomes L. 185.

– Door 856 leading to L. 77 what had been the original L. 86 is now definitively sealed.

Stratigraphy and chronology of L. 86, 89 and 185

The excavation of the room was carried out in six working days from 16/3/54 to 22/3/54. The *Journal*'s notes on L. 86 do not exactly match the course of the excavation which we are attempting to follow. The notes on L. 87-89 should not be juxtaposed

fig. 139.   Reinforcement 869 to the south of Locus 86
   a) Foundation of reinforcement 869 above paving 816.
   b) Block of sandstone engraved with a Greek letter *chi*, inserted in the S-E corner of L. 86 (Photo 2008, after restoration).

a) Loci 77 and 86, to the south

b) Simple levelling in bad mortar in front of door 856 (Loc. 86)

c) The mass of burnt wood sealing the pottery (towards the south-east)

d) Burnt pillar in Locus 86

e) The passage in the door 856 (Locus 86)

f) Burnt pillar in Locus 86

fig. 140. Locus 86

but inserted into those of L. 86. From the first day, 16/3/54, L. 86 was viewed as the sum of compartments 86, 87 and 89, considered together in the walls of the *new L. to the southwest of room 77 (...) pottery in place against the south wall* (L. 86, 16/3/54). It emerges from the notes that the rapid discovery of the stacks of pottery captured all the attention, to become a circumscribed sondage, under new headings: L. 89 then 87. The clearing of the pottery was conducted under 87-89 up to 30/3/54 while, from 22/3/54, the excavation was not completed in L. 185, but still being conducted under the heading L. 86.

Locus 89

A surface identified at a shallow depth was, with some hesitation, viewed as a floor. Its existence is far from obvious. Is floor 89.2, presented as a witness to Period II, anything more than a shepherd's shelter? Under surface layer 89.1 about which nothing is said, a late occupation 89.2 appears although not evident in the stratigraphy; mixed up the chronology of L. 86 as a whole. The first sentence in the *Notes* states right away: *We uncover a layer with much ash, pottery in place* (L. 86, 16/3/54). The first cut, starting from the surface as elsewhere, was rapid and done without much care; excitement triggered by the stack of pottery accelerated the clearance needed to keep up pace in the excavation process. The upper layers were neglected and observations about them in the notes were reduced to a minimum. Excavation was not uniform, it would seem that the southeast corner was the first to be excavated: it would be no suprise if a floor was identified precisely there without having left more traces in the records than: *We stop at a floor matched by a door in the southeast corner, perhaps from period II* (L. 89, 17/3/54) and: *There are (...) two levels in the L.: that of the plastered floor and the small wall containing the pottery, and the higher and thus more recent one with door to the south in the southeast corner* (22/3/54). When one accepts there is a door opening in the wall, the next step would be to look for a corresponding floor. A simple difference in colour or compaction will have been sufficient to identify it, even if this did not mean an occupation. If we accept that floor 89.2 existed, it was not seen anywhere else than in the southeast corner. The evidence, however, is thin. An occupation of this kind would have indicated that it was limited to the unused and sealed L. 89 with rear entrance 875 in wall 868. Towards the southeast corner of L. 86, wall 868 is in fact chipped, but no threshold was seen there. A door is not appropriate, especially as no step or incline facilitates crossing the one metre difference in height to access the outside. We repeat that such a precarious layout in no way corresponds to an organized human occupation contemporary with a *Period II* in full development. Even if floor 89.2 had ever existed, its layout would at best mark the almost obliterated traces of a shelter or a shepherd's hut, to be dated as late as possible, and would certainly not be sufficient to confirm the existence of Period II.

Definition and chronology of Locus 185

One of the main difficulties de Vaux had to face relates to the transition from his Period Ib to Period II. But his idea of an abandonment after the 31 BC earthquake and the community subsequent return from *exile* was not backed up by solid argument. His position was to inaugurate Period II with the return of the group, but such a return is now ruled out by the certainty that neither an earthquake nor an abandonment had taken place. The idea of a clean-up after a long absence impressed itself so much on de Vaux that it would compensate for the weakness of the stratigraphic link: are the layers of collapse caused by the earthquake missing? The argument compensates for the absence of traces. The coherence of the argument makes up for the absence of evidence. Alluvial cones or garbage on the approaches to inhabited premises, construction refuse, agricultural waste, domestic and farming waste, are a function of the extent and density of human occupation. Careful excavation would enable one to distinguish its constituent parts well and date them whatever the situation, which is lacking at Qumran with the exception of Trench A, domestic spoil from Level 2A and B. Without an earthquake, without an abandonment, without a return of exiles, the occupation of L. 77 and L. 86 turns out to be continuous and the means of establishing the chronology have to be sought elsewhere: a better argument may be drawn from the numismatics.

The *Journal* records the collection of fourteen coins in L. 86, twelve of which the *Catalogue* attributes to the upper level. Their precise location requires caution. The *Journal* raises an element of doubt in relation to the different denominations from the upper level. Starting from 17/3/54, the notes on L. 86 relate only to its northern part. L. 185 was excavated after L. 89:

fig. 141. The original space of Locus 86 with its installations have been reconstructed

Clearing of the upper level. We look for the door, which is finally found in the middle door of L. 77 (L. 86, 17/3/54); the mention of the door assures us that the work was still being pursued in L. 185. Then: *Uncovering of the upper layer of 86: this is not a ground surface but the collapsed upper floor* (L. 86, 22/3/54). As mortar floor 881 of the original L. 86 had been revealed, this so-called upper layer corresponds to occupation 185.4, the *collapsed floor*. The apportionment of the objects selected in the *Journal* separates the *upper layer of L. 86, i.e. material fallen from the upper floor* (our floor 185.4) and the *lower layer, i.e. on the floor* (our floor 881, L. 86). We cannot confuse the *upper level* with the improbable floor 89.2: this is floor 185.4.

We must again decide: is floor 185.4 a ground floor in place or does it represent the remains of a fallen upper floor? A photograph (fig. 138a and fig. 31) is the only available document to facilitate the decision. In the southwest corner of L. 185, the photograph fortunately shows in section what has remained of a floor before its removal to clear lime-mortar floor 881 of L. 86 completely. Floor 185.4 represents the normal construction of a floor in place and not that of a floor that has fallen from an upper storey. In the section preserved on the photograph, the heterogeneous, crushed material forms a bed consistent with a solid floor of beaten earth. Is it likely that a floor fallen from a height of three metres, when the rafters give way, can be found in a flat condition, not mixed up as shown in the photo? In a cave-in, the timber breaks and the collapse comes down in disorder; the floor is bound to be broken up by the fall, and the result is not homogeneous as we see it here. Is it likely that pots swept away in such a collapse were found intact on the ground floor, especially when the large pots are vessels with a fine and fragile lining? It is equally important, when ranking the evolution of the items of architecture, to note that ash layer 185.5 is the same as 89.4 (= 883) covering the pottery in L. 89. Ash layer 185.5 does not predate wall 873 but rests on it. The *Journal*, incidentally, says: *The wall which closed the L. on both sides of the central pillar is built directly on the plastered floor, which it has depressed somewhat* (L. 86, 22/3/54). *On this floor, L. 86, remains of burnt beams* (L. 86, 22/3/54). One would not say that the point of wall 873 was to seal movable objects after a fire. Floor 185.4 is that of a box room, accessible from L. 77, after the bottom of the room was condemned. In time, L. 185 closely follows sealed L. 89. During the first day of the dig in L. 86 *(w)e collect many coins in L. 86* (L. 86, 16/3/54). The level of pottery *in situ* and upper floor 882 were reached in a single day without distinguishing anything and without locating the finds over a thickness of a metre : *Clearing of the upper level. We look for the door* (L. 86, 17/3/54). Floor 882 (the upper floor), recorded after the stack of pots, is the only occupation in L. 185, as lower mortar floor 881 is that of the original L. 86. We have to understand that the coins, except for one, were found in association with, or close to, floor 185.4. The homogeneity of the hoard encourages us to believe that the coins were grouped together and not dispersed. The coins cannot have been thrown away or lost gradually in a heap of collapse or an abandonment. This strati-chronological datum will help mark the sequence of L. 86, 87, 89 and 185.

Of the twelve coins that have been read, seven collected in L. 185 are attributed to Herod Agrippa I[st] (40-44 AD) which provides a strong chronological indication. Four other coins are attributed to the Procurators under Nero (54-68 AD). For L. 89, no coin is recorded. L. 87 produced just one coin, again from Herod Agrippa I[st], and the disuse of L. 89 cannot antedate it. We are then able to confirm that our L. 86 was still in activity after the middle of the 1st century. However, de Vaux states: *many coins (...) those which are legible are from Agrippa I and from the First Revolt* (L. 86, 16/3/54), and it is amazing that the coins from the First Revolt do not appear in the catalogue of the *Journal* on L. 86. Did de Vaux make a mistake when attributing coins of the First Revolt to L. 86, while the ones from the procurators under Nero were collected in nearby L. 83? Be that as it may, the chronology is safe as the minting of the procurators under Nero matches up chronologically with the years of the revolt. It would then be necessary to place the architectural modifications in the run-up to 68. The sealing may be linked to the conflict. Though we cannot prove it, the hypothesis is convincing.

Beaten-earth and unrepaired floor 185.4 does not indicate a long occupation. The sealing of L. 89/87 by wall 873 will have occurred after the middle of the century. Since the disuse of L. 185 by the blocking of door 856 to L. 77 is only slightly earlier or later than 68, the pottery remains the same before and after: this does not matter much, since in a short span of time common crockery had not evolved. May we doubt the identity of the occupants of L. 185? If the Roman army camped in the ruins after having overthrown the revolt, would we expect to find *Roman* pottery there? The occupation of L. 185 is Judaean.

fig. 142. The stacks of pots in Locus 89

L. 185 has to be viewed as intermediate between the end of Level 3C and the initial occupation of Level 4. The deposits of pottery of L. 89 are still to be situated in Level 3C (AD 10-68). They cannot be from much before the occupation in L. 185: the layer of ash separates L. 89 from 185. Since L. 87 and 89 had a simultaneous period of occupation, the Herod Agrippa coin collected in L. 87 is contemporary with the pottery, as this L. only has a low layer in place. It will be best to date the stacks of pottery to after the year 40. If the age of the deposit has been obtained, the moment when L. 86 was erected is a mystery; one would hesitate to place it any earlier than Level 3B.

The chronological interpretation of L. 86 was discussed by J.T. Milik, who confirms our proposals. Milik had noted, pertinently, that the storeroom of L. 89 had produced a bowl bearing a lightly engraved name before firing: Eleazar (KhQ 1650, *Catalogue*: *L. 89, lower level,*). Milik confirms that the palaeography cannot be from before the first century of our era. The remark damaged the chronology established by de Vaux and questioned once again the system of the periods. Milik was right, and the epigraphic argument was correct. De Vaux defended his position, while Milik maintained his, and finally de Vaux held firm, reluctant to change his stratigraphy and his chronology.

Apportionment of the layout of Locus 86

Before dealing with the site's internal installations, we tried to find out how the L. 86 and 77 were installed in the space and then built, and how they were modified over time. Now we need to understand how they were used. The stratification-layout combination in L. 86 is the best preserved of the *khirbeh*. The layout is identical to that of L. 77, but it is preserved as it was in L. 86. The loci has been the subject of a rather unconvincing interpretation as refectories, which needs to be revisited. Interpretations differ widely. It is one of the premises from which people claimed to draw arguments in favour of sectarian or simply religious life (a refectory), or evidence of artisanal activities, though they have not been able to discern a Jewish character (a pottery workshop etc.). A sacristy versus a shop, the life of the spirit versus the bustle of a crossroads, both in the name of scientific necessity on which all insist – at any rate, like it or not, a place where history occurs. For the sake of simple honesty, it is best not to harden the downstream effects of an intuition which no one really has the right to deny or insist upon.

The subject of the identity of Qumran remains open. Upstream of interpretations, the idea which would prevail to link or mix profane and sacred. In a site rich with ideology and history it is allowed to reestablish a place where everyday life alternated with the sacredness of festivals, it is logical to weave the warp and woof, as we know life went by in Judaea.

Loci 77 and 86 were each laid out with a row of pillars (fig. 30). We would like to return to the irrationality of their placement and the weakness of arguments as to their support function. Their irregular arrangement was an embarrassment to de Vaux, whose comment is not convincing: the door is not completely in the axis of the two pillars of L. 86 and the circle of stones of 77 (L. 86, 18/3/54). The logic of the construction does not encourage us to set a wooden frame in the length and axis of a door. The *pillars* of L. 77 cover only the east part of the room. One part only of the refectory would have been covered, and the reason – namely the president standing on the stone circle – has no basis. The starting point for questioning the pillars was the observation that the piers, which are not inserted pillars, did not support anything. At best, a prop against a wall is a provisional way of stopping the fall of a broken beam, or one close to breaking, and in such cases the prop would be of wood. To do this one does not carefully construct a pier with raw material, especially when the layout is repeated in L. 77 and L. 86. Would just the east part of the roofing of L. 77 and the whole of the roofing of L. 86 have threatened to collapse, and an easier and less costly repair of the roof not be undertaken? The propping is too well designed not to last. It is difficult to accept that the *pillars* were supports; having recognized the weakness of the proposal, we would like to extend our investigation beyond the banal hypothesis of a propping-up. To clarify the formulations as in L. 77, we prefer from this point on to use the more neutral term *pedestal* rather than *pillar*.

Morphology of the pedestals

Now that we are granting the pedestals an importance they have not hitherto had, must regret our inability, in the situation we find ourselves in today,

338 The archaeology of Qumran – an attempted reassessment

fig. 143.   The stacks of pots in Locus 89

to examine them. Pedestal 872 in L. 86, immersed in masonry, presented the best state of preservation when it was excavated; after excavation, however, it was quickly consolidated and disguised, and there is no photo to attest to its original condition. In L. 77, the series of stands was dismantled, according to oral tradition, at the time of the explorations by J. Allegro. Several times afterwards, the two loci, like the ruin as a whole, were subjected to substantial restoration for purposes of their exploitation in tourism. We still have from the original state some photographs and some plans.

Leaning against south wall 868 in L. 86, pedestal 871 is 65 cm wide and 55 cm deep; pedestal 872 at the centre of the room has the same width, i.e. 65 cm, with a length of 80 cm in the north-south axis. Their height is of importance to establish what they were, if they are to be regarded as pedestals, but nothing was measured and nothing was said about their tops. Pedestal 872 owes its preserved state to the fact that it was included in the masonry of wall 873 with its complete form. The photograph (fig. 138) shows it at the moment when it was discovered, when the wall was notched to clear its top, manifestly flat. Given the mediocre quality of the photograph, the texture of the top cannot be assessed. There is, however, a good chance that the pedestal was complete, as it is hardly likely that both pedestals would have had a flat top at the same height if the pillars had been truncated.

The pedestals are made of rough brick (L. 77, 28/3/54), with correctly plastered faces: *traces of a rectangular pillar, pile of fallen bricks around it* (L. 77, 10/3/54). This material is attested at many locations on the site for the construction of partition walls (L. 23, 61, 63, 121 etc.) or to block doors (L. 77); sections, still upright until a short time ago, attest to important piles of rough brick thrown beyond the east closure of the compound. When examined, brick fragments show a strong degreasant of river sand, making the pedestals resistant but not to the point of competing with stone which is abundant everywhere and better suited to supporting a roof.

The pedestals were without foundation: *The three pillars and the pilaster of the east wall are of rough brick, founded directly on the plaster* (L. 77, 28/3/54). Consideration of the construction procedures may help to explain the different elements recorded. If the *pillars* were supports for a ceiling or an upper floor, the excavation would have found them anchored in some kind of foundation, even if just a lightweight one. Lower floor 880 of L. 77, offering no resistance, was said to be in poor condition; the bed in which it was set, too poor to have been recorded, lies without any real transition on *another deeper coated floor, then ash* (L. 77, 23/3/54). Over time, a weight-bearing support – its own weight added to that of the roofing – would imprint or embed itself in a poorly founded floor; this is the case in L. 86 where wall 873 *is founded directly on the plastered floor which it has depressed somewhat* (L. 86, 22/3/54). The argument militates in favour of the pedestals' not having exerted pressure because they were light, short and made of rough material.

Architectonics, placement in space

The L. 77–86 wing did not have an upper floor. Nor does the layout of the pedestals meet the requirements of a support in this location: there was no point in trying to prevent the sagging of a storey, as an upper floor is improbable here; support of a simple light roof in this type of building does not require such an apparatus: in such an architectural context, one does not support, one repairs. The existence of an upper floor was suggested by de Vaux and repeated by a few commentators, without much insistence. We noted above that the mound of debris from collapsed L. 77–86 was not sufficient in volume to restore an upper level from it whose hypothetical access cannot, by the way, be placed anywhere. The residence had an upper floor in its original state (Level 2) and it is likely that the occupants of Level 3, re-occupying the ruin, restored part of it. The L. 77–86 wing is detached from the central building and too far from the staircases of L. 35.

Intermediate supports to reduce the reach of the timbers are not justified. The width of L. 77 and 86 does not exceed that of the numerous loci which have no need of props, L. 2, 4, 51, 101, 111, not to mention that large pools 71, 91 etc., must also have been covered. The palm tree trunks that provided the material for beams have reaches considerably exceeding the modest width of the rooms of Qumran between 4.5 and 5 m. Remains of palm tree trunks which served as covering were found at the site.

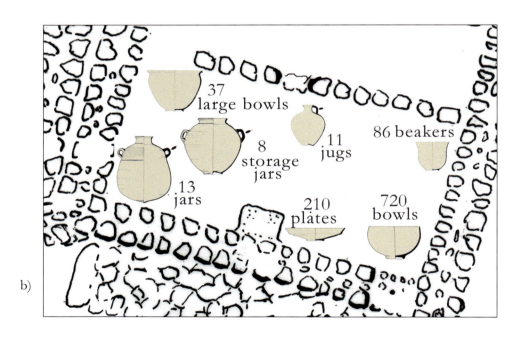

fig. 144. a) The stacks of pots in Locus 89
b) Location of different types of pottery in Locus 89

A staggered or asymmetrical position of pillars in the space to be covered or supported, did not raise any question for the archaeologist (fig. 137c). Each of the two loci accommodates what has been viewed as a pier abutting back wall 852 (L. 77) and 868 (L. 86). A flat beam rests on the long walls of the room and not widthwise on an excrescence from the shorter walls. A beam in the axis of the length of L. 86 would have been placed on the wall itself and not on a pier abutting it, which would be useless in the logic of construction. In addition, the northern support of the frame in the axis of the pillars, falls on the weak point above the door which opens onto L. 77. Such a layout is even more odd in L. 77, as much in length as in width. Such installations do not comply with the rules of architecture; they have no functions, and considerations on this point are futile. Let us abandon the risky, strictly utilitarian hypothesis in favour of a more rational installation. The pedestals, arranged in the same way in both L. 86 and 77, have their place in the space, which seems to correspond to an intentional arrangement. In both cases, the semi-pedestal abutting the back east wall is at the opposite end from the entrance door. The pedestals are arranged like tables, or rather display shelves, whose position implies that one makes one's way towards them on entering the room. In both cases, a low wall reserves the space at the back of the rooms as if to mark a boundary on the floor.

Sealed loci

Loci 77 and 86 are barred by walls. Wall 873 cuts L. 86, and the fact that it is blind, well-constructed, not supporting anything, not repairing anything, obliges us to find another *raison d'être* for it. It clearly condemns the south end of the room. The identical and simultaneous blocking of the back of L. 77 and L. 86 constitutes a remarkable fact which cannot be accidental. If we want to go beyond intuition, we need to suppose that we know hardly anything of the century of daily life at Qumran, on the fringes of what historical sources have given us. Wall 973 is not a support, and we cannot believe that the urgency of the propping-up would have been such that there was no opportunity to evacuate the crockery. Was it desirable one day to seal the back of L. 86 simply to protect objects of domestic value? Or – to mention a more ambitious hypothesis – to seal the objects of a rite which was practised and then interrupted?

In L. 77, a low wall 861, barring the L. at the height of second pedestal 858, is merely indicated. The *Journal* omits to record it on the day when the precise location was excavated: *we find an intermediate pillar associated with the descending step towards the east* (L. 77, 28/3/54). The plans (fig. 125a and 128b) and the photographs (fig. 124b and 129d) are more explicit. In our description of L. 77 we proposed that barrier 861 condemned the east end of the room. The poor inked sketch (fig. 128b) does not show that it was built of stone, and the photograph suggests a partition of rough brick. That the late floor 879 in L. 77 rested on it would indicate – and this is very likely – that it was placed flush with older floor 880, and that the location thus separated had remained lower. Even if one cannot guess what its elevation was, it is preferable not to see it as a barrier but the preserved low part of a blocking. We note also that, as in L. 86, partition 861 has enclosed the first free pedestal.

In L. 86, the sealing is identical but repeated, with two partitions close to each other. Poor partition 874 is botched masonry: *poor partition, constituted half of rough brick, half of pebbles. Perhaps a narrow door in the middle* (L. 87, 18/3/54). The mediocrity of the apparatus and the narrow passageway raised are not contradicted by the photographs (fig. 138a). Partition 874 cannot be homogeneous in construction and the best quality of its base leads us to believe that its bed is older. The fact that de Vaux preserved it, whereas he dismantled 874, reinforces the idea. A passageway is probable against west wall 851, as is suggested by the survey (fig. 137a) and the photographs (fig. 141b, c and d): *The small wall which separates loci 87 and 89 is itself also placed on the plastered floor. One entered L. 89 by a door at the western end of the wall* (L. 89, 22/3/54). We gave the label 884 to the low bed which, in origin, was little more than a screen to protect or reserve the stacks of pottery. More serious is wall 873, which certainly blocks the south part of L. 86. The similarity between the two modifications of the layout is certainly striking. We had suggested seeing it as a rite of offering of first fruits. It is not forbidden to return to this (see the note on the first fruits, p. 71).

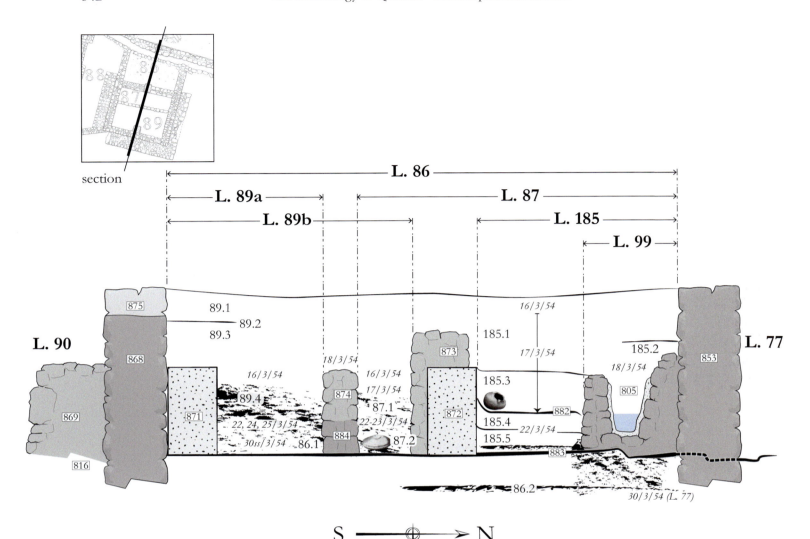

Restored elements	Level	Definition	Journal dates	Coins	Position	N°	Chronology
89.1 185.1	Post 4	Definitive abandonment	16-17/3/54				
89.2 185.2	4	Filling-in of foundation drain 805	18/3/54				
89.3 185.3	Post-68, between 3C and 4	Filling-in by erosion	16-17/3/54	KhQ. 1426.	upper level	1	Antiochus, Ist cent.
185.4	3C (Post 68?)	Occupation on collapse	16-18 and 22/3/54	1424, 1425, 1430, 1431. 1427, 1428, 1429, 1458, 1459, 1480.	upper level (floor 882)	4 6	Proc. under Nero Agrippa Ist
89.4 87.1 185.5	3C	L. 87-89 sealed by the collapse L. 185, collapse under 185.4	16-30/3/54				
86.1 87.2	3C	L. 86 before partition, deposit of pottery	16-17 and 22-30/3/54	1436	upper level (L. 87)	1	Agrippa Ist
86.2	1 (Iron Age IIC)	Traces under 86.1	30/3/54				

Schema and stratigraphic diagram of Loci 86 and 89 (for the chart of symbols, see page 155)

Plate 54

Locus 89, photographs and pottery

N° Pl.	N° Catal.	Position	Comments (archives)	Date	Description	Clay	Exterior
1	1591-i	86.1 (L. 89)	lower level	30/03/54	plate		
2	1591	86.1 (L. 89)	lower level	30/03/54	204 plates		
3	1650	86.1 (L. 89)	in the 1601 series, penultimate of stack 63, lower level	8/04/54	inscribed bowl	° red earth	white wash
4	1601-1	86.1 (L. 89)	lower level	31/03/54	708 bowls	° red earth	white wash
5	1601-2	86.1 (L. 89)	lower level	30/03/54	bowl	° red earth	white wash
6	1601-3	86.1 (L. 89)	lower level	30/03/54	bowl	° red earth	white wash
7	1468	86.1 (L. 89)	upper level	17/03/54	bowl	° red earth, fine	pink wash
8	1546	86.1 (L. 89)	lower level	30/03/54	bowl	° red earth	white wash
9	1591-1	86.1 (L. 89)	lower level	30/03/54	plate		
10	1544	86.1 (L. 89)	lower level	30/03/54	plate	° red earth	white wash
11	1591-a	86.1 (L. 89)	lower level	30/03/54	plate		
12	1591-d	86.1 (L. 89)	lower level	30/03/54	plate		
13	1591-k	86.1 (L. 89)	lower level	30/03/54	plate		
14	1591-f	86.1 (L. 89)	lower level	30/03/54	plate		
15	1543	86.1 (L. 89)	lower level	30/03/54	plate	° red earth	white wash
16	1591-l	86.1 (L. 89)	lower level	30/03/54	plate		
17	1540	86.1 (L. 89)	lower level	30/03/54	plate	° red earth	white wash
18	1591-j	86.1 (L. 89)	lower level	30/03/54	plate		
19	1591-h	86.1 (L. 89)	lower level	30/03/54	plate		
20	1591-c	86.1 (L. 89)	lower level	30/03/54	plate		
21	1542	86.1 (L. 89)	lower level	30/03/54	plate	° red earth	white wash
22	1591-g	86.1 (L. 89)	lower level	30/03/54	plate		
23	1591-e	86.1 (L. 89)	lower level	30/03/54	plate		
24	1591-b	86.1 (L. 89)	lower level	30/03/54	plate		
25	1503	86.1 (L. 89)	lower level	30/03/54	plate	° red earth	white wash
26	1526	86.1 (L. 89)	lower level	30/03/54	plate	° red earth	pink wash
27	1556	86.1 (L. 89)	lower level	25/03/54	goblet	° red earth	white wash
28	1510	86.1 (L. 89)	lower level	30/03/54	goblet	° red earth, fine	traces of white wash
29	1587-4	86.1 (L. 89)	lower level	30/03/54	goblet	° red earth	white wash
30	1587	86.1 (L. 89)	lower level	30/03/54	75 goblets	° red earth	white wash
31	1587-3	86.1 (L. 89)	lower level	30/03/54	goblet	° red earth	white wash
32	1470	86.1 (L. 89)	upper level	30/03/54	goblet	° red earth	white wash
33	1509	86.1 (L89)	lower level	30/03/54	goblet	° red earth, fine	traces of white wash
34	4435	89.2/3?	upper level?	14/03/54?	goblet	red paste	red
35	1587-2	86.1 (L. 89)	lower level	30/03/54	goblet	° red earth	white wash
36	1588	86.1 (L. 89)	lower level	30/03/54	goblet	° red earth	white wash

° *According to de Vaux*

Locus 89, catalogue of pottery

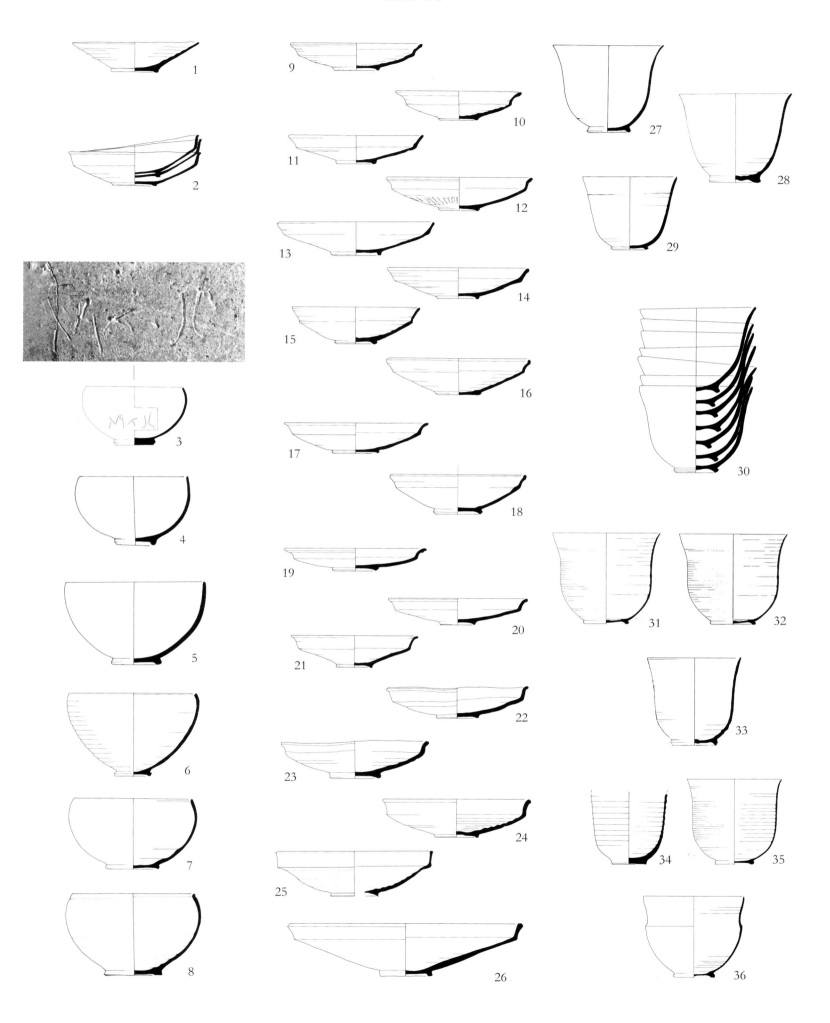

Plate 55

Locus 89, pottery, scale ¼

Plate 56

N° Pl.	N° Catal.	Position	Comments (archives)	Date	Description	Clay	Exterior
1	1676-8	86.1 (L. 89)	lower level	25/03/54	37 large bowls	° pink earth	white wash
2	1539	86.1 (L. 89)	lower level	25/03/54	large bowl	° red earth	white wash
3	1676-3	86.1 (L. 89)	lower level	25/03/54	large bowl	° pink earth	white wash
4	1676	86.1 (L. 89)	lower level	25/03/54	large bowl	° pink earth	white wash
5	1676-4	86.1 (L. 89)	lower level	25/03/54	large bowl	° pink earth	white wash
6	1676-5	86.1 (L. 89)	lower level	25/03/54	large bowl	° pink earth	white wash
7	1676-7	86.1 (L. 89)	lower level	25/03/54	large bowl	° pink earth	white wash
8	1676-6	86.1 (L. 89)	lower level	25/03/54	large bowl	° pink earth	white wash
9	1676-1	86.1 (L. 89)	lower level	25/03/54	large bowl	° pink earth	white wash
10	4438	89.2/3?	upper level?	14/03/54?	large bowl		
11	1574	86.1 (L. 89)	lower level	28/03/54	large bowl	° red earth	white wash
12	1575	86.1 (L. 89)	lower level	28/03/54	two-handled pot	° red earth	white wash

° *According to de Vaux*

Locus 89, pottery and catalogue, scale ¼

Plate 57

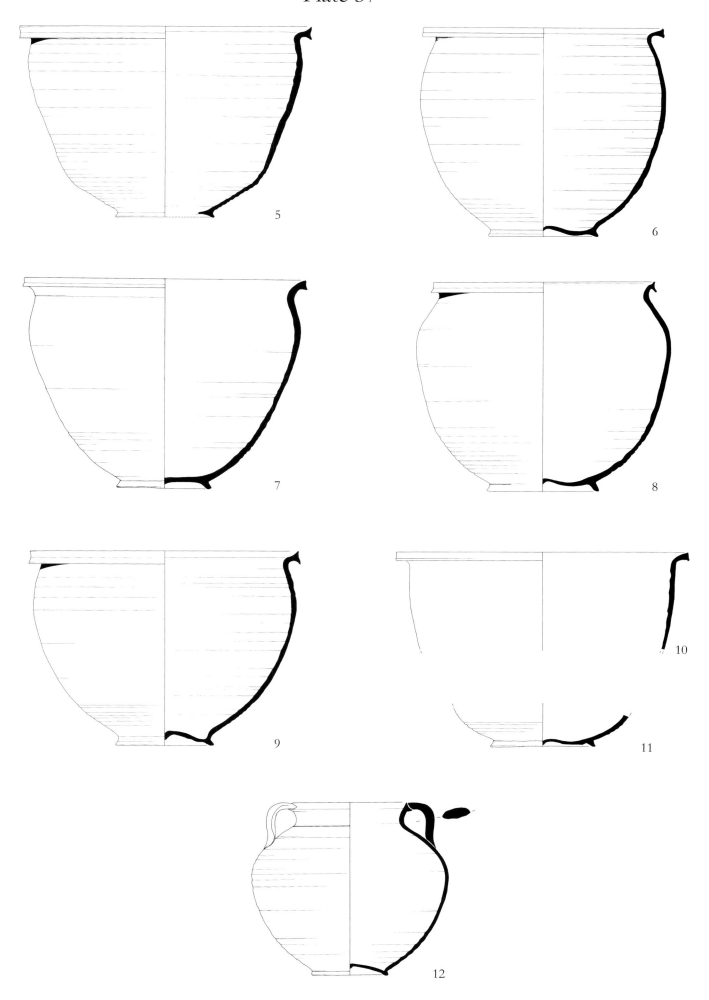

Locus 89, pottery, scale ¼

Plate 58

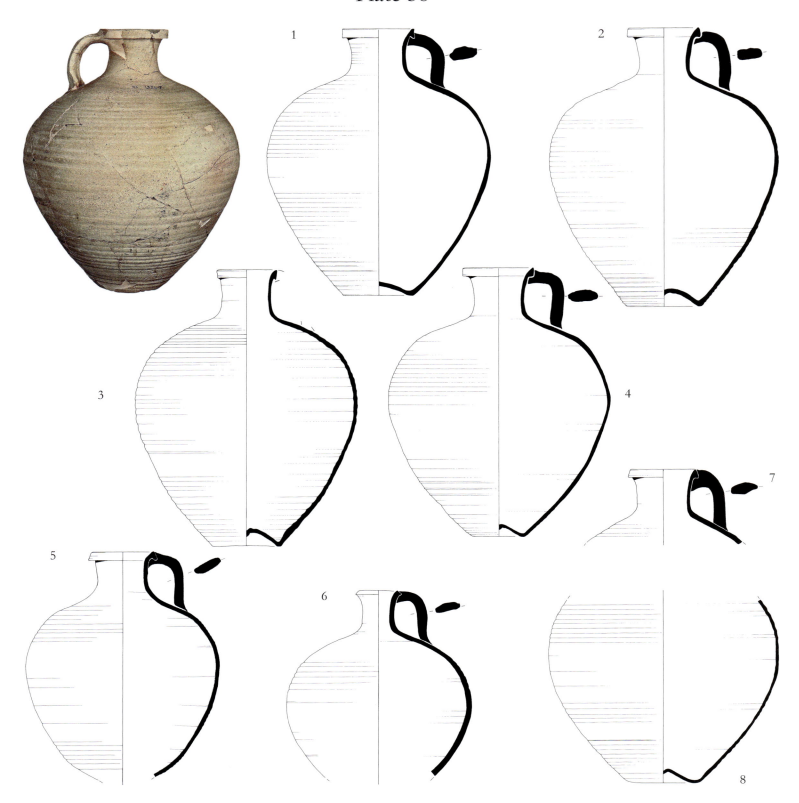

N° Pl.	N° Catal.	Position	Comments (archives)	Date	Description	Clay	Exterior
1	1574-6	86.1 (L. 89)	lower level	28/03/54	11 jugs	° red paste	white wash
2	1574-7	86.1 (L. 89)	lower level	28/03/54	jug	° red paste	white wash
3	1574-3	86.1 (L. 89)	lower level	28/03/54	jug	° red paste	white wash
4	1574-8	86.1 (L. 89)	lower level	26/03/54	jug	° red paste	white wash
5	1574-5	86.1 (L. 89)	lower level	26/03/54	jug	° red paste	white wash
6	1574-2	86.1 (L. 89)	lower level	26/03/54	jug	° red paste	white wash
7	1574-1	86.1 (L. 89)	lower level	26/03/54	jug	° red paste	white wash
8	1574-4	86.1 (L. 89)	lower level	26/03/54	jug	° red paste	white wash

° *According to de Vaux*

Locus 89, pottery and catalogue, scale ¼

Plate 59

N° Pl.	N° Catal.	Position	Comments (archives)	Date	Description	Clay	Exterior
1	1678	86.1 (L. 89)	lower level	26/03/54	jar	° pink earth	white wash
2	1677	86.1 (L. 89)	lower level	26/03/54	jar	° pink earth	white wash

° *According to de Vaux*

Locus 89, pottery, catalogue and photographs, scale ¼

Plate 60

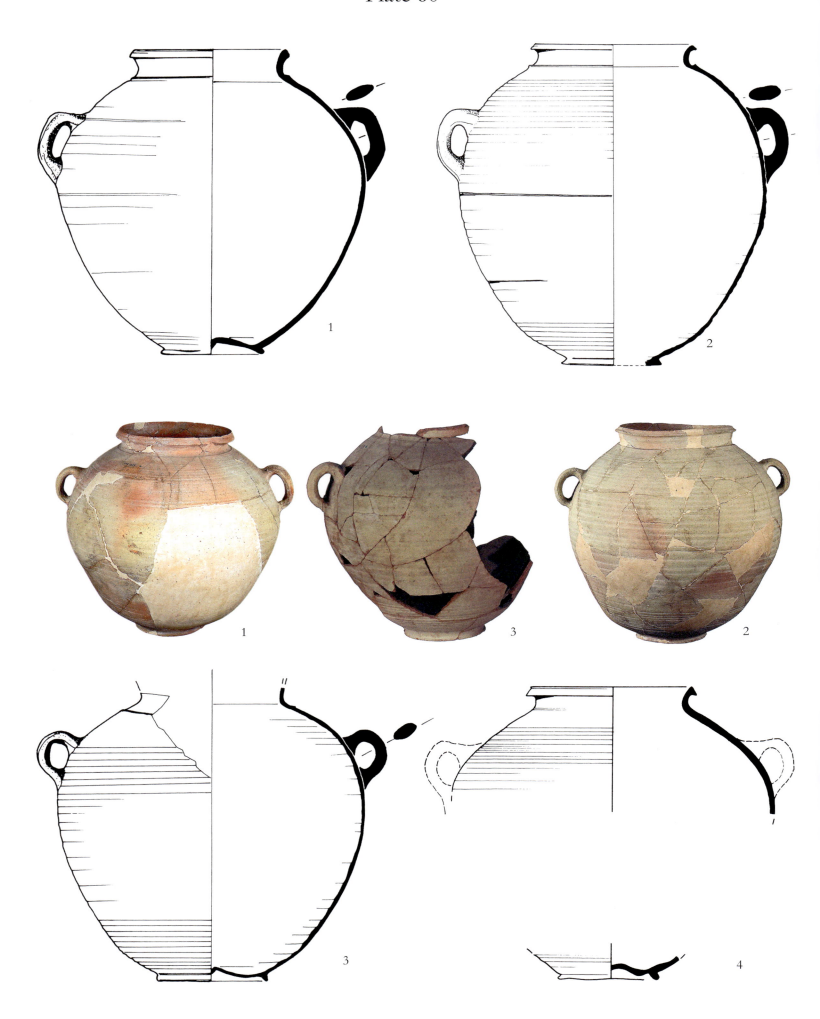

Locus 89, pottery and photographs, scale ¼

Plate 61

N° Pl.	N° Catal.	Position	Comments (archives)	Date	Description	Clay	Exterior
1	1678-D	86.1 (L. 89)	lower level	26/03/54	jar	° pink earth	white wash
2	1678-E	86.1 (L. 89)	lower level	26/03/54	jar	° pink earth	white wash
3	1678-F	86.1 (L. 89)	lower level	26/03/54	jar	° pink earth	white wash
4	1678-AC	86.1 (L. 89)	lower level	26/03/54	jar	° pink earth	white wash
5	1678-AC	86.1 (L. 89)	lower level	26/03/54	8 jars	° pink earth	white wash
6	1678-B	86.1 (L. 89)	lower level	26/03/54	jar	° pink earth	white wash
7	1678-C	86.1 (L. 89)	lower level	26/03/54	jar	° pink earth	white wash

° *According to de Vaux*

Locus 89, pottery, catalogue and photographs, scale ¼

Plate 62

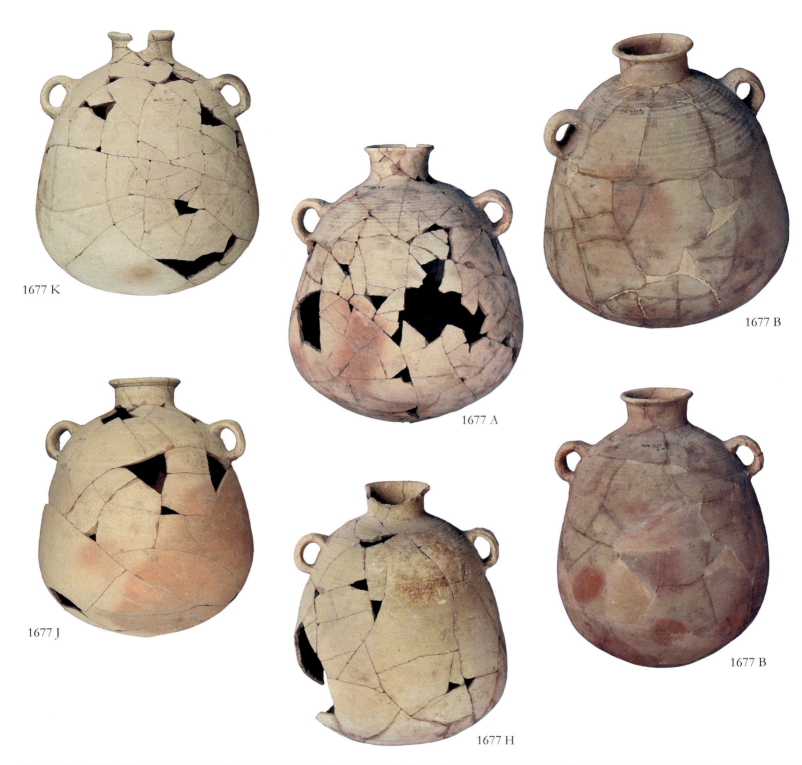

N° Pl.	N° Catal.	Position	Comments (archives)	Date	Description	Clay	Exterior
1	1677-K	86.1 (L. 89)	lower level	26/03/54	13 jars	° pink earth	white wash
2	1677-H	86.1 (L. 89)	lower level	26/03/54	jar	° pink earth	white wash
3	1677-G	86.1 (L. 89)	lower level	26/03/54	jar	° pink earth	white wash
4	1677-F	86.1 (L. 89)	lower level	26/03/54	jar	° pink earth	white wash
5	1677-C	86.1 (L. 89)	lower level	26/03/54	jar	° pink earth	white wash
6	1677-A	86.1 (L. 89)	lower level	26/03/54	jar	° pink earth	white wash
7	1677-D	86.1 (L. 89)	lower level	26/03/54	jar	° pink earth	white wash
8	1677-J	86.1 (L. 89)	lower level	26/03/54	jar	° pink earth	white wash
9	1677-B	86.1 (L. 89)	lower level	26/03/54	jar	° pink earth	white wash
10	1677-E	86.1 (L. 98)	lower level	26/03/54	jar	pink earth	white wash

° *According to de Vaux*

Locus 89, catalogue of pots and photographs

Plate 63

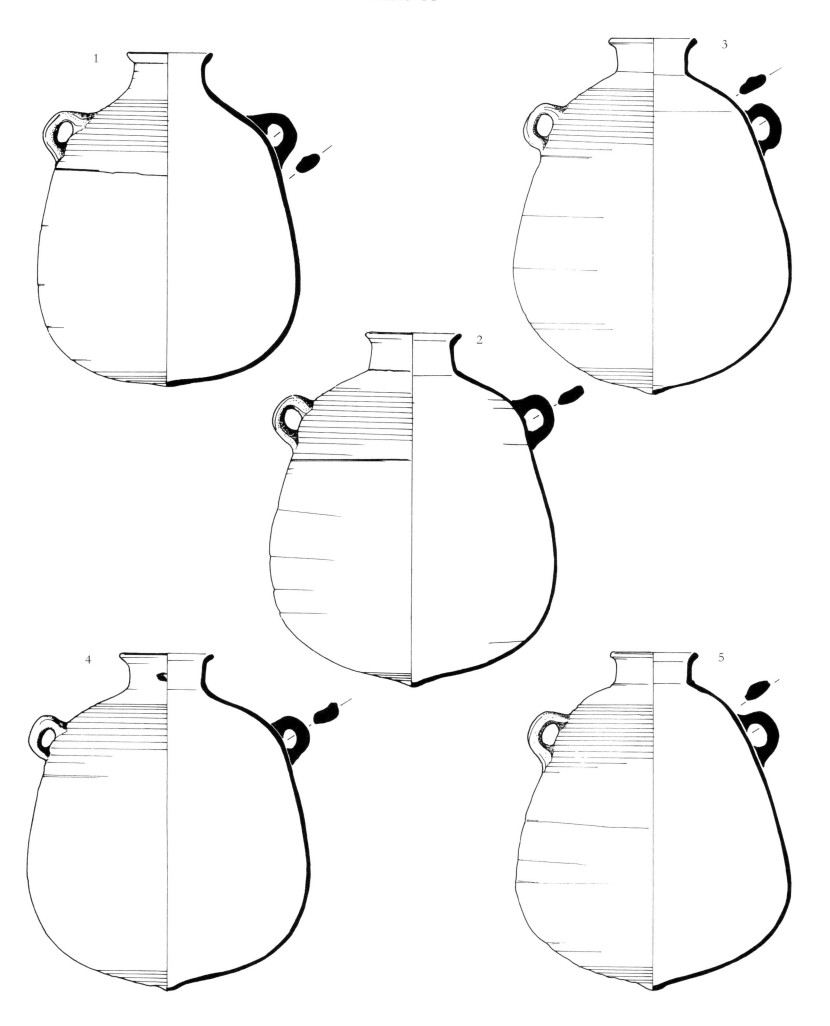

Locus 89, pottery, scale ¼

Plate 64

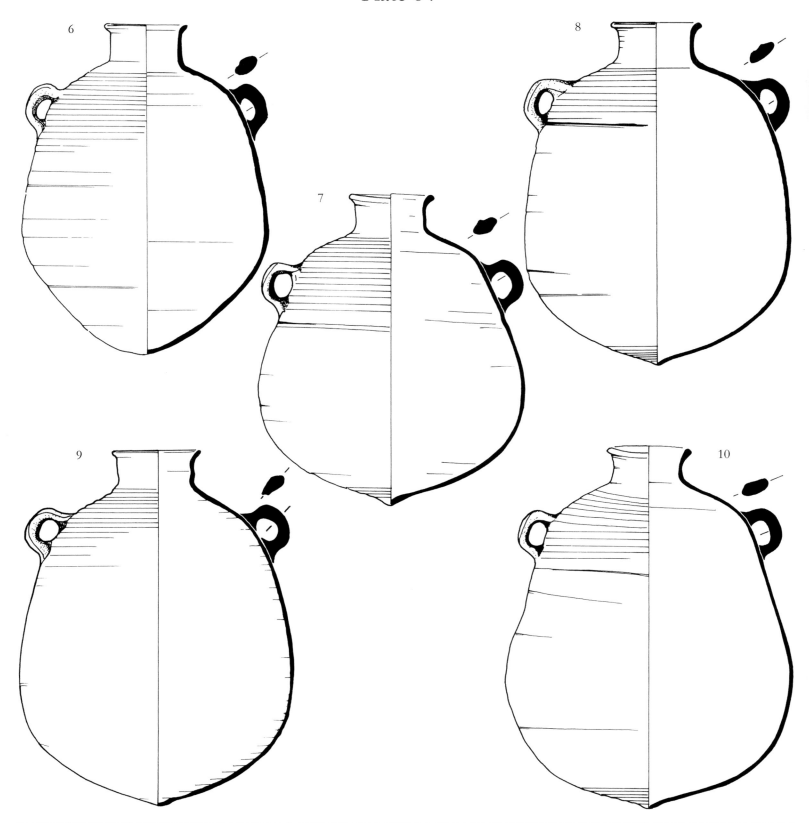

N° Pl.	N° Catal.	Position	Comments (archives)	Date	Description	Clay	Exterior
1	4436	89.3		14/03/54	crater	orange paste	beige wash
2	4439	89.3		14/03/54	jar	brown-grey paste	beige
3	4434	89.3		16/03/54	kettle	red paste	beige

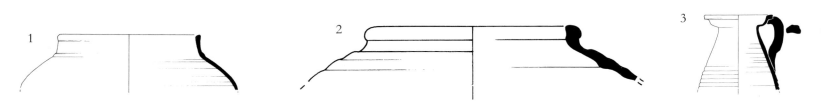

Locus 89, pottery and catalogue, scale ¼

Plate 65

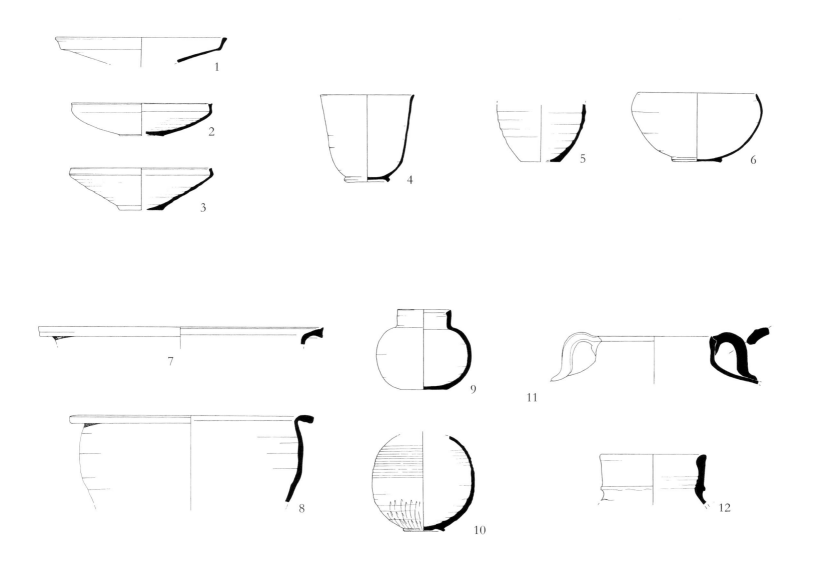

N° Pl.	N° Catal.	Position	Comments (archives)	Date	Description	Clay	Exterior
1	4419	87.2	(L. 87)	23/03/54	small dish	red paste	grey and red
2	1512	87.2	lower level (L. 87)	23/03/54	plate	° grey earth	white wash, burnt
3	1527	87.2	lower level (L. 87)	23/03/54	plate with a pierced hole	° red earth with grey section	white wash, burnt
4	1473	87.2	lower level (L. 87)	18/03/54	goblet	° red earth, fine	white wash
5	4416	87.2	(L. 87)	23/03/54	goblet	light brown paste	light brown
6	1528	87.2	lower level (L. 87)	23/03/54	bowl	° red earth with grey section	red wash
7	4418	87.2	(L. 87)	23/03/54	bowl	brown paste	beige engobe
8	4417	87.2	(L. 87)	23/03/54	bowl	orange paste	red-beige
9	1501	87.2	lower level (L. 87)	22/03/54	globular pot	° red earth	pink wash
10	1513	87.2	lower level (L. 87)	23/03/54	small jug	° red earth	pink wash
11	4421	87.1	(L. 87)	16/03/54	cooking pot	dark red paste	brown
12	4415	87.1	(L. 87)	16/03/54	jar	brown paste	beige, burnt

° *According to de Vaux*

Locus 87, pottery and catalogue, scale ¼

Plate 66

Plate 64, 3

Plate 67, 13

Plate 67, 1

Plate 67, 11

N° Pl.	N° Catal.	Position	Comments (archives)	Date	Description	Clay	Exterior
1	4362	185.1/03/4 ?	upper level (L. 86)	17/03/54	small dish	brownish-red paste	greyish-red
2	1450	185.1/03/4 ?	upper level (L. 86)	16/03/54	plate	° grey earth in section	white wash
3	1449	185.1/03/4 ?	upper level (L. 86)	16/03/54	bowl	° grey earth	white wash
4	1456	185.1/03/4 ?	upper level (L. 86)	17/03/54	plate	° red earth	white wash
5	1451	185.1/03/4 ?	upper level (L. 86)	16/03/54	plate	° grey earth	white wash
6	1476	185.1/03/4 ?	upper level (L. 86)	17/03/54	bowl	° red earth	white wash
7	1454	185.1/03/4 ?	upper level (L. 86)	17/03/54	small jug	° red earth	white wash, burnt
8	1455	185.1/03/4 ?	upper level (L. 86)	17/03/54	small jug	° red earth, coarse	white wash
9	4371	185.1/03/4 ?	upper level (L. 86)	16/03/54	unguentarium	orange paste	beige
10	4374	185.1/03/4 ?	upper level (L. 86)	17/03/54	small jug	brown paste	beige
11	4361	185.1/03/4 ?	upper level (L. 86)	17/03/54	jug	red paste with grey core	beige engobe
12	1457	185.1/03/4 ?	upper level (L. 86)	17/03/54	flask	° grey earth	white wash
13	4373	185.1/03/4 ?	upper level (L. 86)	17/03/54	flask	red paste with grey core	beige
14	4357	185.1/03/4 ?	(L. 86)	17/03/54	pot	orange paste	light red
15	4369	185.1/03/4 ?	(L. 86)	17/03/54	bottle	dark brown paste	dark brown
16	4366	185.1/03/4 ?	(L. 86)	17/03/54	bowl	red paste	light red
17	4367	185.1/03/4 ?	upper level (L. 86)	17/03/54	bowl	red paste with grey core	beige engobe
18	4368	185.1/03/4 ?	upper level (L. 86)	17/03/54	lid	orange paste	beige engobe
19	1452	185.1/03/4 ?	upper level (L. 86)	17/03/54	funnel	° grey earth	white wash
20	1467	185.1/03/4 ?	upper level (L. 86)	17/03/54	cooking pot	° red earth	burnt
21	1453	185.1/03/4 ?	upper level (L. 86)	17/03/54	globular pot	° grey earth	white wash
22	4363	185.1/03/4 ?	upper level (L. 86)	17/03/54	cooking pot	grey-brown paste	brown
23	4356	185.1/03/4 ?	upper level (L. 86)	17/03/54	cooking pot	orange paste	brown
24	4372	185.1/03/4 ?	upper level (L. 86)	17/03/54	jar	red paste with grey core	beige engobe
25	4370	185.1/03/4 ?	(L. 86)	17/03/54	jar	dark brown paste	brown-grey
26	4375	185.1/03/4 ?	upper level (L. 86)	17/03/54	jar support	brown paste	beige

° *According to de Vaux*

Locus 86, catalogue of pots and photographs

Plate 67

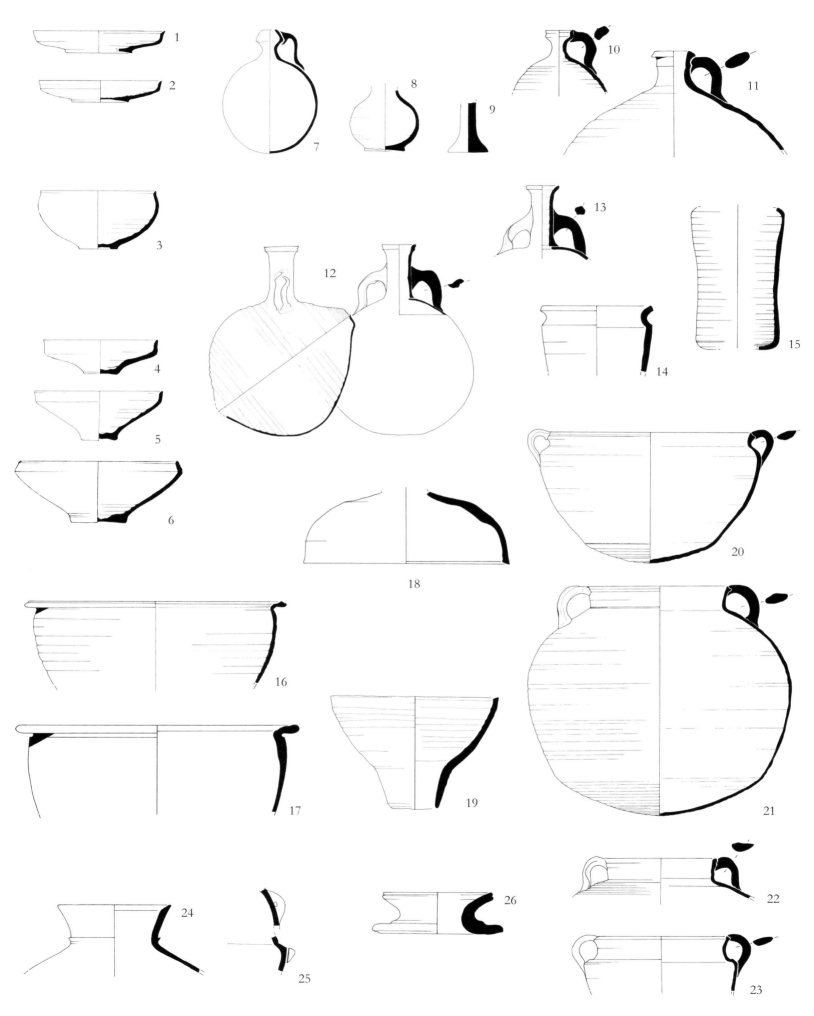

Locus 86, pottery, scale ¼

fig. 145. Paving 816, Loci 90, 93 and 98, and drain 878 on the south boundary, looking east (Photo 2008, after stripping in 2000)

Chapter E

The south platform

Vast paving 816 to the south of the settlement

Loci 90, 93, 94 and 83

A vast paved area 816, which de Vaux called a *platform* or *paving*, extends the settlement to the south. Though being a homogeneous part of the site, the area was excavated under different L. numbers – 90, 93, 94, 98 and 76 – despite its continuous profile. The excavation progressed from known buildings to verify the extension of the site to the south. The work took place between 18/3/54 and 1/4/54. Trenches were dug: the pavement was stripped in L. 93 as far as L. 76 (L. 76, 2/4/55), where it seems to be interrupted; as one leaves door 876, a trench extending L. 98 reaches its limit to the south: *We clear a wide surface of paving to the south, then we stop because it is without interest* (L. 94, 23/3/54) and: *An installed trench must follow the paving up to where it is lost at the outcrop of the terrace* (L. 98, 1/4/54). The clearance made in the year 2000 cleared it completely as far as drain 878 – open, well made and dropping into cesspit 936 (fig. 148).

The southern extension of the settlement, paved for almost 450 m², forms a transition between the constructions and the long terrace, but its function is not easy to see. De Vaux was not interested in it. Pavement 816, made of coarse, medium-sized stones, mixed with strewn pebbles, hugs the slope towards the southeast. Its regular and leveled extent is bordered by a carefully constructed drain 878; it was constructed in one go. It communicates with L. 77 and the connection gives it meaning; it is of a piece, at least at a late date, with the installations of L. 75 and 68 (bath) and opens onto workshop 144. The paving 816 is a work space. Drain 878, which avoids spreading of waste, suggests that people took water from it for laundry or washing. The proximity of an abundance of waste date pits, directly to the south, relates to agricultural work at the palm grove. The pavement would be suitable for desiccation, and press L. 75 for possible pressing. There is no reason why it should not also have served bivouacs, as deposits of buried bones were discovered there on several occasions.

Moreover, the borders of paving 816 raise the question of its place in the sequence of constructions. In the absence of a complete report, a recent photograph allows two remarks at this point: The first is that drain 878 continued to the west and that it was cut, in L. 94, by overflow 799 of pool 91. Overflow 799 is therefore subsequent to pavement 816. The second remark relates to the eastern boundary of 816, rectilinear on a north-south axis which is clearly visible on the photograph[82]. The paving is interrupted here, for some reason. The gravel marks a limit which would, in the axis, join up with the eastern partition of the restored pool L. 72-73 (the furthest to the west and the oldest of the series) to border the constructions before the digging of pool 71. In this case, cesspool 936 precedes pool 71, which is possible because, following the slope, its position matches the outlet of drain 878. Finally, the border of the paving corresponds roughly to the earthquake fracture in an extended line from the crack of pools 72-73 and 48-49; it may indicate a fracture line in the terrace, although the straight line of the border does not militate in favor of this. We would go so far as to suspect that the two north-south lines which affect the paving might be signs of other fractures; the limit of the pavement towards the east could be one of the edges of collapsed slabs, and the paving might have continued as far as pavement 938. We do not know whether sondages were taken in the intermediate unpaved space between L. 98-76 and 75.

---

82. Y. MAGEN, Y. PELEG, JSP 18, fig. 51, p. 47

fig. 146. Paving 816; a) and b) Loci 93/98, looking northeast and east (2008)
c) under the reinforcement around Locus 89, to the east (2014, Lionel Mochamps)

The stratification in L. 93 associated with L. 86 – The constructed elements can be sequenced without too much hesitation, even though the *Journal* makes no comment on their succession. The sequence is logical enough and is evident in Level 3B – the level of the reoccupation of the premises and the rapid development of its fixtures – with the exception of aqueduct 805, which borders L. 77 at Level 4, the digging of it having cut the stratification along the central building. The sherds collected in its proximity came from a mixed-up context; it makes no sense to take account of a coin of Alexander Jannaeus (KhQ 1534, from the surface). On the other hand, the stratification seems in place next to L. 86. Starting from the bottom:

93.8 – The oldest element must be Iron Age ash-scattering 86.2, which may spill out this far; 93-8 may be the extension of 81-7.

93.7 – The building of L. 86, the foundation of which was not observed.

93.6 – Paving 816; observation of the premises was possible after clearance of the site in 2004; the pavement stones lean, curving slightly, on the base of east wall 867 of L. 86; the paving therefore postdates the erection of L. 86.

93.5 and 93.4 – Layer 93.4 is more or less restored; sealing paving 93.6 (816), it contained *buried deposits*. Spoil deposit 93.5 is an extension of 93.4 up to the wall of L. 86. We isolated the material (93-5) as the *Journal* specified on 27/3/54 that east reinforcement 870 *is built on the spoil which produced two plates and a large pot with a wide opening* (L. 93, 27/3/54). The *Catalogue* adds as a note, on 25/3/54 and for plate KhQ 1537: *L. 93, under the reinforcement of the wall of 89*. The dating to 25/3 obliges us to accept that on that day the excavation had already recognized spoil 93-5 under the reinforcement.

93.3 – The square reinforcement, 869 and 870, surrounding the southeast part of L. 86, was to protect or contain walls 867 and 868. The foundation of 870 will have cut into the upper part of spoil 93-3. The pottery of 93-5 constitutes the *terminus a quo* for situating the construction of the reinforcement in the chronology. As a precaution, and to the extent possible, we have separated the pottery of layers 93-4 and 93-5, even though they are contemporary.

Reconstruction of the stratigraphy

93-1 surface layer

93-2 erosion heap; indeterminate thickness

93-3 reinforcement L. 86 with heaps 869 and 870

93-4 layer sealing 93.6

93-5 spoil sealed by 93.3

93-6 paving 816 to the south of the constructions

93-7 foundation of L. 86

93-8 restored layer: the old buried deposits

The casing of L. 86 – The encasement of the southern half of L. 86 by three stretches of stone masonry was viewed as the reinforcement of a weakened L. 86. The morphology of the masonry is surprising as it plays a role of discontinuous support for the building. To the west, in L. 81-88, support wall 801 has clearly slipped in the sequence of constructions. L. 86 initially stood in isolation, L. 92 then joined its southwest corner, and finally support wall 801 (L. 88) was placed in the corner of L. 92. Support 869, to the south of L. 86, against wall 868, extends as a square with east support 870 against wall 867. The two extremities of the square finish at a sharp right angle. Element 869 is interrupted to the west and east with heavy bond stones. The size of the three walls is not identical: to the west 801 displays a thickness of 1.05 m, 1.20 m for 869 to the south and 0.80 m for 870 to the east. Their preserved height varies between 0.80 and 1 m. Their surface is so uniform and even in jonction to each other that one has to suppose that the superstructure was of crude earth like that of the supporting walls of L. 86. We see them as a reinforcement rather than a buttress.

The reasons for a reinforcement of L. 86 are not clear, but there is a convergence of indications. De Vaux interpreted side by side walls as the restoration necessary after the earthquake, which the stratification does not show and the chronology does not allow. We have said that L. 86 was in active use in the middle of the first century and very probably up to

fig. 147. a) and b) Paving along the east front of the settlement (Photo 2014)

the run-up to the revolt, but we know nothing of its foundation. Might the casing of L. 86 go back to the last third of the first century BC as per the proposal that was made?

We have to accept that it does not. First, the earthquake did not take place and the building remained intact; there is no indication of any weakness in the masonry. A violent shaking could have destabilized the southern part of an unsupported L. 86 like other buildings to the north. However, the remains of the walls have suffered neither fissure due to a seismic tremor. The supporting walls are wide, solid and compact. In the visible low beds, there is nothing to suggest an emergency containment; nothing was restored there, and L. 86 is in good condition.

The arrangement of the succession of constructed elements convinces us that the encasing was late. A careful examination on site in 2004 has allowed us to confirm that the base of support wall 869 (south) is made of small stones, while the mass of the heap contains large pebbles (fig. 146a and c). The small stones must constitute a foundation which is imprinted or depressed in layer 93-4/5. For L. 81, we noted that the support wall on the north side (801) had converted tanks 802 and 803, attributed to phase 81-3 of Level 3B. Spoil 93-5, sealed by the casing, antedates the latter, which *is constructed on the spoil which produced two plates and a large pot with a wide opening* (L. 93, 27/3/54). The *Journal* does not describe spoil 93.5 – neither its composition nor its compact or layered nature. The spoil may, on the contrary, be of a piece; the accumulation would have taken a long time. It is above paving 816, *much lower than the foundation of the reinforcement (...) a wide pavement begins* (L. 90, 21/3/54). The reinforcement around L. 89 rests on paving 816 (fig. 146c).

The approximate date of spoil 93.3 can be defined by the large, complete cooking pot (pl. 70:11). This kind of pot was manufactured over a long period: R. Bar-Nathan situates it at Masada in the slot AD 66/74[83]. Her proposal matches the late date of the reinforcement which seals the spoil. The various arguments invite us to lower the chronology of the casing: a later work, probably from the last phase of the occupation before 68, and in any case after decommissioning of the L. 88.

---

83. R. Bar-Nathan, *Masada VII*, Jerusalem 2006, p. [164] et pl. 30: 51 to 55

The blocking wall 873 and support walls 801-869-870 would be contemporaneous. We recall that transverse blocking wall 873 sealed L. 89. The plan (fig. 137d) neatly shows that the casing encloses only L. 89, as if to confirm the sealing. So, wall 873 closes off the fourth side. It may be that this is a coincidence. Nonetheless, there is a high probability that this can be seen as the result of protection or preservation of a particular room with its objects. The great care evidently taken lends the location and the objects it contains a value which was not solely domestic. Protecting and preserving was an evident concern not only in the hiding places of the area.

Buried meals left-overs – We note, and we regard this as settled, that layer 93-8 shows signs of deep buried deposits. Meal left-overs were interred in the south of the settlement. The clearance carried out by the Israeli army uncovered a few more *on the floor and between the paving stones*. We have several times assigned the buried deposits to deep layers: L. 130-131 for the northern sector and 80-60 for the eastern sector. It would be logical for them to be found there. That the recent clearance recognized some above paving 816 and *between the stones* does not oblige us to modify the other stratigraphic attributions. Oral tradition collected at the *École Biblique* reported that, during the digging of the trenches for recognizing the boundaries of the paving, the buried deposits were so numerous that it was decided not to record them on the surveys. They clearly lay on top of the paving, but some, earlier, might still lie underneath. Another oral tradition reported that a deposit in a large complete pot was found during the uncovering of the *pillars* of L. 77 by the English team which made sondages in the early 1960s. We may draw two conclusions from these observations that are of interest for the stratigraphy: First, that the custom of burying meal left-overs was continued for quite some time well after laying of the paving. Then, that paving 816 had been covered by repeated accumulations so that the deposits could be interred there. These accumulations lend credibility to the existence of layer 93-4.

Postscript – Against the northeast front of the *khirbeh*, the excavations conducted in 2002 stripped a paved area laid in the same manner as that which borders the south front in L. 93. The paving is still visible today, although its contours have worn away, as recent

Plate 68

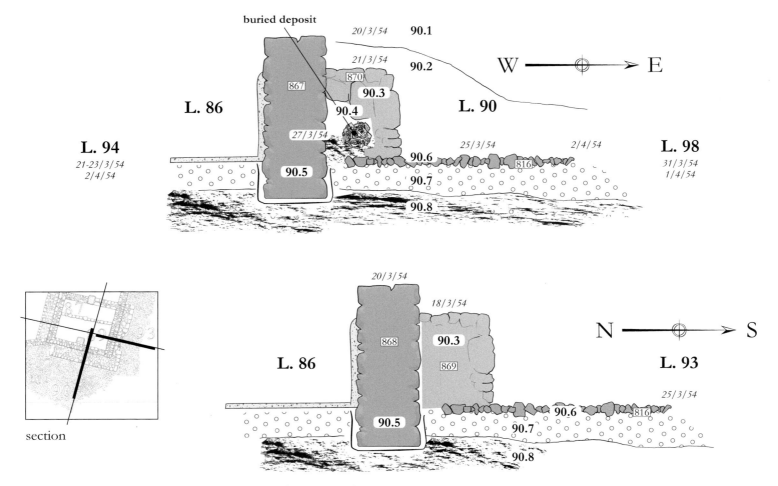

Schema and stratigraphic diagram of Locus 90 (for the chart of symbols, see page 155)

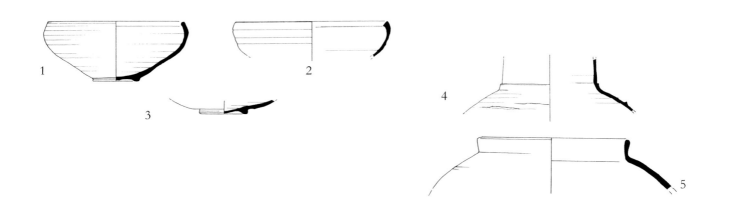

N° Pl.	N° Catal.	Position	Comments (archives)	Date	Description	Clay	Exterior
1	1596	90.6	(L. 98, catalogue)	31/03/54	bowl	° grey earth	white wash
2	3614	90.6	(L. 98, catalogue)	31/03/54	bowl	red paste	beige-red
3	3560	90.6	(L. 98, catalogue)	31/03/54	plate	red paste	red
4	3561	90.6	(L. 98, catalogue)	31/03/54	jar	red paste	beige
5	3562	90.2?	(L. 98, catalogue)	23/03/54	jar	red paste with grey core	red-beige

° *According to de Vaux*

Locus 98, pottery and catalogue, scale ¼

Restored elements	Level	Definition	Journal dates	Coins	Position	N°.	Chronology
90.1	Post 4	Erosion level (L93)	20/3/54				
90.2	Post 4	Levelling of walls (L90)	18/3/54				
90.3	3C	Reinforcement of L86	18-20/3/54 (L. 90) 21-25/3/54 (L. 93)	KhQ. 1518 1463 1519 1535	upper level surface to the south upper level upper level	1 1 1 1	Dora (68/69) Proc./Tiberius Proc./Tiberius Herod
90.4	3B/C	Buried deposits	27/3/54 (L. 93)				
90.5	3B/C	Construction of locus 86	see on L86				
90.6	3B/C	Metalling on the south front	21-23/3/54 (L. 94) 25/3/54 (L. 90)				
90.7	2 (?)	Leveling at the approaches to the south front	Restored				
90.8	1	Layer of ash	at L. 77 = 77.8				

Stratigraphic diagram of Locus 90

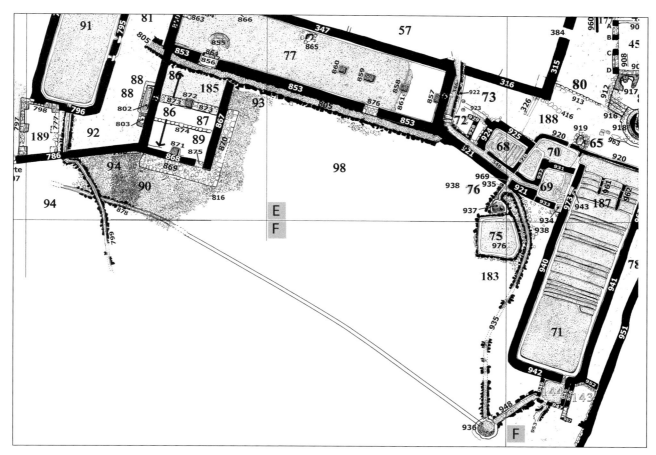

fig. 148.   The general layout of the south paving, surrounded by drains

photographs show (fig. 147). Some published photographs give a better, if approximate, view of it[84]. The paving, fractured by long parallel faults on the eastern front of the ruin, borders them to the east. It is cut by drain 910 which issues from L. 61. It is possible that it is interrupted to the south at the height of door 909, which we are trying to restore. Such an eventuality would lend credibility to L. 45 being considered a lobby. The paved areas to the south and east may be in front of the busy access points.

---

84. Y. Magen and Y. Peleg, JSP 18, figs. 69-70, p. 64.

Plate 69

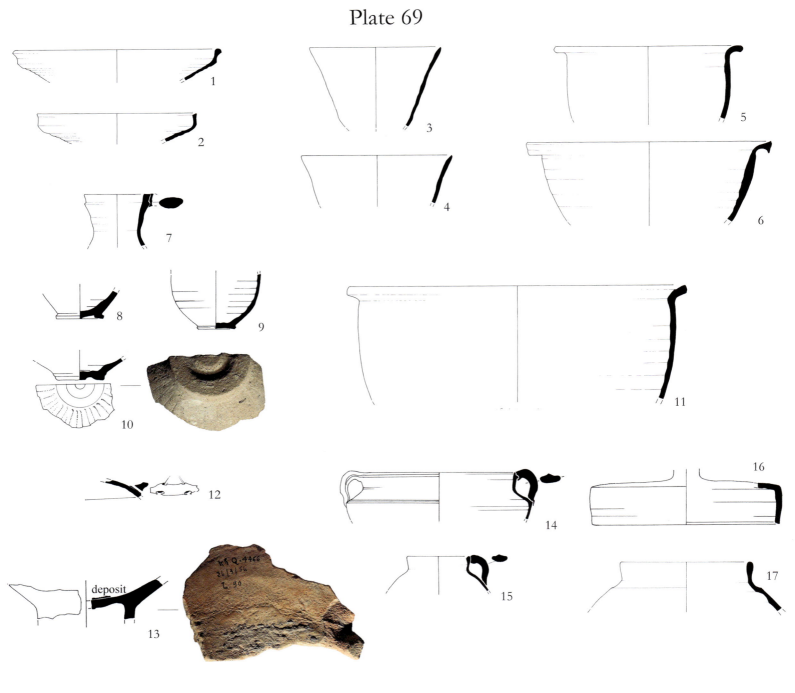

N° Pl.	N° Catal.	Position	Comments (archives)	Date	Description	Clay	Exterior
1	4479	90.2	L. 90 (catalogue)	21/03/54	small dish	orange paste	beige
2	4470	90.1	L. 90 (catalogue)	20/03/54	small dish	orange paste	beige
3	4472	90.6	L. 90 (catalogue)	31/03/54	goblet	dark red paste	beige
4	4478	90.1	L. 90 (catalogue)	20/03/54	goblet	grey paste	beige
5	4471	90.2	L. 90 (catalogue)	21/03/54	bowl	brown-red paste	beige
6	4465	90.2	L. 90 (catalogue)	21/03/54	bowl	brownish-red paste	beige
7	4468	90.2	L. 90 (catalogue)	24/03/54	jug	brownish-red paste	beige
8	4469	90.2	L. 90 (catalogue)	21/03/54	bowl	dark grey paste	burnt
9	4512	90.2	L. 90 (catalogue)	21/03/54	goblet	dark red paste	red
10	4474	90.6?	L. 90 (catalogue)	28/03/54	bowl	brown-red paste	beige engobe
11	4473	90.2?	L. 90 (catalogue)	no date	bowl	orange paste	beige engobe
12	4475	90.2	L. 90 (catalogue)	24/03/54	jar lid	red paste	beige-red
13	4466	90.2	L. 90 (catalogue)	24/03/54	incense burner	brownish-red paste with residue	red-beige
14	4467	90.2	L. 90 (catalogue)	21/03/54	cooking pot	brown-red paste	brown
15	4398	90.6	L. 90 (catalogue)	31/03/54	cooking pot	orange paste	light brown
16	4477	90.2?	L. 90 (catalogue)	no date	jar lid	dark brown paste	beige engobe
17	4476	90.6	L. 90 (catalogue)	30/03/54	jar	light brown paste	light brown

Locus 90, pottery and catalogue, scale ¼

Plate 70

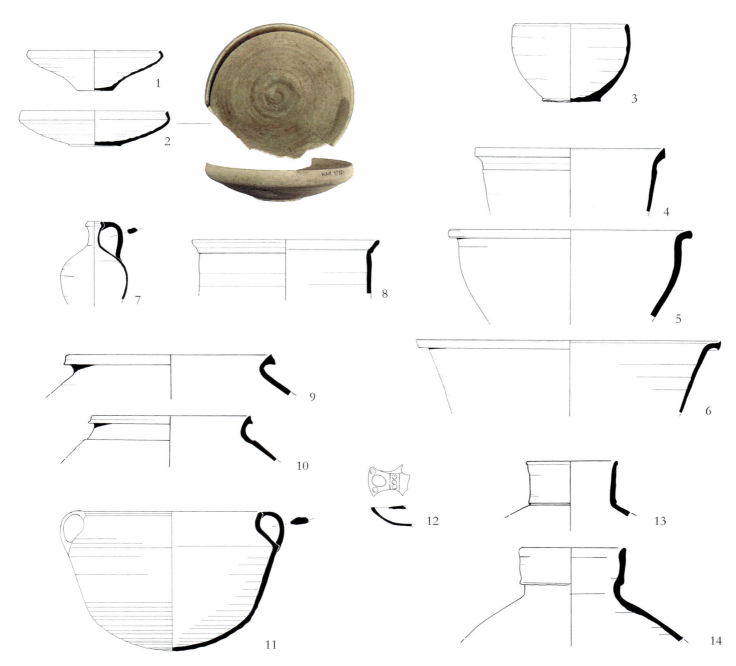

N° Pl.	N° Catal.	Position	Comments (archives)	Date	Description	Clay	Exterior
1	1538	90.5	L. 93	25/03/54	plate	° red earth	pink wash
2	1537	90.5	L. 93, upper level, under the reinforcement of the wall of 89 (870)	25/03/54	plate	° red earth	pink wash
3	3568	90.2	L. 93 (catalogue)	24/03/54	bowl	brownish-yellow paste	beige
4	3571	90.5	L. 93 (catalogue)	27/03/54	bowl	brownish-red paste	beige
5	3574	90.5	L. 93 (catalogue)	27/03/54	bowl	brownish-red paste	beige engobe
6	3577	90.6	L. 93 (catalogue)	26/03/54	bowl	red paste	beige engobe
7	1561	90.6	L. 93	25/03/54	small pyriform jug	° grey earth	white wash
8	3576	90.6	L. 93 (catalogue)	25/03/54	small vat	brownish-red paste	beige engobe
9	3573	90.5	L. 93 (catalogue)	27/03/54	crater	greyish-brown paste	beige engobe
10	3572	90.5	L. 93 (catalogue)	27/03/54	crater	brownish-red paste	beige engobe
11	1565	90.6	L. 93, lower level	27/03/54	cooking pot	° red earth	burnt
12	1571	90.5	L. 93	27/03/54	lamp		
13	3570	90.5	L. 93 (catalogue)	27/03/54	neck of jar	red paste	beige
14	3569	90.5	L. 93 (catalogue)	27/03/54	jar neck and shoulder	red paste	brown

° *According to de Vaux*

Locus 93, pottery and catalogue, scale ¼

fig. 149.　　Aerial view of the western edge of the site (photograph: Jordan Air Force, 1953)

Chapter F

The western boundary

Loci 95, 96 and 97

Loci 95, 96 and 97 occupy the southwest corner of the settlement. The excavated space extends between pool 91 and the edge of the ravine to the west. The crest of it being more fragile, a large part of the constructions was swept away and we think the earthquake fractured the terrace at exactly this point: fault 4 crosses it diagonally from the southwest to the northeast (fig. 8). The clearance of the three loci, covering roughly 190 m², was conducted in less than ten days between the 10th and 30th March, 1954. No photograph was taken of it.

The series of separate curtain walls completes the enclosure of the settlement at this point. The steep slope of the ravine was first reinforced by two ranked parallel terraces; external terrace wall 426, lower on the slope, supports crest wall 785. The reinforcement of the line of the plateau continues towards the north, bordering L. 103 until it joins heap 598 at the north corner of the western annexes. In the overall project of enclosing the site, consolidation work was considered necessary at the point where it dominates the ravine. Especially so when it was intended to manage the reentrant of the corner and to bed L. 97. In an effort to give the extension towards the west manageable space, wall 786 joins up with the right-hand corner of wall 785. The most economical means of achieving this was to follow the straight line of the corner of L. 86 at the point closest to the ravine.

The archaeological sediment is not thick here and the natural gravel of the terrace was struck 40 cm below the surface: *the east-west wall is founded on the gravel roughly 0.40 m under the floor of L. 96* (L. 96, 30/3/54); as de Vaux did not find any occupation floor, *floor* here means the *surface* of the floor. We may deduce that the layout in the southwest corner is recent in the chronology and that it cannot be attributed to the origins of the settlement, as is proposed by the *Plan* of Period Ib. Activity there was not intense; the layer was thin and no stratigraphy could be described.

L. 96 is an open-air space which does not really set out a specific walking area. The space was defined to complete the south front of the establishment as its western flank remained open to the countryside. The south front then closed, a useful door towards the esplanade was inserted in wall 786, and we do not know why lock chamber/lobby L. 189 seemed necessary. L. 96 and 97, although enclosed, would have been viewed as exteriors to a more private inner core of the settlement.

L. 95 barely exists. The investigation progressed from the east starting at L. 92 and the space worked was labeled 95 after the ends of the lobby, renamed L. 189, were recognized. Starting from L. 92, the excavation conducted under the heading 95 spilled over to the west, L. 189. At the time of the works, the sherds collected in L. 189 were recorded under L. 95, and again under the same cipher those of the south part of L. 96. The pottery recorded under L. 96 relates only to the northern part of the L.. The junction between L. 96 north and L. 103 was not defined while L. 103 is a lost space in the form of a possible corridor. At the end of the occupation, remains of a precarious wall 749 and the first section of wall 557 at the northern end, trace out a L. 192 in the middle of L. 103, with the advantage of isolating the conveniences, L. 112.

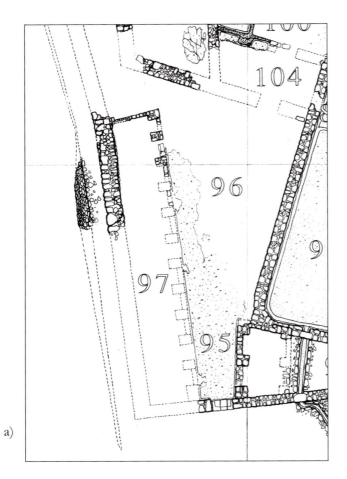
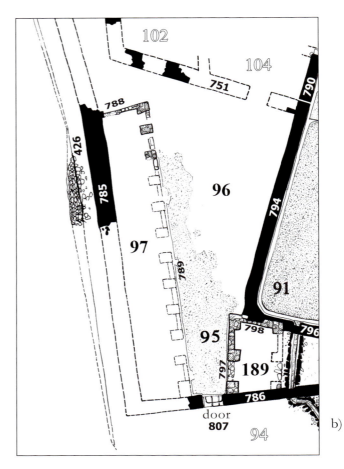

fig. 150. The late extension of the southwest of the site.
  a) Coüasnon plan, Period Ib
  b) Designation of the constructed elements
  c) Reconstruction according to plans, placed on the photogrammatic model of the terrace, looking east (the scree on the slope of the ravine is spoil earth from the excavation)

The L. 97 area is the most destroyed of the whole site: *The structures were here carried off by the very steep slope* (L. 97, 20/3/55). Careful to give the whole an architectural coherence, Coüasnon reconstructed L. 97 by symmetry, reproducing in the south what he had drawn in the north. As represented on the *Plans*, it attracts attention because of the configuration restored to it from Period Ib onwards: a sort of narrow gallery open to courtyard L. 96 through twelve pillars (*L'archéologie*, pl. VI). The gallery does not feature on the *Plan* of Period II (*ibid.*, pl. XVII), indicating that de Vaux apparently decided, at least when he was drawing up the plan, that the gallery, destroyed by the earthquake, was not restored on the return from exile, Period II. The reconstitution is in any case hypothetical as two-thirds of the construction has disappeared. Further on, *in a line of stones we distinguish the remains of a threshold opening towards the west* (L. 96, 27/3/54). A door provided access to the gallery, between the second and third pillars from the north, and not in the axis of the construction. That a door closed one of the intercolumniations means that the passage was not free in the other openings of the series, as the long stones placed in the spaces framing the door suggest. What remains upright of L. 97 could be just an aedicule opened by three or four pillars at the height of the threshold, and the continuation of the gallery could be blind. The restoration measures 19 m and was probably modeled on the twelve-pillar long gallery of L. 17, 18, 19, 20 at Ain Feshkha, L. 33[85], although this was much bigger, reaching 30 m in length. Gallery 97 of Qumran would be a replica on a reduced scale as there was a lack of space here unlike at Ain Feshkha.

The question of its function remains unanswered. A few proposals have been advanced brought forward. In the *Journal*, de Vaux makes no pronouncement on it. In *L'archéologie*, he proposes seeing it as *a light building (...) loc. 97 (...) is interpreted, conjecturally, as a stable for beasts of burden* (p. 6). The internal width of the gallery is only two metres, and just a metre for that of the door, which is insufficient for passage and stabling of horses or donkeys. The subsidiary question of the presence of animals at Qumran cannot be solved; it is only in the modern period and in evolved societies that animals have disappeared from daily life. It would be surprising if the group living at Qumran, between fifteen and twenty persons, we think, did not have at least some sheep or goats to provide dairy products as a staple. L. 135, however, is not a sheep pen. Flocks had to graze and be placed in the palm grove and not on the escarpment plateau upward. Mounted or pack animals remain, but space L. 97, set out as it is, is not suitable. In any case, entrance to Qumran was from the north and it is hardly likely that animals were used to cross the site from area to area. The gallery of Ain Feshkha was linked to a workshop, but we cannot be more specific than this. L. 97, whatever extension might be restored to it, must have been something similar.

---

85. *Qumrân*, Vol. I, pl. XLVII, p. 261.

fig. 151. Sector of Locus 96 partly destroyed by the earthquake. In the background, pillars of Locus 97.

fig. 152. Locus 130 with exposed deposits, in the foreground, the mass of ash filling pool 173, in the middle distance, the yellow sediment on wall 501 of Locus 123.

Section III

The north enclosure

An extension for a communitarian function?

*Loci 134, 130 – 131, 132, 138, 135,
136 – 137, 172 (129 – 133), 140, 141*

General observations on the north enclosure

The north enclosure extends to the northwest of the main body of the settlement inside its walls. The plan shows it as an planned extension. Its layout is linked to the diversification of human activities after the Hasmonaean house was converted into a permanent establishment. It is possible to insert it into the chronology. The enclosure occupies an area crossed by the system of water collection which disturbs its unity, which is why we are right to suppose that the layout of the aqueduct will have put the enclosure out of use; or at least interrupted its primary function. The founding of aqueduct 500, at least in its final layout, would thus be more recent. The enclosure of almost 1000 m² divides the spaces without apparent regularity; it was formed in successive stages, and at first sight the reasons for them are difficult to understand. Four irregular quadrants may be distinguished. We start from the logical principle that the site extended to the north from wall 501. In general, the management of the space develops from what is built. Generally speaking, we may surmise its chronological progression as follows: 1) to the southwest, L. 130 and L. 131, originally an open space outside the built-up perimeter; 2) to the southeast, the trapezoid space of L. 129, L. 133 and L. 134; 3) to the northeast, the vast open space of L. 135 which includes the store separated from L. 141; 4) to the northwest, as an outgrowth to the west, L. 132 and L. 138 (and L. 136, L. 137, L. 139 and L. 142?). De Vaux thinks the enclosure was abandoned in Period III, after 68, and this is quite likely.

The general set-up

Even when built, the enclosure separated from the main block *intra muros*, remained an exterior adjoining the north front of the main building extended by the annexes and the west wing (L. 111, L. 120, L. 121 and L. 122). Its irregular layout responds to different demands. The short southwest segment, bayonet wall 656 of L. 132, follows the crest of the ravine. The northwest segment, wall 655 of L. 139, to receive the aqueduct, bars at right angles the narrow cordon of the plateau between the ravine to the west and the small wadi to the north. The north segment, wall 657 of L. 135, towards the east, curves to the south, respecting the path which came from the west and ends in front of L. 27. Previous late L. 27, a recess in the north front was the main entrance of the residence. Later, at small door 399 (L. 27-152) on the same path should have been the principal access to the main building following the conversion of the premises.

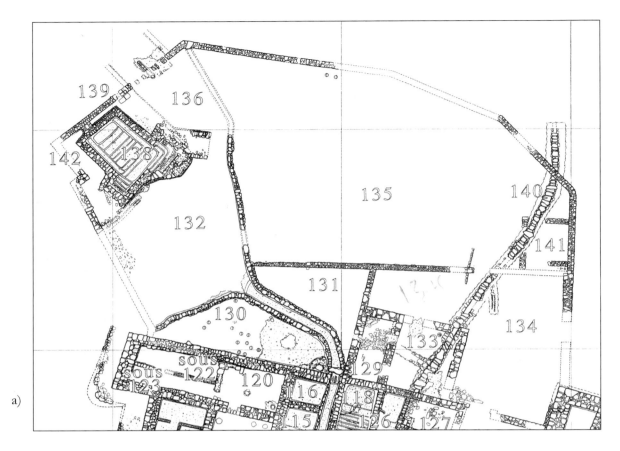
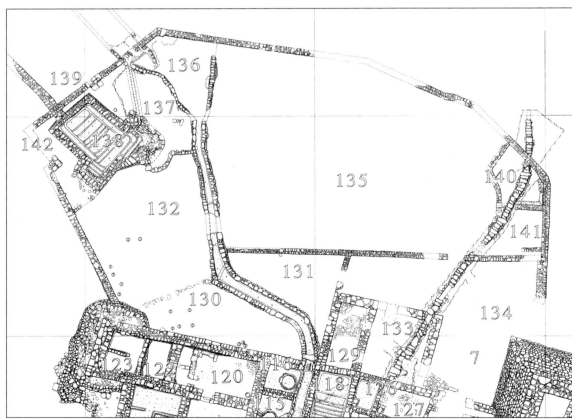

fig. 153. The north enclosure
 a) From Coüasnon Plan, period Ib
 b) From Coüasnon Plan, period II

Layout and the question of circulation

The location extends in the open air with low walls, as we shall see, but the circulation is not easy to recreate as, traffic patterns have been modified. It The open space even seems congested, and in the end the final conversions confirm a virtual abandonment.

On the outside, the reception platform of the Hasmonaean period, Level 2, to the north of the residence, had remained in use at Level 3 as the culmination of the west path which, after the mouth of the gorge, came from the Beqaʿ (and Jerusalem). Originally, one entered the enclosure by way of L. 134 at the foot of the tower. Coüasnon's *Plan* of Period Ib restores the entrance in breach 704 in wall 660; we do not demur, as it respects the early organization of the enclosure. Door 705 of the settlement *intra muros* was still that of the outbuildings of the Hasmonaean residence; there is nothing left of it but a fragment of the displaced threshold, because it is situated on one of the earthquake faults. With evacuation drain 564 buried, access towards L. 135 was straightforward, by means of passageway 703 in wall 678. Aedicule L. 141 was dependent on L. 134 and will have been linked to the activities conducted in L. 135; we shall see below that a destination can be attributed to it.

The western front of the enclosure manifests an expansion of the inhabited surface towards the ravine. The extension responded to the concern to approach the ravine better and to place L. 138 there, the final architectural addition to the enclosure. Such an expansion linked the space *intra muros* with the most practical path, which drops into the western ravine. L. 138 is within reach of entrance 702.

Entry occurred via door 702, itself served by the path from the west. However, internal progression towards door 582 (705), L. 128/L. 134, is impeded: the drain blocks the way. Everything suggests that wide drain 500, possibly in its final state in Level 4, brought circulation in the space to a standstill. In the western sector of the enclosure, it had been subjected to a radical reordering at the time when large pools L. 91, L. 56-58 and L. 71 were filled with water, which required a more effective means of supply; all these works may correspond to the construction of the dam, from the gorge to the foot of the drop, which promised an increased water supply. The sometimes rather unconvincing restorations on Coüasnon's plans of Periods Ib and II reveal the excavators' reluctance to link the constructed elements. The hypothesis of a gangway has been raised; though not very credible, it does have the advantage of replying to the question of passage: block 668, encroaching under the masonry of bath L. 138, would have been the first stone-built section of a crossing over aqueduct 500. But the eastern fallout from the supposed gangway is missing, and we shall see below that, on the contrary, the setting of the aqueduct entailed the demolition of part of block 668. The aqueduct rendered obsolete the block 668. The best thing is still to imagine a more modest supply drain leaving the passage free.

Another solution has the advantage of being the simplest and most logical: that aqueduct 500 and bath L. 138 were linked in a conjoined project and that their realization involved abandoning the original function of the entire north enclosure. The proposal raises the question of the water supply to Hasmonaean Qumran. Would collecting rainwater from the roof have sufficed to supply cistern L. 110? It all depends on the surface exploited. A quick calculation, only approximate of course, provides a satisfactory answer.

Round cistern L. 110 has a capacity of some 100 m^3 without being filled to the top, i.e. 100,000 litres. For an average of 100 mm/m^2 of annual rainfall, i.e. 100 litres/m^2, a collection surface of 1000 m^2 is required. Not all the rainwater that fell was collected, and we would estimate that a third of it was lost. We have to find 1500 m^2. The surface of the roofs of the western annexes amounts to 310 m^2. The courtyard between the annexes and the large central building has an area of 275 m^2. The roofs of the large central building cover 1100 m^2. The total available surface is a little over 1700 m^2. The result is that old Qumran Level 2 was easily capable of supplying cistern L. 110. It is probable that the converted site, Level 3, first developed before the digging of the large pools, and that the construction of the aqueduct was part of the same project. We cannot be precise as to its chronology, Level 3A and B. Finally, the whole space to the north of the *khirbeh* was available long-term to establish the large enclosure.

Functions

The vast enclosed north space, outside the walls, had a function linked to the settlement; it cannot have been a separate feature. The remains betray an occupation of some duration. As reading only the plan may lead to mistakes, we have to insist on the fact that

a) Level (2 ?) -3A

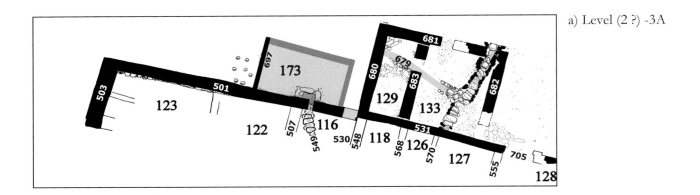

b) Level 3A/Bel 3B/C

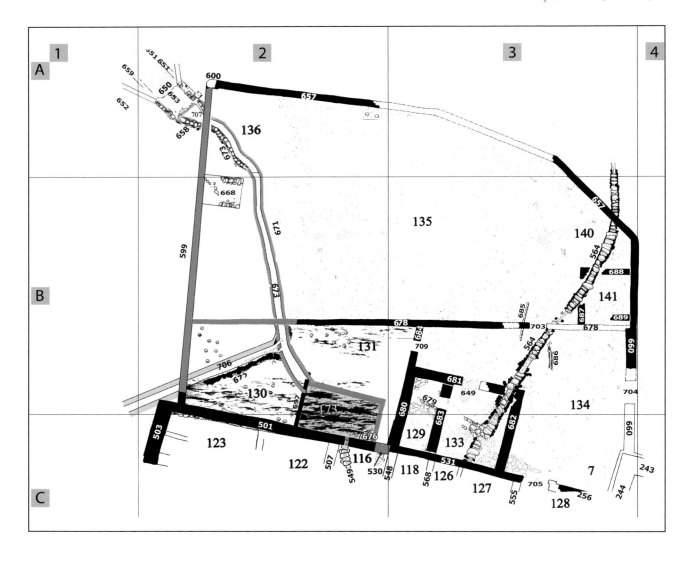

fig. 154. Stages of occupation of the space of the north enclosure

The western boundary 377

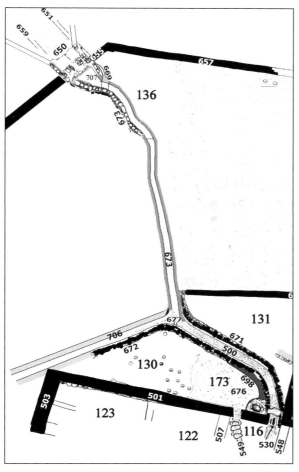

c) Level 3B

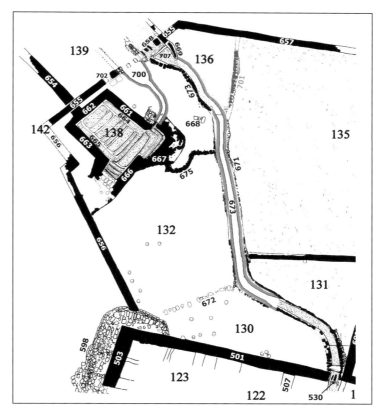

d) Level 3B/C

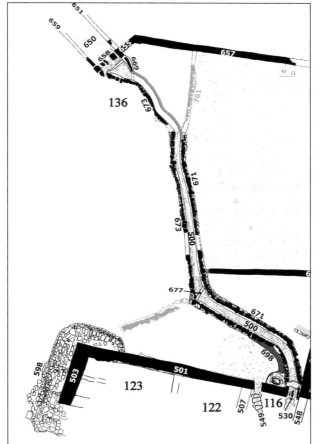

e) Level 4

Following opposite page

the limits of the enclosure, 656, 655, 657 and 660, were low walls. They are narrow, but built of coarse stones. As the site was never pillaged, the walls collapsed in on themselves and the fallen stones remained unplundered in place at the foot of the wall until the excavations. The structure had not been elevated by rough brick as we had suggested on the south front of the site, without which their collapsed mass would have formed a more pronounced projecting slope. The aerial photograph shows the north sector of the *khirbeh* before clearance: we see this as the bed of stones, stacked with some regularity, and on the only south side where we might suspect a fall due to the earthquake (fig. 156). Their elevation may be recreated at roughly one metre fifty. Those who saw the enclosure as a garden or a vegetable patch and those who saw it as an animal enclosure are wrong. When there are no neighbours a vegetable garden has no need of protection, and goats jump such simple obstacles. It cannot have been an enclosing wall and we see it as the delimitation of a boundary (the *eruvim*).

The limits of the enclosure recall long wall 951 which marks out the southern terrace. Long wall 951 was not a higher curtain, defence or separation, but again a simple barrier. The succession of barriers which surround the palm grove as far as Ain Feshkha seems to restore the fiction of a town within its ramparts, by *eruvim*: the low walls would include the north enclosure in the symbolic town; door 702 which opens onto the settlement towards L. 139 leads directly to the west ravine, the shortest path by which to reach Ain Feshkha. The dimensions of the space of L. 135 are surprising, especially when recreated in its state before being made obsolete by large aqueduct 500. Its extent obliges us to find a reason for it. It is probable that it was linked to L. 130, and its particular function would come from the link between the two spaces.

Finally, L. 130 contains the densest concentration of bone deposits in disused pots. The hesitant and controversial explanations proposed as to their purpose are null and void. None of them has gained support. De Vaux was tempted to see them as left-overs from sacrificial meals; then he abruptly changed his mind: *We need to find an explanation for all these deposits: clearly a rite, but which we can link with nothing, neither in the sectarian documents nor in the Bible. Does this imply sacrifices?* (L. 135, 7/3/55). By this comment, he confirmed that such an important phenomenon deserved the greatest interest, but he simply put off the moment to interpret it. He just did not have the time. The hastily abandoned festive meal proposed by E. Laperrousaz does not rely on any archaeological argument; the sanitary measure suggested by Y. Magen would be the fruit

fig. 155.   Locus 130 after clearing, showing the pillaging hole in pool 173

of a unique initiative which loses credibility because of its very uniqueness – flies being elsewhere too – and finally those who have nothing to propose accept failure and put up with it.

The chronology of the north enclosure

The enclosure, which provides exceptional archaeological documentation for the history of Qumran, deserves our full attention. We have the benefit of the careful surveys of the 1955 campaign, which was not the case for earlier campaigns. It is to be regretted, however, that the buried deposits were granted no more than a freehand sketch, without a precise indication of the location of the pots and bones. The survey at least has the merit that it exists.

The lack of stratigraphy of the enclosure, which has occupation levels that are scattered and thin, is compensated for by a fairly certain chronology of the sequence of successive layouts of the space. The buried the animal bone deposits are the pivot of the stratigraphy and the chronology of de Vaux, here again impeded by the 31 BC date provided by the assumed earthquake, the effects of which are being interpreted disputed. The whole chronological edifice stands on a rupture of the aqueduct at the time of a violent flood. Now, a fairly quick assessment confirms that, as the earthquake did not take place, the rupture of the drain and muddy flood are empty arguments. The key thing is that the buried deposits do not constitute a one-off event but instead prove an enduring practice. The historical bolt of 31 BC had fixed the chronology of a varied and consistent collection of pottery. A numismatic link, however, allows us to set the earliest date of the level of the deposits at around the middle of the first century BC.

We propose a succession of phases of occupation of the premises with provisional chronological identifications. From the oldest to the most recent:

1) Restoration of the Hasmonaean residence, north front: Level 3A

2) The bone deposits in broken pots: Level 3A

3) Construction of the north enclosure, L. 130, 131 and 135: Level 3A/B?

4) Extension to the west with L. 138 and disuse of the enclosure: Level 3A/B

5) Establishment of aqueduct 500 and abandonment of the enclosure: Level 3(B/C?)

fig. 156.   Aerial view of the north enclosure, 1953

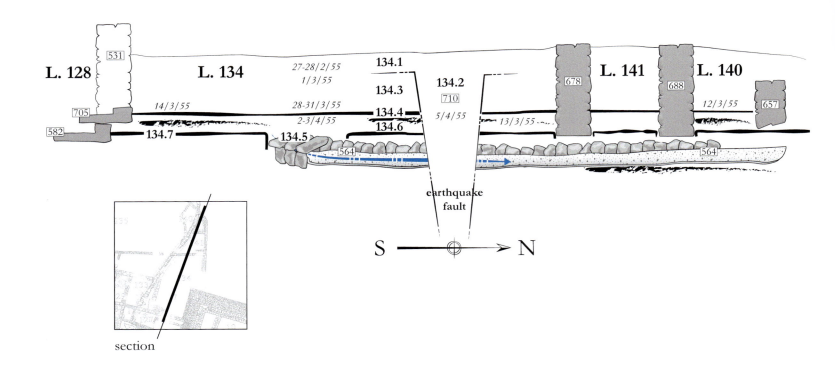

Restored elements	Level	Definition	Journal dates	Coins	Position	N°	Chronology
134.1	Post-earthquake	Abandonment	27-28/3/55				
134.2	Post 4: earthquake	Earthquake	5/4/55				
134.3	Post 4	Abandonment	28-31/3/55				
134.4	3C	Short lobby L134	14, 28-31/3/55	KhQ. 2402	to the east	1	Antigone Mattathias
				KhQ. 2427	to the east	1	Hyrcanus II
				2261	-	1	Herod
				2406	to the east	1	Agrippa I[st]
				2405	to the east	1	Proc. under Augustus
				2408	to the east	1	Proc. under Tiberius
				2396	L134 northeast corner	8	Alexander Jannaeus
				2403	to the east	1	Alexander Jannaeus
				2404	to the east	1	Alexander Jannaeus
				2429	to the east, lower level	1	Alexander Jannaeus
				2430	to the east, lower level	1	Alexander Jannaeus
				2603	to the east, lower level	1	Alexander Jannaeus
				2262	-	1	Alexander Jannaeus
				2398	to the east	1	Alexander Jannaeus
				2624	floor L134	1	Alexander Jannaeus
134.5	3B/C	evacuation 564	2-3/4/55				
134.6	2B – 3A/B/C	Ash (buried deposits?)	13/3/55				
134.7	2	Threshold 582	14/3/55				

Schema and stratigraphic diagram of Locus 134 (for the chart of symbols, see page 155)

Locus 134
Vestibule of the enclosure

The north enclosure increased the allocated space, backing onto the tower of the residence and its outbuildings. L. 134 occupies the eastern sector, and as the main doors there were maintained, it functioned as entrance hall. Its unity on the plan is visibly broken by evacuation drain 564, which crosses it; but this does not stop us noting its unity because the drain was buried under floor. Its function was to provide access points across the whole settlement. De Vaux did not attach any importance to it and excavated it as an exterior. With varying success he looked for the earthquake fault which he called the *ancient trench* and ends here in the north. The ash that lies strewn on the ground in slabs links it with what was uncovered further to the west in the north enclosure: *We continue to dig in the earth and ash. In the northeast corner, we uncover eight coins (Alexander Jannaeus)* (L. 134, 13/3/55). The find pointed him towards an early chronology of the enclosure.

Eastern wall 660 of L. 134, cannot be built before the glacis of the tower was put in place, is partly destroyed; we have to re-establish a passageway 704 in the gap: at that time, the main entrance to the settlement will have been here. Wall 660 is thick; wall 657 is narrower and extends the enclosure to the north; it is legitimate to restore a certain height to it. We may imagine L. 134 in the open air, surrounded by high walls to screen it from view: to the north 678, and to the west 680 and 684 may also have been surmounted by beds of brick to complete a high enclosure. L. 134 will have been a private space, connecting the core of the settlement by door 582, then L. 130 (131) by door 709 and L. 135 by door 703. L. 134 was a courtyard vestibule and, from the outside, it will have looked like an enclosed space in contrast with the L. 135 that merely was an open-air space marked simply by a low wall.

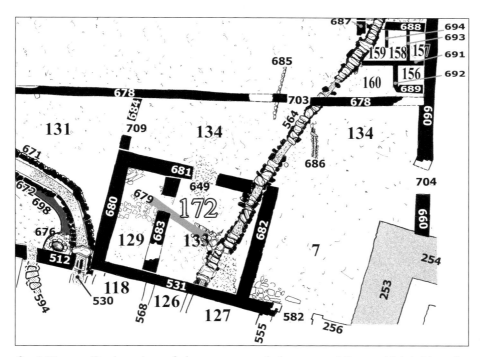

fig. 157. Designation of the constructed elements of Locus 134, lobby of the north enclosure with Locus 172

Plate 71

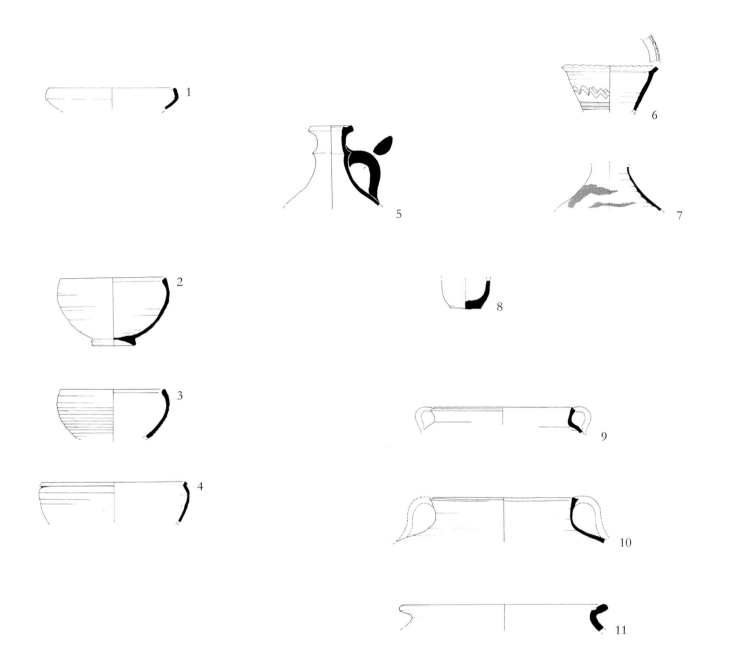

N° Pl.	N° Catal.	Position	Comments (archives)	Date	Description	Clay	Exterior
1	4210	134.1/3	east of 133	05/04/55	small dish	red paste	brown-red
2	2305	134.1/3	-	01/03/55	bowl	° red earth	remains of white wash
3	4236	134.1/3	-	01/03/55	bowl	orange paste	beige
4	4239	134.1/3	-	01/03/55	large bowl	light brown paste	light brown
5	4213	134.1/3	east of 133	05/04/55	jug	orange paste	light red
6	4212	134.1/3	east of 133	05/04/55	jug	white paste	yellowish
7	4209	134.1/3	east of 133	05/04/55	jug	red paste	red remains of red painting
8	4240	134.1/3	-	01/03/55	unguentarium	light brown paste	light brown
9	4211	134.1/3	east of 133	05/04/55	cooking pot	red paste	brownish-red
10	4201	134.1/3	-	01/03/55	cooking pot	red paste	light brown
11	4238	134.3-4	-	14/03/54	crater	brown paste	beige engobe

° *According to de Vaux*

Locus 134, pottery and catalogue, scale ¼

Loci 130–131
The location of the meals and buried deposits

Despite the interest aroused by the concentration of buried deposits and a real effort to conduct a methodical excavation, the observations were then recorded in telegram form. The exceptional character of the level discovered prompted a more systematic exploration; L. 130 was then quartered in two rows (A and B) of squares of 2 x 2 m numbered from 1 to 7. This is our way of assessing the extent of a deposit exposed over an area of 56 m². On this L., the *Synthesis,* which has collated different notes, presents the *Journal*'s longest comments. However, there is little description of the elements by de Vaux, although he was insistent in noting the mixing-up of the layers. The arrangement of the elements constituting the archaeological level is weakened by an *a priori* interpretation of the causes of the formation of layers which guided the description of the phenomenon: where he sees the result of a geological process, we observe the result of human activity. De Vaux imposes his reconstruction to the detriment of a precise observation of the materials of which the level is composed. The earthquake was wrongly brought in to account for an odd move of mishmash layers. The excavator was confronted with the difficulties of a complicated level at this point: he lacked the time and the distance to draw all the consequences. We know that he had doubts about his reconstruction. After all, as he concluded his interpretation, he said: *All this is obscure* (L. 130, 3/3/55).The general interpretation is biaised by a succession of statements that are poorly founded by observations, cleverly linked to produce an unpersuasive explanation. The archaeological level of L. 130 was entirely cleared, and it is impossible for us to identify the constitution and the texture of the different components of the terrain which de Vaux recognized and described in the Journal, L. 130:

a) *ashes and pottery (26/2/55);*
b) *a sediment of yellow earth evidently put down by water, in which large pots are embedded* (27/2/55);
c) *a thin layer of ash and silt* (28/2/55);
d) *a bed of earth and pebbles, about 5 cm thick, insulating (the ash) of a plastered floor* (3/3/55);
e) *this plastered floor stops quite neatly (...) with a slight inclination* (3/3/55);
f) *the entrance of the lower channel* (24/3/55);
g) *below, a floor extends everywhere, which does not seem to be plastered* (27/3/55).

To verify the proposal, it is useful to recall the stratigraphic reconstruction and the succession of the seven phases of the L. according to de Vaux:

1) *The large pool in the north (L. 132), the channel and an empty space between the channel and the building form an open-air sector;*
2) *in this empty space, large pots are deposited, and broken jars with animal bones, Period 1;* 3) *the earthquake, abandonment* (31 BC); 4) *return of the community: abandonment of pool L. 132;*
5) *a plastered floor is made in the western part;* 6) *the building is cleared and ash and broken pots are thrown to the ground;*
7) *(the eastern space) and that of the west are re-used for deposits of bones (3/3/55)* .

He does not find a suitable solution to explain the ancient mixing-up of the archaeological layer: *Objection: why is the sediment not horizontal? The argument is not decisive: the mud spilling from L. 132 flowed towards the east. Why the plastered floor, and why does it stop suddenly? Why are the pots that are immersed in the sediment not at the same height? Lifted by the mud? It is possible. In that case, they were not interred. In any case, pots of bones then continued to be deposited in this sector, and again to the north in the disused pool. All this is very obscure* (L. 130, 3/3/55). And further on: *Worthy of note are two small pots, intact and upside-down, containing bones but not filled with earth. The same was true of the large pot tipped over in A4 (4). This empty space cannot be explained by a progressive sedimentation of the vessel. On the other hand, it may be explained by floating and then depositing with the sediment, the water and the mud spilling suddenly from pool 132* (L. 130, 7/3/55).

A few claims or assessments need to be critiqued and corrected. Its seems that it will be impossible to achieve a clear stratigraphic reconstruction. The *Journal*'s notes are incomplete and there is a lack of photographs. The elements constituting the level are barely, if at all, shown in their sequence. To set them out without gaps is almost impossible. In the tight eastern corner of L. 130, there are seven overlapping elements: aqueduct 500, a kiln 676 associated with a block of ash 130.2, a mortar floor (L. 173), an evacuation outlet 549, a *buried deposit* with six coins, and a possible deep floor.

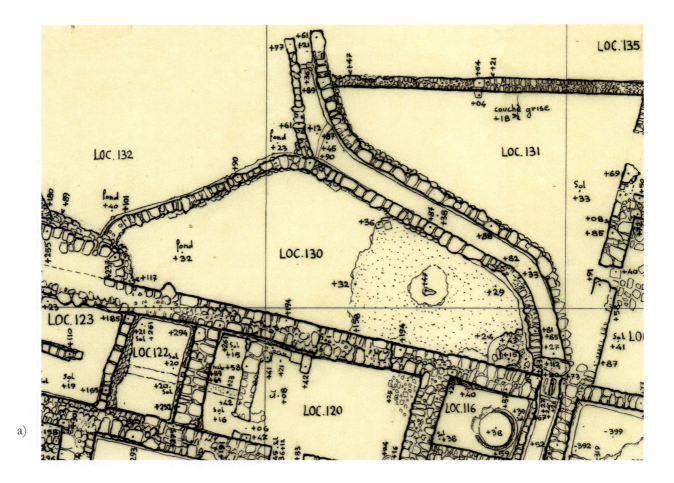

fig. 158. a) Locus 130, from Coüasnon Plan, Period Ib
b) Clearance of kiln 676 to the east of Locus 130

In the upper layers, a sort of circular low wall 676, thick, looks like a kiln or the coping of a cesspool; one survey shows a sketch of it, Coüasnon's *Plan* Ib records it, no note mentions it; according to the photographs (fig. 158b and 159a) in a poorly cleared state, it should be associated with the blanket of ash 130.2; the Coüasnon *Plan* gives it a regular rounded shape leaning against wall 501; the survey (fig. 158a) shows its internal face lined by stones. Does the circular wall have a bottom or not, and what does it rest on? Nothing is said about it. We hesitated to interpret it. Is it what remains of a downpipe for rainwater? We do not know if it had an exit: it is not directly in line with outlet 549. It is more probable that it was a kind of hearth, leaning against the corner, sheltered from the winds, the base immersed in a mass of ash. The workman is extracting a greasy, ashy material on photo fig. 158b.

The notes of the *Journal* from 24 to 27/3/55 plunge the reader into confusion. Nothing is said of the relationship between the plastered floor (bottom of pool L. 173) and the mouth of drain (channel) 549. De Vaux thought *floor* and not *pool*, not recognizing the link between the bottom-floor of mortar and the mouth; he did not try to find out what the mouth might have evacuated. He notes: *The entrance of the channel (...) Coated to the right and left*. It is difficult to decide what was coated to the right and left. Possibly, opening 549, which the photograph (fig. 160c) does not show, may hint at the unscrubbed mortar floor and below the metric scale, the remains of a coating which fills-in the stone of an overflow gully from the right. Coüasnon's survey of 1955 (fig. 160a) aims to prove that the pool did not block the outlet but that the latter was indeed the drain for pool L. 173. Initially, the pool collected the run-off of rainwater towards cistern L. 110 but was no longer in service when the new track of aqueduct 500 was redirected to feed cistern L. 110 from the south.

Completing the clearance at this precise location in front of the entrance of the channel, the excavation reveals a final deposit of bones with fragments of large pots and six coins. *Below, a floor extends everywhere, which does not seem to be plastered* (27/3/55). It is not too important that the bone deposit was not exactly situated in the space; but we do not know whether this floor, which has to be called 130.5, was above the plastered floor or below it. The imprecision is reinforced by a remark on 3/3/55 which seems decisive: The important thing is that the sedimentary deposit (which contains large pots and the bones) of L. 130 west runs under *the floor* – for us, the bottom of pool L. 173. We are convinced that the opposite is the case.

De Vaux had thought that the buried deposits preceded the laying of the *plastered floor* (i.e. of the pool). We shall see that this is based on a mistaken reading of the layers. He had little hesitation to think that the deposit is above the plastered floor, which seems logical in the progress of the excavation. But the last sentence muddles the understanding he had of it: *Below, a floor extends everywhere* (27/3/55). Below the deposit, or below plastered floor 130.4? And where does it extend, as we are told it was *everywhere*? However, the lime-mortar floor occupies the whole space in the closed corner of L. 130, and there is no indication that it was cleared. In the lime-mortar floor of the pool there is in fact an explicit gap on the sketches which is also visible on the photographs (fig. 155, 159b and 162c). The notes refer to it: *To the north of the channel, it [the floor] seems to include two or three large stones* (3/3/55) which are easy to see on the photograph (fig.158b) by the shading of the gap. The evidence points to this being a case of looting, which is impossible to date. The gap punctures mortar floor 130.4 in front of outlet 549 and the location would match what is written in the *Journal*. Perhaps the floor which seems lower and not plastered was just the opening of the gap? However, it does not extend *everywhere* as de Vaux claimed. Or, perhaps, would there have been a real floor lower down, recognized in a sondage confined to the space of the gap?

The uncertainty persists. We shall not make a decision on this and leave open the possibility of a deep floor, which ought then to correspond to the Hasmonaean occupation of Level 2. We would be tempted to link it to a fine layer of ash which runs under the reinforcement of the corner of the ruin: *The reinforcement of the corner (...) is probably secondary, built above a thin layer of ash and silt* (L. 130, 28/2/55). The stratigraphic continuity was not noted.

fig. 159. Overview of the Locus 130 deposits, a) looking east, b) looking west

Commentary

1) A floor 130.5, possibly of Level 2

Our guess must be that in the first half of the first century BC, the sector to the north of the *khirbeh* was an open air space, not divided by walls. On 27 March, in the last week of the 1955 campaign, de Vaux closes the site and excavates the layers still blocking the eastern part of L. 130. The specification *in front of the entrance of the channel the deposit of bones (...) with six coins* points to the place of the gap in the bottom of pool L. 173 (130.4). *Below, everywhere a floor extends* (130.5) suggests the possible presence of a former occupation of the premises, before or after the end of the reign of Alexander Jannaeus. We have seen that the data do not permit us to take this as assured.

2) An older pool L. 173

The occupation on the exterior developed in successive stages starting from wall 501 and moving northwards. The deepest vestige noted is plastered floor 130.4. The plastered floor is in fact the bottom of pool L. 173 coated with mortar which has been dismantled. De Vaux was rightly amazed: *A plastered floor is constructed in the eastern half of L. 130 but not extended as far as the western part – but why?* (L. .130, 3/3/55). In general, a mortar floor binds the adjoining walls with a thicker joint – a detail which, however, the *Journal* had noted: *This plastered floor stops quite neatly at the limit of 3 and 4A and B with a slight inclination.* (3/3/55). The bottom of the pool is cleared against the western rim, looted. Several restorations in the enclosure provided opportunities to dismantle the walls, and pool L. 173, which was affected by this, is not the only example, as we shall see below. On the occasion of a recent restoration, this sector was cleaned and we were able to see for ourselves that the (partly obliterated) mortar filling under low wall 672 of aqueduct 500 presents the same padding. The edges of the pool are clearly seen; it was put out of use and dismantled to enable conversion into the aqueduct.

What was the function of pool L. 173? It could, first of all, have served to collect water from the roofs of the annexes: it supplied cistern L. 110 by subterranean drain 549, the outlet of which opens below wall 501 and is inserted under L. 115 and L. 116. Outlet 549 and the subterranean drain go back to the construction of the annexes at Level 2, as they are integral to a supporting wall 501. By sealing outlet 549, pool L. 173 could, with its size, decant the muddy water that came down from the rough brick terraces. If a decantation pool existed in the north enclosure, it was not L. 132 but L. 173. Aqueduct 500 starts an elbow to connect with pool L. 173, and at some point the drain could not be further extended. In this case, channel 706 would have served as mud outlet through channel 673 towards the west ravine, the sluice derivation 677 in the channel 500 would have stopped back surge. However, the drain, which we suggest is older, running below the late 500, indisputably hinders the harmonious arrangement of an earlier cultic earth platform which we aim to reconstruct by reuniting L. 132 and L. 135. We may resolve the contradiction by postulating that pool L. 173 was initially intended only to collect water from roofing. At a second point in time, the drain predating aqueduct 500 was set up to lead to the passage, instead of heading directly for sluice 530 as logic demands. Confirmation of an underlying earlier drain, which had disappeared, to feed cistern L. 110, would have compensated for collection from roofing. Subsequently, pool L. 173 was put out of use and then demolished and the location abandoned, the sole advantage being that aqueduct 500 would be better adapted to accrued needs. The abandonment is marked by the bed of pebbles immersed in a thin residual layer of earth 130.3 which de Vaux observed at the bottom of the pool; it is due to erosion.

3) The nature of the yellow sediment as alluvial silt

The bottom of pool L. 173 is covered with a thick layer of ash which neatly stops at the edge of A3-B3, directly below the west rim of the pool. It has been shown that the pool was filled with ash before the demolition of its walls. The *Journal* describes a yellow sediment extending the block of ash: *Then, towards the west, a sediment of yellow earth in which large pots are embedded* (L. 130, 28/2/55). As we have mentioned, de Vaux states that the yellow sediment predates pool L. 173: *the sedimentary deposit runs under this (plastered) floor* (L. 130, 3/3/55). Then again, the archaeologist is convinced that the yellow, alluvial sediment had blocked the whole sector of L. 132 and L. 130 during the abandonment which followed the supposed earthquake:

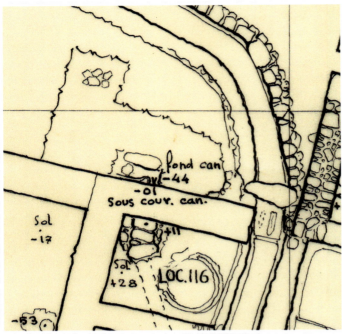

a) Draft excerpt (Coüasnon) of 22/3/1955

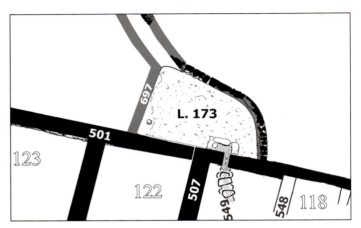

b) Layout restitution of the earliest basin 173

c) Locus 130. Basin 173 and the supply 549 of cistern 110

fig. 160.   Pool 173 in Locus 130

Earthquake which breaks up the water system (...) Inundation, whence sedimentary deposit in L. 130 (3/3/55). De Vaux explained the confusion of pots containing the bones by the violence of the flow during the flooding. We have to conclude that according to him, the pots had been deposited at two points in time, before and after the earthquake. In the de Vaux' stratigraphy, the deposits in the yellow sediment predate the earthquake, and those which were buried in the mass of ash follow it: *Return of the community (...) a plastered floor is constructed in the eastern part of L. 130 (...) Then the building is cleared and ash and broken pots are thrown on this floor*, refuse contradicted by the proposal recorded further on: *In any case, pots of bones then continued to be deposited in this area* (L. 130, 3/3/55), thus in the mass of ash where, on the last day of the excavation (27/3/55), deposits with bones were exposed.

We need to show that the process set out is based on an erroneous reading of the stratigraphy. If the yellow sediment is alluvial, and it may be so, it is unlikely to have been dumped there by a violent flood, spilling out from the drain broken by the earthquake. First of all, there is no earthquake, so the argument fails anyway. Then, the volume of silt is disproportionate for a once-in-a-century flood or several heavy floods in close succession. The surface of L. 130 being 80 m^2, the deposited layer, with a thickness of 50 cm, would amount to 40 m^3. Just a single photograph shows the material (fig. 152): it is indeed yellow, homogeneous and without intrusive pebbles. We recognize this as a lime deposit from a persistent trickle. The geological plateau at the foot of the cliff presents a pronounced incline to the east, and the terrace of Qumran is attached to it by a narrow, flat cordon through which the trickling waters pass. The yellow sediment was seen further to the east, too, retained by low wall 701, an early phase of the end of the aqueduct: *this low wall retains to the west a layer of yellow earth, fine, identical to that of L. 132* (L. 136, 9/3/55). The flow came to a stop against the north front of the constructions where the water accumulated, especially if the L. 129-133 wing barred the slope and caused a pothole. That being the case, wing L. 129-133, preceding the deposits, would belong to Level 2, which is not impossible.

De Vaux thought it decisive that the yellow sediment runs under the plastered floor, which is right. The yellow sediment is a geological accumulation; it would not make sense if the yellow sediment with its deposits and the plastered floor filled with ash was separated by the earthquake. The movement has to be reversed: Pool L. 173 was first dug into the yellow sediment; then it served as a location for burying bones deposits from a kitchen. The L. 173 fell out of use and kiln 676, if it really was a kiln, was installed in the pool and filled progressively with ash from repeated firings; crockery was buried close by. The circular construction could be a kiln when we consider its filling; on the photograph (fig. 158b), a worker is emptying its interior, which looks like black, greasy ash.

4) The buried deposits and their morphology

De Vaux did not exploit the consequences of his interpretation why the yellow sediment was mixed up with the burial of the deposits: he did, however, suspect that it was implausible. The idea of an overflow of rushing water turning the deposits upside-down came to him, but he did not pick it up again later. In the absence of a convincing explanation, the argument of burial, so useful in determining the function of L. 130, has been dismissed. The implausibility of the reconstructed process should have caught his mind. The sparse available photographs are of poor quality.

De Vaux' proposal does not stand up, being weakened by an *a priori* assessment of the site. We have already noted the difficulty of accumulating 40 m^3 of silt in the course of a single flood in an area that was not a watercourse. We should add that a violent flood can only cast up sufficiently diluted sediment, which would have engulfed and dispersed the deposits. We can answer the questions which de Vaux himself noted in his *Journal*, L. 130 on 3-7/3/55: *Why is the sediment not horizontal?* – because pool L. 173 was dug in the yellow sediment and the refuse discarded nearby surrounded it. *Why the plastered floor?* – It is the bottom of pool L. 173. *Why does it stop suddenly?* – Because the low west wall of the pool has been taken down. *Why are the pots that are immersed in the sediment not at the same height?* – because they are the result of multiple individual actions, and a function of the wish to bury with more or less care or more or less deeply. Then he hesitates as to the mode of deposition; he does not affirm that the pots were interred, preferring to think they were deposited: *the pots (…) lifted by the mud? The fact is that they were not interred, (...) pots of bones continued to be deposited* (L. 130, 3/3/55). It is difficult to accept that the deposited bone-filled pots were shaken by the violent flow of a flood, displaced and put back in a horizontal position, keeping the bones together as the available

fig. 161.   a), b) and c) The deposits buried in Locus 130
         d) Clearance of scattered deposits and sherds, looking west.
         e) Clearance of deposits against wall 501, looking west

photographs show (fig. 26 and 27): *Worthy of note are two small pots, intact and upside-down, containing bones but not filled with earth (...) the same for the large upside-down pot (...) explicable by floating followed by depositing with the sediment* (7/3/55); such a movement, which requires that the pot floats on its base before being tipped upside-down while preserving its contents in place, is not plausible. Especially if such an exceptional position was close to other pots, head-to-foot and horizontal. The process flies in the face of the mechanics of liquids.

5) *Conclusion and chronology*

The yellow sediment is a fairly thick layer of silt, already in place when visitors started the custom to abandon pottery on the spot with bones. The deposits are contained in a level which is visibly mixed-up, for the simple reason that the burials were repeated at the same spot; there may well have been a seasonal rhythm. The roughly even distribution of the deposits may indicate that the location was a deliberate choice and that the burials were to some degree planned. Certain pottery fragments may have protruded from the ground to mark their position. The jars remained prone; that the large pots were found upright in almost all cases indicates a certain care in the burials. The large pots, still filled with bones, upside-down, betray a dedicated care to bury the items while avoiding spills of the food left-overs.

The result is that the batch is not chronologically homogeneous. The yellow sediment presents a clear hotch-potch, mixing complete, or more or less complete pots, containing or not containing bones, numerous scattered sherds, pockets and blankets of ash. The repeated digging of holes will probably have scattered some of the deposits. The survey (fig. 163), sketched in 1955, of deposits in varying degrees of preservation, attests to at least 35 burials in L. 130; is their number too small to indicate a custom? It is possible that the practice was maintained only by a few. We may observe at this point that the small number invalidates the suggestion of sanitary reasons discussed above. Moreover, the quantity of ash contained in pool L. 173 seems disproportionate for a practice whose frequency we think was limited. Finally, it is reasonable to assume that all the crockery from all meals was not buried but kept and returned. In any case, the number of burials around the settlement lends plausibility to the custom that we are suggesting (see *supra* Chap. 4, p. 81 s.)

The repeated re-digging of the sediment has destroyed its alluvial structure. There would have been no point in trying to identify layers. We accept that the chronology of the deposits is not identifiable, in the absence of a refined typology of the pottery, which has yet to be done. The quite varied corpus of pottery assembled from L. 130 displays a certain homogeneity consistent with the regularity of a custom; it is also reasonable to accept the limited numbers in view of the duration. The peripheral burials of L. 131, L. 132 and L. 135 confirm a long chronology. Accepting that the corpus is a more or less homogeneous mixture, we may at least hope that in the future we shall be able to discern a typological evolution of the pottery, if not a radical change.

We would contend that the practice of burials at Qumran is ancient: it precedes the successive conversions which affected the north enclosure. *In one location, we find another deposit of bones (...) with six coins*. The batch of six Alexander Jannaeus coins collected near a deposit whose position is poorly identified, would allow us to place the burials around the middle of the first century BC. The coinage of Alexander Jannaeus had not disappeared under Salome Alexandra and was probably still legal tender up to the seizure of Pompey, until first century AD . No argument points to a more precise chronology and we shall not make a decision as to when the custom of burying food remains began. Nor do we know whether the first deposits were episodic or spaced out in time, or indeed whether the custom appeared suddenly and in a concerted way.

We do not confirm that the custom ceased quite early, at least in L. 130. Though a sole coin from the Procurators under Tiberius was collected, the argument in favour of a late burial remains weak. Its position in a precise level is not assured. Would L. 130 have remained a spot that was respected and not walked upon? Surrounded by walls, without real access, the space may have been set aside for reasons of impurity. A first-century deposit cannot be assured.

Did the custom gradually decline before finally stopping? The works conducted in the 2000s by the archaeological service of the Israeli army evidently uncovered the final deposits above the paving 816 of L. 90, L. 93 and L. 98 (see on those loci). Large pots with bones cannot have been abandoned in the open air; they were buried in a layer of earth (93.4) which had already covered the paving. We assign earth layer

fig. 162. The buried deposits in Locus 130

93.4 to Level 3; it precedes reinforcement 870 which was added to protect L. 86-89 and its accumulation of pottery. We think it reasonable to date the period of burials to the end of Level 2, but Level 3A would also be appropriate – there is no need to choose between them, the transition from Level 2 to Level 3 having occurred without a break.

6) Attempted interpretation of the buried deposits

It would be arbitrary to deduce from this that a society used the premises in a regular fashion and with a precise objective; but it is difficult to reject the evidence of an action whose repetition makes sense. The deposits are food left-overs; no one disputes this. It is true that interring meal remains could in some cases and under certain circumstances be thought of as occurring for reasons of hygiene; but it is hardly customary to bury crockery at the same time, not only plates and goblets but also large pots and jars. Our understanding is that this was a practice or the conclusion of a ritual, the reason for which requires investigation. The meal remains were collected together, whereas they could have been thrown into the nearby ravine, where nature would have quickly disposed of them. The practice, repeated in the space all around the walls of the settlement, at least in its former phase, and its maintenance over a fairly long period force us to accept that this was a tradition that had the force of a custom. It would be difficult to dispute its expression.

If one accepts the periodicity of the deposits and the possibility that sacrifices were presented at Qumran (the immolation of animals for Passover having a sacrificial character); if one bears in mind the Hasmonaean penetration of Transjordan under John Hyrcanus in the second century and a probable Essene dispersion on both banks of the Dead Sea; if, furthermore, the likelihood of the Jewish religious character of Qumran is not dismissed out of hand, then it is not inappropriate to suggest that the meal remains were from Passover meals. With the rite desired or intended to be in the Holy Land, the repeated burial of the remains and of the crockery emerging from a religious and probably semitic anthropology, and finally an immolation implying the sacrifice of a lamb, all the conditions are met for a Passover which could have occurred in the context of a pilgrimage.

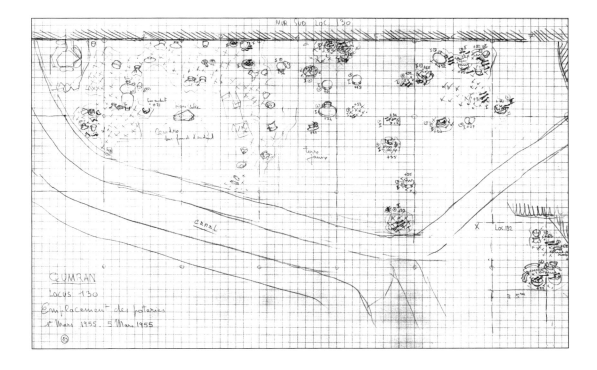

fig. 163.   1955 survey of the main buried deposits of Locus 130 (and Locus 132)

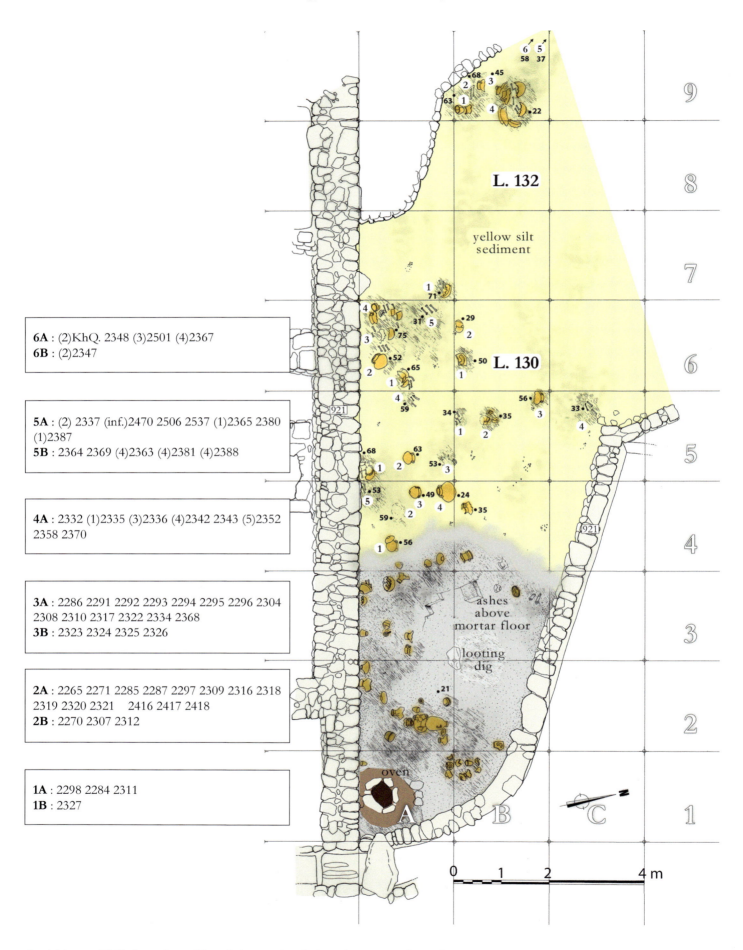

fig. 164. Tidied version of hand-drawn sketch (previous page, fig. 163)

The western boundary

section

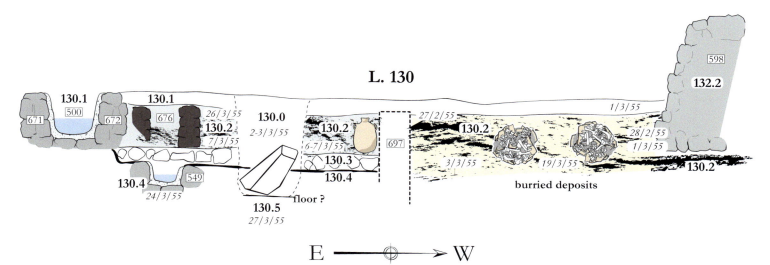

E ⟶ ⊕ ⟶ W

Restored elements	Level	Definition	Journal dates	Coins	Position	N°	Chronology
130.0	4	Surface	26/2/55				
130.1	3C-4	Aqueduct					
130.2	(2B) - 3A/B/C	Kitchen, heap of ash, "yellow sediment" Bone deposits	26-27/2/55, 1-3/3/55, 6-7/3/55, 19/3/55, 26/3/54	KhQ. 2228	L. 130	1	Alexander Jannaeus
				2259	L. 130 6B	1	Alexander Jannaeus
				2260	L. 130 6B	1	Alexander Jannaeus
				2408	L. 130 5A	1	Alexander Jannaeus
				2409	L. 130 5A	1	Alexander Jannaeus
				2410	L. 130 5A	1	Alexander Jannaeus
				2411	L. 130 5A	1	Alexander Jannaeus
				2412	L. 130 5A	1	Alexander Jannaeus
				2413	L. 130 5A	1	Alexander Jannaeus
				2471	L. 130 5A surface	1	Alexander Jannaeus
				2571	L. 131	1	Herod
				2245	L. 131	1	Proc. under Aug.
				2227	L. 130	1	Proc. under Tiberius
				2246	L. 131	1	Proc. under Tiberius
130.3	(2B) - 3A?	Flood deposit	3/3/55				
130.4	(2B) - 3A?	L. 173	24/3/55 26/3/55				
130.5	2?	Floor?	28/2/55				

Schema and stratigraphic diagram of Locus 130 (for the chart of symbols, see page 155)

Plate 72

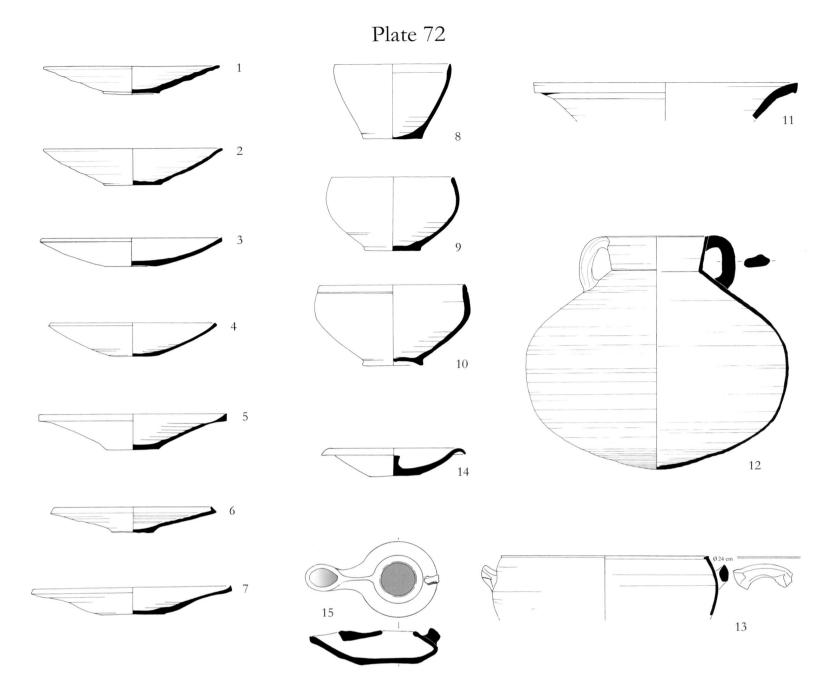

N° Pl.	N° Catal.	Position	Comments (archives)	Date	Description	Clay	Exterior
1	2341	130.2	-	03/03/55	plate	grey earth	pink and white wash
2	2340	130.2	-	02-03/03/55	bowl	° grey earth	white wash
3	2377	130.2	-	03/03/55	plate	° grey earth	
4	2235	130.2	to the east	02/26/55	plate	° red earth, burnt	
5	2339	130.2	-	03/02/55	plate	° pink earth	white wash
6	2349	130.2	-	03/03/55	plate	° grey earth	burnt
7	2234	130.2	-	26/02/55	plate	° burnt earth	
8	2333	130.2	-	03/03/55	goblet	° greyish-black earth	
9	2251	130.2	-	26/02/55	bowl	° buff earth	
10	2344	130.2	-	03/03/55	bowl	° red earth	
11	4207	130.2	lower	24/03/55	bowl	red paste with grey core	beige engobe
12	2348	130.2	-	07/03/55	cooking pot with animal bones	° red earth	
13	4204	130.2	-	06/03/55	saucepan	brown paste	brown
14	2233	130.2	-	26/02/55	lid of jar	° red earth, burnt	
15	2210	130.2	-	26/02/55	lamp	° buff earth	

° *According to de Vaux*

Locus 130, no location on the graph, pottery and catalogue, scale ¼

Plate 73

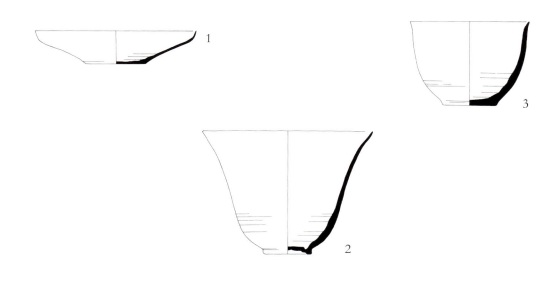

Locus 130-1A

Locus 130-1B

N° Pl.	N° Catal.	Position	Comments (archives)	Date	Description	Clay	Exterior
1	2298	130.2	A1	02/03/55	plate	° red earth with grey section	white and pink wash
2	2311	130.2	A1	02/03/55	goblet	° pink, buff earth, soft	smoothed
3	2284	130.2	A1	02/03/55	goblet	° grey earth	pink wash
4	2327	130.2	B1	02/03/55	bowl	° red earth with grey section	cream wash
5	4649	130.2	B1	no date	bowl	red paste	brownish-red

° *According to de Vaux*

Locus 130 -1A and 1B, pottery and catalogue, scale ¼

Plate 74

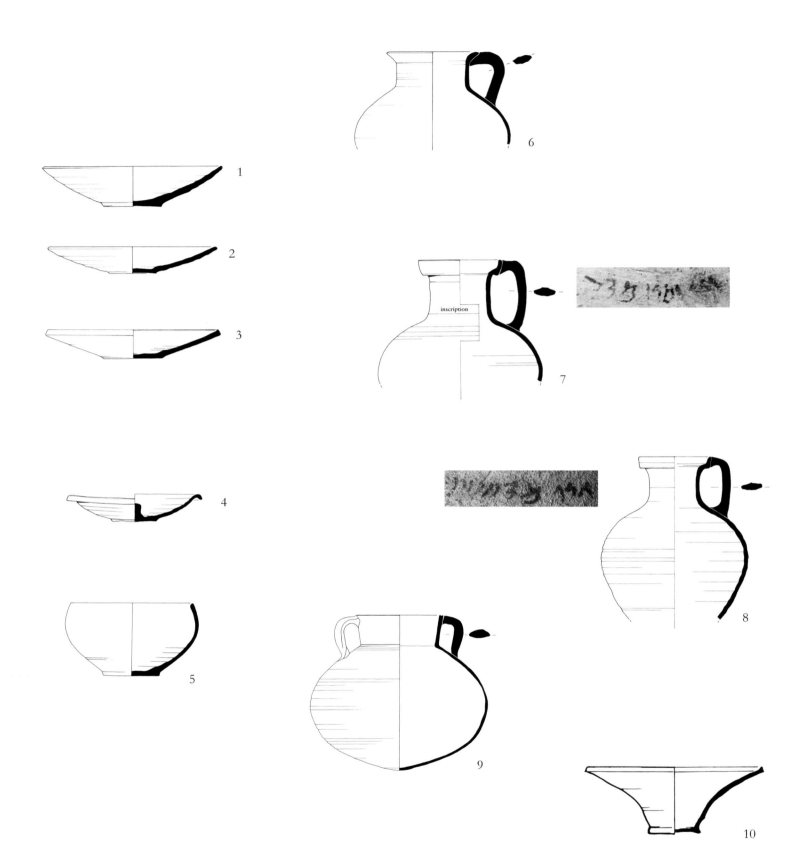

Locus 130-2A, pottery, scale ¼

Plate 75

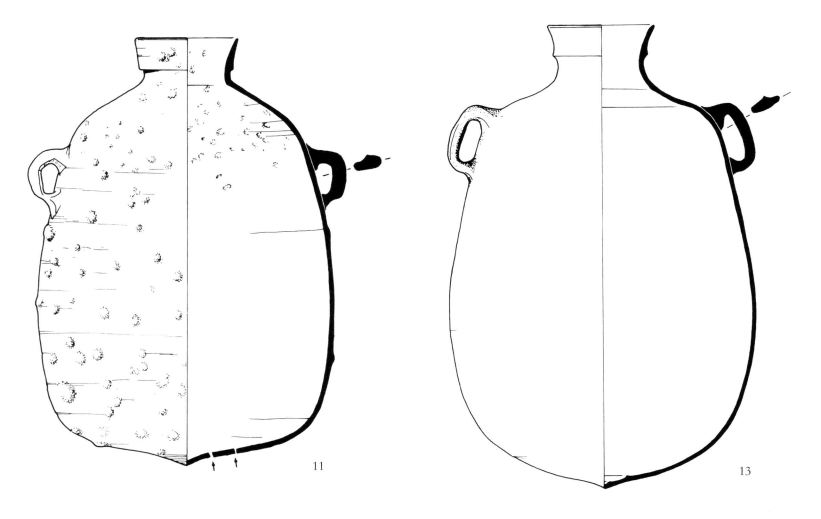

N° Pl.	N° Catal.	Position	Comments (archives)	Date	Description	Clay	Exterior
1	2321	130.2	A2	03/03/55	plate	° red earth, soft	red wash
2	2319	130.2	A2	03/03/55	plate	° red earth, soft	pink wash
3	2297	130.2	A2	02/03/55	plate	° red earth	
4	2320	130.2	A2	02/03/55	lid of jar	° grey earth	red and white
5	2309	130.2	A2	02/03/55	bowl	° red earth	grey, white wash
6	2418	130.2	A2 ash	02/03/55	jug	° red earth with grey section	white wash
7	2417	130.2	A2 ash	02/03/55	jug with a Hebrew inscription on the shoulder	° red earth with grey section	white wash
8	2416	130.2	A2 ash	02/03/55	jug with a Hebrew inscription on the shoulder	° pink earth	white wash
9	2265	130.2	A2 ash	27/02/55	cooking pot	° red earth	
10	2285	130.2	A2	02/03/55	plate/lid	° pink earth, coarse	
11	2287	130.2	A2, to the side of jar n°. 2316	02/03/55	jar	° red earth	white wash
12	2271	130.2	A2 ash	02/03/55	stopper of jar	raw clay	
13	2316	130.2	A2, to the side of jar n° 2287	02/03/55	jar	° grey earth, red in section	white wash

° *According to de Vaux*

Locus 130-2A, pottery and catalogue, scale ¼

N°. Pl.	N° Catal.	Position	Comments (archives)	Date	Description	Clay	Exterior
1	2307	130.2	B2	02/03/55	plate	° red earth with grey section	white wash
2	2312	130.2	B2	02/03/55	bowl	° red and grey earth	white wash
3	2270	130.2	B2	02/03/55	lamp	° buff earth	

° *According to de Vaux*

Locus 130-2B, pottery and catalogue

N° Pl.	N° Catal.	Position	Comments (archives)	Date	Description	Clay	Exterior
1	2318	130.2	A3	02/03/55	plate	° red earth, soft	
2	2310	130.2	A3	03/03/55	plate	° red earth with grey section	
3	2304	130.2	A3	03/03/55	bowl	° grey earth	traces of white wash
4	2322	130.2	A3	03/03/55	goblet	° grey earth	white wash
5	2292	130.2	A3	03/03/55	goblet	° grey earth	white wash
6	2286	130.2	A3	02/03/55	bowl (vertebrae, lambs' bones?)	° red paste	traces of white wash
7	2296	130.2	A3	03/03/55	stopper of jar	° salmon earth (poorly fired)	
8	2334	130.2	A3 on the ash level	03/03/55	cooking pot	° red earth	
9	2317	130.2	A3	03/03/55	cooking pot	° red earth	
10	2291	130.2	A3	03/03/55	lamp	° buff earth	
11	2295	130.2	A3	02/03/55	lamp	° grey and red earth	pink wash
12	2294	130.2	A3	03/03/55	lamp	° buff earth	
13	2308	130.2	A3	03/03/55	lamp	° buff earth	
14	4205	130.2	A3	no date	jar	brownish-red paste	surface with beige engobe

° *According to de Vaux*

Locus 130-3A, pottery and catalogue

Plate 76

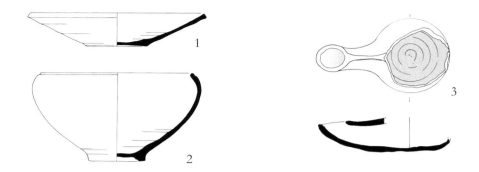

Locus 130-2B, pottery, scale ¼

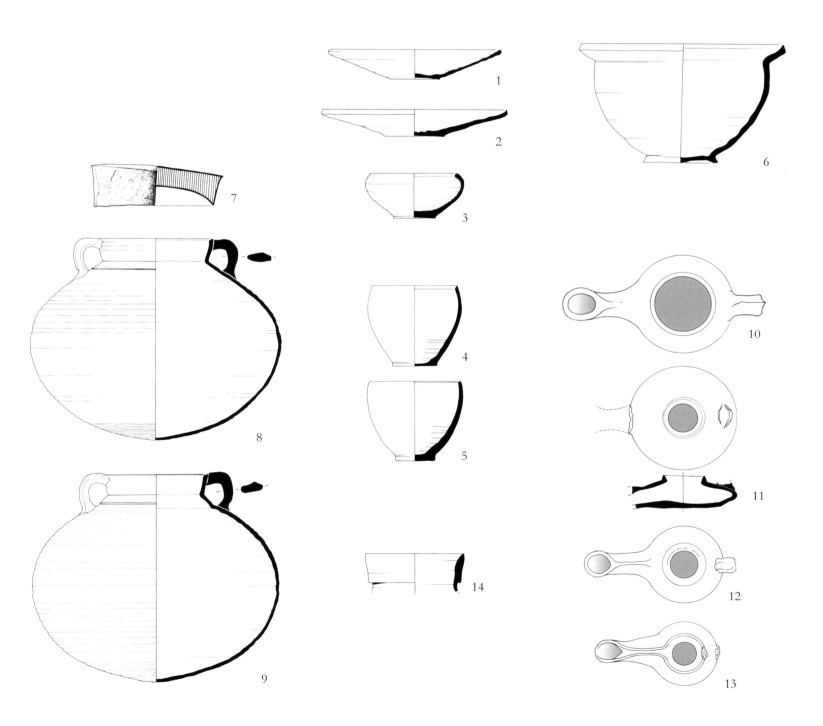

Locus 130-3A, pottery, scale ¼

N° Pl.	N° Catal.	Position	Comments (archives)	Date	Description	Clay	Exterior
1	2323	130.2	B3	02/03/55	plate	° red earth	red wash
2	2325	130.2	B3	02/03/55	plate	° grey-black earth	
3	2324	130.2	B3	02/03/55	bowl	° red earth	pink wash
4	2326	130.2	B3	02/03/55	goblet	° grey-black earth	

° *According to de Vaux*

Locus 130-3B, pottery and catalogue

N° Pl.	N° Catal.	Position	Comments (archives)	Date	Description	Clay	Exterior
1	2343	130.2	A4 (4)	06/03/55	plate/lid of cooking pot n° 2342	° pink earth	
2	2332	130.2	A4	03/03/55	bowl	° red earth	pink wash
3	2342	130.2	A4 (4)	06/03/55	cooking pot	° red earth	
4	2335	130.2	A4 (1)	05/03/55	cooking pot	° red earth	
5	2370	130.2	A4 (5)	06/03/55	cooking pot	° red earth	
6	2336	130.2	A4 (3)	06/03/55	cooking pot	° red earth	
7	2358	130.2	A4 (5)	06/03/55	stewpot	° red earth	
8	2337	130.2	A4 (3)	06/03/55	cooking pot	° red earth	

° *According to de Vaux*

Locus 130-4A, pottery and catalogue

Plate 77

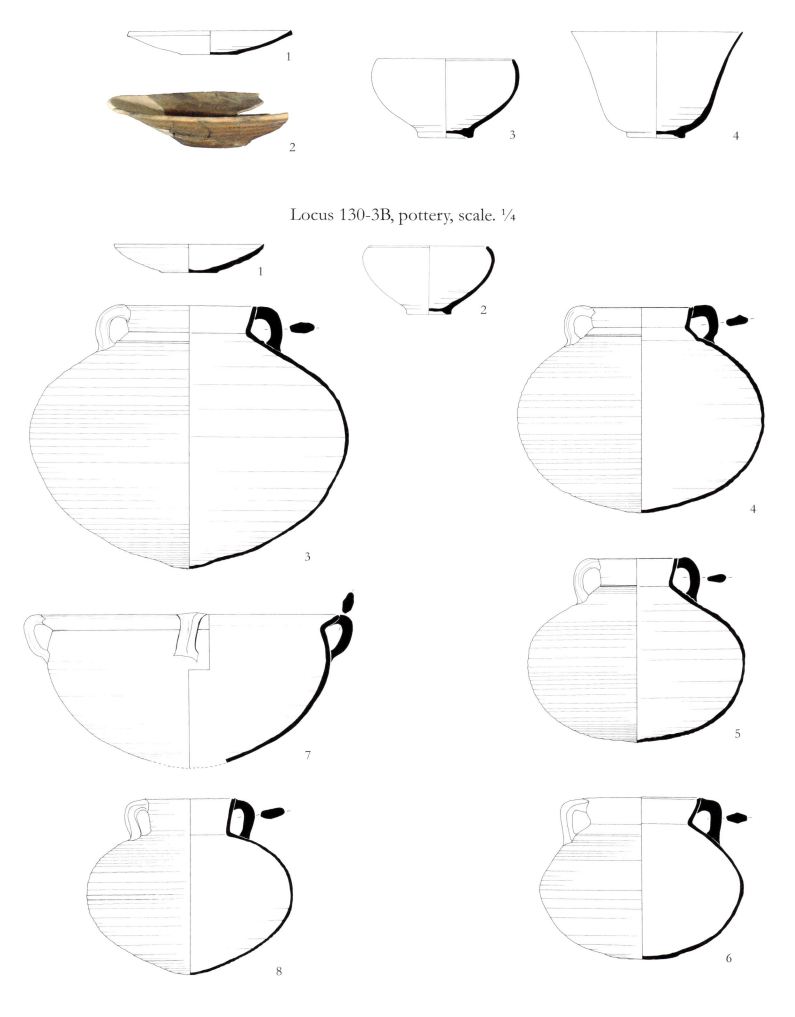

Locus 130-3B, pottery, scale ¼

Locus 130-3B, pottery, scale ¼

N° Pl.	N° Catal.	Position	Comments (archives)	Date	Description	Clay	Exterior
1	5383	130.2	ash	28/02/55	bowl	reddish-brown paste	brownish-red
2	2232	130.2	ash	27/02/55	bowl	° salmon earth	pink wash
3	2205	130.2	ash	26/02/55	bowl	° buff earth	white wash
4	2578	130.2	in the ash hole	26/02/55	bowl	° grey earth	
5	4662	130.2	ash	28/02/55	bowl	brownish-red clay	
6	4661	130.2	ash	28/02/55	bowl	brown paste	beige
7	4659	130.2	ash	28/02/55	bowl	red paste with grey core	red
8	4658	130.2	ash	28/02/55	bowl	orange paste	beige
9	4641	130.2	ash	28/02/55	bowl	reddish-brown paste	brownish-red
10	4643	130.2	ash	28/02/55	cooking pot	red paste with grey core	brownish-grey
11	4644	130.2	ash	28/02/55	cooking pot	red paste	dark red
12	4667	130.2	ash	28/02/55	cooking pot	orange paste	brownish-red
13	4670	130.2	ash	28/02/55	cooking pot	brownish-red paste	brown
14	4642	130.2	ash	28/02/55	cooking pot	brownish-red, dark grey	
15	4660	130.2	ash	28/02/55	bowl	brown paste	brown
16	4669	130.2	ash	28/02/55	bowl	red paste with grey core	beige engobe
17	4650	130.2	ash	28/02/55	small vat	red paste with grey core	brown

° *According to de Vaux*

Locus 130, catalogue of the pottery collected in the ashes

Plate 78

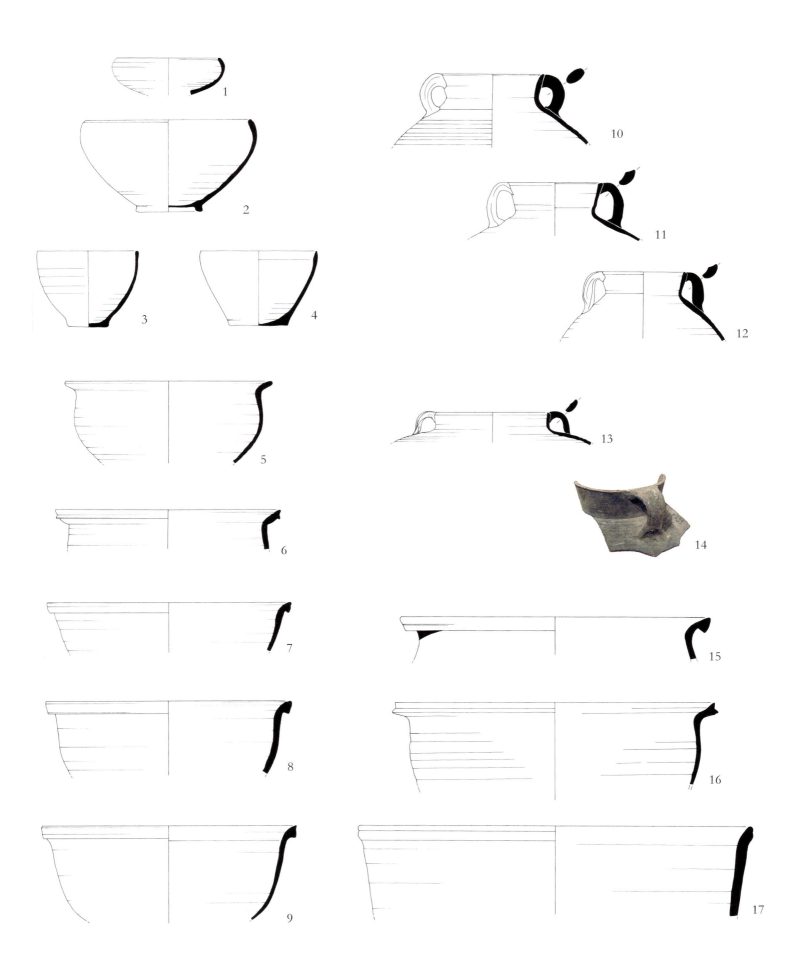

Locus 130, pottery collected in the ashes, scale ¼

N° Pl.	N° Catal.	Position	Comments (archives)	Date	Description	Clay	Exterior
1	4673	130.2	ash	no date	bowl jar	light brown paste	light brown
2	4662	130.2	ash	no date	cooking pot	brownish-red paste	brownish-red
3	4655	130.2	ash	no date	jar with large opening	red paste with grey core	beige-brown
4	4646	130.2	ash	no date	jug	red paste with grey core	beige engobe
5	4666	130.2	ash	no date	jar	red paste	beige engobe
6	4645	130.2	ash	no date	jug	dark brown-red paste	grey
7	5136	130.2	ash	no date	flask	orange paste	beige
8	3503	130.2	ash	no date	jar		
9	4656	130.2	ash	no date	jar	dark grey paste	grey engobe
10	4654	130.2	ash	no date	jar	red paste with grey core	beige engobe
11	4652	130.2	ash	no date	jar	red paste with grey core	grey
12	4648	130.2	ash	no date	jar	dark grey paste	beige engobe
13	4657	130.2	ash	no date	jar	dark grey paste	dark grey
14	4672	130.2	ash	no date	jar	brown paste	beige engobe
15	2206	130.2	ash	26/02/55	lamp	° brown earth	white wash
16	5087	130.2	ash	26/03/55	fragment of lamp	red with grey core	

° *According to de Vaux*

Locus 130, catalogue of the pottery collected in the ashes (continued)

Plate 79

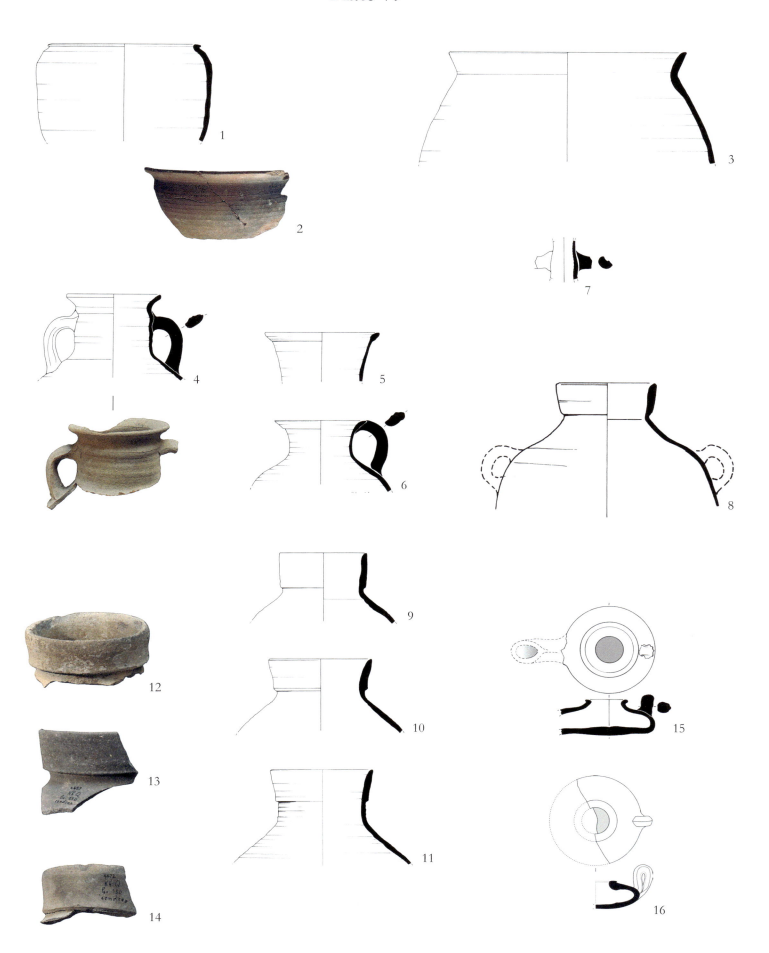

Locus 130, ash, pottery, scale ¼

Plate 80

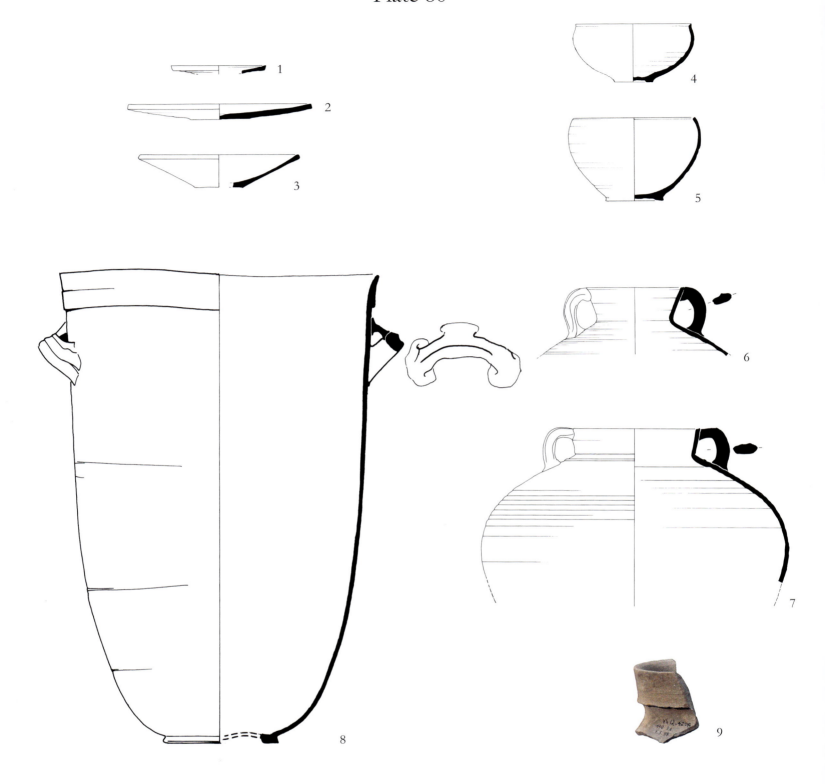

N° Pl.	N° Catal.	Position	Comments (archives)	Date	Description	Clay	Exterior
1	4206	130.2	A5	no date	small dish	red paste	grey-beige
2	2470	130.2	A5 inf.	19/03/55	plate/lid with bones	° red earth with grey section	red wash
3	2387	130.2	A5	07/03/55	plate	° red earth with grey section, coarse	
4	2380	130.2	A5	07/03/55	bowl	° salmon earth, soft	
5	2414	130.2	A5	12/03/55	bowl	° buff earth, soft	
6	4194	130.2	A5	01/03/55	cooking pot	red with grey-brown core	
7	2365	130.2	A5 (1)	07/03/55	cooking pot	° red earth	
8	2537	130.2	A5 inf.	19/03/55	small vat	° white earth	white wash
9	4208	130.2	A5	01/03/55	jar	grey-brown paste	

° *According to de Vaux*

Locus 130-5A, pottery and catalogue, scale ¼

Plate 81

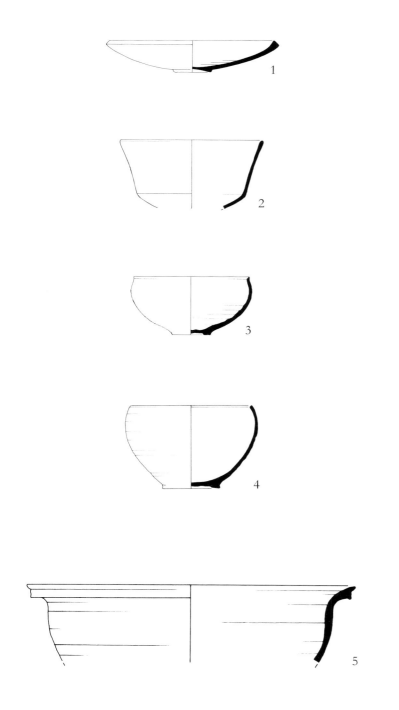
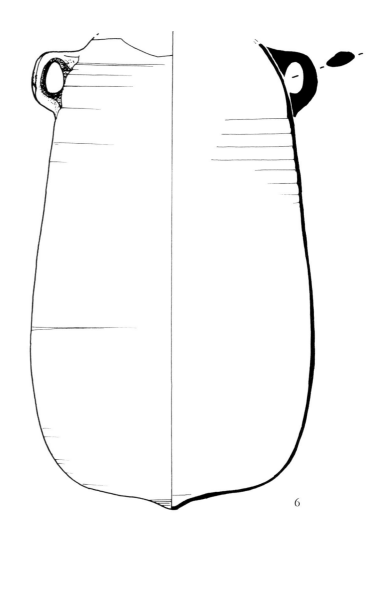

N° Pl.	N° Catal.	Position	Comments (archives)	Date	Description	Clay	Exterior
1	2364	130.2	B5	01/03/55	plate	° buff earth, soft	pink wash
2	2381	130.2	B5	07/03/55	bowl	° buff earth, soft	white wash inside and out
3	2363	130.2	B5	07/03/55	bowl	° red earth	white wash
4	2369	130.2	B5 (1)	07/03/55	goblet?	° red earth with grey section	
5	4671	130.2	B5	no date	bowl	reddish-beige paste	reddish-beige engobe
6	2388	130.2	B5 (4)	07/03/55	jar	° grey-brown earth	white wash

° *According to de Vaux*

Locus 130-5B, pottery and catalogue, scale ¼

Plate 82

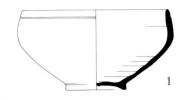

N° Pl.	N° Catal.	Position	Comments (archives)	Date	Description	Clay	Exterior
1	2367	130.2	A6 (4)	08/03/55	bowl	° red earth with grey section	white wash
2	4680	130.2	A6 (4)	08/03/55	flask handle	dark brown paste	burnt
3	2501	130.2	A6	08/03/55	fragment of jar	° red earth	white wash

° *According to de Vaux*

Locus 130-6A, pottery and catalogue

Locus 130-6B, pottery

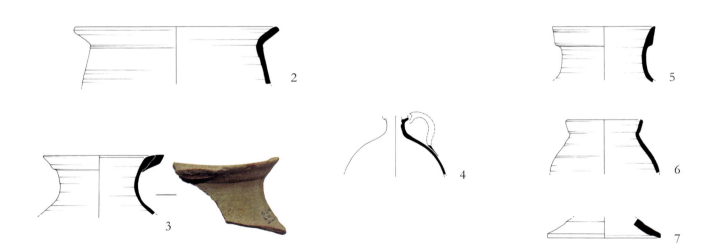

No. Pl.	N° Catal.	Position	Comments (archives)	Date	Description	Clay	Exterior
1	2347	130.2	B6 (2)	07/03/55	plate	° buff earth	pink wash
2	4651	130.2	sediments	no date	large bowl	red paste with grey core	grey
3	4653	130.2	sediments	no date	large jug	red paste	beige
4	4668	130.2	sediments	no date	small jug	orange paste	beige
5	4665	130.2	sediments	no date	jar	orange paste	beige-red
6	4664	130.2	sediments	no date	jar	orange paste	beige
7	4674	130.2	sediments	no date	fragment of support?	brown paste	grey-brown

° *According to de Vaux*

Locus 130, sediments, pottery and catalogue, scale ¼

Plate 83

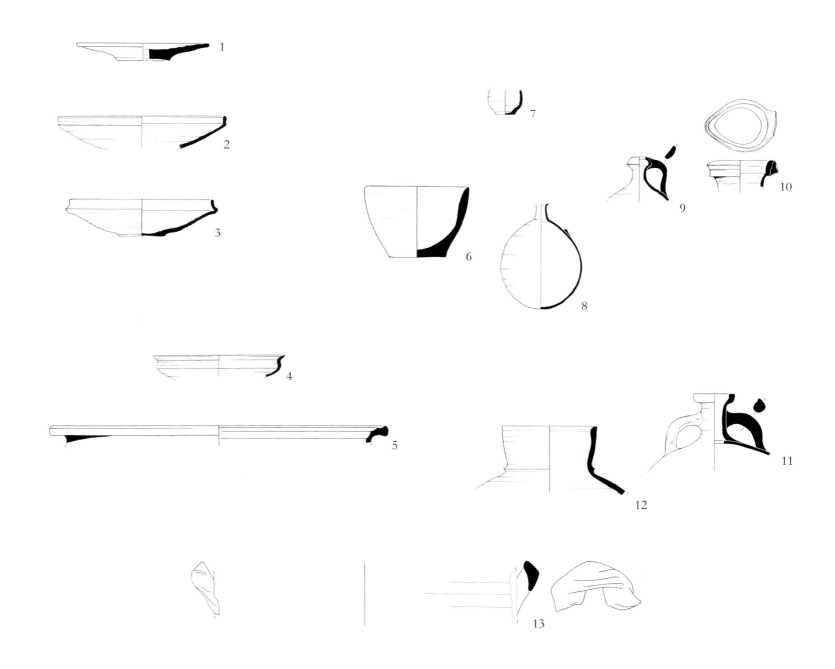

N° Pl.	N° Catal.	Position	Comments (archives)	Date	Description	Clay	Exterior
1	2290	130.2	L. 131	02/03/55	plate	° red earth with grey section	white wash
2	4199	130.2	L. 131 (catalogue)	26/03/55	plate	light brown paste	beige
3	2273	130.2	L. 131	01/03/55	plate	° red earth with grey section	
4	4196	130.2	L. 131 (catalogue)	28/03/55	plate	red paste	beige
5	4895	130.2	L. 131 (catalogue)	02/03/55	edge of large bowl	red paste	red
6	2598	130.2	L. 131	27/03/55	goblet	° grey earth	white wash
7	4200	130.2	L. 131 (catalogue)	28/03/55	unguentarium	red paste	red
8	2268	130.2	L. 131	01/03/55	small globular bowl	° buff earth	pink wash
9	4195	130.2	L. 131 (catalogue)	28/02/55	small globular bowl	red paste	beige
10	4197	130.2	L. 131 (catalogue)	01/03/55	neck of jug	red paste	red
11	4203	130.2	L. 131 (catalogue)	28/03/55	flask	red paste	red
12	4198	130.2	L. 131 (catalogue)	28/03/55	neck of jar	orange paste	beige-red
13	4202	130.2	L. 131 (catalogue)	26/03/55	handle of large jar or vat	red paste	beige

° *According to de Vaux*

Locus 131, pottery and catalogue, scale ¼

Plate 84

Plate 77 4A, 5

Plate 72, 12

Plate 77 4A, 3

Plate 75 2A, 11

Plate 75 2A, 13

Locus 130, photographs of pottery

Plate 85

Plate 80, 2

Plate 76 3A, 1

Plate 72, 4

Plate 76 3A, 2

Plate 76 3A, 6

Plate 77 4A, 7

Plate 80, 8

Locus 130, photographs of pottery

fig. 165. Locus 132
a) Aqueduct 500 hillock on projection 677
b) Survey of Locus 132 (1955)
c) and d) Designation of the constructed elements

Locus 132
A lost space

L. 132 was excavated in the course of the first two weeks of March 1955, then checked again in one of the last days of the same month. The *Journal* is sparing with details, and photographs are sparse, almost nothing. The Coüasnon *Plan* of Period Ib leads us to understand that the pool, with its rather large dimensions, will have extended as far as L. 136 in the north. This lost space, without real coherence, was interpreted by de Vaux as a huge decantation pool built in the first phase of occupation and disused in Period II in favour of aqueduct 500. Such an early date would be at odds with our proposal of seeing the western triangle of the space in the north as a late extension. The interpretation given to L. 132 raises difficulties when the time comes, in the evolution of the architecture, to separate the different walls that mark its limits, and then to interpret its function and its destination. The Coüasnon *Plans* of Periods Ib and II (fig. 153) link it to ritual bath L. 138 by means of an awkward passage; the bath is accessed by an entrance and an exit which would oblige the user to cross a sometimes muddy pool. One could argue that the decantation pool was not filled with water permanently, but the layout does not fit as a pool. The *Journal* comments briefly on L. 132 and is quick to offer the decantation pool interpretation *a priori*, while still noting the buried deposits, which would be incompatible in a pool. It omits to undo the knot of tangled constructions at the external corner of L. 123; but this permits some remarks on the chronology of the north enclosure.

L. 132 was not a pool – The decantation interpretation faces difficulties. The high diversion sluice 677, stops the current of the aqueduct 500 at the elbow where it joins L. 130; de Vaux saw this as the sluice which bars undecanted water. Diversion 677 is not exactly a sluice but the permanent stopper of an overflow. Diversion sluice 677 is too high for the planned pool to be able to empty. Low wall 672 constitutes its southeast edge; photograph fig. 166a shows its coating, and the northwest edge was taken down: *we clear (…) the base of the plaster on the south edge* (L. 132, 7/3/55). The other dividing walls of the L. were not coated with mortar: the photographs show nothing of this and the *Journal* states: *This coating seems destroyed elsewhere* (7/3/55). L. 132, therefore, was not a pool: de Vaux imagined it with stretches of masonry which are not contemporary (fig. 167). The overflow is positioned to discharge water into the western ravine, following the sharp corner of L. 123; it was then cut by the construction of wall 699, preserved as far as the join; the function of the overflow will have been interrupted unless it was crossed by a conduit. The later works on the site were able to re-use the stones of the northwest edge of 706.

The eastern edge (671) of the supposed decantation, L. 132, does not show an earlier phase of aqueduct 500: *a low wall with a poor sill were constructed parallel to its east wall to repair a channel* (L. 132, 2/3/55). There is nothing to show that the latter was designed at one time. An undemonstrated asymmetry between the east and west edges and a *poor sill* may betray an earlier and more modest masonry to supply pool 173. The aqueduct, as shown on Coüasnon *Plan* of Period II, is in fact the latest restoration of the hydraulic system (Level 4). The presentation of the aqueduct on the *Plans* is the same for Periods II and III, which means according to de Vaux's chronology that the state of the visible drain would have been maintained for more than a century – a rather unlikely proposal. We recall that the apparent high preservation of its edges is due to the most recent restoration, when bath L. 138 was already in disuse. L. 132 was no more than a vague terrain.

Enclosure wall 656 which would have closed a pool 132 to the southwest was not coated and was only a protective wall where the ravine commences; this is the latest constructed element: photograph fig. 166a clearly shows that it rests untidily on reinforcement 598, as the sketch shows. It was built when the rim of the supposed pool 132 was put out of use. Finally, further impeding the interpretation of the pool, bath L. 138 has its own overflow, discrete and poorly preserved, which Coüasnon *Plan* of Period Ib has correctly placed. A small overflow 669 runs under the south corner 666 of bath L. 138 and trickles out towards the ravine via a small drain 670 on top of the base of wall 666, passing under wall 656. The fact that drain 669 rests at the same level as the bottom of the claimed pool invalidates even better the decantation function of the location.

a) Reinforcement 598 at the corner of Locus 123 has been indented. It shows the sabre cut of the remnant of wall 599

b) The aqueduct 500 comes up against the rise 677

c) Bones deposit, Locus 132

d) Bones deposit, Locus 132

fig. 166.   Locus 132

We can state that L. 132, with no precise function, was a lost space in the course of the staged conversion of the north enclosure. However, the connection of the constructed elements at this point suggests a sequence linked to the masonry.

Aqueduct 500, at least in its last condition (132.1), represents the most recent restoration on Level 4 of an earlier drain, Level 3B/C (132.2, cf. stratigraphic draft L. 132). Reinforcement 598 (132.2) predates it, although its date cannot be specified; the *Journal* does not describe it: *We also clean the reinforcement of the northwest corner* (L. 124, 15/3/55). Its position is late, as it caps dismantled wall element 599 which leans on supporting wall 501 of L. 123. The latter, unwisely founded at the break in the slope of the ravine, compensated for its fragility with the support by reinforcement 598 which surrounds the first section of wall 599 (132.4); we shall attempt to take advantage of this to argue for a new definition of L. 135. Photograph fig. 166a clearly shows the sabre-cut made by the support of reinforcement 598 against the eastern face of wall 599. The recreation of the track of 599 along a north-south axis extends from the vestige embedded in reinforcement 598. On its axis, towards the north, the first section of 599 ideally links with elbow 600 which joins walls 655 and 657 and testifies to the increasing building up of the site (see on L. 135). The sequence is established as follows: 1) drain 706 was installed as an overflow diversion from aqueduct 500; 2) the first section of 599, not clad and fortunately suggested on Coüasnon's *Plan* of Period Ib (fig. 153a), seems to have obliterated drain 706; 3) Coüasnon's *Plan* supposes, with some credibility, that the erection of enclosure 656 to the southwest joined up with what remained of 599 to create L. 138 – *the coating* (on drain 706) *disappears very quickly and the wall of the pool stops* (L. 132, 27/3/55) – if drain 706 was not put out of use by enclosure 656, a conduit could have crossed it; 4) reinforcement 598 makes the complex obsolete and enclosure 656 is placed or repaired so as to rest on it (fig. 166a). Comment: if enclosure 656 is later than reinforcement 598, a possible hypothesis, then bath L. 138, which justifies enclosure 656, is later than reinforcement 598.

The buried deposits of L. 132

The reinforcement of the corner of the building is probably secondary, constructed on a thin layer of ash and silt (L. 130, 28/2/55), which has a strong chance of being the extension of yellow sediment 130.2 containing the deposits. At L. 130 it is not indicated whether the edge of drain 706 cut the yellow sediment or not. We prefer the hypothesis of the earlier date of the yellow sediment which, we think, accumulated as soon as the main constructions barred the slope. The buried deposits establish a clear continuity between L. 130 and L. 132, and in fact it seems that the construction of a drain did not share them in two. However, wall 599, as restored, has made it (L. 130 and 132) into two separate spaces, and the deposits may have preceded its construction, or followed its demolition. This is not particularly important, as the deposits were spread over a fairly long period. In L. 132, the yellow sediment was found to be less thick: *the filling is of fine earth* (7/3/55), less evident than in L. 130, downstream. A muddy sediment could not have drained into L. 130 by the force of a flood as de Vaux proposed. We may note that these deposits have not been disturbed. Eight of them are indicated: *in the southwest corner lie two accumulations of jar sherds with bones* (L. 132, 7/3/55); *We discover two more nests of sherds with bones against the west wall* (8/3/55); *Two groups of pots with bones (...) one of them, important, on the virgin ground with two coins* (L. 132, 14/3/55). Burial in a pool makes no sense.

The mention of the virgin ground can be misleading. The base of the archaeological sediment cannot be confused with an occupation floor dated by two coins (one of Alexander Jannaeus and the other of Hyrcanus II): the hole for burying the deposit and the coins would have pierced the yellow sediment and hit the sterile, more resistant floor. We may form the logical hypothesis that drain 706 is later than the deposits. Here we would have the deepest archaeological layer, and we think it probable that it leans on long wall 501 of L. 116, 122 and 123. The fact remains that sondages were not made of their floors and that deposits may perhaps underlie them. The date to be assigned to west wing L. 111, L. 121-123, added to the Hasmonaean house, is dependent on this.

fig. 167. Succession of architectural phases at the junction of Loci 130 and 132.

North wall (1) of the western annexes against which wall 599 rests (2) (the western fence of the northern enclosure), dismantled to make way for the diversion 672 of the overflow of the aqueduct 673 (500), cancelled in order to found the reinforcement 598 (4) of the corner of the annexes, against which abuts the late border wall (5) enclosing the bath 138

The western boundary

section

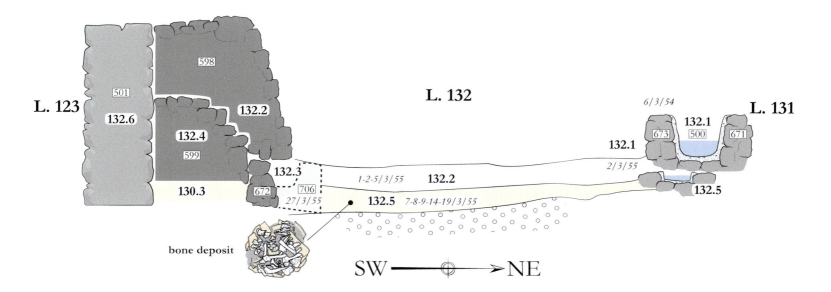

Schema and stratigraphic diagram of Locus 132 (for the chart of symbols, see page 155)

Restored elements	Level	Definition	Journal dates	Coins	Position	N°	Chronology
132.1	4	Aqueduct 500					
132.2	3C	Thin layer indistinct	1-2/3/55 5-6/3/55	KhQ. 2277 -2278 2328 2313	Independent of deposits	2 1 1	Proc. under Nero Agrippa Ist Herod
132.3	3B/C	Reinforcement of 598	27/3/55				
132.4	3B	North wall 599 of L. 135					
132.5	3A/B	Buried deposits drain 673 overflow 706	2-3/3/55 7-8-9/3/55				

fig. 168.   Plate 86, 1

N° Pl.	N° Catal.	Position	Comments (archives)	Date	Description	Clay	Exterior
1	2382	132.5	southwest 1	09/03/55	plate with animal bones	° red earth with grey section	
2	4226	132.2	-	05/03/55	plate?	dark grey paste	grey
3	2421	132.5	south-west 2	09/03/55	broken bowl with animal bones	° red earth with grey section	white wash
4	2391	132.5	south-west 2	09/03/55	broken bowl	° very fine earth, pink, grey section	
5	4225	132?	-	no date	bowl	red paste	beige-red
6	2495	132.5	east-west trench 8	20/03/55	bowl	° red earth	pink wash
7	2389	132.5	south-west 3	09/03/55	broken bowl with animal bones	° grey earth	white wash
8	4229	132.5	-	14/03/55	bowl	brown paste	beige
9	2306	132.2	-	01/03/55	goblet	° grey earth	red with white wash
10	2346	132.2	-	05/03/55	goblet	° buff earth	white wash
11	2366	132.5	-	07/03/55	goblet	° red earth with grey section	white wash
12	2495 bis	132.5	-	19/03/55	broken bowl with animal bones	° coarse, red and grey earth	
13	2541	132.5	south-west 1	09/03/55	broken bowl	° red earth, soft	
14	2420	132.5	south-west 4	10/03/55	broken bowl with animal bones	° red earth with grey section	
15	4233	132.1	-	06/03/55	bowl	orange paste	beige
16	4227	132.2	-	03/03/55	flask	red paste	beige-red
17	4228	132.5	-	08/03/55	unguentarium	red paste	beige
18	2338	132.2	-	05/03/55	lid	° grey earth	white wash

° *According to de Vaux*

Locus 132, catalogue and photograph

Plate 86

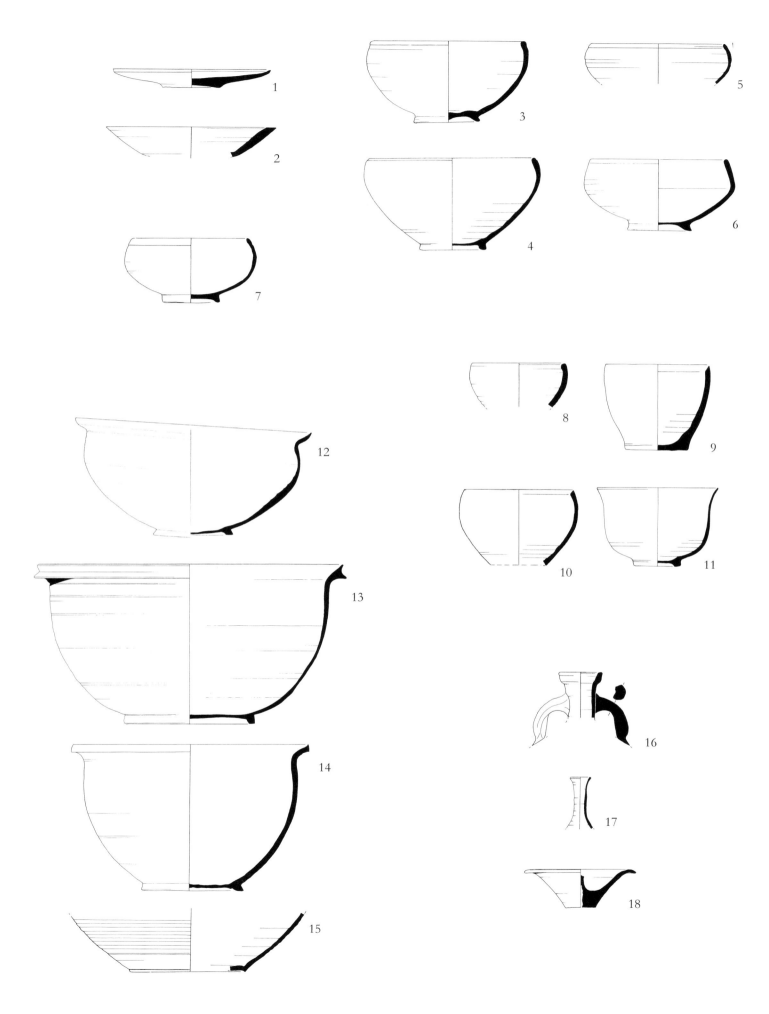

Locus 132, pottery, scale ¼

422   The archaeology of Qumran – an attempted reassessment

fig. 169.   Storage jar, Plate 87, 5

N° Pl.	N° Catal.	Position	Comments (archives)	Date	Description	Clay	Exterior
1	2455	132.5	south-west 4	10/03/55	cooking pot	brownish-red earth	
2	2484	132.5	east-west trench 7	19/03/55	pan handle	° red earth with grey section	white wash
3	4234	132.2	-	05/03/55	bowl	red paste	beige
4	4235	132.1	-	06/03/55	crater	red paste	beige engobe
5	2654	132.5	south-west 4	10/03/55	jar with large opening	° red earth	pink and grey
6	4223	132.?	-	no date	jar	light red paste	beige
7	4231	132.2	-	03/03/55	small jug	red paste	beige
8	4224	132.?	-	no date	jar	brownish-red paste	beige-red
9	4230	132.2	-	01/03/55	jar	red paste	red
10	4232	132.5	-	09/03/55	scroll jar type	orange paste	beige
11	4222	132.?	-	no date	jar	dark grey paste	beige
12	4218	132.2	-	03/03/55	jar	red paste with grey core	beige-red
13	4219	132.?	-	no date	jar	red paste	beige-red
14	4220	132.?	-	no date	jar	brownish-red paste	beige-red
15	4221	132.?	-	no date	jar	brown paste	beige engobe

° *According to de Vaux*

Locus 132, catalogue and photograph

Plate 87

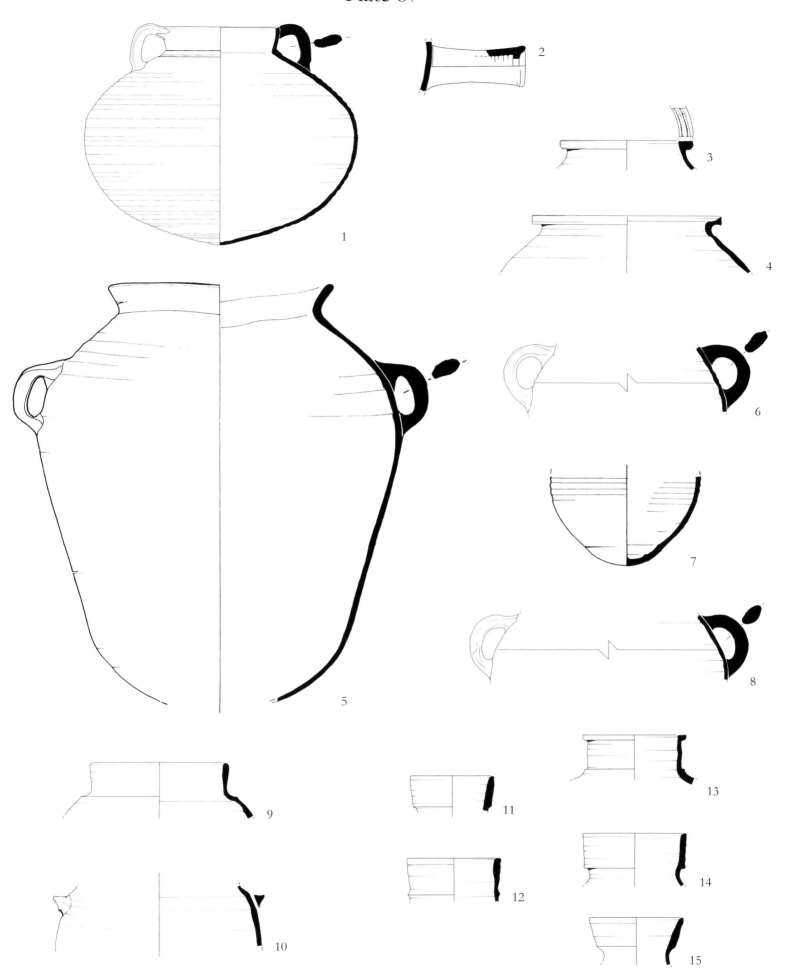

Locus 132, pottery, scale ¼

fig. 170. Locus 138 in the course of excavation and Locus 132 in the background (photo: Fr. Robert Beauvery)

Locus 138
A ritual bath adjoins entrance 702

Aerial photograph fig. 156 suggests an indentation west of the north enclosure where the relief outlined a quadrilateral. The structure collapsed on itself, filling the pool. De Vaux begins the excavation on 8/3/55, and interprets the L. as a bath from 9/3/55 on. The 10th and 12th of March were devoted to emptying the tank; the walls and the immediate surroundings were cleared on the days after this, 13 and 14/3/55, according to the *Journal*, and up to 4/4/55. The exploration extended to the north: *Between the north wall of this bath and the end wall of loci 136 and 137, narrow empty space where the Period I pottery comes from* (L. 138, 9/3/55). The pots preserved come from here, and nothing of what might have come from the bath has been kept. The attribution of the vessels to an early phase of the occupation is arbitrary.

De Vaux's interpretation of the ritual bath is unassailable; L. 138 is a perfect miqveh in both morphology and dimensions. One question remains: What are the reasons for its peripheral position, which is surprising on the plan? We have already emphasized its isolation and we shall return to this[86].

The layout of constructions of the northwest corner of the site has been pulled like the corner of a table cloth. L. 138 is isolated, but the place it occupies can still be explained. It adjoins an entrance to the settlement (by way of L. 137), used by anyone arriving at or leaving from Qumran who needed to perform ritual ablutions. Door 702 opens directly onto the precise point where the ravine bordering the site on its western side rejoins the plateau. This ravine with its slope, steep but easily accessible, was the shortest route and the most convenient to reach the gardens of the palm grove and the spring of Ain Feshkha.

It seems that it was no need to place the ritual bath towards the entrance to the ravine. It would have found its place better in L. 129-133, contiguous with door 705 which opened to the core of the settlement. The approach of aqueduct 500 provided its water. The proximity of the door opening onto the ravine is not the ultimate reason for moving aside bath 138. At a certain moment in Qumran's history, the decision was taken to redefine the boundaries of the settlement to place it in a coherent, more extensive complex. The project required that the opening to the ravine should be included within the constructed perimeter. To do this, it was necessary to extend the occupied space by creating the triangle to the west of wall 599. We discern traces of a constructed extension which would have included the entrance to the ravine, L. 139; wall 654 secured the connection with the base of the slope. The location was heavily eroded and a makeshift set-up at the start of the slope may have been swept away.

Wall 599, of which only the end attachments remain, was removed, and the material may have served in the construction of bath L. 138 (see on L. 132). Its dismantlement confirms the abandonment of L. 135. It is notable that podium 668, in the longitudinal axis of L. 135 and abutting wall 599, was not completely taken down: its remains are inserted in the masonry of buttress 667 which contains the east corner of the bath; 668 therefore antedates the bath. Coüasnon's *Plan* of Period Ib interpreted this as a sort of ramp for a bridge which, leaving the pool, would have crossed drain 500. The proposal, not taking account of the integrity of the complex, does not solve the difficulties of circulation in the north enclosure, divided at a late stage by the obstacle of an aqueduct. Previously, the enclosure will have had a more harmonious configuration. Heap 668, even cut short, is preserved high. It merges as far as the top into block 667, which encloses it; such a height was of no use in crossing aqueduct 500, the linings of which seem to jut out on the photographs because the approaches were dug-over during the excavation. We may note that in its final form, aqueduct 500 was a rather rough restoration, carried out after 68, and it finds its counterpart in the terminal diversion which skirts L. 77 to the south, *Plan* Period III – Level 4. It was probably designed with a lesser height before the abandonment following AD 68 (Level 3), and it was easily crossed to get back to the settlement.

The conversions in this sector responded to the desire to organize a closed circuit linking the complex of buildings at Qumran with the palm grove and the dependency of Ain Feshkha. The closed circuit is marked by *eruvim*, closing elements to facilitate movements during sabbath within a defined territory. On sabbath the law limited a walk *extra muros* to

---
86. J.-B. Humbert, *Archaelogical Interpretations*, p. 23-24.

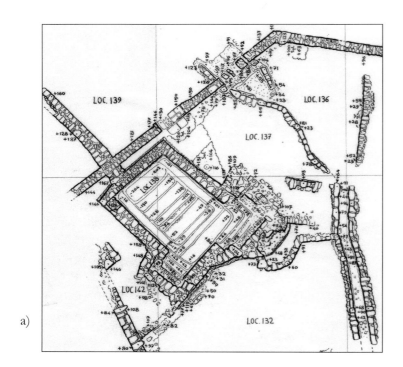
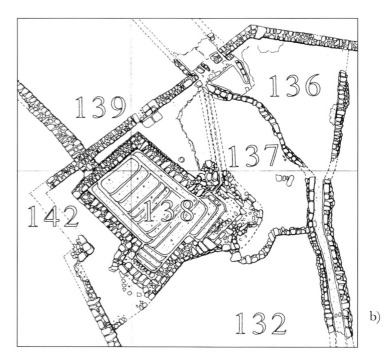
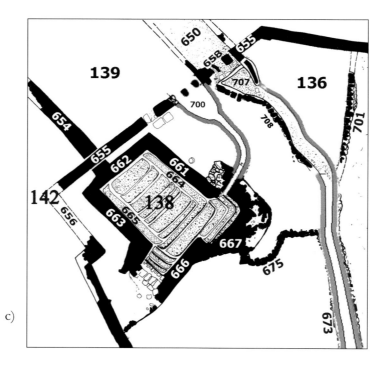

fig. 171. Locus 138
a and b) Surveys (1955)
c) Designation of the constructed elements

a thousand steps or two thousand cubits, with no restrictions on distances *intra muros*. We trace the boundaries of the *eruv* in our note on the *long walls* (p. 35). Accepting *eruvim* concept at Qumran allows us to take account of units which have hitherto failed to convince: the long wall at the eastern edge of the southern promontory, without a function unless it is to mark a space, then the separation of bath L. 138. The two units belong to the same phase of the extension of the site.

Bath L. 138 is incompatible with L. 132 as a decantation pool. De Vaux may have thought that this was where one entered the pool and that one left by way of block 667, which would have functioned as a pavement. Having climbed the steep slope of the ravine and passed through doorway 702, one entered by the east corner. One left, at the opposite end, through the well-preserved doorway in the south corner, dropping into L. 132. We cannot conclude that the decantation was episodic. An overflow 670 poured into the ravine; the small run-off channel follows wall 666 of the bath, on the level of L. 132, erroneously described as a pool because channel 670 will have been embedded and the two water circulations are incompatible. Leaving L. 138, the bather was able to walk into L. 132 without water, and to walk towards door 705 by crossing L. 135 and L. 134.

The sometimes violent arrival of run-off water has damaged the outlet exiting from sluice 658 in L. 137: *Impossible to find the point where water arrives in bath/cistern L. 138* (4/4/55). Feed 700 of the pool was recreated implausibly and Coüasnon's *Plan* of Period II notes what remains of a conduit. We modify another track of the drain in our comments on L. 136-137. Bath L. 138 could not have been fed otherwise than from upstream; nothing remains of the capture which we prefer to link to the mouth of the supply upstream of sluice 658 in pool 650, at the opening furthest to the right in the direction of flow, easily handled. In either case, bath L. 138 could not have been filled other than by water from the channel which starts from the dam in the cliff gorge. This, with the obstruction of sluice 669, poses the problem of maintenance of a symbolic, permanent flow to preserve the ritual function of the bath.

Coüasnon *Plan* of Period II tried to place the supply to the bath near the east entrance to the bath. The result is not clear, but the drain cannot have been constructed anywhere else. The sketch indicates the pipe, possibly coated with mortar, which passes through the right of the threshold as it enters. De Vaux then examined the sluice of overflow 669 which passes through wall 666. He was right to call it an *overflow, then blocked by a very hard cement when the pool was put out of service* (L. 138, 2/4/55). He may have thought that the sluice sent water to the west from decantation pool L. 132, which was a possibility; we examined sluice 669 before the recent heavy restorations, and noted that it widens on the side of L. 132; the stopper was placed from L. 132, against the flow of an overflow. But L. 132 was not a pool, and the sluice, although in the opposite direction, indeed functions as an overflow of L. 138. The plugging of sluice 669 provoked comment: *Thus bath 138 would be earlier than the earthquake* (L. 138, 2/4/55). De Vaux imagined that the bath was abandoned at the end of his Period Ib, which is a surprise. We do not see why condemnation of the pipe would have provoked the abandonment of the pool.

We reject the option, retained on Coüasnon's *Plan* of Period II, according to which the bath was maintained from the beginning of Period Ib to 68. The sequence of the phases does not link up well. The question of the supply to the bath is not consistent with the chronology. The *Plan* of Period Ib shows only a dotted line; there is nothing to indicate that two phases of supply in Ib and II were distinguished during the excavation; the plan of Period II placed it downstream of sluice 658, without suggesting the mode of capture, arbitrarily shifting its route northwards. The formula adopted by Coüasnon is an adaptation to lend credibility to the modification of the sluice. It is probable that there was only one supply system and it would have been best to place bath L138 only in Period II, which brings us back to the option we retain: the bath, in our view, was a late installation, dependent on the *eruvim* (see our note on *The long walls*). L. 138 probably remained in operation up to 68. It was enclosed by walls 655 and 656 when it was constructed. Enclosure 656, which closes it to the southwest, leans on reinforcement 598 which, in turn, seals overflow 706 of main aqueduct 500. L. 138 closes the sequence. It seems difficult to put its foundation back before Level 3C.

No stratification is identifiable in L. 138. After abandonment, its upper part collapsed. A partial fill was able to furnish some pots. A coin of the procurators under Tiberius (KhQ 2359) collected in the fill is without significance.

428 The archaeology of Qumran – an attempted reassessment

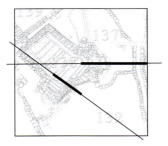

section

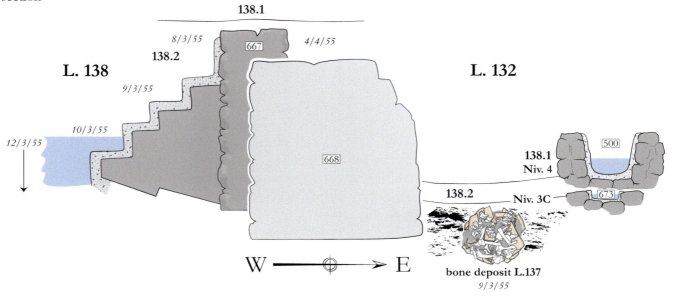

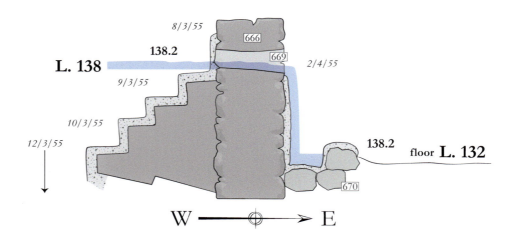

Restored elements	Level	Definition	Journal dates	Coins	Position	N°	Chronology
138.1	3C-4	Aqueduct 500 filling-in of the bath	See locus 132				
138.2	3B/C	Construction of bath 138 Aqueduct 673	8-12/3/55 2-4/4/55	KhQ. 2359	L138	1	Proc. under Tiberius
138.3	2 - 3A/B/C	Buried deposits	9/3/55 (L137)				

Schema and stratigraphic diagram of Locus 138 (for the chart of symbols, see page 155)

Plate 88

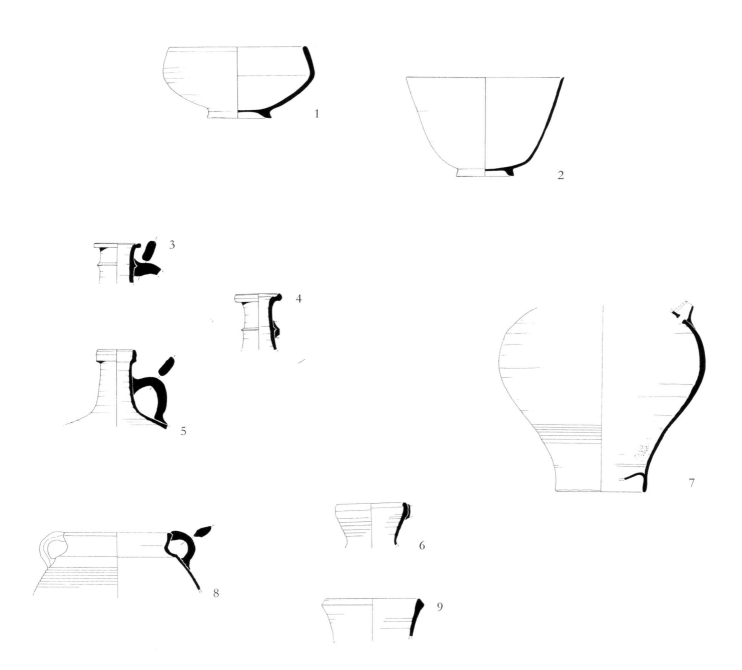

N° Pl.	N° Catal.	Position	Comments (archives)	Date	Description	Clay	Exterior
1	2378	138.2	-	3/8/1951	bowl	° grey earth	white wash
2	2379	138.2	-	3/8/1951	goblet	° red earth	white wash
3	4264	138.2	-	3/9/1951	jug	brownish-red paste	light red
4	4262	138.2	-	10/03/55	jug	brownish-red paste	light red
5	4263	138.2	-	3/8/1951	jug	orange paste	beige engobe
6	4261	138.2	-	09/03/55	jug	beige-red paste	beige-red
7	2419	138.2	-	10/03/55	jug	° whitish earth, soft	white
8	4259	138.2	-	10/03/55	cooking pot	red paste	red
9	4260	138.2	-	12/03/55	jar	brownish-red paste	brownish-red

° *According to de Vaux*

Locus 138, pottery and catalogue, scale ¼

430 The archaeology of Qumran – an attempted reassessment

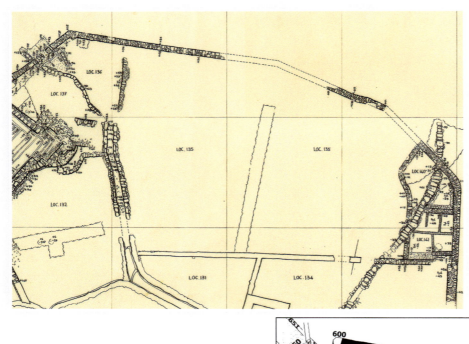

fig. 172. a) Coüasnon survey 1955
b) Designation of the constructed elements

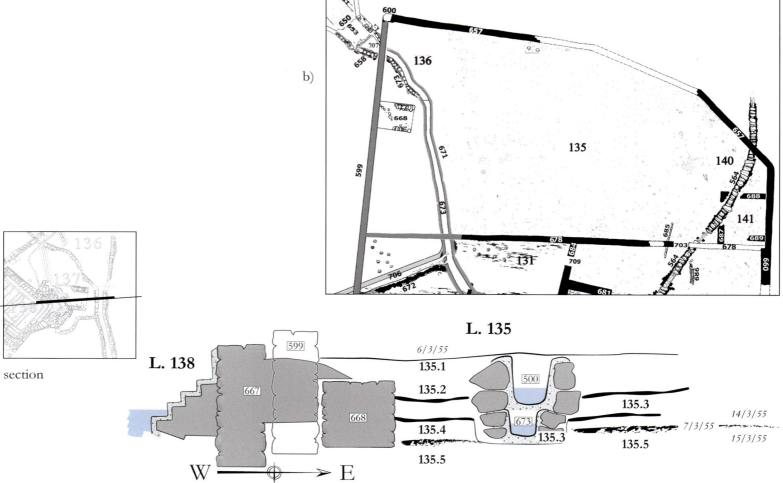

Restored elements	Level	Definition	Journal dates	Coins	Position	N°	Chronology
135.1	Post 4	Abandonment	6/3/55	KhQ. 2276		1	Proc. under Nero
				2301		1	Agrippa Ist
				2302		1	Herod Archelaus
135.2	3C-4	Drain 500	See locus 133				
135.3	3C	Drain 673	See locus 136				
135.4	3A/B	Construction of enclosure 135	1-9/3/55				
135.5	2–3A	Buried deposits	7, 14-15/3/55	2356	In the ash	1	First Revolt
				2361	To the east	1	Proc. under Claudius

Schema and stratigraphic diagram of Locus 135 (for the chart of symbols, see page 155)

Locus 135
An assembly area? (fig. 172)

L. 135, the site's most extensive delimited space, occupies the major part of the north enclosure[87]. Because of its size, it took two weeks to excavate it, from the 1st to 15/3/55. There is a high probability that its construction responded to the need to extend the inhabited perimeter northwards: L. 135 is the original heart of the enclosure and the constructions that surround it depended on its evolution. A number of archaeological indicators show that it was subject to re-purposing and that it was created with a particular objective which, stage by stage, will have been lost. We would like to help giving it back its *raison d'être* and the interest it deserves.

Its irregular plan narrows towards the east: north wall 657 followed, via two successive corners, the former path from the west, ending at the main entrance to the former residence (fig. 173). The wall was a low one, marking out an enclosure rather than a courtyard, *The wall, not very thick, seems not to have a foundation, probably a simple enclosure* (L. 135, 6/3/55).

The original spot was reworked several times, with the modification of access points to reach the top of the ravine, construct bath 138, and finally to found aqueduct 500. As we said, L. 132 and 138 constituted an extension of L. 135 at the time when a closed domain was formed by *eruvim*. When it was built, it did not have the configuration shown on the *Plans*, so one wonders what the purpose was of a space which seems to expand towards the north. It has no apparent use and gives the impression of being a cattle pen. Which it is not. L. 135 was designed with a western enclosure which we have good grounds to restore: wall 599 was built and then dismantled. The south attachment remains, leaning against wall 501 of the western annexes, clearly marked on Coüasnon's *Plan* Ib; there was no reason to construct masonry in a Y: wall 599 was not completely cleared and its attachment to wall 501 was preserved; the latest remains, wall 656 (west of L. 132) and what remains of drain 706 were subsequently attached. The north attachment is at elbow 600 which, on the *Plans*, articulates walls 657 and 655; the latter, with its very open corner, is shown on the *Plans* as a clear addition; the large foundation stone is that of a right angle formed by wall 657 and the restored 599. This complex was dismantled to build L. 138.

Closed to the west by full wall 599, L. 135 was marked off to the south by wall 678, the construction of which fits at an angle in the site's general right-angled grid. Its staggered position cannot be the fruit of an error and we need to look for its cause. The surveyors who laid out the site knew their work and did not set it up haphazardly: the three walls 599, 678 and 660 fit in a right-angled grid independent of that of the site. The slant affecting 678 gives the plan of L. 135 the form of a trapeze extended to the west. The space thus opens in the right direction, i.e. towards Jerusalem. *This is very probably a large open space in front of the buildings* (L. 135, 7/3/55). But a space like this is not simply an open space. An understanding of its original layout reveals an enclosure with an internal organization, and we may see it as an assembly point adjoining L. 130 with its furnace and its buried left-overs. It would have had a part to play in the course of the activities that have been proposed. The orientation to Jerusalem is not fortuitous, as it was known.

Block of stones 668, which was not commented upon by the excavator, deserves to be considered with more attention. Today, all that is left to see is two thin lines of stones which again fix what Coüasnon *Plan* Ib had made of it. We must emphasize that its position and its orientation immediately link it with L. 135 and that it has nothing to do with bath L. 138. The building of bath L. 138 has surrounded the western part in the masonry of block 667: 668 predates 667 (see on L. 138). The Coüasnon *Plans* reveal that it must have leaned exactly on wall 599, before the latter was taken down. We can recreate its dimensions: 2 m from east to west and 2.5 m in a north-south direction. We do not think it served as a podium to stand on, but as a dais for depositing objects which people did not want to leave on the ground, spoiled by the buried bone deposits and rendered powdery by being walked on. It is positioned in the east-west axis of L. 135 and we believe that it was one of the units of the layout in this cleared space: it marks the direction of Jerusalem, which must have been known to the people using Qumran.

---

87. Here we resume the subject raised in: *Qumrân*, Vol. II, p. 434-5.

L. 135 has produced a number of buried deposits: *(I)n the northwest corner, we clear a large accumulation of sherds, fragments of several jars, several goblets, two large pots, two bowls surrounding animal bones* (L. 135, 7/3/55). *The location is ashy, (...) level of ashy earth (7/3/55);* to the east *brown and black ash* (9/3/55); *Clearing to the east in the ash* (14/3/55); *clearance in the ash to the northeast and the southeast* (L. 135, 15/3/55). The fire-linked activities are the same as those in L. 130 and L. 132. Coüasnon *Plan* Ib noted burials against north wall 657; they do not precede the founding of L. 135. Assembled in the background are the few data relating to the paschal pilgrimage that we suspect: an assembly point would not have been out of place there. The state of the remains does not allow us to recreate the circulation paths with any certainty. However, even if the walls are low, passageways are necessary. L. 134 distributed the walkways. L. 130, a sort of open-air kitchen, was at the far end in the distribution of the spaces. From L. 134 one entered it by L. 131, which forms a unit with L. 130; east wall 684 of L. 131 shows passage 709 on Coüasnon *Plan* II. From L. 134 one then entered L. 135 by door 703, inserted in wall 678. We may suppose that an opening allowed communication between L. 130 and L. 135 not far from the southwest corner: the deposits are mainly scattered in this area.

The reading of the spaces on the *Plans* is impeded by the drawing of the aqueduct and the drains, which lay an artificial partition on the original layout. We recall that de Vaux wrongly proposed a complex and ramified hydraulic system from the very beginning of the installation. In L. 135, aqueduct 500 drawn on Coüasnon *Plans* Ib and II is heavily reconstructed and belongs to Level 4 (Period III, post-68). If L. 135 accommodated the activities we would like to attribute to it, to return a correct space we can restore a modest lower drain 673, according to some poor elements; it supplied only pool 173, upstream of cistern 110 and could be covered without projecting too far and without impeding circulation. L. 135 then recovers its unity. The sequence of the different constructions, however, testifies to a complex evolution. In its original state, L. 135 would be quite ancient and this is appropriate as we want to link it to the episode of the buried deposits of L. 130, some of the pots from which date from before the turn of the era. However, we cannot take the development of the hydraulic system too far down in the chronology. We infer a progressive disuse or a fairly rapid decline of L. 135. The digging of the large reservoirs and other pools necessitated a more voluminous aqueduct which doubled small pool L. 173, then out of use, and penetrated into the settlement by crossing wall 512, which is a resumption of masonry. We have to imagine that the new arrangements for the supply of water prompted the reallocation of L. 135 for the construction of bath L. 138, which in turn triggered the demolition of wall 599. All this movement did not necessarily interrupt the custom of open-air meals there. We suspect that pilgrimage was the object of an organization that subsequently declined.

fig. 173. General view of Loci 134 and 135, looking west

Plate 89

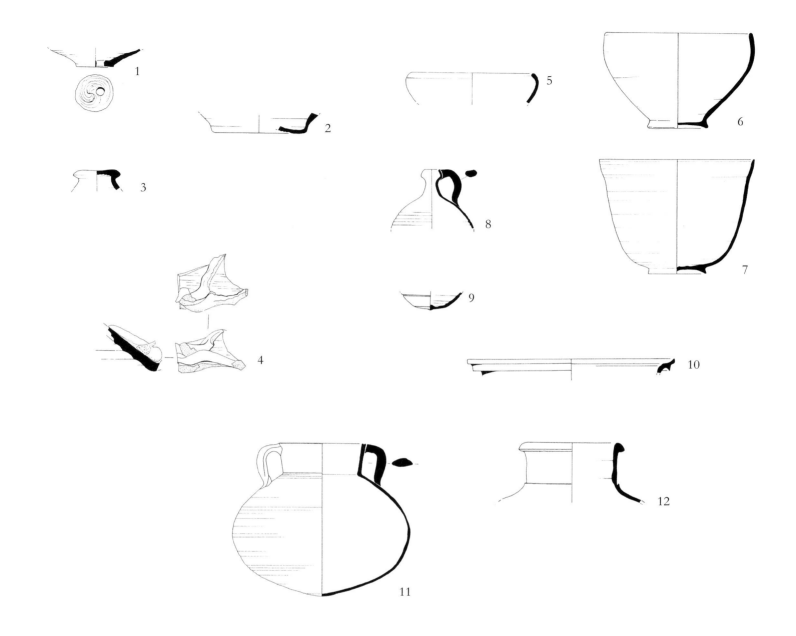

N° Pl.	N° Catal.	Position	Comments (archives)	Date	Description	Clay	Exterior
1	4243	135.1	-	02/03/55	plate, pierced after firing	red paste	light brown
2	4247	135.1	-	02/03/55	jug	red paste	brown-red
3	4246	135.1	-	02/03/55	knob of scroll type jar lid	red paste	light brown
4	4218	135.1	-	03/03/55	jar with formed decoration	red paste with grey core	beige-red
5	4244	135.5	ash	13/03/55	bowl	red paste	brownish-red
6	2353	135.5	northwest with bones	07/03/55	bowl	° grey earth in section	traces of white wash
7	2351	135.5	northwest with bones	07/03/55	goblet	° pink earth, grey in section	pink wash
8	4245	135.?	-	12/03/55	small jug	red paste	brownish-red
9	4248	135.5	ash	14/03/55	small jug	red paste with grey core	red
10	4242	135.5	ash	14/03/55	crater?	red paste with grey core	burnt
11	2500	135.5	northwest with animal bones	07/03/55	cooking pot	° red earth	
12	4241	135.5	ash	14/03/55	jar	red with grey core	brownish-red

° *According to de Vaux*

Locus 135, out of the grid, pottery and catalogue, scale ¼

Loci 136 (and 137)
Collection at the point of arrival of the water

Loci 136, L. 137 and L. 139 encircle the aqueduct at the point where it reaches the border of Qumran. Two millennia of trickling water and floods have distorted the layout. De Vaux tried hard to form a picture of the organization of the premises. *The sector between the pool and cistern 138 remains confused* (L. 137, 10/3/55); *We continue to dig without seeing much of importance* (L. 137, 12/3/55); *work without result* (L. 137, 13/3/55); *We clear in front of the lining of bath 138 to find where the water arrives,* and *nothing clear* (L. 137, 14/3/55). On the other hand, the Coüasnon *Plans* propose a simple restoration of the layout, inadequate for a serious intent to give the best coherence to his presentation of the site. First of all, the distinction into two loci separated by a drain was not useful. The drain crosses a defined space, L. 136. L. 137 has no place in the list of loci.

At first sight, the restorations of the arrival of water on the *Plans* simplify and satisfy; at the same time, they muddle the succession of phases of the north enclosure which we are trying to set out. The first difficulty comes from having placed bath L. 138 and the route of the aqueduct to the very beginning of the installation. The late triangular extension of bath L. 138 enlarged the enclosure towards the west in the last half of the occupation. The arrival and transit of the water had to be adapted. From sluice 658 to its opening, aqueduct 673, which precedes its restoration under number 500, crosses the north enclosure and bars it diagonally, following the unevennesses found on its route.

Coüasnon *Plan* Ib sets out sluice 658 in its full width, while it is narrowed on *Plan* II. Neither of the two plans proposes a satisfactory restoration of the supply to bath L. 138. The absence of an upstream drain on *Plan* Ib indicates that the bath will first have been filled from L. 132 through small sluice 669, inserted in wall 666 of the bath. But given its high position, the sluice would have necessitated a very high water level in decantation pool L. 132 to cater for the considerable capacity required by the bath. We must repeat that L. 132 was not a pool and that sluice 669 was an overflow, in the opposite direction to a feed; the bath emptied into the ravine by way of small drain 670 on the ground level of L. 132. A water-filled L. 132 would have drowned it. *Plan* II drew the feed as a dotted line, sloping from sluice 658, necessary after the abandonment of the principle of decantation. The argument falls at the same point as that for decantation. No further element supports the proposal.

Qumran's hydraulic system is complex and on another occasion we shall undertake a detailed study of it. The system is important for an overall interpretation of the site, as it dominated buildings which it served and modified those which it bordered on. It seems clear that its evolution was progressive and, with regard to L. 136, its opening was first a simple drain in a northern space that was as yet unallocated; it was adapted in line with the constraints that followed. To consider the position of the sluice, its modifications and the survey of the constructed units separately, will allow us to reassess the water system in L. 136. We propose it was in four phases:

1 – Fig. 174a: Before the ambitious project of damming the gorge of wadi Qumran and of a long drain to provide for the site, the collection of water came from a single stream. Its capture occurred at the point of issue of the ring of the plateau which empties upstream of the sluice. The water retained, directed by small low walls 701 and 708 forming collector 709, was directed *intra muros* by a drain 673 sealed by the more substantial drain 500, of Level 4. De Vaux distinguished the restoration of drain 500: *a low wall with a bad slope were constructed (...) to repair a channel* (L. 132, 2/3/55).

2 – Fig. 174b: The moment came when L. 135 more or less defined the north enclosure. Before the building of L. 138, L. 135 was limited to the west by restored wall 599, the construction of which had put collector 709 out of use. Renovations were needed, and work on the hydraulic system began here. The place of the collector with its position dictated by the slope will have been maintained up to Level 4 after 68, despite successive conversions. East boundary 701, quickly rendered obsolete, remained an isolated vestige, cut off from its attachments: the building of wall 599 had put it out of use. Another more modest catchment 707, was installed to permit the flow cross wall 599. It was even equipped with upstream sluice 658, narrowed by two nozzle points. The water entered the drain 673, which had not to be prominent, so as not to spoil levelling the floor of L. 135.

3 – Fig. 174c: The desire to include the top of the west ravine inside the inhabited perimeter (see L. 138 and the note on *The long walls*) triggered a second restoration of the system. With wall 599 then making a barrier, it was taken down to free up space. All we now have is the attachments, one of them on the nearby elbow 600. Bath L. 138 had been set up on the approach to door 702 which opens onto L. 138, anteroom towards the ravine. Because of increased traffic at this location, the ritual bath was added closest to the aqueduct; together, they form a tight unit here. It was thought necessary to expand the size of the sluice to distribute the flow; the inlet of the external aqueduct was doubled, approached from L. 138, to feed the bath. The sector was ravaged by erosion but the new sluice remained in place and it is here alone that missing feed 700 can be restored. Avoiding extrapolations, we simply reproduce collector 707. The waste pipe of 700, which still exists, runs to the right of the threshold of the entrance to the bath. The proposal is rational.

4 – Fig. 174d: At Level 4, the reoccupation of Qumran neglected the whole of the northwest sector and bath 138 was disused. The aqueduct was restored, the new sluice was given an outlet and the former one renewed with collector 707. Channel 500 was able to cross the former, abandoned north enclosure without obstacles.

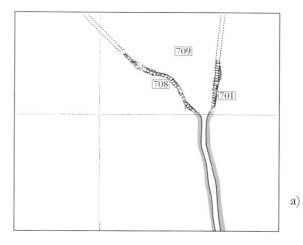

a)

b)

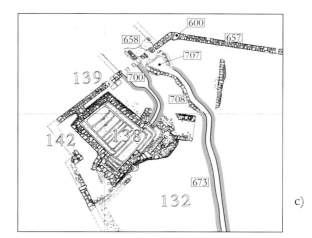

c)

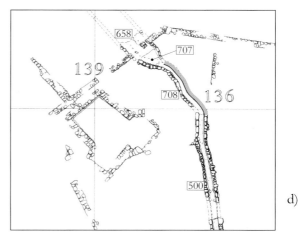

d)

fig. 174. Evolution of the water supply, according to the surveys and plans

436 The archaeology of Qumran – an attempted reassessment

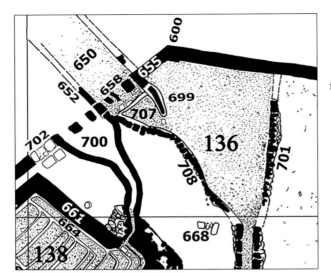

fig. 175. Designation of the constructed elements of L. 136

Location

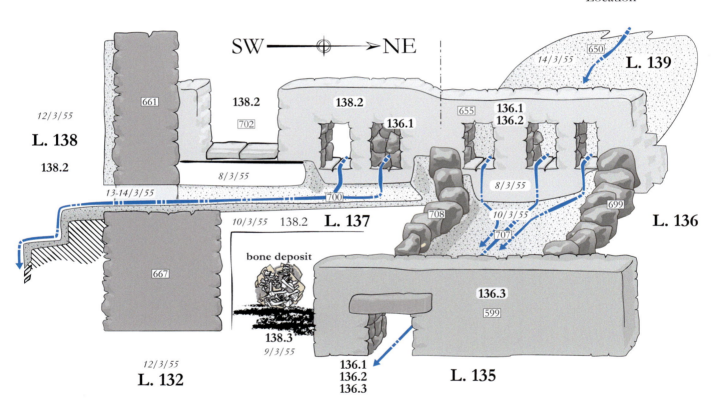

Restored elements	Level	Definition	Journal dates
136.1	4	collector 709 (collector 700 condemned)	8, 10/3/55
136.2 (138.2)	3C	collectors 700 and 709	8, 10/3/55
138.2	3B/C	Construction of bath 138	8-12/3/55 2-4/4/55
136.3	3A/B	Construction of enclosure 135	1-9/3/55 (L 135)
138.3	2 - 3A/B/C	Buried deposits	9/3/55 (L. 137)

Schema and stratigraphic diagram of Loci 136 and 137
(for the chart of symbols, see page 155)

Plate 90

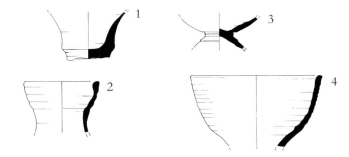

N° Pl.	N° Catal.	Position	Comments (archives)	Date	Description	Clay	Exterior
1	4251	136.2	-	13/03/55	lid of jug or jar	brownish-red paste	brownish-red
2	4257	136.2	-	12/03/55	jug	brownish-red paste	beige
3	4256	136.2	-	12/03/55	jug	brown paste	beige-red
4	4253	136.2	-	13/03/55	funnel	brownish-red paste	beige engobe

N° Pl.	N° Catal.	Position	Comments (archives)	Date	Description	Clay	Exterior
1	4250	136.2	-	08/03/55	unguentarium	red paste	light brown
2	4249	136.2	-	14/03/55	flask (L. 139)	red paste	yellow engobe

Loci 136 and 137, pottery and catalogue, scale ¼

Locus 172 (129 and 133)
A gatehouse or a stable?

In the north enclosure, the siting and mode of construction make L. 172 a structure that was linked to the outbuildings of the former residence: it antedates the north enclosure; the Coüasnon *Plans* show it resting on the walls of the outbuildings. L. 172 may go back to Hasmonaean Level 2 and will have been added before the end of that occupation. De Vaux, who already placed it in his Coüasnon *Plan* Period Ia, was right to consider L. 172 an ancient part of the network of constructions. However, the *Plan* of Period Ia where L. 172 appears, was worked out without reordering the space, placing both L. 138 and, to the northeast and without any connection, L. 141 which are contemporary. L. 172 is then an unexpected construction outside the perimeter of the Hasmonaean residence; we shall take account of this when we investigate its precise function.

We have renamed the complete building L. 172 (47 m²) as L. 129 could have been added by L. 133: the survey confirms that the northeast corner of L. 129 is sharp, and it is not impossible that L. 129 fisrt had an opening on the overflow in front of the entrance to the outbuildings. On L. 129 and L. 133 the *Journal* is sparing with details, as nothing in this excavation gives any indications that would be useful to the communitarian theory. They were not commented upon at all. L. 172 being earlier than the installation of the north enclosure, it should have received more attention as the only building erected outside the walls.

De Vaux notes on L. 129: *L. exactly in the north axis of cistern 118* (L. 129, 24/2/55). Is he suggesting they were linked? Such an arrangement must be fortuitous, as the size of L. 129, including the 3.80 m thickness of the walls, is roughly the same as the 4 m average size of the loci of Qumran. Further, there is no communication between L. 129 and L. 118. L. 172 communicates with outside the complex only before the setting-up of the north enclosure and the protection of L. 134. Its exposure made it vulnerable.

Two observations guide our interpretation. The first notes that L. 129 was paved – *We clear the paving* (L .129, 27/2/55) – and the survey shows irregular stone paving, laid without great care: L. 129 was a location that was repeatedly cleaned. The second observation indicates that the drains cross the basement of L. 172: we are inclined to think that the building was sited at precisely this spot for the benefit of the route of evacuation drain 564. Especially as the basement of L. 133 is crossed b y short drain 679, which connects with evacuation drain 564. *A branch of the drain separates to the west and is quickly lost and may be an abandoned project* (L. 133, 5/3/55). The Coüasnon Period Ib sketch plan has drawn it as it was seen and dots outline a pointless extension of it towards the west. The excavators did not think it could help to clean out the interior of rooms L. 129-133. They thought the drain would have connected with a disappeared installation, but towards the west the state of the remains in the north enclosure did not allow it to be restored. The drain also seemed to take the direction of bath L. 138, though too far away did have the advantage of an overflow towards the nearer ravine. It is true that nothing in L. 133 remains of an opening, the location of which has not been found. The simplest solution is that drain 679 drained waste water from L. 129 which was paved; or that it served to clean only L. 133 since nothing is preserved as far as L. 129. The *Journal* rather laconically concludes with two lines on 5/3/55, and on this date large jar KhQ 2649 was recorded. Nothing is said of the setting in which it was found; but the record states that it was intact. L. 133 has apparently been excavated in stages. De Vaux would have noted the fact if jar 2649 had been buried. Consequently, it can only have come from the abandonment level at the end of Level 3C.

It is not easy to recreate the circulation paths as the walls are not complete; fractures adjacent to fault 4 of the earthquake (fig. 8) may have disfigured the building. The Coüasnon sketch plans (fig. 176) propose nothing convincing. An opening in wall 680 is implausible. Openings made in wall 683 are simply suppositions. The door sketched to the east, against wall 531, may be imagined because of a pavement that will have preceded it. Just one sufficiently wide access point may have been inserted in the north wall; the remains of a mortar floor make this possible. We suggest that L. 172, which benefits from its situation outside the settlement, will have accommodated the frames at a suitable point, to the right before penetrating into the courtyard of the outbuildings.

The western boundary

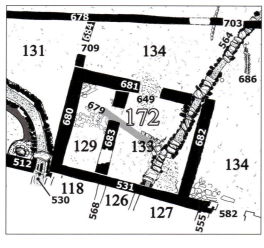

a) Designation of constructed elements

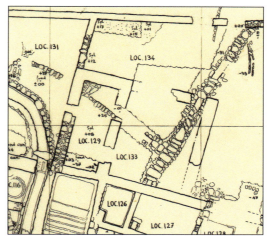

b) Channels survey (Coüasnon 1955)

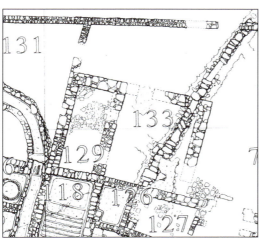

c) Excerpt from plan Period II, 1955

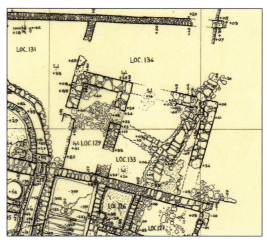

d) Plan with elevation data

fig. 176. Locus 172, Coüasnon surveys

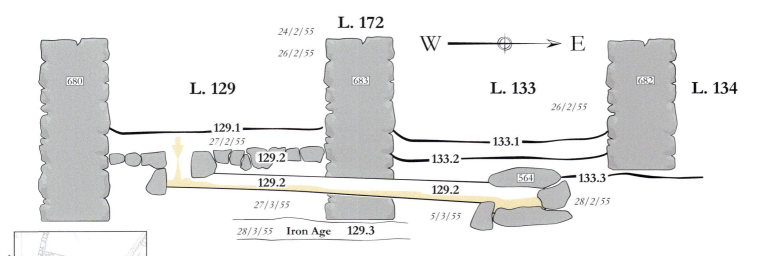

Restored elements	Level	Definition	Journal dates
133.1	3C	upper floor L. 133	26/2/55
133.2	3C	Drain 129.2	26/2/55
133.3	3B/C?	Evacuation drain 679 linked to collector 564	28/2/55 5/3/55

Schema and stratigraphic diagram of L. 172 (129, 133)
(for the chart of symbols, see page 155)

Plate 91, 18

Plate 91, 8

N° Pl.	N° Catal.	Position	Comments (archives)	Date	Description	Clay	Exterior
1	4619	129.1	-	26/02/55	small dish	brown paste	beige
2	4622	129.1	-	26/02/55	goblet	brown paste	grey
3	4637	129.1	-	29/03/55	unguentarium	light brown paste	beige engobe
4	4632	129.1	-	26/02/55	goblet	brown paste	brown-red
5	4625	129.1	-	26/02/55	bowl	red paste	beige
6	4635	129.1	-	26/02/55	painted sherd	red paste with grey core	traces of red paintwork
7	2215	129.2	-	24/02/55	small dish, lid of 2252	° fine earth, pink, grey in section	pink wash
8	2252	129.2	-	24/02/55	jar (with inscription ?)	° red earth with grey section	white wash
9	4631	129.2	-	27/02/55	support of the type of L. 77, N° 17	red paste	beige
10	4624	129.2	-	27/02/55	goblet	brown paste	beige
11	4629	129.2	-	27/02/55	flask	dark grey paste	beige
12	4621	129.2	-	27/02/55	small cylindrical jar	red paste	red
13	2217	129.1	-	24/02/55	fragment of painted jar	° grey earth, pink wash	hasty decoration, washed-off red paintwork
14	4627	129.3	-	28/02/55	small dish	light brown paste	beige
15	4633	129.3	-	28/02/55	small jug	red paste	red-beige
16	4630	129.3	-	28/02/55	flask	dark grey paste	beige
17	4640	129.3	-	28/02/55	small pedestal	red paste with grey core	beige-red
18	4639	129.3	-	28/02/55	fenestrated vessel	dark grey paste	beige
19	4623	129.3	-	28/02/55	jar	dark grey paste	dark grey
20	4620	129.3	-	28/02/55	jar	red paste	beige-red
21	4638	129.3	L. 129 lower	27/03/55	inkwell?	light brown paste	brownish-red, residue of black ink

Catalogue of pottery Locus 129   ° *According to de Vaux*

Plate 91

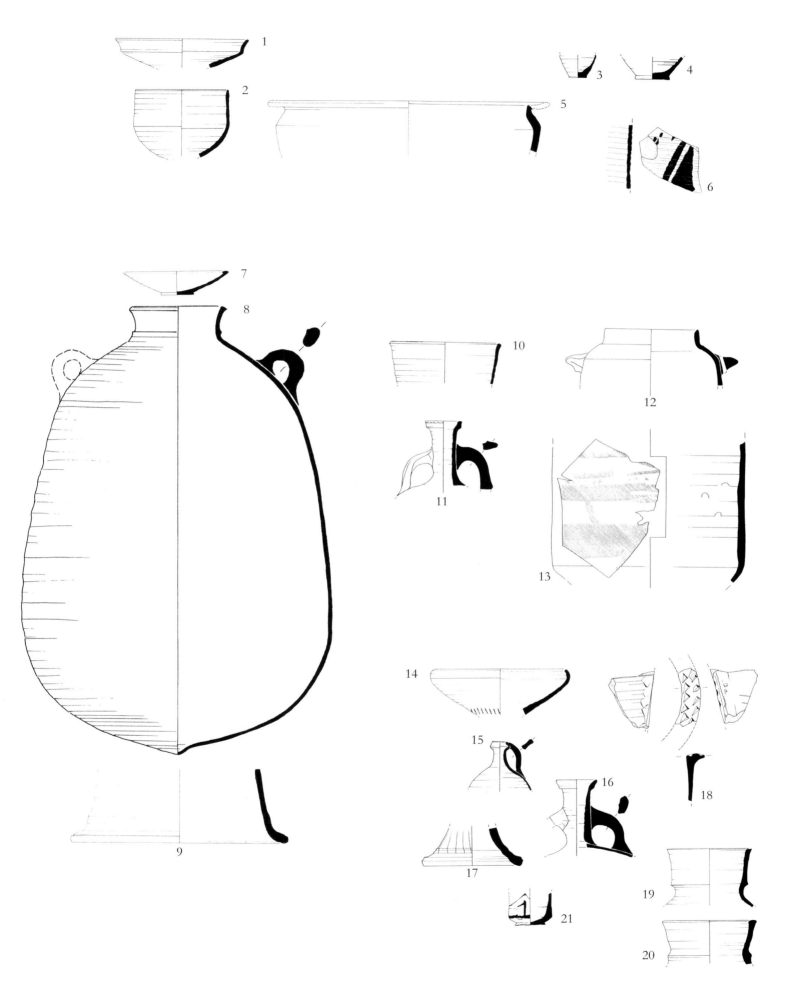

Locus 129, pottery and catalogue, scale ¼

Plate 92

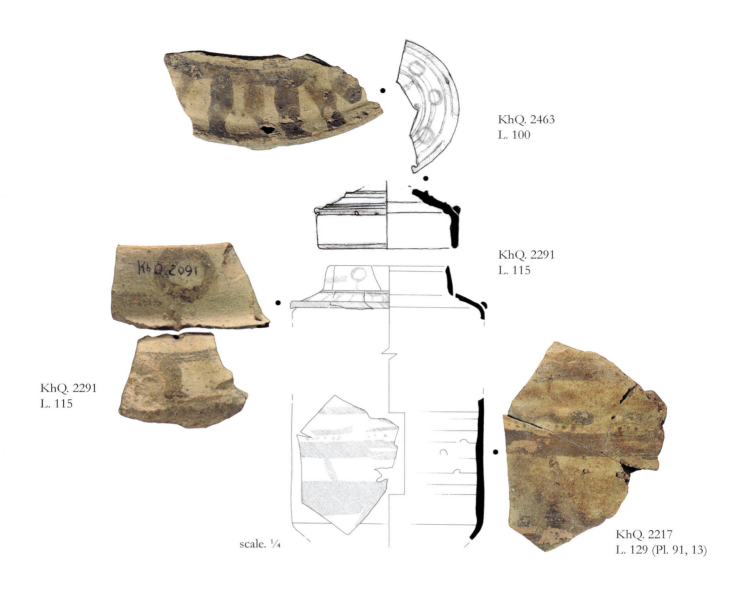

KhQ. 2463
L. 100

KhQ. 2291
L. 115

KhQ. 2291
L. 115

KhQ. 2217
L. 129 (Pl. 91, 13)

scale. ¼

scale ½

Photo after PAM, 1956

Loci 100, 115 and 129, collection of painted sherds of type pl. 91, 13

Plate 93

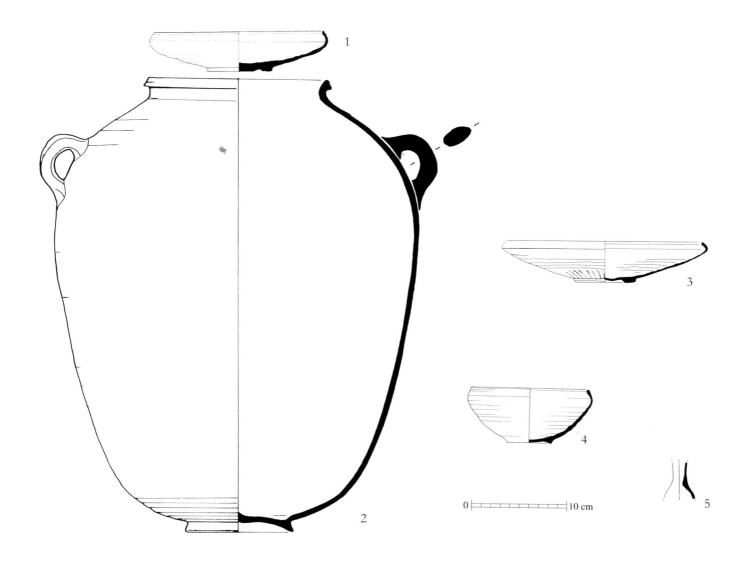

N° Pl.	N° Catal.	Position	Comments (archives)	Date	Description	Clay	Exterior
1	2253	133.3	-	28/02/55	small dish, lid of 2649	° buff earth	white wash
2	2649	133.1	-	05/04/55	jar	° red earth with grey section	remains of white wash
3	2254	133.3	-	28/02/55	small dish	° red earth with grey section	white wash
4	2255	133.3	-	28/02/55	bowl	° pink earth, grey in section	white wash
5	4214	133.3	-	28/02/55	unguentarium	light brown	light brown

° *According to de Vaux*

Locus 133, pottery and catalogue, scale ¼

Loci 140 and 141
A slaughterhouse?

Loci 140 and 141 were cleared towards the end of the 1955 campaign and finishing touches were made on 30 and 31/3/55. On L. 140 and 141 the *Journal* begins only on 10/3, whereas the objects were recorded from 9/3. The *Journal* mentions little more than the clearance of drain 564, which monopolized all efforts. On L. 141, the *Journal* confines itself to a few lines on a modified room. In fact, neither is described. The two last days were devoted to opening the east of wall 657, L. 152 (north of the main building). A floor was hit which produced a coin of Agrippa I[st], attesting to the end of the occupation.

L. 141 occupies an eccentric position and not much attention was paid to it for the good reason that the north enclosure, setting aside bath L. 138, was recognized as a collection of precarious installations, grafted on outside the settlement walls. Their interest seemed secondary. They did not provide evidence for the communitarian theory. The best understanding of L. 135, which restores an organic role to the north enclosure, may integrate L. 141 in the layout. The carefully constructed small square room is correctly inserted in the corner of the right-angled line of L. 135, and as such it was part of the project that erected it. It leans to the east against wall 660, which then closes the enclosure at the corner of the tower and, as far as we can tell from the plan, it opened onto L. 134. We should note further that it was placed in such a way as to benefit from evacuation channel 564: the northwest corner of the L. overhangs the drain. It is probable that L. 135 was extended to the east so that L. 141, which it integrates, could benefit from the drain. Loci 135 and 141 are connected. As in L. 133, the evacuation opening was not discovered; it could not open onto the drain itself because the survey on the Coüasnon *Plans* shows an intact cover to it; as in L. 133, the connection with the evacuation channel must have been lateral. It is possible that the collector was demolished by the earthquake, as we find ourselves on fault 3 (fig. 8) Despite the distance away from the pools, the water evacuated by the drain was used there. We propose that the premises could also have been a place for slaughtering animals. In the context of the Passover pilgrimage, it is possible that the throat-cutting was controlled so as not to spill blood carelessly. The animals may have been penned in L. 140. The proximity of L. 130 to the kitchen lends coherence to this hypothesis.

L. 141 was converted with partitioning of the space by thin pisé clay partition walls. Four rather large caissons, L. 156–159, were laid out in a orthogonal disposal, the recess L. 160, left free as an easy access. The whole complex suggests a workshop or a granary with silos. The conversion of L. 141 assumes the disuse of L. 135.

fig. 177.   Loci 140 and 141, looking south, in the course of the excavations

The western boundary

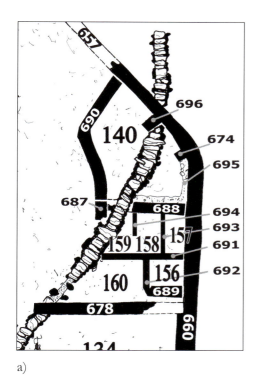 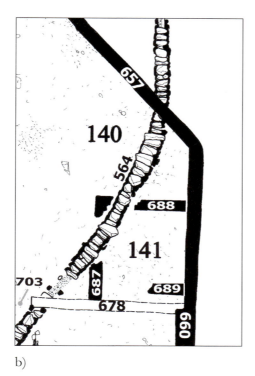 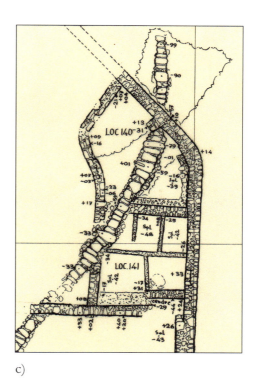

fig. 178.
a) Designation of the constructed elements, L. 140 and 141
b) From Coüasnon, Plan of Period II
c) Survey of Loci 140 and 141, Coüasnon, 1955

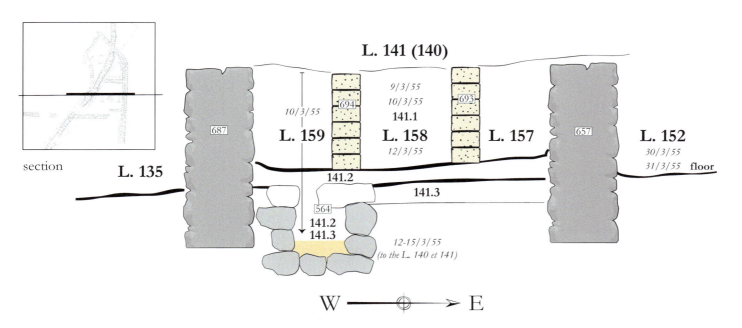

Restored elements	Level	Definition	Journal dates	Coins	Position	N°	Chronology
141.1	3C	Arrangement in three compartments, 157–158–159	10-12/3/55				
141.2	3B/C	Erection of locus 141 Possible evacuation, drain 564	Restoration	KhQ. 2382	on drain	1	Herod Archelaeus
141.3	3A/B	Installation of drain 564	10-15/3/55 (L. 140)				

Schema and stratigraphic diagram of Loci 140 and 141 (for the chart of symbols, see page 155)

Plate 94

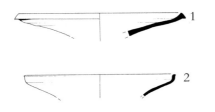

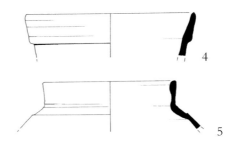

N° Pl.	No. Catal.	Position	Comments (archives)	Date	Description	Clay	Exterior
1	4269	141.3	northern exterior of L. 140	15/03/55	lid of cooking pot	red with grey core	red
2	4270	141.1 upper	L. 140	09/03/55	small dish	dark red	grey
3	4271	141.1 upper	L. 140	09/03/55	flask	grey	beige
4	4268	141.3	northern exterior of L. 140	15/03/55	small vat	red	beige-pink
5	4267	141.1 upper	L. 140	09/03/55	jar	dark red	beige engobe
6	2390	141.3	L. 140 on the drain	13/03/55	lamp (L. 140)	° red earth	red

° *According to de Vaux*

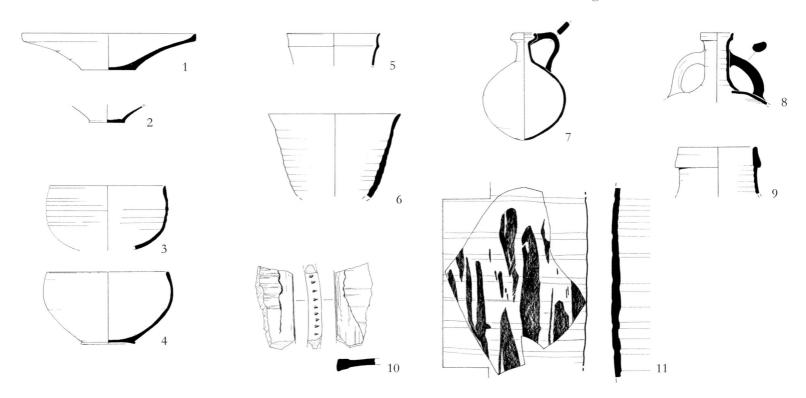

No. Pl.	No. Catal.	Position	Comments (archives)	Date	Description	Clay	Exterior
1	2415	141.3	-	12/03/55	plate	° red earth with grey section	white wash
2	4274	141.1-2-3	-	10/03/55	dish	red paste, fine	light beige
3	4277	141.1-2-3	-	10/03/55	bowl	grey paste	beige
4	2414	141.3	-	12/03/55	bowl	° buff earth, soft	light beige
5	4278	141.1-2-3	-	10/03/55	goblet	grey paste	beige
6	4275	141.3	-	12/03/55	goblet	red paste with grey core	beige engobe
7	2376	141.1-2-3	-	10/03/55	juglet	° grey earth	light red
8	4273	141.1-2-3	-	10/03/55	flask	brown paste	light brown
9	4272	141.3	-	12/03/55	jar	brown paste	red-beige
10	4237	141.3	-	13/03/55	fragment of niche?	grey paste	off-white
11	2422	141.3	L. 134 east	13/03/55	sherd of painted jar?	° red earth	white wash, blackish colours, splashes of paint or burnt oil?

° *According to de Vaux*

Loci 140 and 141, pottery and catalogue, scale ¼

Quatrième Partie

Qumran Terracotta Oil Lamps

R. de Vaux Excavations at Khirbet Qumran,
Ain Feshkha and Caves

Jolanta Młynarczyk
*Institute of Archaeology,
University of Warsaw, PL*

Typology and Catalogue of Finds

Introduction

An assemblage of *ca.* 200 oil lamps, preserved mostly in fragments, was discovered at Qumran, both at the settlement itself and in the caves (1951-1956) as well as at Ain Feshkha (1958), by the team of the École Biblique et Archéologique Française directed by R. de Vaux, O.P. The study of these objects has been carried out by the present author in the framework of the Andrew W. Mellon Fellowship in the Albright Institute of Archaeological Research (AIAR) in Jerusalem during January-March 2012, as a research project entitled "Terracotta Oil Lamps from Qumran and Ein Feshkha (R. de Vaux's Excavations, 1951-1958): Typology, Chronology and the Question of Manufacturing Centers". The study in question has first resulted in two papers dealing with the Qumran lamps, specifically, with their formal/chronological typology (Młynarczyk 2013) and with those lamps that were found in the Qumran caves (Młynarczyk, Lugano).

In this very place I would like to express my sincere thanks to Jean-Baptiste Humbert, O.P. (Ecole Biblique et Archéologique Française de Jérusalem), for having entrusted me with the study of the Qumran lamps; to the AIAR Fellowship Committee for having granted me the funding for the research project in question; to Dr. Sy Gitin, the then Director of the AIAR, as well as the Staff of the Institute, for having made my stay there both fruitful and most agreeable. The lamp drawings, belonging to the archives of the EBAF, have been prepared for the present chapter (as well as for my previous papers) by Mr. Kiyoshi Inoue and by Dr. Mariusz Burdajewicz who also composed the figures; I am most grateful for their dedicated work.

The Qumran lamp material published earlier has been limited to some lamp examples quoted and illustrated in the excavation reports by R. de Vaux and in the publications of the Qumran Caves (DJD I and III), included in the ceramic typologies by P. Lapp (1961) and F. Diez Fernandez (1983) respectively, in a series of synthesis articles on Palestinian lamps by Smith (1961, 1964, 1966) and in a paper by R. Donceel (1998). Single objects have occasionally been mentioned and illustrated in other publications as well; one example is a mention about main categories of lamps present at Qumran made by J. Magness (2002, 79).

An "official inventory" of the Qumran lamps that were then stored in the Ecole Biblique in Jerusalem was prepared by R. Donceel in 1995 (Donceel ms, see also Donceel and Donceel-Voûte 1994, 6-7). The material from Khirbet Qumran and Ain Feshkha dealt with by R. Donceel was divided into two basic categories (wheel-made and mould-made lamps respectively), and then presented in the order of their inventory numbers, without any attempt at creating a typology. In his manuscript, Donceel has also omitted the lamps found in the Caves. In the paper that followed, R. Donceel contained a summary of a very limited stratigraphic information regarding the lamps (Donceel 1998, 89, n. 8), even if *de facto* slightly larger number of lamps seemed to have some stratigraphic indication. Nonetheless, unfortunately, the statement of R. Donceel (*La façon dont la fouille de Khirbet Qumrân a été conduite limite malheuresement l'utilisation des lampes du site dans le débat chronologique, en ce sens que fort peu d'entre elles sont localisées verticalement et horizontalement avec précision dans le "locus" de provenance*) cannot be contested.

As many as 25 lamps originally registered during R. de Vaux' excavations, be they entire or fragmentary, have disappeared since the end of the field work; in the text of the catalogue presented below, those lamps are identified by an asterisk. Their drawings come from the original register books of R. de Vaux' expedition, while their rudimentary description (fabric, dimensions) follows that provided by R. Donceel (Donceel ms), gathered by him in 1995 from excavation and post-excavation documentation available by that time. While referring to them, the present author decided to quote the fabric colour identifications in the language of their original description (French).

On the other hand, there are a few lamp fragments that have remained unregistered(?) and cannot be identified in excavation records. However, since they still have some statistical value, we decided to include them in the catalogue. It is to be noted that all the dimensions in the catalogue are given in centimeters. The Munsell colour chart notations occur only in the cases when the author found it difficult to decide upon the individual fabric colour.

Principles of typological classification

The lamps have been divided on the obvious basis of different manufacturing technique into two categories:

– wheel-made lamps (030),

– mould-made lamps (040).

To each of these categories, a different hierarchy of typological elements had to be applied, in accordance with the mentioned basic difference in the lamp shaping technique.

For the wheel-made lamps (Qumran Types 031-037), these diagnostic elements are the following:

1) wall profile

2) shape of the base

3) shape of the rim to the filling hole

4) shape and decoration (in case there is any) of the nozzle

5) shape of the handle.

For the mould-made lamps (Qumran Types 041-048), the typological elements are:

1) plan of the body and the nozzle

2) shape of the top of the nozzle (whether flat or convex)

3) shape of the base

4) decorated parts of the lamp

5) decoration motives employed.

Wheel-Made Lamps (031-037)

031. Folded-rim lamps

Shape description:

The lamps stand on a flat (string-cut) base, sometimes slightly concave inside, and they have a flaring simple rim pinched or folded at one point to form a nozzle.

They can be identified as Lapp type 81.1 ("open" nozzle) and 81.2 ("closed" nozzle; Lapp 1961, 192); Kennedy type 1, Group D (Kennedy 1961, 70, pl. XX:481), Masada type A ("folded wheel-made lamp": Barag and Hershkovitz 1994, 11-12, no. 1, fig. 1); Jericho type J-LP1A (with "closed" nozzle: Bar-Nathan 2002, 103-104, no. 284; Bar-Nathan 2006, fig. 15.2:4); Jerusalem Jewish Quarter Type LP 1b – LP 1c (Geva 2003, 139-140, pls. 5.1:42, 5.3:35-38, 5.5:20, 5.7:15, 5.9:1-3, 34, 5.10:45), of which LP 1b may have the "nozzle" sides either meeting or not, while in LP 1c the nozzle sides are pinched firmly together. The latter variant, described as "Late Hasmonean lamp", typical of the 1st century BC assemblages in Jerusalem, is believed by H. Geva to have been still in use at the beginning of the second half of the 1st century BC, although it is also known by the late 2nd century BC examples from Beth-Zur and early 1st century BC examples from Gezer (Geva 2003, 140, with references). Three examples of the type, all with pinched-in rim, occur in the tomb of Jason known to have been abandoned at *ca.* 37/31 BC (Rahmani 1967, 100 and fig. 9:3).

A fragmentary lamp of this type (with "closed" nozzle) comes from one of the caves in the Quruntul ridge west of Jericho (Wolff 2002, 78-79, fig. 5). In the nearby Jericho palaces, these lamps were found in late Hasmonean contexts, dated to 85/75 – 31 BC (Bar-Nathan 2002, 103; cf. Bar-Nathan 2006, fig. 15.2). A much wider time-range for the type ("beginning in the 2nd century BCE and going out of use in the times of Herod the Great") has been proposed by Rosenthal-Heginbottom (Rosenthal-Heginbottom 2003, 218, pl. 6.4:9 and pl. 6.12:5) who claims they were co-occurring with the "Judean radial lamp" type.

The lamp type classified at Qumran as 031, described as the "cornucopia" lamp by Smith (1964, 117-118, fig. 16, with "closed" nozzle, from Tell en-Nasbeh, dated to *ca.* 2nd century BC) and considered as characteristic of the southern and central part of the country (…) "stands within the saucer lamp tradition, for it is made by folding the rim of a wheel-made bowl". Smith 1964, 121-122: "the cornucopia lamp (…) apparently grew in popularity in the vicinity of Jerusalem" (Smith 1964, fig. 20, dated early to middle 1st century BC). For other Jerusalem examples, see Geva and Hershkovitz 2006, 98, 112-113, pls.4.6:1, 4.9:19. Indeed, a lamp of this type found at Masada allegedly comes, according to NAA tests, from the Jerusalem area (Barag and Hershkovitz 1994, 11-13).

Out of three lamps from Qumran representing this form, all of them clearly in the same ware, two lamps (*1* and *3*) have their nozzles pinched-in (type 81.2 in Lapp 1961, 192) and the third one (no. *2*) has its nozzle open (type 81.1 in Lapp 1961, loc. cit.). Despite this formal difference, the latter lamp, with its small size, thin wall and the ware, seems to fit description of Geva's type LP 1c which would be "the final stage of development of the folded-rim lamp", dated mostly to the first half of 1st century BC (Geva 2003, 140, with abundant *comparanda* from Jerusalem, Beth-Zur and Gezer; he proposes to replace a commonly used name of the "Hasmonean lamp" by a "Late Hasmonean lamp").

The fabric of our Qumran and Ain Feshka lamps is not only macroscopically the same; petrographic and chemical analyses of two of them confirmed they were made from the same raw material and according to the same technology (PG group 2; for Petrographic Groups (PG) distinguished by J. Michniewicz among the samples of lamps from Qumran and Jericho, see Michniewicz 2009, 37-51) which means they have come from the same workshop.

1. KhQ 538 (fig. 179, 1).

   Fragmentary pinched-rim lamp, missing *ca.* 0.5 of the rim. Wheel marks inside and out, dense soot at wick part of rim.
   Fabric: hard fired, light red (2.5 YR 6/6) with partial grey core, many small and few medium-sized white grits; wet-smoothed pink surface (between 5 YR 8/4 and 7/4). Petrographic group (henceforth: *PG) 2* (Michniewicz 2009, 42-45).
   L. 8.0, extant W. 4.0, H. 3.4.
   Found: Loc. 22, lower level;
   Cf. Qumran 1, 304 (and Qumran 1B, 26, mistakenly mentioned as found in Loc. 36).
   Cf. Donceel ms, pl. I and VIII; cf. Młynarczyk 2013, 102, fig. 1.
     Similar to: Rahmani 1967, fig. 9:3.

2. KhQ 5110 (fig. 179, 2).

   Fragmentary folded-rim lamp: portions of base, wall and nozzle preserving full profile. Wheel marks inside and out. Nozzle wide open.
   Fabric: light red, hard and dense; smooth yellowish pink surface with occasional tiny white grits, apparently the same fabric as previous, more thin-walled. *PG 2* (Michniewicz 2009, 42-45).
   Extant L. 6.9 cm, extant W. 3.0 cm, H. 3.6.
   Found: Trench A, Layer 5.

3. AF 310 (fig. 179, 3).

   Lamp nozzle, closed; traces of burning at wick hole.
   Fabric (and ware) exactly the same as with the previous two examples, with a few small white grits.
   Extant L. 4.2.
   Found: Loc. 21; lower level of Loc. 16 (room to the north-west of the court).

031.

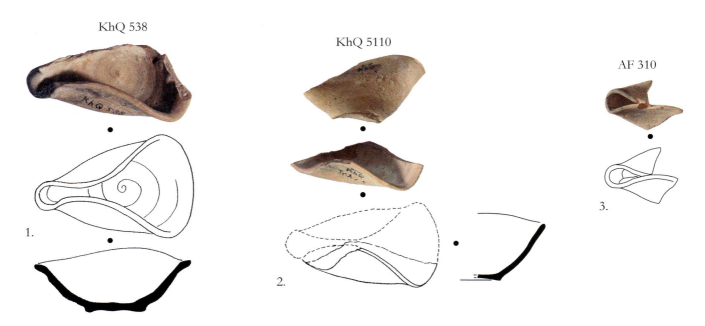

fig. 179.   Pinched-rim lamps

032. Deep bi-conical lamps with flat base and long ridged nozzle attached to lower body

Shape description:

The lamps of this type, represented by five objects, have a bi-conical body on a well-defined small circular base (either flat or slightly concave) and thickened or everted rim. The nozzle is elongated, tilted up, with ridged top and oval end provided with flat rim to the wick hole. In this type, as well as in Types 033-034 (see below), the nozzle, attached to below the carination of the body, was shaped by folding-in two sides of a clay piece (like in the "open" lamps of Type 031), so that its joining edges formed a ridge. The lamps were provided with a handle shaped by hand and added to the body. In three recorded cases that was a loop handle, made of a roll of clay, with its two ends joining at the lower shoulder. Macroscopically, they appear to have been made of the same fabric and probably are the products of a local workshop.

Type 032 belongs to a cluster of five types (032 – 035-Prime) tentatively identified as "Qumran lamp family" and hardly attested elsewhere. They fall into Bar-Nathan's type J-LP3 from Jericho (Bar-Nathan 2002, 110-112, Ill. 87-88 and Pl. 18), further divided into J-LP3A1 (represented by two objects, corresponding to our 032 and 035 respectively) and J-LP3A2 (with two other objects corresponding to our 033 and 034, see below), so in fact the Jericho type embraces as many as four Qumran types. Bar-Nathan supposes that her J-LP3 "may have emerged already in the mid-first century B.C.E.", but at the same time she questions the attribution of comparable Qumran lamps (our Types 032-035) to the Hasmonean period only, since in Jericho they occur in the Herodian-period contexts. However, both their scarce number and fragmentary state of preservation in Jericho may suggest that they were residual there. Also the very fact that Masada yielded just a single sherd of a lamp pertaining to this "Qumran family" is in favour of its pre-Herodian (or early Herodian) dating. Indeed, the examples of virtually all the "Qumran family" types were found in Loc. 130 of the Qumran settlement (Humbert 2003, 434-436; Donceel 2005, 35), indicating that they were being manufactured during the same period. According to J.-B. Humbert (*ibidem*), "the artifacts from *locus* 130 can date from 50 BC, possibly later". Specifically, Loc. 130 yielded the lamps of Qumran Types 032 (cat. no. *6:* KhQ 2294), 033 (cat. no. *12:* KhQ 2210 and no. *17:* KhQ 2270), 034 (cat. no. *29:* KhQ 2206, no. *30:* KhQ 5088 + 5129, no. *31:* KhQ 2295, no. *33:* KhQ 2291, no. *34:* KhQ 5087) and 035-Prime (no. *39:* KhQ 2308). N.b., Donceel mentions four other lamps from Locus 130 with register numbers which do not exist in the Qumran documentation of the Ecole Biblique (specifically, KhQ 3054, 3055, 3057, 3058: Donceel 2005, note 120).

Bar-Nathan has rightly stated that her two Jericho sub-types, in spite of differences in their shape, probably belong to the same lamp family, attested (until 2002) only in Qumran, Jericho and at Masada, therefore it "can be associated with a pottery workshop in the Jericho Valley and the Dead Sea area". However, upon comparing the sheer number of finds from Qumran and the other two sites, one can hardly look for a workshop manufacturing these lamps elsewhere than in Qumran itself, even if Humbert (2003, 435) used to be in favour of considering the "Qumran family" lamps from Loc. 130 as having been imported from Egypt.

R. Bar-Nathan (2002, 110-112) seems to go too far in regarding these lamps as local imitations of the "Ephesus Lamp of Asia Minor". Actually, already Smith (1964, 124) spoke about "apparent traces of the influence of the Ephesian lamp" but, on the other hand, he rightly recognized "some connection with wheel-made closed lamps of the 2nd century and the cornucopia lamp" in terms of the manufacturing technique. Indeed, the ridged nozzle is very obviously a development of pinched nozzles of the "folded-rim" lamps (Type 031) and its similarity to that common in Ephesian lamps seems to be a pure coincidence.

The "Qumran family" of lamps (our Types 032 through 035-Prime) has been characterized by Smith fairly accurately: "Although differing widely in form, these lamps have a similarity of ware – gray to buff clay, usually wet-smoothed or having a slip similar to the body color – and a similarity of style and technique of manufacture. There can be no doubt that these lamps are the products of the potter's shop at Qumran" (Smith 1964, 124).

As far as Qumran Type 032 is concerned, the only parallel from Jericho is fragment no. 300 of J-LP3A1 found in a context dated to 15 BC – AD 6 (Bar-Nathan 2002, Ill. 87 and pl. 18 for the profile). Another similar lamp from a private collection is equipped with a heavy loop handle; it has been published by Smith who tentatively dated it to the 2nd century BC (Smith 1964, 119, fig. 18, from a private collection, a buff-orange ware, originally covered "with a rich red slip"). A third example of the type, also with a loop handle, was found at the site of Umm Hadar in al-Kufrayn area (western Jordan) and dated (following Lapp 1961, type 84:B) to between 50 and 31 BC (Zayadine 2011, 173 and 180, pl. 4).

The possible predecessors of the type, in terms of the body profile (and not the nozzle type), could be sought among the Hellenistic lamps like those from Beth-Zur and Tell en-Nasbeh (Smith 1964, 106, fig. 5).

4. KhQ 171 (Pl. 95).

    Lamp lacking parts of nozzle and body as well as a loop(?) handle once attached right above the carination of body; base slightly concave. Pronounced wheel-marks on body.
    Fabric: gritty grey (10 YR 6/1) with some small white (and black?) grits and fine voids; surface: pale beige (10 YR 7/2 "light grey"), wet-smoothed yet coarse in feel.
    L. 13.0, max. Diam. of body 8.0, H. 5.3.
    Found: Trench A, Layer 2;
Cf. Qumran 1, 339-340 (in this layer, two coins of Alexander Jannaeus); Qumran 1B, 62.
Cf. *RB* 1954, fig. 2:16 (with graphic reconstruction of the handle); Lapp 1961 type 84 ("loop-handled lamps"), variant B. cf. Donceel ms, pl. I and VIII; Młynarczyk 2013, 103-104, fig. 1; Młynarczyk, Lugano, Ill. 2.

5. KhQ 1645* (Pl. 95).

    Lamp lacking end of nozzle. Ring handle from right below filling hole rim to carination.
    Fabric: *terre rouge, brûlée, couverte blanche* (register book).
    Extant L.10.9; H. 5.0.
    Found: Loc. 40, "lower";
Cf. Qumran 1, 306; Qumran 1B, 27.
Cf. Donceel ms, pl. III and X.

6. KhQ 2294* (Pl. 95).

    Complete lamp with loop handle.
    Fabric: *terre chamois*.
    L. 15.4, Diam. 8.2, H. 5.4.
    Found: Loc. 130 – 3A;
Cf. Qumran 1, 334; Qumran 1B, 56.
Cf. Donceel ms, pl. IV and XI.
    See also *RB* 1956, 552-553, fig. 1:2 (*période* Ib); Lapp 1961, Type 84:B.

7. KhQ 2034 (Pl. 95).

    Part of lamp body, showing full profile but lacking both nozzle and handle; flat disc base.
    Fabric: very hard light brown (7.5 YR 6/4) with some tiny white grits; surface: pale beige (between 10 YR 8/2 and 8/3 "white" to "very pale brown"), wet-smoothed yet semi-coarse in feel. PG ?3 (Michniewicz 2009, 46-48).
    Diam.(est.) 6.4; H. 4.7.
    Found: Loc. 104;
Cf. Qumran 1, 325; Qumran 1B, 47.
Cf. Donceel ms, pl. III.

8. KhQ 5094 + 5109 (Pl. 95).

    Two joining parts of lamp body at nozzle, preserving full profile. Wheel-marks outside; part of top sooted. Flat disc base.
    Fabric: finely gritty light brown (7.5 YR 6/4) with tiny white, grey(?) and black grits; surface: fired unevenly, from light beige on top (10 YR 8/3 "very pale brown") to pink on lower half (near 5 YR 7/4), partly discoloured to dark grey (soot?), wet-smoothed yet coarse in feel. The same fabric and finishing as nos. *7* (KhQ 2034) and *4* (KhQ 171) of the same shape.
    Diam. (est.) *ca.* 8.0; H. 4.6.
    Found: Trench A, Layer 2.

Plate 95

032.

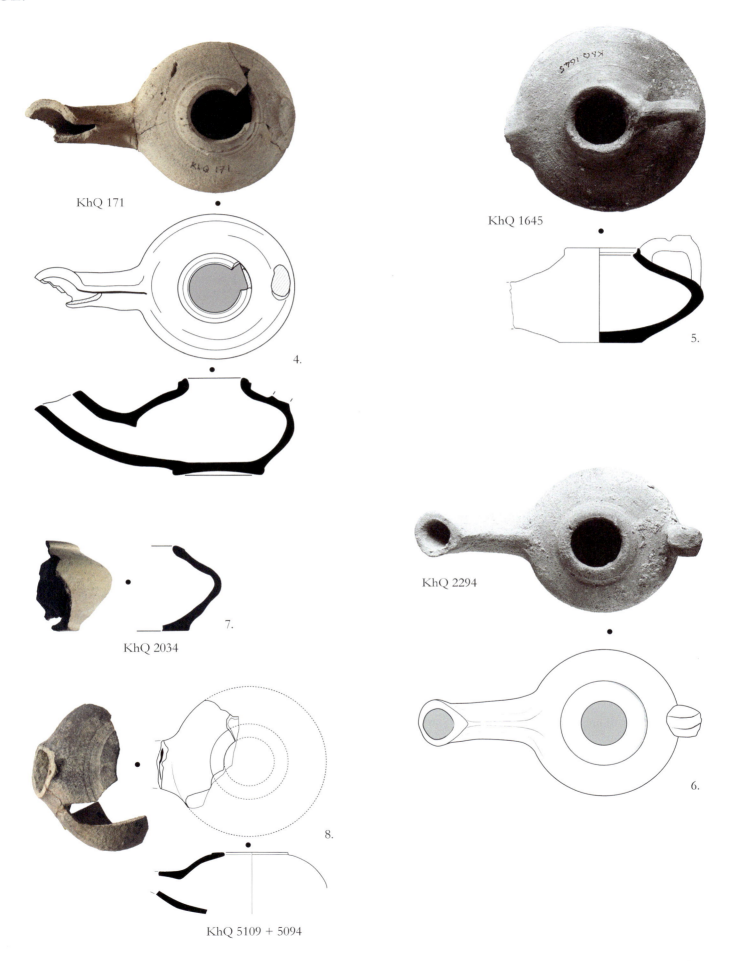

KhQ 171

4.

KhQ 1645

5.

KhQ 2034

7.

KhQ 2294

6.

KhQ 5109 + 5094

8.

Lamp type 032

033. Shallow lamps with body bi-conical or rounded in section and long ridged nozzle attached to upper body

Shape description:

The lamps of this type, represented by nine (or eight? If we count our no. *11* as a part of no. *10*, see below) objects, have shallow body, rounded or bi-conical in section and thick out-folded rim to filling hole. Long ridged nozzle has an oval end and flattened edge to wick hole. Unlike in Type 032, the nozzle ridge joins the rim of the filling hole (probably in order to improve stability of the lamp) in such a way that the nozzle top makes a horizontal line in side view. According to the form of the base, two subtypes can be distinguished. Subtype 033.1 (represented by a single example) has a pseudo-base ring, while in Subtype 033.2 the base is flattened, but not defined. The handle in most cases is either of loop or of lug type; possibly also strap handle may have been used. Besides nine lamps classified by us with Type 033, at least one other similar lamp comes from the excavations conducted at the "northwestern refuse dump" in Qumran by Magen and Peleg (Magen and Peleg 2006, 69, fig. 3.14, left). The Type is represented by a single fragment from Jericho (type J-LP3A2, in reddish yellow ware), found in a context dated to 31 BC - AD 6 (Bar-Nathan 2002, 110-112, Ill. 88 and pl. 18, no. 302; Bar-Nathan 2006, fig. 15.3:1) and by a lamp nozzle from Masada in "light grey-brown ware" (Barag and Hershkovitz 1994, 71-72, no. 124, fig. 21), its wick hole framing identical to that of our lamp no. *9* (Gr 1Q-43). The Masada fragment is dated by Barag and Hershkovitz to the end of the Hasmonean period or to the reign of Herod, on the basis of its affinity with "similar wheel-made lamps" from Qumran Level Ib, which would correspond to 50-31 BC. In the present author's opinion, this dating seems to be more correct than that proposed for the Jericho fragment, which may have been just a residual object in a later context.

033.1. Lamp on pseudo ring base

This is a single object, Gr 1Q-43, once with a loop handle attached to the body carination. Pseudo ring base is created by a double deep and irregular groove made free-hand. Root of the nozzle ridge at the wick hole is flanked by two angular projections. This feature, present also on the above-mentioned lamp nozzle from Masada and on two other nozzles from Qumran, must have been borrowed from metal (bronze) lamps such as an ornate lamp from Tell Sandahannah (Maresha) illustrated by Smith who has also suggested that the Qumran lamps might have had "metallic prototypes" (Smith 1964, 117 and 124, fig. 15: "possibly of 2nd century B.C."). It occurs also in a lamp fragment from Masada (Barag and Hershkovitz 1994, 71-72, no. 124, fig. 21).

9. Gr 1Q-43 (Pl. 96).
    Lamp lacking handle. Dense burning traces at wick hole. Turning marks on
    shoulder interrupted by the nozzle ridge. Pseudo ring base (double irregular
    groove). Two angular projections flanking the rim of the wick-hole.
    Fabric: dense, fired dark grey, with tiny white grits; surface: beige-grey to very pale brown (10 YR
    5/1 "gray" to 7/3 "very pale brown"). Gunneweg and Balla 2003, 23 and table 9, sample Qum 286:
    similar to the pottery of Chemical Group III ("this chemical composition is local to Jericho").
    L. (handle fragment included) 12.6, body Diam. 8.0, body H. 4.0.
    Found: Cave 1Q (also cited as GQ 14);
Cf. Qumran 1B, 66.
Cf. DJD I, 11 and 16, fig. 3:5 and pl. III:3; Smith 1964, 123, fig. 23 ("*ca.* second and third quarters
    of 1st century B.C."); Donceel 1998, 103, note 36, fig. 11; Magness 2002, fig. 21:3; Bar-
    Nathan 2006, fig. 15.3:6; Młynarczyk 2013, 105, fig. 1; Młynarczyk, Lugano, Ill. 1-2.

Plate 96

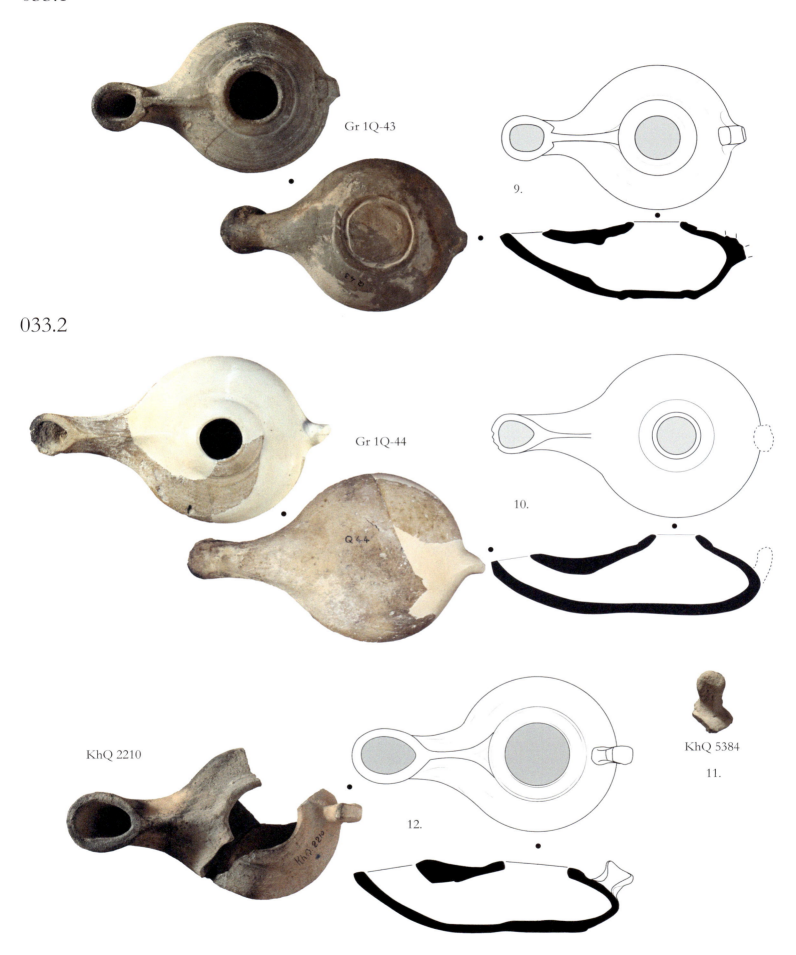

Lamp types 033.1 and 033.2

033.2. Lamps with undefined (rounded or slightly depressed) base

10. Gr 1Q-44 (Pl. 96).

    Lamp restored in plaster. Rounded base, thick out-folded rim to filling hole, the handle form is not certain (rendered in plaster as lug handle); wheel-marks on shoulder, soot on rim of wick hole.
    Fabric: break not available (*terre rose*, according to DJD I, 16); surface: beige with pink spots (10 YR8/3 "very pale brown" to 7.5 YR 8/4 "pink") with some white grits' eruptions, semi-rough in feel.
    L. body 14,2; Diam. body 9.0; H. 4.1.
    Found: Cave 1Q (also cited as GQ 14);
    Cf. Qumran 1B, 66.
    Cf. DJD I, 11 and 16, fig. 3:4 and pl. III:1 (before reconstruction in plaster); Donceel 1998, 103, note 36, fig. 12; Magness 2002, fig. 21:4; Bar-Nathan 2006, fig. 15.3:5; Młynarczyk 2013, 106, fig. 1; Młynarczyk, Lugano, Ill. 1.

11. KhQ 5384 *(registration 2015)*, (Pl. 96).

    Lug handle ("18" written in pencil), pertaining to a lamp of Type 033 (alternatively, of Type 034); such handle has been reconstructed in plaster on lamp no. *10* (Gr 1Q-44), and it is actually possible that the fragment no. 11 comes from this specific lamp.
    The same fabric like Gr 1Q-44: hard, dense, dark grey (10 YR 5/1 "gray") with some tiny white grits; surface beige (10 YR 7/2 "light gray").
    Extant H: 2.9.

12. KhQ 2210 (Pl. 96).

    Two joining parts of lamp (burnt after it was broken), lacking fragment of body; dense soot on nozzle and body (including interior). Slightly flattened base, irregularly shaped rim to filling hole, nozzle with large wick hole; angular lug handle. Sides of relatively short nozzle with very large wick hole bear traces of smearing clay by means of a cloth or a small stick(?).
    Fabric: rather hard light brick-red (5 YR 6/6 "reddish yellow"), with many small voids and rare small white grits; surface: pink to pale pink (5 YR 7/4 to 7.5 YR 8/2 "pinkish white"), partly discolored to light grey, occasional lime eruptions.
    L. 14.0, H. 3.8.
    Found: Loc. 130 *cendres;*
    Cf. Qumran 1, 334; Qumran 1B, 55-56 (with the pottery of Period I in the eastern part of locus 130, "in the ashes").
    Cf. *RB* 1956, 552-553, fig. 1:1 (Loc. 130, *période* Ia); Lapp 1961, type 84 A ("loop handled lamps"); Smith 1964, 123, fig. 23: in all three cases, the lamp was published as a whole object, apparently broken afterwards? (Or graphically reconstructed?).
    See also: Donceel ms, pl. IV (drawing copied from the register book) and pl. XI (photo, present state?); Donceel 1998, 102, fig. 9 (already lacking a part of body, but not as much as it is now); Młynarczyk 2013, 106, fig. 1; Młynarczyk, Lugano, Ill. 2.
    An exact parallel comes from excavations by Magen and Peleg (Magen and Peleg 2006, 69, fig. 3.14, left) of the "northwestern refuse dump" of Qumran.

13. KhQ 5092 + KhQ 5084 (Pl. 97).

    Two non-joining parts: KhQ 5092 (half of body with root of square-sectioned lug(?) handle, wheel-marks inside) and KhQ 5084 (nozzle with part of base; sooted rim of wick hole), most probably belong to the same lamp with rounded base.
    Fabric: very gritty, hard, fired brown (7.5 YR 5/2), with tiny voids and some tiny white grits; surface: brown (as the break) covered with a very pale brown (to almost white in places) thin coating (2.5 Y 7/2 "light gray" to 8/2 "white"), coarse in feel. Gunneweg and Balla 2003, 23 and table 9, sample Q 289 (KhQ 5084): "may belong to Chemical Group I, thus local to Qumran".
    a) KhQ 5092 (Loc. 60): Diam. est. 8.6-8.8; H. 3.6.
    b) KhQ 5084 (Loc. 62): L. extant 8.5; H. extant 3.0.
    Found in two adjacent *loci*: Loc. 60 and Loc. 62 respectively.

Plate 97

033.2

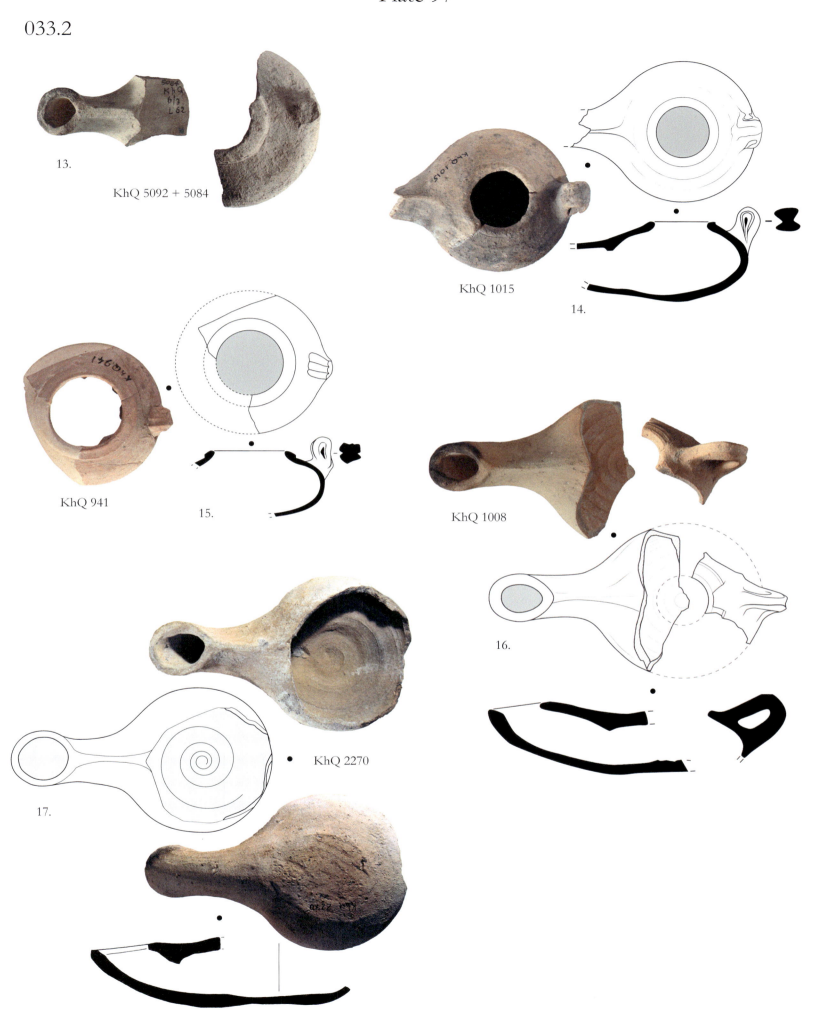

Lamp type 033.2

14. KhQ 1015 (Pl. 97).
   Fragmentary lamp, recomposed of two parts (broken in antiquity), missing most of nozzle and a part of body. Gently rounded base, very narrow and flat rim to filling hole, flat-sectioned loop handle (with just cavity on both sides instead of a true opening) attached to the lower shoulder; traces of wheel wet-smoothing on body.
   Fabric: medium-hard, pink (7.5 YR 6/6 "reddish yellow"), with tiny voids; surface: thick wet-smoothing pale yellowish pink (7.5 YR 8/4 "pink"), discoloured to grey on one of the two parts, coarse in feel. Gunneweg and Balla 2003, 23 and table 9: sample QUM 287: "chemical outlier".
   Extant L. 9.5, Diam. 7.7, H. 4.1.
   Found: ancient fill to the east of Loc. 44;
Cf. Qumran 1, 307; Qumran 1B, 23.
Cf. Donceel ms, pls. III and X; Młynarczyk 2013, 106, fig. 1; Młynarczyk, Lugano, Ill. 2.
   Parallel: Jericho (Bar-Nathan 2006, fig. 15.3:2).

15. KhQ 941 (Pl. 97).
   Fragmentary lamp, preserving full body profile; nozzle missing along with the body part to where it was attached and which was restored in plaster. Wheel-marks on shoulder. Vertical loop/lug handle (folded, but without opening), rather oval-sectioned, with triple delicate ridge and a knife incision on one side. Body surface partially knife-pared.
   Fabric: dense, hard, reddish yellow (7.5 YR 6/6 "reddish yellow") with occasional minute white grits; surface: smooth pale pink (near 7.5 YR 7/4). *PG 1* (Michniewicz 2009, 38-42).
   Diam. body 7.8, Diam. filling hole 3.8, H. body *ca.* 3.7, H. with handle 4.1.
   Found: Loc. 52;
Cf. Qumran 1, 309; Qumran 1B, 31.
Cf. *RB* 1956, 220-221, fig. 3:16.
Cf. Donceel ms, pl. II and VIII; Młynarczyk 2013, 107, fig. 2 (mistakenly attributed there to Type 034.2).
   A close parallel comes from the excavations by Magen and Peleg (2006, 69, fig. 3.14, right) at the "northwestern refuse dump" in Qumran.

16. KhQ 1008 (Pl. 97).
   Two non-joining parts: a) nozzle with small part of body including slightly depressed base, and b) fragment of body top with handle. Thick band handle, square in section and concave along its top part, is attached at body carination and at rim of filling hole. Wheel marks inside. Sides of nozzle bear traces of smearing clay by means of a cloth or a small stick(?). Dense soot at the wick hole.
   Fabric: dark grey (7.5 YR 6/0 "gray") banded pink with many tiny white and black grits; surface: thickly wet-smoothed, pink on top (5 YR 7/4) to very pale brown on bottom (10 YR 8/2 "white"), with some medium-size to large lime eruptions, wet-smoothed yet semi-rough in feel. Gunneweg and Balla 2003, 23 and table 9, sample Q 288, "may belong to Chemical Group I, thus local to Qumran".
   Extant L. 10.6, extant W. 7.5, extant H. 3.3
   Extant L. 5.7, extant H. 3.0.
   Found: Trench B, Layer 2, north;
Cf. Qumran 1, 340; Qumran 1B, 63.
Cf. Donceel ms pl. II and X.

17. KhQ 2270 (Pl. 97).
   Fragmentary lamp, lacking most of upper part of body and handle. Irregular flattened (to slightly concave) base. Wheel-marks inside. Faint burning traces at wick hole.
   Fabric: granular light red (5 YR 7/6 reddish yellow) with some tiny voids, rather many medium-sized dark grey/black grits and occasional tiny white ones; surface fired from pink (7.5 YR 7/4) on base through pink to mostly beige and pale beige (10 YR 7/2 "light gray" and 8/2 "white"), wet-smoothed, semi-coarse in feel, like no. *8* (KhQ 5094, Type 032). *PG 3* (Michniewicz 2009, 46-48).
   Extant L. 14.2, Diam. 8.4, extant H. 3.8.
   Found: Loc. 130-2B;
Cf. Qumran 1, 334; Qumran 1B, 56.
Cf. Donceel ms, pls. IV and XI; Donceel 1998, 102, fig. 10.

Fragments attributed to 032-033.

18. KhQ 5385 (Pl. 98) *(registration 2015)*.

    Two long tubular nozzles. No traces of burning visible.
    The same fabric as no. *20* (KhQ 5086):
    a) Fabric: very hard, dense, grey (7.5 YR 5/0) with small white
    grits; surface: beige (10 YR 7/3 "very pale brown").
    Extant L. 8,0, Extant W. 3,5
    b) Fabric: light grey (10 YR 6/1 "gray") with some tiny dark
    grey(?) grits; surface: beige (10 YR 7/2 "light grey")
    Extant L.6.8, Extant W. 4,7
    They parallel the nozzle shape of no. *9* (Gr 1Q-43) of Type 033.1,
    with decorative projections at the wick hole.
    Provenience not recorded; perhaps Loc. 130.

19. KhQ 5386 (Pl. 98) *(registration 2015)*.

    Two long tubular nozzles, unregistered. Faint traces of burning at the nozzle tip of the two(?).
    The same fabric as no. *20* (KhQ 5086):
    a) Fabric: hard and dense greyish brown (10 YR 5/1 "gray") with some minute white grits and
    small dark grey ones; surface: light greyish beige (10 YR 7/2 "light gray"), semi-coarse in feel.
    Extant L. 7,4, Extant W. 2,9.
    b) Nozzle restored of two parts, lacking a small fragment at wick hole.
    Fabric: very hard grey (10 YR 6/1 "gray") with some tiny white grits;
    surface pale beige (10 YR 7/2 "light gray"), semi-coarse in feel.
    Extant L. 7,8; Extant W. 2,7.
    They parallel the nozzle shape of nos. *10* (Gr 1Q-44) and *16* (KhQ 1008), both of Type 033.2,
    Provenience not recorded; perhaps Loc. 130.

20. KhQ 5086 (Pl. 98).

    Fragment of deep nozzle with dense soot at wick hole, its form similar to that
    of nos. *10* (Gr 1Q-44) and *16* (KhQ 1008), both of Type 033.2.
    Fabric: hard, dense, fired dark brown (7.5 YR 3/2), with occasional tiny white grits; surface
    greyish beige with thin pale brown self-slip(?) (10 YR 7/1 light grey), of coarse feel.
    Extant L. 4.3, extant H. 3.3.
    Found: Loc. 74.

21. KhQ 5085 (Pl. 98).

    Nozzle with flat circular rim to wick hole and pared ridge along the top, once
    attached to upper body (Type 033). Dense burning traces at wick hole.
    Fabric: medium-hard, orange-pink (near 5 YR 6/6 reddish yellow) with some voids and
    many tiny white grits, especially on surface where they create "salted" effect, as well as some
    grey ones visible in section; surface pink to yellow (5 YR 7/6 reddish yellow) turning pale
    brown towards base. *PG 1* (Michniewicz 2009, 38-42). Gunneweg and Balla 2003, 23 and
    table 9, sample QUM 290: "similar to Jericho pottery (…) thus coming from there".
    Extant L. 8.5, extant W. 4.2, extant H. 3.3.
    Found: Loc. 66.

22. KhQ 5090 (Pl. 98).

    Fragment of upper half of lamp body with part of ring handle attached to carination; base not
    preserved; body profile closely similar to both KhQ 2034 (Type 032) and Gr 1Q-43 (Type 033).
    Fabric: dark greyish brown (5 YR 4/1 "dark grey") banded brown with many
    small white grits; surface: wet-smoothed, pale beige (10 YR 7/3 "very pale
    brown") with occasional white eruptions, semi-rough in feel.
    Extant W. 6.7, extant H. 3 cm.
    Found: Loc. 134.

23. KhQ 3385 (Pl. 98).
    Fragment of broad flattened base at the root of nozzle, with wheel marks
    inside, partly obliterated by attaching the nozzle. Type 032 or 033.
    Fabric: rather hard and dense, pale red (5 YR 5/6 "yellowish red") with partial light
    grey core where thick, with lots of small white grits; surface: wet-smoothed, light
    pink outside (5 YR 7/4 "pink"), orange-pink inside (7.5 YR 7/4 "pink").
    Extant L 6.0, extant W. 6.8.
    Found: Loc. 46.

24. KhQ 5091.
    Fragment of lamp body at the root of nozzle. Shallow bi-conical body,
    undefined base, wheel-marks inside. Apparently Type 033.2.
    Fabric: pinkish brown (7.5 YR 6/4 "light brown") with mineral inclusions of all sizes
    (including large piece of rock), white and dark grey. Surface: wet-smoothed, pale beige (10
    YR 8/4 "very pale brown"), of a semi-coarse feel. *PG 3* (Michniewicz 2009, 46-48).
    Extant L. 7.1, extant H. 3.1
    Found: Loc. 60.

25. KhQ 5158.
    Fragment of body near the root of nozzle. Bi-conical body,
    fairly thin-walled, wheel-marks inside. Type 033.
    Fabric: dense, dark grey (10 YR 4/1 dark grey) banded brown, with lots of tiny white grits. Surface:
    wet-smoothed beige to pale beige (between 10 YR 7/3 and 7/4 "very pale brown"), semi-coarse in feel.
    Extant L. 5.4, extant H. 2.9
    Found: Loc. 22.

26. KhQ 3263 (Pl. 98).
    Fragment of lamp top with broad out-folded rim to filling hole and root of an
    oval/angular-sectioned band handle, its one end attached to the rim of filling
    hole; flattened shoulder. Similar to no. *16* (KhQ 1008) of Type 033.2.
    Fabric: medium-hard, fired dark greyish brown (10 YR 3/2 "very dark grayish brown"), occasional
    tiny white grits; surface: beige (10 YR 7/2 "light gray"), soot inside (secondary burning?).
    Extant W. 3.8, Diam.(est.) of filling hole 3.0.
    Found: Loc. 27.

27. KhQ 5114 (Pl. 98).
    Fragment of lamp, burnt after it was broken, preserving full body profile (base),
    low body, shoulder, filling hole with a moulded rim. Apparently, Type 033.2.
    Fabric: granular brown to (mostly) very dark grey (burnt) (10 YR 4/1 "dark gray") with fine white grits;
    surface: rough, grayish beige (10 YR 7/2 "light gray") to orangish (7.5 YR 6/4 "light brown") on base.
    Diam. (est.) 7.0, H 3.1.
    Found: east of Loc. 45/78.

28. KhQ 5089 (Pl. 98).
    Fragment of rather deep spherical body with loop handle; delicate wheel-marks inside and out. Body
    profile corresponding to Type 032. Handle oval-sectioned with tiny opening, attached to shoulder.
    Fabric: rather hard, beige-pink (5 YR 6/3 "light reddish brown"), with fairly many
    oblong voids, some tiny white grits and small dark grey ones; surface: pale beige (self
    slip? 10 YR 8/2 "white") with pink spots, wet-smoothed, semi-rough in feel.
    Extant W. 6.1; extant H. (incl. handle) 4.4.
    Found: Loc. 91.

Plate 98

032-033

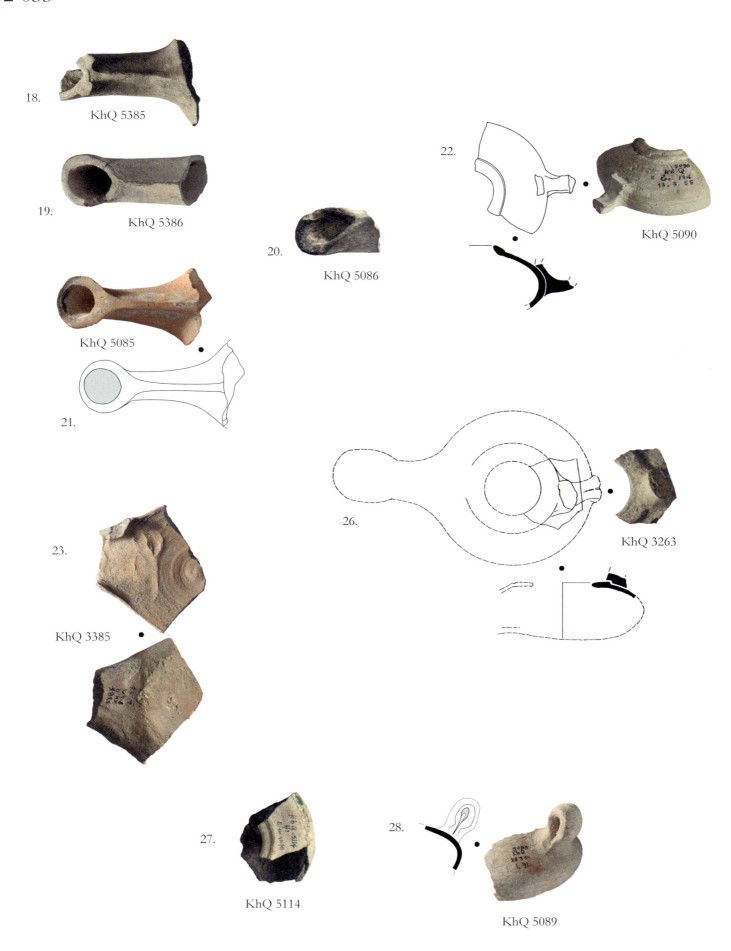

Lamp types 032-033

034. Large and flat circular lamps

Shape description:

Discoid body, shallow to very shallow, perfectly circular in outline, standing on undefined base; out-turned or out-folded (everted) rim to the filling hole; vertical loop handle, sometimes simplified to a mere upright lug, or (in one case) band handle. No lamp preserves its nozzle; it seems they were of long ridged type as in Types 032-033, but (like in Type 032) their top ridge didn't continue on the body. According to the shape of the rim to the filling hole, the lamps are divided into two subtypes: 034.1 (with upright or everted rim) and 034.2 (with wide out-folded rim). To the lamps excavated by the team of R. de Vaux, one should add at least one lamp of the same type excavated at Qumran by Magen and Peleg (2006, 69, fig. 3.14, right).

The Qumran lamps of this group are paralleled by a single object from Jericho, classified as J-LP3A2, which falls into our Type 034.2, and which is said to have come from a context of 31 – 15 BC (Bar-Nathan 2002, 110-111, no. 301, Ill. 88 and pl. 18; Bar-Nathan 2006, fig. 15.3:2).

034.1. Lamps with upright or everted (out-turned) rim of filling hole; usually lug handle; in one case, band handle

29. KhQ 2206 (Pl. 99).
    Lamp lacking nozzle and parts of rim to filling hole. Wheel-marks on shoulder. Upright lug handle, made of band of clay, folded into two and then pressed together, attached to lower shoulder.
    Fabric: rather hard, very gritty, brown (near to 7.5 YR 5/4 "brown") with lots of tiny white grits; surface beige (10 YR 7/2 "light gray"), wet-smoothed, yet semi-coarse in feel. Gunneweg and Balla 2003, 23 and table 9, sample QUM 291: chemical outlier, but: "similar to Jericho pottery (…) thus coming from there".
    Diam. 10.1, H. body 3.9, H. (including handle) 4.3.
    Found: eastern part of Loc. 130, "in the ashes";
    Cf. Qumran 1, 334; Qumran 1B, 56.
    Cf. Donceel ms, pl. IV and XI; Młynarczyk 2013, 107, fig. 1; Młynarczyk, Lugano, Ill. 2.

30. KhQ 5088 (Pl. 99) + KhQ 5129 (Pl. 99).
    Two non-joining parts.
    a) KhQ 5088: fragment of lamp body, its strap handle missing (preserving body profile, closely similar to KhQ 2206, with oval-sectioned band handle extending from carination to rim of filling hole); extant L. 4.4, H. body 3.9;
    b) KhQ 5129: fragment of rim/shoulder. Everted rim upon kind of short neck; sloping shoulder with wheel-marks upon it; extant W. (L.) 3.8; extant H. 2.6.
    Fabric: hard reddish brown (5 YR 5/3 "reddish brown"), with rare voids and occasional small white grits; grey core at handle; surface: pale beige (10 YR 8/1 "white") coarse in feel.
    Found: Loc. 130, "in the ashes".

31. KhQ 2295 (Pl. 99).
    Fragmentary lamp restored of several parts, lacking nozzle, small parts of body, and lug (or loop?) handle. Wheel-marks on shoulder. Plain rim triangular in section, with outer face vertical.
    Fabric: granular brown (7.5 YR 5/2); surface fired yellow-beige (10 YR 7/3 "very pale brown") at top and brown (10 YR 6/3 "pale brown") at bottom, wet-smoothed, yet semi-coarse in feel. *PG 3* (Michniewicz 2009, 46-48).
    Diam. 11.2, H. body 3.9.
    Found: Loc. 130-3A;
    Cf. Qumran 1, 334; Qumran 1B, 56.
    Cf. Donceel ms, pl. V and XI; Bar-Nathan 2006, fig. 15.3:4.

Plate 99

034.1

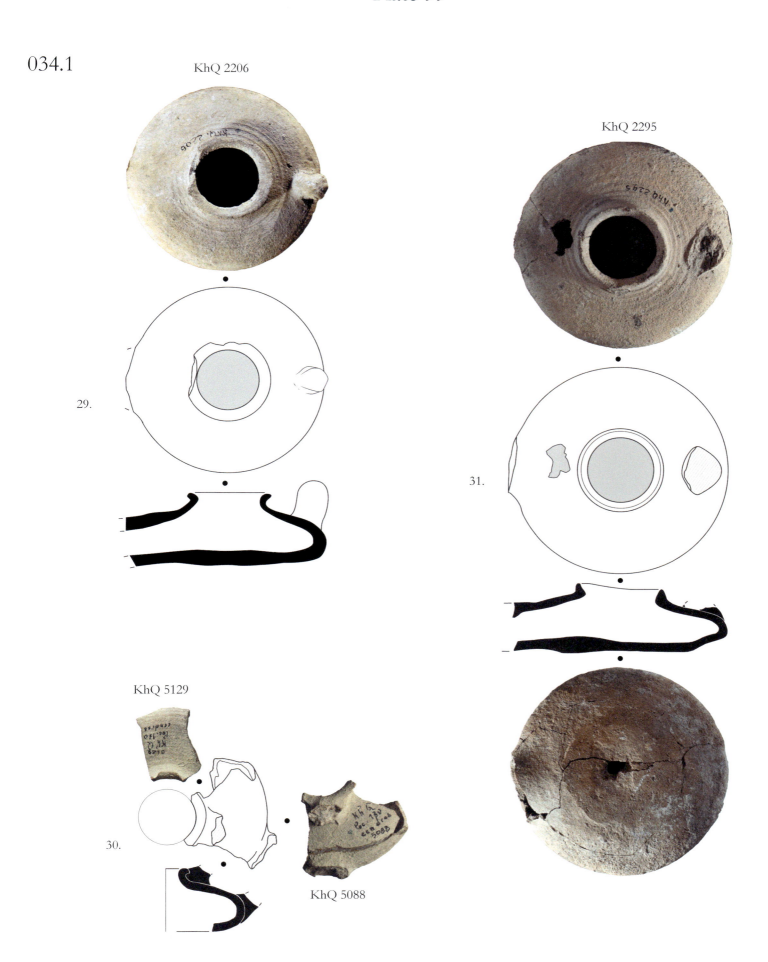

Lamp type 034.1

32. KhQ 5105.

> Fragment of upper body of lamp; upright rim to the filling hole with relatively narrow shoulder. Fabric: hard and dense, pink/light brown (7.5 YR 6/6 "reddish yellow") with small white grits; surface yellowish pink (between 7.5 YR 7/4 and 7/6 "pink" to "reddish yellow"), wet-smoothed (traces of cloth, fingerprints). Fabric similar to that of many "Herodian" lamps (Type 036, below). Extant L. 5.6, Diam. est. 7.0 cm.
> Found: Loc. 62.

034.2. Lamps with wide out-folded ("collared") rim of filling hole

33. KhQ 2291* (Pl. 100).

> Complete lamp. The way of attaching the nozzle is not quite clear: to judge by the drawing (*RB* 1956, fig. 1:4), the latter seems to be meeting the lower part of body. Wick hole within flat rim. Loop handle apparently attached at the mid-height of body.
> Fabric: *terre chamois*.
> L. 20.1, Diam. body 10.9, Diam. filling hole 7.0, H. not given.
> Found: Loc. 130-3A;
> Cf. Qumran 1, 334; Qumran 1B, 56.
> Cf. *RB* 1956, 552-553, fig. 1:4 (Loc. 130, *période* Ia); Lapp 1961 type 84 D; Smith 1964, 123, fig. 23 bottom.
> Cf. Donceel ms, pl. IV: copy of the drawing in the register book.

34. KhQ 5087 (Pl. 100).

> Fragmentary lamp, lacking a half of body and nozzle. Wheel-marks inside and on shoulder. Upright loop handle (oval to square-sectioned).
> Fabric: hard, pink (5 YR 7/4) to reddish brown (5 YR 5/3) with thin grey core; some circular voids, some tiny white grits. Outer surface wet-smoothed, fired light grey-brown (10 YR 6/2 "light gray/gray"), slightly coarse in feel. *PG 1* (Michniewicz 2009, 38-42); Gunneweg and Balla 2003, 23 and table 9, sample Qum 292: similar to pottery of Chemical Group III ("this chemical composition is local to Jericho").
> Diam. body 9.8, Diam. filling hole 3.0, H. body 3.0, H. with handle 5.5.
> Found: Loc. 130, *trou cendres*;
> Cf. Młynarczyk 2013, 107, fig. 2; Młynarczyk, Lugano, Ill. 2.

35. KhQ 5099 (Pl. 100).

> Part of upper body of lamp with "loop" handle (devoid of any opening).
> Fabric: light pinkish brown (7.5 YR 6/4 "light brown") with some oblong voids and some minute dark brown and white (?) grits (plus a large piece of grey-coloured rock); surface pale pinkish beige (near 7.5 YR 8/4 "pink") of coarse feel with occasional white eruptions.
> Extant H. (handle included) 4.4, extant W. 4.6.
> Found: Trench A, Layer 3;
> Cf. Qumran 1, 315

35-bis.

> Two joining fragments of lamp body, preserving full body profile; upper part has "10" written in pencil inside, lower part has "KhQ 1257, L 74" (clearly, an erroneous attribution; see no. *36* below). Wheel marks inside and on shoulder. Doubtlessly coming from the same lamp as fragment KhQ 5099; however, due to allegedly different find spots, these two objects are presented as separate catalogue entries.
> Fabric: cf. no. *35* (KhQ 5099).
> Diam. (estimated) 9,0; H. (body) 4.9;
> Cf. Qumran 1, 315; Loc. 74, 1257: *lampe hellénistique*.

Plate 100

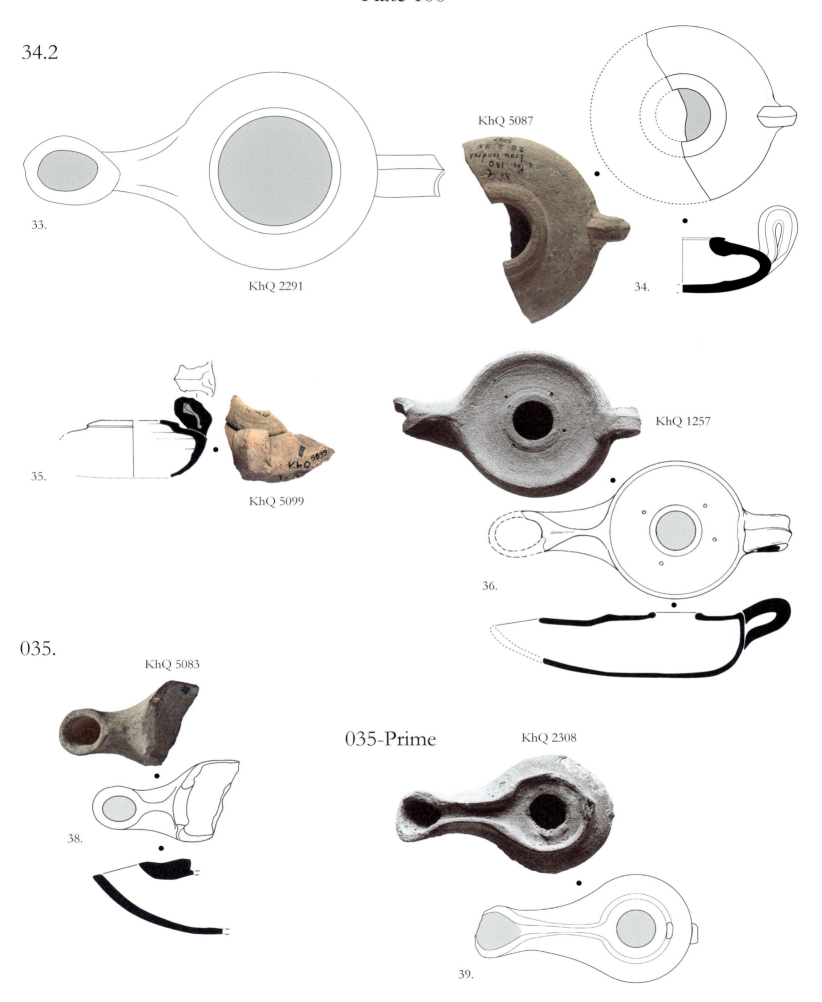

Lamp types 034.2, 035, 035-Prime

035. Ridged nozzle attached to the outer rim of flattened top of the lamp

Shape description:

The lamps of this type, represented by three objects, stand on undefined(?) base; the filling hole is in the middle of a sunken area which is encircled by a protruding rim joined by an indistinct nozzle ridge. Similar protruding rim around the lamp top occurs also in one of the variants of the "Herodian" lamp type, specifically, Qumran Type 036.6.

A lamp apparently falling into Qumran Type 035 comes from Jericho; classified as J-LP3A1, it was found in a context dated to 31-15 BC (Bar-Nathan 2002, 110-111, no. 299, Ill. 87 and pl. 18; cf. also Bar-Nathan 2006, fig. 15.3:3). This type may, indeed, have been influenced by some "Ephesus" lamps, with which it shares both the ridge on the nozzle top and an upright rim around the sunken "discus" (pierced with four tiny holes in lamp KhQ 1257), as well as a band/strap handle. The "Ephesus" lamps have been dated by Bailey to the period from the last quarter of the 2nd century BC into the 1st century AD (Bailey 1975, 89 and 110, Q 198 – Q 199, pl. 38). The "Ephesus" lamps with ridged nozzle were indeed present in Jerusalem, both as importations (Rosenthal-Heginbottom 2003, pl. 6.4:8 and pl. 6.7:27) and as local(?) imitations *(ibidem*, fig. 6.4:15).

36. KhQ 1257* (Pl. 100).
    Lamp nearly complete, missing only tip of nozzle. Four small circular holes in the flattened discus-like area around the filling hole. Strap handle attached at the mid-height of body and at rim.
    Fabric: *terre rouge, grise dans la masse; engobe chamois* (Donceel, ms).
    Dimensions (register book): L. 13.2, Diam. 7.5, H. 3.3.
    Found: Loc. 74;
    Cf. Qumran 1B, 37.
    Cf. Donceel, ms, pls. III and X; Młynarczyk 2013, 107, fig. 2; Młynarczyk, Lugano, Ill. 2.

37. KhQ 5387 *(registration 2015)*.
    Fragment of lamp body with loop handle square in section ("No. 5" written in pencil). Lamp very closely similar to no. *36* (KhQ 1257*); however, to judge by the photo of the latter, they do not seem to have belonged together.
    Fabric: dense (very tiny circular voids?), with "sandwich" section, brown (10 YR 5/2 "grayish brown") banded reddish brown inside, with some minute white grits; surface: pale grey, coated with a white (10 YR 8/2) slip.
    Found: ?

38. KhQ 5083 (Pl. 100).
    Nozzle with fragment of lamp body. Fairly deep body apparently on undefined(?) base. Relatively short nozzle with indistinct ridge on top connecting the rim of wick hole to flattened rim which encircles the sunken area around filling hole.
    Fabric: (macroscopically, the same as no. *37* above) dark brownish grey (near 10 YR 5/1 "gray") with tiny voids and minute white grits; surface: light grey (sizeable white eruptions, coarse feel) with partly worn whitish slip and whitish deposit (sediment?) all over, including breaks. *PG 3* (Michniewicz 2009, 46-48).
    Extant L. 7.7, extant W. 4.5, H. 4.0.
    Found: Loc. 52.

035-Prime

Shape description:

In this Type, represented by a single lamp no. *39* (KhQ 2308) standing on an undefined base, the long nozzle is attached to the upper body; the nozzle sides, however, instead of ending up in a ridge on the top (as with the previously discussed types), form a channel all along the nozzle and around the filling hole area. Most probably, there was a strap handle (broken), once attached to the mid-body and to the ridge encircling the top. Unfortunately, the body profile remains unknown, as the only record available for this lamp has been the top view drawn in the original field register. However, it seems obvious that also this lamp's shape reflects some influence from the "Ephesus" lamps (see for instance Bailey 1975, Q 301, pl. 38 from Ephesus).

> 39. KhQ 2308* (Pl. 100).
>> Lamp complete, except for the handle (strap? handle).
>> Fabric: *terre chamois, tendre*.
>> L. 11.6, Diam. 6.6, H. 3.3.
>> Found: Loc. 130- 3A;
> Cf. Qumran 1, 334; Qumran 1B, 56.
> Cf. *RB* 1956, 552-553, fig. 1:3 (*loc. 130, période Ib*); Lapp 1961, type 84C; Donceel ms, pl. V (drawing from register book), and pl. XI (photo); Młynarczyk 2013, 108, fig. 2; Młynarczyk, Lugano, Ill. 2.

036. Knife-pared ("Herodian", spatulate) lamps

The typology of the "Herodian" lamps, a name which (even if not quite correct in terms of chronology) is still a very convenient one to use, is partly based on that proposed by Smith (1961) who, describing the "Herodian" lamps as "attractive, inexpensive lamps which could compete successfully with moulded lamps", divided them into two basic types, one succeeding the other (Smith 1961, 60-65; Smith 1966,5). The "Herodian" lamps were included into the Palestinian ceramics typology by P. Lapp as his type 82:1 (Lapp 1961, 193), embracing all the "Herodian" lamps, either plain or with some ornament (such as grooves and circlets) on the nozzle. Lapp listed the sites known to him which had yielded this type of lamps, all of them (with the exception of Samaria) situated in the south (a picture that has changed since then to embrace today a number of the northern sites as well). At the same time P. P. Kahane (1961, 135-138) provided an overview of the wheel-made "Herodian" lamps (dividing them into varieties a-c) and mould-made lamps of related shape. The "Herodian" lamp type also corresponds to Kennedy type 3 (Kennedy 1961, 71-72), and to Diez Fernandez (1983) type L 3.1 (plus at least one example in type L 3.2? specifically lamp no. 38).

In the nineties of the 20th century the Kennedy's typology was applied to the material from Machaerus by S. Loffreda (1996). At the same time, however, it was rejected by Barag and Hershkovitz (1994) who upon studying the material from Masada created an independent typology: they changed the name "Herodian" lamps to "wheel-made knife-pared lamps" and distinguished as many as nine types (Barag and Hershkovitz 1994, 24-55, types C I-IX). The methodologically weak side of their typology was that the lamps were considered two-dimensionally, in their top view.

The great majority of the "Herodian" lamps coming from Machaerus were just nozzles which became a basis for distinguishing five different groups (Loffreda 1996, 108-112, figs. 49-50). Two of them, Machaerus groups 75 and 76, share plain (undecorated) nozzles, yet according to Loffreda, they can be divided between the two types of Smith, type 1 and type 2 respectively. Unfortunately, it is only their plans and not profiles that were illustrated in the publication of Machaerus, which renders any verification impossible. Further groups, 77 through 79, all of them falling into Smith's type 2, have been distinguished by Loffreda on the basis of different kinds of the nozzle decoration.

R.H. Smith was among the first to suggest the chronology for the "Herodian" lamps: type 1 in exclusive use between *ca*. 37 BC and AD 35; transitional period in *ca*. 35-50 AD, and type 2 in exclusive use between *ca.* 50 and 135 AD (Smith 1961, 65). According to P.P. Kahane, the "Herodian" lamps would be manufactured from the times of Herod the Great to *ca.* 70 AD (Kahane 1961, 138). Diez Fernandez even proposed to date Smith type 1 (his own type L 3.1) to as early as the second third of the 1st century BC through the early 1st century AD (Diez Fernandez 1983, 66-72) which, however, did not find confirmation in the archaeological record.

On the base of the Machaerus contexts, S. Loffreda has agreed with Smith that the latter's type 1 seems to be indeed earlier than type 2 and that the beginning of the former might have coincided with the early years of Herod the Great (Loffreda 1996, 111-112). The evidence from the Jericho palaces suggests that the "Herodian" lamps (classified there as J-LP4) appeared already by the "Herodian 2" period (*ca.* 15 BC – AD 6); they were still present there in the "Herodian 3" period (AD 6 – 48) as well as in post-Herodian contexts (Bar-Nathan 2002, 112 and 188-189, nos. 303 and 543-548). The finds from the Lower Herodion have confirmed the presence of the lamps of Smith's type 2 in a context of AD 48-70 (Bar-Nathan 1981, 138, note 88). In the case of the "Herodian" lamp finds from Machaerus and its dependent Callirrhoe, it is clear that they antedate the fall of Machaerus in AD 72 (Clamer 1997, 110-111). The same is true about the "Herodian" lamps found in the northern Jewish settlements of Iotapata and Gamala, destroyed by the Romans in AD 67 (Adan-Bayewitz *et al.* 2008, 69, with examples of lamps from the two sites illustrated in Fig. 3:1-12). As to the terminal date of the "Herodian" lamps production, it is generally agreed that they were still present in the contexts of the Bar-Kochba Revolt (for a useful summary of the history of the study of the "Herodian" lamps and of their dating, see Barag and Hershkovitz 1994, 44-47 and notes 30-47).

In recent years, a number of doubts have arisen as to the early (Herodian-period) dating of the "Herodian" lamps. R.H. Smith himself, in his second overview of the Palestinian lamps, has tended to date his type 1 to the early decades of the 1st century AD, considering it as a dominating lamp type during the first third of that century (Smith 1964, 4-5, fig. 2). Indeed, the evidence from the Jewish Quarter in Jerusalem and from Jericho "demonstrates that it first appeared at the very end of the 1st century BCE or at the very beginning of the 1st century CE" (Geva and Hershkovitz 2006, 115; see also Hadad 2002, 13). The same view has recently been accepted by J. Magness who summed up the discussion on these lamps' general chronology as spanning the period from the late 1st century BC to at least the Bar Kokhba revolt (Magness 2009, 80-81).

The "Herodian" lamps and their fragments account for 64.5% of the Qumran lamps from all the periods; R. Donceel (1998, 93) has been mistaken in evaluating their proportion as amounting to 50% only. Claiming to have distinguished *10 groupes et sous-groupes des lampes "hérodiennes" nettement distincts* (where the present writer cannot see more than *maximum* seven sub-types) expressed also the view that they, in fact, have come from a number of workshops the majority of which were located outside Qumran (Donceel 1998, 93-94 and note 17). There can be no doubt indeed that such lamps were being made in a number of Judaean workshops, perhaps also in Idumaea. For instance, 31 "Herodian" lamps found at the necropolis of Maresha have been reported by Oren and Rappaport (1984, 123, fig. 14:3-4 and pl. 14:B) who also state that "numerous examples were found by the North Sinai Expedition in Nabataean sites of the first-second centuries C.E. along the North Sinai coast and as far afield as Pelusium(…) A few such lamps were discovered in Nabatean contexts at some of the major sites in the Negev."

R.H. Smith (1964, 4) has been the first to suggest that the "Herodian" lamps "may have evolved in Jerusalem or nearby" (Smith 1964, 4). Scientific research on such lamps from some sites in the north of Palestine that had a Jewish (Iotapata, Gamala) or largely Jewish (Sepphoris) population proved that most of those objects did come from the Jerusalem area (Adan-Bayewitz *et al.* 2008, 55 and 77, figs. 6 and 12). Bringing them to the northern Jewish sites over a long period "suggests that these lamps may have had some socio-religious or ritualistic significance" (Adan-Bayewitz *et al.* 2008, 75). On the other hand, the research in question has made it clear that the "Herodian lamps account for the majority of the lamps dating to the first century C.E. (until 70 C.E.)" also at predominantly gentile (Dora) or largely gentile (Scythopolis) towns. However, at those places, only a part of them were of a Jerusalem origin; several examples of the "Herodian" lamps were made "from a variety of locally available raw materials" (Adan-Bayewitz *et al.* 2008, 45 and 72). They were popular objects of daily use which was probably not confined to the Jewish population alone.

Given the short distance between Jerusalem and Qumran, it is quite obvious that a good number of the "Herodian" lamps found at Qumran have been made in the Jerusalem area. It seems, however, very logical that at least some of the lamps of Type 036 were made in Qumran itself, be it from imported or from locally acquired raw material.

Gunneweg and Balla (2003,16) have mentioned NAA analysis of three "Herodian" lamps of which one "was locally made in Jerusalem" (sample Qum 294, KhQ 2541: missing from the present evidence at the EBAF!). Of four "Herodian" lamps sampled by Michniewicz (2009, 37), one was of *PG 2* (a fabric attested both among Jericho and Qumran products), one of *PG 3* (a Qumran workshop?), while the petrography of two remaining samples was unidentified.

For discussion of the "Herodian" ("knife-pared", "spatulate") lamps, see also (in chronological order): Bar-Nathan 2002, 112-113 and 188-189; Grawehr 2006, 356-357 (ten fragments and one complete lamp from Petra ez Zantur, not local); Sussman 2008, 219-220 (type R6 at Caesarea where their number is said to have amounted to 350 fragments); Adan-Bayewitz *et al.* 2008, 38-40.

According to our typological study, the "Herodian" lamps family as represented at Qumran embraces seven shape variants (036.1-7) distinguished by their body profile and, additionally, by their nozzle characteristics. This division, of course, considers only those lamps that preserve full body profile. The chronology of specific variants, however, deserve further in-depth studies, and the statement of R. Donceel that *les représentants de différentes familles de lampes hérodiennes étaient en usage à Khirbet Qumran de manière strictement contemporaine* (Donceel 1998, 93) may be a matter of some dispute.

036.1. Machaerus group 75 (fig. 49:17-24), Smith type 1; Masada group CI

Shape description:

The lamps, which most often are rather small, stand on undefined, slightly convex base; they present a rounded wall profile, with the filling hole surrounded by a ridge with a long inner flange; the nozzle is short, fairly splayed, with pronouncedly concave sides and with plain, downward sloping top. This variety, represented in Qumran by eight objects, has been considered by Smith as the early one (Smith 1961, 60-61; Smith 1966, 4, fig. 2).

V. Sussman has agreed that the pronounced flange and rounded body profile are early features in the "Herodian" lamps (Sussman 2008, 220, nos. 21-22 from Caesarea, both "light red": 2.5 YR 6/6). This subtype has been recorded among the lamp finds from the Jewish Quarter excavations in Jerusalem; commenting on them, R. Rosenthal-Heginbottom supposes that this variant may indeed have been the early one because it is apparently rare at Masada (Rosenthal-Heginbottom 2003, 219, pl. 6.8:4 and pl. 6.9:43). They are attested by some fragments from the site of the Jerusalem International Convention Center, dated to between the early 1st century AD to AD 70 (Berlin 2005, 48-49, fig. 17:15-16; Rosenthal-Heginbottom 2005, 240-241, nos. 2-3). This is also the only "Herodian" group occurring in the tombs on the French Hill in Jerusalem, as published by J.F. Strange (Strange 1975, 61-62 and fig. 16:7-11). On the contrary, only one such lamp was retrieved from the tombs at Akeldama site in Jerusalem (Ben-Arieh and Coen-Uzzielli 1996, 83 and 85, fig. 4.8:2). Of the two lamps found in the Sanhedriyya tombs in Jerusalem (Rahmani 1961, 100, fig. 5:24-25), no. 25 seems to represent Qumran Type 036.1, while the profile of no. 24 places it in a transition from 036.1 to 036.2.1.

R. H. Smith who initially dated his type 1 to the period of 37 BC – 35 AD, and later emphasized that its *floruit* covered the first third of the first century AD, described the fabric of this early variant as "thin buff or light brown clay fired medium-hard" and self-slipped (Smith 1961, 65; Smith 1966, 4-5). According to him, this variety "dominated a major portion of Palestine (a disputable statement, according to the present author) during the first third of the first century A.D."

Chronological indications for this group of lamps recorded at Qumran itself are rather limited. Lamp no. *44* (KhQ 1391*) was found (according to de Vaux's records) with the coins of "procurators under Tiberius", but two other lamps appear to have come from secondary contexts. One of them is no. *42* (KhQ 757) found in an aqueduct, and believed by

R. Donceel to have been placed there towards AD 68 when the aqueduct went out of use, hence the lamp would have been manufactured close to that date (Donceel 1998, 97, n. 29, fig. 6). However, one can hardly figure out a reason for intentional placing of the lamp in the channel, while it is much more probable that the lamp made its way there by pure accident. This means that its original context remains unknown and it could be much earlier. The same can be said about another lamp of subtype 036.1, no. *45* (KhQ 2662*), which was found in the fill of a shaft tomb 26, that is, in a context that probably contained an accidental (disturbed) material.

Of the other sites, among the published lamps from Maresha necropolis, there are two objects that could be classified with this type, were it not for their extremely short flange of the filling hole framing (Oren and Rappaport 1984, fig. 14:4 and pl. 14:B); one should consider them as examples of a transition between types Smith 1 and Smith 2 (corresponding to Qumran Types 036.1 and 036.2, respectively). The only complete "Herodian" lamp from Petra ez Zantur (Grawehr 2006, 357, no. 560), no doubt of Judean/Idumaean origin, pertains to our Type 036.1. As far as the northern sites are concerned, it is interesting to note the presence of three entirely preserved lamps of this type, found in a tomb at Shaar ha-Amakim in western Lower Galilee (unpublished; IAA inventory nos. 66-742, 98-3383, 98-3384).

40. KhQ 1285 (Pl. 101).

> Fragmentary lamp, recomposed of several pieces; lacking part of body. Traces of burning at wick hole. Fabric: hard, granular grey-beige (10 YR 7/3: very pale brown) with some tiny voids(?) and mineral inclusions; surface coarse, light grey (10 YR 7/2). *PG undetermined* (Michniewicz 2009, 37)
> L. 8.2, Diam. 6.0, H. 2.8.
> Found: eastern trench, exterior of Loc. 45;
> Cf. Qumran 1, 308; Qumran 1B, 29.
> Cf. Donceel ms, pl. X.

41. KhQ 2473 (Pl. 101).

> Lamp recomposed of several pieces; missing part of body. Faint traces of burning at wick hole. Fabric: medium-hard, light red (5 YR 7/8) with many small white grits; surface: smooth pinkish orange (5 YR 7/6: reddish yellow) with white grits' eruptions. Macroscopically, the same fabric as nos. *37* and *38* (KhQ 5083) of Type 035.
> L. 8.4, W. 5.9, H. 2.8.
> Found: L 102, *niveau inférieur* (Donceel ms),
> Cf. Qumran 1, 324; Qumran 1B, 46.
> Cf. Młynarczyk 2013, 111, fig. 2.

42. KhQ 757 (Pl. 101).

> Lamp recomposed of several pieces; missing small parts of body. Dense burning traces at wick hole. Fabric: fine granular pale orange; surface: smooth, fired unevenly, from orange-beige on bottom to dark grey on top and nozzle; transitional from "grey metallic" firing at top (10 YR 5/1 "grey") to "pink metallic" at the lower part (7.5 YR 7/4, with beige spots: 10 YR 7/4).
> L. 8.5, H. 2.7.
> Found: Loc. 42, "in the channel" (register book);
> Cf. Qumran 1, 306; Qumran 1B, 27.
> Cf. Donceel 1998, 97, n. 29, fig. 6.

43. KhQ 1619 (Pl. 101).

> Fragmentary lamp recomposed of several pieces, lacking large part of body; dense burning at nozzle. Fabric: medium-hard, orange-pink both at break and surface (5 YR 7/6: reddish yellow), with tiny voids and some small white grits; surface weathered, semi-rough in feel. *PG undetermined* (Michniewicz 2009, 37).
> L. 8.4, W. 6.0, H. 2.3.
> Found: Loc. 40, "lower";
> Cf. Qumran 1, 306 (*niveau intermédiaire*); Qumran 1B, 27.

Plate 101

036.1

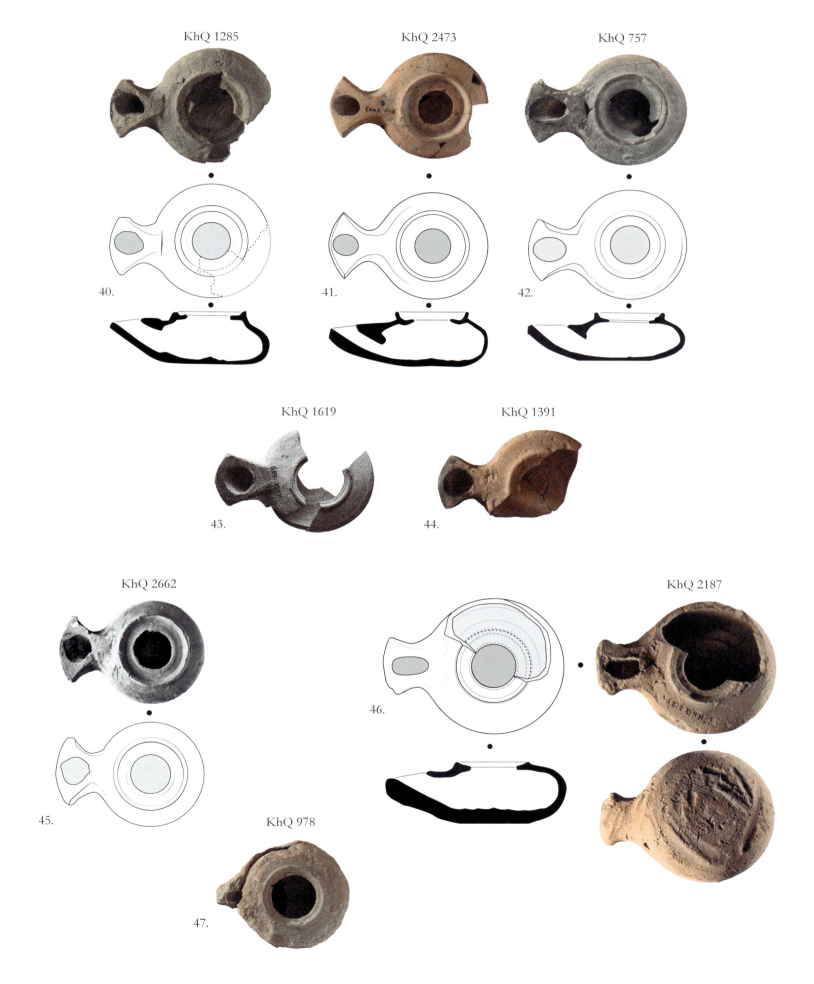

Lamp type 036.1

44. KhQ 1391* (Pl. 101).
   Fragmentary lamp, lacking ca. 0.5 of body.
   Fabric: *terre rouge*.
   L.max. 8.0 cm.
   Found: Loc. 81, "upper";
   Cf. Qumran 1, 317; Qumran 1B, 39 (accompanied by coins of procurators under Tiberius).
   Cf. Donceel ms, pl. X.

45. KhQ 2662* (Pl. 101).
   Complete lamp.
   Fabric: *terre rouge*.
   L. 8.1, Diam. 5.7, H. 2.6.
   Found: tomb 26, in the fill;
   Cf. Qumran 1, 350; Qumran 1B, 77.
   Cf. Donceel ms, pl. VI; Donceel 1998, 92-95, n. 21 and fig. 3 (the lamp being part of the filling of the tomb shaft which sealed the inhumation, and NOT of any funerary equipment).

46. KhQ 2187 (Pl. 101).
   Complete lamp with slight burning traces at wick hole. Fabric: heavy and coarse; rather hard and dense, light reddish brown (5 YR 6/40) with many small white grits, "sandwich" firing: pink outside, beige inside; surface: pink (7.5 YR 7/4) to beige on top, with many white grits' eruptions, coarse in feel. The fabric macroscopically resembles that occurring with lamps of Types 032-035.
   L. 9.4, W. 7.2, H. 4.2.
   Found: Loc. 123;
   Cf. Qumran 1, 330; Qumran 1B, 53.
   Cf. Donceel ms, pl. IV and XI.

47. KhQ 978 (Pl. 101).
   Fragmentary lamp, recomposed of several fragments, its surface mutilated in many places, lacking most of the nozzle, the plan of which remains unknown. To judge by the body shape, the lamp pertains to 036.1.
   Fabric: very hard and dense reddish brown (7.5 YR 6/4: light brown) with lots of medium-size to small white grits; surface of similar colour as break, with light grey patina.
   L.max. 7.2; H. 2.8.
   Found: Loc. 54, "upper locus";
   Cf. Qumran 1, 310; Qumran 1B, 32.
   Cf. Donceel ms, pl. X.

036.2. Machaerus groups 76.1 (plain nozzle) 77 (single incision across the nozzle top) and 78 (double incision across the nozzle top); Masada group C II-III, falling into Smith type 2

Shape description:

The body in this lamp variety, represented by 26 objects among the Qumran material, is usually lower in relation to the length/diametre than it is in 036.1; the profile is more or less angular, with flattened shoulder, "often with a distinct carination and always with some suggestion of it" (Smith 1961, 61 and fig. 2). The inner flange around the filling hole is usually much shorter or it is absent. According to the modified description of the same type by Smith (1966, 15 and fig. 5), "a humped nozzle (when seen in profile), a wide and often carelessly-formed wick-hole, and a small ridge around the filling-hole but little or no flange". The sides of the nozzle are less concave, and its top is almost always "decorated". To this type also some Machaerus lamps with undecorated nozzle have been assigned by Loffreda (1996, 109-110, fig. 49, nos. 25-35: group 76), but since only one of his lamps (no. 31) preserves a little bit more than a mere nozzle, this attribution remains uncertain.

The appearance of Smith's type 2 has been dated by him to the mid-1st century AD (Smith 1966, 15 and fig. 5), following a period of transition from type 1 to type 2 during ca. AD 35-50 (Smith 1961, 65). Qumran Type 036.2 certainly matches a part of this type, at the same time corresponding to major part of type L.3.2 and to type L.3.3 in Diez Fernandez' classification, which cover the period from the end of the 1st century BC till after AD 75 (Diez Fernandez 1983, 72-78). A fragmentary plain-nozzle lamp from the Tomb of Jason in Jerusalem, which apparently belongs to this type, most probably dates from the final episode of this tomb's use, associated with the coins of AD 30/31 (Rahmani 1967, 78-79, 100 and fig. 9:10).

Among eight "Herodian" lamps published from Dor (distinguished there as type 22 and broadly dated to *ca.* 25 BC - AD 150), as many as six appear to match Qumran Type 036.2 (Rosenthal-Heginbottom 1995, 243-244, fig. 5.21: nos. 1-5 and 7). A typologically early example of the type from Dor, still standing close to Qumran 036.1, but not of Jerusalem manufacture, has been illustrated by Adan-Bayewitz *et al.* (2008, fig. 2:1, accompanied by an example of the "mature" type: fig. 2:2). Lamps of Qumran Type 036.2 are also attested in Caesarea (Sussman 2008, 220 and 264, no. 20, while no. 19 appears to be transitional from 036.1 to 036.2). Single examples come from the sites in the south (e.g. Maresha: Oren and Rappaport 1984, fig. 14:3, and pl. 14:B centre), with a groove across the nozzle; and the north, where a tomb at Shaar ha-Amakim in western Lower Galilee yielded a lamp apparently of this type, but with plain nozzle top (IAA inventory no. 98-3386) and another one with a groove across the nozzle (IAA inventory no. 98-3385).

The dating evidence from Qumran points toward the mid-1st century AD till AD 68/70: lamp cat. no. *61* (KhQ 1437*) contained two coins from the time of Nero (AD 54-68) (Qumran 1B, 27) while no. *65* (KhQ 2168) is said to have come from the layer associated with coins of Herod Agrippa I and procurators under Nero (Qumran 1, 330). Two lamps (today lost), nos. *63-64* (KhQ 729*-730*) were found together on the floor of Loc. 41 (Qumran 1, 306; Qumran 1B, 27).

A more detailed division of Type 036.2 into two Subtypes can be introduced as regards the shape of the lamp base.

036.2.1. No defined base (14 objects)

This group resembles Type 036.1 in having slightly rounded edges of the base, often with traces of a shaping tool. Most often, a single line is incised across the nozzle above the wick hole; just few examples have a double incised line rather than a single one (as specified in the catalogue below). However, some examples of this subtype may have their nozzle top plain, such as a lamp from Jason's Tomb in Jerusalem (Rahmani 1967, fig. 9:10) or a lamp from Cave 1 at Murabba'at (*RB* 1953b, fig. 4:11 and pl. XI b, 3).

48. KhQ 65* (Pl. 102).
    Complete lamp. Nozzle apparently plain.
    Fabric: pink; traces of burning at wick hole.
    L. 8.4, Diam. 6.2.
    Found: Loc. 4, "near the north door" (*devant la porte nord*), together with KhQ 66, KhQ 67, KhQ 68;
    Cf. Qumran 1, 293; Qumran 1B, 13.
    Cf. Donceel ms, pls. I: drawing from the register book, and VII: photo, in fragmentary state!
    Cf. *RB* 1953, fig. 3:4; Diez Fernandez 1983, no. 41 (his type L 3.2).

49. KhQ 362* (Pl. 102).
    Complete lamp. A single incision at mid-length of the nozzle(?).
    Fabric: *terre chamois*.
    L. 8.0; W. 6.4; H. 2.6.
    Found : Loc. 10, "upper";
    Cf. Qumran 1, 296; Qumran 1B, 16.
    Cf. Donceel ms, pl. I and IX.

50. KhQ 267 (Pl. 102).

Fragmentary lamp, lacking most of the upper part of body, a non-joining top part obviously belongs here; no traces of use. Single incision across the nozzle.
Fabric: red to reddish brown (near 5 YR 6/6 reddish yellow) with partial grey core in places and small white grits; surface with thin slip(?) fired whitish (near 10 YR 8/2 "white") with pink spots, rather smooth.
Extant L. 8.9; W. 6.3.
Found: Loc. 4;
Cf. Qumran 1B, 13: "under the upper level".
Cf. Donceel ms, pl. I and VIII.

51. KhQ 584 (Pl. 102).

Complete lamp with only slight damage to the edge of filling hole; traces of dense burning at wick hole and on part of body. Single incision across the nozzle top, above the wick hole.
Fabric: pink (2.5 YR 6/8) with abundant white grits (eruptions), surface wet-smoothed, pink (5 YR 7/6 to 8/4), semi-smooth.
L. 9.2, W. 6.5, H. 2.6.
Found: Loc. 31, *sous le mur E;*
Cf. Qumran 1B, 24.
Cf. Młynarczyk 2013, 112, fig. 2.

52. KhQ 228 (Pl. 102).

Two joining fragments, virtually giving full body profile, but lacking nearly whole bottom and major part of wall; slight traces of burning at wick hole. Single incision across the nozzle.
Fabric: hard, fired dark pink (5 YR 6/4: light reddish brown) banded beige, with fine voids, some white grits and small dark (brown?) ones; surface: grayish beige (10 YR 7/2) with white grits' eruptions, semi-rough in feel.
Extant L. 8.9, W. *ca.* 5.5, H. 2.2.
Found: Loc. 9;
Cf. Qumran 1, 295; Qumran 1B, 15.
Cf. *RB* 1954, 222-223, fig. 4:8 (Qumran Niv. II), clearly a whole lamp by then; Lapp 1961, Type 82.1:D (dated AD 50-68); Diez Fernandez 1983, no. 44, his type L 3.3.

53. KhQ 704 (Pl. 102).

Whole lamp, except for a circular hole in the wall; traces of dense burning at wick hole. Single incision across the nozzle top, above the wick hole.
Fabric: pink (2.5 YR 6/8) with abundant white grits (eruptions), surface pink (5 YR 7/6 to 8/4) partly worn out, wet-smoothed and semi-glossy on nozzle.
L. 9.0, W. 6.4, H. 2.6.
Found: Loc. 39, "upper";
Cf. Qumran 1, 305; Qumran 1B, 26.

54. KhQ 619 (Pl. 102).

Fragmentary lamp lacking large part of shoulder. Traces of burning at wick hole. Single incision across the nozzle top.
Fabric: pink (2.5 YR 6/8) with abundant white grits (eruptions) and some fine brown ones; surface: wet-smoothed, pink (5 YR 7/6 to 8/4), semi-smooth.
L. 9.0, W. 6.4, H. 2.4.
Found: Loc. 34, "upper";
Cf. Qumran 1, 304; Qumran 1B, 25.

55. KhQ 5058 (Pl. 102).

Lamp nozzle with small part of body showing virtually full profile; traces of burning at wick hole. Single incision across the nozzle top, above the wick hole.
Fabric: hard and clean ("metallic"), ash-grey; surface: pale beige (10 YR 8/2 to 8/3: white to very pale brown) with white grits' eruptions, smooth.
Extant L. 5.8, extant W. 3.4.
Found: Loc. 15.

Plate 102

036.2.1

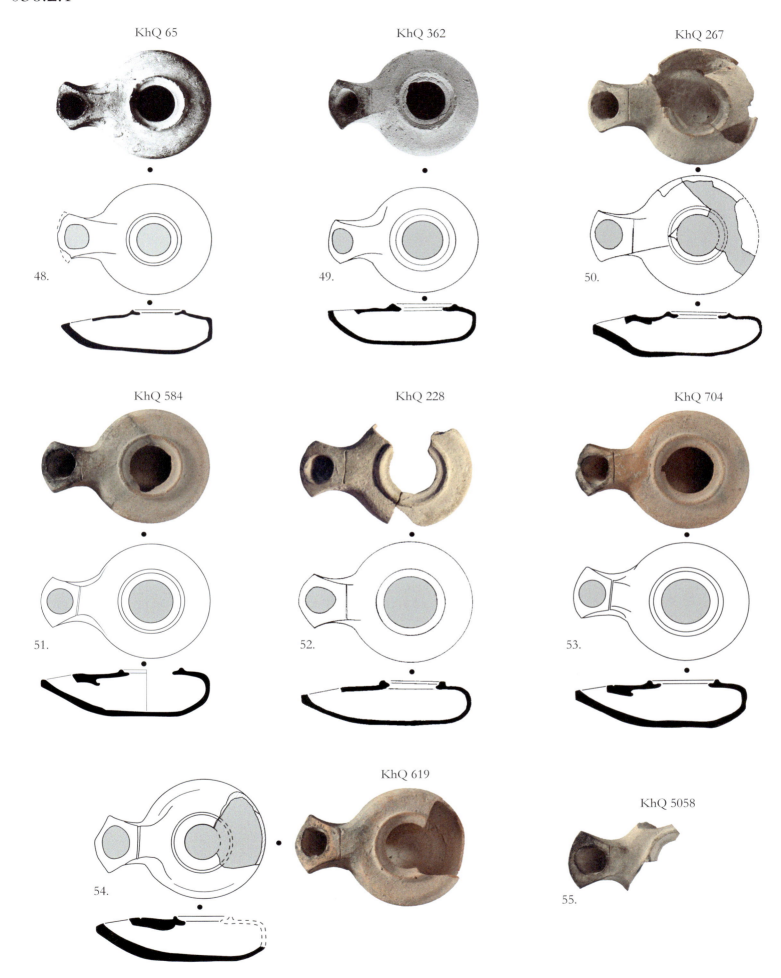

Lamp type 036.2.1

56. KhQ 1169 (Pl. 103).

Lamp nozzle (lacking one edge) with a part of body; wheel marks on floor, dense burning traces at wick hole. Single incision across the nozzle top, above the wick hole.
Fabric: dark brown (10 YR 4/1: dark grey), with some voids, occasional tiny white and black grits; surface: yellowish brown (10 YR 6/4), with white grits' eruptions, semi-smooth to smooth.
Extant L. 7.7, Diam. (est.) 6.5, H. 2.5.
Found: Loc. 45 South, *cendres;*
Cf. Qumran 1, 308; Qumran 1B, 29.

57. KhQ 5128 (Pl. 103).

Lamp nozzle with large part of bottom; traces of burning at wick hole. Single incision across the nozzle top, above the wick hole.
Fabric: brown-grey (7.5 YR 5/2), with many tiny white grits; surface: pink to grey (7.5 YR 7/4 and 6/2), smooth.
Extant L. 7.8, extant W. 6.0, extant H. 2.8.
Found: Loc. 34.

58. KhQ 1141 (Pl. 103).

Fragmentary lamp: nozzle with *ca.* one third of body; faint traces of burning at wick hole. Single incision across the nozzle top, above the wick hole. Marks of a tool on bottom. Two small scrolls impressed on the shoulder flanking the nozzle which has a single deep incision across the top.
Fabric: very hard with tiny white grits, red (10 R 5/4 "weak red") to overfired dark greyish brown at bottom; surface: red (2.5 YR 6/6 "light red") with dark grey spots, smooth.
Extant L. 7.0; extant W. 5.1, H. 2.8.
Found: Loc. 45 South, "upper";
Cf. Qumran 1, 308; Qumran 1B, 29: Loc. 45.

59. KhQ 527 (Pl. 103).

Four joining parts of lamp, lacking *ca.* one third of body as well as the end of nozzle. Single incision across the nozzle top.
Fabric: hard and clean ("metallic"), beige (10 YR 7/3: "very pale brown"); surface: pale beige (10 YR 8/2 to 8/3: "white" to "very pale brown") with large white grits' eruptions, smooth.
Extant L. 7.8, W. (est.) 6.0, H. 2.5.
Found: Loc. 13, *niveau supérieur (du four);*
Cf. Donceel ms
Cf. Qumran 1, 297; Qumran 1B, 18.

60. KhQ 541 (Pl. 103).

Two joining parts of lamp giving virtually full profile; *ca.* two thirds of body are missing; dense burning at wick hole. Double incised line across the nozzle top. Untypically high body.
Fabric: dense yellowish beige (10 YR 8/4 "very pale brown") with occasional rather large grits (white, red); similar surface (10 YR 8/3), very smooth.
Extant L. 9.0, W. 6.2, H. 2.8.
Found: Loc. 9A (NW room of the tower);
Cf. Qumran 1, 295; Qumran 1B, 15.

61. KhQ 1437* (Pl. 103).

Complete lamp; some traces of burning. Double incised line across the nozzle top.
Fabric: grayish pink, with many small grey and black grit (Donceel, ms).
L. 9.4, H. 2.7.
Found: Loc. 40 "upper";
Cf. Qumran 1, 305-306 (with two copper coins: from the time of the First Revolt and minted at Caesarea under Nero); Qumran 1B, 27 ("Herodian lamp containing two coins": Tyre AD 53 and Caesarea under Nero).
Cf. Donceel ms, pl. X.

Plate 103

036.2.1

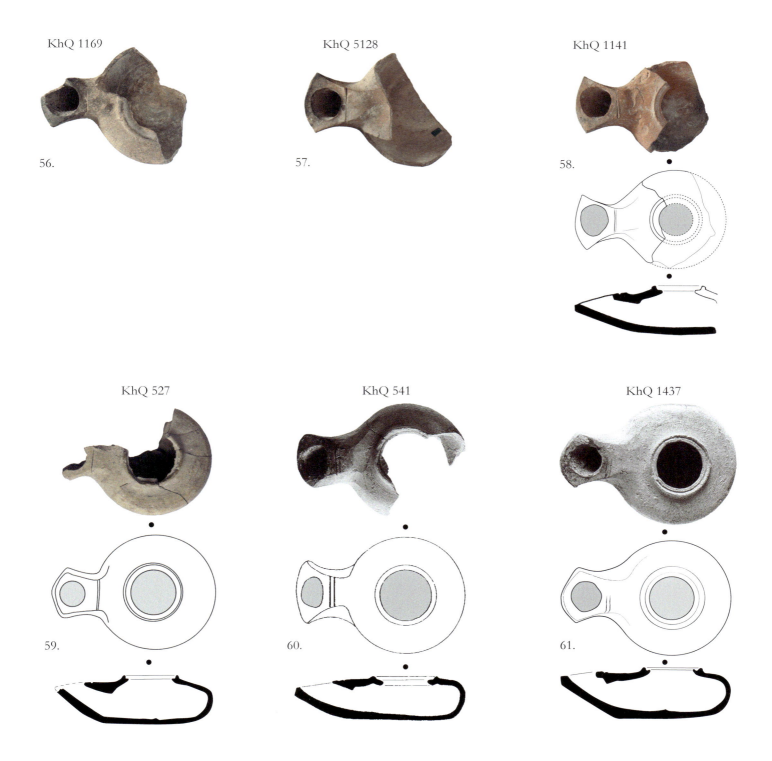

Lamp type 036.2.1

036.2.2. Flattened base with angular edges (nine objects)

The lamp's wall is nearly vertical, and the shoulder flat; the body can be very shallow. Nozzle adornment consists of a single (Machaerus group 77) or double (Machaerus group 78) transverse line, usually continuous, but occasionally punctured, sometimes with two dotted circlets above it (Machaerus group 79). The full profile is illustrated by four lamps in this subtype (cat. nos. *62-65*), three of which are, unfortunately, lost. Other lamps are fragmentary, preserving their nozzles together with parts of base and displaying their wall profile; they appear to belong to the same variant. A lamp from the Jewish Quarter in Jerusalem, found in a stratum dated to *ca.* 1-30 AD (Rosenthal-Heginbottom 2003, 200, pl. 6.8:4: "light grey clay, many white and grey grits"), by its angular base, low body and the nozzle end just slightly splayed would also belong to this subtype. However, its wall profile is rounded and the ledge around the filling hole is rather wide: the features which, together with the plain nozzle top, better match Qumran Type 036.1, thus the lamp may be considered as transitional between 036.1 and 036.2.

The Qumran lamps still available for study seem to include two varieties which share the same body profile:

With large heavy nozzle pertaining to Machaerus group 77: single transverse incision (at its mid-length): nos. *65* (KhQ 2168) and *67* (KhQ 5057).

With the nozzle more slender in proportion to the body and pertaining to Machaerus groups 78 and 79: nos. *68* (KhQ 661), *69* (KhQ 2093) and *70* (KhQ 5124).

62. KhQ 618* (Pl. 104).
   Complete lamp; single incision across the nozzle top, *ca.* at its mid-length (?).
   Fabric: *terre beige*.
   L. 8.9; Diam. 5.9; H. 2.3.
   Found: Loc. 31, *sup* (register book); *sous le mur O* (Donceel ms);
   Cf. Qumran 1B, 24.
   Cf. Donceel ms, pl. II and IX.

63. KhQ 729* (Pl. 104).
   Complete lamp; single incision across the nozzle, *ca.* at its mid-length (?).
   Fabric: *terre chamois*.
   L. 9.0; W. 6.4; H. 2.3.
   Found: Loc. 41, on floor;
   Cf. Qumran 1, 306; Qumran 1B, 27.
   Cf. Donceel ms, pl. II and IX.

64. KhQ 730* (Pl. 104).
   Complete lamp; traces of burning; single incision across the nozzle, *ca.* at its mid-length (?).
   Fabric: *terre chamois*.
   L. 8.6; Diam. 6.3; H. 2.4.
   Found: Loc. 41, on floor;
   Cf. Qumran 1, 306; Qumran 1B, 27.
   Cf. Donceel ms, pl. II and IX.

65. KhQ 2168 (Pl. 104).
   Complete lamp; dense burning traces at wick hole. Transverse incision at mid-length of the nozzle.
   Unbroken; surface thickly wet-smoothed with a piece of cloth (judging by the traces),
   fired to very pale yellow (between 2.5 Y 8/2 "white" and 2.5 Y 8/4 "pale yellow"),
   with white (including a large rock piece) and dark grits, semi-rough in feel.
   L. 8.8; W. 5.8, H. 2.5.
   Found: Loc. 121 "lower",
   Cf. Qumran 1, 330 (the coins from that level belong to procurators under
     Nero and to Herod Agrippa I); Qumran 1B, 52.
   Cf. Młynarczyk 2013, 112, fig. 3.

Plate 104

036.2.2

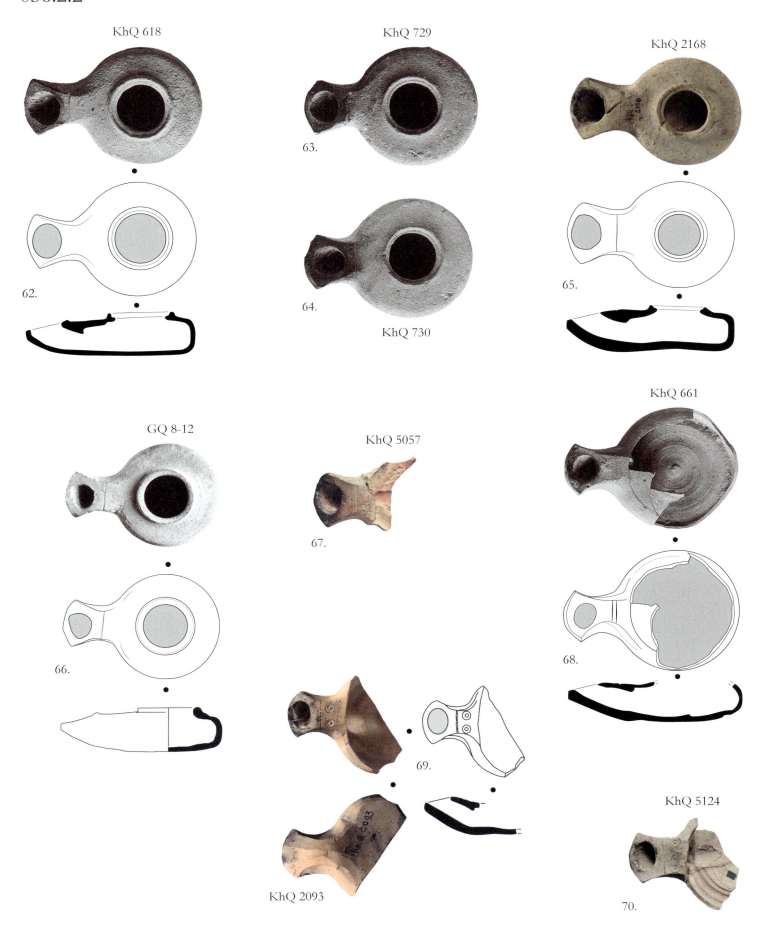

Lamp type 036.2.2

66. GQ 8-12 (?) (Pl. 104).

Erroneously marked as KhQ 1619. This seems to be a fragment surviving from lamp that was found entire. Preserved is nozzle with a part of wall and top; traces of burning at wick hole. Single incision across the nozzle top above the wick hole.
Fabric: gritty but dense, dark reddish brown (5 YR 4/3 "reddish brown") with partial dark grey core and many minute white grits; surface: beige to light grey (7.5 YR 6/2 "pinkish gray"), rather smooth.
Extant L. 4.9, extant W. 4.6 ; W. nozzle 2,9
Found : GQ 8(?).
If our identification is correct, this is what has remained of a lamp published as entire object in: DJD III, fig. 5:6, pl. VII; Qumran 1B, 66;
Cf. Młynarczyk, Lugano, Ill. 6.
For comparable lamp nozzles from En-Gedi, see Vincenz de 2007, pl. 78:23-24.

67. KhQ 5057 (Pl. 104).

Lamp nozzle with part of base; dense burning at wick hole. Single incision across the nozzle top at its mid-length (cf. no. *65:* KhQ 2168 above, also for the nozzle proportions). Fabric: light red (2.5 YR 6/6) with thin grey core in places, voids and few small white grits; surface smooth, light reddish brown (2.5 YR 6/4) on top to light brown underneath (with black spot on base: burning?), smooth, semi-glossy.
Extant L. *ca.* 6.6, extant W. 4.6.
Found: Loc. 15.

68. KhQ 661 (Pl. 104).

Lamp fragment (nozzle with lower part of body); traces of burning at wick hole. Double punctured line across the nozzle top at its mid-lenght (Machaerus group 78).
Fabric: pink (5 YR 7/4) rather hard, dense, with tiny white grits; surface: pink (5 YR 8/3 – 8/4) with large white grits' eruptions, semi-rough in feel to smooth on top. *PG 2* (Michniewicz 2009, 42-45).
L. 9.3, W. 6.8, extant H. 2.0.
Found: Loc. 34, "lower";
Cf. Qumran 1, 304; Qumran 1B, 25.

69. KhQ 2093 (Pl. 104).

Lamp fragment (nozzle and lower body part); dense burning at wick hole. Single punctured line across the nozzle with two circlets above it (Machaerus group 79).
Fabric: pink (5 YR 7/4), rather hard and dense, with tiny white grits; surface: semi-glossy, pink (7.5 YR 8/4) with white grits' eruptions, very smooth.
Extant L. 6.0, extant W. 5.0, H. 1.7.
Found: Loc. 115;
Cf. Qumran 1, 328; Qumran 1B, 50.
One of the samples analyzed by Gunneweg and Balla 2003, 16 and 35-38 (note that one register number has been given twice as two different samples: Qum 194 and Qum 293!).

70. KhQ 5124 (Pl. 104).

Lamp fragment (nozzle and lower body part); wheel-marks inside; faint traces of burning at wick hole. Double grooved line across the nozzle top with two (three?) indistinct circles above it (Machaerus group 79).
Fabric: light beige (10 YR 7/3: very pale brown), very dense; surface: pale beige (10 YR 8/2: white) with white grits' eruptions, very smooth, semi-glossy.
Extant L. 6.0, extant W. 5.0, extant H. 2.3.
Found: Loc. 13, oven.

036.2.

Additionally, three lamp fragments, with their nozzles entirely preserved, definitely show an angular (carinated) body profile, therefore should be classified with Qumran Type 036.2. Lack of the bases, however, prevents one from further assigning them to Subtype 036.2.1 or 036.2.2.

71. KhQ 5097 (Pl. 105).
   Lamp fragment preserving *ca.* one third of the body and entire nozzle; no traces of use. Single incision across the nozzle top, above wick hole.
   Fabric: thin-walled, red (2.5 YR 5/6) with tiny white grits; surface: pink (2.5 YR 6/4 "light reddish brown" to 5 YR 7/4 "pink") to pinkish brown under the nozzle, rather smooth.
   Extant L. 6.1, Diam. (est.) *ca.* 7.0, H. (est.) 2.8; W. nozzle 2,9.
   Found: Loc. 8.

72. KhQ 5066 (Pl. 105).
   Lamp nozzle with small part of body top; dense burning at wick hole. Thin single incision across the nozzle top, at its mid-length.
   Fabric: medium hard, unevenly fired from dark brown to pink (mostly 5 YR 6/3 "light reddish brown"), with some small white and fewer dark grits plus a single large white rock; surface: fired pink (near 7.5 YR 7/4) to dark grey under the nozzle (5 YR 4/2 "dark reddish gray") semi-glossy. *PG 3* (Michniewicz 2009, 46-48).
   Extant L. 4.6, W. nozzle 2,9.
   Found: Loc. 25.

73. KhQ 5064 (Pl. 105).
   Lamp nozzle with fragment of wall and top; dense burning at wick hole. Nozzle very short, with single incision across its top.
   Fabric: very hard and dense, clean, ash grey (7.5 YR 5/0 "gray"); surface: light grey (10 YR 6/1), smooth.
   Extant L. 4.8, extant W. 3.9, W. nozzle 2,7.
   Found: Loc. 37.

035.3.

Shape description:

Represented by four fragmentary objects (pertaining perhaps to three lamps), the type is characterized by wide flat shoulder and rather narrow inner flange around the filling hole. The lamps are similar in profile to those of Subtype 036.2.1, from which they differ by their larger size and the presence of elaborate ring/strap handle (decorated with ribs alternating with grooves), applied onto the shoulder. Of two objects with nozzle, no. *74* (GQ 29-1*) had the nozzle top plain, while the nozzle of no. *77* (Gr 1Q-56) bore a double groove.

Qumran Type 036.3 seems to correspond to type L 4 of Diez Fernandez (dated by him, definitely too early, to the second and third quarters of the 1st century BC) and partly to type L 5 (dated to *ca.* 50 BC – AD 25; cf. Diez Fernandez 1983, 80-82). It matches also Masada type C VIII, described by the authors as "grey ware knife-pared lamps with handle" (Barag and Hershkovitz 1994, 54-55, fig. 13). Indeed, Smith who illustrated an example of the type in question, provided with a handle "in the old Hellenistic style", stated that such lamps were always black and may have even been products of a single workshop (Smith 1966, 14 and fig. 4, centre: grey clay, black slip). However, Qumran Type 036.3, in which only two out of four lamps (specifically, nos. *75:* KhQ 5125 and *77:* Gr 1Q-56*) match this ware description, proves that they were not confined to grey ware.

74. GQ 29-1* (Pl. 105).
    Lamp almost complete; just tip of nozzle missing; nozzle top plain.
    Fabric: *terre rouge*.
    Extant L. 11.3, W. 7.3; H. body 2.8.
    Found: GQ (Survey Cave) 29;
    Cf. Qumran 1B, 71.
    Cf. *RB* 1953, fig. 3:4 and pl. XXII b, 1; DJD III, fig. 5:2 (top view and section), pls. V and VII (phots.); Diez Fernandez 1983, no. 77 (his type 3.4c); Młynarczyk 2013, 113, fig. 3; Młynarczyk, Lugano, Ill. 5.

75. KhQ 5125 (Pl. 105).
    Fragment of lamp body and of handle.
    Fabric: pinkish grey (2.5 YR 5/2: weak red), hard and dense, with many white grits; surface fired pale grey (10 YR 7/2) with remains of matt dark grey slip (10 YR 5/1 to 4/1) on top, sides and partly inside.
    Extant W. 6.3, Diam. (est.) *ca.* 7.2.
    Found : Loc. 46.

76. KhQ 5082 (Pl. 105).
    Fragment of lamp body with handle.
    Fabric: medium hard, very dense and clean, beige (10 YR 7/3 "very pale brown"); surface light pink (between 5 YR 8/4 and 7/3), smooth.
    Extant L. 3.5.
    Found: Loc. 115.

77. Gr 1Q-56* (Pl. 105).
    Two non-joining parts: wall fragment with strap handle (double longitudinal groove, resembling that of Type 036.7, see below), and nozzle with a double groove across the top (Machaerus group 78). By the shape, it could be the same object as *76* (above) for which, however, a different find spot has been indicated.
    Fabric: *terre grise, fine et très cuite*.
    Estimated L. *ca.* 11 cm.
    Found: Gr 1Q.
    Cf. DJD I, fig. 3:1; Magness 2002, fig. 21:1; Młynarczyk, Lugano, Ill. 4.

Plate 105

036.2

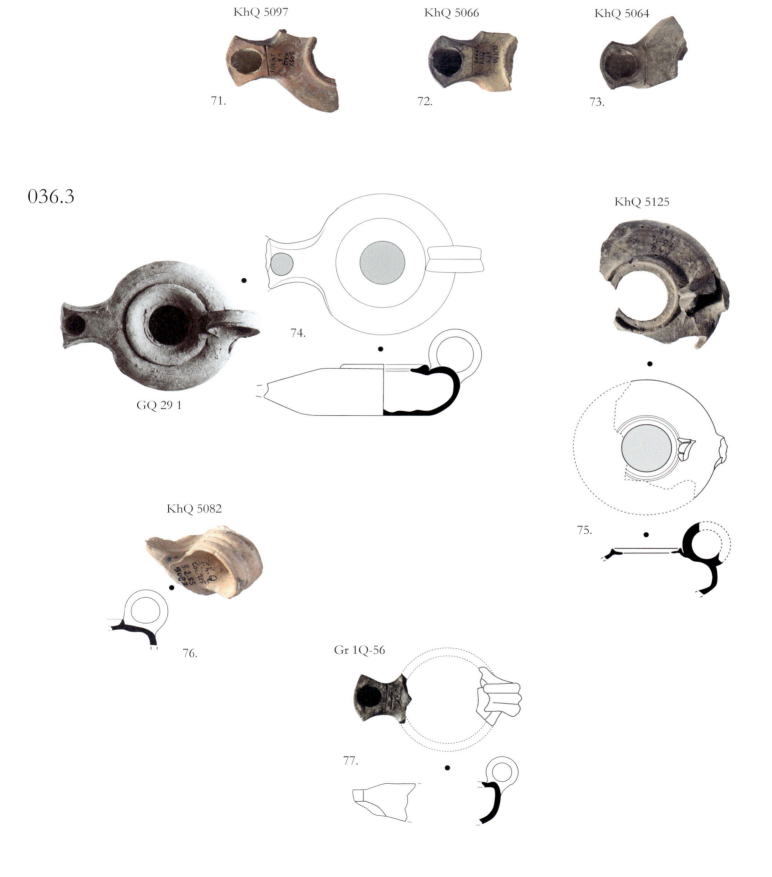

Lamp types 036.2 and 036.3

036.4.

Shape description:

The six objects (four of them lost!) that pertain to this type, have low angular body (like that in 036.2.2) with a narrow ridge around the filling hole; nozzle end is only slightly splayed. Included in Diez Fernandez type L 3.3 (dated by him to *ca.* 20-70 AD: Diez Fernandez 1983, 76-78, specifically, nos. 45, 47, 51) and partly also into L 3.2 (dated to between the late 1st century BC and beyond AD 50: Diez Fernandez 1983, no. 33), this group corresponds to Masada type C VI (Barag and Hershkovitz 1994, 52-53, fig. 11). Most importantly, however, an example of Qumran Type 036.4/5 was found in a sealed context of Cave X/35, in association with two lamps of Qumran Type 045.1 (see below) and with a *pruta* of the First Revolt (Itah, Kan and Ben-Haim 2002, part 1, fig. 11:1 and part 2, 172; the authors obviously made a mistake in dating all the three lamps to the 2nd century AD). The same cave was initially marked as Cave (P)13 by J. Patrich, who discovered there a "Herodian" lamp pertaining to Qumran Type 036.2 (Patrich and Arubas 1989, 43, fig. 3:12, pl. 5C; see also Młynarczyk, Lugano, notes 12 and 47). There can be no doubt that the four lamps found in Cave X/35 = (P)13 are contemporaneous and were deposited there during the First Jewish Revolt.

As far as the Khirbet Qumran contexts are concerned, it is probably meaningful that three lamps, allegedly of the same shape, were found together in Loc. 114. Unfortunately, they have not only been given just one inventory number (KhQ 2579 a-b-c, our cat. nos. *78 a-b-c*), but also have been lost since then.

78. KhQ 2579* (a-b-c) (Pl. 106).
    In this group, also at least two photographed lamps out of three complete lamps registered as KhQ 2579 (a-b-c) with common description ("base convexe, terre rouge"): only one illustrated in the register book (cf. Donceel ms, pl. V), two of them photographed (cf Donceel ms, pl. XI). Gunneweg and Balla 2003, 10 and pl. 3, Q 199, mention lamp KhQ 2579 from Loc. 114 as pertaining to Chemical Group I, that is, the Qumran production.
    Dimensions, according to the register book (the same for all the three lamps?), are as follows: L. 9.2, Diam. 7.6.
    Found: Loc. 114;
    Cf. Qumran 1, 328; Qumran 1B, 50: "deposit locus 114 (…) three Herodian lamps".
    Cf. *RB* 1956, 558-559, fig. 4:14 (*période II*) and pp. 562-563; Lapp 1961, Type 82.1:C (dated to AD 50-68).

79. KhQ 1184* (Pl. 106).
    Complete lamp, with traces of burning at nozzle(?). Top lacks any flange and the nozzle is only slightly splayed; body profile, however, is rather rounded (to judge by the drawing).
    Fabric: *terre chamois*.
    L. 8.8; Diam. body 6.4; H. 2.2.
    Found: Loc. 58 NW, northwest corner;
    Cf. Qumran 1, 311; Qumran 1B, 33.
    Cf. Donceel ms, pl. III and X.

80. GQ 9-1 (Pl. 106).
    Several fragments of thin-walled lamp preserving nearly full profile; surface severely mutilated; dense burning at nozzle; nozzle top apparently plain(?). Small and low, by its profile the lamp might have also been classified with 036.2.1. However, the sides of rather slim nozzle are only slightly concave, giving the lamp a look different from that of the "standard" knife-pared lamps.
    Fabric: hard, light red (2.5 YR 6/8) with light grey core at the bottom and with abundant tiny white grits; surface: light reddish brown (2.5 YR 6/4), with occasional white grits' eruptions, smooth.
    L. 7.9, Diam. (est.) 5.2, H. (est.) 2.6.
    Found: GQ 9
    (Survey Cave 9, cf. Qumran 1B, 69).
    Cf. *RB* 1953, fig. 4:5 (described as *lampe moulée en terre cuite, du type "hérodien"*);
    DJD III, fig. 5:5 and pl. VII; Młynarczyk, Lugano, Ill. 7.

Plate 106

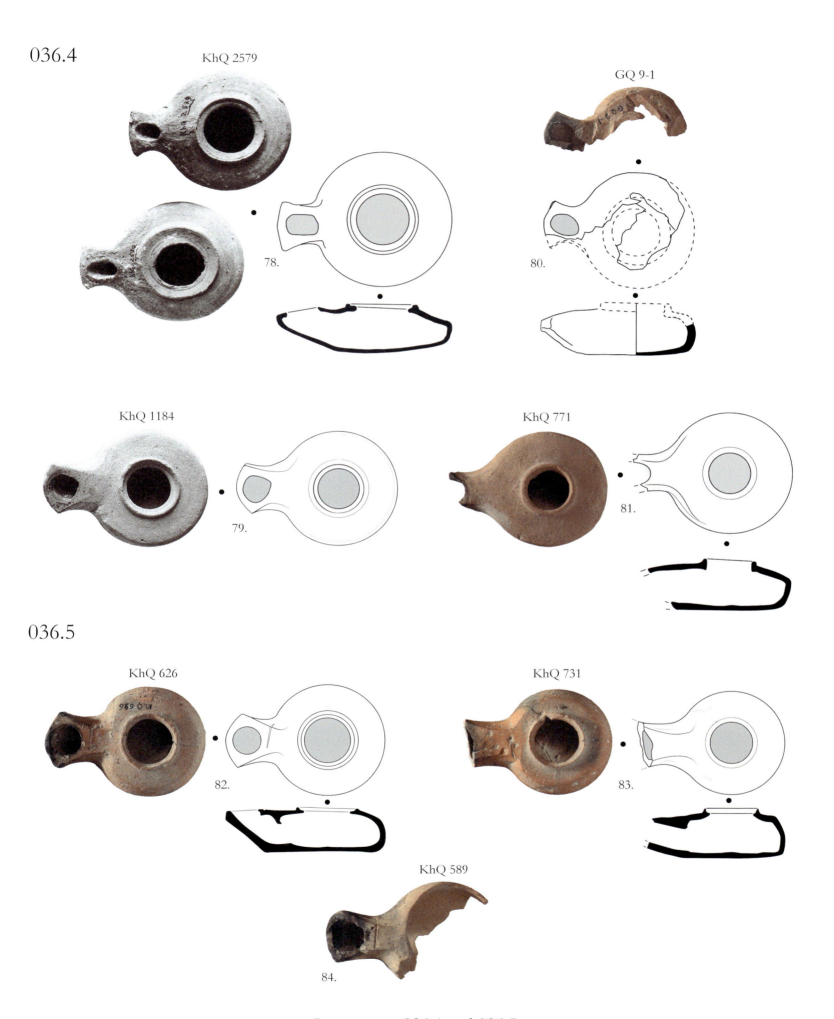

Lamp types 036.4 and 036.5

81. KhQ 771 (Pl. 106).
   Lamp lacking tip of nozzle. Some fingerprints on the shoulder; traces of burning at wick hole.
   Fabric: medium-hard, pink (5 YR 7/4), with some circular voids and occasional dark red grits;
   surface pink (5 YR 8/3 – 8/4), smooth (traces of cloth on upper part), of slightly powdery feel.
   Extant L. 8.1, Diam. 6.3, H. 2.7.
   Found: Loc 36, "lower, on the wall";
Cf. Qumran 1, 304; Qumran 1B, 25-26.
Cf. Młynarczyk 2013, 114, fig. 3; corresponding to Masada group C VI (e.g., no. 74).

036.5.

Shape description:

The type is represented by three Qumran objects, with the wall profile tapering upwards from a broad, flat base. The filling hole is surrounded by a ridge with a vestigial inner flange, similar to that present in Qumran 036.2. The nozzle may be slightly tilted either up or down towards the wick hole. It seems that a lamp from the Jerusalem International Convention Center (Berlin 2005, 48, fig. 17:14) may have belonged to this type; however, its profile has not been provided. A fragmentary grey-ware Masada lamp (its top not preserved) seems to have represented the same shape (Barag and Hershkovitz 1994, 53, fig. 12:80). It is interesting to note that at Tel Dor this variety is represented by just one out of eight "Herodian" lamps in the assemblage published by Rosenthal-Heginbottom (1995, fig. 5.21, no. 6). This perhaps suggests that this lamp variety may have been characteristic of a region more distant from the coastal Dor, presumably of the Judean workshops.

82. KhQ 626 (Pl. 106).
   Complete lamp; dense traces of burning; nozzle with double
   (narrowly spaced) groove across top, above wick hole.
   Fabric: very hard and dense, grey (2.5 YR 6/0) banded light red, with some
   white and dark grits; surface light red (10 R 6/6) where polished, paler red (10
   R 6/4) where not polished, with some sizeable white grits' eruptions.
   L. 8.0, H. 2.5; W. nozzle 2,9.
   Found: Loc. 31, "upper";
Cf. Qumran 1B, 24.
Cf. Młynarczyk 2013, 114, fig. 3.

83. KhQ 731 (Pl. 106).
   Lamp recomposed of two parts; nozzle lacking end and bearing traces of
   burning. Nozzle top undecorated, with two accidental incisions.
   Fabric: dense, light red with grey core and some minute white grits; surface light red (10
   R 6/6) where polished, pale red (10 R 6/4) where more rough, with some sizeable white
   grits' eruptions. Apparently the same workshop as that of *82* (KhQ 626) above.
   Extant L. 7.6, H. 2.5.
   Found: Loc. 41, on floor;
Cf. Qumran 1, 306; Qumran 1B, 27.

84. KhQ 589 (Pl. 106).
   Two joining fragments of lamp preserve full profile, parts of body are missing;
   dense burning at wick hole. Single groove across the nozzle top.
   Fabric: light red (2.5 YR 6/8), medium-hard, with tiny voids and rather abundant very small white
   grits; surface: unevenly fired from pink (5 YR 7/4) to pale yellow (7.5 YR 8/4 "pink"), smooth.
   L. 9.4, Diam. estimated 6,0, H. 2.6, W. nozzle 2,9
   Found: Loc. 33 "upper";
Cf. Qumran 1, 393; Qumran 1B, 24-25.

036.6.

Shape description:

In this type, represented by five objects from Qumran, the body's vertical wall ends in a short ridge or protruding rim around the lamp top. The top part can be either flattened (as in no. *85:* AF 161, the only complete example of the type, which is now lost) or convex (as in no. *89:* KhQ 5127); the base is not defined. The nozzle end develops only slight flukes; wherever its decoration is preserved, it can be classified with Machaerus group 79 (for an entire lamp of this type from Machaerus, see Loffreda 1996, fig. 50:121 and phot. 51).This type corresponds to a couple of lamps included in Masada group C V ("knife-pared lamps, body with straight sides") where they are dated to the time of the First Revolt (Barag and Hershkovitz 1994, 51-52, fig. 10, nos. 67-68).

85. AF 161* (Pl. 107).

   Complete lamp, with nozzle of Machaerus group 79 (punctured line across top with two dotted circlets above).
   Fabric: *terre rouge*.
   L. 9.0, Diam. 6.3, H. 2.7.
   Found: Loc. 16, east;
   Cf. *RB* 66 (1959), fig. 2:3, *période II* (mistakenly described as *lampe moulée*!); Qumran 1, 358 (again mentioned as *lampe moulée*!); Qumran 1B, 85.
   Cf. Diez Fernandez 1983, no. 74; Donceel ms, pl. V and VII; Młynarczyk 2013, 114, fig. 3. Lamp with similar nozzle decoration comes from Jerusalem Jewish Quarter (Rosenthal-Heginbottom 2003, pl. 6.9, of different fabric).

86. KhQ 5062 (Pl. 107).

   Fragmentary nozzle of lamp; traces of dense burning at wick hole. Punctured double line across the nozzle top with two dotted circlets above it (Machaerus group 79); an air-hole at the edge of the flat body top ("discus").
   Fabric: hand, ash-grey banded pink, with some tiny white grits (and some tiny voids?); surface: pale beige (near 10 YR 8/4 "very pale brown"), with occasional fine white grits' eruptions, very smooth.
   Extant L.4.3, W. nozzle 2.3.
   Found: Loc. 35 "lower".

87. KhQ 3097.

   Fragment of lamp nozzle; traces of dense burning at wick hole. Depression of the "discus" is clearly visible. Single incision across the nozzle with two dotted circlets above it (Machaerus group 79).
   Fabric: medium-soft, pink (2.5 YR 6/6: light red) with some tiny white grits (including eruptions to the surface) and fewer black ones; surface: slightly paler than break.
   Extant L. 3.8.
   Found: Loc. 41.

88. KhQ 5096.

   Mutilated nozzle of lamp with part of body; no traces of burning preserved. Depression of the "discus" is clearly visible; blurred decoration of the nozzle seems to have consisted of a double punctured line across the nozzle above an incised one.
   Fabric: medium-hard light red (2.5 YR 6/6) with pale grey core and lots of fine white grits; surface pale red, weathered, with poor remains of smooth beige slip.
   Extant L. 3.0.
   Found: Loc. 75 (?).

89. KhQ 5127 (Pl. 107).

   Fragmentary body of lamp. Flattened undefined base, vertical wall (slightly tapering upwards and ending in a ridge); lamp top raises in a convex line towards (unpreserved) filling hole.
   Fabric: dark brown (10 YR 4/2 "dark greyish brown") with some tiny voids(?) and tiny white grits; surface: grey (10 YR 6/1), rather smooth, with occasional black particles. Extant L. 5.2; H. 1,8; Diam. (est.) 5.8.
   Found: Trench A, Layer 2.

Lamp fragments of Qumran Type 036

A large number of lamp fragments, some of which would appear to have been broken after they were excavated, may present just one of the set of diagnostic features as established by us for the above-distinguished types. Even if some of them can be assigned to individual types with a fairly high degree of probability, we consider it more prudent to present these fragments simply as three morphological groups: 1) nozzles, 2) body top/wall fragments, 3) base/wall fragments.

The nozzles of Type 036

The group consists of 50 nozzles pertaining to lamps the body profile of which is not known. Therefore, they have been classified after their decoration, that is, following the division applied to the lamps from Machaerus (Loffreda 1996, 108-114).

Plain nozzles attributed to Type 036.1 (Machaerus groups 75 and 76, Diez Fernandez types L 3.1 and L 3.2)

It seems that 19 nozzles devoid of any kind of ornamentation or marks should be attributed to Qumran Type 036.1. However, even if this may be basically true, one should bear in mind that a nozzle, which was an element shaped by hand and added to the wheel-thrown body of the lamp, cannot be considered as a leading typological feature. Therefore, for the sake of methodological correctness, the author decided to detach the undecorated nozzles from their presumed typological place, thus refraining from attempt to establish any sound connection between the nozzle ornamentation and the shape of the lamp body.

Confer undecorated spatulate nozzles from Jerusalem, Jewish Quarter, found in a stratum dated to between *ca.* 50 and 70 AD, in which they might have been residual (Rosenthal-Heginbottom 2003, 201, 219, pls 6.9.:43 and 6.10:21, made of "reddish yellow clay, grey core, white and black grits" and of "light red clay, white grits"); two nozzles ("of well-levigated pink clay") from Jerusalem Convention Center (Hershkovitz 2005, 290-291, fig. 11:1-2) and a nozzle ("clay buff") from the same area (Rosenthal-Heginbottom 2005, 240, no. 1). They are present on the sites around the Dead Sea, e.g. in En-Gedi (Vincenz de 2007, pl. 68:3, fabric "red with many small white inclusions"; pl. 68:4, fabric "yellowish red with small white inclusions", and pl. 78:22, fabric "brown with thick core and many white inclusions"), in Callirrhoe (Clamer 1997, pl. 6:12, pl. 15:12-17). In the coastal gentile towns they are known from Caesarea (Sussman 2008, 220 and 287, no. 23a, "black ware") and Dor/Dora (Adan-Bayewitz *et al.* 2008, fig. 2:3-4). As far as the northern sites are concerned, at Nabratein synagogue (where only lamp nozzles were found), the majority represents the group of lamps with undecorated nozzles (Lapp 2009, 278-279, Plate A: nos. 1-2, 4-5, 8, 11, 13-16). A single fragment comes from one of the Jewish tombs at Huqoq in eastern Galilee, (Kahane 1961, 135-136, fig. 3:18), and more examples are known from Scythopolis and Sepphoris as well as from Jewish settlements of Gamala and Iotapata (Adan-Bayewitz *et al.* 2008, fig. 2, nos. 7-8 and 11 from Scythopolis, and nos. 14-15 and 17-18 from Sepphoris; fig. 3, nos.1-3 from Gamala and nos. 8-9 from Iotapata).

90. KhQ 5075.
    Nozzle short and wide, its top slightly convex. Faint traces of burning at wick hole.
    Fabric: light red (2.5 YR 6/6), very dense, with some tiny white grits; surface: pale red to pink, smooth, semi-glossy.
    Extant L. 4.2; extant W. 4.9 ; W. nozzle 3,3.
    Found : Trench A, Layer 3.

91. AF 308 (Pl. 107).
    Nozzle with strongly concave sides and flat top. Traces of burning at wick hole.
    Fabric: light red (2.5 YR 6/6), medium-soft, with rare minute white and black grits; surface: yellowish red (near 5 YR 7/6 "reddish yellow"), very smooth (where not weathered).
    Extant L. 4.9; H. 2.3; W. nozzle 3,8.
    Found: Loc. 19.

92. AF 303 (Pl. 107).

   Nozzle with strongly concave sides and flattened top; dense burning at wick hole. Fabric: light red (2.5 YR 6/6), rather soft; surface: smooth, with remains of pale yellow slip (10 YR 8/4 "very pale brown").
   Extant L. 2.8; W. nozzle 3,2
   Found: Loc. 4.

93. AF 302 (Pl. 107).

   Short and broad nozzle with flattened top; traces of burning at wick hole.
   Fabric: medium soft, light red (2.5 YR 6/6) with white and red grits; surface: yellowish pink, with small white and red eruptions, very smooth.
   Extant L. 3.8; W. nozzle 3,4.
   Found: Loc. 4.

94. AF 309 (Pl. 107).

   Short nozzle with narrow flat top; traces of burning at wick hole. Fabric: light red (near 2.5 YR 6/6), medium soft, with many tiny to small white grits and rare red ones; surface reddish yellow (7.5 YR 8/6), with many small red and white (up to very large) eruptions, yet very smooth. The same fabric/workshop as no. 93 (AF 302).
   Extant L. 3.5.
   Found: Loc. 4.

95. Gr 7Q-10 *(17.2.55)* (Pl. 107).

   Short nozzle with flat top; dense burning on nozzle.
   Fabric: light red (2.5 YR 6/6), medium hard, with small to medium-size white grits; surface smooth, pale orange (7.5 YR 7/6 "reddish yellow") with some large white eruptions; dense traces of burning on nozzle. Fabric: as nos. *93-94* (AF 302 and 309).
   Extant L. 3.2; W. nozzle 3,0.
   Found: Cave 7Q.
  Cf. Młynarczyk, Lugano,

96. KhQ 5069 (Pl. 107).

   Nozzle with strongly concave sides and narrow flat top; traces of burning at wick hole.
   Fabric: light red (2.5 YR 6/6), hard and dense, with some minute white grits; surface smooth, beige-pink to pink (near 5 YR 7/6 reddish yellow).
   Extant L.3.4; W. nozzle 3,2
   Found: Loc. 88.

97. KhQ 5076 (Pl. 107).

   Rather long nozzle with flat top; faint traces of burning at wick hole.
   Fabric: light red (2.5 YR 6/6), medium hard, with small white grits; surface pink (between 2.5 YR 6/6 "light red" and 5 YR 7/4 "pink"), with medium to large-sized white eruptions, smooth.
   Extant L. 5.0, H. *ca.* 2.8 ; W. nozzle 2,8.
   Found: Trench A, Layer 4.

98. KhQ 5095 (Pl. 107).

   Rather long nozzle with flat top; dense burning at wick hole.
   Fabric: dense light red (2.5 YR 6/6), with some minute white grits; surface smooth, semi-glossy, pink (near 5 YR 7/6 "reddish yellow").
   Extant L. 4.2.; W. nozzle 2,7.
   Found: Loc. 13, oven.

99. KhQ 5074 (Pl. 107).

   Rather long nozzle with wide flat top; traces of burning at wick hole.
   Fabric: dark grayish brown (10 YR 4/2) banded pink, very hard and dense, with some minute white grits; surface: beige-pink (7.5 YR 6/4 "light brown") smooth, semi-glossy.
   Extant L. 3.4; W. nozzle 4,1.
   Found: Trench A, Layer 3.

100. KhQ 5046 (Pl. 107).
   Nozzle with flattened top; traces of burning at wick hole.
   Fabric: yellowish pink (7.5 YR 8/6 "reddish yellow"), medium soft, rather
   porous, with occasional tiny white grits and some "black" ones; surface: pinkish
   beige (7.5 YR 7/4 "pink") medium smooth, partly weathered.
   Extant L. 3.0.; W. nozzle 2,9.
   Found: Loc. 88.

101. KhQ 5045 (Pl. 107).
   Nozzle with un-symmetrically splayed flukes and wide flat top; dense burning at wick hole.
   Fabric: pale yellow (5 Y 8/3), medium hard, rather porous (circular voids), occasional small
   black grits and minute white ones; surface: pale yellow (5Y 7/3), smooth, semi-glossy.
   Extant L. 3.2; W. nozzle 3,2.
   Found: Loc. 4.
   Cf. Młynarczyk 2013, fig. 4.

102. KhQ 5063 (Pl. 107).
   Nozzle with strongly splayed end and flat top; traces of burning at wick hole. Fabric:
   hard and dense, dark grey (7.5 YR 3/0 "very dark gray"), with some minute white
   grits; surface: greyish brown (7.5 YR 6/2 "pinkish gray"), smooth, semi-glossy.
   Extant L. 3.1; W. nozzle 4,5.
   Found: to the east of Loc. 45/78.

103. KhQ 5119 (Pl. 107).
   Short nozzle with broad flat top; some traces of burning at wick hole.
   Fabric: hard, dense and clean, greyish brown (5 YR 3/1 "very dark gray"); surface smooth, semi-glossy.
   Extant L. 4.2; extant W. 4.6; W. nozzle 3,0.
   Found: Loc. 37.

104. KhQ 5053 (Pl. 107).
   Nozzle with rather broad flat top; no traces of burning.
   Fabric: hard, light reddish brown (5 YR 5/4 "reddish brown"), with few tiny white grits and
   occasional deep circular voids; surface: light brown (5 YR 6/2 "pinkish gray"), smooth, semi-glossy.
   Extant L. 2.8; W. nozzle 3,0.
   Found: Loc. 30.

105. KhQ 5115 (Pl. 107).
   Nozzle with ill-developed flukes and flattened top; dense burning at wick hole.
   Fabric: dark grayish brown (5 YR 4/2 "dark reddish gray"), dense, with occasional tiny white
   grits; surface: dark grayish brown (the same colour as the break) smooth, semi-glossy.
   Extant L. 3.5; W. nozzle 2,4.
   Found: *inconnue*.

106. AF 301.
   Middle fragment of nozzle with flat top, missing tip; some traces of burning.
   Fabric: hard, light red (2.5 YR 6/6), with many small white grits and occasional tiny
   circular voids; surface pinkish yellow (near 5 YR 8/4 "pink"), very smooth.
   Extant L. 3.4.
   Found: Loc. 4.

107. KhQ 5080.
   Middle fragment of lamp nozzle with broad flat top, missing tip; some traces of burning.
   Fabric: medium hard grayish beige (10 YR 5/3 "brown") with occasional
   minute white grits and some oblong voids; surface fired light beige (10 YR 8/2
   "white") to pale pink (5 YR 8/2 "pink"), with some gloss on top.
   Extant L. 3.1.
   Found: Trench S.

108. KhQ 4529.
   About one half of lamp nozzle, rather elongated, with slight flukes
   only. Faint traces of burning; fingerprints underneath.
   Fabric: very hard and dense, light reddish brown (5 YR 5/4), with an
   oblong large white grit; surface very smooth, beige to pink.
   Extant L. 3.5.
   Found: Trench A, Layer 1.

Plate 107

036.6

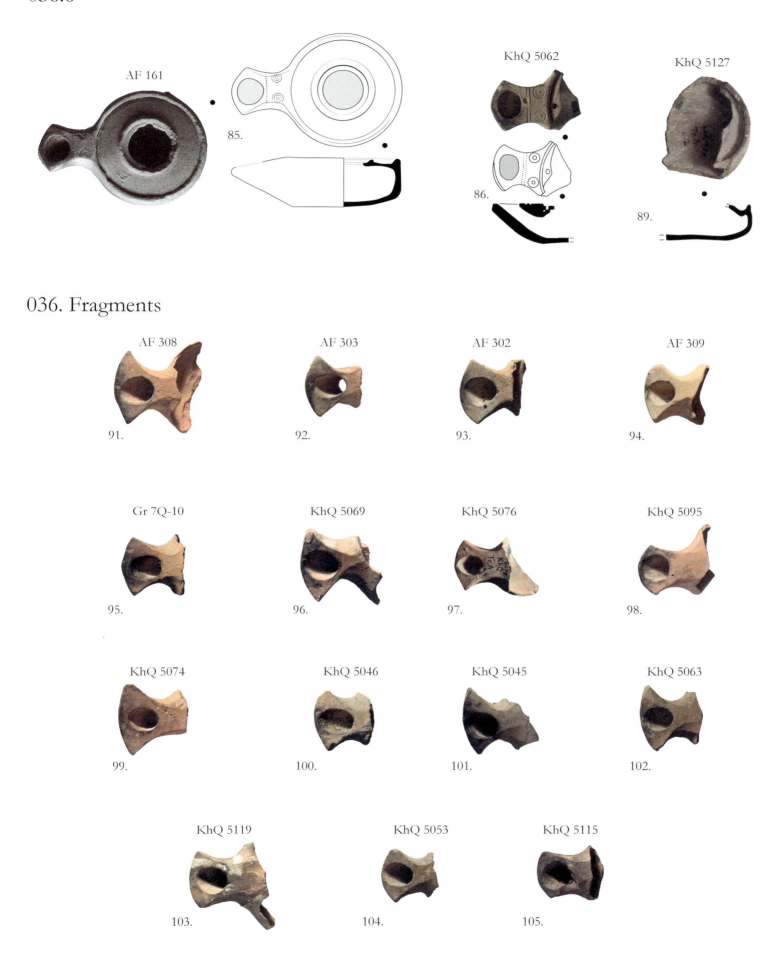

036. Fragments

Lamp types 036.6 and 036 (fragments)

Nozzles that can be attributed to any "Herodian" lamp variant between 036.2 and 036.6

Machaerus group 77, with a single incised line across top of the nozzle, is represented by ten objects. In Diez Fernandez' typology, this kind of the nozzle mark occurs with his types L 3.3 and L.3.4. At least five such nozzles were found in Callirrhoe (Clamer 1997, pl. 6:11 and pl. 15:7, pl. 15:9-11). Such lamps are absent from the Nabratein synagogue (Lapp 2009, 279, Pl. A), but relevant finds are known from Dor/Dora, Scythopolis, Sepphoris and Iotapata (Adan-Bayewitz *et al.* 2008, fig. 2, no. 5 from Dor, nos. 9 and 12 from Scythopolis, no. 13 from Sepphoris; fig. 3, no. 10 from Iotapata).

109. KhQ 5081 (Pl. 108).
   Lamp nozzle with part of convex base and rather angular wall (presumably Subtype 036.2.1); dense traces of burning at wick hole. Thick-walled body.
   Fabric: pink (5 YR 7/4), hard, with tiny voids and few white grits; surface: pale beige (10 YR 8/2 "white"), with white grits' eruptions, thickly wet-smoothed, semi-glossy.
   Extant L. 5.8, extant W. 5.3; W. nozzle 3,6.
   Found: Trench *voie*.

110. KhQ 5044 (Pl. 108).
   Lamp nozzle with slight traces of burning.
   Fabric: hard, fired unevenly from brown to dark grey, with some tiny white grits; surface: light brown to beige (near 7.5 YR 7/2 "pinkish gray"), smooth.
   Extant L. *ca.* 3.7; W. nozzle 3,0.
   Found: Loc. 32.

111. KhQ 5079.
   Lamp nozzle with very dense burning traces around wick hole.
   Fabric: gritty medium-hard, red (2.5 YR 5/6) with many white grits; surface semi-smooth, fired to very pale brown (10 YR 8/3) with pale red part underneath.
   Extant L. *ca.* 3.9; W. nozzle 3,0.
   Found: Trench W.

112. KhQ 5071 (Pl. 108).
   Lamp nozzle with traces of burning at wick hole.
   Fabric: medium-hard light red (2.5 YR 6/6) with occasional tiny white grits; surface: light orange-red (near 5 YR 7/6) smooth, semi-glossy.
   Extant L. *ca.* 4.6; W. nozzle 3,2.
   Found: Loc. 88 ("9.4.53")

113. KhQ 5047 (Pl. 108).
   Lamp nozzle with dense burning traces.
   Fabric: hard, dark brownish grey (5 YR 3/2 "dark reddish brown") with tiny white grits; surface: from dark reddish brown on top to brown and light brown underneath, smooth.
   Extant L. *ca.* 3.8; W. nozzle 3,0.
   Found: Loc. 38.

114. KhQ 5060 (Pl. 108).
   Lamp nozzle with traces of burning all over.
   Fabric: hard, red (2.5 YR 5/6), with thin grey core and minute white grits (plus some tiny voids?); surface: reddish brown (2.5 YR 5/4), smooth, semi-glossy.
   Extant L. 3.4; W. nozzle 2,9
   Found: Loc. 19.

115. KhQ 5043.
   Lamp nozzle with faint traces of burning at wick hole.
   Fabric: hard, light reddish brown (5 YR 5/4 "reddish brown"), with some tiny white grits; surface: pink to pinkish brown and beige, smooth. The same "hand" as that of no. *114* (KhQ 5060).
   Extant L. *ca.* 3.6; W. nozzle 2,9.
   Found: Loc. 38.

116. KhQ 5052 (Pl. 108).
   Lamp nozzle with dense burning all over.
   Fabric: hard, dark grey (5 YR 4/1), with minute white grits; surface: pale brown (10 YR 6/3), smooth. Apparently the same "hand" as that of nos. *114-115* (KhQ 5060 and KhQ 5043).
   Extant L. 3.9; W. nozzle 2,9.
   Found: Loc. 37.

117. KhQ 5051 (Pl. 108).
   Lamp nozzle with a small part of flattened base; traces of burning at wick hole. Transverse incision at mid-length of the nozzle.
   Fabric: pink (5 YR 7/3), medium hard, dense, with tiny white grits; surface smooth pale beige (10 YR 8/3) with white grits' eruptions.
   Extant L. 5.3; extant W. 4.7; W. nozzle 2,8.
   Found : Loc. 31.

118. KhQ 5056 (Pl. 108).
   Lamp nozzle with traces of burning. Transverse incision at mid-length of the nozzle.
   Fabric: medium hard orange-red (5 YR 6/6 "reddish yellow"), with tiny black grits (and occasional white ones?); surface: light reddish brown (near 5 YR 6/4), smooth.
   Extant L. 4.8; extant W. 4.4; W. nozzle 3,0.
   Found: Loc. 13.

Machaerus group 78, with a double line across the nozzle top, either incised or punctured, is represented by eight objects; like Machaerus group 77, they are included in Diez Fernandez type L 3.3 and L 3.4.

a) for two incised lines across the nozzle top, see for instance examples: from Cave 1 at Murabba'at (*RB* 1953b, fig. 4:12); Diez Fernandez type L 3.4a (1983, no. 55); from Masada (Barag and Hershkovitz 1994, lamps nos. 41-43 and 51-55 pertaining to Qumran Types 036.2.1-2, 036.4, 036.5); from Callirrhoe (Clamer 1997, pl. 15:8); from En-Gedi (Vincenz de 2007, pl. 50:1-2); from Caesarea (Sussman 2008, 220 and 287, nos. 23c-d); from Sepphoris, Gamala and Iotapata (Adan-Bayewitz *et al.* 2008, fig. 2, no. 16 from Sepphoris, fig. 3, no. 6 from Gamala and no. 11 from Iotapata).

119. KhQ 5078 (Pl. 108).
   Lamp nozzle with dense burning traces. Double (widely spaced) groove deeply incised across the nozzle top.
   Fabric: hard red (2.5 YR 5/6) with white grits (including sizeable ones); surface: pink (between 5 YR 7/4 "pink" and 7/6 "reddish yellow"), smooth, semi-glossy.
   Extant L. 3.8; W. nozzle 2.9.
   Found: Trench E.

120. KhQ 5072 (Pl. 108).
   Lamp nozzle with dense burning traces. Double (widely spaced) groove deeply incised across the nozzle top.
   Fabric: dark grey (5 YR 4/2 "dark reddish gray") with some tiny white grits; surface: beige (10 YR 7/2 "light gray"), smooth, semi-glossy.
   Extant L. 3.4; W. nozzle 2.5.
   Found: Loc. 110.

121. KhQ 5067 (Pl. 108).
   Lamp nozzle with traces of burning. Double (widely spaced)
   groove deeply incised across the nozzle top.
   Fabric: pale brown (7.5 YR 8/4 "pink") with many fine white grits and fine voids;
   surface: pale beige (darker than 7.5 YR 8/2 "pinkish white"), smooth.
   Extant L. 3.6, W. nozzle 2.7.
   Found: Loc. 78.

122. KhQ 5050 (Pl. 108).
   Lamp nozzle with faint traces of burning. Double (widely spaced) groove incised across
   the nozzle top. This element is particularly interesting as it seems that the potter initially
   intended to make punctured lines but then he decided to change them into continuous
   incisions: apparently, the nozzle ornamentation was not that meaningless.
   Fabric: medium soft gritty light red (2.5 YR 6/6) with lots of white grits and some
   black ones(?); surface: smooth, with remains of pale beige self-slip(?)
   Extant L. 3.3, W. nozzle 2.7.
   Found: Loc. 38;
   Cf. Młynarczyk 2013, fig. 4.

123. KhQ 5070 (Pl. 108).
   Lamp nozzle with a small part of bottom; traces of piercing the wick hole
   against pronounced wheel-marks on floor; dense burning at wick hole. Double
   groove (rather narrowly-spaced) incised across the nozzle top.
   Fabric: pink (7.5 YR 7/4) with white grits, surface smooth to semi-
   glossy, fired to pink (7.5 YR 8/4), with whitish and orange spots.
   Extant L. 5.3; W. nozzle 2,9.
   Found: Loc. 95.

124. KhQ 5055 (Pl. 108).
   Lamp nozzle, short and large, with very large wick hole bearing traces of dense burning.
   Double narrowly spaced groove, delicately incised across the nozzle top.
   Fabric: very dark grey (5 YR 3/2 "dark reddish brown") with lots of tiny white grits,
   surface: fired from very dark grey ("black") on top to light brown underneath.
   Extant L. 3.9, W. nozzle 3.0.
   Found: Loc. 12.

b) for two punctured lines; see, for instance, two nozzles from the Jerusalem Convention Center excavations (Hershkovitz 2005, 290-291, fig. 11:3-4); a single example from the Nabratein synagogue (Lapp 2009, 278-279, Pl. A: no. 10) and another one from Iotapata (Adan-Bayewitz *et al.* 2008, fig. 3, no. 12).

125. KhQ 5042 (Pl. 108).
   Lamp nozzle without traces of use. Double line (rather narrowly
   spaced) of fine punctures across the nozzle top.
   Fabric: hard pink (5 YR 7/6 "reddish yellow") with many tiny white grits; surface
   pink (7.5 YR 8/4) with occasional white eruptions, smooth, semi-glossy. Fabric
   and finishing seem to be the same as with no. *123* (KhQ 5070) above.
   Extant L. 4.5, W. nozzle 2.7.
   Found: Loc. 16;
   Cf. Młynarczyk 2013, fig. 4.

126. KhQ 5098 (Pl. 108).
   Lamp nozzle with part of flattened base; traces of burning. Double line
   (widely spaced) of fine punctures across the nozzle top.
   Fabric: pink (5 YR 7/4), rather hard and dense, with tiny white grits and some big irregular
   black ones (and voids?); surface pink (5 YR 8/4) with white grits' eruptions, smooth.
   Extant L. 5.8, W. of nozzle 2.3.
   Found: Loc. 13, oven.

Machaerus group 79 that is, the nozzles bearing combinations of punctured lines and stamped dotted circlets, is represented by ten objects, seven of which are in the reduced-firing ware (grey to dark grey fabric with black slip). This group would correspond to Diez Fernandez' types L 3.4b, L 3.4c and L 5, of which L 3.4b and L 3.4c have been dated by him to between *ca.* 40/50 and 70/75 AD (and later), while type L 5, with much the same decorative elements of the nozzles, has been assigned a date between 50 BC(!) and AD 20 (Diez Fernandez 1983, 105). More reliably, the find contexts of comparable nozzles in Jerusalem Jewish Quarter have been dated to AD 1-30 and AD 50-70 (Rosenthal-Heginbottom 2003, 200-219, pl. 6.8:5 and pl. 6.9:44; see also *ibidem*, 205, pl. 6.12:18; additionally, Geva and Hershkovitz 2006, pl. 4.13:20). Three lamp nozzles from the same excavations, all of them in one fabric ("light brownish grey clay and dark grey slip, white and grey grits, some large white") display a rather complex combination of circlets and lines, not represented at Qumran (Rosenthal-Heginbottom 2003, 205, pl. 6.12:15-17).

Besides Jerusalem, the lamp nozzles paralleling those from Qumran have also been found, among others, in En-Gedi (Vincenz de 2007, pl. 50:4), in Callirrhoe close to Machaerus (Clamer 1997, pl. 15:1-6), in Beth Shean-Scythopolis (Hadad 2002, no. 9 and Adan-Bayewitz *et al.* 2008, fig. 2, no. 10), Caesarea (Sussman 2008, 220 and 287, nos. 23e-f), Dor (Rosenthal-Heginbottom 1995, fig. 5.21, no. 8 and Adan-Bayewitz *et al.* 2008, fig. 2:6, the latter made in the Jerusalem area), Nabratein (Lapp 2009, 278-279, pl. A, nos. 3, 9 and 12), the settlement site of Shaar ha-Amakim in western Lower Galilee (several nozzles, not published, at least two of them apparently of local manufacture) as well as in Gamala (Adan-Bayewitz *et al.* 2008, fig. 3, no. 7).

127. KhQ 66 (Pl. 108).

> Complete nozzle and entire bottom with convex base, recomposed of two parts; wheel marks on bottom with a trace of opening the wick hole across them; traces of dense burning around wick hole. Decoration: two dotted circlets above a punctured line.
> Fabric: medium hard light red (near 2.5 YR 6/6) with pale grey core at base; some tiny white and "black" grits, fine oblong voids; surface: pink (7.5 YR 8/4), smooth, semi-glossy.
> L. 9.5, extant H. 2,0. W. nozzle 2.6.
> Found: Loc. 4, "near the north door" (together with nos. *128:* KhQ 67 and *156:* KhQ 68);
> Cf. Qumran 1, 293; Qumran 1B, 13.
> Parallels: from Jerusalem: Rosenthal-Heginbottom 2003, 248-249, pl. 6.9:44 ("pinkish-white") and 254-255, pl. 6.12:18 ("light red"); from En-Gedi: de Vincenz 2007, pl. 50:5 ("7.5 YR 8/4 to 7/4 pink"); from Caesarea: Sussman 2008, 220 and 287, no. 23e ("pink ware").

128. KhQ 67* (Pl. 108).

> Complete nozzle and fragment of body recomposed of nine parts; decorated like no. *127* (KhQ 66).
> Fabric: (after Donceel, ms: *terre fine mais assez tendre, de couleur rouge dans la masse, orange en surface, assez lisse en surface (engobe?), avec quelques particules blanches et noires, parfois grandes*): red, fine, rather soft, with some white and black grits up to large; surface rather smooth (self-slip?), orange-coloured.
> L.max. 9.0, H.max. 2.5.
> Found: Loc. 4, together with no. *127:* KhQ 66 and no. *156:* KhQ 68;
> Cf. Qumran 1, 293; Qumran 1B, 13.
> Cf. Donceel ms, pl. VII.
> Similar lamp nozzles come from Jerusalem Jewish Quarter (Rosenthal-Heginbottom 2003, pl. 6.9:44 "pinkish white" and 254-255, pl. 6.12:18 "light red").

129. AF 311 (Pl. 108).

> Lamp nozzle with dense traces of burning. On the nozzle top, a double (concentric) dotted circlet above a deeply punctured line.
> Fabric: medium hard light red (2.5 YR 6/6) with some tiny white grits; surface: light orange-red (near 5 YR 7/6 "reddish yellow"), very smooth, semi-glossy.
> Extant L. 3.0; W. nozzle 2.8.
> Found: ?

130. KhQ 5061 (Pl. 108).

Lamp nozzle with faint traces of burning. On the nozzle top, two
dotted circlets in between two punctured lines;.
Fabric: medium-hard, light grey (10 YR 7/1) with some voids and some tiny white grits; surface: self-slip greyish brown (10 YR 5/1-5/2) on top and dark grey (10 YR 4/1) on bottom, with slight gloss.
Extant L. 3,5; W. nozzle 3,0.
Found: Loc. 34.
Closely related to nos. *127* (KhQ 66) and *128* (KhQ 67); Similar
to: Lapp 2009, 278-279, pl. A:3, from Nabratein.

131. KhQ 5049 (Pl. 108).

Lamp nozzle with some traces of burning at the tip; adorned with two dotted circlets in
between two punctured lines with a pair of such circlets filling the flukes of the nozzle.
Fabric: hard and dense, grey (7.5 YR 6/0) with lots of white grits (including
sizeable ones); surface: dark grey (7.5 YR 4/0) self-slip with metallic gloss.
Extant L. 3.4; W. nozzle 3.3.
Found: Loc. 4.
See similar nozzle from Beth Shean (Hadad 2002, no. 9, in a comparable ware); also related
nozzle from the Jewish Quarter excavations in Jerusalem (Geva and Hershkovitz 2006, pl.
4.13:20, "light grey, dark grey slip", adorned with circlets only, without punctured lines).

132. KhQ 5059 (Pl. 108).

Lamp nozzle with slight traces of burning(?) at the tip; adorned with two dotted circlets in
between two punctured lines with a pair of such circlets filling the flukes of the nozzle.
Fabric: hard and dense, grey (7.5 YR 6/0) with lots of white grits, including big ones; surface:"black'
self(?) slip (7.5 YR 4/0), semi-glossy, partly exposing light grey surface (10 YR 7/2).
Extant L. 2.8, W. nozzle 3,0.
Found: Loc. 4.
Comparable to no. *131* (KhQ 5049) above.

133. KhQ 5048 (Pl. 108).

Lamp nozzle; no traces of burning visible. Nozzle adorned with three dotted circlets in
between two punctured lines with a pair of such circlets filling the flukes of the nozzle.
Fabric: hard and dense, grey (7.5 YR 6/0) with lots of white grits, including big ones; surface: "black"
(7.5 YR 4/0) (self?) slip with faint gloss, partly worn exposing light grey surface (10 YR 7/2).
Extant L. 3.5, W. nozzle 3.1.
Found: Loc. 38.
Parallel: Sussman 2008, 220 and 287, no. 23f ("black ware, black slip":
apparently the same ware as KhQ 5048) from Caesarea.

134. KhQ 1571 (Pl. 108).

Lamp nozzle of elongated proportions, with traces of burning faintly visible;
the same nozzle decoration scheme as in the previous one (KhQ 5048).
Fabric very hard and dense, dark grey (5 YR 4/1) with tiny white grits;
remains of semi-glossy self(?) slip of the same colour, the same workshop
(ware, proportions and the nozzle decoration) as *133* (KhQ 5048).
Extant L. 4.2, extant H. 2.3. W. nozzle 3.1.
Found: Loc. 93;
Cf. Qumran 1, 321; Qumran 1B, 43.
Cf. Mlynarczyk 2013, fig. 4.

Plate 108

Lamp nozzles attributed between 036.2 to 036.6

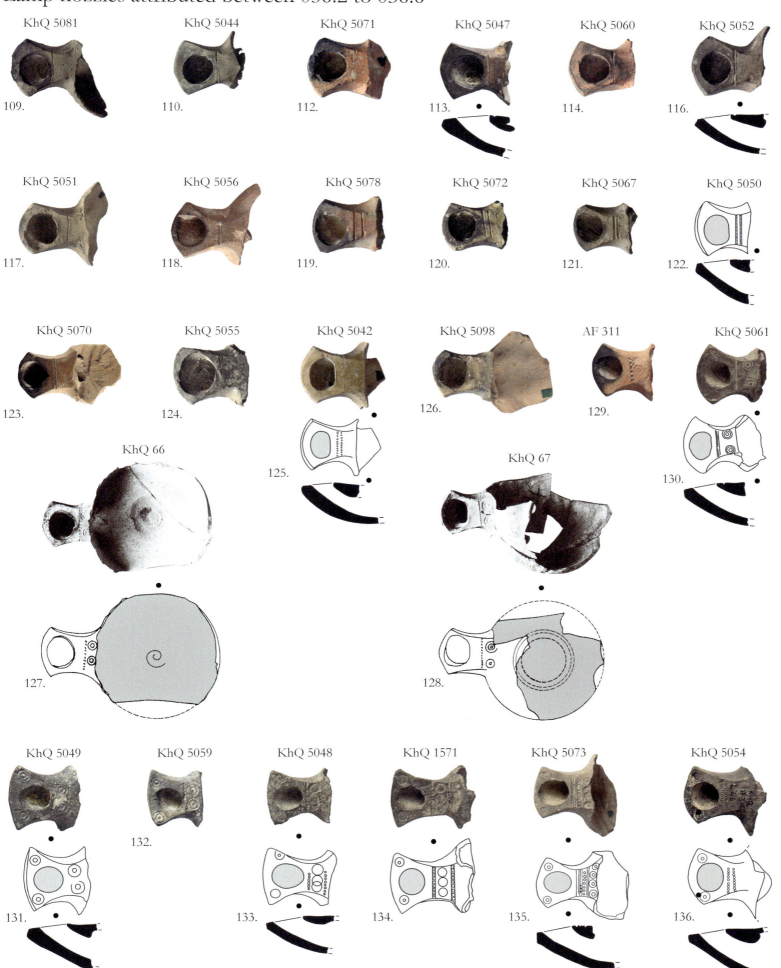

Lamp nozzles attributed to type 036.2 to 036.6

135. KhQ 5073 (Pl. 108).
> Lamp nozzle with part of bottom; pronounced wheel marks on floor with a trace of opening the wick hole; very faint traces of burning(?) at wick hole. On nozzle top, faintly impressed four dotted circlets above a series of five transverse grooves with a punctured line in the middle, and a pair of such circlets filling the nozzle's flukes.
> Fabric: hard, dense, fired with grey core banded brownish red, with many small white grits; surface: light brown (10 YR 6/2 "light brownish grey") with occasional large white eruptions, smooth.
> Extant L. 4.6; W. nozzle 2.6.
> Found: Loc. 111.

136. KhQ 5054 (Pl. 108).
> Lamp nozzle with faint traces of burning(?). On nozzle top, a double punctured line above wick hole and a pair of dotted circlets filling the nozzle flukes.
> Fabric: hard grey (7.5 YR 6/0), with tiny white grits; surface grey (10 YR 6/1), with darker grey slip (10 YR 5/1) with slight gloss.
> Extant L. 4.2, W. nozzle 3.0.
> Found: Loc. 46;
> Cf. Młynarczyk 2013, fig. 4.
> Similar fragments come from Jerusalem (Rosenthal-Heginbottom 2003, pl. 6.8:5, in different fabric), Dor (Rosenthal-Heginbottom 1995, fig. 5.21, no. 8), En-Gedi (Vincenz de 2007, pl. 50:4, "grey to dark grey") and Nabratein (Lapp 2009, 278-279, pl. A:9, fabric 10 YR 6/1).

036.1-6 Mutilated nozzles

137. AF 306.
> Lamp nozzle lacking top and end (shape details unknown).
> Fabric: light red, dense with tiny white grits, surface semi-smooth, beige-pink with occasional white eruptions; traces of burning.
> Extant L. 3.6.
> Found: *Tr ouest* (West trench).

138. AF 312.
> Small fragment of nozzle (shape details unknown).
> Fabric: light red, dense with tiny white grits, surface semi-smooth pale red.
> Extant L. 3.7.
> Found: ? (illegible note on surface of lamp).

139. AF 307.
> Small fragment of wall with inner opening of nozzle.
> Fabric dense light brown with tiny white and "black" grits; surface smooth, pink.
> Extant L/W 3,4.
> Found: *Tr ouest* (West trench)

Body top/wall fragments attributed to 036.1 - 3.

140. KhQ 5107.
> Fragment of lamp top and wall, partly burnt after it was broken. Wall profile rounded, fairly long flange at filling hole framing: apparently Type 036.1.
> Fabric: beige (7.5 YR 7/4 "pink"), porous, with many mineral grits (white, dark and red); surface of the same colour as break, gritty in feel.
> Extant L. 5.7, Diam.(est.) *ca.* 6.0.
> Found : Loc. 28.

141. KhQ 5093.
   Two joining parts of lamp top and wall, profile closely similar to KhQ 5107: apparently Type 036.1.
   Fabric: light (porous) and "sandy" (white, dark and red grits), fired very
   pale brown (10 YR 8/2 "white"), both at break and surface.
   Extant L. 5.8; Diam. (est.) *ca.* 6.2.
   Found : Loc. 20.

142. KhQ 5388 *(registration 2015) (marked as "no. 30" on surface)*.
   Two joining fragments of top and wall. Lamp shoulder sloping, wall fairly high: apparently Type 036.1
   Fabric: dense pink (2.5 YR 6/4 "light reddish brown"), with some tiny white grits and
   occasional red ones; surface: yellowish pink (5 YR 8/4), smooth, semi-glossy.
   Extant L. 4.3.
   Found: ?

143. KhQ 5113.
   Fragment of lamp top with complete filling hole within its tall ridge and fairly
   long flange; shoulder pronouncedly sloping; apparently Type 036.1.
   Fabric: reddish brown (near 5 YR 4/3), fairly dense, with small white grits and
   occasional crystals(?); surface greyish brown (near 5 YR 4/2 "dark reddish gray")
   with fairly large white eruptions, semi-rough; traces of burning inside.
   Extant L. /W. 4.2.
   Found: Loc. 110.

144. KhQ 5112.
   Fragment of lamp top with a pronounced ridge and a fairly long
   flange which would suggest an attribution to Type 036.1.
   Fabric: medium hard, pinkish orange (5 YR 7/6 "reddish yellow"), with
   occasional large voids, otherwise dense; some minute white (and black?)
   grits; surface yellowish pink (7.5 YR 7/4 "pink"), smooth.
   Extant L. 4.2.
   Found: Loc. 19.

145. AF 304.
   Fragment of lamp top with ridge and flange, closely similar to no. *144* (KhQ 5112): Type 036.1(?).
   Fabric: very thin-walled, pink (5 YR 7/4), dense, with some small white grits;
   surface smooth, yellowish pink (7.5 YR 8/6 "reddish yellow").
   Extant L/W 3.5.
   Found: Loc. 5.

146. KhQ 5106.
   Lamp fragment with fairly long flange at the filling hole framing and with rather vertical wall. The
   flange suggests attribution to Type 036.1, while the wall profile would rather speak for Type 036.2.
   Fabric: light (porous) and "sandy" (white, dark and red grits), very pale brown
   (10 YR 8/3), both at break and at surface, the latter semi-rough in feel.
   Extant L. 5.7, Diam. (est.) *ca.* 6.0.
   Found : Loc. 5, "upper" (on the lamp: *Niv Sup*).

147. KhQ 5132.
   Lamp fragment closely comparable to no. *146* (KhQ 5106) both in
   terms of body profile and the fabric; Type: 036.1-2.
   Fabric: light (porous) and "sandy" (white, dark and red grits), very
   pale brown, both at break and at semi-rough surface.
   Extant L. 4.5.
   Found: Loc. 138.

148. KhQ 5134 (Pl. 109).
   Fragment of lamp body, burnt after it was broken. Wall rather low and convex; well-developed flange to filling hole (profile close to Type 036.1, but with slight carination at shoulder): transitional 036.1-2.
   Fabric: light (porous) and "sandy" (tiny white, dark and red grits, also eruptions), fired unevenly: reddish brown with partial grey core to light red; surface semi-rough, fired light brown to brown. The same fabric as nos. *146-147* (KhQ 5106 and KhQ 5132).
   Extant L. 5.8, Diam. (est.) 6.0.
   Found: Loc. 19.

149. KhQ 5135 (Pl. 109).
   Lamp fragment with convex wall, closely similar to KhQ 5134: Type 036.1-2.
   Fabric: hard, fired dark brown (7.5 YR 4/2), with some tiny white and small black grits, surface semi-rough, fired light brown to brown (7.5 YR 6/2 to 5/2 "pinkish gray" to "brown").
   This fragment may have possibly come from the same lamp as no. *148* (KhQ 5134).
   Extant L. 4.9.
   Found: Loc. 19.

150. KhQ 5133.
   Fragment of lamp body (top and wall profile lacking base) and part of nozzle with traces of burning. Nozzle very short, tilted upwards, with a single incision across its top: apparently Type 036.2. The same profile as in nos. *148* (KhQ 5134) and *149* (KhQ 5135).
   Fabric: red (2.5 YR 5/6) with partial thin grey core, small white grits and occasional black ones; surface: beige (10 YR 8/3 "very pale brown") to grayish beige (10 YR 7/2 "light gray") with white eruptions, rather rough in feel.
   Extant L. 5.4, extant W. 3.0.
   Found: Loc. 11.

151. KhQ 25 (Pl. 109).
   Three joining parts of top and wall; traces of secondary burning on body. Rather deep body, convex wall, short and flat shoulder, filling hole rim devoid of flange. Type 036.2(?).
   Fabric: light (porous) and sandy (white, dark and red grits), very pale brown (10 YR 8/3), both at break and surface, the latter coarse in feel. Apparently the same fabric as no. *141* (KhQ 5093).
   Diam. (est.) 6.0 ; extant H. 1.7.
   Found: Loc. 1;
   Cf. Qumran 1, 292; Qumran 1B, 12 (found together with coins from the time of Claudius and Herod Agrippa I).

152. KhQ 5103.
   Two joining parts of top of large lamp. Shoulder wide and flat, carinated; narrow flange at filling hole framing. The lamp might have pertained to Type 036.3, there is, however, no room for attaching a handle.
   Fabric: very dense pink (5 YR 7/4) with pale grey core and minute white grits; surface: beige- pink (7.5 YR 7/4 "pink"), semi-smooth.
   Diam. 7.2.
   Found: Loc. 13, oven.

153. KhQ 5104.
   Lamp fragment with vertical wall and short flange at filling hole framing.
   The same type (shape and fabric) as no. *152* (KhQ 5103).
   Fabric: very dense pink with pale grey core and minute white grits. Surface semi-smooth, pale pink.
   Extant L. 5.9, Diam. (est.) *ca.* 6.4.
   Found: Loc. 41.

154. KhQ 5108.
   Fragment of lamp body with flattened shoulder, low vertical wall and short flange at filling hole framing. The same type (shape and fabric) as nos. *152-153* (KhQ 5103 and 5104). The fabric is shared also with no. *76* (KhQ 5082) of Subtype 036.3.
   Fabric: very dense pink with pale grey core and minute white grits.
   Surface pale pink (7.5 YR 7/4 "pink"), wet-smoothed.
   Extant L. 6.5; Diam. 6.5.
   Found: Trench *voie*.

Plate 109

Fragments attributed to 036.1 - 3

036.7

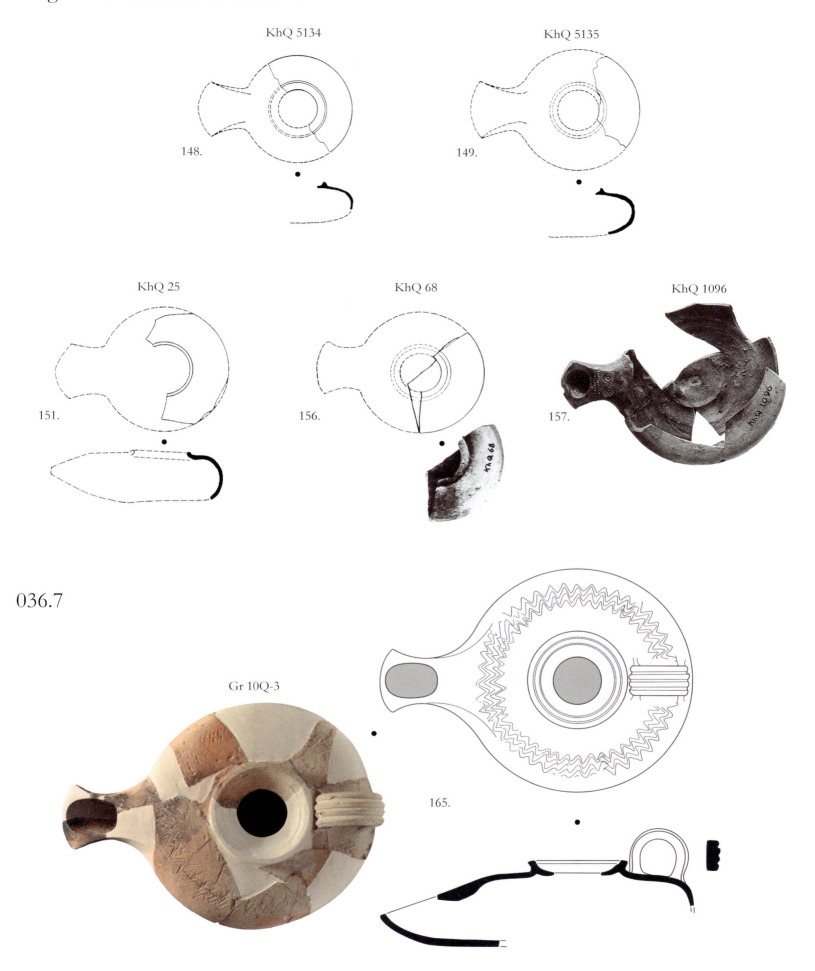

Lamp type 036.7 and fragments attributed to 036.1 to 036.3

155. KhQ 5111.
   Fragment of lamp body with wide, flat carinated shoulder and minimal flange at filling hole framing. Apparently the same form as nos. *152-154* (Subtype 036.2-3), different fabric.
   Fabric: dense red (2.5 YR 6/6) with some minute white (and black?) grits; surface semi-smooth with fine white eruptions.
   Extant L. 5.6; Diam. (est.) *ca.* 7.2.
   Found: Loc. 30.

156. *(Probably also)* KhQ 68* *(not illustrated in the register book)* (Pl. 109).
   Recomposed of several fragments, incomplete, with traces of burning.
   Fabric: *terre fine, de couleur rose.*
   Extant L. 6.0; Diam. 6.2 ; extant H. 2.5.
   Found: Loc. 4, "near the north door" (together with no. *127:* KhQ 66 and no. *128:* KhQ 67*);
   Cf. Qumran 1, 293; Qumran 1B, 13 .
   Cf. Donceel ms, pl. VII (photo).

157. KhQ 1096 (Pl. 109).
   Six fragments of a fairly large lamp in grey ware; burnt after it was broken;
   flat base and very low slightly convex wall. Type 036.2 or 036.3.
   In the register book and in Donceel ms (pl. III: drawing from the reg. book; pl. X: phot., erroneously marked as 1069), they were still joining nozzle of Machaerus group 79.
   Fabric: hard, grayish brown (10 YR 5/2), with some minute white (and black?) grits and rare fine voids; surface light grey (10 YR 7/2) where not burnt, smooth.
   L. 12.1; H. max. 2.6 (Donceel ms); actual dimensions: extant L. 8.7, extant H. 2.2.
   Found: Loc. 44, "floor";
   Cf. Donceel 1998, 94, n. 19 (considered as possibly local product); Qumran 1, 307; Qumran 1B, 28, listed as "Herodian lamp".

Base/wall fragments attributed to Type 036.

158. KhQ 5131.
   Fragment of lamp body with flat base and tall convex wall.
   Fabric: reddish brown (2.5 YR 6/4: light reddish brown), medium-hard with tiny white grits and tiny dark ones (or voids?); surface pinkish brown (5 YR 7/3: pink).
   Extant L. 5.2; extant H. 2.4.
   Found: Trench A, Layer 5.

159. KhQ 3852.
   Fragment of flattened base and vertical wall.
   Fabric: hard light red with lots of small to tiny white grits; surface smooth, pale pink with brown spots.
   Extant L. 6,6; est. Diam 6,0; extant H. 1,8.
   Found: Loc. 9.

160. KhQ 5130.
   Fragment of slightly convex base; angular joint with vertical wall.
   Fabric: hard, dense light red with some tiny white grits; surface: light reddish brown, very smooth.
   Extant L. 5,2.; est. Diam. 6,4
   Found: Loc. 4.

161. KhQ 3456.
   Fragment of gently convex base with wheel marks giving an "undulate" profile.
   Fabric: hard, dense, light red, with some tiny white grits and some red ones; surface pink. The same fabric as no. *160* (KhQ 5130).
   Extant L. 5,7; Diam. estimated 6,4.
   Found: Loc. 30 North.

162. KhQ 5137.
> Fragment of convex base with a part of vertical(?) wall.
> Fabric: very dense, pinkish brown (5 YR 6/3 "light reddish brown") with some small white grits; surface: pale brown (6.5 YR 7/2 "pinkish gray") with dark grey spots, smooth.
> Extant L. 5,7; Diam. estimated 6,0.
> Found: Loc. 13, oven.

163. KhQ 3420.
> Fragment of rather flattened base with spiral wheel marks at the centre of bottom.
> Fabric: very hard, dense, grey with minute white grits; surface pale brown with dark grey spots, smooth. The same fabric as no. *162* (KhQ 5137).
> Extant L. 6,3; Diam. estimated *ca.* 7,4(?).
> Found: Loc. 34.

164. KhQ 3155.
> Fragment of slightly convex base with traces of a tool.
> Fabric: hard and dense orange (7.5 YR 6/6 "reddish yellow") with some minute white grits; surface pinkish grey (7.5 YR 7/2 to 8/2), smooth.
> Extant L. 5,1.
> Found: Loc. 38.

036.7. Large lamp with strap handle and decorated shoulder

A single object (Gr 10Q-3) classified as a separate type of the "Herodian" lamps family, is a fragmentary large-sized lamp with elaborate strap handle and decorated shoulder.

This lamp, apparently related to the "Herodian" Type 036.1, may at the same time have been inspired by the "Ephesian" lamps of the 1st century BC. A somewhat comparable object comes from Beth Shean (Smith 1966, 14-15, fig. 4); it resembles our lamp by its size, the form of the handle and the zig-zag decoration on the shoulder incised by hand; unlike our lamp, however, it has two nozzles adorned with punctured lines and stamped dotted circlets. On the other hand, the Qumran lamp recalls also a large-sized Knidian lamp in the British Museum collection (Bailey 1975, 151, Q 325).

165. Gr 10Q-3 (Pl. 109).
> Several fragments of an upper part of a large lamp, including parts of shoulder with handle, parts of central depression and of slightly splayed nozzle; restored in plaster (2011); traces of burning on nozzle. Shoulder decorated with three to two (partly overlapping) rows of grooved zig-zags or chevrons made *à la roulette*. The strap handle is adorned with alternating ribs and grooves.
> Fabric: hard and dense, light red (2.5 YR 6/6) with some small white grits; surface of "metallic" feel, fired from glossy red (2.5 YR 5/6) to pale beige (10 R 8/3: very pale brown) with many white grits' eruptions.
> L. 17.2, Diam. 12.2, extant H. (with handle) 5.5.
> Found: Cave 10;

Cf. DJD III, fig. 6:4 and pl. VIII:4; Qumran 1B, 67.
Cf. Młynarczyk 2013, 116, fig. 4; Młynarczyk, Lugano, Ill. 8-9.

037. Unclassified wheel-made lamps

This "type" (or, more properly, group) embraces five fragments of wheel-made lamps that represent different types the identification of which with any certainty, however, is not possible. They include two band (strap) handles (037.1) added to the wheel-made bodies of lamps the form of which is unknown (presumably, either Qumran Type 036.3 or 036.7), fragments of two different lamps' bodies (037.2 and 037.3) and a lamp nozzle (037.4).

037.1. Two band handles

Added to wheel-made bodies of lamps the form of which is unknown. To judge by the size of the handles, they might have pertained to large lamps of our Type 036.7 the more so that, macroscopically, all the three items seem to be of the same fabric. Another type of Qumran wheel-made lamps provided with similar handles is 036.3 in which, however, the objects are definitely smaller.

166. KhQ 5068 (Pl. 110).
Fragment of lamp body with band (strap) handle, its section featuring three ribs alternating with two grooves, similarly to lamp Gr 10Q-3 of Type 036.7.
Fabric: medium hard (7.5 YR 7/6 reddish yellow) with some fine oblong voids and occasional small white grits; surface pink, semi-rough in feel.
Extant W. 4.7, extant H. *ca.* 4.0.
Found : Loc. 87.

167. KhQ 5065 (Pl. 110).
Ring handle of a wheel-made lamp (fine wheel marks inside), attached to sloping shoulder; its section featuring two ribs divided by a deep groove.
Fabric: dense reddish brown, with tiny white grits and occasional black ones; surface light reddish brown, semi-rough in feel.
Extant H. *ca.* 4.0.
Found: Loc. 40.

037.2. Lamp top

168. KhQ 5116 (Pl. 110).
Fragment of top of a big-size lamp, with very large filling hole inside a moulded low ridge with internal flange. By its profile and diameter it resembles no. *27* (KhQ 5114), probably of Type 033.2; it is possible that both lamps pertained to the same type.
Fabric: granular, but dense, dark brown, medium-hard, with small to minute white grits some small black ones; surface smooth, very dark brownish grey (5 YR 4/1 "dark gray").
Extant L. 5.4.
Found: Loc. 111.

037.3. Top/wall fragment of lamp

169. KhQ 5126 (Pl. 110).
Fragment of deep double-convex body with large filling hole surrounded by an inward-sloping rim.
Fabric: gritty, orange-red (5YR 7/6) with many small white grits (including eruptions, up to large) and occasional circular voids; surface covered with thin matt dark grey ("black") slip, partly worn.
Extant L. 4.7, extant H. 2.8, Diam. est. 5.4 (?).
Found : Trench A, Layer 5.

037.4. Nozzle

170. KhQ 5077 (Pl. 110).
Lamp nozzle; traces of burning at wick hole. Nozzle rectangular in outline (straight sides, straight end, just slight suggestion of nozzle flukes) with perfectly flat top;.
Fabric: dense, reddish brown (5 YR 6/4), very gritty (tiny white grits, crystals); surface pink (5 YR 7/4) with many small and medium-sized white grits, rough in feel.
Extant L. 4.4; W. of nozzle 2.4.
Found: Trench A, Layer 5.

Plate 110

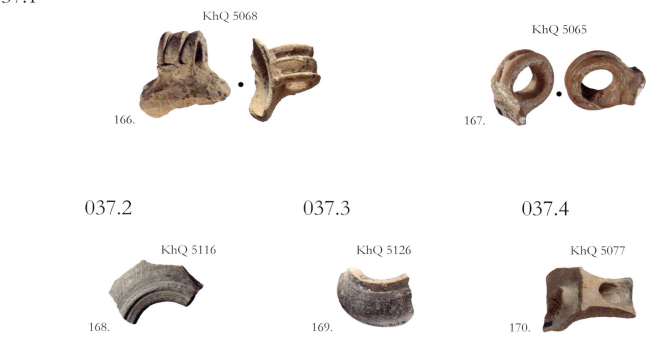

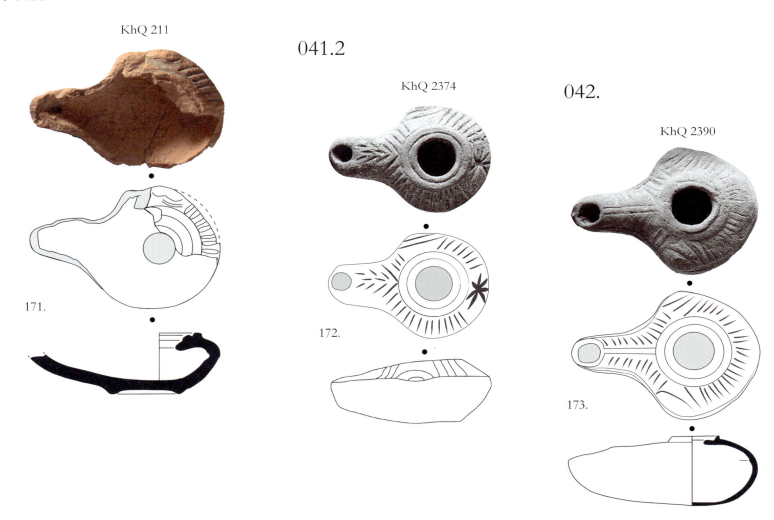

Lamp types 037.1 to 037.4, 041.1 - 041.2 and 042

Mould-made lamps (041-048)

041.

Lamps with a deep body bi-conical in section, with side lug and nozzle either tapering to a rounded end or straight-sided (Alexandrian lamps scheme: A-I/2, according to Młynarczyk 1997, 128, fig. 2; Lapp 1961, type 83.2). Two varieties can be distinguished, each represented at Qumran by a single object only. One of them, Subtype **041.1**, has a kind of concave "discus" within a rather narrow and steep shoulder, while in Subtype **041.2** the filling hole is bordered by a convex ring. Both lamp patterns share the simplest and the most common shoulder decoration: that of "rays" (alternately convex and concave).

041.1. Concave "discus" around filling hole

Our example of Subtype **041.1** (KhQ 211) seems to be comparable to a fragmentary lamp from Jerusalem which, however, has a handle (cf. Rosenthal-Heginbottom 2003, 205, pl. 6.12:3, in a rather similar fabric). Curiously enough, as far as the shape is concerned, this seems also to be paralleled by a group of fragments of hand-shaped(!) lamps from Petra ez Zantur with which it shares elongated nozzle and narrow "rayed" shoulder; they are dated on stratigraphic grounds to between the late 2nd and the mid-1st century BC (Grawehr 2006, 272-273).

171. KhQ 211 (Pl. 110).
   Lower half of lamp with small fragment of the upper part, recomposed of several fragments. No traces of burning preserved. Ring base; narrow shoulder with series of oblique grooves, concave top within double ridge; S-shaped lug on the left-hand side. Fabric: soft reddish yellow (5 YR 6/6), rather clean, with some tiny voids and occasional tiny white grits; surface reddish yellow (5 YR 7/6) weathered, with faint traces of dark red slip. *PG 2* (Michniewicz 2009, 37: misidentified as "Herodian")
   L. 9.6, W. 6.7, H. 3.5.
   Found: Trench A, Layer 4;
   Cf. Qumran 1B, 62.
   Cf. *RB* 1954, 218-219, fig. 2:15; Donceel 1998, 91, fig. 1 (with findspot erroneously given as *locus* 130); Młynarczyk 2013, 118, fig. 4.

041.2. No "discus" around filling hole

Subtype **041.2**, with a convex ring around the filling hole, corresponds to Levantine/Alexandrian type A-Prime (Młynarczyk 1997, 22-25 and 130, figs. 14-18) dated to the 2nd and through the early 1st century BC; to Kennedy type 2 (Kennedy 1961, 71, pl. XX:484); to type BI ("Hellenistic Radial Lamp") at Masada (Barag and Hershkovitz 1994, 13-14, no. 2); type 12 at Dor (Rosenthal-Heginbottom 1995, fig. 5.16: 11-13 and fig. 5.17:1-3); to some examples of group 74 at Machaerus (Loffreda 1996, 108-109, specifically lamp 3253, fot. 50 and fig. 49:3, found in a Hasmonean-period context) and to type 2 at Beth Shean (Hadad 2002, 13-14). Three lamps of this subtype were found in Jason's Tomb in Jerusalem alongside the "folded" lamps Qumran 031 (Rahmani 1967, 77, fig. 9:4-6), which means they had been of a pre-Herodian date. A similar object from Samaria has been illustrated by Smith as "sunburst" lamp of *ca.* first half of the 1st century BC (Smith 1961, 122, fig. 21).

172. KhQ 2374* (Pl. 110).
> Complete lamp with deep body. Filling hole within a double(?) ridge, shoulder with ray ornament divided by a rosette at the rear (on the axis of nozzle); shell-shaped side lug (concentric double-arched groove) on the left; incisions on nozzle may be rather careless imitation of "herring bone" ornament. The kind of base is not known.
> Fabric: *terre rouge*.
> L. 8.6, H. 3.5.
> Found: Loc. 140;
> Cf. Qumran 1, 337; Qumran 1B, 60 ("Hellenistic lamp").
> (cf. Donceel ms, pls. VI and XI) cf. Donceel 1998, 90 and n.14; Młynarczyk 2013, 118, fig. 4. Not later than first half of 1st century BC.
> For related lamp (with a double ring around the filling hole, though), see Rosenthal-Heginbottom 2003, pl. 6.4:11.

042. Lamp with two side lugs and nozzle tapering to rounded end

This type, represented in Qumran by a single lamp no. *173* (KhQ 2390, lost), pertains to the Alexandrian lamps scheme C-I/3b or 4, dated to not later than the first half of 1st century BC. (Młynarczyk 1997, 13 and 128, fig. 2). A similar, but stylistically later lamp (short nozzle, side projections on the axis of body) comes from the Jewish Quarter excavations in Jerusalem (Geva and Hershkovitz 2006, pl. 4.12:21).

173. KhQ 2390* (Pl. 110).
> Complete lamp; rounded profile; ridge and groove around filling hole; type of base not known. Body outline slightly kite-shaped, with unsymmetrical side lugs (the left-hand one more protruding from the outline of body). Ray decoration on shoulder. Deep nozzle with rounded tip and apparently ridged/convex top, decorated with a sort of schematic herring bone (oblique grooves on either side of the ridge).
> Fabric : *terre rouge*.
> L. 10.0, H. 3.6.
> Found: L 140 (*sur le drain*);
> Cf. Qumran 1, 337 (*lampe hellénistique*); Qumran 1B, 60.
> Cf. Donceel ms, pls. VI and XI; Donceel 1998, 90, n. 14; Młynarczyk 2013, 118, fig. 4.

043. Lamps with circular body and straight-sided convex-topped nozzle with rounded end

The type corresponds to Lapp type 83.2 (Lapp 1961, 194, lamp D) and to scheme A-I/1 in Hellenistic mould-made lamps of Alexandria and Egypt (Młynarczyk 1997, 13 and 128, fig. 2). The nozzle is rather slim and relatively long; it may be plain or decorated with incised ornaments. Shoulder decoration may include linear imitations of side lugs proving that this type of lamp is a development of a lamp pattern like Qumran Type 042 (see above). The filling hole is surrounded, like in Qumran Types 041-042, by a single or double convex ring. The lamps corresponding to Qumran Type 043, along with those of Type 044 (the latter pertaining to "Judean Radial Lamps", see below) have been classified by V. Sussman as the "Jerusalem workshop", embracing several varieties (her H36 – H41), with general dating from the 2nd-1st centuries BC to 1st century AD (Sussman 2009, 59-65, nos. 287-347). In the Herodian palaces in Jericho lamps J-LP2C1-2 corresponding to Qumran 043 are dated to "only slightly before the last decade" of the 1st century BC, although Bar-Nathan admits a possibility that at other sites they may go back to mid-1st century BC (Bar-Nathan 2002, 108, nos. 295-296, pl. 18, with references to its distribution at: Jerusalem, Kypros, Masada, Marissa, Ashdod). Indeed, the context of our lamp no. *174* (KhQ 1012), specifically, the layer with a coin of Alexander Jannaeus (Qumran 1, 340), points to not later than the first half of the 1st century BC. This agrees well with the evidence from Jason's Tomb in Jerusalem, where a lamp of this type (Rahmani 1967, 77-78, fig. 9:7) occurred together with lamps of Qumran Types 031 and 041.2.

043.1. Single ring around the filling hole

174. KhQ 1012 (Pl. 111).
Fragmentary lamp, missing *ca.* half of body and end of nozzle; traces of burning at wick hole. Biconical body on indistinct low ring base. Decoration of the upper part possibly comes from a re-worked mould(?): ray ornament on shoulder, seven-arms dotted star on top of nozzle; star-shaped incision on shoulder imitates side-lug.
Fabric: hard light red (near 2.5 YR 6/6) with some voids and rather few tiny white grits; surface fired very pale brown (10 YR 8/6) with poor remains of matt slip, red mottled black on nozzle and in orange-brown runs on base. *PG 2* (Michniewicz 2009, 37: misidentified as "Herodian").
Extant L. 6.9, Diam. of body 6.5, H. 3.2.
Found: Trench B, Layer 2, middle;
Cf. Qumran 1, 340 (in this layer, coin of Alexander Jannaeus); Qumran 1B, 63.
Cf. Młynarczyk 2013, 119, fig. 5.
For a similar lamp from Jerusalem, see Geva and Hershkovitz 2006, pl. 4.6:7 ("pinkish brown, reddish brown slip", with double ring around filling hole, different nozzle decoration and two more rosettes on shoulder) and pl. 4.10:25 (fragment of body, "light brown"). Indeed, there can be no doubt that the lamps of this type found in the Jewish Quarter in Jerusalem were of local manufacture. They were occurring there in the layers "from the 1st century BCE to the beginning of the 1st century CE" (Geva and Hershkovitz 2006, 113). Also Sussman describes a lamp comparable to KhQ 1012 as representing "Jerusalem workshop" and found in context with 1st century BC objects (Sussman 2009, 151, no. 310). A comparable lamp from Samaria has been dated to 75-25 BC (Lapp 1961, 194, lamp D). No exact parallels to the mentioned examples were found in Jericho.

043.2. Double ring around the filling hole

This group includes three objects from Qumran, one of them (once found entire), now unfortunately lost. Lamps representing the same combination of shape and decoration are known from Jerusalem (Rosenthal-Heginbottom 2003, 196-197, pl. 6.8:3; Sussman 2009, 151-152, type H38, nos. 312-315, dated to the 1st century BC).

175. KhQ 5100 (Pl. 111).
Fragment of shoulder with top of nozzle; shoulder with ray decoration (or side bands, each composed of two convex "rays"?); nozzle plain. From fresh mould.
Fabric: medium hard light red (near 2.5 YR 6/6), dense, with few fine white grits; surface deep pink, apparently unslipped. *PG 2* (Michniewicz 2009, 38: misidentified as "Herodian").
Extant L. 4.0, extant W. 3.7.
Found: Trench S.

176. KhQ 5102 (Pl. 111).
Fragmentary lamp preserving about a half of upper body; shoulder with ray decoration, no specific side bands(?), nozzle apparently plain. From rather worn mould.
Fabric: hard, grey (10 YR 5/2: grayish brown), fairly dense (some tiny voids), with occasional tiny white grits; surface. pinkish beige (*ca.* 10 YR 7/4: very pale brown), unslipped, with rare fine white eruptions.
Extant L. 5.4, Diam. (est.) *ca.* 7.0
Found: Loc. 56.

177. KhQ 2116* (Pl. 111).
Complete lamp on ring base. Shoulder decorated with "rays" and a pair of concentric arches in imitation of side-lugs flanking the root of rather short nozzle with schematic "herring-bone" pattern on top. The graphic imitation of two (rather than one) side lugs may be an echo of models in scheme A-I/3b (Młynarczyk 1997, 128, fig. 2).
Fabric: *terre rouge*.
L. 8.8, Diam. 6.4, H. 3.9.
Found: Loc. 111, floor level;
Cf. Qumran 1, 327; Qumran 1B, 49.
Cf. Donceel ms, pls. VI and XI; cf. Młynarczyk 2013, 119, fig. 5.

Plate 111

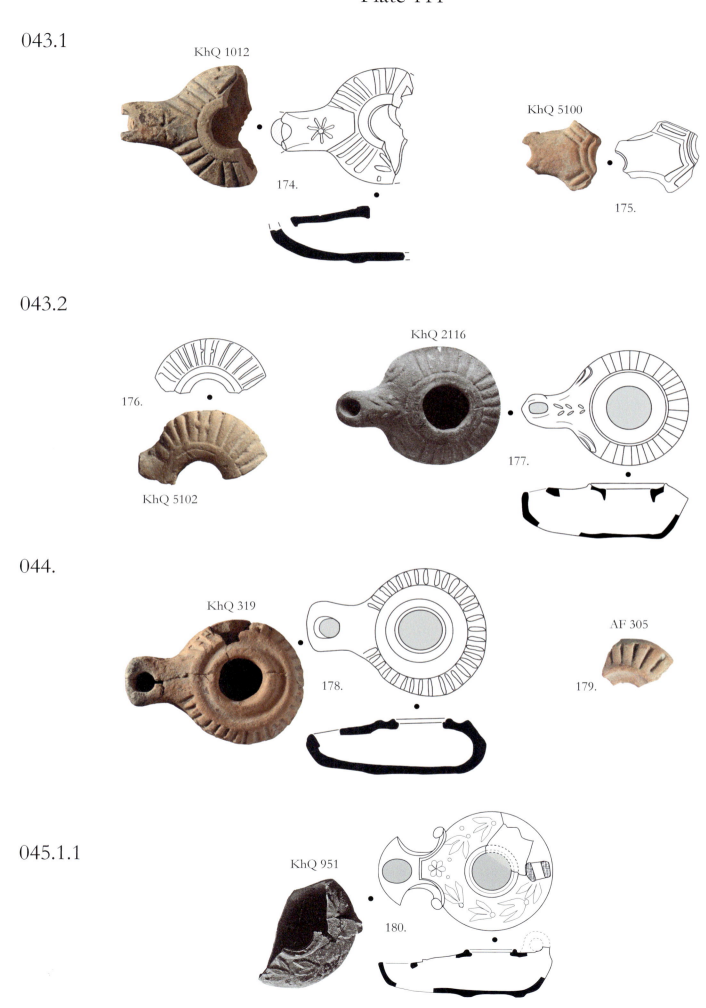

Lamp types 043.1, 043.2, 044, and 045.1.1

044. "Judean radial lamps"

The type, represented at Qumran by two objects, corresponds to Masada type B II ("First Century B.C.E. Judaean Radial Lamps") and to a part of Sussman's type H40 (Barag and Hershkovitz 1994, 14-15, nos. 3-8; Sussman 2009, 154-155, nos. 334-335 from Jerusalem). The lamps' outline mirrors the scheme A-I/1 of Hellenistic mould-made lamps of Alexandria and Egypt (Młynarczyk 1997, 128, fig. 2).

The lamps have circular shallow body with rounded profile and broad flat base. The nozzle is shorter than that in Qumran 043 and it has a blunt end that may develop very slight flukes. The body has steep shoulder decorated with "rays" bordering a flat area between two concentric ridges on top; occasionally, the side lugs "are indicated not so much by the shape of the lamp as by incised lines" (Smith 1964, 122). This type has first been distinguished by Smith who dated it to *ca.* third quarter of the 1st century BC (*ibidem*, 122-123, fig. 22: a lamp "from the vicinity of Jerusalem"). Indeed, even if the first occurrence of the type in question is dated by Barag and Hershkovitz to the first half of the 1st century BC, from the parallels they quote it is clear that the type must have become popular only during the reign of Herod the Great (Barag and Hershkovitz 1994, 22). Nevertheless, they must be right in stating that the type "evidently developed locally in Judaea and replaced the local Hellenistic radial types like No. 2" (that is, the forerunner of our Qumran Type 043). Recently published evidence from the Jewish Quarter in Jerusalem suggests for the "Judean radial lamps" a date in the second half of the 1st century BC and the beginning of the 1st century AD (Geva and Hershkovitz 2006, 113; cf. also Rosenthal-Heginbottom 2003, pl. 6.12:6). However, while publishing fragments of similar lamps found in a tomb on the French Hill in Jerusalem, J.F. Strange followed V. Tzaferis in attributing them to the first rather than the second half of the 1st century BC (Strange 1975, 61 and fig. 16:1-5, with references). Similarly, the dating assigned to such lamps by Diez Fernandez is from the beginning of the 1st century BC and into the time of Herod (Diez Fernandez 1983, 64-65, type L 2).

Lamps of this type belong to the group of products of a "Jerusalem workshop" described by Sussman, with a broad dating in the 1st century BC – 1st century AD (Sussman 2009, 64-65 (specifically, type H40). At Jericho, they were classified as J-LP2B embracing several variations; according to Bar-Nathan, they apparently came into production in the second half of the 1st century BC, were a dominant lamp type in Herod's Third Palace and continued to be made "until at least the first decade of the first century C.E." (Bar-Nathan 2002, 107-110, nos. 293-294, Ill. 85 and pl. 17 with references to other sites). Two fragments of Judean Radial Lamps discovered at Petra ez Zantur, however, do not come from stratified contexts (Grawehr 2006, 357-358).

The present author is of the opinion that the *floruit* of the type covered the second half of the 1st century BC. Qumran Type 044 seems to have shortly preceded and announced the wheel-made "Herodian" lamp type, with its broad undefined base, nozzle with flukes and the "inner flange" around the filling hole.

178. KhQ 319 (Pl. 111).
   Lamp recomposed of several pieces, lacking a part of shoulder; mutilated broad base was probably flat and undefined. From a fresh plaster mould. Traces of burning at wick hole.
   Fabric: rather soft light red (near 2.5 YR 6/6), rather clear, with some tiny voids; surface deep pink (5 YR 7/6 reddish yellow) with poor remains of dark red slip. Most probably Michniewicz *PG 2*.
   L. 9.3, Diam. 6.8, H. 3.0.
   Found: Loc. 19 "upper";
Cf. Qumran 1, 299 (Qumran 1B, 20: "upper level").
Cf. *RB* 1954, 226-227, fig. 6:3; Młynarczyk 2013, 120, fig. 5.

179. AF 305 (Pl. 111).
   Fragment of lamp top, its filling hole within inner flange and a ridge separating it from shoulder. From fresh mould.
   Fabric: medium-hard reddish yellow (5 YR 7/6) with some tiny voids and some fine mineral grits (dark and tiny white ones); surface pink (5 YR 7/4), unslipped. *PG 2* (Michniewicz 2009, 38: misidentified as "Herodian").
   Extant L. 3.8 ; Diam. (est.) 6.4.
   Found: Feshkha Loc. 5.

045. Lamps with circular body on base ring and spatulate (splayed) nozzle; ring handle *(as a rule, provided with a longitudinal groove)*

In terms of the shape, these lamps are clearly a mould-made counterpart/development of the wheel-made "Herodian" lamps. Their shoulder is usually adorned with a floral wreath (but in some lamps the shoulder appears to be plain), and they have volutes or fins projecting at the joint with the body and repeated also on the nozzle's underside. Indeed, P. Lapp describes the type as the decorated "Herodian" lamp and dates it to 50-31 BC (Lapp 1961, type 82.2). Also Smith, while illustrating a lamp of Qumran of the type in question (no. *180:* KhQ 951*), not only stated that it had been found in a pre-31 B.C. level(?!), but also pointed to a number of Hellenistic features it displayed, including the decoration of laurel leaves and berries recalling that of some Ephesian-type lamps (Smith 1966, 3 and fig. 1). Contrary to that, Rosenthal and Sivan dated the type's beginning much later, to AD 70-75 (Rosenthal and Sivan 1978, 82-85). A single lamp of the type found in one of the Jewish tombs at Huqoq was tentatively dated to the "second half of first cent. C.E., possibly shortly after 70 C.E." (Kahane 1961, 139, fig. 3:19)

Type 045 is the best represented one among the mould-made lamps found in the Qumran area, amounting to ten items. It corresponds to some lamps of type D.I-III from Masada ("Moulded Lamps with Floral Decoration", usually made of grey fabric with black slip), which are considered by Barag and Hershkovitz (1994, 64-71, nos. 102-118) as Jerusalem products of *ca.* 50-68 AD. In Masada, they were used during the period of the Zealots, and probably date from the last decade or two before the siege of Masada; in Jerusalem, they were found in the burnt destruction level of 70 AD at the Citadel (ibidem, 67-68). This dating matches perfectly well that of two lamps of this type found in cave X/35, sealed by rocks and stratigraphically associated with a "Herodian" lamp of Qumran Subtype 036.4-5 and with a *pruta* of the First Revolt (Itah, Kan and Ben Haim, 2002, part 1, fig. 11:2-3 and part 2, 172). This cave deposit must have come from the period of the First Revolt, but the authors erroneously dated all the three lamps to the 2nd(!) century AD. Another example of a late dating is a single lamp from Tel Dor, paralleling Qumran Type 045, dated by Rosenthal-Heginbottom to as late as *ca.* 75 – 150/200 AD (Rosenthal-Heginbottom 1995, 244 and fig. 5.21:11, type 23.3). In Beth Shean publication, the type is represented by just one fragmentary lamp of light grey fabric (Hadad 2002, 15-16, type 5, no. 11). A Transjordan counterpart of this type, of a slightly later (late Traianic?) date, with a solid "stub" handle instead of a ring handle, was found in a potter's store in Jerash (Iliffe 1945, nos. 155-156 and plaster mould no. 160; in terms of the lamp pattern, it seems to stand mid-way between Qumran Types 045 and 046).

In terms of the pattern details, Qumran Type 045 embraces several varieties, as listed below.

045.1. No border to the shoulder *(no structurally marked division between the shoulder and the lower wall)*.

Diez Fernandez (1983, 82-83) assigns them to his type L 6, dated to between 30 BC and 60 AD.

045.1.1. Filling hole framed by a ridge

180. KhQ 951* (Pl. 111).
Nearly complete lamp on ring base (lost and located in 1988 in kibbutz Almog), lacking mould-made (ring) handle. Spatulate nozzle flanked by narrow volutes encroaching on shoulder that is decorated with laurel wreath composed of two branches running towards nozzle above which they are separated by a rosette.
Fabric: *terre grise fine* (register book); *terre dure, grise; restes d'un engobe brillant, brun chocolat sur l'avant* (Donceel, ms, note 30, pl. VI and VIII).
L. 9.5, W. 6.4, H. body 2.5.
Found: "north of locus 52": Qumran 1, 309; Qumran 1B, 31;
Cf. *RB* 1954, 220-221, fig. 3:17; Lapp 1961, Type 82:2; Smith 1966, 3 and fig. 1; Donceel and Donceel-Voûte 1994, 7-8 and 22, fig. 1; Młynarczyk 2013, 122, fig. 5.
For the shape and related decoration, see Rosenthal and Sivan 1978, 83, no. 337; Barag and Hershkovitz 1994, nos. 102 and 107 (the two in grey fabric with black slip); Rosenthal-Heginbottom 1995, type 23, 244 and fig. 5.12:11, dated to *ca.* 75 – 150/200 AD.

045.1.2. Filling hole in the centre of small flat "discus" surrounded by ridge

181. AF 8 (Pl. 112).

Lamp recomposed of several fragments, lacking small parts of body and of nozzle top; traces of burning at wick hole. Ring base, mildly curved wall, mould-made handle with single groove on front part. On shoulder, scrolls of ivy leaves alternating with berries; ring ornament above the nozzle; side volutes reproduced also on the lower half of body. From worn mould. Fabric: metallic-hard, with ash-grey core banded light red. Surface (self-slip?) very smooth, beige (unevenly fired between 10 YR 7/2 light gray and 7/3) with whitish spots on upper half.
L. body 10.2, Diam. body 7, H. of body 3.2, H. including handle 4.1.
Found: Loc. 3;
Cf. Qumran 1, 353; Qumran 1B, 80.
Cf. Młynarczyk 2013, 122, fig. 5.
Similar shoulder decoration on lamp of type 045.2: Rosenthal and Sivan 1978, 84, no. 343. Closely similar lamp (differing only in some details of the floral scroll) comes from Masada, cf. Barag and Hershkovitz 1994, no. 105 (possibly the same fabric as no. *181* with a different firing?).

182. Gr 8Q-12 (Pl. 112).

Fragments of lamp, missing large part of body and handle. Ring base, low body of mildly curved profile, filling hole within a "discus", voluted nozzle with a dotted circlet on either fluke; shoulder decorated with vegetal scrolls. Thin walled, from fresh mould.
Fabric: hard, very dark grey/black (5 YR 3/1) both at break and
surface (the latter with semi-glossy self-slip).
L. (est.) 12.3, Diam.body 9.2, H. 3.3.
Found: Cave 8Q;
Cf. Qumran 1B, 67.
Cf. DJD III, fig. 6:3 and pl. VIII:12; Diez Fernandez 1983, no. 85, his type L 6; Młynarczyk, Lugano, Ill. 10. For the same lamp shape and similar decoration, see Rosenthal and Sivan 1978, 84, no. 345. Several parallel features are found in the lamps from Masada, such as Barag and Hershkovitz 1994, no. 111 (form and decoration of nozzle), shoulder fragment no. 106 and two-nozzled no. 120 (both with scroll decoration on shoulder closely similar to that of our lamp); see also a fragment from the "Miqveh House" in En-Gedi, found in context with two nozzles of "Herodian" lamps of Qumran Type 036.1-2 (Vincenz de 2007, pl. 68:2, fabric "grey with white inclusions").

183. KhQ 1409 (Pl. 112).

Fragment of lamp body, possibly from the same (fresh) mould as Gr 8Q-12.
Gently rounded shoulder, decorated with scrolls filled with rosettes.
Fabric: very dense dark grey (5 YR 4/1), with occasional tiny white grits; slightly paler smooth surface (brownish shade). *PG* undetermined (Michniewicz 2009, 37).
Extant L. 4.2, extant H. 2.0.
Found: Loc. 81;
Cf. Qumran 1, 317; Qumran 1B, 39.
Cf. DJD III, 31, n. 2; Donceel ms, pl. VI and X.

184. KhQ 5121 (Pl. 112).

Fragment of lamp nozzle and shoulder. Preserved right-hand fin of nozzle and part of floral scroll(?) on shoulder: apparently the same decoration as Gr 8Q-12 and KhQ 1409. From fresh mould.
Fabric: hard and dense, grey (2.5 YR 5/0), with occasional tiny white grits; slightly paler surface with runs(?) of dark grey slip (2.5 YR 4/0), thin and matt.
Extant L. 4.7
Found: Loc. 91.

185. KhQ 5123 (Pl. 112).

Two non-joining fragments of lamp: a) fragment of top,
b) fragment of nozzle/body with small section of base.
Ring base, low body of gently curved profile, shoulder plain, with part of right-hand volute of nozzle; the inner edge of the volute decorated with a row of fine incisions. Thin-walled, from fresh mould.
Fabric: hard, very dense and clean, ash-grey (near 2.5 YR 5/0 gray); semi-matt black slip (2.5 YR 3/0 very dark gray), partly worn.
a) extant L. 6.2, Diam. (est.) 6.6.
b) extant L. 6.4, extant H. 2.7
Found: Loc. 46.

Plate 112

045.1.2

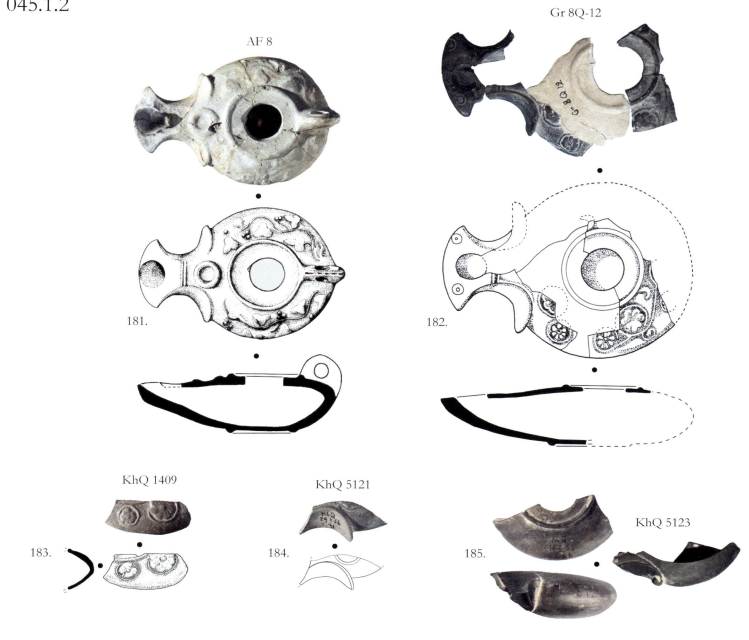

045.2

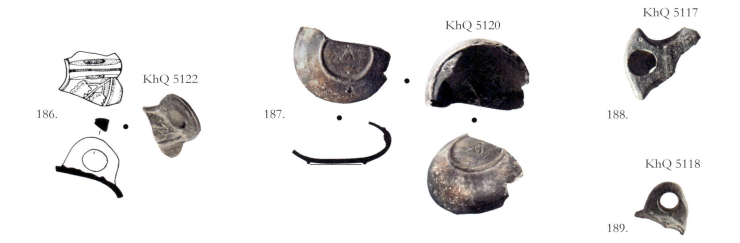

Lamp types 045.1.2 and 045.2

045.2. Decorated shoulder surrounded by a ridge

This Subtype, represented by fragments of two lamps from Khirbet Qumran, is dated by Smith to the 1st century AD, and by Diez Fernandez to between the late 1st century AD and the Hadrianic period (Smith 1966, 12, fig. 3; Diez Fernandez 1983, 83, type L 8.1); they correspond to Kennedy type 7 (Kennedy 1961, 76, pl. XXIII: 516 and 518). The assemblage of nearly 35 lamps of this kind found in the necropolis of Maresha have been identified by Oren and Rappaport (1984, 124, fig. 14:1-2, 15:1-4, 16:1-25 and pl. 14:C) as the "southern" (Darom) type, which would postdate the fall of the Second Temple and be manufactured until mid-2nd century AD (the same date-range as that accepted by Diez Fernandez), apparently in the Beth Govrin – Hebron region. The "Darom" type of lamps was earlier described by Sussman (1982,15-16) and dated to *ca.* AD 70 – 135. In terms of the shape and decoration, the Qumran examples are particularly closely paralleled by the lamps from Masada (Barag and Hershkovitz 1994, nos. 113 and 114).

186. KhQ 5122 (Pl. 112).
> Fragment of lamp shoulder with ring-handle. The shoulder is decorated with oak(?) leaves; the handle has a median groove. From fresh mould.
> Fabric: medium-hard, grey (2.5 YR 5/0) with tiny white grits (and tiny voids?); glossy self-slip 2.5 YR 3/0 (very dark gray) to 5 YR 4/1 (dark gray).
> Extant L. 3.4, extant H. 3.3(?)
> Found: ? (locus unknown);
> Cf. Młynarczyk 2013, 122, fig. 5.
> For oak leaves on the shoulder of a Masada lamp equipped with a ring handle, see Barag and Hershkovitz 1994, no. 113, fig. 19 (apparently, in the same ware as our lamp, so possibly coming from the same source).

187. KhQ 5120 (Pl. h) (Pl. 112).
> About half of lower body with small part of shoulder decorated with rosettes (scrolls?). Inside ring base, workshop mark: A (incuse: delicately incised on archetype). From fresh mould.
> Fabric: hard, greyish brown (5 YR 4/2 dark reddish gray) with rare voids and rare tiny white grits; surface with matt slip, black (5 YR 3/1) mottled brown.
> Diam. 5.6; extant H. 2.3.
> Found: Loc. 111;
> For comparable shape and decoration, see lamp from Masada pertaining to a group dated "from the last decade or two before the siege and fall of Masada" (Barag and Hershkovitz 1994, 62 and 67, no. 114). The mark "A" parallel to that on the Qumran lamp appears inside the ring base of one of the lamps of undetermined pattern found in a refuse of a Traianic/early Hadrianic period workshop in Jerash (Iliffe 1945, pl. IX, no. 171, no fabric description provided).

Fragments attributed to 045.

188. KhQ 5117 (Pl. 112).
> Fragment of nozzle with strongly splayed end; perfectly flat top, with double line of very faint punctures, almost invisible. On the left-hand side, at the junction with shoulder, traces of convex ornament (a volute root?) can be seen.
> Fabric: hard and dense, clean, light grey; thin semi-glossy black slip.
> Extant L. 4.2, W. nozzle 3.7.
> Found : Loc. 13, oven.

189. KhQ 5118 (Pl. 112).
> Ring handle, from worn mould, with partial median groove.
> Fabric: medium-hard, grey (2.5 YR 5/0) with semi-glossy dark grey slip.
> Extant H. 2.9.
> Found: Loc. 13, oven.

046. Decorated shoulder framed on both sides by multiple fine ridges; large filling hole; lug handle

To this type there pertains a single lamp fragment from Khirbet Qumran (no. *190:* KhQ 5101). It is paralleled by type 6 of Beth Shean, described as the northern version of the "Darom" lamps and represented there by 57 objects, dated to AD 70-135 (Hadad 2002, 16-17); this northern counterpart of the "Darom" lamps was identified earlier by Sussman (1982, 16). The same type is attested at Tel Dor as type 23.1, with the suggested date of *ca.* 75 – 150/200 AD (Rosenthal-Heginbottom 1995, 244, fig. 5.21:9).

It also corresponds to "Jerash lamps" named after some examples found at a potter's workshop in Jerash, whose activity has been dated to the Traianic/Hadrianic period (Iliffe 1945, nos. 155-156 and plaster mould no. 160; see also Rosenthal and Sivan 1978, 96-97, no. 393) and to Diez Fernandez type L 8.2, placed by him in between the end of the 1st century AD and the Hadrianic period (Diez Fernandez 1983, 83). Also Smith (1966, 24 and fig. 14, left) has been in favour of a pre-135 AD date for the type.

190. KhQ 5101 (Pl. 113).
Two joining fragments of lamp top with flat lug handle. Large filling hole inside moulded rim; shoulder adorned with a series of relief *ovuli* and bordered by a groove and ridge. From rather worn mould.
Fabric: medium hard, with tiny white grits; surface unslipped; it is probably due to different conditions of deposition that each of the fragments presents different colour: one is 5 YR 6/6 (reddish yellow) at break, its surface fired unevenly beige to light grey, while the other is 2.5 YR 6/6 (light red) both at break and surface.
Diam. (est.) 6.0-6.4.
Found: Loc. 10;
Cf. Donceel 1998, 90-93, fig. 2 (published as no. 3149); Młynarczyk 2015, 123, fig. 5.

047. Two versions of Italian type lamps (Loeschcke type VIII), imported and local/regional respectively

047.1. Roman relief lamp of Loeschcke type VIII

This Subtype is represented by a single fragment of lamp (KhQ 3136) which, to judge by the ware, is a product of a foreign source, perhaps southern Phoenicia or Northern Syria (rather than Italy itself). Very close (and likewise fragmentary) parallels come from Masada Camp F established in AD 72/73 or 73/74 (Magness 2009, pl. 9:7-8). A fragment of another apparently imported (although not necessarily Italian) lamp comes from the caves at Murabba'at (*RB* 1953, 255, fig. 5). The manufacturing of such rather faithful imitations of Italian Loeschcke type VIII lamps in Syro-Palestine have been confirmed, among others, by the finds from a Traianic/Hadrianic-period workshop in Jerash (Iliffe 1945, pl. VIII, nos. 140, 145, 157 and plaster mould no. 161, as well as pl. IX, no. 167).

191. KhQ 3136 (Pl. 113).
Fragment of shoulder and discus of lamp. Outer part of discus, surrounded by a double convex ring, is decorated with a frieze of "millings"; ovolo border on shoulder. From fairly fresh mould.
Fabric: soft, whitish, with many voids (2.5 Y 8/2 white), covered with semi-matt brown slip (10 YR 5/3). Extant L. 3.1.
Found: Loc. 39;
Cf. Młynarczyk 2013, 123, fig. 5.
The lamp, made in a fresh mould and very close to the Italian prototypes, should be dated to last third of the 1st century AD rather than to the early 2nd century.

047.2. Circular lamp of Syrian type (Levantine version of Loeschcke type VIII)

A single example, no. *192* (Gr 4Q-22, lost), was found in the entrance to Cave 4Q. Fairly closely paralleled by a lamp fragment from Jerusalem (Rosenthal-Heginbottom 1981, 24, Abb. X:4), it represents a Levantine type very common in Cyprus/Cilicia and Syro-Palestine, from the Phoenicia and Galilee in the north to Idumaea in the south (for relevant Palestinian finds see, a.o., Kahane 1961, 129; Hayes 1980, nos. 355-356, pl. 42; Rosenthal-Heginbottom 1981, *passim*). This type was dependent on the Italian Loeschcke type VIII, which had started in Italy around the mid-1st century AD (Bailey 1980, 294 and pl. 56: Type O, group I).

Initially dated by Smith to the late 1st to 2nd century AD (Smith 1966, 25 and fig. 16), this Levantine type corresponds to Kennedy's type 5 dated to the 2nd and 3rd centuries (Kennedy 1961, 73-75), to Dor type 26, dated to between the late 1st century AD to AD 150 (and later) (Rosenthal-Heginbottom 1995, 244-245, fig. 5.22, type 26), to Beth Shean type 7, Variant 1, dated to the late 1st and the 2nd centuries AD (Hadad 2002, 16-22) and to Diez Fernandez type L 9.1a, dated to *ca.* 60 – 130 (?) AD (Diez Fernandez 1983, 85-87). The eight examples from the tombs at Huqoq (close to Tiberias and Magdala) were "attributed to the earliest phase, the second half of the first cent. C.E., with a possible extension into the early IInd cent." (Kahane 1961, 130). Many examples of the type ("more than one hundred lamps") were found at the necropolis of Maresha and dated to the 1st/2nd century AD "with a possible extension into the third century" (Oren and Rappaport 1984, 123, figs. 14:5-6, 17:3-4, pl. 14:A). The introduction of the type to Judea has been linked to the presence of the Roman soldiers (Rosenthal-Heginbottom 1981, 8, 26-27, 131). Several examples have been found in Jerusalem, e.g. in the Akeldama tombs (Ben-Arieh and Coen-Uzielli 1996, 84-85, fig. 4.9:1-4)., at the Jerusalem Convention Center site (Hershkovitz 2005, 290-293, fig. 11:5-7 and figs. 12-13: the type dated from the end of the 1st century AD and widespread in the 2nd and 3rd centuries). An in-depth study of the legionary pottery workshop place at the Jerusalem Convention Center by J. Magness, allowing to place its activity in the 2nd century AD (Magness 2005, 104), gives two examples of such lamps apparently manufactured there (*ibidem*, 101 and 154, photo 31 and fig. 32:8-9).

Our lamp no. *192* (Gr 4Q-22) appears to be connected with the Roman presence at Qumran well after AD 68. Indeed, this object seems to have been used by the pagan rather than the Jewish population; the latter, before handling a lamp of the "discus type", would break its discus, probably out of need to observe the rules of ritual purity. It is significant to note that all the lamps of this type found in the Jewish tombs at Huqoq in eastern Galilee (Kahane 1961, 129, 134-135, 141-142, figs. 3: 21-26 and 4:5-6) have their *disci* intentionally broken. In terms of the type's chronology, it is highly improbable that lamp Gr 4Q-22 made its way to the Cave earlier than during de Vaux's Period III ("Roman outpost at Qumran") or Level 4 of the *khirbeh* according to J.-B. Humbert (2003). The widespread use of this lamp type in Judea should be placed not earlier than the first quarter of the 2nd century AD. Actually, J.W. Hayes attributes the "model" South Syrian/North Palestinian series (to which Gr 4Q-22* doubtlessly belongs) to the first half of the 2nd century AD (Hayes 1980, 86-87 and nos. 355-356), while Bailey (1988, 280, pl. 58), dates the beginning of the type in the Levant to not earlier than the end of the 1st century AD.

This chronology has been confirmed by the fact that three fragmentary lamps of this very type were found in a perfectly narrowly dated context of the Cave of the Letters (Yadin 1963, 114, fig. 42, lamps: 3.1, B.1, II.2, 114), and a fragment of a similar (imported?) lamp, dated to the end of the 1st century AD (perhaps too early), comes from Cave 1 at Murraba'at (DJD II, 31-34, fig. 8:13). A lamp of exactly the same type as Gr 4Q-22* and clearly of the same dating (its discus broken, no doubt by a Jewish user) was discovered in Cave (P)24, at short distance to the north of Cave 11Q; it has been attributed by Patrich to "even a post-70 C.E. date" (Patrich 1994, 90, fig 10, the cave considered as having been inhabited). Therefore, we may forward the hypothesis that lamp no. *192* (Gr 4Q-22*) would have been left by a Roman "visitor" searching the Qumran caves sometime during the Second Revolt.

Plate 113

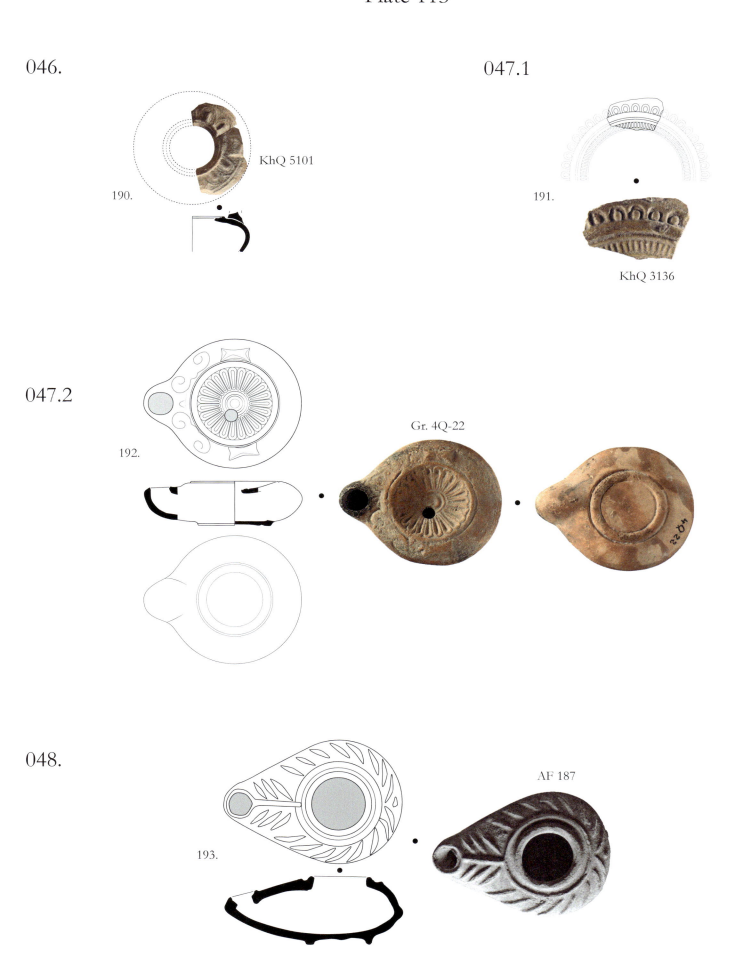

Lamp types 046, 047.1, 047.2 and 048

192. Gr 4Q-22* (Pl. 113).

    Complete lamp. Double-convex circular body on ring base, with small rounded nozzle; discus (with filling hole off the centre) adorned with multi-petalled rosette; shoulder with symmetrical "double axes"; a pair of double volutes flanking the root of the nozzle.
    Fabric: *pâte rosée en dessous avec des traces plus rouges (coulées de peinture du dessus?)*
    L. 8.5, W. 7.0, H. 2.4.
    Found in the entrance to Cave 4Q;
Cf. Qumran 1B, 66.
Cf. Młynarczyk 2013, 123-124 and fig. 5; Młynarczyk, Lugano, Ill. 11.

048. "Candlestick" lamp type

This well-known, common Byzantine-period type is represented by a single lamp from Feshkha, AF 187 (lost), its presence connected with the re-occupation of the site in the Byzantine times (for comparable finds from the nearby En-Gedi, see Vincenz de 2007, 267-268, pl. 53:1-3, 5 and 9; pl. 73:2). It corresponds to Kennedy type 19 (Kennedy 1961, 83-87) dated by Rosenthal and Sivan to between the 5th and early 8th century (Rosenthal and Sivan 1978, 116-120 with nos. 476-479 providing close parallels to our lamp), and by Bailey to *ca.* 450-600 AD (Bailey 1988, 287-288, Q 2330 OA, pl. 60, with abundant *comparanda*). According to J. Magness typology, the dating of lamp AF 187 can be narrowed down to the 6th/7th century AD (Magness 1993, 251-252, "large candlestick lamp" form 3A, cf. p. 252 no. 1). More recently, J. Magness (2005, 159-160, fig. 35:4-5) has precised the dating to between mid-6th and late 7th/early 8th centuries, the more so the dating given to lamp no. *193* (AF 187*) by Donceel (1998, 89, n. 9) as the 5th or 6th century is too early.

193. AF 187* (Pl. 113).

    Complete lamp of the "candlestick" type.
    Fabric: *terre rouge*.
    L. 9.5, H. 3.9,
    Found: *contre la face S du mur de clôture nord, assez haut dans la couche d'alluvion*;
Cf. Qumran 1, 364-365; Qumran 1B, 92: Loc. 30, ("Southern Enclosure").
Cf. Donceel ms, pl. V and VII; Donceel 1998, 89, n. 9; Młynarczyk 2013, 124, fig. 5.

Summary of the chronology of the mould-made lamps:

041: late 2nd - first half of the 1st century BC

042: as 041

043: (development of 041.2): first half(?) of the 1st century BC

044: second half of the 1st century BC (mostly Herod the Great's reign) till the early 1st century AD

045: AD 50-70

046: AD 70-135

047.1: last third of the 1st century AD (or slightly earlier)

047.2: late 1st century AD till 3rd century AD

048: 6th to 7th century AD

Conclusions

In conclusion, it seems important to sum up the distribution of the Qumran lamp types among the chronological phases of the Qumran settlement according to the two systems established in the scholarly literature: the original one, proposed by R. de Vaux (*RB* 1954), and the modified one, introduced by J.-B. Humbert (2003).

a) "Periods" by R. P. de Vaux, *RB* 61 (1954), 254

- **Period I:** 135/104-31 BC: Types **031, 032-035, 041-044**

- **Period II:** 4 BC/AD 6 to AD 68: Types **036.1-7,** continuation(?) of **044,** introduction of **045**

- **Period III:** AD 68 to end of the 1st century AD (Roman outpost at Qumran):

- Types **036.2-5**(?), continuation(?) of Type **045,** introduction of Types **046-047.1**

- + habitation during the Second Revolt, AD 132-135: Type **047.2**

b) "Levels/Phases" by J.-B. Humbert (2003): a reassessment of the chronology of Qumran as compared with de Vaux's synthesis, in correlation with historical events in the region

- **Level 2, Phase A:** 104-63/56 BC (*an aristocratic Hasmonean residence*): Types **031, 032-035, 041-043**

- **Level 2, Phase B:** 56-34/31 BC (*after one of the three possible destructions: 56 BC, 40 BC or 31 BC, Qumran re-settled as a refugee camp*): probably continuation of the use of the above-mentioned Types and the beginning of Type **044**

- **Level 3, Phase A:** 31/30 BC (*occupation by "a new group"*): the same lamp types as in Level 2, Phase B

- **Level 3, Phase B:** 30-10/1 BC (*a sectarian center; worship?) sectarian installations Loci 77, 86, 111, 120, 121, 122, 135 and elaborated water system*: Type **044** (continued?); towards the latter part of the Phase, introduction of Type **036.1**

- **Level 3, Phase C:** 1-60/68 AD (*from c. 1 to 50 AD, climax of the site; Essenism(?) according to the historical sources*): Types **036.1-7;** towards the end of this Phase, introduction of Type **045**

- **68 AD:** destruction and dispersion

- **Level 4:** 68 - 132/135 AD (*Roman outpost, reduction in size*): possibly Types **036.2-5** and continuation(?) of Type **045;** usage of Types **046-047.**

Another important question is that concerning the number and location of the workshops that were supplying Qumran with oil lamps. It is beyond any doubt that at least some of the lamps must have been made in Qumran like much of its domestic pottery, the production of which at Qumran may have started as early as the first half of the 1st century BC (Magen and Peleg 2006, 68-70, 110-111 and note 21). However, attempts have been made to tell more precisely which lamp types were made locally, and which were manufactured outside of Qumran, and during what period of time? This, of course, is a part of a wider discussion about the place of Qumran in the regional economic system of Judea in the Hasmonean and Late Second Temple periods.

Archaeometric studies of select Qumran lamps aimed at detecting their provenance were carried out in the framework of at least three different projects, specifically, petrographic readings referred to by Donceel (1998, 94), NAA analysis by Gunneweg and Balla (2003, 16); and physico-chemical analyses by Michniewicz (2009, 37-83). The obtained results, however, do not always seem to be compatible with each other (to say the least), and the choice of the sampled material may appear random.

In his paper, R. Donceel (1998) has referred to the results of the examination of thin sections of six lamps, of which just three (two of them mentioned by their register numbers: KhQ 1096 "hérodienne noire" and KhQ 3159 of a different type "du locus 130", the latter missing from the lamps record kept at the Ecole Biblique) might have come, according to him, from the same workshop, possibly located in Qumran. The other three lamps (KhQ 3063, 3115, 3157: again, all of these numbers missing from the records kept in the EBAF) would have originated elsewhere (Donceel 1998, 94 and notes 18-20). Since as many as four register numbers have clearly been mistaken, it is impossible to verify the results of this research.

The NAA study by Gunneweg and Balla (2003) resulted in distinguishing five Chemical Groups among sampled Qumran and Jericho pottery, including eight samples of the lamps from Khirbet Qumran and one from Gr 1Q (Gunneweg and Balla 2003, 23 and table 9). Of those nine lamps, two were linked up with Chemical Group I (our cat. nos. *13* and *16*, both of Qumran Type 033.2, see above) which the authors considered as local to Qumran. Three or four lamps have been said to be close to Chemical Group III (our cat. nos. *9, 21, 34* and possibly *29*, all of the "Qumran family" Types 032-034, see above), which the authors identify as characteristic of Jericho workshop; the remainder have been described as "chemical outliers". The quoted results seem to suggest that the "Qumran family" lamps would be manufactured either in two different places (Qumran and Jericho) or in one place (apparently, Qumran), but from two different raw materials.

Shortly after that, Michniewicz (2009, 37-60) examined 18 lamp samples from Qumran and one from Ain Feshkha, comparing them to five samples of lamps found at the Herodian palaces of Jericho. He distinguished three petrographic groups (*PG 1*-3) among them, leaving three samples unassigned (Michniewicz 2009, 37-38, Table 4).

Three lamp samples from Qumran, defined by Michniewicz as pertaining to his *PG 1* (Michniewicz 2009, 37-42), come from the "Qumran family" lamps (our cat. nos. *15, 21* and *34*, specifically Types 033 and 034, see above). However, five other sampled lamps of the same "Qumran family" have been made of *PG 3* (our cat. nos. *7, 17, 24, 31, 38* of Types 032 through 035, see above) which is described as "chemically dissimilar" to *PG 1*. Actually, this picture resembles that provided by the study of Gunneweg and Balla (2003): the lamps pertaining to one formal category (the "Qumran family"), their fabrics and finishing similar to each other on macroscopic examination, turn out to have been made from two different kinds of raw material. Beside the representatives of the "Qumran family", *PG 3* was identified only in one "Herodian" lamp (cat. no. *72,* Type 036.2).

On the contrary, *PG 2* of Michniewicz (2009, 42-45), identified in seven lamp samples, was used in manufacturing of a most wide range of the lamp types, specifically, Qumran Types 031 (cat. nos. *1-2*), 036.2 (cat. no. *68*), 041 (cat. no. *171*), 043 (cat. nos. *174 - 175*) and 044 (cat. no. *179*). What seems to be worthy of note, is the absence of the "Qumran family" representatives from this petrographic group and the fact that, except for Type 036.2, all the other types made of *PG 2* (that is, the "folded-rim" wheel-made lamps and a variety of the mould-made lamps) occur at Qumran/Feshkha in a strictly limited number of examples: a fact suggestive of their non-local origin. Their source should probably be looked for in Jerusalem, where the types in question find a number of parallels. If, indeed, *PG 2* (and *PG 3*, which chemically belongs to the same raw material as *PG 2*) should be identified as derived from the Motza Formation (Michniewicz 2009, 140-141), they may safely be linked up with the production of pottery in and around Jerusalem, which included "various types of lamps" (Berlin 2005, 47).

To sum up the results of the recent archaeometric research: it has been demonstrated beyond any doubt that Qumran, throughout its history, was supplied with lamps by a number of workshops the location of which remained hypothetical. One has to bear in mind that for the manufacturing of small ceramic objects such as the oil lamps, the raw material could have been easily brought from elsewhere. This is probably why the lamps of the "Qumran family" (Types 032-035), almost all of them very similar to each other in macroscopic appearance of both the fabric and surface finishing, turned out to have been made of chemically dissimilar *PG 1* (local to Qumran?) and *PG 3* (imported from the Motza Formation clay?).

In the pre-Herodian (to early Herodian?) Qumran, the local production of the "Qumran family" lamps using two kinds of raw material (*PG 1* and *PG 3*) was supplemented by occasional importations from Jerusalem ("folded-rim" lamps of Type 031 and mould-made lamps of Types 041-043) as testified by the presence of *PG 2*. An interesting case is that of un-sampled lamp cat. no. *32* (Type 034.1) which is macroscopically very different from the remaining "Qumran family" lamps, since its pink fabric of a "metallic" firing closely resembles examples of *PG 2*.

With the introduction of the "Herodian" lamp type, greatly prevalent at Qumran and throughout Judea from the late 1st century BC to *ca.* 70 AD, we probably deal with a multitude of workshops represented by their respective output. Michniewicz' research included just two examples of "Herodian" lamps from Qumran, one of which represented *PG 2*, and another *PG 3* (both based on the same Motza Formation? material), but several more fabric groups can be distinguished on the basis of macroscopic examination; in the catalogue above, the present author tried to indicate some of the (possibly meaningful) fabric/ware similarities between individual objects. It has been also suggested that different kinds of "decoration" present on the "Herodian" lamp nozzles in Machaerus groups 77, 78, 79 (see Loffreda 1996) may have been meant as the workshop marks. There is no doubt that many of the unsampled "Herodian" lamps discovered at Qumran must have come from the Jerusalem area, but the question of distinguishing them from the production of other Judean centres (with Jericho in the first place) remains to be examined within a framework of a much more extensive project combining archaeology and science.

(Warszawa, 19 April 2015)

Bibliographical References and Abbreviations:

Adan-Bayewitz *et al.* 2008: D. Adan-Bayewitz, F. Asaro, M. Wieder and R.D. Giauque, "Preferential Distribution of Lamps from the Jerusalem Area in the Late Second Temple Period (Late First Century B.C.E.- 70 C.E.)", *BASOR* 350 (May 2008), 37-85.

Aviam 2004: M. Aviam, "First-Century CE Earthworks at Gischala (Gush Halav)", in *Jews, Pagans and Christians in the Galilee*, University of Rochester Press 2004, 106-109.

Bailey 1975: D.M. Bailey, *A Catalogue of the Lamps in the British Museum* I, *Greek, Hellenistic and Early Roman Pottery Lamps,* British Museum, London 1975.

Bailey 1980: D.M. Bailey, *Catalogue of the Lamps in the British Museum* II, *Roman Lamps made in Italy*, London 1980.

Bailey 1988: D.M. Bailey, *Catalogue of the Lamps in the British Museum* III, *Roman Provincial Lamps*, London 1988.

Bar-Adon 1977: P. Bar-Adon, "Another Settlement of the Judean Desert Sect at 'En el-Ghuweir on the Shores of the Dead Sea", *BASOR* 227 (October 1977), 1-25.

Barag and Hershkovitz 1994: D. Barag and M. Hershkovitz, "Lamps from Masada", in D. Barag (ed.), *Masada* IV, *The Yigael Yadin Excavations 1963-1965. Final Report,* Jerusalem 1994, 1-147.

Bar-Nathan 2002: R. Bar-Nathan, *Hasmonean and Herodian Palaces at Jericho. Final Reports of the 1973-1987 Excavations* III: *The Pottery*, Jerusalem 2002.

Bar-Nathan 2006: R. Bar-Nathan, "Qumran and the Hasmonean and Herodian Winter Palaces of Jericho: the implication of the pottery finds on the interpretation of the settlement at Qumran", in K. Galor, J.-B. Humbert and J. Zangenberg (eds), *Qumran, The Site of the Dead Sea Scrolls: Archaeological Interpretations and Debates,* Leiden – Boston 2006, 263-277.

Ben Arieh and Coen-Uzzielli 1996: R. Ben Arieh and T. Coen-Uzzielli, "The Pottery", in G. Avi and Z. Greenhut, *The Akeldama Tombs. Three Burial Caves in the Kidron Valley, Jerusalem.* IAA Reports no. 1, Jerusalem 1996, 73-93.

Berlin 2005: A. M. Berlin, "Pottery and pottery production in the Second Temple period", in B. Arubas and H. Goldfus (eds), *Excavations on the Site of the Jerusalem International Convention Center (Binyanei ha'Uma). The Pottery and other Small Finds*, *JRA* Supplementary Series no. 60, Portsmouth, Rhode Island 2005, 29-60.

Clamer 1997: Ch. Clamer, *Fouilles archéologiques de 'Aïn ez-Zâra/Callirrhoé, villégiature hérodienne*, Beyrouth 1997.

Diez Fernandez 1983: F. Diez Fernandez, *Ceramica comun romana de la Galilea*, Jerusalén – Madrid 1983.

DJD I: D. Barthélemy, O.P. and J.T. Milik, *Qumran Cave I, Discoveries in the Judaean Desert of Jordan* I, Oxford 1955.

DJD II: P. Benoit, J. T. Milik, R. de Vaux, *Les grottes de Murabba'at, Discoveries in the Judaean Desert of Jordan* II, Oxford, 1961.

DJD III: M. Baillet, J.T. Milik et R. de Vaux, O.P., *Les «petites grottes» de Qumran. Discoveries in the Judaean Desert of Jordan* III, Oxford 1962.

Donceel 1998 : R. Donceel, «Poursuite des travaux de publication du matériel archéologique de Khirbet Qumrân. Les lampes en terre-cuite», in Z. Kapera ed, *Mogilany 1995. Papers on the Dead Sea Scrolls*, Kraków 1998, 87-104.

Donceel ms: R. Donceel: *Inventaire officiel des lampes en terre-cuite de Khirbet Qumrân et de 'Ain Feshkha* , EBAF, Jerusalem 1995.

Donceel 2005 : R. Donceel, *Khirbet Qumrân (Palestine) : Le Locus 130 et les « ossements sous jarre ». Mise à jour de la documentation*, The Qumran Chronicle, vol 13, No. 1, Cracovie/Cracow 2005.

Donceel and Donceel-Voûte, « The Archeology of Khirbet Qumran », in M.O. Wise, N. Golb, J.J. Collins, and D.G. Pardee (eds.), *Methods of Investigation of the Dead Sea Scrolls and the Khirbet Qumran Site,* Annals of the New York Academy of Sciences 722 (1994), 1-38.

Geva 2003: H. Geva, "Hellenistic Pottery from Areas W and X-2", in H. Geva, *Jewish Quarter Excavations in the Old City of Jerusalem conducted by Nahman Avigad, 1969-1982,* II, Jerusalem 2003, 113-175.

Geva and Hershkovitz 2006 : H. Geva and M. Hershkovitz, "Local Pottery of the Hellenistic and Early Roman Periods", in H. Geva, *Jewish Quarter Excavations in the Old City of Jerusalem, conducted by Nahman Avigad, 1969-1982*, Jerusalem 2006, 94-143.

Grawehr 2006: M. Grawehr, *Die Lampen der Grabungen auf ez Zantur in Petra. Petra Ez Zantur* III, Teil 2, Main am Rhein 2006.

Gunneweg and Balla 2003: J. Gunneweg and M. Balla, "The Provenance of the Pottery", in J.-B. Humbert and J. Gunneweg eds, *Khirbet Qumran and Ain Feshkha,* vol. II, Göttingen 2003, 3-53.

Hadad 2002: S. Hadad, *The Oil Lamps from the Hebrew University Excavations at Bet Shean,* Jerusalem 2002.

Hayes 1980: John W. Hayes, *Ancient Lamps in the Royal Ontario Museum*, Toronto, 1980.

Hershkovitz 2005: M. Herskovitz, "The pottery of the late 1st and 2nd c. A.D. from the 1949 excavations", in B. Arubas and H. Goldfus (eds), *Excavations on the Site of the Jerusalem International Convention Center (Binyanei ha'Uma). The Pottery and other Small Finds*, JRA Supplementary Series no. 60, Portsmouth, Rhode Island 2005, 283-296.

Hirschfeld 2004: Y. Hirschfeld, *Qumran in Context. Reassessing the Archaeological Evidence*, Hendrickson Publishers (Peabody, Massachusetts) 2004.

Humbert 1994: J.-B. Humbert, «L'espace sacré à Qumrân: Propositions pour l'archéologie», *RB* 101/102 (1994), 161-214.

Humbert 2003: J.-B. Humbert, "The Chronology during the First Century B.C., de Vaux and his Method: a Debate", in: J. B. Humbert and J. Gunneweg eds, *Khirbet Qumran and Ain Feshkha,* vol. II, Göttingen 2003, 425-444.

Iliffe 1945: J.H. Iliffe, "Imperial Art in Transjordan. Figurines and lamps from a potter's store at Jerash", *QDAP* 1945 (XI), 1-26.

Itah, Kan and Ben-Haim 2002: M. Itah, Y. Kan and R. Ben-Haim, "Survey and Excavations of Caves in the Fault Excarpment South of Almog Junction and West of Qalya", *'Atiqot* XLI (1999), part 1 (Hebrew), 175-187 and part 2 (English), 169-176.

Kahane 1961: P.P. Kahane, "Rock-Cut Tombs at Huqoq, Notes of the Finds", *'Atiqot* III (1961), 126-147.

Kennedy 1961: Ch. A. Kennedy, "The Development of the Lamp in Palestine", *Berytus* 14 (1961), 67-115.

Killebrew 1998: A. E. Killebrew, "The Pottery", in: R. Hachlili and A.E. Killebrew, *Jericho: The Jewish Cemetery of the Second Temple Period*, Jerusalem 1998, 115-133.

Lapp 2009: E. Lapp, "Material Culture: Lamps", in: E.M. Meyers and C.L. Meyers, *Excavations at Ancient Nabratein: Synagogue and Environs*, Winona Lake, Indiana 2009, 252-283.

Lapp 1961: P. Lapp, *Palestinian Ceramic Chronology 200 B.C. – A.D. 70*, New Haven 1961.

Loffreda 1996: S. Loffreda, *La ceramica di Macheronte e dell'Herodion (90 a.C.-135 d.C.)*, Jerusalem 1996.

Magen and Peleg 2006 : Y. Magen and Y. Peleg, "Back to Qumran : Ten years of Excavation and Research, 1993-2004", in K. Galor, J.-B. Humbert, and J. Zangenberg eds, *Qumran, The Site of the Dead Sea Scrolls: Archaeological Interpretations and Debates,* Leiden – Boston 2006, 55-113.

Magness 1993 : J. Magness, *Jerusalem Ceramic Chronology circa 200-800 CE*, Sheffield 1993.

Magness 2002 : J. Magness, *The Archaeology of Qumran and the Dead See Scrolls*, Grand Rapids, Michigan/Cambridge, U.K, 2002.

Magness 2005 : J. Magness, "The Roman legionary pottery", in B. Arubas and H. Goldfus (eds), *Excavations on the Site of the Jerusalem International Convention Center (Binyanei ha'Uma). The Pottery and other Small Finds, JRA* Supplementary Series no. 60, Portsmouth, Rhode Island 2005, 69-191.

Magness 2009 : J. Magness, "The Pottery from the 1995 Excavations in Camp F at Masada", *BASOR* 353 (February 2009), 75-107.

Michniewicz 2009 : J. Michniewicz, *Qumran and Jericho Pottery : a Petrographic and Chemical Provenance Study*, Poznań 2009.

Młynarczyk 1997: J. Młynarczyk, *Alexandrian and Alexandria-influenced Mould-made Lamps in the Hellenistic Period*, Oxford 1997.

Młynarczyk 2013: J. Młynarczyk, "Terracotta Oil lamps from Qumran: the Typology", *RB* 120 (2013), 99-133.

Młynarczyk, Lugano: J. Młynarczyk, "Terracotta oil lamps (R. de Vaux's excavations of the caves)", in: proceedings of the conference in Lugano, in print.

Oren and Rappaport 1984: E. Oren and U. Rappaport, "The Necropolis of Maresha – Beth Govrin", *IEJ* 34 (1984), 114-153.

Patrich 1994: J. Patrich, "Khirbet Qumran in Light of New Archaeological Explorations in the Qumran Caves" in M.O. Wise, N. Golb, J.J. Collins, and D.G. Pardee (eds.), *Methods of Investigation of the Dead Sea Scrolls and the Khirbet Qumran Site,* Annals of the New York Academy of Sciences 722 (1994), 73-95.

Patrich and Arubas 1989: J. Patrich and B. Arubas, "A juglet containing balsam oil(?) from a cave near Qumran", *IEJ* 39 (1989), 43-59.

Qumran 1: J.-B. Humbert and A. Chambon eds, *Fouilles de Khirbet Qumrân et de Ain Feshkha* vol. 1: *Album de photographies. Répertoire du fonds photographique. Synthèse des notes de chantier du Père Roland de Vaux*, Fribourg, Göttingen 1994.

Qumran 1B: J.-B. Humbert and A. Chambon (eds), *The Excavations of Khirbet Qumran and Ain Feshkha, Synthesis of Roland de Vaux's Field Notes*, translated and revised by Stephen J. Pfann, Novum testamentum et orbis Antiquus Series Archaeologica 1B, Fribourg 2003.

Rahmani 1961: L.Y. Rahmani, "Jewish Rock-cut Tombs in Jerusalem", '*Atiqot* III (1961), 93-120.

Rahmani 1967: L.Y. Rahmani, "Jason's Tomb", *IEJ* 17:2, 1967, 61-100.

RB 1953a : R. P. de Vaux, « Exploration de la région de Qumrân », *RB* 60 (1953), 540-561.

RB 1953b : R. P. de Vaux, « Les grottes de Murabba'at et leurs documents », *RB* 60 (1953), 245-267.

RB 1954: R. P. de Vaux, « Fouilles au Khirbet Qumrân. Rapport préliminaire sur la deuxième campagne », *RB* 61 (1954), 206-236.

RB 1956: R. P. de Vaux, « Fouilles au Khirbet Qumrân. Rapport préliminaire sur les 3, 4, et 5 campagnes », *RB* 63 (1956), 533-577.

RB 1959 : R. P. de Vaux, « Fouilles de Feshkha. Rapport préliminaire », *RB* 66 (1959), 224-255.

Rosenthal-Heginbottom 1981: R. Rosenthal-Heginbottom, *Römische Bildlampen aus Östlichen Werkstätten*, Wiesbaden 1981.

Rosenthal-Heginbottom 1995: R. Rosenthal-Heginbottom, "Imported Hellenistic and Roman Pottery", in E. Stern *et al.* eds, *Excavations at Dor, Final Report.* volume IB: *Areas A and C: The Finds*, Jerusalem 1995, 183-288.

Rosenthal-Heginbottom 2003: R. Rosenthal-Heginbottom, "Hellenistic and Early Roman Fine Ware and Lamps from Area A", in: H. Geva, *Jewish Quarter Excavations in the Old City of Jerusalem conducted by Nahman Avigad, 1969-1982,* vol. II, Jerusalem 2003, 192-223 and 232-255 (plates).

Rosenthal-Heginbottom 2005: R. Rosenthal-Heginbottom, "The 1968 excavations", in B. Arubas and H. Goldfus (eds), *Excavations on the Site of the Jerusalem International Convention Center (Binyanei ha'Uma). The Pottery and other Small Finds, JRA* Supplementary Series no. 60, Portsmouth, Rhode Island 2005, 229-282.

Rosenthal and Sivan 1978: R. Rosenthal and R. Sivan, *Ancient Lamps in the Schloesinger Collection, Qedem* 8, Jerusalem 1978.

Smith 1961: R.H. Smith, "The "Herodian" lamp of Palestine: Types and Dates", *Berytus* 14 (1961), 53-65.

Smith 1964: R.H. Smith, "The Household Lamps of Palestine in Intertestamental Times", *Biblical Archaeologist* XXVII:4, December 1964, 101-124.

Smith 1966: R.H. Smith, "The Household Lamps of Palestine in New Testament Times", *Biblical Archaeologist* XXIX:1, February 1966, 2-27.

Strange 1975: J.F. Strange, "Late Hellenistic and Herodian Ossuary Tombs at French Hill", Jerusalem, *BASOR* 219 (October 1975), 39-67.

Sussman 1982: V. Sussman, *Ornamented Jewish Oil Lamps,* Warminster 1982.

Sussman 2008: V. Sussman, "The Oil Lamps", in: J. Patrich, *Archaeological Excavations at Caesarea Maritima, Areas CC, KK and NN. Final Report* Volume I: *The Objects,* Jerusalem 2008, 209-292.

Sussman 2009: V. Sussman, *Greek and Hellenistic Wheel- and Mould-Made Closed Oil Lamps in the Holy Land. Collection of the Israel Antiquities Authority,* Oxford 2009.

Yadin 1963: Y. Yadin, *The Finds from the Bar Kokhba Period in the Cave of Letters,* Jerusalem 1963.

Vincenz de 2007 : A. de Vincenz, "The Pottery", in Y. Hirschfeld, *En-Gedi Excavations* II, *Final Report (1996-2002),* Jerusalem 2007, 234-427.

Wolff 2002 : S.R. Wolff, "The Excavation of Cave IV/12", *'Atiqot* XLI:2 (2002), 73-83.

Zayadine 2011: F. Zayadine, "Hellenistic pottery from the Estate of the Tobiads", in D. Frangié and J.-F. Salles eds, *Lampes antiques du Bilad es Sham. Jordanie, Syrie, Liban, Palestine.* Actes du Colloque de Pétra-Amman (6-13 novembre 2005), Paris 2011, 167-181.

Afterword to the English version

This is an English translation of our Qumran IIIA volume. I would like to express my deepest thanks to Mr. David Orton for his courage in undertaking it and for transcribing the sustained rhythm of a text in its idiomatic form; and to our colleague Jürgen Zangenberg for conducting a careful proofreading. The book would have deserved a revised version, but the time to do so has not yet come. The best thing is to provide the material for debate. As for the substance, some readers regretted that the volume published in French did not bring anything new. What did they expect? A batch of archives and documentation that had been neglected or lost?[1] Is the 'archaeology' dossier so surrounded by fantasy? At the risk of disappointing people, we must remember that the Vaux legacy has been delivered. We can hardly add anything more. Fortunately, Qumran is more promising than what de Vaux has given us, and we feel it is necessary to make progress. Qumran has now become a heavy dossier. It is not futile to say how we entered into a stalled enterprise and how we tried to revive the movement. Let us outline some of the already known but often neglected lineaments of the obstacles encountered, some of them functional, some of them scientific.

The initiative

The fall of Jerusalem in 1967 had burdened the publication with the diplomatic recommendation to postpone its continuation until the *corpus separatum* of the city was settled, which never came. In 1971, the death of de Vaux, then director of the publication of Qumran, manuscripts and archaeology, slowed down the process. Pierre Benoit, who succeeded him, inherited a delicate situation and made efforts to maintain a link between the different researchers in charge of the manuscripts. John Strugnell, having taken over, and sensing that the time had come to ignore the diplomatic injunction, had convinced Luc Vesco, then director of the École Biblique, to resume the study of archaeology in 1987. Since Vesco had invested himself in directing it, the École Biblique could not relinquish the task of publishing Qumran to a researcher from outside the institution; that would have been an admission of incapacity. He had personally entrusted me with the project, a choice that may have been disconcerting for some. My first task was to form a team. I invited a few faithful collaborators to join us, and then I asked Robert Donceel, professor of Middle East archaeology at Louvain-la-Neuve, in the hope of an academic collaboration. Often held up in Belgium by his teaching, he had agreed to coordinate, albeit from a distance, the research of the scholars approached[2].

The research was undertaken on the basis of the foundations already laid and was part of a continuum. John Strugnell, who had been promoted to the position of director of manuscript publishing, was anxious to show the recovery, and mistakenly believed that archaeology would be quicker to publish. He asked me to produce a booklet as soon as possible. I accepted the principle and proposed the reasoned repertory of the "manuscript jars" in the form of a simple typology intended for archaeologists. However, opening the archaeology of Qumran required learning, and it took time. I had thought the task was easy, but it was not, because of the disorder of the abandoned documentation in the Rockefeller Museum's basement and its poor state of preservation. Nor was it easy, because mastering the de Vaux archive required understanding how he moved from investigation to publication, and the thread was not continuous. First, a complete inventory had to be made and a long restoration of the pottery had to be undertaken. Finally, in response to Strugnell's urgent request, we proposed that the photographic archives[3], which were easier to collect, be made available, accompanied by a summary of the minutes of the excavations. A summary was in de Vaux's hand and was certainly not intended for publication. His mode of expression was concise. Re-reading his excavation diary, he had simply eliminated the unnecessary sentences. He had taken notes for his own use, in a telegraphic and idiomatic style. In the version we intended to print, we saw fit to insert an occasional verb to make it more accessible to English-speaking readers. We have been accused of falsifying the content. A separate English version by Stephen Pfann, useful for English-speaking readers, was required, which is also not free of rough translations[4]. Our simple compilation of photographs and notes from the site does not yet lead to interpretation. Once the excavation was completed, the hundreds of photographs from the site were, later and for us, the indispensable documentation for the re-examination of the stratigraphy. The album was freely available, and what we tried to do could be have been tried by others.

As for the delay, have we forgotten that Qumran was born and raised in the throes of war? It is worth recalling this and seeking the causes, variously commented upon, for the delay in delivering the final report; political reasons that some avoid considering; natural reasons, the death of the pioneers; simply human reasons, Qumran has become the object of covetousness mixed with legitimate ambitions; academic reasons, caution before engaging in a sensitive scientific field, with poorly defined edges. The publication of the Qumran IIIA volume is not the result of a choice but the obligation to finally present the archaeology of the site in the form of a final report. The complaint has been repeated, printed over and over again, and certainly heard, that the lack of a publication of the archaeology of the site has deprived two generations of researchers. We will not deny this by separating the true from the false. True, since the material documentation and especially the corpus of pottery had not been delivered; false, since the essential part of the dossier was not unknown and we worked hard to print more than five hundred photographs of the site; we published the synthesis of the "Field Notes". The base was in place. This was not true either, since de Vaux published his preliminary reports, offered his interpretation, made reviews, and conducted a dialogue with colleagues, commentators, and opponents in the Revue Biblique of the 1950s. We had once envisaged making a volume of translations of his preliminary reports, articles, notes and reviews, intended for an Anglo-Saxon society and other speakers unfamiliar with the French publications, since they had read little or nothing of them. Much of the flaw lies in the question of language. Little more than the English version of the Schweich Lectures is cited today, the rest remains almost ignored. To enter the foundation of Qumran archaeology, the younger generation of scholars would have benefited from the research of the 1950s and the particular spirit of those who, as pioneers and alongside de Vaux, forged the interpretation. Twenty years later we have re-read it. Without too much surprise, we have noticed, in friendly exchanges or in reviews, that what we said was misunderstood or that we were made to say what we did not say. Let us blame the failure on language, which for many is an obstacle. It is therefore useful to provide an English version here to help the English-speaking community. It was not scientifically necessary, but it will comfort those who, concerned with the debate, will not seek to defend their convictions or to defend themselves, because to seek is to understand and the only way to move forward. In science, nobody is owner.

The subject of Qumran was born in the specific Jerusalem crucible of the 1950s. Our French version follows in its Franco-Jordanian footsteps, treated in French since all the documentation concerning the excavation was recorded in that language. It is also a question of homogeneity, because changing the language obliges us to change the way we look at things and possibly our method; each language conveys its own way of thinking and we do not go to Qumran by the same route in English as in French. We have already emphasised certain differences. In short, French favours an anthropological approach through the form of the gesture and the meaning of the object; English, pragmatic, derives a truth from the result of technologies which, without always being confined to it, leads to a deterministic vision of history. In both cases, the approach to the archaeological site is not identical, the means of conceiving it differ and the goal to be reached is not exactly the same.

The question of method

The complexity of an exhaustive publication of the archaeology of Qumran became apparent over time. We had the archives, we had to classify them, understand them, organise them. The report on an excavation that had been left unfinished for a long time required the identification of abundant material documentation and its comparison with the minutes of the site; the articulation of the graphic and photographic documentation in order to caption it; and the harmonization of the collected file with the document of the Schweich Lectures, whose authority did not seem to be questionable a priori. Or almost, because the French version of the Lectures had already raised criticisms that de Vaux welcomed in the English version, a revised edition[5]. The task was not easy for him, he struggled to arrange the reconstruction of the site and still hesitated to formulate the interpretation. This is not surprising, since in field archaeology certainties do not appear at once.

We perceive that de Vaux and his disciples conceived Qumran within the envelope of the Jewish and pious society that had been placed there without procrastination. We respected their option because the choice of another path seemed neither necessary nor legitimate. The search was done and the expected publication could not or should not deviate from the framework already established. In fact, we are not publishing a "different" Qumran than the one that de Vaux delivered, reconsidered without deviating from it as some have tried to do by purging the interpretation of its religious side: *villa rustica*, Zealot fortress, commercial warehouse on the Dead Sea, pottery workshop, etc. It is remarkable that all those who have tried to distance themselves from the first interpretation have evacuated its religious character. Qumran can be considered without its Jewish trappings, which some see as unjustifiably or arbitrarily imposed. It must be understood, however, that the archaeology of Qumran, without the sectarian structure that is attributed to it, has little meaning for the archaeologist. This is at least what de Vaux quickly and clearly understood. All the arguments that seemed reasonable to those who felt able to deviate remain at odds with each other, and it is surprising that these visions have benefited from the benevolence they have aroused. Secularising Qumran forced arguments and documents from the excavations and forced a simplification. On the other hand, our poorly accepted way of approaching the task has not always been known or understood: we are doing an autopsy of the file that de Vaux left, we are extending it in its established form of the Essene Qumran. In short, the most exact definition of our approach is to reinterpret an interpretation, with the firm decision to conduct our investigation independently of the manuscripts, because the archaeological site must speak for itself. The option may be surprising, but our intuition is confirmed: that those who lived there did not write manuscripts that came from elsewhere. We at least accept that they have read them. The reformulation of the archaeology of the site can in no way come from being impregnated by their content.

We have undertaken to verify the statement of the archaeology and its formulation. It was difficult to publish de Vaux as it was, as some researchers requested or demanded. Could we publish assertions that we felt were forced without setting out them, errors in reconstruction that had already been pointed out without checking them? We made proposals. The original interpretation, which remains the foundation, has been sifted to deliver a more readable evolution of the site, and we are looking for an internal coherence that is more free of conventions. De Vaux had articulated his version with skill, we have tried to better arrange the mechanism. Our aim is not to disqualify de Vaux, his work as it stands is still available, but to verify the anthropological framework he has drawn up. The dossier, which had aged and had to be reworked, which had changed envelope without corresponding to the progress obtained in the knowledge of the archaeological and historical context, had to be confronted with new excavations in the same discipline and in the same region. It was necessary to review how the original plans had been arranged and to reconstitute the criteria for the sequence of the architectures, with regard to what could still be seen on the site. The best thing to do, after careful examination of the installations, was to review their function or sometimes to extend the proposal that had been made. We tried to recompose the stratification of the sediments, which led us to the obvious conclusion that two built complexes were intertwined: an ancient, well-planted central square, which a less well-founded crown came to enclose. It follows that Qumran is made up of two successive periods and imposes two distinct societies. What had been given as a history of the place was no longer as well linked as it had been thought, and the use of sources did not appear as convincing as expected. The chronology rectified according to stratigraphy proved to be simpler.

The volume we are presenting is therefore in two parts. While the second part compiles retrospective observations of the excavation, the first part explains the sometimes radical changes to the main points of the original interpretation. Those who are bothered by it are not obliged to read it. Some have reproached us for disqualifying de Vaux's lesson and replacing it with an extrapolation whose abuse would be the one we denounce, and we know that the reproach is perhaps not without reason. It remains true that questioning some of the premises of the original lesson breaks the continuity of the original interpretation in several places, and it is precisely on the break that the reproach is directed. Basically, the reproach is not so much directed at our proposals as at having weakened or broken the logic of a primitive narrative. Whoever dismantles the mechanism undertakes to reassemble it by considering all pieces of it. What, coming from us and concerning the interpretation of the site, simply proposes to restore the fractures in order to safeguard the original form. The frame remains unharmed. In view of the other fanciful interpretations that have arisen, we feel that our readjustments respect the line drawn by de Vaux, in a kind of fidelity. The proposals are worth what they are worth and when they are rejected, the author must demonstrate that they are false. The truth is approached by successive corrections.

In order to accept the validity of our re-reading, it is useful to understand how de Vaux proceeded. When the archaeologist worked with the methods of his time, we have no doubt that he was a good practitioner. We assure you that the Qumran excavation was carried out quickly but correctly and we have no choice but to rely on it. We have at our disposal what he has written: the sum remains modest. We have to follow the thread he followed from the recorded observations of the excavation to the preliminary reports and then, in a second stage, to the Schweich Lectures[6]. We examine the composition of a confidently painted picture.

The brevity of the Excavation Diary has been emphasised: the Diary is an account of the progress of the work, a day-to-day observation; sometimes a reflection is the outline of an explanation retained later on. The reports of each seasons in the Revue Biblique provide us with a commentary on the excavation. Their sum constitutes a description arranged with the embryo of a story that was already present in the commentary. An excavation report must be based on a commented iconography, but de Vaux rarely provided the figurative evidences for his commentary; he often showed without demonstrating. Did he feel that reports were not the place to do this, perhaps wanting to take the time to expound it later? In the Schweich Lectures, he finally sensed that the subject was ripe enough to deliver a coherent narrative.

Reasons to move on

Between 1949 and 1951, in the effervescence of the irruption of the manuscripts and then the discovery of the 'Cave of Manuscripts' (1Q), de Vaux multiplied articles and notes in order to articulate a chronology with the historical data[7]. The foundation quickly contained the history of Qumran. The demand for an interpretative account, which he thought he had to deliver, never left him. As early as 1949, he placed archaeology in the crucible of interpretation. He buried the seeds and waited for the germination. He had said, and he was not afraid to correct: *I was also wrong in saying that the jars had been made for the purpose of depositing the manuscripts*[8]; *I was also wrong in linking the Roman shards found in the cave to a later violation ....*[9] As an archaeologist, his thinking progressed in two stages. He showed great intellectual honesty in the analysis, and yet the distinction between cause and effect is not systematic. Interpretation was tied up in the Schweich Lectures, written after the lectures were given, in the composition of an overall narrative, modelled on what was known about the Essenes. The historian has, by right, taken precedence over the archaeologist. His narrative must be held as a framework history. We had grasped the outline in the preliminary reports of each campaign where he elaborates his interpretation in the course of the excavation. But with the Lectures, priority was given to a crystallisation of the narrative in which the archaeologist's hesitations were attenuated. If we recognise that de Vaux has drawn the definitive outline, all in straight lines, we must return to the analysis without the interpretation. In de Vaux's case, the intuitions in the analysis are often better founded than the Schweich Lectures.

De Vaux explains this without hesitation: "*All these discoveries have aroused enormous interest, and it is justifiable that interest in them should be concentrated above all on the texts which have in this way been made available to us. But the archaeologist can make a contribution to the understanding of the texts by indicating the nature of the setting in which they were discovered and so perhaps making it possible to reconstruct the character of the human group from which they emerged"*, p. viii. *"The book makes no pretence ? to be anything more than a synthesis, or to provide more than a general orientation arising from the preliminary reports..."*, p. ix[10]. And in the conclusion of the Lectures: *"(...) it is apparent that the same lack of certainty hangs over all the archaeological evidence which we might be tempted to invoke in order to establish that the Qumran community was Essene in character. (...) The solution to the question is to be sought from the study of the texts, and not from that of the archaeological remains"*[11].

What conclusions are to be drawn from this? That those who follow de Vaux are not amateurs or adventurers. De Vaux considered that the proximity of the site and the manuscripts was the most likely option for linking the whole: *"... it remains for us to establish what bearing these discoveries have upon the texts and upon history"*. From the moment he was almost certain that the Qumran question would nevertheless have an Essene answer, he put archaeology at the service of the sources, as a theory that would be affirmed with time. The benefit that he felt entitled to draw from it was the opportunity offered that should not be missed. Clearly, there was a priority "manuscript event" and archaeology was only the subsidiary part: *"It is quite certain that in the study of the Qumran documents archaeology plays only a secondary role"*. In the harmony sought, it was archaeology that was easier to conform, an option that seemed legitimate to him when, by deduction, one followed from the other. The interpretation is a crystallisation of all that had been learned from the manuscripts, the sources and what he had retained from the excavation. He constructed Qumran as a rigorous, rational whole that convinced. We must accept it as a hypothesis.

As a hypothesis de Vaux formulated an Essene account, even though he wrote that the evidence for Essenism is missing. However, we have little doubt about the sectarian option because Qumran is probably Essene, a matter of probability. However, we would like to stress the arbitrariness and the risk of an "Essene archaeology" based on a "literary Essenism". Superimposing the one on the other, or confusing them, proceeds from associations by analogy that raise almost insoluble questions because the two are not of the same nature: it was necessary to distinguish, from what was recorded, the way of life of a group, its particularity in a wider society. The Vaux vulgate sometimes relies on undocumented arguments: the conception of a community settlement and its *sui generis* foundation as such; a community that camped in tents or troglodytes; the continuous occupation of the site by a homogeneous group[12]; the use of the earthquake in 31 BC; the local conception of the library of a society in autarky in a place cut off from the rest of the world; a cemetery for strictly internal use. It is legitimate to restate some of the outstanding questions in different terms.

Jean-Baptiste Humbert

Endnotes

1 Some people feared that we had hidden it.

2 It is highly regrettable that Reverend Puech, who was not without knowledge, thought he was authorized to state in a reputable journal that the École Biblique ... *had charged R. Donceel, in 1986 (sic), with the task of carrying out this project, and then, due to unexplained circumstances the "Notes de chantier"* (field notes), *sometimes reworked and inaccurate, were first published by J.-B. Humbert and A. Chambon*. We publicly regret the lack of respect for academic morality. The motives are obscure that we do not want to know. The breach was repeated. R. Donceel, attentive but prevented, his wife Pauline Donceel-Voûte subtly attributed the Qumran archaeology file to herself. A few media echoed the news. In 1990, having broken off, without explanation, all contact with the École Biblique, she nevertheless committed, in collaboration with R. Donceel, but without the approval of the École Biblique, a parallel inventory of glasses, stone vases and lamps. The proposed incomplete catalogue is rendered obsolete by random references to the excavation archives. This publication, outside of an academic consultation, is not authorised by the École Biblique: R. DONCEEL and P. DONCEEL-VOUTE, *Matériel archéologique de Khirbet Qumrân et 'Aïn Feshkha sur la mer Morte*, Louvain 2017.

3   J.-B. HUMBERT and A. CHAMBON, *Qumran* Vol. I. offers the 538 best pictures of the excavation. A well-deserved reproach has been made about the presentation of the extract of the plans. To have captioned the presentation of the architecture according to the de Vaux Periods was to suggest that it had evolved. The diagrams presented are in fact taken from the three Coüasnon plans but without any stratigraphic or chronological indication. Their rearrangement and repetition were intended to help the reader understand the location and the angle from which the photographs were taken.

4   Steven Pfann, having undertaken the English version of the Field Notes published in *Qumran* I, perceptively detected that R. Donceel had completed the missing loci in the Vaux synthesis by inserting the entries from the Excavation Diary. The notes published in *Qumran* I are not our own and thus entirely in de Vaux's hand: S. PFANN, *The Excavations of Khirbet Qumran and Ain Feshkha, Synthesis of Roland de Vaux's Field Notes*, Vol. IB, Freiburg and Göttingen, 2003. His English and revised edition could help.

5   R. de VAUX, *Archaeology and the Dead Sea Scrolls*, London 1973.

6   De VAUX, *L'archéologie et les manuscrits de la mer Morte*, London 1961. And the English revised version, London, 1973.

7   R. de VAUX, *RB* 1949, p.234-7 and 586-609; *RB* 1950, p. 417-429. Review by DUPONT-SOMMER, *RB* 1951, pp. 437-443.

8   Definition and function of the scroll jar, J.-B. HUMBERT, « Revoir la jarre à manuscrits de Qumrân », *RB* 2020, p. 260-294.

9   R. de VAUX, « Fouilles au Khirbet Qumran », *RB* 1953, p. 104.

10 *Archaeology*, p. ix

11 *idem*, p. 133

12 For an Hasmonaean level at Qumrân, see: J.-B. HUMBERT, « Qumran and Machaerus on a Hasmonean Axis », in Chemnitz conference proceedings : *Life at the Dead Sea*, Chemintz 2020, p. 317-338.

Index

Lists and bibliography

List of figures

fig. 1.	The Qumran site in its untouched environment, in 1951	6
fig. 2.	The Qumran plateau	12
fig. 3.	Khirbet Qumran during the 1955 campaign	14
fig. 4.	Photogrammetric reconstruction of the environment of the Qumran site, From the Jordan Air Force aerial photographs, 1953	16
fig. 5.	Photogrammetric reconstruction, views towards the northwest and north, From the Jordan Air Force aerial photographs, 1953	18
fig. 6.	Photogrammetric reconstruction, views towards the south and east, From the Jordan Air Force aerial photographs, 1953	20
fig. 7.	Pool 48–49, broken by fault 2a of the earthquake	24
fig. 8.	Illustration of the different faults o f the earthquake	26
fig. 9.	Faults 1 and 1a of the earthquake in Locus 145. The upper layers of ash, the latest ones, have flowed into the crevice (2002)	30
fig. 10.	A possible Essene domain situated in the northern basin of the Dead Sea	33
fig. 11.	The long wall of the Qumran terrace viewed toward the south close to the *khirbeh*.	34
fig. 12.	Ain Feshkha with the long wall running towards the north	36
fig. 13.	The ravine and the long wall of the terrace form a closed space	38
fig. 14.	Long wall 951 bordering the terrace to the east	40
fig. 15.	The Qumran domain defined by the *erubim*	42
fig. 16.	The western ravine links Qumran to the palm grove to form the closed domain.	43
fig. 17.	Plan and photographs of the long wall of ez-Zara, Transjordan bank a) General plan of the palm grove of ez-Zara. *Archaeological excavations of Ain ez-Zara/Callirrhoe*, p. 9 b, c and d) Remains of the long wall in the eastern sector of the site *With the kind permission of C. Clamer*	44
fig. 18.	Locus 130, the block of ash in pool 173	46
fig. 19.	Examples of wood carbonized by slow combustion: a) Locus 4, carbonized wood of the door b) Tomb 17, carbonized wood of a coffin	48
fig. 20.	Locus 35, fragments of a carbonized piece of furniture	49
fig. 21.	Ash deposit	50
fig. 22.	Fallen roofing	52
fig. 23.	Spreading of ashes	54
fig. 24.	Evidence of ash or charcoal produced by slow combustion	56
fig. 25.	Slaughtering of sheep at Qumran for the festive meal at the end of the excavation, 1956	58

fig. 26.	Photographs of the deposits in place, Locus 130	60
fig. 27.	Photographs of the deposits in place, Locus 130	62
fig. 28.	Buried deposit, Locus 130, large cooking pot KhQ. 2342 (Grid A4)	64
fig. 29.	a) Photograph of a buried deposit of Locus 130 b) Identification of fauna	66
fig. 30.	Arrangement of the display stand of Locus 77, viewed towards the east	70
fig. 31.	Display stand 872 of Locus 86. a) At the time of its discovery, its top in the indentation of partition wall 873; b) Locus 86 during the excavation, state of display stand 872 (photo Leo Boer, with the kind permission of the Leo Boer Archive, *Archaeology in the Land of Tells and Ruins*, Oxford 2014, p. 158)	72
fig. 32.	Display stands 871 and 872 in Locus 86, after restoration	74
fig. 33.	The Qumran cemetery, aerial views (Jordan Air Force, Amman)	76
fig. 34.	Report of Henri V. Vallois, 14 November 1952. Musée de L'Homme, Paris.	78
fig. 35.	The main cemetery in 1952	82
fig. 36.	Covering of the loculi in the graves	84
fig. 37.	*Journal* of the excavation of graves 24 and 32, in 1956	86
fig. 38.	Excavation of the graves and the state of the human remains	88
fig. 39.	Excavation of the graves and the state of the human remains	90
fig. 40.	Examples of delayed burial: secondary interments (a, b, c); in wooden coffins (d, e)	92
fig. 41.	The state of Locus 112 in 2014	94
fig. 42.	Installation of Locus 51 as cesspool	96
fig. 43.	Surveys and plans of the sector around Locus 112 and designation of the constructed elements	98
fig. 44.	Locus 112, discharge of the toilet	99
fig. 45.	Survey plan and elevation of the installation of baths, Locus 34 (Coüasnon 1954)	102
fig. 46.	Plans and surveys of Loci 34 and 35	104
fig. 47.	Locus 34 in the stages of excavation a) Terracotta pipe 621 of workshop L. 34 b) The long bath, original lining remoulded, covering of mortar supporting part of a small tank c) The bath viewed towards the east; to the left the thin dividing wall 306 d) The small seated bath	106
fig. 48.	Examples of African baths. a) Associated tub and seated bath, Tabiet el-Ramleh (Aboukir, Egypt) (photo Paolo Gallo, by author's permission) b and c) Seated Hellenistic baths of Kerkouane (Tunisia), partly restored (photos Humbert 2011)	108
fig. 49.	The cesspool pipe of the workshop of Locus 34	110
fig. 50.	Proposal for a new chronology	114
fig. 51.	Coüasnon Plan, Period Ib, shaded	120
fig. 52.	Western annexes of the residence, C.H. Coüasnon, 1956	122
fig. 53.	Examples of types of survey in the course of the excavations a) The central building, Du Buit and Rousée, 1953 b) The central building, details of the constructions, Du Buit and Rousée, 1953	125
fig. 54.	Plan Period Ib, Coüasnon 1956	126
fig. 55.	Plan Period II, Coüasnon 1956	127
fig. 56.	Plan Period III, Coüasnon 1956	128
fig. 57.	Location of the loci added for publication purposes	139
fig. 58.	The sun dial KhQ 1229 from the upper layers of Locus 45 (sub 84) Publication: Paul Tavardon, *Le disque de Qumrân*, Pendé 2010	152
fig. 59.	Chart of the symbols used in the illustration of the stratigraphic diagrams	155
fig. 60.	Survey of the southeast triangle with elevations, 1953	156
fig. 61.	Overview of the southeast workshops (from Coüasnon Plan of IIb and III)	158
fig. 62.	Southeast annexes, designation of the constructed elements	160
fig. 63.	a) Overview of the southeast workshops (from Coüasnon Plan of Ib) b and c) Surveys with the option of the passage between L. 45 and 145, 1953 d) Preparatory survey of the south segment of wall 900	162
fig. 64.	Locus 44 towards the south, open towards Locus 61 (left) and towards Locus 59 (right)	164
fig. 65.	Locus 44 on the 1953 survey	165

List of figures

fig. 66. Locus 44
 a) Burnt layer, towards the northwest
 b) Rafters of the collapsed roofing, towards the south
 c) The mouth of the channel and its cover 169

fig. 67. Pottery from Locus 61:
 a) Buried jar to the north of pool 905, a slab of mortar from which can be made out in the left lower corner.
 b) Buried jar in the northwest corner.
 c) Jar KhQ 1474 fitted into a cylinder of crude earth
 d) The crude earth cylinder against the east wall 174

fig. 68. Niche 905, Locus 61:
 a) towards the northwest
 b) towards the west 175

fig. 69. Passage from locus 60 to locus 61; the silos and the location of the buried jar. 176

fig. 70. Locus 59 181

fig. 71. Locus 59 towards the northeast. Wall 902, from the front, on which wall 901 rests. 182

fig. 72. Locus 60
 a) Top of the stack of pottery of Level 3C
 b) Buried jar KhQ 1679 surrounded by a circle of stones (according to the catalogue: actually Locus 61?)
 c and d) Jar KhQ 1630 buried in front of the door of Locus 61 184

fig. 73. Locus 45
 a) Designation of the constructed elements, (b) of Coüasnon's survey, (c and d) of the restoration 190

fig. 74. Locus 45a and b 192

fig. 75. Locus 45a, towards the west 193

fig. 76. a) Locus 45 a, b, c, Coüasnon survey at 1:100, 1953
 b) Hand-drawn sketch on the preparatory survey of 1954. Locus 177 was wrongly positioned by Coüasnon.
 The elevations correspond to different zero references. 202

fig. 77. a) Layers of ash in Loci 52 and 62, from the photo PAM 40427
 b) Two upper layers above wall 315 are separated by ash 62.2
 c) Loci 52 and 53 and Locus 43 in the background. 206

fig. 78. Numbering of constructed elements (late levels) of the triangle 207

fig. 79. Initial location of Loci 62 and 63 208

fig. 80. Locus 80 212

fig. 81. Locus 80: elevation of west wall 913 and section 214

fig. 82. Locus 80: small jar KhQ 1465 and its lid KhQ 1466 215

fig. 83. The buttress of Locus 65 containing kiln 918 218

fig. 84. Section of Locus 64, north-south (de Vaux, 1954) 220

fig. 85. a) Survey of Loci 64 and 84, from Coüasnon Plan (Period II)
 b) Diagram section from the pottery kiln 917, L 84 (1954 survey) 222

fig. 86. French Gallo-Roman lime kiln
 Arnaud Coutelas, *Le Mortier de chaux*,
 Edition Errance, Paris 2009, p. 43 223

fig. 87. Locus 64 and Locus 71 in the background 226

fig. 88. Southeast annexes, designation of the constructed elements 238

fig. 89. Series of pools:
 a) Coüasnon Plan (Period II)
 b) From survey of work with elevations 239

fig. 90. Loci 72 and 73, stratification 240

fig. 91. a) Designation of the constructed elements
 b, c, d) Concise surveys of late remains to the south of the southeast annexes
 e) Reconstruction of Loci 180-186 according to the 1954 surveys
 f) Reconstitution of original pool 72/73 242

fig. 92. a) Locus 72 fractured by the earthquake
 b) South face of wall 921 (L76)
 c) and d) Photo and survey of the ash under Loci 72 and 68 244

fig. 93. First part of the elbow for condemned feed to pool 72-73. Towards the west. 246

fig. 94. Earthquake fracture in Loci 72 and 73 248

fig. 95. Bath L. 68, towards the east 252

fig. 96. Locus 68 253

fig. 97.	Locus 69 towards the southeast.	255
fig. 98.	Final constructions in the southeast annexes: Locus 180 Level 4/5?	256
fig. 99.	Loci 69 and 71, from plan Ib	257
fig. 100.	a) Survey 1, 1954 b) Correction of wall 967	259
fig. 101.	Reservoir L. 71 before the excavation work	260
fig. 102.	Coüasnon surveys and plan of the L. 71 sector	262
fig. 103.	Proposed reconstruction of Loci 187 and 188	263
fig. 104.	Reservoir L. 71	264
fig. 105.	Planned and axonometric reconstruction of reservoir L. 71	265
fig. 106.	The outside workshops to the southeast, Coüasnon plans and designation of the constructed elements a) First installation b) Late installation c and d) Designated walls	266
fig. 107.	Locus 75	268
fig. 108.	Locus 75, towards the south. Note the back-lit flap in the partition wall of the pool.	269
fig. 109.	Locus 183, surveyed in 1954	270
fig. 110.	Surveys of Loci 143 and 144	273
fig. 111.	The southwest corner of L. 143, dismantled to clear drain 944	274
fig. 112.	Locus 81 a) Wall 800 and aqueduct 805, Levels 3 and 4 b) and on the photograph, projecting to the Left of reservoir 91	276
fig. 113.	a) Locus 91, numbering of the walls and surroundings b) On the Coüasnon plan with supply outlets	278
fig. 114.	Locus 91 fill-in, crossed by late drain 805, 81.1	279
fig. 115.	Buried jars in Locus 81 a) Clearing of the buried jars b) Jars deprived of the Level that contained them	280
fig. 116.	a) Slabs of wall coating in Locus 81 and the raised passage towards Locus 79 b) Installation 802 seals the older levels: ash 81.7 (Level 3A)	282
fig. 117.	Arrangement of the buried jars of Locus 81	283
fig. 118.	Locus 82, jar KhQ 1634	293
fig. 119.	Reservoir 91 looking towards the east with the staircase discovered in 2000 (photo 2015, Lionel Mochamps)	295
fig. 120.	Loci 83 and 85, designation of the walls	299
fig. 121.	Loci 83 and 85, plans	300
fig. 122.	Smashed jars at the foot of the steps of Locus 85	303
fig. 123.	Axonometries of Loci 77, 86, 91	304
fig. 124.	Locus 77	306
fig. 125.	Survey of the side of Loci 77 and 86 a) survey 1 south sector b) survey 2 - 1954	308
fig. 126.	Designation of the walls and of some constructed elements (L. 77 and 86)	309
fig. 128.	a) Periods Ib and b) II (Coüasnon 1954)	310
fig. 127.	South front of the settlement: Locus 79 to the foreground and 77 then 86 to the rear	310
fig. 129.	Floors and mortars of the walls, Loci 77 and 86	312
fig. 130.	The blocked doors of Locus 77	314
fig. 131.	Construction and condemnation of supply 356 of Locus 77	316
fig. 132.	a) Aqueduct 805 crossing Locus 185 (86) b) Stone circle 855 in front of threshold 856 and reduced sondage. c) Debris from kiln 865 in L. 77	318
fig. 133.	Appearance of Loci 77 and 86 before the dig, 1953, aerial photograph, Jordan Air Force (JAF 6)	321
fig. 134.	Locus 77 after the dig	322
fig. 135.	Arrangement of the display stands of Locus 86, looking south	326
fig. 136.	Loci 86, 87, 89, then 185, designation of the elements	327
fig. 137.	Locus 86	328

List of figures

fig. 138.	a) Locus 86 east, set in which is Locus 185 b) The two stands, at the time of the dig, are flat-topped	330
fig. 139.	Reinforcement 869 to the south of Locus 86 a) Foundation of reinforcement 869 above paving 816. b) Block of sandstone engraved with a Greek letter *chi*, inserted in the S-E corner of L. 86 (Photo 2008, after restoration)	331
fig. 140.	Locus 86	332
fig. 141.	The original space of Locus 86 with its installations have been reconstructed	334
fig. 142.	The stacks of pots in Locus 89	336
fig. 143.	The stacks of pots in Locus 89	338
fig. 144.	a) The stacks of pots in Locus 89 b) Location of different types of pottery in Locus 89	340
fig. 145.	Paving 816, Loci 90, 93 and 98, and drain 878 on the south boundary, looking east (Photo 2008, after stripping in 2000)	358
fig. 146.	Paving 816; a) and b) Loci 93/98, looking northeast and east (2008) c) under the reinforcement around Locus 89, to the east (2014, Lionel Mochamps)	360
fig. 147.	a) and b) Paving along the east front of the settlement (Photo 2014)	362
fig. 148.	The general layout of the south paving, surrounded by drains	365
fig. 149.	Aerial view of the western edge of the site (photograph: Jordan Air Force, 1953)	368
fig. 150.	The late extension of the southwest of the site. a) Coüasnon Plan, Period Ib b) Designation of the constructed elements c) Reconstruction according to plans, placed on the photogrammatic model of the terrace, looking east (the scree on the slope of the ravine is spoil earth from the excavation)	370
fig. 151.	Sector of Locus 96 partly destroyed by the earthquake. In the background, pillars of Locus 97.	371
fig. 152.	Locus 130 with exposed deposits, in the foreground, the mass of ash filling pool 173, in the middle distance, the yellow sediment on wall 501 of Locus 123.	372
fig. 153.	The north enclosure a) From Coüasnon Plan, period Ib b) From Coüasnon Plan, period II	374
fig. 154.	Stages of occupation of the space of the north enclosure	376
fig. 155.	Locus 130 after clearing, showing the pillaging hole in pool 173	378
fig. 156.	Aerial view of the north enclosure, 1953	379
fig. 157.	Designation of the constructed elements of Locus 134, lobby of the north enclosure with Locus 172	381
fig. 158.	a) Locus 130, from Coüasnon Plan, Period Ib b) Clearance of kiln 676 to the east of Locus 130	384
fig. 159.	Overview of the Locus 130 deposits, a) looking east, b) looking west	386
fig. 160.	Pool 173 in Locus 130	388
fig. 161.	a), b) and c) The deposits buried in Locus 130 d) Clearance of scattered deposits and sherds, looking west. e) Clearance of deposits against wall 501, looking west	390
fig. 162.	The buried deposits in Locus 130	392
fig. 163.	1955 survey of the main buried deposits of Locus 130 (and Locus 132)	393
fig. 164.	Tidied version of hand-drawn sketch (previous page, fig. 163)	394
fig. 165.	Locus 132 a) Aqueduct 500 hillock on projection 677 b) Survey of Locus 132 (1955) c) and d) Designation of the constructed elements	414
fig. 166.	Locus 132	416
fig. 167.	Succession of architectural phases at the junction of Loci 130 and 132.	418
fig. 168.	Plate 86, 1	420
fig. 169.	Storage jar, Plate 87, 5	422
fig. 170.	Locus 138 in the course of excavation and Locus 132 in the background (photo: Fr. Robert Beauvery)	424
fig. 171.	Locus 138 a and b) Surveys (1955) c) Designation of the constructed elements	426
fig. 172.	a) Coüasnon survey 1955 b) Designation of the constructed elements	430
fig. 173.	General view of Loci 134 and 135, looking west	432

fig. 174. Evolution of the water supply, according to the surveys and plans 435
fig. 175. Designation of the constructed elements of L. 136 436
fig. 176. Locus 172, Coüasnon surveys 439
fig. 177. Loci 140 and 141, looking south, in the course of the excavations 444
fig. 178. a) Designation of the constructed elements, L. 140 and 141
b) From Coüasnon, Plan of Period II
c) Survey of Loci 140 and 141, Coüasnon, 1955 445
fig. 179. Pinched-rim lamps 450

List of plates

Plate 1: Locus 103, catalogue and pottery, scale ¼ 101
Plate 2: Locus 34, pottery, scale ¼ 113
Plate 3: Locus 153, pottery and catalogue scale ¼ 166
Plate 4: Locus 44, pottery, scale ¼ 171
Plate 5: Locus 44, photographs and pottery 172
Plate 6: Locus 61, photographs and pottery 177
Plate 7: Locus 61, pottery, scale ¼ 179
Plate 8: Locus 61, pottery, scale ¼ 180
Plate 9: Locus 59, pottery and catalogue scale ¼ 183
Plate 10: Locus 60, catalogue of pots and photographs 188
Plate 11: Locus 60, pottery, scale ¼ 189
Plate 12: Locus 45, catalogue of pots, recorded before 15/3/54 and photographs 194
Plate 13: Locus 45, pottery, recorded before 15/3/54, scale. ¼ ...195
Plate 14: Locus 45a, pottery and catalogue scale ¼ 196
Plate 15: Locus 45a, pottery, scale ¼ 197
Plate 16: Locus 45a, pottery, scale ¼ 198
Plate 17: Locus 45a and 45b, photographs of pottery 199
Plate 18: Locus 45b, catalogue of pots and photographs 200
Plate 19: Locus 45b, pottery, scale ¼ 201
Plate 20: Locus 177 (45c), catalogue of pots and photographs ...203
Plate 21: Locus 177 (45c), pottery, scale ¼ 204
Plate 22: Locus 63, pottery and catalogue 209
Plate 23: Locus 62, catalogue of pots and photographs 210
Plate 24: Locus 62, pottery, scale ¼ 211
Plate 25: Locus 80, catalogue of pots and photographs 215
Plate 26: Locus 80, pottery, scale ¼ 216
Plate 27: Locus 65, pottery and catalogue scale ¼ 219
Plate 28: Locus 84, catalogue of pots and photographs 227
Plate 29: Locus 84, pottery, scale ¼ 228
Plate 30: Locus 145, pottery, scale ¼ 231
Plate 31: Locus 145, pottery, scale ¼ 233
Plate 32: Locus 145, pottery, scale ¼ 235
Plate 33: Locus 145, photographs and pottery........................236
Plate 34: Loci 72 and 73, pottery and catalogues, scale ¼ 250
Plate 35: Locus 68, pottery and catalogue, scale ¼ 254
Plate 36: Locus 69, pottery and catalogue, scale ¼ 258
Plate 37: Locus 75, pottery and catalogue, scale ¼ 271
Plate 38: Locus 143, pottery and catalogue, scale ¼.................275
Plate 39: Locus 81-1, pottery and catalogue, scale ¼ 285
Plate 40: Locus 81-2, catalogue of pots and photographs 286
Plate 41: Locus 81-2, pottery, scale ¼ 287
Plate 42: Locus 83-3, pottery and catalogue, scale ¼ 288
Plate 43: Locus 81-3, pottery, scale ¼ 289
Plate 44: Locus 81-3, pottery, scale ¼ 290
Plate 45: Locus 83 -3, photographs of pots 291
Plate 46: Locus 81-4, pottery and catalogue, scale ¼ 292
Plate 47: Locus 82, pottery and catalogue, scale ¼ 293
Plate 48: Locus 91, pottery, scale ¼ 297
Plate 49: Locus 91, pottery, scale ¼ 298
Plate 50: Locus 83, pottery, catalogue and photographs, scale ¼ ...302
Plate 51: Locus 85, pottery and catalogue, scale ¼ 303
Plate 52: Locus 77, catalogue of pots 324
Plate 53: Locus 77, pottery, scale ¼ 325
Plate 54: Locus 89, photographs and pottery 343
Plate 55: Locus 89, pottery, scale ¼ 345
Plate 56: Locus 89, pottery and catalogue, scale ¼ 346
Plate 57: Locus 89, pottery, scale ¼ 347
Plate 58: Locus 89, pottery and catalogue, scale ¼ 348
Plate 59: Locus 89, pottery, catalogue and photographs, scale ¼ ...349
Plate 60: Locus 89, pottery and photographs, scale ¼ 350
Plate 61: Locus 89, pottery, catalogue and photographs, scale ¼ ...351
Plate 62: Locus 89, catalogue of pots and photographs 352
Plate 63: Locus 89, pottery, scale ¼ 353
Plate 64: Locus 89, pottery and catalogue, scale ¼ 354
Plate 65: Locus 87, pottery and catalogue, scale ¼ 355
Plate 66: Locus 86, catalogue of pots and photographs 356
Plate 67: Locus 86, pottery, scale ¼ 357
Plate 68: Locus 98, pottery and catalogue, scale ¼ 364
Plate 69: Locus 90, pottery and catalogue, scale ¼ 366
Plate 70: Locus 93, pottery and catalogue, scale ¼ 367
Plate 71: Locus 134, pottery and catalogue, scale ¼.................382
Plate 72: Locus 130, no location on the graph, pottery and catalogue, scale ¼ 396
Plate 73: Locus 130 -1A and 1B, pottery and catalogue, scale ¼ ...397
Plate 74: Locus 130-2A, pottery, scale ¼ 398
Plate 75: Locus 130-2A, pottery and catalogue, scale ¼ 399
Locus 130-2B, pottery and catalogue........................400
Locus 130-3A, pottery and catalogue 400
Plate 76: Locus 130-2B, pottery, scale ¼ 401
Locus 130-3A, pottery, scale ¼ 401
Locus 130-3B, pottery and catalogue........................402
Plate 77: Locus 130-3B, pottery, scale. ¼ 403
Locus 130, catalogue of the pottery collected in the ashes...404

Plate 78: Locus 130, pottery collected in the ashes, scale ¼ 405
Locus 130, catalogue of the pottery collected in the ashes (continued) 406
Plate 79: Locus 130, ash, pottery, scale ¼ 407
Plate 80: Locus 130-5A, pottery and catalogue, scale ¼ 408
Plate 81: Locus 130-5B, pottery and catalogue, scale ¼ 409
Plate 82: Locus 130-6A, pottery and catalogue 410
Locus 130-6B, pottery 410
Locus 130, sediments, pottery and catalogue, scale ¼ ...410
Plate 83: Locus 131, pottery and catalogue, scale ¼ 411
Plate 84: Locus 130, photographs of pottery 412
Plate 85: Locus 130, photographs of pottery 413
Locus 132, catalogue and photograph 420
Plate 86: Locus 132, pottery, scale ¼ 421
Locus 132, catalogue and photograph 422
Plate 87: Locus 132, pottery, scale ¼ 423
Plate 88: Locus 138, pottery and catalogue, scale ¼ 429
Plate 89: Locus 135, out of the grid, pottery and catalogue, scale ¼ 433
Plate 90: Loci 136 and 137, pottery and catalogue, scale ¼ 437
Plate 91: Locus 129, pottery and catalogue, scale ¼ 441
Plate 92: Loci 100, 115 and 129, collection of painted sherds of type pl. 91, 13 442

Plate 93: Locus 133, pottery and catalogue, scale ¼ 443
Plate 94: Loci 140 and 141, pottery and catalogue, scale ¼ 446
Plate 95: Lamp type 032 453
Plate 96: Lamp types 033.1 and 033.2 455
Plate 97: Lamp type 033.2 457
Plate 98: Lamp types 032-033 461
Plate 99: Lamp type 034.1 463
Plate 100: Lamp types 034.2, 035, 035-Prime 465
Plate 101: Lamp type 036.1 471
Plate 102: Lamp type 036.2.1 475
Plate 103: Lamp type 036.2.1 477
Plate 104: Lamp type 036.2.2 479
Plate 105: Lamp types 036.2 and 036.3 483
Plate 106: Lamp types 036.4 and 036.5 485
Plate 107: Lamp types 036.6 and 036 (fragments) 491
Plate 108: Lamp nozzles attributed to type 036.2 to 036.6 497
Plate 109: Lamp type 036.7 and fragments attributed to 036.1 to 036.3 501
Plate 110: Lamp types 037.1 to 037.4, 041.1 - 041.2 and 042....................................505
Plate 111: Lamp types 043.1, 043.2, 044, and 045.1.1 509
Plate 112: Lamp types 045.1.2 and 045.2 513
Plate 113: Lamp types 046, 047.1, 047.2 and 048....................517

Bibliography

Authors cited

BAR-ADON, Pessah, "Another Settlement of the Judean Desert Sect at En el-Ghuweir, on the Shores of the Dead Sea", *ASOR* 227 (1997), p. 1-25; and *Eretz-Israel 10* (1971), p. 72-89 (Heb.).

BENNETT-ELDER, Linda, "The Woman Question and Female Ascetics among Essenes", *Biblical Archaeologist*, 57, no. 4 (1994).

BLAKE, Ian, «Rivage occidental de la mer Morte", *RB* 61 (1966), p. 564-566.

BOUSSAC, Marie-Françoise, Thibaud FOURNET and Bérangère REDON, *Le bain collectif en Égypte, Études urbaines 7*, IFAO, Cairo 2009.

BURDAJEWICZ, Mariusz, *L'Age du Fer à Qumrân* (forthcoming).

CINTAS, Pierre, "Une ville punique au Cap Bon en Tunisie", *CRAI,* 97 no. 3 (1953), p. 256-260.

CLAMER, Christa, *Fouilles archéologiques de Ez-Zara/Callirrhoé, villégiature hérodienne*, IFPO, Beirut 1997.

COLLINS, John J. and Robert A. KUGLER, "Rewriting Rubrics: Sacrifice and the Religion of Qumran", in *Religion in the Dead Sea Scrolls*, Grand Rapids 2000, p. 90-112.

CROSBY, Henry Lamar, in *Dio Chrysostom vol. V*, Cambridge, MA and London, 1951.

CROSS, Frank Moore, *The Ancient Library of Qumrân and Modern Biblical Study, 3rd ed.,* Sheffield 1994.

FANTAR, Mohamed Hassine, *Kerkouane, Cité punique au pays berbère de Tamezrat*, Tunis 2007.

GALLO, Paolo, "Un bain à la grecque dans l'île de Nelson", in BOUSSAC *et al., Le bain*...

GALOR, Katharina, Jean-Baptiste HUMBERT and Jürgen ZANGENBERG, *The Site of the Dead Sea Scrolls. Archaeological Interpretations and Debates*, Leiden and Boston 2006. Cited: *Archaeological Interpretations*.

GOLB Norman, "The Qumran-Essene Hypothesis: A Fiction of Scholarship", *Christian Century* 109 (1992).

GOLB, Norman, "Khirbet Qumran and the Manuscript Finds of the Judean Wilderness", *Methods of Investigation of the Dead Sea Scrolls and the Khirbet Qumran Site*, New York 1994.

GOODMAN, Martin, cf. VERMES, Geza, *The Essenes* ...

GUNNEWEG Jan, cf. HUMBERT, Jean-Baptiste, *Fouilles de Khirbet Qumrân…, vol. II*

MISGAV, Haggai, "The Ostraca", in Győző VÖRÖS, *Machaerus I*, Milan 2013.

HIRSCHFELD, Yizhar, *Qumran in Context, Reassessing the Archaeological Evidence*, Peabody MA 2004.

HUMBERT, Jean-Baptiste, "L'espace sacré à Qumrân. Propositions pour l'archéologie", *RB* 101 (1994), p. 161-214.

HUMBERT, Jean-Baptiste and Alain CHAMBON, *Fouilles de Khirbet Qumrân et de 'Aïn Feshkha, vol. I, Album de photographies, répertoire du fonds photographique, synthèse des notes du Père Roland de Vaux*, Editions universitaires, Fribourg and Göttingen 1994. Cited: *Qumrân vol. I*.

HUMBERT, Jean-Baptiste, "Some Remarks on the Archaeology of Qumran", in GALOR *et al., Archaeological Interpretations*, p. 19-39.

HUMBERT, Jean-Baptiste and Jan GUNNEWEG, eds., *Fouilles de Khirbet Qumrân et de 'Aïn Feshkha, vol. II, Etudes d'Anthropologie, de physique et de chimie*, Fribourg and Göttingen 2003. Cited: *Qumrân vol. II*.

HUMBERT, Jean-Baptiste, "Cacher et se cacher à Qumrân: grottes et refuges", in Marcello FIDANZIO, *The Caves of Qumran*, Leiden, 2016, p. 34-63.

HUMBERT, Jean-Baptiste, "Revoir la jarre à manuscrits de Qumrân ", *RB* 127 (2020), p. 260-294.

HUMBERT, Jean-Baptiste, "Qumran and Machaerus on a Hasmonean Axis ", in *Life at the Dead Sea,* Chemnitz 2020, p. 317-338.

HUMBERT, Jean-Baptiste and FIDANZIO Marcello, eds., *Khirbet Qumrân and Aïn Feshkha IVA, Qumrân Cave 11Q, Archaeology and New Scrolls Fragments*, Göttingen 2019.

JONES, Christopher Prestige, *The Roman World of Dio Chrysostom*, Cambridge MA and London 1978.

KUGLER, Robert A., cf. COLLINS... "Rewriting Rubrics…"

LAPERROUSAZ, Ernest-Marie, *Qoumrân, L'établissement essénien des bords de la mer Morte,* Paris 1976.

LEMAIRE, André, "Inscriptions et graffiti", in *Qumrân vol. II*, p. 341-388.

MACALISTER, Robert Alexander Stewart, *The Excavation of Gezer 1902-1905 and 1907-1909*, London 1912.

MAGEN, Yitzhak and Yuval PELEG, "Back to Qumran: Ten Years of Excavation and Research, 1993-2004", in GALOR, *Archeological Interpretations* ... p. 55-113

MAGEN, Yitzhak and Yuval PELEG, "The Qumran Excavations 1993-2004, Preliminary Report, Appendix", in MAGEN, Y., *Judea and Samaria, Researches and Discoveries,* Judea and Samaria Publications 6, Jerusalem 2008, p. 353-426. Cited: JSP 6.

MAGEN Yitzhak, Yuval PELEG, *Back to Qumran. Final Report (1993-2004)*, Judea and Samaria Publications 18, Jerusalem, 2018. Cited: JSP 18.

MAGNESS, Jodi, *The Archaeology of Qumran and the Dead Sea Scrolls,* Grand Rapids, MI/Cambridge UK, 2002.

NAVEH, Joseph, "Seven New Epitaphs from Zoar", *Tarbiz 1999-2000*, p. 619-635.

NODET, Étienne, "De Josué à Jésus via Qumrân et le 'Pain quotidien'", *RB* 114 (2007), p. 208-236.

NORTON, Jonathan, "Reassessment of the Controversial Studies on the Cemetery", in *Qumrân vol. II*.

NORTH, Robert, "The Damascus of Qumran Geography", *PEQ* 1955, p. 34-48.

PELEG, Yuval, cf. MAGEN, Yitzhak, "The Qumran Excavations ..."

PELEG, Yuval, cf. MAGEN, Yitzhak, "Back to Qumran ..."

PELEG, Yuval, cf. MAGEN, Yitzhak, "Back to Qumran ..."

PFANN, Stephen, in J.-B. HUMBERT, "L'espace sacré …", Annexe, *RB 101 (*1994), p. 212-214.

PFANN, Stephen, "A Table prepared in the Wilderness", *Archaeological Interpretations*, p. 159-178.

PUECH, Émile, "Ossuaires inscrits d'une tombe du mont des Oliviers", *LA 32* (1982) p. 355-372.

SELLERS, Ovid Rogers and William Foxwell ALBRIGHT, "The First Campaign of Excavation at Beth-Zur", *BASOR* 43 (1931), p. 2-13.

STECKOLL, Salomon, "Preliminary Excavations Report in the Qumran Cemetery", *RQ vol. 6, no. 23* (1968), p. 323-336.

de VAUX, Roland,

- "Fouilles au Khirbet Qumrân. Rapport préliminaire", *RB* 60 (1953), p. 540-561.

- "Fouilles de Khirbet Qumrân. Rapport préliminaire sur la deuxième campagne", *RB* 61 (1954), p. 206-236.

- "Fouilles de Khirbet Qumrân. Rapport préliminaire sur les 3e, 4e et 5e campagnes" *RB* 63 (1956), p. 533-577.

- *L'archéologie et les manuscrits de la mer Morte, The Schweich Lectures of the British Academy 1959*, London, *Archaeology and the Dead Sea Scrolls, The Schweich Lectures of the British Academy 1959*, London 1973. Revised edition.

VERMES, Geza and Martin D. GOODMAN , *The Essenes, acccording to the Classical Sources*, Sheffield 1989.

YADIN Yigael, *The Temple Scroll*, Jerusalem, 1983.

ZIAS, Joseph , "The Cemeteries of Qumrân, and Celibacy: Confusion Laid to Rest?", *Dead Sea Discoveries* 7/2, 2000.